The Bilingualism Reade₁

'Li Wei has put together . . . an absolutely essential minimal foundation for any serious student of bilingualism. It contains major classics that form the basis of courses at whatever level, . . . covering a wide range of issues central to the major concerns of the study of the bilingual individual. No fundamental issue of current interest in the field has been omitted. The methodology chapter contains very useful warnings and advice.'

Hugo Baetens Beardsmore, *Vrije Universiteit, Brussel*

'This is a very well judged selection of classic articles on bilingualism. The Introduction provides a most comprehensive advance organizer to the subject and is joined by valuable study questions and activities for each section.'

Colin Baker, *University of Wales at Bangor*

The Bilingualism Reader is a comprehensive collection of key classic articles in the study of bilingualism. Designed as a structured student reader, it covers:

- definitions and typology of bilingualism
- language choice and bilingual interaction
- grammar of code-switching and bilingual acquisition
- the bilingual brain and bilingual production and perception
- methodological issues in the study of bilingualism.

Invaluable editorial material guides the reader through the different sections. Critical discussion of research methods, graded study questions and activities, a comprehensive glossary, and an up-to-date resource list make *The Bilingualism Reader* an essential introductory text for students.

Contributors: Peter Auer, Michael Clyne, Kees de Bot, Charles Ferguson, Joshua Fishman, Fred Genesee, David Green, François Grosjean, John Gumperz, Li Wei, William Mackey, Jürgen Meisel, Lesley Milroy, Carol Myers-Scotton, Loraine Obler, Michel Paradis, Shana Poplack.

Li Wei is Professor of Applied Linguistics in the Department of Speech, and Director of the Centre for Research in Linguistics at the University of Newcastle upon Tyne. He is author of *Three Generations Two Languages One Family* (1994) and co-editor of the *International Journal of Bilingualism*.

The Bilingualism Reader

Edited by Li Wei

London and New York

First published 2000
by Routledge
11 New Fetter Lane, London EC4P 4EE

Simultaneously published in the USA and Canada
by Routledge
29 West 35th Street, New York, NY 10001

Routledge is an imprint of the Taylor & Francis Group

This collection and editorial matter © 2000 Li Wei

Typeset in Perpetua and Bell Gothic by
RefineCatch Limited, Bungay, Suffolk
Printed and bound in Great Britain by
T.J. International Ltd, Padstow, Cornwall

British Library Cataloguing in Publication Data
A catalogue record for this book is available from the British Library

Library of Congress Cataloging in Publication Data
The Bilingualism reader/edited by Li Wei.
p. cm.
Includes bibliographical references and index.
1. Bilingualism. I. Wei, Li
P115.B553 2000
306.44′6–dc21   99–056043

ISBN 0–415–21335–5 (hbk)
ISBN 0–415–21336–3 (pbk)

CONTENTS

PREFACE

ONE INCIDENT DURING my years as a PhD student changed my views on academic research considerably: I was drafting a joint paper with my supervisor Lesley Milroy and in it I cited a textbook writer's comments on William Labov's work which included a quote from Labov. Lesley, who knows Labov's work well, asked me, 'Have you read Labov's original paper?' and pointed out that the comments by the textbook writer were in fact misguided and misguiding. Rather sheepishly I had to admit that I had not read that particular paper of Labov's. When I did read the paper, I was astonished to find what Labov meant in the original paper was very different from what the textbook writer suggested in his comments. Since then, I have been rather suspicious of authors' interpretations and comments, especially the sharply worded ones, on other people's work. I have learnt the benefit of reading the originals.

I am often amazed to see many of our otherwise quite brilliant students readily base their arguments on 'second-hand' interpretation and remarks. I understand that once on that 'degree assembly line', students do not have much choice but to turn out essays and reports very quickly. They do not normally have the time to delve into a wide array of publications, ranging from history and anthropology to neurology and artificial intelligence, in which research papers on bilingualism typically appear. I am nevertheless concerned that a new generation of 'scholars' might be emerging out of a 'hear-say' tradition.

I have also learnt from my visits to Central America, and East and Southeast Asia, that many of the books and journals which we use routinely in our teaching and learning and which we take for granted are not always readily available in those places, because of inadequate library facilities. I have become concerned that research on bilingualism which deals with linguistic and cultural diversity is in fact inaccessible to the very people we wish to represent.

It is with these concerns that I have decided to compile the present Reader. The main objective of the Reader is to make available in a single, affordable volume a selection of the most important research papers on bilingualism. I have focused primarily on the 'classics' in bilingualism research – papers that every newcomer to the field must read and the more established researchers frequently cite. Constraints of budget and space mean that it has not been possible to include all the papers I would like. I have deliberately excluded papers on bilingual education, language planning, language maintenance and language shift, and language attitude. A good reader on policy and practice in bilingual education already exists (Garcia and Baker, 1995), and the sociolinguistics readers edited by Coupland and Jaworski (1997) and Trudgill and Cheshire (1997) both contain key articles on language planning, language maintenance and language shift, and language attitude. Consequently, most of the papers in the present Reader focus on the micro aspects of bilingualism, especially on the language behaviour of bilingual individuals. All the chosen papers are journal articles or book chapters. Extracts from single authored monographs are not included, as a decontextualised digest is deemed inappropriate for student use. Some of the more recent papers published in easily accessible journals and books are also excluded. They, and the important single authored monographs, are listed under Further Reading at the end of each section of the Reader.

Recently, handbooks have become a popular commodity. They are usually compilations of specially commissioned survey-type articles. There is no doubt that they provide a handy resource for students and lecturers. However, handbooks do not address the concerns I have specified above. In fact, handbook users may be more at risk of believing that they knew the subject without actually consulting, let alone understanding, the original formulation of ideas. I therefore declined the suggestion that was put to me to compile a handbook of bilingualism and chose instead to edit a reader of classic articles. Some of the recent state-of-the-art collections are listed in the Resource List section.

In theory, a reader represents a diversity of voices rather than a single authorial one as is normally the case with a textbook. But I am fully aware of the fact that I, as the editor, imprint my views via selection of the papers and the leading comments in the introductory remarks and even in the suggested study activities and Further Reading. I must confess, however, that I do not agree with all the views expressed in the papers included in this Reader. Nevertheless I believe that all these papers are essential reading for anyone interested in bilingualism and hope the Reader as a whole gives a good representation of the various dimensions of bilingualism research.

ACKNOWLEDGEMENTS

I am grateful to Colin Baker, Margaret Deuchar, Anthea Fraser Gupta, Mark Sebba, Jeanine Treffers-Daller and several anonymous readers commissioned by the publisher who read and commented on the Introduction and Conclusion and on the selection of papers. Hugo Baetens Beardsmore provided an almost word-by-word commentary on the editorial material I have written and offered many interesting and useful examples, without which the Reader would be much duller and poorer in quality. Michael Clyne spent a significant amount of time during his brief stay in Newcastle in April 1999 going through the details of the papers and making helpful suggestions. Many of the authors of the original papers went out of their way to help me negotiate copyright permission and suggested feasible alternatives; in this respect François Grosjean, Shirley Brice Heath (executrix of Charles Ferguson's estate) and Carol Myers-Scotton deserve very special thanks. My colleagues Nigel Armstrong, Karen Corrigan and Nick Miller and several of the postgraduate students in Newcastle offered their users' comments on the selection of papers; they include: Rob Davies, Debbie Friedland, Emily Lam-Kwok, Sherman Lee and Miyako Takagi. Special thanks go to Brigid O'Connor who proofread a considerable amount of the material very quickly and efficiently. Thanks also to Louisa Semlyen and her team at Routledge for all the work they have done. As always, my wife Zhu Hua has been the most important source of inspiration and understanding without which this Reader would not be possible.

The editor and publisher would like to acknowledge the copyright holders for permission to reprint the following material:

Mackey, W.F. (1962) The description of bilingualism. *Canadian Journal of Linguistics.* 7: 51–85, by permission of the author.

Ferguson, C.A. (1959) Diglossia. *Word* 15: 325–40, by permission of the International Linguistics Association.

Fishman, J.A. (1967) Bilingualism with and without diglossia; diglossia with and without bilingualism. *Journal of Social Issues* 23(2): 29–38, by permission of Blackwell Publishers.

Fishman, J.A. (1965) Who speaks what language to whom and when? *La Linguistique* 2: 67–88, by permission of the author.

Blom, J.-P. and Gumperz, J.J. (1972) Social meaning in linguistic structure: code-switching in Norway. In J.J. Gumperz and D. Hymes (eds) *Directions in Sociolinguistics*. New York: Holt, Rinehart and Winston, pp. 407–34, by permission of the authors.

Myers-Scotton, C. (1988) Code-switching as indexical of social negotiations. In M. Heller (ed.) *Codeswitching*. Berlin: Mouton de Gruyter pp. 151–86, by permission of Mouton de Gruyter. N.B. This paper was originally published under the name C.M. Scotton.

Auer, J.C.P. (1988) A conversation analytic approach to code-switching and transfer. In M. Heller (ed.) *Codeswitching*. Berlin: Mouton de Gruyter pp. 187–214, by permission of Mouton de Gruyter.

Li Wei, Milroy, L. and Pong, S.C. (1992) A two-step sociolinguistic analysis of code-switching and language choice. *International Journal of Applied Linguistics* 2(1): 63–86, by permission of Novus Press.

Poplack, S. (1979/80) Sometimes I'll start a sentence in Spanish *y termino en español*. *Linguistics* 18: 581–618, by permission of Mouton de Gruyter.

Clyne, M. (1987) Constraints on code-switching: how universal are they? *Linguistics* 25: 739–64, by permission of Mouton de Gruyter.

Myers-Scotton, C. and Jake, J. (1995) Matching lemmas in a bilingual competence and production model. *Linguistics* 33: 981–1024, by permission of Mouton de Gruyter.

Genesee, F. (1989) Early bilingual language development: one language or two? *Journal of Child Language* 16: 161–79, by permission of Cambridge University Press.

Meisel, J.M. (1989) Early differentiation of languages in bilingual children. In K. Hyltenstam and L. Obler (eds) *Bilingualism across the Lifespan*. Cambridge: Cambridge University Press pp. 13–40, by permission of Cambridge University Press.

Obler, L.K., Zatorre, R.J., Galloway, L. and Vaid, J. (1982) Cerebral lateralization in bilinguals. *Brain and Language* 15: 40–54, by permission of Academic Press.

Paradis, M. (1990) Language lateralization in bilinguals. *Brain and Language* 39: 570–86, by permission of Academic Press.

Green, D.W. (1986) Control, activation, and resource. *Brain and Language* 27: 210–23, by permission of Academic Press.

de Bot, K. (1992) A bilingual production model: Levelt's 'speaking' model adapted. *Applied Linguistics* 13: 1–24, by permission of Oxford University Press.

Grosjean, F. (1997) Processing mixed language: issues, findings, and models. In A.M. De Groot and J.F. Kroll (eds) *Tutorials in Bilingualism*. Mahwah, NJ:

Lawrence Erlbaum, pp. 225–54, by permission of Lawrence Erlbaum Associates.

Every effort has been made to obtain permission to reproduce copyright material. If any proper acknowledgement has not been made, or permission not received, we would invite copyright holders to inform the editor and publishers of that oversight.

All the original papers and chapters are reproduced as faithfully as possible. The authors' original writing styles and conventions, whether in British or North American norms, have been kept. This policy results, in some cases, in maintaining the sexist-pronoun usage. Given the inevitable restrictions of space and the need to produce a coherent and readable collection, the editor has changed or omitted references to other papers in the same original collection (e.g. 'see Chapter 6 in this volume' has been changed to 'see XXX, date'), and put all the bibliographical details of the original papers at the end of the Reader. Where a work exists in different editions which have been variably cited by the original authors, the different dates are all listed with the later ones given in parenthesis. Other minor textual changes and omissions are indicated by the insertion of [. . .] in the text. The only paper that has been 'updated' is Shana Poplack's article, to which a short preface is added. This was done by the author at her insistence.

HOW TO USE THE READER

The Reader is intended for use as a teaching text, either on its own or as a secondary source-book, on a variety of courses. All the papers are selected from journals and collected volumes. No extracts from single authored monographs are included here. The papers are grouped into different parts, each having a brief introduction highlighting its theme. They are further divided into sections within the main parts, according to topics. Within each section, the papers are arranged, as far as possible, in a chronological order. The general Introduction and Conclusion which I have written aim to provide links between the sections.

The Introduction and Mackey's article together aim to place the other papers in this Reader in a wider context, and thus should be read first. Users can then choose to read the papers in different parts and sections which interest them most, although I have organised the papers in such a way that the focus of discussion moves from the macro-external (social and sociolinguistic) to the micro-internal (linguistic and psychological) aspects of bilingualism. The editorial material I have added, in the form of sectional introductions, points out the differences and similarities in the theoretical and methodological stances of individual papers. I have followed the models of successful readers such as Garcia and Baker (1995) and provided a set of Study Questions and Study Activities at the end of each section. The Study Questions are intended for reviewing some of the essential themes and concepts in the individual papers and can be used on beginners' level courses or for self study. The Study Activities aim to extend reading by generalisation to the user's own locality or experience. Some of the activities require research, and may be used as topics for essays or dissertation projects. These are particularly suitable for use at an intermediate level. There is also a short list of Further Reading which suggests additional sources of material for those who are interested in following up particular issues and ideas. The Conclusion chapter highlights some of the methodological issues in bilingualism research. Although it is placed at the end of the volume, it can (and perhaps should) be read before reading the individual papers.

I have also provided a Resource List and a Glossary. The Resource List contains the state-of-the-art collections, the important journals, book series, reference books and textbooks, as well as key websites and electronic mailing lists. The Glossary contains the key terms in bilingualism research. A full Bibliography, listing all the references for the individual chapters in this Reader, is provided at the end.

Introduction

Dimensions of bilingualism

LI WEI

Languages in contact

Estimates vary as to how many languages are spoken in the world today. Most reference books give a figure of around 6,000 (e.g. Crystal, 1987; Baker and Prys Jones, 1998). This is in fact a conservative estimate, as many parts of the world have been insufficiently studied from a linguistic point of view. We simply do not know exactly what languages are spoken in some places. What we do know, however, is that there are fewer than 200 countries – that politico-geographic unit to which most of us belong – in the world. It is inevitable perhaps that an enormous amount of 'language contact' takes place.

There is a popular metaphor in linguistics that language is a living organism, which is born, grows and dies. However, language is a human faculty: it co-evolves with us, *homo sapiens*; and it is we who give language its life, change it and, if so desired, abandon it. When we speak of 'language contact', we are therefore talking about people speaking different languages coming into contact with one another.

There are many reasons for speakers of different languages to come into contact. Some do so out of their own choosing, while others are forced by circumstances. Key external factors contributing to language contact include (for further discussion, see Crystal, 1987; Baker and Prys Jones, 1998):

- *Politics*: Political or military acts such as colonisation, annexation, resettlement and federation can have immediate linguistic effects. People may become refugees, either in a new place or in their homeland, and have to learn the language of their new environment. After a successful military invasion, the indigenous population may have to learn the invader's language in order to prosper. Colonisation is exemplified by the former British, French, Spanish, Portuguese and Dutch colonies in Africa, Asia and South America, most of which achieved independence in the nineteenth century. A modern example of annexation can be found in the absorption of the Baltic republics – Lithuania, Latvia and Estonia – into the Soviet Union after the Second World War. In the latter part of the twentieth century military conflicts in Central Africa and the former Yugoslavia have seen the resettlement of people of different ethnic backgrounds. Examples of federation where diverse ethnic groups or nationalities are united under the political control of one state include Switzerland, Belgium and Cameroon.

- *Natural disaster*: Famine, floods, volcanic eruptions and other such events can be the cause of major movements of population. New language-contact situations then emerge as people are resettled. Some of the Irish and Chinese resettlements in North America were the result of natural disasters.
- *Religion*: People may wish to live in a country because of its religious significance, or to leave a country because of its religious oppression. In either case, a new language may have to be learned. The Russian speakers in Israel are a case in point.
- *Culture*: A desire to identify with a particular ethnic, cultural or social group usually means learning the language of that group. Minority ethnic and cultural groups may wish to maintain their own languages, which are different from the languages promoted by the governing state or institution. Nationalistic factors are particularly important.
- *Economy*: Very large numbers of people across the world have migrated to find work and to improve their standard of living. This factor accounts for most of the linguistic diversity of the US and an increasing proportion of the bilingualism in present-day Europe.
- *Education*: Learning another language may be the only means of obtaining access to knowledge. This factor led to the universal use of Latin in the Middle Ages, and today motivates the international use of English.
- *Technology*: The availability of information and communication technologies (ICT), such as the internet, has led to a further expansion of the use of English across the world. The vast majority of ICT users are non-native speakers of English.

From the above list we can see that one does not have to move to a different place to come into contact with people speaking a different language. There are plenty of opportunities for language contact in the same country, the same community, the same neighbourhood or even the same family. The usual consequence of language contact is bilingualism, or even multilingualism, which is most commonly found in an individual speaker.

Who is a bilingual?

People who are brought up in a society where monolingualism and uniculturalism are promoted as the normal way of life often think that bilingualism is only for a few 'special' people. In fact, one in three of the world's population routinely uses two or more languages for work, family life and leisure. There are even more people who make irregular use of languages other than their native one; for example, many people have learnt foreign languages at school and only occasionally use them for specific purposes. If we count these people as bilinguals then monolingual speakers would be a tiny minority in the world today.

The question of who is and who is not a bilingual is more difficult to answer than it first appears. Table 0.1 is a list of terms which have been used to describe bilingual speakers (for further discussions, see Baetens Beardsmore, 1982: Chapter 1; see also Chapter 1 of this volume). Baker and Prys Jones (1998: 2) suggest that in defining a bilingual person, we may wish to consider the following questions:

- Should bilingualism be measured by how fluent people are in two languages?
- Should bilinguals be only those people who have equal competence in both languages?
- Is language proficiency the only criterion for assessing bilingualism, or should the use of two languages also be considered?
- Most people would define a bilingual as a person who can *speak* two languages. What about a person who can understand a second language perfectly but cannot speak it? What about a person who can speak a language but is not literate in it? What about an individual who cannot speak or understand speech in a second language but can read and write it? Should these categories of people be considered bilingual?
- Should self-perception and self-categorisation be considered in defining who is a bilingual?
- Are there different degrees of bilingualism that can vary over time and with circumstances? For instance, a person may learn a minority language

Table 0.1   A variety of bilinguals

---

achieved bilingual   same as *late bilingual.*

additive bilingual   someone whose two languages combine in a complementary and enriching fashion.

ambilingual   same as *balanced bilingual.*

ascendant bilingual   someone whose ability to function in a second language is developing due to increased use.

ascribed bilingual   same as *early bilingual.*

asymmetrical bilingual   see *receptive bilingual.*

balanced bilingual   someone whose mastery of two languages is roughly equivalent.

compound bilingual   someone whose two languages are learnt at the same time, often in the same context.

consecutive bilingual   same as *successive bilingual.*

co-ordinate bilingual   someone whose two languages are learnt in distinctively separate contexts.

covert bilingual   someone who conceals his or her knowledge of a given language due to an attitudinal disposition.

diagonal bilingual   someone who is bilingual in a non-standard language or a dialect and an unrelated standard language.

dominant bilingual   someone with greater proficiency in one of his or her languages and uses it significantly more than the other language(s).

dormant bilingual   someone who has emigrated to a foreign country for a considerable period of time and has little opportunity to keep the first language actively in use.

early bilingual   someone who has acquired two languages early in childhood.

equilingual   same as *balanced bilingual.*

functional bilingual   someone who can operate in two languages with or without full fluency for the task in hand.

horizontal bilingual   someone who is bilingual in two distinct languages which have a similar or equal status.

incipient bilingual   someone at the early stages of bilingualism where one language is not fully developed.

late bilingual   someone who has become a bilingual later than childhood.

maximal bilingual   someone with near native control of two or more languages.

minimal bilingual   someone with only a few words and phrases in a second language.

natural bilingual   someone who has not undergone any specific training and who is often not in a position to translate or interpret with facility between two languages.

passive bilingual   same as *receptive bilingual*.

primary bilingual   same as *natural bilingual*.

productive bilingual   someone who not only understands but also speaks and possibly writes in two or more languages.

receptive bilingual   someone who understands a second language, in either its spoken or written form, or both, but does not necessarily speak or write it.

recessive bilingual   someone who begins to feel some difficulty in either understanding or expressing him or herself with ease, due to lack of use.

secondary bilingual   someone whose second language has been added to a first language via instruction.

semibilingual   same as *receptive bilingual*.

semilingual   someone with insufficient knowledge of either language.

simultaneous bilingual   someone whose two languages are present from the onset of speech.

subordinate bilingual   someone who exhibits interference in his or her language usage by reducing the patterns of the second language to those of the first.

subtractive bilingual   someone whose second language is acquired at the expense of the aptitudes already acquired in the first language.

successive bilingual   someone whose second language is added at some stage after the first has begun to develop.

symmetrical bilingual   same as *balanced bilingual*.

vertical bilingual   someone who is bilingual in a standard language and a distinct but related language or dialect.

---

as a child at home and then later acquire another, majority language in the community or at school. Over time, the second language may become the stronger or dominant language. If that person moves away from the neighbourhood or area where the minority language is spoken, or loses contact with those who speak it, he or she may lose fluency in the minority language. Should bilingualism therefore be a relative term?

The word 'bilingual' primarily describes someone with the possession of two languages. It can, however, also be taken to include the many people in the world who have varying degrees of proficiency in and interchangeably use three, four or even more languages. In many countries of Africa and Asia, several languages co-exist and large sections of the population speak three or more languages. Individual multilingualism in these countries is a fact of life. Many people speak one or more local or ethnic languages, as well as another indigenous language which has become the medium of communication between different ethnic groups or speech communities. Such individuals may also speak a foreign language – such as English, French or Spanish – which has been introduced into the community during the process of colonisation. This latter language is often the language of education, bureaucracy and privilege.

Multilingualism can also be the possession of individuals who do not live within a multilingual country or speech community. Families can be trilingual when the husband and wife each speak a different language as well as the common language of the place of residence. People with sufficient social and educational advantages can learn a second, third or fourth language at school or university, at work or in leisure time. In many continental European countries, children learn two languages at school – such as English, German or French – as well as being fluent in their home language – such as Danish, Dutch or Luxembourgish.

It is important to recognise that a multilingual speaker uses different languages for different purposes and does not typically possess the same level or type of proficiency in each language. In Morocco, for instance, a native speaker of Berber may also be fluent in colloquial Moroccan Arabic, but not be literate in either of these languages. This Berber speaker will be educated in modern standard Arabic and use that language for writing and formal purposes. Classical Arabic is the language of the mosque, used for prayers and reading the Qur'an. Many Moroccans also have some knowledge of French, the former colonial language (for further discussion, see Bentahila, 1983).

What's in a language?

The above discussions of the causes of language contact and types of bilingual or multilingual people presuppose a definition of language. But what exactly is a language? This question has troubled linguists for decades.

One way of thinking about language is as a systematic combination of smaller units into larger units to create meaning. For example, we combine the sounds of our language (*phonemes*) to form meaningful words (*lexical items*) and we do so according to the rules of the language we speak. Those lexical items can be combined to make meaningful structures (*sentences*) according to the syntactic rule of our language. Language is hence a rule-governed system. Many linguists have devoted their lives to the scientific study of the rules that govern our language.

However, this kind of approach only works in a general, abstract way. As soon as we focus on a specific language of a specific speech community, we find that many other factors, mostly non-linguistic, have to be considered. For instance, when we want to work out the rules of English, we need to have some kind of agreement as to what English refers to. The *Concise Oxford Dictionary* defines English as 'the language of England'. What then is the language spoken by a large number of people in Australia, Canada, South Africa and the USA? What is the language spoken by people from Adelaide, Houston or Liverpool? Questions such as these have led some linguists to suggest that the notion of 'language' is essentially a social one in the sense that it is defined in terms of the people who speak it, and that as people vary in terms of their social character-istics – such as age, gender, place of origin and ethnicity – the language they speak will have various manifestations.

Traditionally, linguists make a distinction between 'language' and 'dialect', based on two criteria: *size* and *prestige* (for a more detailed discussion, see Hudson, 1996 (1980): Chapter 2). A language is believed to be larger than a dialect. That is, a variety called a language would contain more items than one called a dialect. In this sense we may refer to English as a language, containing the sum total of all the terms in all its dialects, such as Texan English and Yorkshire English. A language is also thought to have prestige which a dialect lacks. English as a language, for example, is supported institutionally through schools and the mass media; however, Appalachian and Geordie are not, and are hence often classified as dialects.

However, the two criteria of size and prestige sometimes contradict each other in distinguishing language and dialect. For example, the so-called 'standard English' must be a dialect if we consider its size only, as it does not contain items from many other varieties of English. Yet standard English has far more prestige than other English dialects because its use is encouraged in formal contexts. It should therefore be regarded not as a dialect but a language. In fact, standard English, or any standard language, is a result of a direct and deliberate, and in some cases prolonged, intervention by society. This intervention – known as 'standardisation' – produces a standard language where before there were just dialects.

There are many counter-examples for the language and dialect distinction based on size and prestige. For instance, Luxembourgish is a language according to the constitution of Luxembourg, but linguistically it is a Rhennish dialect. Philipino is a language in the process of corpus building, but it is unclear whether it is bigger than Tagalog or Ilocano or any other Philippine languages/dialects. There are some very prestigious 'dialects' which may also be supported institutionally. For example, the European Charter of Minority Languages of the Council of Europe gives institutional support to a number of what used to be called dialects across the European Union.

One obvious candidate for an extra criterion for distinguishing language and dialect is that of *mutual intelligibility*. If the speakers of two linguistic varieties can understand each other, then the varieties concerned are dialects of the same language; otherwise they are separate languages. This is a widely used criterion. However, it cannot be taken seriously because there are a number of problems with its application.

First, even popular usage does not correspond consistently to this criterion. There are varieties which we as lay people call different languages but which are mutually intelligible – such as Danish, Norwegian and Swedish – and varieties which we call dialects of the same language but which may not be mutually intelligible; for example, the so-called dialects of Chinese (see Figure 0.1 for an illustration). Popular usage tends to reflect a prestige-based definition of language. If two varieties are both standard languages, or are subordinate to different standards, they must be different languages and, conversely, if they are both subordinate to the same standard, they are considered as the same language.

Second, mutual intelligibility is a matter of degree, ranging from total intel-ligibility down to total unintelligibility. How high up on the intelligibility scale do two varieties need to be in order to count as members of the same language? Unfortunately the answer to this question must be arbitrary.

Third, mutual intelligibility is not really a relationship between linguistic varieties, but between people, since it is they, and not the linguistic varieties, that understand one another. This being so, the degree of mutual intelligibility depends not just on the amount of overlap between the linguistic items in the two varieties, but also on the perceptions of the people concerned. For instance, how much does speaker X want to understand speaker Y? How much experience have they had of the variety to which they are listening? And how strongly do they want to identify themselves as speakers of the same language?

Another popular way of delimiting languages is by the names they have. All the 'major' languages of the world have a single name which translates neatly into other languages, such as Arabic, English, French, German, Russian and Spanish. If we want to refer to a particular variety of these languages, we can simply attach a place name; for instance, Moroccan Arabic, Australian English and Puerto Rican Spanish. Dialects, on the other hand, tend not to have a proper name or at least tend not to have one that is easily translatable into other languages. For example, many communities in Africa have no specific names for their languages. The names they use are the same as a common word or phrase in the language, such as the word for 'our language' or 'our people'. The various English names for the Chinese dialects – such as Mandarin and Cantonese – are virtually unknown to native speakers of these varieties, and the London dialect,

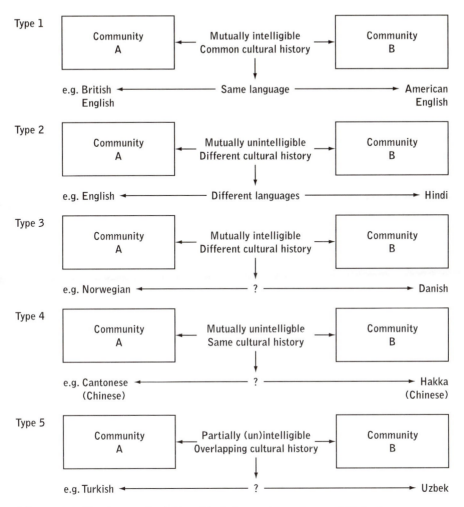

Figure 0.1 Five types of relationship between language and dialect
Source: adapted from Crystal, 1997 (1987): 289.

Cockney, would be known as the 'dialect of London' to speakers of French, German, Chinese and Japanese, rather than by its name. It is also as common to find a community whose language has numerous names as it is to have the same name applied to two different languages. Sometimes speakers from different backgrounds disagree as to which language they are speaking or if the varieties they are speaking are related at all.

To complicate the matter even further, there are what have been called 'mixed languages' whose sources are diverse and sometimes unknown (e.g.

Bakker and Mous, 1994). They are, as the linguists who study them point out, not pidgins or creoles, nor relexified languages. While a large amount of borrowing and mixing can be traced in them, they do not fit into any of the models of bilingual speech. They did not have names, until linguists provided them. They are a product of contacts between people and a symbol of an emerging social identity.

So there is no simple answer to the question 'what is a language'. There is no pure linguistic definition of a language, nor is there a real distinction to be drawn between language and dialect. Language is a social notion; it cannot be defined without reference to its speakers and the context of its use. Language boundaries are boundaries between groups of people, as language contacts are contacts between people. Thus, language is not simply a system of sounds, words and sentences. Language also has a social function, both as a means of communication and as a way of identifying social groups.

Language as a socio-political issue

In many countries of the world a lot of the social identification is accomplished through language choice. By choosing one or other of the two or more languages in one's linguistic repertoire, a speaker reveals and defines his or her social relationships with other people. At a societal level, whole groups of people and, in fact, entire nations can be identified by the language or languages they use. Language, together with culture, religion and history, becomes a major component of national identity.

Multilingual countries are often thought to have certain problems which monolingual states do not (see Fasold, 1984: Chapter 1; Edwards, 1994). On the practical level, difficulties in communication within a country can act as an impediment to commerce and industry. More seriously, however, multilingualism is a problem for government. The process of governing requires communication both within the governing institutions and between the government and the people. This means that a language, or languages, must be selected as the language for use in governing. However, the selection of the 'official language' is not always easy, as it is not simply a pragmatic issue. For example, on pragmatic grounds, the best immediate choice for the language of government in a newly independent colony might be the old colonial language, since the colonial governing institutions and records are already in place in that language, and those nationals with the most government experience already know it. The old colonial language will not, however, be a good choice on nationalist grounds. For a people which has just acquired its own geographical territory, the language of the state which had denied it territorial control would not be a desirable candidate for a national symbol. Ireland has adopted a strategy whereby both the national language, Irish, and the language of the deposed power, English, are declared as official; the colonial language is used for immediate, practical purposes while the national language is promoted and developed. However, in many other multilingual countries which do not have a colonial past, such as China, deciding which language should be selected as the national language can sometimes lead to internal, ethnic conflicts.

Similarly, selecting a language for education in a multilingual country is often problematic. In some respects, the best strategy for language in education is to use the various ethnic languages. After all, these are the languages the children already speak, and school instruction can begin immediately without waiting until the children learn the official language. Some would argue, however, that this strategy could be damaging for nation-building efforts and disadvantage children by limiting their access to the wider world.

It should be pointed out that there is no scientific evidence to show that multilingual countries are particularly disadvantaged, in socio-economic terms, compared to monolingual ones. In fact, all the research that was carried out in the 1960s and 1970s on the relationship between the linguistic diversity and economic well-being of a nation came to the conclusion that a country can have any degree of language uniformity or fragmentation and still be underdeveloped; and a country whose entire population speaks the same language can be anywhere from very rich to very poor. It might be true that linguistic uniformity and economic development reinforce each other; in other words, economic well-being promotes the reduction of linguistic diversity. It would, however, be too one-sided, to say the least, to view multilingualism as the cause of the socio-economic problems of a nation (Coulmas, 1992).

Multilingualism is an important resource at both the societal and personal levels. For a linguistically diverse country to maintain the ethnic-group languages alongside the national or official language(s) can prove to be an effective way to motivate individuals while unifying the nation. Additionally, a multi-ethnic society is arguably a richer, more exciting and stimulating place to live in than a community with only one dominant ethnic group.

For the multilingual speaker, the availability of various languages in the community repertoire serves as a useful interactional resource. Typically, multilingual societies tend to assign different roles to different languages; one language may be used in informal contexts with family and friends, while another for the more formal situations of work, education and government. Imagine two friends who are both bilingual in the same 'home' and 'official' languages. Suppose that one of them also works for the local government and that her friend has some official business with her. Suppose further that the government employee has two pieces of advice to give to her friend: one based on her official status as a government representative, and one based on their mutual friendship. If the official advice is given in the 'government' language and the friendly advice in the 'home' language, there is little chance that there would be any misunderstanding about which advice was which. The friend would not take the advice given in the 'home' language as official (for specific examples, see Chapter 5).

There is a frequent debate in countries where various languages co-exist concerning which languages are a resource. The favoured languages tend to be those that are both international and particularly valuable in international trade. A lower place is given in the status ranking to minority languages which are small, regional and of less perceived value in the international marketplace. For example, French has traditionally been the number one modern language in the British school curriculum, followed by German and Spanish, and then a choice between Italian, Modern Greek and Portuguese. One may notice that all of these are European languages. Despite large numbers of mother-tongue Bengali, Cantonese, Gujarati, Hakka, Hindi, Punjabi, Turkish and Urdu speakers, these languages occupy a very low position in the school curriculum. In the British National Curriculum, the languages Arabic, Bengali, Chinese (Cantonese or Mandarin), Gujarati, Modern Hebrew, Hindi, Japanese, Punjabi, Russian, Turkish and Urdu are initially only allowed in secondary schools (for 11 to 18 year olds) if a major European language such as French is taught first (Milroy and Milroy, 1985).

Clearly, multilingualism as a national and personal resource requires careful planning, as would any other kind of resource. However, language planning has something that other kinds of economic planning do not usually have: language has its own unique cultural symbolic value. As has been discussed earlier, language is a major component of the identity of a nation and an individual. Often, strong emotions are evoked when talking about a certain language. Language planning is not simply a matter of standardising or modernising a corpus of linguistic materials, nor is it a reassignment of functions and status. It is also about power and influence. The dominance of some languages and the dominated status of other languages is partly understandable if we examine who are in positions of power and influence, who belong to elite groups that are in control of decision-making, and who are in subordinate groups, upon whom decisions are implemented. It is more often than not the case that a given arrangement of languages benefits only those who have influence and privileges (Kaplan and Baldauf, 1997).

For the multilingual speaker, language choice is not only an effective means of communication but also an act of identity (Le Page and Tabouret-Keller,

1985). Every time we say something in one language when we might just as easily have said it in another, we are reconnecting with people, situations and power configurations from our history of past interactions and imprinting on that history our attitudes towards the people and languages concerned. Through language choice, we maintain and change ethnic group boundaries and personal relationships, and construct and define 'self' and 'other' within a broader political economy and historical context.

What does it mean to be a bilingual?

A frequently asked question is whether a bilingual speaker's brain functions differently from that of a monolingual's brain. A more technical way of asking the question is whether language is differently organised and processed in the brain of a bilingual compared with the monolingual. In the majority of right-handed adults, the left hemisphere of the brain is dominant for language processing. There is some evidence to suggest that second language acquisition, especially adult second language acquisition, involves the right hemisphere more than first language acquisition in language processing. As proficiency in a second language grows, right hemisphere involvement decreases and left hemisphere involvement increases. However, quantitative analyses of the existing data often show that the left hemisphere strongly dominates language processing for both monolinguals and bilinguals, and that differences between them are the exception rather than the rule. Bilinguals do not seem to vary from monolinguals in neurological processes; the lateralisation of language in the brains of the two groups of speakers is similar (see Chapters 14 and 15).

A related issue concerns the mental representation of a bilingual's two languages and the processing emanating from such representation. Evidence exists for both separate storage and shared storage of the two languages in the bilingual's brain, resulting in the suggestion that bilinguals have a language store for each of their two languages and a more general conceptual store. There are strong, direct interconnecting channels between each of these three separate stores. The interconnections between the two languages comprise association and translation systems, and common images in the conceptual store act as mediators. Furthermore, speakers of different proficiency levels or at different acquisitional stages vary in the strength and directness of the interconnections between the separate stores in language processing; for instance, those who are highly proficient in two languages may go directly from a concept to the target language, while those whose second language is weaker than their first tend to use the first language to mediate (see Chapters 17 and 18).

Although the more general definitions of bilingualism would include people who understand a second language – in either spoken or written form or both – but do not necessarily speak or write it, a more common usage of the term refers to someone who can function in both languages in conversational interaction. We have already mentioned that bilingual speakers choose to use their different languages depending on a variety of factors, including the type of person addressed (e.g. members of the family, school-mates, colleagues, superiors, friends, shop-keepers, officials, transport personnel, neighbours), the subject matter of the conversation (e.g. family concerns, schoolwork, politics, entertainment), location or social setting (e.g. at home, in the street, in church, in the office, having lunch, attending a lecture, negotiating business deals), and relationship with the addressee (e.g. kin, neighbours, colleagues, superior–inferior, strangers). However, even more complex are the many cases when a bilingual talks to another bilingual with the same linguistic background and changes from one language to another in the course of conversation. This is what is known as code-switching. Figure 0.2 illustrates a decision-making process of the bilingual speaker in language choice and code-switching.

There is a widespread impression that bilingual speakers code-switch because they cannot express themselves adequately in one language. This may be true to some extent when a bilingual is momentarily lost for words in one of his or her languages. However, code-switching is an extremely common practice among bilinguals and takes many forms. A long narrative may be divided into different parts which are expressed in different languages; sentences may begin in one language and finish in another; words and phrases from different languages may succeed each other. Linguists have devoted much attention to the

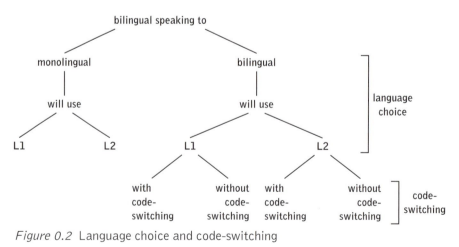

Figure 0.2 Language choice and code-switching

Source: adapted from Grosjean, 1982: 129.

study of code-switching. It has been demonstrated that code-switching involves skilled manipulation of overlapping sections of two (or more) grammars, and that there is virtually no instance of ungrammatical combination of two languages in code-switching, regardless of the bilingual ability of the speaker. Some suggest that code-switching is itself a discrete mode of speaking, emanating from a single code-switching grammar.

One important aspect of the code-switching grammar is that the two languages involved do not play the same role in sentence making. Typically one language sets the grammatical framework, with the other providing certain items to fit into the framework. Code-switching therefore is not a simple combination of two sets of grammatical rules but grammatical integration of one language in another. Bilingual speakers of different proficiency levels in their two languages or speaking two typologically different languages can engage in code-switching and indeed vary it according to their needs (see Chapters 9, 10 and 11).

The possible existence of a code-switching grammar calls into question the traditional view of the bilingual as two monolinguals in one person (for further discussions, see Grosjean, 1985). One consequence of the 'two-in-one' perspective is that bilingual speakers are often compared to monolinguals in terms of their language proficiency. For example, some researchers have suggested that bilingual children had smaller vocabularies and less developed grammars than their monolingual peers, while their ability to exploit the similarities and differences in two sets of grammatical rules to accomplish rule-governed code-switching was not considered relevant. In some experimental psycholinguistic studies, tests are given without taking into account that bilingual speakers may have learnt their two languages under different conditions for different purposes, and they only use them in different situations with different people. It is important to emphasise that bilingual speakers have a unique linguistic and psychological profile; their two languages are constantly in different states of activation; they are able to call upon their linguistic knowledge and resources according to the context and adapt their behaviour to the task in hand.

In addition to the social use of code-switching, some bilinguals regularly change their speech production from one language to another in their professional life. Interpreters and translators, for example, switch between languages as a routine part of their job. They typically do so by reiterating in one language a message which was originally in a different language, either in the oral or written mode. They also tend to operate at the sentence level, rather than mixing two languages within sentences. Often we think of professional interpreters and translators as special people with highly developed language skills in each of their languages. In fact, even they are rarely perfectly balanced in two languages. More often than not, interpreters use one language actively and with greater ease than the other which they understand perfectly but in which their production is weaker. They are trained to translate from the 'passive' to the 'active' language. They are also trained to think rapidly of appropriate wording of ideas and produce words from a restricted area of meaning.

Another group of bilinguals engage themselves in cross-modality language production. This is the case with speech-sign bilinguals who, in addition to the oral modality, use the manual-visual modality in everyday communication. They are special in one aspect, i.e. the two different modalities allow for the simultaneous production of the two languages. In other words, one can speak and sign at the same time. Research has shown that such simultaneous bi-modal production is typically exemplified by the use of lexical items from both languages but only one set of grammatical rules which is usually from the spoken language. At the end of the twentieth century we know relatively little about how the two linguistic systems interact in the language production and processing of speech-sign bilinguals (for a review of existing studies of sign bilingualism, see Dufour, 1997). Indeed, much more work needs to be undertaken before we can fully appreciate the complexity of the language behaviour of bilinguals generally.

Changes in attitudes towards bilingualism

From the early nineteenth century to about the 1960s, there was a widespread belief that bilingualism has a detrimental effect on a human being's intellectual and spiritual growth. Stories of children who persisted in speaking two languages in school having had their mouths washed with soap and water or being beaten with a cane were not uncommon. The following is a quote from a professor at Cambridge University which illustrates the dominant belief of the time, even among academics and intellectuals:

> If it were possible for a child to live in two languages at once equally well, so much the worse. His intellectual and spiritual growth would not thereby be doubled, but halved. Unity of mind and character would have great difficulty in asserting itself in such circumstances.
>
> (Laurie, 1890: 15)

This view of Professor Laurie represented a commonly held belief through the twentieth century that bilingualism disadvantages rather than advantages one's intellectual development. The early research on bilingualism and cognition tended to confirm this negative view point, finding that monolinguals were superior to bilinguals on intelligence tests. One of the most widely cited studies was done by Saer (1923) who studied 1,400 Welsh–English bilingual children between the ages of seven and 14 in five rural and two urban areas of Wales. A 10-point difference in IQ was found between the bilinguals and the monolingual English speakers from rural backgrounds. From this Saer concluded that bilinguals were mentally confused and at a disadvantage in intelligence compared with monolinguals. It was further suggested, with a follow-up study of university students, that 'the difference in mental ability as revealed by intelligence tests is of a permanent nature since it persists in students throughout their university career' (1924: 53).

Controversies regarding the early versions of IQ tests and the definition and measurement of intelligence aside, there were a number of problems with Saer's study and its conclusions. First, it appeared to be only in the rural areas that the correlation between bilingualism and lower IQ held. In urban areas monolinguals and bilinguals were virtually the same; in fact the average IQ for urban Welsh–English bilingual children in Saer's study was 100, whereas for monolingual English-speaking children it was 99. The urban bilingual children had more contact with English both before beginning school and outside school hours than did the rural bilinguals. Thus the depressed scores of the rural population were probably more a reflection of lack of opportunity and contexts to use English and were not necessarily indicative of any socio-psychological problems.

More important, however, is the issue of statistical inference in this and other studies of a similar type. Correlations do not allow us to infer cause and effect relationships, particularly when other variables – such as rural versus urban differences – may be mediating factors. Another major factor is the language in which such tests were administered, particularly tests of verbal intelligence. Many such studies measured bilinguals only in the second or non-dominant language.

At around the same time as Saer conducted studies on bilinguals' intelligence, some well-known linguists expressed their doubts about bilingual speakers' linguistic competence. The following is Bloomfield's characterisation of a Menomini Indian man in the US who he believed to have 'deficient' knowledge of Menomini and English:

> White Thunder, a man around 40, speaks less English than Menomini, and that is a strong indictment, for his Menomini is atrocious. His vocabulary is small, his inflections are often barbarous, he constructs sentences of a few threadbare models. He may be said to speak no language tolerably.
>
> (Bloomfield, 1927: 395)

This is one of the early statements of a view which became fashionable in educational circles; namely, that it was possible for bilinguals not to acquire full competence in any of the languages they spoke. Such an individual was said to be 'semilingual'. They were believed to have linguistic deficits in six areas of language (see Hansegard, 1975; Skutnabb-Kangas, 1981):

1   Size of vocabulary;
2   Correctness of language;
3   Unconscious processing of language;
4   Language creation;
5   Mastery of the functions of language;
6   Meanings and imagery.

It is significant that the term 'semilingualism' emerged in connection with the study of language skills of people belonging to ethnic minority groups. Research which provided evidence in support of the notion of 'semilingualism' was conducted in Scandinavia and North America and was concerned with accounting for the educational outcomes of submersion programmes where minority children were taught through the medium of the majority language. However, these studies, like the ones conducted by Saer, had serious methodological flaws and the conclusions reached by the researchers were misguided.

- First, the educational tests which were used to measure language proficiencies and to differentiate between people were insensitive to the qualitative aspects of languages and to the great range of language competences. Language may be specific to a context; a person may be competent in some contexts but not in others.
- Second, bilingual children are still in the process of developing their languages. It is unfair to compare them to some idealised adults. Their language skills change over time.
- Third, the comparison with monolinguals is also unfair. It is important to distinguish if bilinguals are 'naturally' qualitatively and quantitatively different from monolinguals in their use of the two languages, i.e. as a function of being bilingual.
- Fourth, if languages are relatively underdeveloped, the origins may not be in bilingualism *per se*, but in the economic, political and social conditions that evoke under-development.

The disparaging and belittling overtone of the term 'semilingualism' itself invokes expectations of under-achievement in the bilingual speaker. Thus, rather than highlighting the apparent 'deficits' of bilingual speakers, the more positive approach is to emphasise that, when suitable conditions are provided, languages are easily capable of development beyond the 'semi' state (for a critical analysis of the notion of semilingualism, see Martin-Jones and Romaine, 1986).

One of the specific issues Bloomfield raised in his comments on the language behaviour of members of the Menomini Indians in North America was the frequent mixing of their own language and English. It has been described as 'verbal salad', not particularly appealing but nevertheless harmless, or 'garbage' which is definitively worthless and vulgar. Unfortunately, although switching and mixing of languages occurs in practically all bilingual communities and all bilingual speakers' speech, it is stigmatised as an illegitimate mode of communication, even sometimes by the bilingual speakers themselves. Haugen (1977: 97), for example, reports that a visitor from Norway made the following comment on the speech of the Norwegians in the United States: 'Strictly speaking, it is no language whatever, but a gruesome mixture of Norwegian and English, and often one does not know whether to take it humorously or seriously'. Gumperz (1982: 62–3) reports that some bilingual speakers who mixed languages regularly still believe such behaviour was 'bad manners' or a sign of 'lack of education or improper control of language'. One of the Punjabi–English bilinguals Romaine interviewed said: 'I'm guilty as well in the sense that we speak English more and more and then what happens is that when you speak your own language you get two or three English words in each sentence . . . but I think that's wrong' (Romaine, 1995 (1989): 294).

Attitudes do not, of course, remain constant over time. At a personal level, changes in attitudes may occur when there is some personal reward involved. Speakers of minority languages will be more motivated to maintain and use their languages if they prove to be useful in increasing their employability or social mobility. In some cases, certain jobs are reserved for bilingual speakers only. At the societal level, attitudes towards bilingualism change when the political ideology changes. In California and elsewhere in the south-western United States, for instance, *pocho* and *calo* used to serve as pejorative terms for the Spanish of local Chicanos. With a rise in ethnic consciousness, however, these speech styles have become symbolic of Chicano ethnicity and are now increasingly used in contemporary Chicano literature.

Since the 1960s, there has been a political movement, particularly in the US, advocating language rights. In the US, questions about language rights are widely discussed, not only in college classrooms and language communities but also in government and federal legislatures. Language rights have a history of being tested in US courtrooms. From the early 1920s to the present, there has been a continuous debate in US courts of law regarding the legal status of language minority rights. To gain short-term protection and a medium-term guarantee for minority languages, legal challenges have become an important part of the language rights movement. The legal battles concerned not just minority language vs. majority language contests, but also children vs. schools, parents vs. school boards, state vs. the federal authorities, etc. Whereas minority language activists among the Basques in Spain and the Welsh in Britain have been taken to court by the central government for their actions, US minority language activists have taken the central and regional government to court.

The language rights movement has received some support from organisations such as the United Nations, UNESCO, the Council of Europe and the European Union. Each of these four organisations has declared that minority language groups have the right to maintain their languages. In the European Union, a directive (77/486/EEC) stated that member states should promote the teaching of the mother tongue and the culture of the country of origin in the education of migrant workers' children. The kind of rights, apart from language rights, that minority groups may claim include: protection, membership of their ethnic group and separate existence, non-discrimination and equal treatment, education and information in their ethnic language, freedom to worship, freedom of belief, freedom of movement, employment, peaceful assembly and association, political representation and involvement, and administrative autonomy.

However, real changes in attitudes towards bilingualism will not happen until people recognise, or better still experience, the advantages of being bilingual. Current research suggests that there are at least eight overlapping and interacting benefits for a bilingual person, encompassing communicative, cognitive and cultural advantages (adapted from Baker and Prys Jones, 1998: 6–8):

Communicative advantages

1   *Relationships with parents*: Where parents have differing first languages, the advantage of children becoming bilingual is that they will be able to communicate in each parent's preferred language. This may enable a subtler, finer texture of relationship with the parent. Alternatively they will be able to communicate with parents in one language and with their friends and within the community in a different language.

2   *Extended family relationships*: Being a bilingual allows someone to bridge the generations. When grandparents, uncles, aunts and other relatives in another region speak a language that is different from the local language, the monolingual may be unable to communicate with them. The bilingual has the chance to bridge that generation gap, build closer relationships

with relatives and feel a sense of belonging and rootedness within the extended family.

3   *Community relationships*: A bilingual has the chance to communicate with a wider variety of people than a monolingual. Bilingual children will be able to communicate in the wider community and with school and neighbourhood friends in different languages when necessary.

4   *Transnational communication*: One barrier between nations and ethnic groups tends to be language. Language is sometimes a barrier to communication and to creating friendly relationships of mutual respect. Bilinguals in the home, in the community and in society have the potential for lowering such barriers. Bilinguals can act as bridges within the nuclear and extended family, within the community and across societies.

5   *Language sensitivity*: Being able to move between two languages may lead to more sensitivity in communication. Because bilinguals are constantly monitoring which language to use in different situations, they may be more attuned to the communicative needs of those with whom they talk. Research suggests that bilinguals may be more empathic towards listeners' needs in communication. When meeting those who do not speak their language particularly well, bilinguals may be more patient listeners than monolinguals.

Cultural advantages

6   Another advantage of being a bilingual is having two or more worlds of experience. Bilingualism provides the opportunity to experience two or more cultures. The monolingual may experience a variety of cultures; for example, from different neighbours and communities that use the same language but have different ways of life. The monolingual can also travel to neighbouring countries and experience other cultures as a passive onlooker. However, to penetrate different cultures requires the language of that culture. To participate and become involved in the core of a culture requires a knowledge of the language of that culture.

7   There are also potential economic advantages to being bilingual. A person with two languages may have a wider portfolio of jobs available. As economic trade barriers fall, as international relationships become closer, as unions and partnerships across nations become more widespread, an increasing number of jobs are likely to require a person to be bilingual or multilingual. Jobs in multinational companies, jobs selling and exporting, and employment prospects generated by transnational contact make the future of employment more versatile for bilinguals than monolinguals.

Cognitive advantages

8   More recent research has shown that bilinguals may have some advantages in thinking, ranging from creative thinking to faster progress in early cognitive development and greater sensitivity in communication. For example, bilinguals may have two or more words for each object and idea; sometimes corresponding words in different languages have different connotations. Bilinguals are able to extend the range of meanings, associations and images, and to think more flexibly and creatively. Therefore, a bilingual has the possibility of more awareness of language and more fluency, flexibility and elaboration in thinking than a monolingual.

It would be misleading to suggest that there is no disadvantage to bilingualism. Some problems, both social and individual, may be falsely attributed to bilingualism. For instance, when bilingual children exhibit language or personality problems, bilingualism is sometimes blamed. Problems of social unrest may unfairly be attributed to the presence of two or more languages in a community. However, the real possible disadvantages of bilingualism tend to be temporary. For example, bilingual families may be spending significantly more of their time and making much greater efforts to maintain two languages and bring up children bilingually. Some bilingual children may find it difficult to cope with the school curriculum in either language for a short period of time. However, these are challenges that bilingual people have to face. The individual, cognitive, social, cultural, intellectual and economic advantages bilingualism brings to a person make all the efforts worthwhile.

A more complex problem associated with bilingualism is the question of identity of a bilingual. If a child has both a French and an English parent and speaks each language fluently, is he or she French, English or Anglo-French? if a child speaks English and a minority language such as Welsh, is he or she Welsh, English, British, European or what? It has to be said that for many bilingual people, identity is not a problem. While speaking two languages, they are resolutely identified with one ethnic or cultural group. For example, many bilinguals in Wales see themselves as Welsh first, possibly British next but not English. Others, however, find identity a real, problematic issue. Some immigrants, for instance, desperately want to lose the identity of their native country and become assimilated and identified with the new home country, while some others want to develop a new identity and feel more comfortable with being culturally hyphenated, such as Chinese–American, Italian–Australian, Swedish–Finn or Anglo-French. Yet identity crises and conflicts are never static. Identities change and evolve over time, with varying experiences, interactions and collaborations within and outside a language group.

Bilingualism is not a static and unitary phenomenon. It is shaped in different ways, and it changes depending on a variety of historical, cultural, political, economic, environmental, linguistic, psychological and other factors. People's attitudes towards bilingualism will also change as the society progresses and as our understanding of bilingual speakers' knowledge and skills grows. However, one thing is certain: more and more people in the world will become bilinguals, and bilingualism will stay as long as humankind walks the earth.

The description of bilingualism

WILLIAM F. MACKEY

BILINGUALISM IS NOT A phenomenon of language; it is a characteristic of its use. It is not a feature of the code but of the message. It does not belong to the domain of "langue" but of "parole".[1]

If language is the property of the group, bilingualism is the property of the individual. An individual's use of two languages supposes the existence of two different language communities; it does not suppose the existence of a bilingual community. The bilingual community can only be regarded as a dependent collection of individuals who have reasons for being bilingual. A self-sufficient bilingual community has no reason to remain bilingual, since a closed community in which everyone is fluent in two languages could get along just as well with one language. As long as there are different monolingual communities, however, there is likelihood of contact between them; this contact results in bilingualism.

The concept of bilingualism has become broader and broader since the beginning of the twentieth century. It was long regarded as the equal mastery of two languages; and this is the definition still found in certain glossaries of linguistics, e.g., "Qualité d'un sujet ou d'une population qui se sert couramment de deux langues, sans aptitude marquée pour l'une plutôt que pour l'autre" (Marouzeau, 1951). Bloomfield considered bilingualism as "the native-like control of two languages" (Bloomfield, 1933: 56). This was broadened by Haugen to the ability to produce "complete meaningful utterances in the other language" (Haugen, 1953: vol. 1, p. 7). And it has now been suggested that the concept be further extended to include simply "passive-knowledge" of the written language or any "contact with possible models in a second language and the ability to use these in the environment of the native language" (Diebold, 1961: 111). This broadening of the concept of bilingualism is due to realization that the point at which a speaker of a second language becomes bilingual is either arbitrary or impossible to determine. It seems obvious, therefore, that if we are to study the phenomenon of bilingualism we are forced to consider it as something entirely relative (Mackey, 1956: 8). We must, moreover, include the use not only of two languages, but of any number of languages (Mackey, 1959). We shall therefore consider bilingualism as the alternate use of two or more languages by the same individual.

What does this involve? Since bilingualism is a relative concept, it involves the question of DEGREE. How well does the individual know the languages he uses? In other words, how bilingual is he? Second, it involves the question of FUNCTION. What does he use his languages for? What role have his languages played in his total pattern of behaviour? Third, it includes the question of ALTERNATION. To what extent does he alternate between his languages? How does he change from one language to the other, and under what conditions? Fourth, it includes the question of INTERFERENCE. How well does the bilingual keep his languages apart? To what extent does he fuse them together? How does one of his languages influence his use of the other? Bilingualism is a behavioural pattern of mutually modifying linguistic practices varying in degree, function, alternation, and interference. It is in terms of these four inherent characteristics that bilingualism may be described.[2]

Degree

The first and most obvious thing to do in describing a person's bilingualism is to determine how bilingual he is. To find this out it is necessary to test his skill in the use of each of his languages, which we shall label A and B. This includes separate tests for comprehension and expression in both the oral and written forms of each language, for the bilingual may not have an equal mastery of all four basic skills in both languages. He may indeed be able to understand both languages equally well; but he may be unable to speak both of them with equal facility. Since the language skills of the bilingual may include differences in comprehension and expression in both the spoken and written forms, it is necessary to test each of these skills separately if we are to get a picture of the extent of his bilingualism. If, however, we are only interested in determining his bilingualism rather than in describing it, other forms of tests are possible: word-detection tests, word-association and picture-vocabulary tests, for example, have been used for this purpose (Peal and Lambert, 1962: 76).

The bilingual's mastery of a skill, however, may not be the same at all linguistic levels. He may have a vast vocabulary but a poor pronunciation, or a good pronunciation but imperfect grammar. In each skill, therefore, it is necessary to discover the bilingual's mastery of the phonology (or graphics), the grammar, the vocabulary, the semantics, and the stylistics of each language. What has to be described is proficiency in two sets of related variables, skills, and levels. This may be presented as in Table 1.1.

Table 1.1   Degree

	Levels									
	Phonological–graphic		Grammatical	Lexical			Semantic		Stylistic	
Skills	*A*	*B*	*A*	*B*	*A*	*B*	*A*	*B*	*A*	*B*
Listening										
Reading										
Speaking										
Writing										

If we consider Table 1.1, it is easy to see how the relation between skills and levels may vary from bilingual to bilingual. At the phonological–graphic level, for example, we have the case of the Croatian who understands spoken Serbian but is unable to read the Cyrillic script in which it is written. At the grammatical level, it is common to find bilinguals whose skill in the use of the grammatical structures of both languages cannot match their knowledge of the vocabularies. At the lexical level it is not unusual to find bilinguals whose reading vocabulary in Language B is more extensive than it is in Language A, and far beyond their speaking vocabulary in either language. At the semantic level a bilingual may be able to express his meaning in some areas better in one language than he can in the other. A bilingual technician who normally speaks Language A at home and speaks Language B indifferently at work may nevertheless be able to convey his meaning much better in Language B whenever he is talking about his specialty. Finally, a bilingual's familiarity with the stylistic range of each language is very likely to vary with the subject of discourse.

To get an accurate description of the degree of bilingualism it is necessary to fill in the above framework with the results of tests. Types and models of language tests have now been developed.[3] On these models it is possible to design the necessary tests for each of the languages used by the bilingual in the dialects which he uses.

Function

The degree of proficiency in each language depends on its function, that is, on the uses to which the bilingual puts the language and the conditions under which he has used it. These may be external or internal.

External functions

The external functions of bilingualism are determined by the number of areas of contact and by the variation of each in duration, frequency, and pressure. The areas of contact include all media through which the languages were acquired and used: the language-usage of the home, the community, the school, and the mass media of radio, television, and the printed word. The amount of influence of each of these on the language habits of the bilingual depends on the duration, frequency, and pressure of the contact. These may apply to two types of activity: either comprehension (C) alone, or expression (E), as well. These variables plotted against the areas and points of contact give Table 1.2.

If we examine Table 1.2 we note that it lists a number of contact areas and points, each of which appears opposite a number of columns of variables. Let us first consider the contacts.

Contacts

The bilingual's language contacts may be with the languages used in the home, in the community, in the school, in the mass media of communication, and in his correspondence.

Home languages

The language or languages of the home may differ from all or any of the other areas of contact. Within the home the language of the family may differ from that of its domestics and tutors. Some families encourage bilingualism by engaging a domestic worker or governess who speaks another language to the children. Others send their children as domestic workers into foreign families for the purpose of enabling them to master the second language. This is a common practice in a number of bilingual countries. Another practice is the temporary exchange of children between families speaking different languages. There are even agencies for this purpose.[4] Some families who speak a language other than that of the community insist on keeping it as the language of the home.

Within the family itself the main language of one member may be different from that of the other members. This language may be used and understood by the other members; or it may simply be understood and never used, as is the practice of certain Canadian Indian [i.e. Native American] families where the children address their parents in English and receive replies in the native Indian language of the parents.

In families where one of the parents knows a second language, this language may be used as one of two home languages. Studies of the effects of such a practice have been made by Ronjat (1913), Pavlovitch (1920), and Leopold (1939–49) to test the theory that two languages can be acquired for the same effort as one. Each

Table 1.2 Variables plotted against areas and points of contact

Contacts	Variables				Pressure															
	Duration				Frequency				Economic				Administrative				Cultural				...
	A		B		A		B		A		B		A		B		A		B		...
	C	E	C	E	C	E	C	E	C	E	C	E	C	E	C	E	C	E	C	E	...
1. Home																					
Father																					
Mother																					
Siblings																					
Other relatives																					
Domestics, etc.																					
2. Community																					
Neighbourhood																					
Ethnic group																					
Church group																					
Occupation group																					
Recreation group																					
3. School																					
Single medium																					
Dual media:																					
Parallel																					
Divergent																					
Subjects:																					
Private tuition																					
Group																					
Individual																					
Self																					
4. Mass media																					
Radio																					
Television																					
Cinema																					
Recordings																					
Newspapers																					
Books																					
Magazines																					
5. Correspondence																					

Additional Pressure columns continuing to the right: Political (A, B), Military (A, B), Historical (A, B), Religious (A, B), Demographic (A, B) — each with C E sub-columns.

experiment used Grammont's formula "une personne – une langue", (Grammont, 1902), whereby the same person always spoke the same language to the child, the mother limiting herself to one of the languages and the father to the other.

Community languages

These include the languages spoken in the bilingual's neighbourhood, his ethnic group, his church group, his occupation group, and his recreation group.

1   *Neighbourhood*: A child is surrounded by the language of the neighbourhood into which he is born, and this often takes the place of the home as the most important influence on his speech. A corrective to this has been the periods of foreign residence which bilinguals have long found necessary in order to maintain one of their languages.

2   *Ethnic group*: The extent to which the bilingual is active in the social life of his ethnic group is a measure of the possibility of maintaining his other language. This may be the most important factor in a community with no other possible contact with the language.

3   *Church group*: Although church groups are often connected with ethnic groups, it is possible for the bilingual to associate with one and ignore the other. Although he may attend none of the activities of his ethnic group, he may yet bring his children to the foreign church or Sunday school, where sermons and instructions are given in a language which is not that of the community.

4   *Occupation group*: The bilingual's occupation may oblige him to work with a group using a language different from that which he uses at home. Or, if he lives in a bilingual city like Montreal, the language of his place of work may be different from that of the neighbourhood in which he lives. Or, if he is engaged in one of the service occupations, he may have to use both his languages when serving the public.

5   *Recreation group*: A bilingual may use one of his languages with a group of people with whom he takes part in sports, in music, or in other pastimes. Or he may attend a club in which the language spoken is not that of his home or his neighbourhood. Or the foreign children in a unilingual school may be in the habit of playing together, thus maintaining the use of their native language.

School languages

A person's language contact in school may be with a language taught as a subject or with a language used as a medium of instruction. Both may be found in three instructional media: single, dual, and private.

1   *Single medium*: Some parents will go to a lot of trouble and expense to send their children to a school in which the instruction is given in another language: schools in foreign countries, foreign ethnic communities, or bilingual areas (Mackey, 1952).

In bilingual areas, the language of single-medium schools must be determined by the application of some sort of language policy. This may be based on one of the four following principles: nationality, territoriality, religious affiliation, or ethnic origin.

According to the principle of nationality, a child must always take his schooling in the language of the country, regardless of his ethnic origin, religious affiliation, or of the language which he speaks at home. This is the policy of most of the public school systems in the United States.

According to the principle of territoriality, the child gets his schooling in the language of the community in which he happens to be living. This is the practice in Switzerland, for example.

The principle of religious affiliation may be applied in countries where linguistic divisions coincide to a great extent with religious ones. A sectarian school system may take these language divisions into account. In Quebec, for example, there are French Catholic schools, English Protestant schools, and English Catholic schools. The French Protestants in some areas may not be numerous enough to warrant a separate school system, in which case a French Protestant family might send their children to an English Protestant school rather than to a French Catholic one.

The principle of ethnic origin takes into account the home language of the child. In countries where bilingual communities are closely inter-mingled the policy may be to have the child do his schooling in the language which he normally speaks at home. This is the policy, for example, in many parts of South Africa.

2   *Dual media*: The bilingual may have attended schools in which two languages were used as media of instruction. Dual-media schools may be of different types. In their use of two languages they may adopt a policy of parallelism or one of divergence.

Parallel media schools are based on the policy that both languages be put on an equal footing and used for the same purposes and under the same circumstances. The parallelism may be built into the syllabus or into the time-table. If it is part of the syllabus, the same course, lesson, or teaching point will be given in both languages. This has been the practice in certain parts of Belgium. If the parallelism is built into the time-table, the school makes exclusive use of one of the languages during a certain unit of time – day, week, or month – at the end of which it switches to the other language for an equal period, so that there is a continual alternation from one language to the other. This is the practice of certain military and technical schools in Canada.

Another type of dual-media school is governed by a policy of divergence, the use of the two languages for different purposes. Some subjects may be taught in one language, and some in the other. This is the practice in certain parts of Wales. In describing the influences of such practices on a person's bilingualism it is important to determine which subjects are taught in which language. If one of the languages is used for religion, history, and literature, the influence is likely to be different from what it would be if this language were used to teach arithmetic, geography, and biology instead (Mackey and Noonan, 1952).

3   *Private tuition*: Schooling may be a matter of private instruction, individually or in small groups. This may be in a language other than that of the community. The second language may be used as a medium of instruction or simply taught as a subject.

Some people may prefer to perfect their knowledge of the second language by engaging a private tutor in the belief that they thus have a longer period of direct contact with the language than they would otherwise have.

Finally, there is the bilingual who tries to improve his knowledge of the second language through self-instruction. This may involve the use of books and sound recordings (see below).

Mass media

Radio, television, the cinema, recordings, newspapers, books, and magazines are powerful media in the maintenance of bilingualism. Access to these media may be the main factor in maintaining one of the languages of a bilingual, especially if his other language is the only one spoken in the area. Regular attendance at foreign film programmes and the daily reading of foreign books and magazines may be the only factors in maintaining a person's comprehension of a foreign language which he once knew. Reading is often the only contact that a person may have with his second language. It is also the most available.

Correspondence

Regular correspondence is another way by which the bilingual may maintain his skill in the use of another language. He may, for business reasons, have to correspond regularly in a language other than the one he uses at home or at work. Or it may be family reasons that give him an occasion to write or read letters in one of his languages. The fact that immigrants to the New World have been able to correspond regularly with friends and relatives in Europe is not to be neglected as a factor in the maintenance of their native languages.

Variables

Contacts with each of the above areas may vary in duration, frequency, and pressure. They may also vary in the use of each language for comprehension (C) only, or for both comprehension and expression (E).

Duration

The amount of influence of any area of contact on the bilingualism of the individual depends on the duration of the contact. A 40-year-old bilingual who has spent all his life in a foreign neighbourhood is likely to know the language better than one who has been there for only a few years. A language taught as a school subject is likely to give fewer contact hours than is one which is used as a medium of instruction.

Frequency

The duration of contact is not significant, however, unless we know its frequency. A person who has spoken to his parents in a different language for the past 20 years may have seen them on an average of only a few hours a month, or he may have spoken with them on an average of a few hours a day. Frequency for the spoken language may be measured in average contact-hours per week or month; for the written language it may be measured in average number of words.

Pressure

In each of the areas of contact, there may be a number of pressures which influence the bilingual in the use of one language rather than the other. These may be economic, administrative, cultural, political, military, historical, religious, or demographic.

1   *Economic*: For speakers of a minority language in an ethnic community, the knowledge of the majority language may be an economic necessity. Foreign parents may even insist on making the majority language that of the home, in an effort to prevent their children from becoming economically under-privileged. Contrariwise, economic pressure may favour the home language, especially if the mastery of it has become associated with some ultimate monetary advantage.

2   *Administrative*: Administrative workers in some areas are required to master a second language. A bilingual country may require that its civil servants be fluent in the official languages of the country. Some countries may require that foreign service personnel be capable of using the language of the country in which they serve. A few governments have been in the practice of granting an annual bonus to the civil servant for each foreign language he

succeeds in mastering or maintaining; this is the case in some branches of the German Civil Service.

3   *Cultural*: In some countries, it may be essential, for cultural reasons, for any educated person to be fluent in one or more foreign languages. Greek and Latin were long the cultural languages of the educated European. Today it is more likely to be French, English, or German. The quantity and quality of printed matter available in these languages constitute a cultural force which an educated person cannot afford to ignore.

4   *Political*: The use of certain languages may be maintained by the pressure of political circumstances. This may be due to the geographical contiguity of two countries or to the fact that they are on especially friendly terms. Or the pressure may be due to the influence of the political prestige of a great world power. Political dominance may result in the imposition of foreign languages, as is the case for certain colonial languages. After many years of such dominance the foreign colonial language may become the dominant one, develop a regional standard, and be used as the official language of the country.

5   *Military*: A bilingual who enters the armed forces of his country may be placed in situations which require him to hear or speak his second language more often than he otherwise would. People serving in a foreign army must learn something of the language which the army uses. The fact that two countries make a military treaty may result in large-scale language learning such as that witnessed in Allied countries during the Second World War. Military occupation has also resulted in second language learning, either by the populace, by the military, or by both.

6   *Historical*: Which languages the bilingual learns and the extent to which he must learn them may have been determined by past historical events. If the language of a minority has been protected by treaty, it may mean that the minority can require its children to be educated in their own language. The exact position of the languages may be determined by the past relations between two countries. The important position of English in India is attributable to the historical role of Great Britain in that country.

7   *Religious*: A bilingual may become fluent in a language for purely religious reasons. A person entering a religious order may have to learn Latin, Greek, Coptic, Sanskrit, Arabic, or Old Church Slavonic, depending on the religion, rite, or sect of the particular order into which he enters. Some languages, also for religious reasons, may be required in the schools which the bilingual may have attended; Latin and Hebrew are examples of such languages.

8   *Demographic*: The number of persons with whom the bilingual has the likelihood of coming into contact is a factor in the maintenance of his languages. A language spoken by some five hundred million people will exert a greater

pressure than one used by only a few thousand. But number is not the only factor; distribution may be equally important. Chinese, for example, may have a greater number of native speakers than does English; but the latter has a greater distribution, used, as it is, as an official and administrative language in all quarters of the globe.

Internal functions

Bilingualism is not only related to external factors; it is also connected with internal ones. These include non-communicative uses, like internal speech, and the expression of intrinsic aptitudes, which influence the bilingual's ability to resist or profit by the situations with which he comes in contact.

Uses

A person's bilingualism is reflected in the internal uses of each of his languages. These may be tabulated as in Table 1.3. Some bilinguals may use one and the same language for all sorts of inner expression. This language has often been identified as the dominant language of the bilingual. But such is by no means always the case. Other bilinguals use different languages for different sorts of internal expression. Some count in one language and pray in another; others have been known to count in two languages but to be able to reckon only in one. It would be possible to determine these through a well-designed questionnaire.

Table 1.3   Internal uses

	Auto-language	
Uses	A	B
Counting		
Reckoning		
Praying		
Cursing		
Dreaming		
Diary-writing		
Note-taking		

Aptitude

In describing bilingualism it is important to determine all those factors which are likely to influence the bilingual's aptitude in the use of his languages or which in turn may be influenced by it. These may be listed as follows:

1	Sex	4	Memory
2	Age	5	Language attitude
3	Intelligence	6	Motivation

Sex

If sex is a factor in language development, as past research into the issue seems to indicate, it is also a factor in bilingualism (see Peal and Lambert, 1962).

Age

Persons who become bilingual in childhood may have characteristics of proficiency and usage different from those who become bilingual as adults. Studies of cases where two languages were learned simultaneously in childhood have given us some indication of the process (see Ronjat, 1913; Pavlovitch, 1920; Leopold, 1939–49). Although Leopold's (1939–49) study reveals an effort on the part of the child to weld two phoneme systems into one, it does not indicate any lasting effect on either language. It does, however, show a great deal of forgetting on the part of the child. Indeed, the child's reputed ability to remember is matched by his ability to forget. For him, bilingualism may simply mean a transition period from one native language to another. Children can transfer from one mother-tongue to another in a matter of months. This has been demonstrated by Tits (1959: 36) in his experiment with a six-year-old Spanish girl who was suddenly placed in a completely French environment and, after only 93 days, seems to have lost her Spanish completely; in less than a year, she had a knowledge of French equal to that of the neighbourhood children.

The child's adaptability has been related to the physiology of the human brain. Penfield and other neurologists have put forth theories to explain the child's linguistic flexibility (Penfield and Roberts, 1959). Before the age of nine, the child's brain seems particularly well suited to language learning, but after this age the speech areas become "progressively stiff" and the capacity to learn languages begins to decrease. Some experienced teachers and psychologists, however, have claimed that there is no decline in language-learning capacity up to the age of 21 (West, 1958).

Intelligence

We are here concerned more with the relation of intelligence to bilingualism than with the influence of bilingualism on intelligence (Darcy, 1953). A number of testable mental traits such as figure-grouping ability, number, space and pattern perception, and others have already been tested on groups of bilinguals (see Peal and Lambert, 1962).

Although it seems safe to include intelligence as a factor in bilingualism, we have as yet been unable to discover its relative importance. Experimental research into the problem has mostly been limited to selected samples of persons of the same intellectual level and has often been based on the assumption that the ability to speak is simply a motor-skill which can be measured by tests of imitation and reading aloud. One would expect intelligence to play some sort of role, nevertheless, in such a skill as comprehension, where a bilingual's reasoning ability and general knowledge should help him guess meanings from context.

Memory

If memory is a factor in imitation, it is also a factor in bilingualism; for the auditory memory span for sounds immediately after hearing them is related to the ability to learn languages. An analogy may be taken from the learning of sound-codes like those used in telegraphy. It has been demonstrated that the span of auditory comprehension is the main difference between the beginner in telegraphy and the expert; whereas the beginner can handle only one word at a time, the expert can deal with 10, keeping them all in his memory before interpreting them (Taylor, 1943). As his degree of proficiency increases, the bilingual keeps more and more words in his memory before deciding on the meaning of an utterance. There is conflicting evidence, however, on the exact role of rote memory in language learning.

Attitude

The attitude of a bilingual towards his languages and towards the people who speak them will influence his behaviour within the different areas of contact in which each language is used. It may in turn be influenced by his hearer's attitude towards him as a foreign speaker. In certain situations he may avoid using one of his languages because he is ashamed of his accent. In other situations he may prefer to use his second language because his first language may be that of an unpopular country or community. It has been said that some speakers of minority languages even harbour an attitude of disrespect toward their first language and an admiration for their second.

Because of such influences as these, the attitude of the speaker may be regarded as an important factor in the description of his bilingualism. The attitudes of bilinguals towards their languages have been tested directly by questionnaire and indirectly by having the bilinguals list traits of speakers whose recorded accent reveals their ethnic origin (Lambert *et al.*, 1958).

Motivation

It seems obvious that the motivation for acquiring the first language is more compelling than the motivation for learning a second. For once the vital purposes of communication have been achieved, the reasons for repeating the effort in another language are less urgent. In the case of simultaneous childhood bilingualism, however, the need for learning both languages may be made equally compelling. This may not be so for the person who becomes bilingual as an adult. Yet, a need or desire of the adult to master a second language may be strong enough to enable him to devote the necessary time and energy to the process of becoming bilingual.

Alternation

The function of each language in total behaviour and the degree to which the bilingual and his hearers have mastered both languages determine the amount of alternation which takes place from one language to the other.

The readiness with which a bilingual changes from one language to the other depends on his fluency in each language and on its external and internal functions. There seems to be a difference in alternation, for example, between bilinguals brought up on Grammont's "une personne – une langue" formula and bilinguals conditioned at an early age to speak two different languages to the same person (Smith, 1935).

Under what conditions does alternation from one language to another take place? What are the factors involved? The three main factors seem to be topic, person, and tension. Each of these may vary both the rate of alternation and the proportion of each language used in a given situation – oral or written. We may present the variables as in Table 1.4. If we examine the alternation in the speech or writings of bilinguals we notice that it may vary in both rate and proportion. The switch may occur only once, or it may take place every few sentences, within sentences, or within clauses. The rate may be measured by establishing a ratio between the number of units in the stretch of text examined and the number of switches which take place.

Alternation in the speech or writings of a bilingual will also vary in proportion. For example, a French–English bilingual when speaking English may, in a given situation, switch from time to time to French. But the amount of French used may be less than 5 per cent of the entire text. On the other hand, his interlocutor, who switches less often, but for longer stretches, may use as much as 50 per cent French in his replies.

Table 1.4   Alternations

	Topics				Persons				Tensions			
	1	*2*	*3*	*4*	*1*	*2*	*3*	*4*	*1*	*2*	*3*	*4*
Rate:												
Oral												
Written												
	A B A B A B A B				*A B A B A B A B*				*A B A B A B A B*			
Proportion:												
Oral												
Written												

Rate and proportion of alternation may vary greatly in the same individual according to the topic about which he is speaking, the person he is speaking to, and the tension of the situation in which he speaks. A German–English bilingual speaking in English to a close friend who he knows understands German may permit himself to lapse into German from time to time in order to be able to express himself with greater ease. On the other hand, when speaking to a person with whom he is less well acquainted he may avoid the use of German switches except when forced to speak about topics which his English does not adequately cover. Or his control of English may break down and he may switch frequently to German only when speaking in a state of tension due to excitement, anger, or fatigue.

Interference

The foregoing characteristics of degree, function, and alternation determine the interference of one language with another in the speech of bilinguals. Interference is the use of features belonging to one language while speaking or writing another.

The description of interference must be distinguished from the analysis of language borrowing. The former is a feature of "parole"; the latter of "langue". The one is individual and contingent; the other is collective and systematic. In language borrowing we have to do with integration (Haugen, 1956: 40); features of one language are used as if they were part of the other. These foreign features are used by monolingual speakers who may know nothing of the language from which such features originated. The loans, however, may be integrated into only one of the dialects of the language and not the others. If loan-words are integrated into the French of Switzerland, for example, they do not necessarily become part of the

French of Belgium. And the loan-words of Belgium are not necessarily those of Canada; and in Canada, the loans current in Acadian are not necessarily those of the French of Quebec. Indeed, the integration of borrowed features may be limited to the language of a village community. A good example of this may be found by studying the varieties of German spoken in the multilingual Banat, where German ethnic groups are scattered among non-German language groups speaking Hungarian, Serbian, and Rumanian. If we look at the use of the article among the Banat Germans we find that it may vary from village to village. One German village may use *die Butter*, while another village may use *der Butter;* one village may use *das Auto*, while another may use *der Auto*. In some cases, the borrowed feature may be integrated into the language of a section of a village. No matter how small the area concerned, a borrowed feature may be distinguished by its integration into the speech of the community.

In contradistinction to the consistency in use of borrowed features in the speech of the community is the vacillation in the use of foreign features by its bilingual individuals. In the speech of bilinguals the pattern and amount of interference is not the same at all times and under all circumstances. The interference may vary with the medium, the style, the register, and the context which the bilingual happens to be using.

The medium used may be spoken or written. Bilinguals seem to resist interference when writing to a friend more than they do when speaking to him.

Interference also varies with the style of discourse used, e.g., descriptive, narrative, conversational, etc. The type and amount of interference noted in the recounting of an anecdote may differ considerably from that noted in the give-and-take of everyday conversation.

Interference may also vary according to the social role of the speaker in any given case. This is what the Edinburgh School has called REGISTER.[5] A bilingual may make sure that all his words are French if he is broadcasting a French speech over the radio; but at the same time he may be quite unconscious of many cases of syntactic interference which have crept into his speech. If, however, he is telling the contents of the speech to his drinking partner, he may be far less particular about interlarding his account with non-French words; yet the proportion of syntactic interference may be considerably less.

Within each register, there are a number of possible contexts, each of which may affect the type and amount of interference. The bilingual may be speaking to the above drinking partner in the presence of his superiors or in the company of his colleagues.

In each of these contexts the interference may vary from situation to situation. A French–Canadian businessman just back from a sales conference in Atlantic City will tell his friends about it with more English interference immediately upon his return than will be noticed when he recounts the same events three months later.

In the last analysis, interference varies from text to text. It is the text, therefore, within a context or situation used at a specific register in a certain style and medium of a given dialect, that is the appropriate sample for the description of interference. Since each text may vary in length, this also must be taken into account if, in addition to the different sorts of interference, we are to get an idea of the proportion of each sort and the total percentage of interference.

In each text, or sample of speech, we analyse the interference of only one of the languages with the predominant language or dialect. If the predominant language is French, we look for elements which are foreign to the particular dialect of French used. We look for the elements which have not been integrated into the dialect.

The first thing to do, therefore, in analysing a case of interference in a text is to identify its model[6] in the dialect of the language from which it comes. This model may be from the cultural, semantic, lexical, grammatical, phonological, phonetic, or graphic levels of the dialect. At each of these levels, what is imported may be a separate item or an arrangement of items; in other words, it may be a unit or a structure. By discovering whether the imported form is a unit or a structure and then identifying the level to which it belongs, we are able to locate the TYPE of interference. This may occur once in the text; or it may recur many times; each time it recurs it is a TOKEN of interference and should be indicated as such.

After having identified the model in the interfering language we compare it with its replica in the text. This enables us to determine the sort of substitution which has taken place. It may be a substitution in level or in structure. A substitution in level takes place when, for example, the foreign word is modified at the phonological level by an adaptation of its phonemes to those of the text. A substitution in structure takes place when a structure in the model becomes a unit in the replica, or a unit in the model becomes a structure in the replica.

These interrelated factors appear in Table 1.5 in tabulated form. If we examine Table 1.5 we notice that it distinguishes two main treatments of interference: the sort of material which the bilingual imports into his speech (importation) and what he does with it (substitution).[7]

The importation columns list only the units and structures of the text which are attributable exclusively to the bilingual's use of another language. In each case it is necessary to identify the model and to compare it, not with the replica, but with all possible equivalents in the dialect of the monolingual community to which the text under analysis belongs. If the text is in the French of Quebec, any English elements are compared with equivalents in the French of the same area, including English loans that have already been integrated into the speech of the area. Only in this way can we distinguish between integration and interference, between the foreign elements existing in the dialect and those attributable to the speaker, between the influences of language contact in "langue", and the effects of bilingualism on "parole".

Table 1.5 Interference

Language ....
Dialect ....
Medium g ....
Style ....
Context ....
Situation ....

Length of text ....
A—B .... √
B—A ....

Levels	Importation				Substitution											Proportion	
	Unit		*Structure*		*Units*					*Structures*						*Percentages*	
	Type	*Token*	*Type*	*Token*	*C*	*S*	*L*	*G*	*P*	*C*	*S*	*L*	*G*	*P*		*Units*	*Structures*
1. Cultural																	
Phenomena																	
Experience																	
2. Semantic																	
3. Lexical																	
4. Grammatical																	
Parts of Speech																	
Grammatical categories																	
Function																	
Forms																	
5. Phonological																	
Intonation																	
Rhythm																	
Catenation																	
Articulation																	

The description of interference requires three procedures:

1   the discovery of exactly what foreign element is introduced by the speaker into his speech;
2   the analysis of what he does with it – his substitutions and modifications; and
3   a measurement of the extent to which foreign elements replace native elements.

The first of these procedures consists in identifying the foreign element, checking it with its counterparts in the monolingual speech of the area, and discovering the model in the foreign language responsible for the interference. This procedure depends on an accurate and complete description of the two languages involved and on an analysis of the differences between them. Unfortunately there are very few differential descriptions available (Gage, 1961); most of those in existence are far too sketchy for the sort of analysis of the cultural, semantic, lexical, grammatical, and phonological levels which we shall now exemplify.

Cultural interference

Although cases of interference may be found in the speech of the bilingual, their causes may be found, not in his other language, but in the culture which it reflects. The foreign element may be the result of an effort to express new phenomena or new experience in a language which does not account for them.

Phenomena include the result of the introduction of unfamiliar objects, obliging the bilingual speaker to use whatever resources his two languages put at his disposal. He may have to talk about such things as hot-dogs and cornflakes, for which the dialect he is speaking may have no equivalent. Such unit phenomena are to be distinguished from the structure or patterning of phenomena occasioned, for example, by the introduction of a new technology such as a railway system, or a culture pattern based on the automobile, with its motels, filling stations, and kerb-service.

In addition to new phenomena, cultural interference includes new types of experience such as the introduction of the custom of greeting and thanking into the speech habits of Amerindian [i.e. Native American] bilinguals. Here again we must distinguish between the units of experience and their structure. For example, both German and English have behaviour units for greeting and thanking; but these are patterned differently. The German *Bitte*, for instance, includes not only English *Please* but parts of English *Thanks, Not at all, Pardon*, or silence. A case of cultural interference in the behavioural structure of experience might consequently appear in the speech of X, a German–English bilingual, as shown in Table 1.6.

Table 1.6   Comparing English and German

	English counterpart	German model	English replica
X	Here's a seat.	Bitte.	Please.
Y	Thanks!	Danke!	Thanks!
X	(silence)	Bitte.	Please.

Semantic interference

Cultural interference due to new phenomena or experience is to be distinguished from semantic interference, which is due to familiar phenomena and experience being classified or structured differently in the other language. The classic example here is the division of the colour spectrum into units. The bilingual speaker has a single experience of colour, but his two languages may have a different number of colour units, some of which may overlap. If the speaker is a Welsh–English bilingual, he will have one unit in Welsh but two units in English for blue and green (= Welsh *glas*) and grey and brown (= Welsh *llwyd*) (Vinay and Darbelnet, 1958: 261). If he is a French–English bilingual he may use *pain brun* (English *brown bread*) for *pain bis*, and *papier brun* (English *brown paper*) for *papier gris* (Darbelnet, 1957). And if he is an English–Spanish bilingual he may be tempted to use *oficina* (English *office*) for a doctor's office (*consulta*), a lawyer's office (*bufete*), an individual office (*despacho*), and a group office (*oficina).*

In addition to the incorporation of new units of classification into the speech of bilinguals, there is the introduction of new semantic structures. Even though the semantic units may be the same in both languages, a foreign way of combining them may be introduced as a new semantic structure. Both English and French, for example, have comparable units for hat (*chapeau*), talk (*parler*), and through (*à travers)*; but when the bilingual speaker uses the figurative *Il parle à travers son chapeau* he introduces into his speech a foreign semantic structure based on the English model *He's talking through his hat*. Similarly, when the German–English bilingual says that *Winter is before the door*, or *He was laughing in his fist*, he is using in his English speech semantic structures based on the German models *Winter steht vor der Tür* in place of the English *Winter is around the corner*, and *Er hat sich ins Fäustchen gelacht* in place of the English *He was laughing up his sleeve*.

Lexical interference

Lexical interference involves the introduction of foreign forms into the speech of the bilingual, either as units or as structures. We must here distinguish between lexical items which have been integrated into the dialect (loan-words) and those which occur in the utterances of a particular bilingual. A Belgian using the word *goal-keeper* in a French-language sports broadcast, or a Frenchman using *goal* (for the same person) may be using an integrated English loan-word; while a Canadian French–English bilingual who listens to his hockey broadcasts in French might prefer the term *gardien de but*, although his compatriot who listens to the same broadcasts in English might from time to time use the word *goalie*, with an anglicized pronunciation. It is this latter case that would constitute an instance of interference.

Resistance to lexical interference results in the elimination of integrated loans, since the bilingual is not always able to make the distinction between what is "accepted" and what is not. It is in this way that bilinguals contribute to the "purification" of the language. The monolingual, on the other hand, being unable to identify the foreign loans, is unable to eliminate them. The use of *gardien de but* and *fin de semaine* for integrated loans like *goal* and *week-end* may be instances of resistance to interference. A study of the vocabulary of French sports broadcasts on the national radio networks of France and Canada might well reveal that the latter's conscious resistance to lexical interference results in a sports vocabulary which is less anglicized.

What applies to isolated lexical units also applies to the grouping of such items into collocations. Here again we must distinguish between integration and interference. An English–French bilingual who does all his shopping in French may, when speaking English at home, use such lexical structures as *gigot d'agneau* instead of *leg of lamb*. Yet this French collocation may never enter the speech of the English-speaking community; indeed, it may never be used by any other English–French bilingual.

Grammatical interference

Grammatical interference includes the introduction into the speech of bilinguals of units and structures of foreign parts of speech, grammatical categories, and function forms.

The interference may involve the creation of new items belonging to a different part of speech. For example when the French–English bilingual says *Je n'ai pas pu le contacter* he is making a new verb out of the French noun *contacte* on the model of the American English *I wasn't able to contact him*.

Two languages often have the same parts of speech, but they may differ considerably in the way they put them together into structures. This is one of the domains of interference of which bilingual speakers are most unconscious. And the extent of such interference varies greatly from region to region. Thus, Acadian bilinguals tend to put more adjectives before the noun in French than do French speakers in other parts of Canada. Some Acadians who can identify these English structures may tend to resist them. But the more complex structures will escape the notice of even the most perceptive Probus. The bilingual who says *une des plus grande jamais vue dans la région* may not notice that he is using the English model *one of the biggest ever seen in the area.*

Grammatical interference also includes the introduction of features from different grammatical categories. The simplest of these is in the category of gender. The bilingual speaker may tend to carry over the gender of one language into that of another, as when the Serbian–German bilingual uses *der* or *dieser Zwiebel* on the model of the Serbian *taj luk.*

Structural interference in grammatical categories has to do with the use of concord and government. When an English–French bilingual says *Vos montagnes sont beaux*, his indifference to concord is influenced by the fact that English has no system of agreement between noun and adjective.

The third type of grammatical interference concerns the function forms of the two languages. Function forms may be free or bound. Free forms include such units as prepositions, conjunctions, determinatives, and so on. A French–English bilingual who says *sur le comité, dans quinze jours*, and *sous étude* is probably modelling these prepositions on those of English, as they appear in such expressions as *on the committee, in fifteen days*, and *under study.* Free forms appear in a number of compulsory structures in some languages which require such things as the marking of classes of nouns by determinatives. This is the case for English, the use of whose function forms differs from that of French. So that when a French–English bilingual uses the article in such expressions as *on the page five*, he is applying the French model *à la page cinq.* Whereas when the Russian–English bilingual leaves out the article in an English sentence like *Where is meeting of committee?* his model is the Russian *Gdje sobranie komitjeta?*

Bound function forms, which result from such inflectional and derivational processes as affixation, internal change, zero modification, and reduplication, are also subject to bilingual interference. When a French–English bilingual says *Those Sunday driver there block my way and I couldn't see*, he is being influenced by the lack of inflected /-s/ for plurals in spoken French. The structure of bound forms may also be carried over by bilingual speakers from one language to another, both in their order and in their boundness (Mackey, 1953). Hungarian–German bilinguals, for example, tend to carry over the patterns of the structure of the Hungarian prepositional prefixes into their German, as the attested individual instance in Table 1.7 illustrates.

Phonological interference

Phonological interference affects the units and structures of intonation, rhythm, catenation, and articulation.

Table 1.7   Comparing German and Hungarian

German counterpart	Hungarian model	German replica
Hat er es zerbrochen? Ja.	Megmondta? Meg.	Hat er es zerbrochen? Zer.
Haben Sie es gesagt? Ja.	Kiment? Ki.	Haben Sie es gesagt? Ge.
Hat er es bekommen? Ja.	Bejött? Be.	Hat er es bekommen? Be.

Intonation

Of all phonological features, intonation is often the most persistent in interference and the most subtle in influence. Welsh and Anglo-Indian bilinguals may often be identified as such only by their intonation, since both the range of their tone units and their patterns are carried over into English.

The tone-groups, or structures of intonation, are more readily identified as causes of interference than are the individual tone units. When the English-French bilingual suggests *C'est 'très 'util*, he is carrying over into his French the implicative intonation structure of English as used suggestively in such sentences as *It's 'very 'useful*.

Rhythm

Not all languages have the same number of stress levels. A speaker of a language with no tertiary level is likely to leave this out of his speech in other languages. Identification of interference at this level, however, is hampered by lack of research findings into the nature and number of stress units.

More is known about rhythm structures, or stress-patterns, as they are often called. Interference in stress patterning can readily be spotted. A French–English bilingual who uses *I think 'so* (for *I 'think so*) and *examina'tion pa'per* or *exami'nation 'paper* (for *exami'nation p'aper*) is obviously transferring his French stress-pattern into English. If interference in stress-patterning is easy to identify, it is not always easy to explain. When the above bilingual also pronounces *deve'lopment* for *de'velopment*, the replica is as far removed from the model as it is from the counterpart.

Catenation

Catenation has to do with the linking together of speech sound into the chain of speech. This includes the units specially used for linking and separating sounds: units of junction and syllabation; it also includes the structures used for this purpose. These differ from language to language.

Like other phonological features, catenation is subject to interference in the speech of bilinguals. This includes interference in junction and syllabation.

Junction

Interference in junction may take the form of the incorporation of foreign junction units into the chain of speech. When a German–English bilingual says /meʔ ai ʔ ask hau ʔ its dʌn/ (*May I ask how it's done?*) he is introducing into his English the glottal junction unit of his German, that is, the German *Grenzsignal* (Trubetzkoy). Conversely, if an English–German bilingual says /viliʲ ist grauʷ abə niçt alt/ (*Willi ist grau, aber nicht alt*) he is placing into the German junction points the palatal and velar glides of his English.

Interference in the mechanism of junction involves the changes which take place when two units are linked. It also involves the direction of such changes. For example, both French and English use assimilation as a linking mechanism, but not in the same direction; so that when a French–English bilingual speaks English he tends to introduce the regressive assimilation of French while ignoring the progressive assimilation of English. Thus, he pronounces the sentence *Take this bag, not those ones* as /teg ðiz bæg, nɔd ðoz wʌns/ instead of /tek ðis bæg, nɔt ðoz wʌnz/.

Syllabation

The division of the chain of speech into syllable units may not be the same in both of the languages spoken by the bilingual. A French–English bilingual may tend to make two syllables out of the English monosyllable *tire* /taiə/ and pronounce it /tajœːr/. When such adaptations become loanwords, however, they sometimes are phonematically homophonous with native words. In such cases the bilingual may endow certain allophonic differences with the distinctive function of phonemes, so that *tire* is pronounced /tajœːr/ and *tailleur* is pronounced /tajœːr/ or /tɔjœːr/.

In syllabic structure the extent of interference depends on the degree of difference between the languages spoken by the bilingual. This may be small, as it is between English and French; or it may be a much wider difference, as it is between English and Japanese. So that when a Japanese–English bilingual says /gurando/ for English *ground*, he is replacing the English syllabic structure /CCVCC/ by the more familiar Japanese /CVCVCV/; similarly, when he says /sisutema/ (/CVCVCVCV/) for English *system* /CVCCVC/.

Articulation

This includes many of the features of interference, popularly identified as comprising a foreign accent. The foreign element may be a unit of articulation, as when a German–English bilingual uses the German velar fricative or uvular trill /ʀ/, as in *ready* pronounced /ʀedi/, instead of the English retroflex. Or the interference may be in the structure of these units of articulation, as when the /-gst-/ structure of English phonemes is replaced by /-gɛst-/ in the speech of certain Spanish–English bilinguals who pronounce *drugstore* as /drɔgɛstɔr/.

Allophones as well as phonemes may be responsible for cases of interference. This is the case when English [ɬ] is introduced into post-vocalic positions in French. An allophone may exist as such in both the languages; or it may exist as an allophone in one and as a phoneme in the other. These may differ, however, in the position in which each may occur. Thus, the nasal trio /m, n, ŋ/ occurs in both English and Spanish; the difference is that, while they all occur finally in English, only /n/ occurs finally in Spanish. This difference produces interference in the speech of Spanish–English bilinguals which results in a tendency to reduce to /rʌn/ or /rɔn/, for example, the pronunciation of the three English words *rum*, *run*, and *rung*. Haugen has elegantly formulated such transfers as ENGLISH/-m, -n, -ŋ > -n/SPANISH.

The identification of foreign units and structures is one thing; the description of what the bilingual does with them is something else. This is the second procedure in the description of interference. It involves the analysis and classification of the different types of substitution made by the speaker.

In introducing a foreign element into his speech, a bilingual may use it exactly as he would in the foreign language, or he may modify it in two ways:

1   by changes in structure;
2   by changes in level.

The change in structure may consist in taking a structure from one language and using it as a unit in the other, or it may consist in taking a unit from one language and using it as a structure in the other. For example, Sicilian–Americans may use the English collocation *son of a gun* as the unit adjective *sonamagonga* in their Italian speech, or reduce highly frequent sentences like *I don't know* and *What's the matter* to units like *aironò* and *vazzumàra* (Menarini, 1939). Contrariwise, a unit in one language may be used as a structure in the other. For example, a unit like the monosyllabic English word *club* may be rendered by a Chinese–English bilingual as three units /kü₁-lö₄-pu₄/, which, if used in Chinese, would be a structure of three signs, meaning "all-joy-section" (Frei, 1936: 79).

Second, the bilingual may change the characteristics of the foreign item at one or more of the following levels: cultural, semantic, lexical, grammatical, or phonological. Only a few examples of the many possibilities may be given here. Let us take the most obvious: the modification of the foreign words. Their introduction into the text (spoken or written) is accounted for under the "importation" column; it now remains for us to list their modifications under the "substitution" column.

The bilingual may modify the foreign word or collocation by changing its cultural content, its meaning, its grammatical role, or its pronunciation. An example of a change in cultural content is the use of cursing and other such expressions as ordinary nouns or content words in the other language, as when the

English expression *God damn it* is used as a French verb *godamer*. This is to be distinguished from a modification in semantic content such as takes place when a Canadian French–English bilingual uses the English word *sport* in French only in the sense of agreeable, cordial, or fair-dealing as when he says *Il est bien sport!* However, the same speaker is altering the foreign word at the grammatical level when he says *Il faut bien que je le toffe encore quelques semaines* (I'll just have to put up with it for another couple of weeks), where the English adjective *tough* is used as a French verb (*toffer*).

Finally, the foreign word may undergo changes at the phonological level. This occurs regularly in the speech of certain types of bilinguals. Like other sorts of interference, this is often the result of what Weinreich has called interlingual identification (Weinreich, 1953: 7), the practice of bilinguals of equating features of one language with those of the other. English speakers of French, for example, will tend to equate the French /e/ with their native /ei/. This equation is applied whenever words like *cours d'été* are pronounced /kuːə dei tei/. The bilingual speaker, however, will not necessarily modify the pronunciation of all the foreign words he introduces. The above bilingual who introduced *sport* and *tough* into his French may well pronounce the first as in English, complete with vocalic *r*, and the second as in French, as [tɔf].

The phonological analysis of foreign words must not be confused with the analysis of foreign accents. This latter begins at the phonological level. When speaking his second language, the bilingual may treat all or some of the foreign phonetic features in terms of those of his first language. In describing what he does we must determine how many of these are changed and the extent to which each is modified. The modification may take the form of equating two distinctive elements of the second language with one distinctive element in the first, as when a French–English bilingual pronounces both English /ʌ/ and English /ɑ/ as /ɔ/, making both *nut* and *knot* homophonous; or he may classify both /d/ and /ð/ as /d̪/, reducing *udder* and *other* to the same pronunciation. The modification may also take the form of the introduction into one language of distinctions which are necessary only in the other, resulting in such effects as the staccato impression created by certain German bilinguals. Third, he may rearrange the features of the second language on the model of his first, as when the German–English bilingual aspirates and devoices all his initial plosives, pronouncing *building* as [pʰildiŋ]. These three types of substitution have been variously called dephonemization, phonemization, and transphonemization (Jakobson) or under-differentiation, overdifferentiation, and reinterpretation (Weinreich).

For the ultimate analysis of what constitutes interference in pronunciation, however, we must go deeper than the phonological level. We can only get a complete picture of what happens by resorting to the use of instrumental phonetics. For such features as the lack of synchronization and variations in muscular tension noted in the speech of certain bilinguals may well be attributable to the habitual use of two languages.

It seems likely that the measurable differences in range of articulatory movement, latitude of variation, distribution of articulatory energy, and synchronization of phonetic variables may become basic elements in the study of interference. A person, for example, whose first language is one with a narrow range of articulatory movement – a language like English, for instance – is likely to narrow the wider articulatory range of a language like German whenever he attempts to speak it; similarly with the relative latitude of variation, distribution of articulatory tension, and synchronization of different speech movements.[8]

The synchronizing of voicing and closure seems to differ from language to language. An example of the extent to which languages may differ may be seen by comparing the amount or voicing of the /b/ in German, English, Spanish, French, and Russian. A bilingual who has a /b/ in his first language which is voiced during only half of the closure time may tend to devoice part of the /b/ of his second language which monolinguals pronounce almost entirely voiced. This sort of interference is illustrated in Table 1.8.

If the text analysed, however, is based not on the spoken but on the written form of the language, we will have to look for evidence of another sort of interference, i.e. graphic interference, the transfer of writing habits from one language to the other. This may take the form of differences in script and differences in spelling. A Serbian–German bilingual with no knowledge of the Roman alphabet may be faced with the alternative of writing his second language in Cyrillic. The use of a foreign writing system may become standardized, however, as is the case when Yiddish is written in Hebrew characters.

The most usual form of graphic interference seems to be in the realm of spelling. The presence of a great number of cognate words in English and French encourages bilinguals to transfer the spelling from one language to the other or to adopt spellings which appear in neither language. Some bilinguals will confuse such pairs as *homage* and *hommage, rhythm* and *rythme, development* and *développement*.

The third procedure in the analysis of interference is a quantitative one. For it is necessary to know, not only the sort of interference which takes place, but also the extent of such interference.

Table 1.8   Illustration of frame for interference

	Russian counterpart	German model	Russian replica
Closure:	————	————	————
Voice:	————	——	————

If 10 per cent of a text is constituted of imported elements, it obviously represents a degree of interference greater than that of a text which reveals only 2 per cent. To determine such proportions, we count all cases of interferences (total tokens) and calculate what percentage of the total text these represent. This gives us our first, rough picture of the amount of interference in the text. But this is not sufficient and may even be misleading. A text dealing with some subject where the same foreign technical term comes up again and again – say 20 tokens – indicates less interference than does a text in which different foreign terms, 20 different types, occur each only once. We must therefore calculate, not only the total tokens, but also the total types.

Finally, we want to know not only the total amount of interference, but where it predominates. We therefore must calculate the type–token figures for each level, distinguishing the units from the structures. This is indicated in the final column of Table 1.5. Other relationships within the text may be discovered by the application of mathematical procedures for type–token calculations, which have now been developed for the use of linguists (Herdan, 1960).

Conclusion

Bilingualism cannot be described within the science of linguistics; we must go beyond. Linguistics has been interested in bilingualism only in so far as it could be used as an explanation for changes in a language, since language, not the individual, is the proper concern of this science. Psychology has regarded bilingualism as an influence on mental processes. Sociology has treated bilingualism as an element in culture conflict. Pedagogy has been concerned with bilingualism in connection with school organization and media of instruction. For each of these disciplines bilingualism is incidental; it is treated as a special case or as an exception to the norm. Each discipline, pursuing its own particular interests in its own special way, will add from time to time to the growing literature on bilingualism (see bibliographies in Weinreich, 1953; Haugen, 1956; Jones, 1960). However, it seems to add little to our understanding of bilingualism as such, with its complex psychological, linguistic, and social interrelationships.

What is needed, to begin with, is a perspective in which these interrelationships may be considered. What I have attempted in this study is to give an idea of the sort of perspective that is needed. In order to imagine it, it was necessary to consider bilingualism as an individual rather than a group phenomenon. This made possible a better and more detailed analysis of all that it entails; and the object of our analysis appeared as a complex of interrelated characteristics varying in degree, function, alternation, and interference. By providing a framework of analysis for each of these, we hope to have contributed to a more accurate description. For this to be complete, however, there are three remaining steps.

First, we have to test our frameworks through extensive use in the description of a variety of cases of individual bilingualism. [. . .] Second, we must discover the extent to which factors in each framework need to be correlated with factors in the others. Finally, we must quantify those factors which remain unquantified so as to arrive at a method for the complete description of bilingualism.

Notes

1   It is important not to confuse bilingualism – the use of two or more languages by the individual – with the more general concept of language contact, which deals with the direct or indirect influence of one language on another resulting in changes in *langue* which become the permanent property of monolinguals and enter into the historical development of the language. Such foreign influences may indeed be due to past periods of mass bilingualism, as in the case of the Scandinavian element in English. But bilingualism is not the only cause of foreign influence; the presence of words like *coffee* and *sugar* in English does not argue a period of English–Arabic bilingualism. Language contact includes the study of linguistic borrowing.

2   We must not confuse "bilingual description" with the "description of bilingualism". "Bilingual description" is a term which has been used to denote the contrastive analysis of two languages for the purpose of discovering the differences between them. This is also known as "differential description". Differential description is a prerequisite to the analysis of one of the most important characteristics of billngualism – interference.

3   For a study of test making, see Lado (1961).

4   Examples of this are the Canadian *visites interprovinciales*, a description of which may be found in "French or English – with Pleasure!" in *Citizen*, 7.5 (1961), pp. 1–7.

5   I wish to thank M.A.K. Halliday and J.C. Catford for introducing me to this term and to the important variable it represents in language description.

6   The terms "model" and "replica" were established by Haugen to distinguish the feature introduced from the other language (the model) from its rendition into the language being used (the replica); see Haugen, 1956: 39.

7   Here again I am following Haugen's terminology; see also Haugen, 1950: 212.

8   I am grateful to Georges Straka for giving me evidence of mutual French–Czech interference which could be resolved only by the use of instrumental techniques. During his term as visiting professor in the experimental phonetics laboratory of Laval, he demonstrated techniques of analysis which will permit the realization of our plans for an instrumental study of phonetic interference.

Source: Mackey, W.F. (1962) The description of bilingualism. *Canadian Journal of Linguistics* 7: 51–85, by permission of the author.

Notes for students and instructors

Study questions

1 Of the names and labels of bilingual speakers listed in the Introduction and in Chapter 1, which describes yourself and your bilingual friends most appropriately, and why?

2 In your view, how useful are the terms 'balanced bilingual' and 'semilingual'? Can you see any problems when you apply them to anyone you know?

3 Why is it important to distinguish language 'proficiency' and language 'use' in defining a bilingual? How important is it to consider bilingual ability across the four language skills: listening, speaking, reading and writing?

Study activities

1 Select five individuals each of whom you would describe as bilingual. Ask each of them whether he or she would consider himself or herself to be bilingual and why. Compare your definition with theirs, and make a table or diagram to illustrate the important factors that need to be taken into account in defining bilingual speakers.

2 Investigate the history of language contact and attitudes towards bilingualism in a community or region of your choice. You may need to consult historical documents and design a short questionnaire on language attitudes. Pay particular attention to how politico-economic changes have affected people's attitudes towards bilingualism.

3   Using a local school (this could be state or private), find out what lan-
       guages are spoken by the children, their parents and the teachers. What
       tests or assessment, if any, does the school use to measure language ability
       of the children whose 'home' language is different from the 'school' lan-
       guage? If it is a bilingual school, how are the different languages being
       used (e.g. is one language confined to one setting/subject?)?

Further reading

Perhaps the most comprehensive introductory text on bilingualism is S.
Romaine, 1995, *Bilingualism* (2nd edn), Blackwell. It contains discussions of all
aspects of bilingualism ranging from the bilingual brain and code-switching to
bilingual education and attitudes towards bilingualism. A highly readable introduction to bilingualism which is written from a bilingual speaker's point of view
is F. Grosjean, 1982, *Life with Two Languages*, Harvard University Press. A
jargon-free introduction to bilingualism, suitable for general reading is K. Hakuta,
1986, *Mirror of Language: The debate on bilingualism*, Basic Books, New York.
       Chapter 1 of R. Fasold, 1984, *The Sociolinguistics of Society*, Blackwell
discusses how multilingual nations develop. A good general introduction to societal multilingualism is J. Edwards, 1994, *Multilingualism*, Routledge.
       Specific discussions of the definitions and typologies of bilingualism are
found in H. Baetens Beardsmore, 1986, *Bilingualism: Basic Principles* (2nd
edn), Multilingual Matters; C. Baker, 1996, *Foundations of Bilingual Education
and Bilingualism* (2nd edn), Multilingual Matters; and J. Hamers and M. Blanc,
2000, *Bilinguality and Bilingualism* (2nd edn), Cambridge University Press.

Sociolinguistic dimensions of bilingualism

Introduction to Part One

LI WEI

The articles reprinted in Part One of this Reader serve to illustrate what may be called the sociolinguistic approach to bilingualism. There are seven articles altogether; three are grouped under 'Language choice' and four under 'Bilingual interaction'.

Language choice

Researchers of bilingualism generally agree that language choice is an 'orderly' social behaviour, rather than a random matter of momentary inclination. Where perspectives differ is in the conceptualisation of the nature of achievement and management of that orderliness. Charles A. Ferguson's article on diglossia (Chapter 2) is a true classic in that it not only defines a concept but also develops an approach to bilingualism which has been extremely influential. It originates from the fact that the co-existing languages of a community are likely to have different functions and to be used in different contexts. The notion of diglossia describes the functional differentiation of languages in bilingual and multilingual communities. A distinction is made between High (H) and Low (L) language varieties and Ferguson noted nine areas in which H and L could differ. One important implication of Ferguson's conception of diglossia is that bilingual speakers' language choice is seen to reflect a set of society-wide norms.

The concept of diglossia can be usefully examined alongside the notion of bilingualism, as Joshua A. Fishman does in Chapter 3. Bilingualism, argues Fishman, is the subject matter for linguists and psychologists and refers to an individual's ability to use more than one language; diglossia, on the other hand, is a concept for sociologists and sociolinguists to study. He describes four language situations where bilingualism and diglossia may exist with or without each other. In doing so, Fishman has incorporated the factor of change in language use. According to Fishman, relative stability can be maintained as long as societal compartmentalisation of language lasts. When two languages compete for use in the same situations, as in the case of bilingualism without diglossia, language shift – a process in which a speech community collectively gives up a language in favour of some other – may occur.

The second article by Fishman (Chapter 4) asks the now famous question 'Who speaks what language to whom and when?', a question which not only set the agenda for bilingualism research but also for the study of language in society in general. The way in which Fishman proposes to answer this question is through what he calls *domain analysis*. Domain refers to a cluster of characteristic situations around a prototypical theme which structures both the speakers' perception of the situation and their social behaviour, including language choice. Extending Weinreich's (1953) earlier work, Fishman tries to link the analysis of societal norms and expectations with language use in face-to-face encounters, using the concept of *domain* as a pivot. His analysis concentrates on stable systems of choice, or 'proper' usage as he calls it, and relates specific language choices to general institutions and spheres of activity, both in one society and between societies comparatively.

Bilingual interaction

The second section of Part One focuses more specifically on the micro-interactional aspects of language choice. The article by Jan-Petter Blom and John J. Gumperz (Chapter 5) is one of the most frequently cited articles on bilingualism. It introduces the now widely used dichotomy of 'situational' versus 'metaphorical' code-switching. On the basis of extensive participant observation in a bi-dialectal community in Hemnesberget, Norway, Blom and Gumperz identify two types of linguistic practice which they argue have different social meanings:

1   changes of language choice corresponding to changes in the situation, particularly participant, setting and activity type, i.e. situational code-switching; and

2   changes in language choice in order to achieve special communicative effects while participant and setting remain the same, i.e. metaphorical code-switching.

They regard metaphorical code-switching as symbolic of alternative inter-personal relationships; in other words, choices of language are seen as a 'metaphor' for the relationship being enacted. This study of the meaning of language choice exemplifies what is meant by an integrated sociolinguistic approach. Both ethnography and linguistics are drawn upon. The outcome is an understanding of social constraints and linguistic rules as parts of a single communicative system.

The idea that language choice and code-switching are symbolic of the social relationships between individuals is further developed in Carol M. Scotton's (later as Myers-Scotton) paper (Chapter 6). She proposes the notion of *markedness* as a basis for understanding the effectiveness of code-switching in defining social rights and obligations. She shows how certain sets of rights and obligations are conventionally associated with certain social situations, and how language use in those situations is unmarked. She goes on to discuss two ways in which situation and language use co-vary: externally motivated language choice signals changes in situation and, therefore, change in unmarked language choice. However, within single encounters participants can deviate from conventional verbal behaviour, and through such marked switches redefine role relations and, consequently, situations.

The article by Peter Auer (Chapter 7) approaches the meaning of language choice and code-switching from a different perspective. Auer uses a framework derived from *conversation analysis* (CA) to account for the ways in which speakers use code-switching either to manage social relations or to accomplish discourse objectives. He argues that the primary function of language alterna-tion – a general term that Auer uses to cover various types of code-switching and transfer – is to establish various kinds of *footing* (in Goffman's terms; Goffman, 1979), which provide the basis for the conversation to be interpretable by parti-cipants. This analysis of bilingual conversation offers a useful alternative to the sociolinguistic studies of language choice and code-switching.

The last chapter in Part One is by Li Wei, Lesley Milroy and Pong Sin Ching, who propose a two-step analysis which integrates language choice at the macro-community level with code-switching at the micro-interactional level. Utilising the analytic concept of *social network* and framework provided by *conversation analysis* (similar to Auer's analysis), they demonstrate, via an analysis of the sociolinguistic patterns of a Chinese community in Britain, that bilingual speakers use code-switching as an organisational procedure for conversational interaction and that the different code-switching practices displayed by speakers of different generations may be described as interactional reflexes of the network-specific language choice preferences. They further argue that while network interacts with a number of other variables, it is capable of accounting

more generally for patterns of language choice than variables such as generation, sex of speaker, duration of stay and occupation with which it intereacts. It
can also deal in a principled way with differences within a single generational
group. In their view, therefore, social network analysis can form an important
component in an integrated social theory of language choice: it links with the
interactional level in focusing on the everyday behaviour of social actors, and
with the economic and socio-political level in that networks may be seen as
forming in response to social and economic pressures.

Language choice

Chapter 2

Diglossia

CHARLES A. FERGUSON

I N MANY SPEECH COMMUNITIES two or more varieties of the same language are used by some speakers under different conditions. Perhaps the most familiar example is the standard language and regional dialect as used, say, in Italian or Persian, where many speakers speak their local dialect at home or among family or friends of the same dialect area but use the standard language in communicating with speakers of other dialects or on public occasions. There are, however, quite different examples of the use of two varieties of a language in the same speech community. In Baghdad the Christian Arabs speak a 'Christian Arabic' dialect when talking among themselves but speak the general Baghdad dialect, 'Muslim Arabic', when talking in a mixed group. In recent years there has been a renewed interest in studying the development and characteristics of standardized languages (see especially Kloss, 1952, with its valuable introduction on standardization in general), and it is in following this line of interest that the present study seeks to examine carefully one particular kind of standardization where two varieties of a language exist side by side throughout the community, with each having a definite role to play. The term 'diglossia' is introduced here, modeled on the French *diglossie*, which has been applied to this situation, since there seems to be no word in regular use for this in English; other languages of Europe generally use the word for 'bilingualism' in this special sense as well. (The terms 'language', 'dialect', and 'variety' are used here without precise definition. It is hoped that they occur sufficiently in accordance with established usage to be unambiguous for the present purpose. The term 'superposed variety' is also used here without definition; it means that the variety in question is not the primary, 'native' variety for the speakers in question but may be learned in addition to this. Finally, no attempt is made in this paper to examine the analogous situation where two distinct (related or unrelated) languages are used side by side throughout a speech community, each with a clearly defined role.)

It is likely that this particular situation in speech communities is very widespread, although it is rarely mentioned, let alone satisfactorily described. A full explanation of it can be of considerable help in dealing with problems in linguistic description, in historical linguistics, and in language typology. The present study should be regarded as preliminary in that much more assembling of descriptive and historical data is required; its purpose is to characterize diglossia by picking out four speech communities and their languages (hereafter called the defining languages) which clearly belong in this category, and describing features shared by them which seem relevant to the classification. The defining languages selected are Arabic, Modern Greek, Swiss German, and Haitian Creole. (See the references at the end of this chapter.)

Before proceeding to the description it must be pointed out that diglossia is not assumed to be a stage which occurs always and only at a certain point in some kind of evolution, e.g., in the standardization process. Diglossia may develop from various origins and eventuate in different language situations. Of the four defining languages, Arabic diglossia seems to reach as far back as our knowledge of Arabic goes, and the superposed 'Classical' language has remained relatively stable, while Greek diglossia has roots going back many centuries, but it became fully developed only at the beginning of the nineteenth century with the renaissance of Greek literature and the creation of a literary language based in large part on previous forms of literary Greek. Swiss German diglossia developed as a result of long religious and political isolation from the centers of German linguistic standardization, while Haitian Creole arose from a creolization of a pidgin French, with standard French later coming to play the role of the superposed variety. Some speculation on the possibilities of development will, however, be given at the end of the chapter.

For convenience of reference the superposed variety in diglossias will be called the H ('high') variety or simply H, and the regional dialects will be called L ('low') varieties or, collectively, simply L. All the defining languages have names for H and L, and these are listed in Table 2.1.

It is instructive to note the problems involved in citing words of these languages in a consistent and accurate manner. First, should the words be listed in their H form or in their L form, or in both? Second, if words are cited in their L form, what kind of L should be chosen? In Greek and in Haitian Creole, it seems clear that the ordinary conversational language of the educated people of Athens and Port-au-Prince respectively should be selected. For Arabic and for Swiss German the choice must be arbitrary, and the ordinary conversational language of educated people of Cairo and of Zürich are used here. Third, what kind of spelling should be used to represent L? Since there is in no case a generally accepted orthography for L, some kind of phonemic or quasi-phonemic transcription

Table 2.1   Terms for H and L in the defining languages

Language	Term for H	Term for L
Arabic		
Classical (=H)	*'al-fuṣḥā*	*'al-ʿāmmiyyah, 'ad-darij*
Egyptian (=L)	*'il-faṣīḥ, 'in-nahawi*	*'il-'ammiyya*
Swiss/German		
Standard German (=H)	*Schriftsprache*	*(Schweizer) Dialekt, Schweizerhdeutsch*
Swiss (=L)	*Hoochtüütsch*	*Schwyzertüütsch*
Haitian Creole		
French (=H)	*français*	*créole*
Greek		
H and L	*katharévusa*	*dhimotikí*

would seem appropriate. The following choices were made. For Haitian Creole, the McConnell–Laubach spelling was selected, since it is approximately phonemic and is typographically simple. For Greek, the transcription was adopted from the manual *Spoken Greek* (Kahane *et al.*, 1945), since this is intended to be phonemic; a transliteration of the Greek spelling seems less satisfactory not only because the spelling is variable but also because it is highly etymologizing in nature and quite unphonemic. For Swiss German, the spelling backed by Dieth (1938), which, though it fails to indicate all the phonemic contrasts and in some cases may indicate allophones, is fairly consistent and seems to be a sensible systematization, without serious modification, of the spelling conventions most generally used in writing Swiss German dialect material. Arabic, like Greek, uses a non-Roman alphabet, but transliteration is even less feasible than for Greek, partly again because of the variability of the spelling, but even more because in writing Egyptian colloquial Arabic many vowels are not indicated at all and others are often indicated ambiguously; the transcription chosen here sticks closely to the traditional systems of Semitists, being a modification for Egyptian of the scheme used by Al-Toma (1957).

The fourth problem is how to represent H. For Swiss German and Haitian Creole standard German and French orthography respectively can be used even though this hides certain resemblances between the sounds of H and L in both cases. For Greek either the usual spelling in Greek letters could be used or a transliteration, but since a knowledge of Modern Greek pronunciation is less widespread than a knowledge of German and French pronunciation, the masking effect of the orthography is more serious in the Greek case, and we use the phonemic transcription instead. Arabic is the most serious problem. The two most obvious choices are (1) a transliteration of Arabic spelling (with the unwritten vowels supplied by the transcriber) or (2) a phonemic transcription of the Arabic as it would be read by a speaker of Cairo Arabic. Solution (1) has been adopted, again in accordance with Al-Toma's procedure.

Characteristic features

Function

One of the most important features of diglossia is the specialization of function for H and L. In one set of situations only H is appropriate and in another only L, with the two sets overlapping only very slightly. As an illustration, a sample listing of possible situations is given, with indication of the variety normally used:

	H	L
Sermon in church or mosque	X	
Instructions to servants, waiters, workmen, clerks		X
Personal letter	X	
Speech in parliament, political speech	X	
University lecture	X	
Conversation with family, friends, colleagues		X
News broadcast	X	
Radio 'soap opera'		X
Newspaper editorial, news story, caption on picture	X	
Caption on political cartoon		X
Poetry	X	
Folk literature		X

The social importance of using the right variety in the right situation can hardly be overestimated. An outsider who learns to speak fluent, accurate L and then uses it in a formal speech is an object of ridicule. A member of the speech community who uses H in a purely conversational situation or in an informal activity like shopping is equally an object of ridicule. In all the defining languages it is typical behavior to have someone read aloud from a newspaper written in H and then proceed to discuss the contents in L. In all the defining languages it is typical behavior to listen to a formal speech in H and then discuss it, often with the speaker himself, in L.

(The situation in formal education is often more complicated than is indicated here. In the Arab world, for example, formal university lectures are given in H, but drills, explanation, and section meetings may be in large part conducted in L, especially in the natural sciences as opposed to the humanities. Although the teachers' use of L in secondary schools is forbidden by law in some Arab countries, often a considerable part of the teachers' time is taken up with explaining in L the meaning of material in H which has been presented in books or lectures.)

The last two situations on the list call for comment. In all the defining languages some poetry is composed in L, and a small handful of poets compose in both, but the status of the two kinds of poetry is very different, and for the speech community as a whole it is only the poetry in H that is felt to be 'real' poetry. (Modern Greek does not quite fit this description. Poetry in L is the major production and H verse is generally felt to be artificial.) On the other hand, in every one of the defining languages certain proverbs, politeness formulas, and the like are in H even when cited in ordinary conversation by illiterates. It has been estimated that as much as one-fifth of the proverbs in the active repertory of Arab villagers are in H.

Prestige

In all the defining languages the speakers regard H as superior to L in a number of respects. Sometimes the feeling is so strong that H alone is regarded as real and L is reported 'not to exist'. Speakers of Arabic, for example, may say (in L) that so-and-so doesn't know Arabic. This normally means he doesn't know H, although he may be a fluent, effective speaker of L. If a non-speaker of Arabic asks an educated Arab for help in learning to speak Arabic, the Arab will normally try to teach him H forms, insisting that these are the only ones to use. Very often, educated Arabs will maintain that they never use L at all, in spite of the fact that direct observation shows that they use it constantly in all ordinary conversation. Similarly, educated speakers of Haitian Creole frequently deny its existence, insisting that they always speak French. This attitude cannot be called a deliberate attempt to deceive the questioner, but seems almost a self-deception. When the speaker in question is replying in good faith, it is often possible to break through these attitudes by asking such questions as what kind of language he uses in speaking to his children, to servants, or to his mother. The very revealing reply is usually something like: 'Oh, but they wouldn't understand [the H form, whatever it is called].'

Even where the feeling of the reality and superiority of H is not so strong, there is usually a belief that H is somehow more beautilul, more logical, better able to express important thoughts, and the like. And this belief is held also by speakers whose command of H is quite limited. To those Americans who would like to evaluate speech in terms of effectiveness of communication it comes as a shock to discover that many speakers of a language involved in diglossia characteristically prefer to hear a political speech or an expository lecture or a recitation of poetry in H even though it may be less intelligible to them than it would be in L.

In some cases the superiority of H is connected with religion. In Greek the language of the New Testament is felt to be essentially the same as the *kathar-évusa*, and the appearance of a translation of the New Testament in *dhimotikí* was the occasion for serious rioting in Greece in 1903. Speakers of Haitian Creole are generally accustomed to a French version of the Bible, and even when the Church uses Creole for catechisms and the like, it resorts to a highly Gallicized spelling. For Arabic, H is the language of the Qur'an and as such is widely believed to constitute the actual words of God and even to be outside the limits of space and time, i.e. to have existed 'before' time began, with the creation of the world.

Literary heritage

In every one of the defining languages there is a sizable body of written literature in H which is held in high esteem by the speech community, and contemporary literary production in H by members of the community is felt to be part of this otherwise existing literature. The body of literature may either have been produced long ago in the past history of the community or be in continuous production in another speech community in which H serves as the standard variety of the language. When the body of literature represents a long time span (as in Arabic or Greek) contemporary writers – and readers – tend to regard it as a legitimate practice to utilize words, phrases, or constructions which may have been current only at one period of the literary history and are not in widespread use at the present time. Thus it may be good journalistic usage in writing editorials, or good literary taste in composing poetry, to employ a complicated Classical Greek participial construction or a rare twelfth-century Arabic expression which it can be assumed the average educated reader will not understand without research on his part. One effect of such usage is appreciation on the part of some readers: 'So-and-so really knows his Greek [or Arabic]', or 'So-and-so's editorial today, or latest poem, is very good Greek [or Arabic].'

Acquisition

Among speakers of the four defining languages, adults use L in speaking to children and children use L in speaking to one another. As a result, L is learned by children in what may be regarded as the 'normal' way of learning one's mother tongue. H may be heard by children from time to time, but the actual learning of H is chiefly accomplished by the means of formal education, whether this be traditional Qur'anic schools, modern government schools, or private tutors.

This difference in method of acquisition is very important. The speaker is at home in L to a degree he almost never achieves in H. The grammatical structure of L is learned without explicit discussion of grammatical concepts; the grammar of H is learned in terms of 'rules' and norms to be imitated.

It seems unlikely that any change toward full utilization of H could take place without a radical change in this pattern of acquisition. For example, those Arabs who ardently desire to have L replaced by H for all functions can hardly expect this to happen if they are unwilling to speak H to their children. (It has been very plausibly suggested that there are psychological implications following from this linguistic duality. This certainly deserves careful experimental investigation. On this point, see the highly controversial article which seems to me to contain some important kernels of truth along with much which cannot be supported; Shouby, 1951.)

Standardization

In all the defining languages there is a strong tradition of grammatical study of the H form of the language. There are grammars, dictionaries, treatises on pronunciation, style, and so on. There is an established norm for pronunciation, grammar, and vocabulary which allows variation only within certain limits. The orthography is well established and has little variation. By contrast, descriptive and normative studies of the L form are either non-existent or relatively recent and slight in quantity. Often they have been carried out first or chiefly by scholars OUTSIDE the speech community and are written in other languages. There is no settled orthography and there is wide variation in pronunciation, grammar, and vocabulary.

In the case of relatively small speech communities with a single important center of communication (e.g. Greece, Haiti) a kind of standard L may arise which speakers of other dialects imitate and which tends to spread like any standard variety except that it remains limited to the functions for which L is appropriate.

In speech communities which have no single most important center of communication a number of regional L's may arise. In the Arabic speech community, for example, there is no standard L corresponding to educated Athenian *dhimotiki*, but regional standards exist in various areas. The Arabic of Cairo, for example, serves as a standard L for Egypt, and educated individuals from Upper Egypt must learn not only H but also, for conversational purposes, an approximation to Cairo L. In the Swiss German speech community there is no single standard, and even the term 'regional standard' seems inappropriate, but in several cases the L of a city or town has a strong effect on the surrounding rural L.

Stability

It might be supposed that diglossia is highly unstable, tending to change into a more stable language situation. However, this is not so. Diglossia typically persists for at least several centuries, and evidence in some cases seems to show that it can last well over a thousand years. The communicative tensions which arise in the diglossia situation may be resolved by the use of relatively uncodified, unstable, intermediate forms of the language (Greek *mikti*, Arabic *al-lugah al-wusṭā*, Haitian *créole de salon*) and repeated borrowing of vocabulary items from H to L.

In Arabic, for example, a kind of spoken Arabic much used in certain semi-formal or cross-dialectal situations has a highly classical vocabulary with few or no inflectional endings, with certain features of classical syntax, but with a funda-mentally colloquial base in morphology and syntax, and a generous admixture of colloquial vocabulary. In Greek a kind of mixed language has become appropriate for a large part of the press.

The borrowing of lexical items from H to L is clearly analogous (or for the periods when actual diglossia was in effect in these languages, identical) with the learned borrowings from Latin to Romance languages or the Sanskrit *tatsamas* in Middle and New Indo-Aryan. (The exact nature of this borrowing process deserves careful investigation, especially for the important 'filter effect' of the pronunciation and grammar of H occurring in those forms of middle language which often serve as the connecting link by which the loans are introduced into the 'pure' L.)

Grammar

One of the most striking differences between H and L in the defining languages is in the grammatical structure: H has grammatical categories not present in L and has an inflectional system of nouns and verbs which is much reduced or totally absent in L. For example, Classical Arabic has three cases in the noun, marked by endings; colloquial dialects have none. Standard German has four cases in the noun and two non-periphrastic indicative tenses in the verb; Swiss German has three cases in the noun and only one simple indicative tense. *Kotharévusa* has four cases, *dhimotikí* three. French has gender and number in the noun, Creole has neither. Also, in every one of the defining languages there seem to be several striking differences of word order as well as a thorough-going set of differences in the use of introductory and connective particles. It is certainly safe to say that in diglossia *there are always extensive differences between the grammatical structures of H and L*. This is true not only for the four defining languages, but also for every other case of diglossia examined by the author.

For the defining languages it may be possible to make a further statement about grammatical differences. It is always risky to hazard generalizations about grammatical complexity, but it may be worthwhile to attempt to formulate a statement applicable to the four defining languages even if it should turn out to be invalid for other instances of diglossia (cf. Greenberg, 1954).

There is probably fairly wide agreement among linguists that the grammatical structure of language A is 'simpler' than that of B if, other things being equal:

1 the morphophonemics of A is simpler, i.e. morphemes have fewer alternants, alternation is more regular, automatic (e.g. Turkish *-lar* ~ *-ler* is simpler than the English plural markers).

2 There are fewer obligatory categories marked by morphemes or concord (e.g. Persian with no gender distinctions in the pronoun is simpler than Egyptian Arabic with masculine–feminine distinction in the second and third persons singular).

3 Paradigms are more symmetrical (e.g. a language with all declensions having the same number of case distinctions is simpler than one in which there is variation).

4 Concord and government are stricter (e.g. prepositions all take the same case rather than different cases).

If this understanding of grammatical simplicity is accepted, then we may note that in at least three of the defining languages, the grammatical structure of any given L variety is simpler than that of its corresponding H. This seems incontrovertibly true for Arabic, Greek, and Haitian Creole; a full analysis of standard German and Swiss German might show this not to be true in that diglossic situation in view of the extensive morphophonemics of Swiss.

Lexicon

Generally speaking, the bulk of the vocabulary of H and L is shared, of course with variations in form and with differences of use and meaning. It is hardly surprising, however, that H should include in its total lexicon technical terms and learned expressions which have no regular L equivalents, since the subjects involved are rarely if ever discussed in pure L. Also, it is not surprising that the L varieties should include in their total lexicons popular expressions and the names of very homely objects or objects of very localized distribution which have no regular H equivalents, since the subjects involved are rarely if ever discussed in pure H. But *a striking feature of diglossia is the existence of many paired items – one H, one L – referring to fairly common concepts frequently used in both H and L, where the range of meaning of the two items is roughly the same, and the use of one or the other immediately stamps the utterance or written sequence as H or L.*

For example, in Arabic the H word for 'see' is *ra'ā*, the L word is *šāf*. The word *ra'ā* never occurs in ordinary conversation and *šāf* is not used in normal written Arabic. If for some reason a remark in which *šāf* was used is quoted in the press, it is replaced by *ra'ā* in the written quotation. In Greek the H word for 'wine' is *ínos*, the L word is *krasí*. The menu will have *ínos* written on it, but the diner will ask the waiter for *krasí*. The nearest American English parallels are such cases as *illuminatian* ~ *light, purchase* ~ *buy*, or *children* ~ *kids*, but in these cases both words may be written and both may be used in ordinary conversation: the gap is not so great as for the corresponding doublets in diglossia. Also, the formal–informal dimension in languages like English is a continuum in which the boundary between the two items in different pairs may not come at the same point, e.g. *illumination*, *purchase*, and *children* are not fully parallel in their formal–informal range of usage.

A dozen or so examples of lexical doublets from three of the sample languages are given in Table 2.2. For each language two nouns, a verb, and two particles are given.

It would be possible to present such a list of doublets for Swiss German (e.g. *nachdem* ≅ *no* 'after', *jemand* ≅ *öpper* 'someone', etc.), but this would give a false picture. In Swiss German the phonological differences between H and L are very great and the normal form of lexical pairing is regular cognation (*kiefli* ≅ *chly* 'small', etc.).

Table 2.2   Lexical doublets

Greek		
H		L
íkos	house	*spíti*
ídhor	water	*neró*
éteke	gave birth	*eyénise*
alá	but	*má*
Arabic		
H		L
ḥiðā'un	shoe	*gazma*
'anfun	nose	*manaxīr*
ðahaba	went	*rāh*
mā	what	*'ēh*
'al'āna	now	*dilwa'ti*
Creole		
H		L
homme, gens	person, people	*moun* (not connected with *monde*)
âne	donkey	*bourik*
donner	give	*bay*
beaucoup	much, a lot	*âpil*
maintenant	now	*kou-n-yé-a*

Phonology

It may seem difficult to offer any generalization on the relationships between the phonology of H and L in diglossia in view of the diversity of data. H and L phonologies may be quite close, as in Greek; moderately different, as in Arabic or Haitian Creole; or strikingly divergent, as in Swiss German. Closer examination, however, shows two statements to be justified. (Perhaps these will turn out to be unnecessary when the preceding features are stated so precisely that the statements about phonology can be deduced directly from them.)

1   *The sound systems of H and L constitute a single phonological structure of which the L phonology is the basic system and the divergent features of H phonology are either a subsystem or a parasystem.*

Given the mixed forms mentioned above and the corresponding difficulty of identifying a given word in a given utterance as being definitely H or definitely L, it seems necessary to assume that the speaker has a single inventory of distinctive oppositions for the whole H–L complex and that there is extensive interference in both directions in terms of the distribution of phonemes in specific lexical items. (For details on certain aspects of this phonological interference in Arabic, cf. Ferguson, 1957.)

2   *If 'pure' H items have phonemes not found in 'pure' L items, L phonemes frequently substitute for these in oral use of H and regularly replace them in* tatsamas.

For example, French has a high front rounded vowel phoneme /ü/; 'pure' Haitian Creole has no such phoneme. Educated speakers of Creole use this vowel in *tatsamas* such as *Luk* (/lük/ for the Gospel of St Luke), while they, like uneducated speakers, may sometimes use /i/ for it when speaking French. On the other hand /i/ is the regular vowel in such *tatsamas* in Creole as *linèt* 'glasses'.

In cases where H represents in large part an earlier stage of L, it is possible that a three-way correspondence will appear. For example, Syrian and Egyptian Arabic frequently use /s/ for /q/ in oral use of Classical Arabic, and have /s/ in *tatsamas*, but have /t/ in words regularly descended from earlier Arabic not borrowed from the Classical (see Ferguson, 1957).

Now that the characteristic features of diglossia have been outlined it is feasible to attempt a fuller definition: DIGLOSSIA *is a relatively stable language situation in which, in addition to the primary dialects of the language (which may include a standard or regional standards), there is a very divergent, highly codified (often grammatically more complex) superposed variety, the vehicle of a large and respected body of written literature, either of an earlier period or in another speech community, which is learned largely by formal education and is used for most written and formal spoken purposes but is not used by any sector of the community for ordinary conversation.*

With the characterization of diglossia completed we may turn to a brief consideration of three additional questions: How does diglossia differ from the familiar situation of a standard language with regional dialects? How widespread is the phenomenon of diglossia in space, time, and linguistic families? Under what circumstances does diglossia come into being and into what language situations is it likely to develop?

The precise role of the standard variety (or varieties) of a language *vis-à-vis* regional or social dialects differs from one speech community to another, and some instances of this relation may be close to diglossia or perhaps even better considered as diglossia. As characterized here, diglossia differs from the more widespread standard-with-dialects in that no segment of the speech community in diglossia regularly uses H as a medium of ordinary conversation, and any attempt to do so is felt to be either pedantic and artificial (Arabic, Greek) or else in some sense disloyal to the community (Swiss German, Creole). In the more usual standard-with-dialects situation the standard is often similar to the variety of a certain region or social group (e.g. Tehran Persian, Calcutta Bengali) which is used in ordinary conversation more or less naturally by members of the group and as a superposed variety by others.

Diglossia is apparently not limited to any geographical region or language family. (All clearly documented instances known to me are in literate communities, but it seems at least possible that a somewhat similar situation could exist in a non-literate community where a body of oral literature could play the same role as the body of written literature in the examples cited.) Three examples of diglossia from other times and places may be cited as illustrations of the utility of the concept. First, consider Tamil. As used by the millions of members of the Tamil speech community in India today, it fits the definition exactly. There is a literary Tamil as H used for writing and certain kinds of formal speaking, and a standard colloquial as L (as well as local L dialects) used in ordinary conversation. There is a body of literature in H going back many centuries which is highly regarded by Tamil speakers today. H has prestige, L does not. H is always superposed, L is learned naturally, whether as primary or as a superposed standard colloquial. There are striking grammatical differences and some phonological differences between the two varieties. (There is apparently no good description available of the precise relations of the two varieties of Tamil; an account of some of the structural differences is given by Pillai (1960). Incidentally, it may be noted that Tamil diglossia seems to go back many centuries, since the language of early literature contrasts sharply with the language of early inscriptions, which probably reflect the spoken language of the time.) The situation is only slightly complicated by the presence of Sanskrit and English for certain functions of H; the same kind of complication exists in parts of the Arab world where French, English, or a liturgical language such as Syriac or Coptic has certain H-like functions.

Second, we may mention Latin and the emergent Romance languages during a period of some centuries in various parts of Europe. The vernacular was used in ordinary conversation but Latin for writing or certain kinds of formal speech. Latin was the language of the Church and its literature, Latin had the prestige, there were striking grammatical differences between the two varieties in each area, etc.

Third, Chinese should be cited because it probably represents diglossia on the largest scale of any attested instance. (An excellent, brief description of the complex Chinese situation is available in the introduction to Chao (1947: 1–17).) The *weu-li* corresponds to H, while Mandarin colloquial is a standard L; there are also regional L varieties so different as to deserve the label 'separate languages' even more than the Arabic dialects, and at least as much as the emergent Romance languages in the Latin example. Chinese, however, like modern Greek, seems to be developing away from diglossia toward a standard-with-dialects, in that the standard L or a mixed variety is coming to be used in writing for more and more purposes, i.e. it is becoming a true standard.

Diglossia is likely to come into being when the following three conditions hold in a given speech community:

1   There is a sizable body of literature in a language closely related to (or even identical with) the natural language of the community, and this literature embodies, whether as source (e.g. divine revelation) or reinforcement, some of the fundamental values of the community.
2   Literacy in the community is limited to a small elite.
3   A suitable period of time, of the order of several centuries, passes from the establishment of (1) and (2).

It can probably be shown that this combination of circumstances has occurred hundreds of times in the past and has generally resulted in diglossia. Dozens of examples exist today, and it is likely that examples will occur in the future.

Diglossia seems to be accepted and not regarded as a 'problem' by the community in which it is in force, until certain trends appear in the community. These include trends toward:

1   more widespread literacy (whether for economic, ideological, or other reasons);
2   broader communication among different regional and social segments of the community (e.g. for economic, administrative, military, or ideological reasons);
3   desire for a full-fledged standard 'national' language as an attribute of autonomy or of sovereignty.

When these trends appear, leaders in the community begin to call for unification of the language, and for that matter, actual trends toward unification begin to take place. These individuals tend to support either the adoption of H or of one form of L as the standard; less often the adoption of a modified H or L, a 'mixed' variety of some kind. The arguments explicitly advanced seem remarkably the same from one instance of diglossia to another.

The proponents of H argue that H must be adopted because it connects the community with its 'glorious past' or with the world community and because it is a naturally unifying factor as opposed to the divisive nature of the L dialects. In addition to these two fundamentally sound arguments there are usually pleas based on the beliefs of the community in the superiority of H: that it is more beautiful, more expressive, more logical; that it has divine sanction, or whatever the community's specific beliefs may be. When these latter arguments are examined objectively their validity is often quite limited, but their importance is still considerable because they reflect widely held attitudes within the community.

The proponents of L argue that some variety of L must be adopted because it is closer to the real thinking and feeling of the people; it eases the educational problem since people have already acquired a basic knowledge of it in early childhood; and it is a more effective instrument of communication at all levels. In addition to these fundamentally sound arguments there is often great emphasis given to points of lesser importance such as the vividness of metaphor in the colloquial, the fact that other 'modern nations' write very much as they speak, and so on.

The proponents of both sides or even of the mixed language seem to show the conviction – although this may not be explicitly stated – that a standard language can simply be legislated into place in a community. Often the trends which will be decisive in the development of a standard language are already at work and have little to do with the argumentation of the spokespeople for the various viewpoints.

A brief and superficial glance at the outcome of diglossia in the past and a consideration of present trends suggests that there are only a few general kinds of development likely to take place. First, we must remind ourselves that the situation may remain stable for long periods of time. But if the trends mentioned above do appear and become strong, change may take place. Second, H can succeed in establishing itself as a standard only if it is already serving as a standard language in some other community and the diglossia community – for reasons linguistic and non-linguistic – tends to merge with the other community. Otherwise H fades away and becomes a learned or liturgical language studied only by scholars or specialists and not used actively in the community. Some form of L or a mixed variety becomes standard.

Third, if there is a single communication center in the whole speech community – or if there are several such centers all in one dialect area – the L variety of the center(s) will be the basis of the new standard, whether relatively pure L or considerably mixed with H. If there are several such centers in different dialect areas with no one center paramount, then it is likely that several L varieties will become standard as separate languages.

A tentative prognosis for the four defining languages over the next two centuries (i.e. to about AD 2150) may be hazarded:

- Swiss German: relative stability;
- Arabic: slow development toward several standard languages, each based on an L variety with heavy admixture of H vocabulary; three seem likely:
  - Maghrebi (based on Rabat or Tunis?);
  - Egyptian (based on Cairo);
  - Eastern (based on Baghdad?);
  - unexpected politico-economic developments might add Syrian (based on Damascus?);
  - Sudanese (based on Omdurman-Khartoum), or others;
- Haitian Creole: slow development toward unified standard based on L of Port-au-Prince;
- Greek: full development to unified standard based on L of Athens plus heavy admixture of H vocabulary.

This paper concludes with an appeal for further study of this phenomenon and related ones. Descriptive linguists in their understandable zeal to describe the internal structure of the language they are studying often fail to provide even the most elementary data about the socio-cultural setting in which the language functions. Also, descriptivists usually prefer detailed descriptions of 'pure' dialects or standard languages rather than the careful study of the mixed, intermediate forms often in wider use. Study of such matters as diglossia is of clear value in understanding processes of linguistic change and presents interesting challenges to some of the assumptions of synchronic linguistics. Outside linguistics proper it promises material of great interest to social scientists in general, especially if a general frame of reference can be worked out for analysis of the use of one or more varieties of language within a speech community. Perhaps the collection of data and more profound study will drastically modify the impressionistic remarks of this paper, but if this is so the paper will have had the virtue of stimulating investigation and thought.

References on the four defining languages

The judgements of this chapter are based primarily on the author's personal experience, but documentation for the four defining languages is available, and the following references may be consulted for further details (see the Bibliography at the end of the book for full details). Most of the studies listed here take a strong stand in favor of greater use of the more colloquial variety since it is generally writers of this opinion who want to describe the facts. This bias can, however, be ignored by the reader who simply wants to discover the basic facts of the situation.

Modern Greek

Hatzidakis, 1905 (Die Sprachfrage in Griechenland)
Kahane et al., 1945 (Spoken Greek)
Krumbacher, 1902 (Das Problem der modernen griechischen Schriftsprache)
Pernot, 1898 (Grammaire Grecque Moderne)
Psichari, 1928 (Un Pays qui ne veut pas sa langue)
Steinmetz, 1936 (Schrift und Volksprache in Griechenland)

Swiss German

Dieth, 1938 (Schwyzertütsch Dialäkschrift)
von Greyerz, 1933 (Vom Wert und Wesen unserer Mundart)
Kloss, 1952 (Die Entwicklung neuer germanischer Kultursprachen von 1800 bis 1950)
Schmid, 1936 (Für unser Schweizerdeutsch)
Senn, 1935 (Das Verhältnis von Mundart und Schriftsprache in der deutschen Schweiz)

Arabic

Al-Toma, 1957 (The teaching of Classical Arabic to speakers of the colloquial in Iraq)
Chejne, 1958 (The role of Arabic in present-day Arab society)
Lecerf, 1932 (Littérature Dialectale et renaissance arabe moderne)
Marçais, 1930–31 (Three articles)
Comhaire-Sylvain, 1936 (Le Créole haitien)
Hall, 1953 (Haitian Creole)
McConnell and Swan, 1945 (You Can Learn Creole)

Other references

Chao, 1947 (Cantonese Primer)
Ferguson, 1957 (Two problems in Arabic phonology)
Greenberg, 1954 (A quantitative approach to the morphological typology of language)
Pillai, 1960 (Tamil: literary and colloquial)
Shouby, 1951 (The influence of the Arabic language on the psychology of the Arabs)

Source: Ferguson, C.A. (1959) Diglossia. Word 15: 325–40, by permission of the International Linguistics Association.

Chapter 3

Bilingualism with and without diglossia; diglossia with and without bilingualism

JOSHUA A. FISHMAN

UNTIL THE 1950s THE psychological literature on bilingualism was so much more extensive than its sociological counterpart that workers in the former field have often failed to establish contact with those in the latter. Since the 1960s a very respectable sociological (or sociologically oriented) literature has developed dealing with bilingual societies. It is the purpose of this chapter to relate these two research traditions to each other by tracing the interaction between their two major constructs: bilingualism (on the part of psychologists) and diglossia (on the part of sociologists).

Diglossia

In the few years that have elapsed since Ferguson (1959) first advanced it, the term diglossia has not only become widely accepted by sociolinguists and sociologists of language, but it has been further extended and refined. Initially it was used in connection with a society that used two (or more) languages for internal (intrasociety) communication. The use of several separate codes within a single society (and their stable maintenance rather than the displacement of one by the other over time) was found to be dependent on each code's serving functions distinct from those considered appropriate for the other. Whereas one set of behaviors, attitudes and values supported – and was expressed in – one language, another set of behaviors, attitudes and values supported and was expressed in the other. Both sets of behaviors, attitudes and values were fully accepted as culturally legitimate and complementary (i.e., nonconflictual) and indeed, little if any conflict between them was possible in view of the functional separation between them. This separation was most often along the lines of a High (H) language, on the one hand utilized in conjunction with religion, education and other aspects of high culture, and a Low (L) language, on the other hand, utilized in conjunction with everyday pursuits of hearth, home and work. Ferguson spoke of H and L as superposed languages.

To this original edifice others have added several significant considerations. Gumperz (1961; 1962; 1964; 1964a; 1966) is primarily responsible for our current awareness that diglossia exists not only in multilingual societies which officially recognize several "languages" but, also, in societies which are multilingual in the sense that they employ separate dialects, registers or functionally differentiated language varieties of whatever kind. He has also done the lion's share of the work in providing the conceptual apparatus by means of which investigators of multilingual speech communities seek to discern the societal patterns that govern the use of one variety rather than another, particularly at the level of small group interaction. On the other hand, I have attempted to trace the maintenance of diglossia as well as its disruption at the national level (Fishman, 1964; 1965a; 1965c; 1965d; 1965e; 1966b; 1966c), and in addition have attempted to relate diglossia to psychologically pertinent considerations such as compound and co-ordinate bilingualism (1965). The present chapter represents an extension and integration of these several previous attempts.

For purposes of simplicity it seems best to represent the possible relationships between bilingualism and diglossia by means of a four-fold table such as that shown in Figure 3.1.

Speech communities characterized by both diglossia and bilingualism

The first quadrant of Figure 3.1 refers to those speech communities in which both diglossia and bilingualism occur. At times such communities comprise an entire nation, but of course this requires very widespread (if not all-pervasive) bilingual-

		+ *Diglossia* −
Bilingualism	+	1. Both diglossia and bilingualism 2. Bilingualism without diglossia
	−	3. Diglossia without bilingualism 4. Neither diglossia nor bilingualism

Figure 3.1 The relationship between bilingualism and diglossia

ism. An example of this type of nation is Paraguay, where almost the entire population speaks both Spanish and Guarani (Rubin, 1962; 1968). The formerly monolingual rural population has added Spanish to its linguistic repertoire in order to talk and write about education, religion, government, high culture and social distance or, more generally, the status stressing spheres; whereas the majority of city dwellers (being relatively new from the country) maintain Guarani for matters of intimacy and primary group solidarity even in the midst of Spanish urbanity.[1] A further example is the Swiss-German cantons in which the entire population of school age and older alternates between High German (H) and Swiss German (L), each with its own firmly established and highly valued functions (Weinreich, 1951; 1953; Ferguson, 1959).

Below the level of nationwide functioning there are many more examples of stable diglossia co-occurring with widespread bilingualism. Traditional (pre-First World War) Eastern European Jewish males communicated in Hebrew (H) and Yiddish (L). In more recent days their descendents have continued to do so, adding to their repertoire a Western language (notably English) for *intragroup* communication as well as in domains of *intergroup* contact (Weinreich, 1951; 1953; 1962; Fishman, 1965d).[2] A similar example is that of upper and upper middle-class males throughout the Arabic world who use classical (koranic) and vernacular (Egyptian, Syrian, Lebanese, Iraqui, etc.) Arabic and, not infrequently, also a Western language (French or English, most usually) for purposes of *intragroup* scientific or technological communication (Ferguson, 1959; Nader, 1962; Blanc, 1964).

All of the foregoing examples have in common the existence of a fairly large and complex speech community in which the members have available to them both a range of *compartmentalized* roles as well as ready *access* to these roles. If the *role repertoires* of these speech communities were of lesser range, then their *linguistic repertoires* would, also be, or become, more restricted in range, with the result that separate languages or varieties would be, or become, superfluous. In addition, were the roles not compartmentalized, i.e., were they not *kept separate* by dint of association with quite separate (though complementary) values, domains of activity and everyday situations,[3] one language (or variety) would displace the other as role and value distinctions merged and became blurred. Finally, were widespread access not available to the variety of compartmentalized roles (and compartmentalized languages or varieties), then the bilingual population would be a small, privileged caste or class (as it is or was throughout most of traditional India or China) rather than a broadly based population segment.

These observations lead to the conclusion that many modern speech communities that are normally thought of as monolingual are, rather, marked by both diglossia and bilingualism if their several registers (speech varieties related to functional specificity; Halliday, 1964) are viewed as separate varieties or languages in the same sense as the examples listed above. Wherever speech communities exist whose speakers engage in a considerable range of roles (and this is coming to be the case for all but the extremely upper and lower levels of complex societies); wherever access to several roles is encouraged or facilitated by powerful social institutions and processes; and finally, wherever the roles are clearly differentiated (in terms of when, where and with whom they are felt to be appropriate), both diglossia and bilingualism may be said to exist. The benefit of this approach to the topic at hand is that it provides a single theoretical framework for viewing bilingual speech communities and speech communities whose linguistic diversity is realized through varieties not (yet) recognized as constituting separate "languages." Thus, it becomes possible for us to note that while nations characterized by diglossia and widespread bilingualism (the latter term being understood in its usual sense of referring to separate languages) have become fewer in modern times, those characterized by diglossia and diversified linguistic repertoires have increased greatly as a consequence of modernization and growing social complexity. The single theory outlined above enabling us to understand, predict and interrelate both of these phenomena is an instance of enviable parsimony in the behavioral sciences.[4]

Diglossia without bilingualism

There are situations in which diglossia obtains whereas bilingualism is generally absent (quadrant 3). Here, two or more speech communities are united religiously, politically or economically into a single functioning unit notwithstanding the socio-cultural cleavages that separate them. At the level of this larger (but not always voluntary) unity, two or more languages or varieties are recognized as obtaining. However, one (or both) of the speech communities involved is (are) marked by relatively impermeable group boundaries such that for "outsiders" (and this may well mean all those not born into the speech community, i.e., an emphasis on ascribed rather than on achieved status) role access and linguistic access are severely restricted. At the same time, linguistic repertoires in one or both groups are limited due to role specialization.

Examples of such situations are not hard to find (see, e.g., the many instances listed by Kloss, 1966). Pre-First World War European elites often stood in this relationship with their countrymen, the elites speaking French or some other fashionable H tongue for their *intragroup* purposes (at various times and in various places: Danish, Salish, Provençal, Russian, etc.) and the masses speaking another, not necessarily linguistically related, language for their intragroup purposes. Since the majority of elites and the majority of the masses never interacted with one another *they did not form a single speech community* (i.e., their linguistic repertoires were discontinuous) and their intercommunications were via translators or interpretors (a certain sign of *intragroup* monolingualism). Since the majority of the elites and the majority of the masses led lives characterized by extremely narrow role repertoires their linguistic repertoires too were too narrow to permit wide-spread societal bilingualism to develop. Nevertheless, the body politic in all of its economic and national manifestations tied these two groups together into a "unity" that revealed an upper and a lower class, each with a language appropriate to its own restricted concerns.

Thus, the existence of national diglossia does *not* imply widespread bilingual-ism amongst rural or recently urbanized African groups (as distinguished from Westernized elites in those settings); nor amongst most lower caste Hindus, as distinguished from their more fortunate compatriots the Brahmins, nor amongst most lower class French-Canadians, as distinguished from their upper and upper middle-class city cousins, etc. In general, this pattern is characteristic of polities that are economically underdeveloped and unmobilized, combining groups that are locked into opposite extremes of the social spectrum and, therefore, groups that operate within extremely restricted and discontinuous linguistic repertoires. Obviously, such polities are bound to experience language problems as their social patterns alter in the direction of industrialization, widespread literacy and educa-tion, democratization, and modernization more generally. Since such polities rarely developed out of initial socio-cultural consensus or unity, the educational, political and economic development of the lower classes is likely to lead to secessionism or to demands for equality for submerged language(s). The linguistic states of Eastern Europe and India, and the language problems of Wales, Canada and Belgium stem from origins such as these.[5] This is the pattern of development that may yet convulse modern African nations if their de-ethnicized Westernized elites and diglossic language policies continue to fail to create bilingual speech communities, incorporating the masses, within their ethnically arbitrary political boundaries.

Bilingualism without diglossia

We turn next to those situations in which bilingualism obtains whereas diglossia is generally absent (quadrant 2 in Figure 3.1). Here we see even more clearly than before that bilingualism is essentially a characterization of individual linguistic behavior whereas diglossia is a characterization of linguistic organization at the socio-cultural level. Under what circumstances do bilinguals of similar cultural extraction nevertheless function without the benefit of a well-understood and widely accepted social consensus as to which language is to be used between which interlocutors, for communication concerning what topics or for what pur-poses? Under what circumstances do the varieties or languages involved lack well-defined or protected separate functions? Briefly put, these are circumstances of rapid social change, of great social unrest, of widespread abandonment of prior norms before the consolidation of new ones.

Many studies of bilingualism and intelligence or of bilingualism and school achievement have been conducted within the context of bilingualism without diglossia, often without sufficient understanding on the part of investigators that this was but one of several possible contexts for the study of bilingualism. As a result many of the purported "disadvantages" of bilingualism have been falsely generalized to the phenomenon at large rather than related to the absence or presence of social patterns which reach substantially beyond bilingualism (Fishman, 1965c; 1968).

The history of industrialization in the Western world (as well as in those parts of Africa and Asia which have experienced industrialization under Western "auspices") is such that the means (capital, plant, organization) of production were often derived from one speech community while the productive manpower was drawn from another. Initially both speech communities may have maintained their separate diglossia-with-bilingualism patterns or, alternatively, that of an overarching diglossia without bilingualism. In either case, the needs as well as the consequences of rapid and massive industrialization and urbanization were frequently such that members of the speech community providing a productive workforce rapidly abandoned their traditional socio-cultural patterns and learned (or were taught) the language of the means of production much earlier than their absorption into the socio-cultural patterns and privileges to which that language pertained. In response to this imbalance some react (or reacted) by further stressing the advantages of the newly gained language of education and industry while others react (or reacted) by seeking to replace the latter by an elaborated version of their own largely pre-industrial, pre-urban, pre-mobilization tongue.

Under circumstances such as these no well-established, socially recognized and protected functional differentiation of languages obtains in many speech communities of the lower and lower middle classes. Dislocated immigrants and their children (for whom a separate "political solution" is seldom possible) are particularly inclined to use their mother tongue and other tongue for intragroup communication in seemingly random fashion (Nahirny and Fishman, 1965; Fishman, 1965c). Since the formerly separate roles of the home domain, the school domain and the work domain are all disturbed by the massive dislocation of values and norms that result from simultaneous immigration and industrialization, the language of work (and of the school) comes to be used at home (just as in cases of more radical and better organized social change the language of the home comes to be established in school and at work). As role compartmentalization and value complementarity decrease under the impact of foreign models and massive change the linguistic repertoire also becomes less compartmentalized. Languages and varieties formerly kept apart come to influence each other phonetically, lexically, semantically and even grammatically much more than before. Instead of two (or more) carefully separated languages each under the eye of caretaker groups of teachers, preachers and writers, several intervening varieties may obtain, differing in degree of interpenetration. Such fused varieties may, within time, become the mother tongue and only tongue of a new generation. Thus, bilingualism without diglossia tends to be transitional[6] both in terms of the linguistic repertoires of speech communities as well as in terms of the speech varieties involved per se. Without separate though complementary norms and values to establish and maintain functional separation of the speech varieties, that language or variety which is fortunate enough to be associated with the predominant drift of social forces tends to displace the other(s). Furthermore, pidginization is likely to set in when members of the workforce are so dislocated as not to be able to maintain or develop significantly compartmentalized, limited access roles (in which they might be able to safeguard a stable mother-tongue variety) and, furthermore, cannot interact sufficiently with those members of the "power class" who might serve as standard other-tongue models.

Neither diglossia nor bilingualism

Only very small, isolated and undifferentiated speech communities may be said to reveal neither diglossia nor bilingualism (Gumperz, 1962; Fishman, 1965e). Given little role differentiation or compartmentalization and frequent face-to-face interaction between all members of the speech community no fully differentiated registers or varieties may establish themselves. Given self-sufficiency no regular or significant contacts with other speech communities may be maintained. Nevertheless, such groups – be they bands or clans – are easier to hypothesize than to find. All communities seem to have certain ceremonies or pursuits to which access is limited, if only on an age basis. Thus, all linguistic repertoires contain certain terms that are unknown to certain members of the speech community, and certain terms that are used differently by different subsets of speakers. In addition, metaphorical switching (Blom and Gumperz, 1972) for purposes of emphasis, humor, satire or criticism must be available in some form even in relatively undifferentiated communities. Finally, such factors as exogamy, warfare, expansion of population, economic growth and contact with others all lead to internal diversification and, consequently, to repertoire diversification. Such diversification is the beginning of bilingualism. Its societal normification is the hallmark of diglossia. Quadrant 4 of Figure 3.1 tends to be self liquidating.

Many efforts are now underway to bring to pass a rapprochement between psychological, linguistic and sociological work on bilingualism. The student of bilingualism – most particularly the student of bilingualism in the context of social issues and social change – may benefit from an awareness of the various possible relationships between individual bilingualism and societal diglossia illustrated in this paper. Since all bilingualism occurs in a social context, and since this context is likely to influence both the manifestations and the concomitants of bilingualism, it is incumbent on the student of bilingualism to differentiate accurately between the particular and the more general phenomena that pertain to his field of study.

Notes

1   Note that Guarani is not an official language (i.e., recognized and utilized for purposes of government, formal education, the courts, etc.) in Paraguay. It is not uncommon for the H variety alone to have such recognition in diglossic settings without this fact threatening the acceptance or the stability of the L variety within the speech community. However, the existence of a single "official" language should not divert the investigator from recognizing the fact of widespread and stable bilingualism at the levels of societal and interpersonal functioning.

2   This development differs significantly from the traditional Eastern European Jewish pattern in which males whose occupational activities brought them into regular contact with various strata of the non-Jewish coterritorial population utilized one or more coterritorial languages (usually involving H and L varieties of their own, such as Russian, German or Polish on the one hand, and Ukrainian, Byelorussian or "Baltic" varieties (e.g. Estonian, Latvian and Lithuanian), on the other), but did so for *intergroup* purposes almost exclusively.

3   The compartmentalization of roles (and of domains and situations as well) requires the redefinition of roles, domains and situations in any encounter in which a seemingly inappropriate topic must be discussed between individuals who normally stand in a given role relationship to each other. Under such circumstances one or other factor is altered (the roles are redefined, the topic is redefined) so as to preserve the cultural norms for appropriateness (grammaticality) of behavior between interlocutors.

4   A theory which tends to minimize the distinction between languages and varieties is desirable for several reasons. It implies that *social* consensus (rather than inherently linguistic desiderata) differentiates between the two and that separate varieties can become (and have become) separate languages given certain social encouragement to do so, just as purportedly separate languages have been fused into one, on the ground that they were merely different varieties of the same language.

5   Switzerland as a whole is not a case in point since it is not an example of discontinuous and hierarchically stratified speech communities under a common political regime. Switzerland consists of geographically stratified speech communities under a common regime. Except for the Swiss-German case there is hardly any societally patterned bilingualism in Switzerland. Only the Jura region, the Romansch area and a very few other small areas have (had) a recent history of diglossia without bilingualism.

6   At an individual level this need not be the case since translation bilingualism can be maintained for intragroup communication purposes and for individual vocational purposes without the formation of natural bilingual speech communities.

Source: Fishman, J.A. (1967) Bilingualism with and without diglossia; diglossia with and without bilingualism. *Journal of Social Issues* 23(2): 29–38, by permission of Blackwell Publishers.

Chapter 4

Who speaks what language to whom and when?

JOSHUA A. FISHMAN

The analysis of multilingual settings

Multilingual settings differ from each other in so many ways that every student of multilingualism must grapple with the problem of how best to systematize or organize the manifold differences that are readily recognizable. This chapter is primarily limited to a formal consideration of several descriptive and analytic variables which may contribute to an understanding of *who* speaks *what* language *to whom* and *when* in those settings that are characterized by widespread and relatively stable multilingualism. It deals primarily with "within-group (or intragroup) multilingualism" rather than with "between-group (or intergroup) multilingualism," that is with those multilingual settings in which a single population makes use of two (or more) separate codes for internal communicative purposes. As a result of this limitation, general knowledge of mother tongue and other tongue may be ruled out as an operative variable since most individuals *could* communicate with each other quite easily in *either* of the available languages. It seems clear, however, that habitual language choice is far from being a random matter of momentary inclination, even under those circumstances when it could very well function as such from a purely probabilistic point of view. "Proper" usage, or common usage, or both, dictate that only *one* of the theoretically co-available languages *will* be chosen by particular classes of *interlocutors* on particular *occasions*.

How can these choice-patterns be described? Our basic conceptual problem in this connection is to provide for the variety of patterns that exist in stable within-group multi-lingual settings throughout the world in such a way as to attain factual accuracy, theoretical parsimony and stimulation of future research. Once we have mastered the problem of how to describe language choice on the level of individual face-to-face encounters, we can then approach the problem of the broader, underlying choice determinants on the level of larger group or cultural settings (Fishman, 1964). Once we have mastered the problem of how to describe language choice in stable within-group bilingual settings (where the limits of language mastery do not intrude), we can then approach the problem of choice determinants in less stable settings such as those characterizing immigrant–host relationships and between-group multilingual settings more generally.

Group, situation, topic

(a) One of the first controlling factors in language choice is *group membership*. This factor must be viewed not only in a purportedly objective sense, i.e., in terms of physiological, sociological criteria (e.g., age, sex, race, religion, etc.), but also, and primarily, in the subjective socio-psychological sense of *reference group membership*. A government functionary in Brussels arrives home after stopping off at his club for a drink. He generally speaks standard French in his office, standard Dutch at his club and a distinctly local variant of Flemish at home.[1] In each instance he identifies himself with a different group to which he belongs, wants to belong, and from which he seeks acceptance. Nevertheless, it is not difficult to find occasions at the office in which he speaks or is spoken to in one or another variety of Flemish. There are also occasions at the club when he speaks or is addressed in French; finally, there are occasions at home when he communicates in standard Dutch or even French. It would be too much to claim that a shift in reference group occurs on *each* of these supposedly atypical occasions. In addition, the very existence of certain reference groups (e.g., club member) seems to depend largely on location, setting or other environmental factors (which, we will see, may deserve recognition in their own right rather than need to remain hidden under a vague "group" rubric), rather than on group-consciousness or group-experience as such. Finally, even were this not to be the case, it seems unnecessarily difficult to analyze language choice within large, complex, literate societies in terms of the enormous repertoire of shifting reference groups which these provide. Thus, while we may admit that the concept of reference group membership enables us to recognize *some* invariables of habitual language choice in stable multilingual settings (e.g., that our hypothetical functionary *is* Flemish and would probably know no Dutch Flemish at all were this not the case), it does so only at a considerable risk, while leaving many exceptional cases in the dark. Obviously, additional clarificatory concepts are needed.

(b) A further regulating factor is recognized via the concept of *situation*.[2] This term has been used to designate a large (and, at times, confusing) variety of considerations. Indeed, it has been used to designate various *separate* considerations as well as their *co-occurrence*. Thus, Ervin (1964) observes that various situations (settings) may be restricted with respect to the *participants* who may be present, the *physical setting*, the *topics* and *functions* of discourse and the *style* employed (my italics). Each of these aspects of "situation" may shed light on certain regularities in language choice on particular social occasions. However, the possible *co-occurrence* of so many variables must also make it exceedingly difficult to use the concept "situation," when so characterized, for analytic purposes. Let us, therefore, limit our use of this term to considerations of "style" alone, and attempt to cope with the other itemized features in other ways and in their own right. Situational styles, following Joos (1962), Labov (1963), Gumperz and Naim (1960) and others, pertain to considerations of intimacy–distance, formality–informality, solidarity–non-solidarity, status (or power) equality–inequality, etc. Thus, certain styles within every language (and, in multilingual settings, certain languages in contrast to others) are considered by particular interlocutors to be indicators of greater intimacy, informality, equality, etc. Not only do multilinguals frequently consider one of their languages more dialectal, more regional, more sub-standard, more vernacular-like, more argot-like than the others, but, in addition, they more frequently associate one of their languages with informality, equality, solidarity than the other. As a result, one is more likely to be reserved for certain situations than the other. Our hypothetical government functionary is most likely to give and get Flemish at the office when he bumps into another functionary who hails from the very same Flemish-speaking town. The two of them grew up together and went to school together. Their respective sets of parents strike them as being similarly "kind-but-old-fashioned." In short, they share many common experiences and points of view (or think they do, or pretend they do) and therefore they tend to speak to each other in the language which represents for them the intimacy that they share. The two do not cease being government functionaries when they speak Flemish to each other; they simply prefer to treat each other as intimates rather than as functionaries. However, the careful observer will also note that the two do not speak Flemish to each other invariably. When they speak about work affairs, or the worlds of art and literature, not to mention the world of government, they tend to switch into French (or to reveal far greater interference in their Flemish), even though (for the sake of our didactic argument) the mood of intimacy and familiarity remains clearly evident throughout. Thus, neither reference group membership nor situational style, alone or in concert, fully explain(s) the variations that can be noted in habitual language choice in multilingual settings. It must also be observed that situational styles, however carefully delineated, may still not provide us with much substantive or procedural insight into the socio-cultural organization of any particular multilingual setting.

(c) The fact that two individuals who obviously prefer to speak to each other in X nevertheless switch to Y (or vacillate more noticeably between X and Y) when discussing certain topics leads us to consider topic per se as a regulator of language use in multilingual settings. It is obviously possible to talk about the national economy (topic) in a thoroughly informal way (situational style) while relating oneself to one's family (reference group). Under such circumstances – even when reference group and situation agree in requiring a particular language – it is not uncommon to find that topic succeeds in bringing another language to the fore.[3]

The implication of topical regulation of language choice is that certain topics are somehow handled better in one language than in another in particular multilingual contexts. This situation may be brought about by several different but mutually reinforcing factors. Thus, some multilingual speakers may "acquire the habit" of speaking about topic *x* in language X partially because that is the language in which they were *trained* to deal with this topic (e.g., they received their university training in economics in French), partially because *they (and their interlocutors)* may *lack the specialized terms* for a satisfying discussion of *x* in language Y, partially because *language Y itself may currently lack as exact or as many terms for handling* topic *x* as those currently possessed by language X, and partially because *it is considered strange* or inappropriate to discuss *x* in language Y. The very multiplicity of sources of topical regulation suggests that *topic* may not in itself be a convenient analytic variable when language choice is considered from the point of view of the social structure and the cultural norms of a multilingual setting. It tells us little about either the process or the structure of social behavior. However, topics usually exhibit patterns which follow those of the major spheres of activity in the society under consideration. We may be able to discover the latter if we enquire why a significant number of people in a particular multilingual setting at a particular time have received certain kinds of training in one language rather than in another; or *what it reveals* about a particular multilingual setting if language X *is* actually less capable of coping with topic *x* than is language Y. Does it not reveal more than merely a topic–language relationship at the level of face-to-face encounters? Does it not reveal that certain socio-culturally *recognized spheres of activity* are, at least temporarily, under the sway of one language (and, therefore, perhaps of one sub-population) rather than another? Thus, while topic is doubtlessly a crucial consideration in understanding language choice variance in our two hypothetical government functionaries, we must seek a means of examining and relating their individual, momentary choices to relatively stable patterns of choice that exist in their multilingual setting as a whole.

Domains of language behavior

(a) The concept of domains of language behavior seems to have received its first partial elaboration from students of language maintenance and language shift among *Auslands-deutsche* in pre-Second World War multilingual settings.[4] German settlers were in contact with many different non-German speaking populations in various types of contact settings and were exposed to various kinds of socio-cultural change processes. In attempting to chart and compare the fortunes of the German language under such varying circumstances Schmidt-Rohr (1963) seems to have been the first to suggest that *dominance configurations* (to be discussed below) needed to be established to reveal the overall status of language choice in various domains of behavior. The domains recommended by Schmidt-Rohr were the following nine: the family, the playground and street, the school (subdivided into language of instruction, subject of instruction, and language of recess and entertainment), the church, literature, the press, the military, the courts, and the governmental administration. Subsequently, other investigators either added additional domains (e.g., Mak, 1935, who nevertheless followed Schmidt-Rohr in overlooking the work-sphere as a domain), or found that fewer domains were sufficient in particular multilingual settings (e.g., Frey, 1945, who required only home, school and church in his analysis of Amish "triple talk"). However, what is more interesting is that Schmidt-Rohr's domains bear a striking similarity to those "generally termed" spheres of activity which have more recently been independently advanced by some anthropologists (Dohrenwend and Smith, 1962), sociologists (Kloss, 1929), social psychologists (Jones and Lambert, 1959) and linguists (Mackey, 1962) for the study of acculturation, intergroup relations, and bilingualism. The latter are defined, regardless of their number,[5] in terms of *institutional contexts* or *socio-ecological co-occurrences*. They attempt to designate the *major clusters of interaction situations that occur in particular multilingual settings*. Domains such as these help us understand that *language choice* and *topic*, appropriate though they may be for analyses of individual behavior at the level of face-to-face verbal encounters, are, as we suggested above, related to widespread socio-cultural norms and expectations. Language choices, cumulated over many individuals and many choice instances, become transformed into the processes of *language maintenance* or *language shift*. Furthermore, if many individuals (or sub-groups) tend to handle topic x in language X, this may well be because this topic pertains to a *domain* in which that language is "dominant" for their society or for their subgroup as a whole. Certainly it is a far different social interaction when topic x is discussed in language Y *although it pertains to a domain in which language X is dominant*, than when the same topic is discussed by the same interlocutors in the language most commonly employed in that domain. By recognizing the existence of domains it becomes possible to contrast the language of topics for individuals or particular sub-populations with the language of domains for larger parts, if not the whole, of the population.

(b) The appropriate designation and definition of domains of language behavior obviously calls for considerable insight into the socio-cultural dynamics of particular multilingual settings at particular periods in their history. Schmidt-Rohr's domains reflect not only multilingual settings in which a large number of spheres of activity, even those that pertain to governmental functions, are theoretically open to both or all of the languages present, but also those multilingual settings in which such permissiveness is at least sought by a sizable number of interested parties. Quite different domains might be appropriate if one were to study habitual language use among children in these very same settings. Certainly, immigrant-host contexts, in which only the language of the host society is recognized for governmental functions, would require other and perhaps fewer domains, particularly if younger generations constantly leave the immigrant society and enter the host society. Finally, the domains of language behavior may differ from setting to setting not only in terms of number and designation but also in terms of level. Thus, in studying acculturating populations in Arizona, Barker (who studied bilingual Spanish Americans; 1947) and Barber (who studied trilingual Yaqui Indians; 1952) formulated *domains at the level of socio-psychological analysis*: intimate, informal, formal and intergroup. Interestingly enough, the domains defined in this fashion were then identified with domains at the *societal-institutional level* mentioned above. The "formal" domain, e.g., was found to coincide with religious-ceremonial activities; the "inter-group" domain consisted of economic and recreational activities as well as of interactions with governmental-legal authority, etc. The inter-relationship between domains of language behavior defined at a societal-institutional level and domains defined at a socio-psychological level (the latter being somewhat similar to situational analyses discussed earlier) may enable us to study language choice in multilingual settings in newer and more fruitful ways. We will present one approach to the study of just such inter-relationships in our discussion of the *dominance configuration*, below.

(c) The "governmental administration" domain is a social nexus which brings people together *primarily* for a certain *cluster of purposes*. Furthermore, it brings them together *primarily* for a certain set of role-relations (discussed below) and in a delimited environment. Although it is possible for them to communicate about many things, given these purposes and contexts, the topical variety is actually quite small in certain media (e.g., written communication) and in certain situations (e.g., formal communication), and is noticeably skewed in the direction of *domain purpose* in most domains. Thus, domain is a socio-cultural construct abstracted from topics of communication, relationships between communicators, and locales of communication, in accord with the institutions of a society and the spheres of activity of a culture, in such a way that *individual behavior and social patterns can be distinguished from each other and yet related to each other.*[6] The domain is a higher order of abstraction or summarization which is arrived at from a consideration of the socio-cultural patterning which surrounds language choices. Of the many factors contributing to and subsumed under the domain concept some are more important and more accessible to careful measurement than others. One of these, topic, has already been discussed. Another, role-relations, remains to be discussed. Role-relations may be of value to us in accounting for the fact that our

two hypothetical governmental functionaries, who usually speak an informal variant of Flemish to each other at the office, except when they talk about technical,
professional or sophisticated "cultural" matters, are themselves not entirely alike
in this respect. One of the two tends to slip into French more frequently than the
other, even when reference group, situational style, topic and several other aspects
of communication are controlled. It would not be surprising to discover that his
role is different, that he is the supervisor of the other for example.

Domains and role-relations

In many studies of multilingual behavior the family domain has proved to be a very
crucial one. Multilingualism often begins in the family and depends upon it for
encouragement if not for protection. In other cases, multilingualism withdraws
into the family domain after it has been displaced from other domains in which it
was previously encountered. Little wonder then that many investigators, beginning with Braunshausen (1928), have differentiated *within* the family domain in
terms of "speakers." However, two different approaches have been followed in
connection with such differentiation. Braunshausen (and also Mackey, 1962) have
merely specified family "members": father, mother, child, domestic, governess and
tutor, etc. Gross (1951), on the other hand, has specified *dyads* within the family:
grandfather to grandmother, grandmother to grandfather, grandfather to father,
grandmother to father, grandfather to mother, grandmother to mother, grandfather to child, grandmother to child, father to mother, mother to father, etc. The
difference between these two approaches is quite considerable. Not only does
the second approach recognize that interacting members of a family (as well as the
participants in most other domains of language behavior) are *hearers* as well as
speakers (i.e., that there may be a distinction between multilingual *comprehension*
and multilingual *production*), but it also recognizes that their language behavior
may be more than merely a matter of individual preference or facility but also a
matter of *role-relations*. In certain societies particular behaviors (including language behaviors) are *expected* (if not required) of *particular individuals vis-à-vis each
other*. Whether role-relations are fully reducible to situational styles for the purpose of describing habitual language choice in particular multilingual settings is a
matter for future empirical research.

The family domain is hardly unique with respect to its differentiability into
role-relations. Each domain can be differentiated into role-relations that are specifically crucial or typical of it in particular societies at particular times. The
religious domain (in those societies where religion can be differentiated from
folkways more generally) may reveal such role relations as cleric–cleric, cleric–
parishioner, parishioner–cleric, and parishioner–parishioner. Similarly, pupil–
teacher, buyer–seller, employer–employee, judge–petitioner, all refer to specific
role-relations in other domains. It would certainly seem desirable to describe and

analyze language use or language choice in a particular multilingual setting in terms of the crucial role-relations within the specific domains considered to be most revealing for that setting. The distinction between one-group-interlocutor and other-group-interlocutor may also be provided for in this way.[7]

Domains and other sources of variance in language behavior

Our discussion thus far has probably succeeded in making at least one thing clear, namely that any simultaneous attempt to cope with *all of the theoretically possible* sources of variance in language behavior in multilingual settings is likely to be exceedingly complex. It is even more complex than indicated thus far, for we have not yet attended to the questions of what *kind of language data to recognize* in a study of multilingualism or of language maintenance and language shift. Should we follow the linguist's dominant tradition of testing for phonetic, lexical and grammatical interference (not to mention semantic interference) in the several interacting languages? Should we follow the psychologist in testing for relative speed or automaticity of translation or response? Should we follow the educator in testing for relative global proficiency? Certainly, each of these traditional approaches is legitimate and important. However, each of them has been set aside in the discussion below, in favor of the sociologist's grosser concern with *relative frequency of use*, a perspective on multilingualism which seems to be particularly appropriate for the study of language maintenance or language shift (Fishman, 1964). However, even when we limit ourselves in this fashion we can barely begin to approximate data collection and analysis in accord with all possible interactions between the many sources of variance and domains of language use mentioned thus far. Any study of multilingualism can select only an appropriate sub-cluster of variables for simultaneous study. Hopefully, all other variables can remain, temporarily, at the level of unexplained error variance until they too can be subjected to study.

For the purpose of illuminating patterns of language choice in multilingual settings, it would seem appropriate to distinguish at least between the following sources of variance:

1   *Media variance: writing, reading and speaking*: Degree of mother tongue maintenance or displacement may be quite different in each of these very different media.[8] Where literacy has been attained *prior* to interaction with an "other tongue" reading and writing use of the mother tongue may resist displacement longer than speaking usage. Where literacy is attained subsequent to (or as a result of) such interaction the reverse more frequently obtains (Fishman, 1964).

2   *Role*[9] *variance*: Degree of maintenance or shift may be quite different in conjunction with *inner speech* (the language of thought, of talking to one's

self, the language of dreams, in short, all of those cases in which ego is both source and target), *comprehension* (decoding, in which ego is the target), and *production* (encoding, in which ego is the source). There is some evidence from individual as well as from group data that where language shift is resisted by multilinguals, inner speech remains most resistant to interference, switching and disuse of the mother tongue. Where language shift is desired the reverse frequently obtains (Fishman, 1964).

3   *Situational variance*: Degree of maintenance or shift may be quite different in conjunction with *more formal, less formal* and *intimate* communication (Fishman, 1965a). Where language shift is resisted more intimate situations seem to be most resistant to interference, switching or disuse of the mother tongue. The reverse obtains where language shift is desired.

4   *Domain variance*: Degree of maintenance or shift may be quite different in each of several distinguishable domains of language behavior. Such differences may reflect differences between interacting populations and their socio-cultural systems with respect to autonomy, power, influence, domain centrality, etc. Domains require sub-analysis in terms of the role-relations that are crucial to them, as well as sub-analysis in terms of topical variance.

A description and analysis of the *simultaneous, cumulative effect* of all of the above-mentioned sources of variance in language choice provides a dominance configuration (Weinrich, 1953). Dominance configurations summarize data on the language choice behavior of many individuals who constitute a defined sub-population. Repeated dominance configurations for the same population, studied over time, may be used to represent the evolution of language maintenance and language shift in a particular multilingual setting. Contrasted dominance configurations may be used to study the relative impact of *various* socio-cultural processes (urbanization, secularization, revitalization, etc.) on the *same* mother tongue group in different contact settings, or the relative impact of a *single* socio-cultural process on *different* mother tongue groups in similar contact settings (Fishman, 1964).

The dominance configuration

Table 1 is primarily intended as a summary derived from an attempt to estimate the relationships obtaining between *domains* of language behavior and the particular *sources of variance* in language behavior specified earlier. The resulting dominance configuration reveals several general characteristics of this mode of analysis:

1   A complete cross-tabulation of all theoretically possible sources and domains of variance in language behavior does not actually obtain. Certain co-occurrences appear to be logically impossible. Other co-occurrences, while

Table 4.1 Yiddish–English maintenance and shift in the United States: 1940–60

Sources of variance			Domains of language behavior					
Media	Role	Situational	Family	Friends	Acquaintances	Mass media	Jewish organizations	Occupations
	Inner*	Formal	X	X	X	X	X	X
		Informal	Y, E	Y, E	Y, E	E, E	Y, E	E, E
		Intimate	Y, E	Y, E	Y, E	E, E	Y, E	E, E
Speaking	Comp.	Formal	X	X	E, E	E, E	Y, E	E, E
		Informal	E, E	E, E	E, E	E, E	Y, E	E, E
		Intimate	Y, E	Y, E	X	X	X	X
	Prod.	Formal	X	X	E, E	X	Y, E	E, E
		Informal	E, E	E, E	E, E	X	Y, E	E, E
		Intimate	Y, E	Y, E	E, E	X	X	X

	Formal	Y,E	X	X	X	Y,E	X
Comp.	Informal	Y,E	X	X	X	Y,E	X
	Intimate	E,E	X	X	X	X	X
	Formal	Y,E	X	X	Y,E	Y,E	X
Prod.**	Informal	Y,E	X	X	Y,E	Y,E	X
	Intimate	E,E	X	X	E,E	X	X
Reading							
	Formal	X	X	X	X	Y,E	X
Writing — Prod.	Informal	E,E	E,E	X	X	Y,E	X
	Intimate	E,E	E,E	X	X	X	X

Notes: Comparisons for immigrant generation "secularists" arriving prior to the First World War (first language shown is most frequently used; second language shown is increasing in use; X indicates no data for this particular population or not applicable).

* For "speaking-inner" combinations the domains imply topics as well as contexts. In all other instances they imply contexts alone.
** For "reading-production" combinations the distinction between "family" and "mass media" domains is also a distinction between reading to others and reading to oneself.

Source: Fishman, 1965a

     logically possible, are either necessarily rare or so rare for the particular population under study that it may not be necessary to provide for them in the dominance configuration.

2   Each cell in the dominance configuration summarizes detailed process data pertaining to the particular role-relations most pertinent to it and the topical range encountered.

3   The domains of language behavior that figure in a particular dominance configuration are selected for their demonstrated utility (or for their theoretical promise) in analyzing language choice in a particular multilingual setting at a particular time.

4   An exhaustive analysis of the data of dominance configurations may well require sophisticated pattern analyses or other mathematical techniques which do not necessarily assume equal weight and simple additivity for each entry in each cell.[10]

5   The integrative summary-nature of the dominance configuration should enable investigators to avoid the reporting of atomized findings although the configuration as such must be based upon refined details. In addition, the dominance configuration does not preclude the combining of domains or other sources of variance in language choice whenever simpler patterns are recognizable (e.g., public vs. private spheres or formal vs. informal encounters). In general, the dominance configuration may best be limited to those aspects of *degree of bilingualism* and *location of bilingualism* which empirical analysis will ultimately reveal to be of greatest *independent importance*.

6   A much more refined presentation of language maintenance or language shift becomes possible than that which is provided by means of traditional mother tongue census statistics (Fishman, 1965c).

     Although the dominance configuration still requires much further refinement, it seems to merit the time and effort that such refinement might necessitate.

Some empirical and conceptual contributions of domain analysis

The domain concept has facilitated a number of worthwhile contributions to the understanding of bilingualism and language choice. It has helped organize and clarify the previously unstructured awareness that language maintenance and language shift proceed quite unevenly across the several sources and domains of variance in habitual language choice. Certain domains appear to be more resistant to displacement than others (e.g., the family domain in comparison to the occupational domain) across all multilingual settings characterized by urbanization and economic development, regardless of whether between-group or within-group comparisons are involved (Fishman, 1964). Under the impact of these same socio-cultural processes other domains (e.g., religion) seem to be very strongly main-tenance oriented during earlier stages of interaction and strongly shift oriented once a decision is reached that their organizational base can be better secured via shift (Fishman, 1965c). The simultaneous, concomitant effect of certain domains and other sources of variance seems to be protective of recessive languages, even when language shift has advanced so far that a given domain as such has been engulfed.[11] On the other hand if a strict domain separation becomes institutional-ized, such that each language is associated with a number of important but distinct domains, bilingualism can become both universal and stabilized even though an entire population consists of bilinguals interacting with other bilinguals (Rubin,1963). The domain concept has also helped refine the distinction between coordinate bilingualism and compound bilingualism (Ervin and Osgood, 1954) by stressing that not only does a continuum (rather than a dichotomy) obtain, but by indicating how one stage along this continuum may shade into another. Thus, as indicated by Figure 4.1, most late nineteenth- and early twentieth-century immi-grants to America from eastern and southern Europe began as compound bilinguals with each language assigned to separate and minimally overlapping domains. With the passage of time (involving increased interaction with English-speaking Americans, social mobility, and acculturation with respect to other-than-language behaviors as well) their bilingualism became characterized, first, by far greater domain overlap (and by far greater interference) and then by progressively greater coordinate functioning. Finally, language displacement advanced so far that the mother tongue remained only in a few restricted and non-overlapping domains. Indeed, in some cases, compound bilingualism once more became the rule, except that the ethnic mother tongue came to be utilized via English (rather than vice-versa as was the case in the early immigrant days). Thus, the domain concept may help place the compound–coordinate distinction in greater socio-cultural perspective, in much the same way as it may serve the entire area of language choice. More generally, we are helped to realize that the initial pattern of acquisition of bilingualism and subsequent patterns of bilingual functioning need not be in agreement (Figure 4.2). Indeed, a bilingual may vary with respect to the compound vs. coordinate nature of his functioning in each of the sources and domains of variance in language choice that we have discussed. If this is the case then several different models of interference may be needed to correspond to various stages of bilingualism and to various co-occurrences of influence on language choice.

Bilingual functioning type	Domain overlap type	
	Overlapping domains	Non-overlapping domains
Compound (interdependent or fused)	2. *Second Stage:* More immigrants know more English and therefore can speak to each other either in mother tongue or in English (still ⟵ mediated by the mother tongue) in several domains of behavior. Increased interference.	1. *Initial Stage:* The immigrant learns English via his mother tongue. English is used only in those few domains (work sphere, governmental sphere) in which mother tongue cannot be used. Minimal interference. Only a few immigrants knew a little English.
Coordinate (independent or discrete)	3. *Third Stage:* The languages function independently of each other. The number of bilinguals is at its maximum. Domain overlap is at its maximum. The second ⟶ generation during childhood. Stabilized interference.	4. *Final Stage:* English has displaced the mother tongue from all but the most private or restricted domains. Interference declines. In most cases both languages function independently; in others the mother tongue is mediated by English (reversal of Stage 1, but same type).

Figure 4.1   Type of bilingual functioning and domain overlap during successive stages of immigrant acculturation

Some remaining problems and challenges for domain analysis

Nevertheless, as is the case with most new integrative concepts, the major problems and the major promises of domain analysis still lie ahead. There are several methodological problems of data collection and data analysis, which cannot be enumerated here, but which do not seem to be in any way unprecedented. The substantive challenges pertaining to domain analysis are more varied, for they will depend on the interests of particular investigators. Domain analysis and the dominance configuration merely seek to provide a systematic approach to descriptive

Bilingual acquisition type	Domain overlap type	
	Overlapping domains	Non-overlapping domains
Compound (interdependent or fused)	Transitional bilingualism: the older second generation. The "high school French" tourist who remains abroad somewhat longer than he expected.	"Cultural bilingualism": the bilingualism of the "indirect method" classroom, whereby one language is learned through another but retained in separate domains.
Coordinate (independent or discrete)	Widespread bilingualism without social cleavage: the purported goal of "responsible" French-Canadians. The "direct method" classroom.	"One-sided bilingualism" or bilingualism with marked and stable social distinctions, such that only one group in a contact situation is bilingual or such that only particular domains are open or appropriate to particular languages.

Figure 4.2 Initial type of bilingual acquisition and subsequent domain overlap type

Source: Fishman, 1964

parameters. Some will wish to utilize these parameters in connection with *other formal features of communication than code-variety*. Thus, the study of "sociolinguistic variants" (i.e., of those linguistic alternations regarded as "free" or "optional" variants *within* a code) may gain somewhat from the greater socio-cultural context provided by domain analysis. Other investigators may seek to establish cross-cultural and diachronic language and culture files in order to investigate the relationship between changes in language behavior (including changes in language choice) and other processes of socio-cultural change. In this connection, domain analysis may facilitate language use comparisons between settings (or between historical periods) of roughly similar domain structure. Still other investigators, more centrally concerned with multilingualism and with language maintenance or language shift, may well become interested in refining the typologies and stages that are currently on record: e.g., Vildomec's (1963) "local" vs. "cultural" multi-lingualism,[12] Kloss's (1929) much earlier five-fold classification of patterns of stabilized multilingualism, Carman's (1962) recent ten-stage analysis of language shift among immigrants settling in Kansas, and many others. Domain analysis (within the context of a dominance configuration) may enable us to see unexpected relationships *between* these several formulations and to improve upon them both on theoretical and empirical grounds.

Conclusions

The concept of "domains of language choice" represents an attempt to provide socio-cultural organization and socio-cultural context for considerations of variance in language choice in multilingual settings. When systematically interrelated with other sources of variance in language behavior (media variance, role variance, situational variance) and when based upon underlying analyses of the role-relations and topics most crucial to them, domains of language behavior may contribute importantly to the establishment of dominance configuration summaries. Domain analysis may be a promising conceptual and methodological tool for future studies of language behavior in multilingual settings and for socio-linguistic studies more generally. Ultimately, a relatively uniform but flexible analytic scheme such as that described here may enable us to arrive at valid generalizations concerning (1) the kinds of multilingual settings in which one or another configuration of variance in language choice obtains and (2) the language maintenance or language shift consequences of particular configurations of dominance or variance.

Notes

1   This example may be replaced by any one of a number of others: Standard German, Schwytzertüsch and Romansch (in parts of Switzerland); Hebrew, English and Yiddish in Israel; Riksmaal, Landsmaal and more local dialectal variants of the latter in Norway; Standard German, Plattdeutsch and Danish in Schleswig, etc.

2   *Situation* and *setting* are frequently used interchangeably in the socio-linguistic literature. In this paper *setting* is intended to be the broader and more multifaceted concept. (Thus, a complete consideration of "the multilingual setting" requires attention to language choice data, socio-cultural process data, historical perspective on the particular intergroup context, data on attitudinal, emotional, cognitive and overt behaviors toward language (Fishman, 1964), etc.) *Situation* is reserved for use in characterizing certain circumstances of communication at the time of communication.

3   This effect has been noted even in normally monolingual settings, such as those obtaining among American intellectuals, many of whom feel obliged to use French or German words in conjunction with particular professional topics. The frequency of lexical interference in the language of immigrants in the United States has also

often been explained on topical grounds. The importance of topical determinants is discussed by Haugen, 1953; 1956; Weinreich, 1953; Gumperz, 1962; and Ervin, 1964. It is implied as a "pressure" exerted upon "contacts" in Mackey's (1962) description of bilingualism.

4   The study of language maintenance and language shift is concerned with the relationship between change or stability in habitual language use, on the one hand, and ongoing psychological, social or cultural processes of change and stability, on the other hand, in multilingual settings (Fishman, 1964).

5   We can safely reject the implication encountered in certain discussions of domains that there must be an invariant set of domains applicable to all multilingual settings. If language behavior is related to socio-cultural organization, as is now widely accepted, then different kinds of multilingual settings should benefit from analyses in terms of different domains of language use, whether defined intuitively, theoretically, or empirically.

6   For a discussion of the differences and similarities between "functions of language behavior" and "domains of language behavior" see Fishman, 1964. "Functions" stand closer to socio-psychological analysis, for they abstract their constituents in terms of individual motivation rather than in terms of group purpose.

7   These remarks are not intended to imply that *all* role-relation differences are necessarily related to language-choice differences. This almost certainly is *not* the case. Just which role-relation differences *are* related to language-choice differences (and under what circumstances) is a matter for empirical determination within each multilingual setting as well as at different points in time within the same setting.

8   Writing and reading are differentiated as separate media not only because they may be pursued in different languages but because each is capable of independent productive and receptive use. In general, the formal dimensions presented here make use of more distinctions than may be necessary in all multilingual settings. Both empirical and theoretical considerations must ultimately be involved in selecting the dimensions appropriate for the analysis of particular settings.

9   Unfortunately, the term *role* is currently employed in several somewhat different ways, e.g., "role in society" (*mayor, untouchable, bank president*), "role relation" vis-à-vis particular others (*husband–wife, father–child, teacher–pupil*), "occasional role" (*chairman, host, spokesman*), and "momentary role" (*initiator of a communication, respondent, listener*). It is in this last sense that the term "role" will be used in connection with "role variance" above, while it is in the sense of "role-relation" that the term "role" has been used previously in our discussion of differentiations within the domains of language behavior.

10   Disregarding this stricture an inspection of Table 4.1 reveals:
    1   there is no cell in which the use of Yiddish is currently increasing in the studied population;
    2   reading is the most retentive area of media variance;
    3   inner speech is the most retentive area of role variance;
    4   formal usage is the most retentive area of situational variance;

5   the organizational context is the most retentive area of domain variance whereas the occupational context is the least retentive.

All in all, this dominance configuration leaves one with the impression of greatest retention of Yiddish in those circumstances that are either most private and subject to personal control or most structured and generationally restricted (Fishman, 1965a).

11   Note, for example, the mass media interaction with either reading-production-formality or with reading-production-informality in Table 4.1.

12   This seems to be the latest in a long tradition of attempts to reduce multilingualism to a dichotomy. For many earlier attempts along such lines see Weinreich, 1953: 9–10, 35, 81–2; Fishman, 1964.

Source: Fishman, J. A. (1965) Who speaks what language to whom and when? *La Linguistique* 2:67–88, by permission of the author.

Notes for students and instructors

Study questions

1   Give two examples from the language contact situations that you know of which may be described in terms of Fishman's model of the four relationships between diglossia and bilingualism.
2   Central to the concept of domain is the notion of congruence on two levels: (a) congruence among domain components (e.g. participant, topic and setting); (b) congruence of domain with specific language or language variety. Give an example from the community you are familiar with and demonstrate how language choice varies across domains.

Study activities

1   Carry out a 'domain analysis' of the language choice patterns of a bilingual family or a small group of bilingual speakers, using a questionnaire or through interview. Summarise your findings in a table or graphical formats.
2   Find a three-generation family from an ethnic minority background (if you live in a multilingual area, find a three-generation multilingual family) and ask one person from each generation about his/her language preference and language use in key domains. Ask them to list ten of their most important and regular contacts who are not members of the family, including the age, sex, occupation and language background of each of the contacts. Can you see any relationship between the three speakers' language preference and language choice patterns and the social characteristics of their key contacts?

Further reading

General introductions to the study of bilingual language choice can be found in Chapter 4 of R. Wardhaugh, 1998, *An Introduction to Sociolinguistics* (3rd edn), Blackwell, and Chapter 7 of R. Fasold, 1984, *The Sociolinguistics of Society*, Blackwell.

On the notion of 'diglossia', see R.A. Hudson, 1992, Diglossia: A bibliographic review, *Language in Society*, 21: 611–74, and M. Fernandez, 1994, *Diglossia: A comprehensive bibliography 1960–1990 and supplements*, John Benjamins.

For Fishman's contributions, see *Language in Sociocultural Change: Essays by J.A. Fishman,* selected by A.S. Dil, 1972, Stanford University Press; *The Rise and Fall of the Ethnic Revival: Perspectives on language and ethnicity,* 1985, Mouton; and *Reversing Language Shift,* 1991, Multilingual Matters.

For classic examples of earlier studies of bilingualism and language contact, see *Languages in Contact: Findings and problems,* 1953, U. Weinreich, Linguistic Circle of New York, and *The Norwegian Language in America,* 1953, by E. Haugen, Pennsylvania University Press.

Examples of community-based studies of language choice include: S. Gal, 1979, *Language Shift: Social determinants of linguistic change in bilingual Austria,* Academic Press; N. Dorian, 1981, *Language Death, The life cycle of a Scottish Gaelic dialect,* Pennsylvania University Press; V. Edwards, 1986, *Language in a Black Community,* Multilingual Matters; and Li Wei, 1994, *Three Generations Two Languages One Family: Language choice and language shift in a Chinese community in Britain,* Multilingual Matters.

For an anthropological perspective on language choice, see J.H. Hill and K.C. Hill, 1986, *Speaking Mexicano: Dynamics of syncretic language in Central Mexico,* University of Arizona Press, and D. Kulick, 1992, *Language Shift and Cultural Reproduction: Socialisation, self and syncretism in a Papua New Guinean village,* Cambridge University Press.

On language choice as a political strategy, see K.A. Woolard, 1989, *Double Talk: Bilingualism and the politics of ethnicity in Catalonia,* Stanford University Press; M. Heller, 1994, *Crosswords: Language, education and ethnicity in French Ontario,* Mouton; and M. Heller, 1999, *Linguistic Minorities and Modernity: A sociolinguistic ethnography,* Longman.

Bilingual interaction

Chapter 5

Social meaning in linguistic structure: code-switching in Norway

JAN-PETTER BLOM AND
JOHN J. GUMPERZ

IN HIS DISCUSSIONS OF the problem of language and society, Bernstein (1961; 1964) explores the hypothesis that social relationships act as intervening variables between linguistic structures and their realization in speech. His formulation suggests that the anthropologists' analysis of social constraints governing interpersonal relationships may be utilized in the interpretation of verbal performances. This chapter attempts to clarify the social and linguistic factors involved in the communication process and to test Bernstein's hypothesis by showing that speakers' selection among semantically, grammatically, and phonologically permissible alternates occurring in conversation sequences recorded in natural groups is both patterned and predictable on the basis of certain features of the local social system. In other words, given a particular aggregate of people engaged in regular face-to-face interaction, and given some knowledge of the speakers' linguistic repertoire (Gumperz, 1964), we wish to relate the structure of that repertoire to the verbal behavior of members of the community in particular situations.

Data on verbal interaction derive from approximately two months' field work in Hemnesberget, a small commercial and industrial town of about 1,300 inhabitants in the center of the Rana Fjord, close to the Arctic circle in northern Norway. The settlement owes its existence to the growth of local trade and industry following the abolition of government-sanctioned trade monopolies covering most of northern Norway in 1858. Since the Middle Ages, these monopolies had kept the area's economy dependent upon a small elite of merchant and landholding families with connections to southern Norway, separated by great differences in wealth, culture, and education from the tenant farmers, fishermen, estate laborers, and servants who formed the bulk of the populace. Apart from a few shop owners and government officials, present-day Hemnesberget residents are mostly descendants of these latter groups. They have been attracted to the town from the surroundings by new economic opportunities there, while around one hundred years of relatively free economic development have splintered the old ruling circles. Many of this former elite have moved away, and the remainder no longer form a visible social group in the region.

Present inhabitants of Hemnesberget earn their livelihood mainly as crafts-men in family workshops or in the somewhat larger boat-building and lumber-processing plants, all of which are locally owned. The area serves as a major source of wood products and fishing equipment for the northernmost part of Norway. A significant group of merchant middlemen deal in locally produced boats and other products, which they ship north for resale, and maintain sales agencies for motors and other appliances and manufactured goods from the south.

While at the beginning of the twentieth century Hemnesberget was the most important communications and commercial center in the area, it was eclipsed in the 1960s by government-sponsored economic development which turned the town of Mo i Rana, at the mouth of Rana Fjord, into Norway's major iron- and steel-producing center. The region of Mo grew from about 1,000 inhabitants in 1920 to almost 9,000 in 1960, largely through immigration from the region of Trøndelag and southern Norway. It now boasts several modern department stores, hotels, restaurants, and cinemas. The railroad from Trondheim in the south through Mo and on north to Bodø was completed shortly after the Second World War, and the road system has steadily improved. All these new communication arteries, however, bypass Hemnesberget, which has all but lost its importance as a communication link for both land and sea traffic.

Although the immediate ecological environment has changed greatly, Hemnesberget remains an island of tradition in a sea of change. There is a regular once-a-day boat service to Mo, buses leave for the railroad station twice a day, and a few people commute to Mo by private automobile or motorcycle. However, the bulk of the residents spend most of their working and leisure time in and around Hemnesberget. Those who can afford it build vacation cabins in the unsettled areas across the fjord a few miles away. Our interviews uniformly show that social events in Mo i Rana are only of marginal interest to local inhabitants.

The community linguistic repertoire

Most residents of Hemnesberget are native speakers of Ranamål (R), one of a series of dialects which segment northern Norway into linguistic regions roughly corresponding to other cultural and ecological divisions (Christiansen, 1962). As elsewhere in Norway, where local independence and distinctness of folk culture are highly valued, the dialect enjoys great prestige. A person's native speech is regarded as an integral part of his family background, a sign of his local identity.

By identifying himself as a dialect speaker both at home and abroad, a member symbolizes pride in his community and in the distinctness of its contribution to society at large.

Formal education, however, is always carried on in the standard language, the language of official transactions, religion, and the mass media. Norwegian law sanctions two standard languages: Bokmål (formally called Riksmål) and Nynorsk (formerly Landsmål), of which only Bokmål (B) is current in northern Norway.

Education is universal and, allowing for certain individual differences in fluency, all speakers of Ranamål also control the standard. Both Bokmål and Ranamål, therefore, form part of what we may call the community linguistic repertoire (Gumperz, 1964), the totality of linguistic resources which speakers may employ in significant social interaction. In their everyday interaction, they select among the two as the situation demands. Members view this alternation as a shift between two distinct entities, which are never mixed. A person speaks either one or the other.

The fact that the two varieties are perceived as distinct, however, does not necessarily mean that their separateness is marked by significant linguistic differences. Pairs such as Hindi and Urdu, Serbian and Croatian, Thai and Laotian, and many others which are regarded as separate languages by their speakers are known to be grammatically almost identical. The native's view of language distinctions must thus be validated by empirical linguistic investigation.

We began our analysis by employing standard linguistic elicitation procedures. A series of informants selected for their fluency in the dialect were interviewed in our office and were asked to produce single words, sentences, and short texts, first in the dialect and then in the standard, for taping or phonetic recording by the linguist. These elicitation sessions yielded a series of dialect features which are essentially identical to those described by Norwegian dialectologists (Christiansen, 1962).

The vowel system distinguishes 10 vowels in three tongue heights:

- high: front unrounded i, front rounded y, central rounded u, back rounded o;
- mid: front unrounded e, front rounded ö, back rounded å;
- low: front unrounded æ, front rounded ø, back a.

Consonants occur either singly or as geminates. Vowels are phonetically short before geminates, consonant clusters, and palatalized consonants. There are two series of consonants: unmarked and palatalized. Unmarked consonants include stops p, b, t, d, k, g; spirants f, v, s, ʃ, j, ç; nasals m, n, ŋ; trill r, lateral l, and retroflex flap ḷ. The palatal series contains tj, dj, nj, and lj. On the phonetic level, a set of cacuminal or retroflex allophones occur for the sequences rs [ʃ], rd [d], rt [t], and rn [ṇ].

The local pronunciation of the standard differs from the "pure" dialect as follows: Bokmål does not have the phonemic distinction between the palatalized and nonpalatalized series of consonants. Only nonpalatalized consonants occur. In addition, it does not distinguish between mid front rounded /ö/ and low front rounded /ø/; only the former occurs. On the purely phonetic level, dialect allophones of the phonemes /æ/ and /a/ are considerably lower and more retracted than their standard equivalents. The dialect furthermore has a dark allophone [ł] of /l/ where the standard has clear [l]. The cacuminal or retroflex allophones of /s/, /d/, /t/, and /n/, and the flap /ļ/, however, which are commonly regarded as dialect features, are used in both varieties, although they tend to disappear in highly formal Bokmål.

Morphological peculiarities of the dialect include the masculine plural indefinite suffix -æ and the definite suffix -an, e.g., (R) hæstæ (horses), hæstan (the horses), contrasting with (B) hester and hestene. In verb inflection the dialect lacks the infinitive suffix -e and the present suffix -er of regular verbs. Further differences in past tense and past participle markers and in the assignment of individual words to strong or weak inflectional classes serve to set off almost every dialect verb from its standard Norwegian equivalent. Some examples of common regular and irregular verbs and their standard equivalents are shown in Table 5.1.

Other important dialect features appear in pronouns, common adverbs of time, place, and manner, conjunctions, and other grammatically significant function words. Some of the most common distinctive forms of personal pronouns and possessive pronouns are shown in Table 5.2. Table 5.3 shows interrogatives, relatives, and indefinites, while Table 5.4 shows adverbs and conjunctions.

Table 5.1   Examples of common regular and irregular verbs and their standard equivalents

Infinitive		Present		Past		Past participle		
Ranamål	Bokmål	Ranamål	Bokmål	Ranamål	Bokmål	Ranamål	Bokmål	English
finj	finne	finj	finner	fanj	fant	fønje	funnet	(find)
vara or va	være	e	ær	va	var	vøre	vært	(be)
få	få	får	får	fekk	fikk	fått	fått	(get)
stanj	stå	står	står	sto	sto	stie	stått	(stand)
jær	jøre	jær	jør	jol	jøre	jort	jort	(do)
læs	lese	læs	leser	læst	leste	læst	lest	(read)
ta	ta	tek	tar	tok	tokk	tatt	tatt	(take)
						or tiçe		

Table 5.2   Examples of personal pronouns and possessive pronouns

Bokmål	Ranamål	English	Bokmål	Ranamål	English
jæjj	*og*	(I)	*hunn*	*ho*	(she)
mæjj	*meg*	(me)	*hanns*	*hanjs*	(his)
dæjj	*deg*	(you)	*hennes*	*hinjers*	(hers)
hann	*hanj*	(he)	*dere*	*dåkk*	(you) (plural)
			di	*dæmm**	(theirs)

Note:
* Sometimes also *di* and *deres*.

Table 5.3   Examples of interrogatives, relatives, and indefinites

Bokmål	Ranamål	English
såmm	*så*	[who, which (relative)]
va	*ke*	[what (interrogative)]
vemm	*kem*	(who)
noe	*nåkka*	(something)
vorfårr	*kefør*	(what for)
vilket	*kefør nokka*	[which (thing)]
vilken	*kefør nann*	[which (person)]
vær	*kvar*	(every)
en	*ein*	(one)

These data constitute empirical evidence to support the view of the dialect as a distinct linguistic entity. By comparing information collected in this manner with local speech forms elsewhere in northern Norway, dialectologists interested in historical reconstruction identify Ranamål as one of a series of northern Norwegian dialects set off from others by the fact that it shows influences of eastern Norwegian forms of speech (Christiansen, 1962). In this discussion however, we are concerned with social interaction and not with history, and this leads us to raise somewhat different problems.

The elicitation sessions which provide the source data for dialect grammars are conducted in the linguist's, and not in the informant's, frame of reference. Although by asking speakers to speak in the dialect, the linguist may be interested in purely descriptive or historical information, the native speaker, mindful of

Table 5.4   Examples of adverbs and conjunctions

Bokmål	Ranamål	English
till	tell	(to, toward)
menn	mænn	(but)
hær	her	(here)
fra	ifra	(from)
mellam	imeljæ	(in between)
vordan	kelesn	(how)
viss	vess	(if)

the association between dialect, local culture, and local identity, is, of course, anxious to present his locality in the best possible light. Consistency of performance in linguistic interview sessions might well be the result of the interviewer's presence; it need not reflect everyday interaction. Furthermore, when comparisons with other forms of speech are made, it is the linguist's analysis which serves as the basis for these comparisons, not the speaker's performance.

Ranamål and Bokmål as codes in a repertoire

In order to understand how natives may perceive the dialect standard language differences, some further discussion of the way in which distinctions between what are ordinarily treated as separate linguistic systems may be manifested in everyday speech is necessary. Thus if we compare a bilingual's pronunciation of the Norwegian sentence *Vill du ha egg og beiken till frokast?* with the same speaker's pronunciation of the English equivalent "Will you have bacon and eggs for breakfast?" the two utterances will show phonetic distinctions in every segment. The Norwegian voiced spirant [v] has much less spirantal noise than its English equivalent, the [i] is tense as compared to the lax English [i], the Norwegian [l] may be clear or dark but it is phonetically different from English [l]. The Norwegian central rounded [u] in *du* has no direct English equivalent. In *egg* the Norwegian has a tense [e] and the [g] has an aspirate release, whereas in English the vowel is lax and [g] has a voiced release. Similarly, the Norwegian has a stressed vowel in *beiken* [æi] whereas the English has [ey]. Bilinguals whose entire articulation shifts in this way can be said to have two distinct articulation ranges in addition to two sets of grammatical rules.

Analysis of recordings of Hemnesberget speakers' switching from the dialect to the standard reveals a different situation. In a sentence pair like *hanj bor på nilsen's paŋʃonat* and its Bokmål equivalent *hann bor pa nilsen's paŋsonat* "He lives in Nilsen's pensionat," only the realizations of /a/, /ɫ/, and /nj/ which appear in our list of dialect characteristics differ. In other relevant respects the two utterances are identical. Furthermore, even in the case of these dialect characteristics, speakers do not alternate between two clearly distinguishable articulation points; rather, the shift takes the form of a displacement along a scale in which palatalized consonants show at least three degrees of palatalization, strong [nj], weak [nʲ], and zero [n] and /a/ and /æ/ each show three degrees of retraction and lowering.

While the switch from Norwegian to English implies a shift between two distinct structural wholes, the Bokmål–Ranamål alternation, in phonology at least, seems more similar to conditions described by Labov (1966) for New York speech. A speaker's standard and dialect performance can be accounted for by a single phonetic system. The bulk of the constituent phones within this system are marked by relatively stable, easily identifiable points of articulation. The palatalized consonants and the vowels listed here differ in that they vary within a much greater articulation range. They are instances of what Labov has called variables (1964). It is the position of such variables along the scale of possible articulations which, when evaluated along with morphological information, signals dialect vs. standard speech.

Not all items identified in our elicitation sessions as Ranamål features, function as variables, however. The contrast between /ø/ and /ö/ was never produced spontaneously. In normal discourse only [ö] occurs. Furthermore, as stated previously, the flap allophone /ļ/ and the retroflex stop allophones which find a prominent place in dialect grammars are also used in local Bokmål as well as in eastern varieties of standard Norwegian; thus their status as dialect markers is doubtful.

Our texts also reveal some individual differences in the pronunciation of the palatalized consonant and vowel variables. While the normal dialect speech of most residents shows strong palatalization of these consonants and extreme vowel retraction, some of the more highly educated younger residents normally have medium palatalization and medium vowel retraction. Regardless, however, the direction of variation is the same for all individuals.

In the realm of morphology–syntax it is also possible to set up a single set of grammatical categories to account for what on the surface seem like striking differences between the two varieties. All nouns, e.g., appear in an indefinite form consisting of the noun stem and in an indefinite form made up of stem plus suffixed article, both of which are inflected for singular and plural. There are three subcategories of noun gender: masculine, feminine, and neuter, and the case categories are shared. Verbs appear in imperative, infinitive, present, past, and past participle forms. Basic function word categories, including pronouns, conjunctions, and adverbs, are shared, etc.

Ranamål shows a few peculiarities in the order of pronouns and verbs in sentences such as (R) *ke du e ifrå*, (B) *vor ær du fra* "Where are you from?" But even without detailed analysis, it is obvious that these differences correspond to relatively low-order syntactic rules. The majority of the distinctions between the dialect and the standard thus do not affect the basic grammar but only what we may call the morphophonemic realization of shared grammatical categories.

Even at the morphophonemic level, variation is not without pattern. Examination of such alternates as the following suggests a general process of lowering of front vowels in the dialect:

- (B) *till*, (R) *tell* "to";
- (B) *fikk*, (R) *fekk* "received";
- (B) *hest*, (R) *hæst* "horse"; and
- (B) *menn*, (R) *mænn* "but."

This lowering process is also found elsewhere in Norway, although it may occur in different linguistic forms. Similarly, other sets of alternates such as *icce/ikke* "not," *dæmm/di* "they," and *ifra/frå* "from" are common in other Norwegian regions.

Leaving aside historical considerations, it is almost as if all dialect variation within Norway were generated by selection of different forms from a common reservoir of alternates. Ranamål differs from other dialects not so much because it contains entirely different features, but because of the way in which it combines features already found elsewhere. Furthermore, Hemnesberget pairs such as (B) *lærer*, (R) *lerar*, and (B) *hær*, (R) *her*, which conflict with the lowering process just mentioned, suggest that here as elsewhere selection may at times be motivated by social pressures favoring maintenance of distinctions (Ramanujan, 1967). No matter what the actual historical facts are, however, the narrow range of variation we find lends support to our view of dialect features as variables within a single grammatical system.

The effect of structural similarities on speakers' perception of speech differences is somewhat counterbalanced by the fact that choice among these variables is always restricted by sociolinguistic selection constraints such that if, for instance, a person selects a standard morphological variant in one part of an utterance, this first choice also implies selection of pronunciation variables tending toward the standard end of the scale. A speaker wishing to ask for another's place of residence may, e.g., start his sentence either with (R) *ke* "where" or (B) *vor*. In the first case, the rest of the sentence will be *hanj e ifrå* "is he from?" In the second case, it will be *ær hann fra*; *vor* and *hanj* do not co-occur. Similarly, selection of *e* "is" requires dialect pronunciation; the form *ær* "is" would sound odd if it appeared in the same sentence with *hanj*.

It is the nature of these selection constraints and the manner in which they cut across the usual boundaries of phonology and morphology to generate co-occurrences among phonetic and allomorphic and lexical variables, which lends the Ranamål–Bokmål variation its peculiar stamp, and sets it off, e.g., from the phonologically similar situation in New York. Sociolinguistic selection rules also account to some extent for the speaker's view of the two varieties as separate entities.

Since the dialect and the standard are almost isomorphic in syntax and pho-netics and vary chiefly in morphophonemics, and since most speakers control the entire range of variables, it would be unreasonable to assume, as is frequently done wherever two distinct dialects are spoken, that selection patterns affecting the above selection rules are motivated by considerations of intelligibility. The most reasonable assumption is that the linguistic separateness between the dialect and the standard, i.e. the maintenance of distinct alternates for common inflectional morphemes and function, is conditioned by social factors.

Some idea of how this came about can be obtained by considering the condi-tions under which the two varieties are learned. The dialect is acquired in most homes and in the sphere of domestic and friendship relations. As a result, it has acquired the flavor of these locally based relationships. However, dialect speakers learn the standard in school and in church, at a time when they are also introduced to national Norwegian values. It has therefore become associated with such pan-Norwegian activity systems.

Since the adult population has equal access to both sets of variants, however, the developmental argument does not provide sufficient explanation for the maintenance of distinctness. Immigrants to urban centers around the world, e.g., frequently give up their languages after a generation if social conditions are favorable to language shift. The hypothesis suggests itself, therefore, that given the initial acquisition patterns, the dialect and the standard remain separate because of the cultural identities they communicate and the social values implied therein. It is this aspect of the problem that we intend to explore in the remaining sections of the chapter. Before we proceed, however, something more needs to be said about the process of social symbolization.

Students of communication usually distinguish between semantics proper, or reference, and pragmatics (Ervin-Tripp, 1964). Reference indicates verbal cat-egorization of objects' actions and experience in terms of their objective proper-ties; pragmatics deals with the effect of symbols of various kinds on speakers and listeners, i.e. with the significance of what is communicated for the actors involved. Most discussions of pragmatics ordinarily do not distinguish between individual intent and interpersonal significance of usage patterns, although it is evident that without such a distinction it would be impossible to explain the fact that the same message may indicate praise in some instances and disapproval in others. Effective communication requires that speakers and audiences agree both on the meaning of words and on the social import or values attached to choice of expression. Our discussions will be confined to the latter. We use the term *social significance*, or *social meaning*, to refer to the social value implied when an utterance is used in a certain context.

In general, the assignment of value to particular objects or acts is as arbitrary as the referential naming of objects. Just as a particular term may refer to a round object in one group and a square object in another, so also the value of actions or utterances may vary. Thus the same term may indicate geographical distinctions in one community and symbolize social stratification elsewhere. Social meanings differ from referential meanings in the way in which they are coded. Whereas reference is coded largely through words, social meaning can attach not only to acoustic signs but also to settings, to items of background knowledge, as well as to particular word sequences. In Hemnes, e.g., values attached to a person's family background or to his reputation as a fisherman are important in understanding what he says and influence the selection of responses to his actions.

It must also be pointed out that referential meanings are at least to some extent recoverable through the study of individual words. They are, to use Pike's (1967) term, segmental, while social meanings are not. A sentence like *ke du e ifrå* "Where are you from?" can be divided into units of reference like *ke* "where," *du* "you," *e* "are," and *ifrå* "from." Social significance attaches to the utterance as a whole; it is not segmentable into smaller component stretches. Sociolinguistic co-occurrence patterns along with intonation contours enable the speaker to group language into larger pragmatic wholes and to interpret them in relation to signs transmitted by other communicative media.

Local organization and values

Social life in Hemnesberget shows a fluidity of class structure quite similar to that described for southern Norway by Barnes (1954). Extremes of poverty and wealth are absent. Expressions of solidarity such as "We all know each other here in Hemnes," and "We are all friends here" recur in our interviews. The majority of those who claim local descent show a strong sense of local identification. To be a *hæmnesværing* "Hemnes resident" in their view is like belonging to a team characterized by commonalty of descent. Members of this reference group act like kin, friends, and neighbors, co-operating in the pursuit of community ideals. In everyday behavior they symbolize this quality of their ties through greetings, exchanges of personal information, and general informality of posture toward fellow members. The dialect is an important marker of their common culture. Residents of neighboring settlements, of Mo i Rana, as well as other Norwegians, stand apart from this local community. They are potential competitors who must at least initially be treated with reserve. Their dialects are said to be different. The linguist interested in structural significance may wish to disregard such variation as minor.

Nevertheless, they have important social meanings for intercommunity communication within the Rana region. They are constantly commented upon and joked about and seem to play an important role in the maintenance of local identity.

Despite the intense sense of local identification, perceptions of closeness within this local group are not everywhere the same among Hemnes residents. More detailed interviews and observations of visiting and recreational patterns and of the exchange of assistance suggest a clear distinction between personal relations and the more general local relations. The range of effective personal relations for any single individual tends to be fairly small and stable over time. For most people it includes only certain near kin, in-laws, neighbors, or fellow workers. The community can thus be described as segmented into small nuclei of personal interaction. Since these groups are not marked linguistically, however, the behavioral signs of friendliness and equality constitute a communicative idiom which applies to both these nuclei and to other relations or shared local identification.

The meaning attached to local descent and dialect use – to being part of the "local team" – is clearly seen when we consider those members of the community who dissociate themselves from this "team." Traditionally, in northern Norway the local community of equals was separated from the landowning commercial and administrative elite by a wide gulf of social and judicial inequality. Since the latter were the introducers and users of standard Norwegian, the standard form was – and to some extent still is – associated with this inequality of status. Many of the functions of the former elite have now been incorporated into the local social system. Individuals who fill these functions, however, continue to be largely of nonlocal descent. Although they may pay lip service to locally accepted rules of etiquette and use the dialect on occasion, their experience elsewhere in Norway – where differences in education, influence, and prestige are much more pronounced – leads them to associate the dialect with lack of education and sophistication. Therefore, they show a clear preference for the standard.

Such attitudes are unacceptable to locals, who view lack of respect for and refusal to speak the dialect as an expression of social distance and contempt for the "local team" and its community spirit. It is not surprising, therefore, that their loyalty to the dialect is thereby reaffirmed. For a local resident to employ (B) forms with other local residents is in their view to *snakk fint* or to *snakk jalat* "to put on airs."

Since the different social meanings which attach to the dialect are regular and persistent, they must in some way be reinforced by the pattern of social ties. This relationship can best be described if we consider the socio-ecological system which sustains the community. There is a correlation between a person's regional background, his reference group, and the niche he occupies in this system (Barth, 1964). This information enables us to segment the local population into three distinct categories:

1   artisans;
2   wholesale–retail merchants and plant managers; and
3   service personnel.

Members of the first two categories are the basic producers of wealth.

The more than 50 percent of the population which falls into the first category includes draftsmen who may or may not own their own shops, as well as workmen employed in the larger plants and their dependents. Most of them are locally born or have been drawn to Hemnes from the surrounding farms by the demand for their skills. Since they live and work among their relatives and among others of the same social background, they tend to choose their friends and spouses from within their own reference group and thus become strong supporters of local values.

Wholesale–retail merchants buy lumber products and finished boats from producers in the Rana area, furnishing them with supplies and gear and appliances in exchange. They sell boats, lumber products, and fishing supplies to customers all the way up to the northernmost tip of Norway. Relationships between merchants and their customers most commonly take the form of long-term credit arrangements based on personal trust in which credit is given to artisans against their future production. Also part of the second category are the managers of large local enterprises who achieve their position partly because of their special commercial and managerial skills and partly through their ability to get along with and keep the confidence of owners, workers, and foremen.

Like artisans, members of category 2 are largely of local descent. Although they tend to be in the higher income brackets, they maintain kin and conjugal relationships among craftsmen and fishermen-farmers. The fact that their livelihood depends to a great extent on their standing within the system of locally based relations leads them to associate more closely with the local values. The circumstances of their commercial enterprises, however, also take them outside this local network. They must be able to act within the urban commercial ethic, and they must also maintain personal ties with their customers in the north and elsewhere. The range of their social connections includes both local and supralocal ties, involving different and sometimes conflicting standards of behavior. The result is that while they maintain strong loyalty to general local values, they tend to avoid close personal ties with their kin in the first category and confine their friendships to others who are in similar circumstances.

The third category is a composite one, consisting of individuals whose position depends on the productivity of others. It includes persons engaged in purely local services – private and administrative – of all kinds such as salesmen, clerks, repairmen, shopkeepers, professionals, and those who are employed in repair shops and in transportation. The socio-cultural background of these people varies. Those who perform manual labor tend to be of local descent and are culturally indistinguishable from members of the first category. The same is true for the lower echelons of employees in stores and in administrative offices. Among the owners of retail businesses – clothing, shoe, pastry, and stationery shops – many belong to families who have moved to Hemnesberget from other urban or semi-urban centers in northern Norway. Their kin and friendship relations tend to be dispersed among these communities, and this leads them to identify with the differentiated nonlocal middle-class value system. Shopowners of local back-ground also aspire to these standards, at the same time trying to maintain their position in the "local team" by showing loyalty to its values. Professionals are similarly drawn to Hemnes from the outside because of their technical expertise. The more stable core of this group, the schoolteachers, tend to be of north Norwegian background. Doctors, veterinarians, dentists, and priests frequently come from the south. Invariably their values are those of the pan-Norwegian elite.

Economic conditions in Hemnes leave little room for the academically trained and those with technical skills outside local niches. Consequently, young people from all categories who aspire to higher education must spend most of their student years away from Hemnes and will eventually have to seek employment somewhere else. While they remain students, however, they are partly dependent on their families. They tend to return home during the summer vacation and seek local employment.

Contextual constraints

Previous sections have dealt with the linguistic repertoire, internal cultural differences, and relevant features of social organization. We have suggested that linguistic alternates within the repertoire serve to symbolize the differing social identities which members may assume. It is, however, evident from our discussion that there is by no means a simple one-to-one relationship between specific speech varieties and specific social identities. Apart from the fact that values attached to language usage vary with social background, the same individual need not be absolutely consistent in all his actions. He may wish to appear as a member of the local team on some occasions, while identifying with middle-class values on others. In order to determine the social significance of any one utterance, we need additional information about the contextual clues by which natives arrive at correct interpretations of social meaning.

Recent linguistic writings have devoted considerable attention to speech events as the starting point for the analysis of verbal communication. It has been shown that aside from purely linguistic and stylistic rules, the form of a verbal message in any speech event is directly affected by:

1   the participants, i.e. speakers, addressees, and audiences;
2   the ecological surroundings; and
3   the topic or range of topics (Hymes, 1964; Ervin-Tripp, 1964).

In visualizing the relationship between social and linguistic factors in speech events, it seems reasonable to assume that the former restrict the selection of linguistic variables in somewhat the same way that syntactic environments serve to narrow the broader dictionary meanings of words. For the purpose of our analysis, we can thus visualize verbal communication as a two-step process. In step 1, speakers take in clues from the outside and translate them into appropriate behavioral strategies. This step parallels the perceptual process by which referential meanings are converted into sentences. In step 2, these behavioral strategies are in turn translated into appropriate verbal symbols. The determinants of this communicative process are the speaker's knowledge of the linguistic repertoire, culture, and social structure, and his ability to relate these kinds of knowledge to contextual constraints. For Hemnesberget, it seems useful to describe these constraints in terms of three concepts representing successively more complex levels of information processing.

We will use the term *setting* to indicate the way in which natives classify their ecological environment into distinct locales. This enables us to relate the opportunities for action to constraints upon action provided by the socially significant features of the environment. First, and most important among local settings in Hemnesberget, is the home. Homes form the center for all domestic activities and act as meeting places for children's peer groups. Houses are well built and provide ample space for all. Also, friends and kin prefer the privacy of meetings at home to restaurants or other more public places.

Workshops and plants where productive activity is carried on are separated for the most part from residential areas, although some families continue to live next to their workshops along the shore of the fjord. The workforce normally consists of male members of the group of owners, whether managed by a single nuclear family or by a group of families connected by filial, sibling, or in-law ties. Employees in the larger plants frequently also include groups of kin who work together as work teams. In view of the homogeneity of workers, it is not surprising that the place of work frequently forms the center for informal gathering among males. In offices, shops, and merchant establishments, however, where the expertise requirements favor socially more differentiated personnel, work relations tend to be less colored by pre-existent social ties.

A second group of settings lacks the specific restrictions on personnel which mark those just mentioned. These include the public dock, where visiting boats and the steamer are moored, as well as a few of the larger stores, e.g., the co-operative society store located near the central square, the square itself, and the community park. Here all local residents may meet somewhat more freely without commitments, subject, of course, to the constraints imposed by lack of privacy. The primary school, the junior high school, the church, and community meeting hall all form somewhat more restricted meeting grounds for more formal gatherings, such as classroom sessions, religious services, political meetings,

meetings of various voluntary associations, and occasional movies. The church is used only for church services.

The socio-ecological restrictions on personnel and activities still allow for a wide range of socially distinct happenings The school, e.g., is used for class sessions during the day and for meetings of voluntary associations during the evening. Similarly, in the town square, men gather for discussions of public affairs, women shoppers stop to chat with acquaintances, adolescent peer groups play their various games, etc. A closer specification of social constraints is possible if we concentrate on activities carried on by particular constellations of personnel, gathered in particular settings during a particular span of time. We will use the term *social situation* to refer to these. Social situations form the background for the enactment of a limited range of social relationships within the framework of specific status sets, i.e. systems of complementary distributions of rights and duties (Barth, 1966).

Thus alternative social definitions of the situation may occur within the same setting, depending on the opportunities and constraints on interaction offered by a shift in personnel and/or object of the interaction. Such definitions always manifest themselves in what we would prefer to call a *social event*. Events center around one or at the most a limited range of topics and are distinguishable because of their sequential structure. They are marked by stereotyped and thus recognizable opening and closing routines. The distinction between situation and event can be clarified if we consider the behavior of Hemnes residents who are sometimes seen in the community office, first transacting their business in an officially correct manner, and then turning to one of the clerks and asking him to step aside for a private chat. The norms which apply to the two kinds of interaction differ; the break between the two is clearly marked. Therefore, they constitute two distinct social events, although the personnel and the locale remain the same.

The terms setting, social situation, and social event as used here can be considered three successively more complex stages in the speaker's processing of contextual information. Each stage subsumes the previous one in such a way that the preceding one is part of the input affecting the selection rules of the next stage. Thus, a speaker cannot identify the social situation without first having made some decision as to the nature of the setting. To demonstrate how these factors influence language usage in Hemnesberget, we turn now to some examples drawn from participant observation.

The fact that the dialect reflects local values suggests that it symbolizes relationships based on shared identities with local culture. Casual observations and recording of free speech among locals in homes, workshops, and the various public meeting places where such relationships are assumed do indeed show that only the dialect is used there. However, statuses defined with respect to the superimposed national Norwegian system elicit the standard. Examples of these are church services, presentation of text material in school, reports, and announcements – but not necessarily informal public appeals or political speeches – at public meetings. Similarly, meetings with tourists or other strangers elicit the standard at least until the participants' identity becomes more clearly known.

Situational and metaphorical switching

When within the same setting the participants' definition of the social event changes, this change may be signaled among others by linguistic clues. On one occasion, when we, as outsiders, stepped up to a group of locals engaged in conversation, our arrival caused a significant alteration in the casual posture of the group. They took their hands out of their pockets and their expressions changed. Predictably, our remarks elicited a code-switch marked simultaneously by a change in channel cues (i.e. sentence speed, rhythm, more hesitation pauses, etc.) and by a shift from (R) to (B) grammar. Similarly, teachers report that while formal lectures – where interruptions are not encouraged – are delivered in (B), the speakers will shift to (R) when they want to encourage open and free discussion among students. Each of these examples involves clear changes in the participants' definition of each other's rights and obligations. We use the term *situational switching* to refer to this kind of a language shift.

The notion of situational switching assumes a direct relationship between language and the social situation. The linguistic forms employed are critical features of the event in the sense that any violation of selection rules changes members' perception of the event. A person who uses the standard where only the dialect is appropriate violates commonly accepted norms. His action may terminate the conversation or bring about other social sanctions. To be sure, language choice is never completely fixed; sociolinguistic variables must be investigated empirically. Furthermore, situations differ in the amount of freedom of choice allowed to speakers. Ritual events, like the well-known Vedic ceremonies of South Asia, constitute extreme examples of determination, where every care is taken to avoid even the slightest change in pronunciation or rhythm lest the effectiveness of the ceremony be destroyed. The greetings, petitions, and similar routines described by Albert (1972) similarly seem strictly determined.

In Hemnesberget, as our example below shows, speakers are given relatively wide choice in vocabulary and some choice in syntax. Selection rules affect mainly the variables discussed previously. Values of these variables are sociolinguistically determined in the sense that when, on the one hand, we speak of someone giving a classroom lecture or performing a Lutheran church service or talking to a tourist, we can safely assume that he is using (B) grammatical forms. On the other hand, two locals having a heart-to-heart talk will presumably speak in (R). If instead they are found speaking in (B), we conclude either that they do not identify with the values of the local team or that they are not having a heart-to-heart talk.

In contrast with those instances where choice of variables is narrowly constrained by social norms, there are others in which participants are given considerably more latitude. Thus, official community affairs are largely defined as nonlocal and hence the standard is appropriate. But since many individuals who carry out the relevant activities all know each other as fellow locals, they often interject casual statements in the dialect into their formal discussions. In the course of a morning spent at the community administration office, we noticed that clerks used both standard and dialect phrases, depending on whether they were talking about official affairs or not. Likewise, when residents step up to a clerk's desk, greeting and inquiries about family affairs tend to be exchanged in the dialect, while the business part of the transaction is carried on in the standard.

In neither of these cases is there any significant change in definition of participants' mutual rights and obligations. The posture of speakers and channel clues of their speech remain the same. The language switch here relates to particular kinds of topics or subject matter rather than to change in social situation. Characteristically, the situations in question allow for the enactment of two or more different relationships among the same set of individuals. The choice of either (R) or (B) alludes to these relationships and thus generates meanings which are quite similar to those conveyed by the alternation between *ty* or *vy* in the examples from Russian literature cited by Friedrich (1972). We will use the term *metaphorical switching* for this phenomenon.

The semantic effect of metaphorical switching depends on the existence of regular relationships between variables and social situations of the type just discussed. The context in which one of a set of alternates is regularly used becomes part of its meaning, so that when this form is then employed in a context where it is not normal, it brings in some of the flavor of this original setting. Thus, a phrase like "April is the cruelest month" is regarded as poetic because of its association with T.S. Eliot's poetry. When used in natural conversation, it gives that conversation some of the flavor of this poetry. Similarly, when (R) phrases are inserted metaphorically into a (B) conversation, this may, depending on the circumstances, add a special social meaning of confidentiality or privateness to the conversation.

The case of the local who, after finishing his business in the community office, turns to a clerk and asks him to step aside for a private chat further illustrates the contrast between metaphorical and role switching. By their constant alternation between the standard and the dialect during their business transaction, they alluded to the dual relationship which exists between them. The event was terminated when the local asked the clerk in the dialect whether he had time to step aside to talk about private affairs, suggesting in effect that they shift to a purely personal, local relationship. The clerk looked around and said, "Yes, we are not too busy." The two then stepped aside, although remaining in the same room, and their subsequent private discussion was appropriately carried on entirely in the dialect.

The experiment

Our discussion of verbal behavior so far has relied largely on deductive reasoning supported by unstructured ethnographic observation. Additional tests of our hypothesis are based on controlled text elicitation. We have stated that gatherings among friends and kin implying shared local identities must be carried on in the dialect. If we are correct in our hypothesis, then individuals involved in such friendly gatherings should not change speech variety regardless of whether they talk about local, national, or official matters.

In order to test this, we asked local acquaintances whom we knew to be part of the network of local relationships to arrange a friendly gathering at which refreshments were to be served and to allow us to record the proceedings as samples of dialect speech. Two such gatherings were recorded, one in the living room of our local hosts, and the other in the home of an acquaintance. The fact that arrangements for the meeting were made by local people means that the groups were self-recruited. Participants in the first group included two sisters and a brother and their respective spouses. One of the men was a shopkeeper, one of the few in this category who claims local descent; his brothers-in-law were employed as craftsmen. All three men are quite literate compared to workmen elsewhere in the world and well read in public affairs. They are active in local politics and experienced in formal committee work. The second group included three craftsmen, friends and neighbors who worked in the same plant, and their wives. One of these had served as a sailor on a Norwegian merchant vessel for several years and spoke English. Participants were all quite familiar with standard Norwegian, and our recorded conversations contain several passages where the standard was used in quoting nonlocal speech or in statements directed at us.

Methodologically, self-recruitment of groups is important for two reasons. It ensures that groups are defined by locally recognized relationships and enables the investigator to predict the norms relevant to their interaction. Furthermore, the fact that participants have pre-existing obligations toward each other means that, given the situation, they are likely to respond to such obligations in spite of the presence of strangers. Our tape recording and our visual observations give clear evidence that this in fact was what occurred.

Our strategy was to introduce discussion likely to mobilize obligations internal to the group, thus engaging members in discussion among themselves. This proved to be relatively easy to do. When a point had been discussed for some time, we would attempt to change the subject by injecting new questions or comments. In doing this we did not, of course, expect that our own interjections would predictably affect the speakers' choice of codes. Participants were always free to reinterpret our comments in any way they wished. Nevertheless, the greater the range of topics covered, the greater was the likelihood of language shift.

As a rule, our comments were followed by a few introductory exchanges directed at us. These were marked by relatively slow sentence speeds, many hesitation pauses, and visual clues indicating that people were addressing us. Linguistically, we noted some switching to the standard in such exchanges. After a brief period of this, if the topic was interesting, internal discussion began and arguments that referred to persons, places, and events we could not possibly be expected to have any knowledge about developed. The transition to internal discussion was marked by an increase in sentence speed and lack of hesitation pauses and similar clues. The tape recorder was run continuously during the gatherings, and after some time participants became quite oblivious to its presence.

Only those passages which were clearly recognizable as internal discussion were used in the analysis; all others were eliminated. The texts obtained in this way consist of stretches of free discussion on diverse topics. The following passages show that our hypothesis about the lack of connection between code-switching and change in topic was confirmed.

Group I   Topic: Chit-chat about local events

Gunnar: *ja de va ein så kåmm idag – ein så kåmm me mælka – så så hanj de va så varmt inj på mo i går – ja, sa eg, de va no içe vent anjæ dåkk må no ha meir enn di anjrann bestanjdi.*

(Yes, there was one who came today – one who came with milk – so he said it was so warm in Mo yesterday. Yes, I said, there is nothing else to be expected, you people must always have more than anybody else.)

Topic: Industrial planning

Alf: *her kunj ha vore eit par sånn mellomstore bedreftæ på ein førtifæmti manu so ha befæftigæ denna fålke detta så ha gådd ledi amm vinjtærn.*

(There might have been here some medium-size plants employing forty to fifty men which then could offer work to those who have nothing to do in winter.)

Topic: Governmental affairs

Oscar: *vi jekk inj før denn forste injstiljingæ ifrå Seikommitenn.*

(We supported the first proposal made by the Schei Committee.)

The first item in Group I deals with a local topic in a somewhat humorous way; the second and third items concern planning and formal governmental affairs. All these passages are clearly in the dialect. Of the phonological variables, [nj] and [lj] show the highest degree of palatalization and [a] and [æ] the highest degree of retraction throughout. Morphophonemic dialect markers are (R) *ein* "one," *så* "who," *içḉe* "not," *dåkk* "you," *meir* "more," *her* "here," *jekk* "went," *ifrå* "from." Even lexical borrowings from the standard such as *injstiljing* "proposal" and *bedreftæ* "plants" are clearly in dialect phonology and morphology. We find one single instance of what seems to be a standard form: (B) *mellom* / (R) *imelja* "middle." But this only occurs as part of the borrowed compound *mellomstore* "medium-size." In several hours of conversation with both groups, marked by many changes in topic, we have found a number of lexical borrowings but not a clear instance of phonological or grammatical switching, in spite of the fact that all informants clearly know standard grammar.

While our hypothesis suggests that switching is constrained in those situations which allow only local relationships to be enacted, it also leads us to predict that whenever local and nonlocal relationships are relevant to the same situation, topical variation may elicit code-switching. To test this, we selected members of a formerly quite active local peer group. For the last few years these individuals had all been at universities in Oslo, Bergen, and Trondheim. They returned home in the summer either for vacation or to take up local employment. In conventional interview sessions, all participants claimed to be pure dialect speakers and professed local attitudes about dialect use. They thus regarded themselves as members of the local "team." As fellow students, however, they also shared statuses that are identified with pan-Norwegian values and associated with the standard. Our assumption, then, is that if topical stimuli are introduced which elicit these values, switching may result.

Three gatherings were arranged in the home of one of our informants. Refreshments were again served. Elicitation strategies were similar to those employed with the first two groups, and similar ranges of topics were covered. The examples cited here show that our hypothesis was again confirmed.

> *Group II*   Topic: Chit-chat about drinking habits
> *Berit:* *ja, ja, mæn vi bjynjt anjer veien du — vi bjynjt i barnelofen — så vi har
> de unjajort.*
> (Yes, yes, we started the other way, we started in the children's
> anti-alcoholic league. So we have finished all that.)
>
> Topic: Industrial development
> *Berit:* *jo da viss di bare fikk de te lønn seg — så e i værtfall prisnivåe hær i
> Rana skrudd høger enn de e vanligvis anner stann i lanne.*
> (Yes, if they could only manage to make it profitable — so in any
> case the prices tend to be higher here in Rana than is common
> in other places in the country.)

Topic: Informal statement about university regulations

Ola: *mænn no ha dæmm læmpæ pa de.*

(But now they have relaxed that.)

Topic: Authoritative statement about university regulations

Ola: *de voel du mellom en faemm saeks.*

(You choose that from among five or six.)

Comparison of Berit's and Ola's first statement with their second statements shows considerable shifting in each case. Thus, Berit's second utterance has such unpalatalized forms as *anner* (vs. *anjer*), and raised and less retracted [a] in *da*. She also uses standard variables (B) *fikk* / (R) *fekk*, (B) *viss* / (R) *vess*, (B) *værtfall* / (R) *kvartfall*, (B) *hær* / (R) *her*, etc. Ola's second statement is characterized by (B) *mellon* / (R) *imelja* and (B) *en* / (R) *ein*. Similarly, his [æ] in *fæm* and *sæks* is raised and fronted. In neither case is the shift to the standard complete; after all the situation never lost its informality. Berit's statement still contains dialect words like (R) *lønn* / (B) *lønne* "to be profitable," (R) *stan* / (B) *steder* "places," and Ola has (R) *væl* / (B) *velger* "to choose." What we see then is a breakdown of co-occurrence rules, an erosion of the linguistic boundary between Ranamål and Bokmål. The tendency is to switch toward standard phonology while preserving some morphophonemic and lexical dialect features of (R). Features retained in this manner are largely those which also occur in other local dialects and to some extent also in standard Norwegian. They have thus gained some acceptance as proper dialect forms. Those characteristics which locals refer to as broad speech – i.e. those that are known as local peculiarities – tend to be eliminated.

It must also be noted that Berit and Ola also differ in their pronunciation of the phonological variables. Ola's normal pronunciation shows the strong palatalization of consonant and extreme vowel retraction characteristic of most residents. Berit's normal pronunciation has medium palatalization and medium retraction. Both, however, switch in the same direction, in response to similar situational and topical clues, and this agreement on the rules of stylistic manipulation is clearly more important in this case than the mere articulatory difference in Berit's and Ola's speech.

The social character of the style switch was clearly revealed when the tape-recorded conversations were played back to other Hemnes residents. One person who had been working with us as a linguistic informant at first refused to believe that the conversations were recorded locally. When he recognized the voices of the participants, he showed clear signs of disapproval. Apparently, he viewed the violation of co-occurrence rules as a sign of what is derogatorily called *knot* "artificial speech" in colloquial Norwegian. Some of the participants showed similar reactions when they heard themselves on tape. They promised to refrain from switching during future discussion sessions. Our analysis of these later sessions, however, revealed that when an argument required that the speaker validate his status as an intellectual, he would again tend to use standard forms in the manner shown by Berit and Ola. Code selection rules thus seem to be akin to grammatical rules. Both operate below the level of consciousness and may be independent of the speaker's overt intentions.

Additional information about usage patterns was provided through an accident. One of our sessions with this group was interrupted by a somewhat mentally retarded young person, who has the habit of appearing in people's homes to solicit assistance for his various schemes. Here are some examples of remarks addressed to him by Berit and Solveig. Of all the members of the group, Solveig was the most prone to use standard forms. Her normal pronunciation shows the least amount of consonant palatalization. She is socially more marginal to Hemnes than other members of the group.

> *Group III*   Topic: Talking to a retarded local youth
> *Berit*:   *e de du så vikarier førr hanj no.*
>   (Are you a stand-in for him now?)
> *Solveig*: *hanj kanj jo jett gåte, haj kanj no va me.*
>   (He is good at word games, he should participate.)

Both Berit and Solveig's pronunciation in these examples become identical with the ordinary speech of Ola and of the members of Group I. The extreme palatalization of [nj] and the lowering of [a] is not normal for them; they are clearly talking down in this case. Their stylistic range, as well as their facility in switching, seem to be greater than those of the others.

In comparing the behavior of the first two groups with that of Group III, we find two different kinds of language-usage patterns. All three groups speak both the dialect and the standard. Groups I and II, however, show only situational switching. When members talk to each other, differences of formality or informality to topic are reflected only in the lexicon. Pronunciation and morphology do not change. Those groups shift to (B) phonology and grammar only when remarks are addressed directly to us who count as outsiders or in indirect quotes on such matters as government rules, on officials' statements, etc. In such instances of situation switching, therefore, Ranamål and Bokmål are kept separate throughout by strict co-occurrence restrictions. In Group III, however, deviation from the dialect results both from metaphorical and situation switching. Metaphorical switching, furthermore, involves a breakdown of the co-occurrence restrictions characteristic of situational shifts.

The dialect usage of locals, on the one hand, corresponds to their view that the two varieties are distinct, and to their insistence on maintaining the strict separation of local and nonlocal values. For the students, on the other hand, the distinction between dialect and standard is not so sharp. Although they display the same general attitudes about the dialect as the team of locals, their behavior shows a range of variation rather than an alternation between distinct systems. It reflects a de facto recognition of their own nonlocal identification.

A fourth conversational group further illustrates the internal speech diversity in the community. The principal speakers here were two men (A and B) and a woman (C), married to A. All came from families who tended to dissociate themselves from the egalitarian value system of the local team. Their normal style of speech was Bokmål for remarks directed at us, as well as for in-group speech. Only in a few instances when A began telling local anecdotes did he lapse into Ranamål. (R) forms were introduced as metaphorical switches into what were basically (B) utterances to provide local color, indicate humor, etc., in somewhat the same way that speakers in Group III had used (B) forms in (R) utterances.

In the course of the evening A and C's teenage daughter joined the conversation. She expressed attitudes toward the dialect which are quite similar to those of the students in Group III and thus are somewhat different from those of her parents. The few samples we have of her speech show (R) phonology similar to that of Berit and Solveig in Group III.

Although the picture of language usage derived from the four groups seems at first highly complex, it becomes less so when viewed in relation to speakers' attitudes, interactional norms, and local values. All Hemnes residents have the same repertoire. Their linguistic competence includes control of both (R) and (B) rules. They vary in the way in which they use these rules. Expressed attitudes toward (R) and (B) do not provide an explanation for these differences in speech behavior. The most reasonable explanation of the ways in which these groups differ seems to be that the dual system of local values, differences in individual background, and the various social situations in which members find themselves operate to affect their interpretation of the social meaning of the variables they employ.

Conclusion

Our analysis in this chapter is based on the assumption that regularities in behavior can be analyzed as generated from a series of individual choices made under specifiable constraints and incentives (Barth, 1966). This position implies an important break with previous approaches to social structure and to language and society. Behavioral regularities are no longer regarded as reflections of independently measurable social norms; on the contrary, these norms are themselves seen as communicative behavior. They are reflected in what Goffman (1959) calls the rules of impression management or, in our terms, in the social meanings which constrain the actor's adoption of behavioral strategies in particular situations.

In interactional sociolinguistics, therefore, we can no longer base our analyses on the assumption that language and society constitute different kinds of reality, subject to correlational studies. Social and linguistic information is comparable only when studied within the same general analytical framework. Moving from statements of social constraints to grammatical rules thus represents a transformation from one level of abstraction to another within a single communicative system.

As Bernstein (1961) has pointed out, verbal communication is a process in which actors select from a limited range of alternates within a repertoire of speech forms determined by previous learning. Although ultimately this selection is a matter of individual choice, this chapter shows that the rules of codification by which the deep structure of interpersonal relations is transformed into speech performances are independent of expressed attitudes and similar in nature to the grammatical rules operating on the level of intelligibility. They form part of what Hymes (1972b) has called the speaker's communicative competence. Sociolinguistic constraints on the selection of variables seem to be of central importance in this codification process. We argued that they determine the speaker's perception of the utterances as a unit of social meaning. By accepting the native's view of what is and what is not properly part of a dialect or language, linguists have tended to assume these co-occurrences rather than investigate them empirically. We have attempted to develop descriptive procedures suitable for the empirical investigation of these rules by combining various ethnographic field techniques with conventional linguistic elicitation methods.

In Hemnes, where Ranamål and Bokmål communicate the same objective information, we were led to ask how the apparent separateness of the dialect and the standard can exist and be maintained. Ethnographic investigation suggests the hypothesis that Ranamål has social value as a signal of distinctness and of a speaker's identification with others of local descent. This social significance of the dialect can only be understood by contrast with the meanings which locals assign to the standard, the language of nonlocal activities. The standard is associated with education and power on the national scene and carries connotations of differences in rank which are unacceptable in the realm of informal local relations. When used casually among Hemnes residents, therefore, it communicates dissociation from the "local team."

Since most Hemnes natives live, marry, and earn their livelihood among others of their own kind, their values are rarely challenged. Their personal relations have all the characteristics of network closure (Barnes, 1954). On the other hand, those with nonlocal background and who maintain significant ties in other communities tend to seek their friends among those in similar circumstances, even though they may have resided in Hemnes for more than a generation. Their contacts with members of the "local team" remain largely nonpersonal, focusing around single tasks, and are thus similar in kind to nonlocal contacts. This lack of personal ties between individuals of dissimilar backgrounds and cultural identification reinforces the general social meanings ascribed to the dialect by those who share local background and identity, and thus contributes to maintaining the separateness of dialect and standard.

While this information provides the background for our study, it does not explain the fact that all residents frequently switch between the dialect and the standard. This can only be explained through the analysis of particular speech events. The concepts of setting, social situation, and social event represent an attempt to explain the natives' conception of their behavioral environment in terms of an ordered set of constraints which operate to transform alternative lines of behavior into particular social meanings. Our distinction between metaphoric and role switching shows how constraints at different levels of inclusiveness produce appropriate changes in the way speech performances are interpreted.

Although locals show an overt preference for the dialect, they tolerate and use the standard in situations where it conveys meanings of officiality, expertise, and politeness toward strangers who are clearly segregated from their personal life. In private gatherings where people meet as natives and equals, a speaker's use of standard variables suggests social dissociation, an attitude which is felt to be out of place. Although the students in our experimental sessions meet as locals and friends, they differ from other members of the local team because they share the additional status of intellectuals. This fact modifies the social meaning of standard forms when they are used among the students. To refrain from using standard forms for these topics which elicit participants' shared experience as intellectuals would constitute an unnatural limitation on their freedom of expression. Group IV demonstrates the effect of intracommunity differences in value systems on language-usage patterns. Because of this identification with the urban middle classes, the adult members of this group use (B) as their normal form of speech while employing (R) only for special effect. Such usage distinctions, however, are not necessarily very stable. The teenage daughter of the adult members seems to follow local usage, thus symbolizing her identification with her peer group rather than with her family.

Our experiments, and the analysis presented in this chapter, demonstrate the importance of social or nonreferential meaning for the study of language in society. Mere naturalistic observation of speech behavior is not enough. In order to interpret what he hears, the investigator must have some background knowledge of the local culture and of the processes which generate social meaning. Without this it is impossible to generalize about the social implication of dialect differences. The processes studied here are specific to particular small communities. Predictions of language maintenance or language shift in larger societies will, of course, have to depend on statistical generalizations. More studies along the lines suggested here, however, should materially improve the validity of such generalizations. For Hemnesberget, the fate of the dialect seems assured as long as local identification maintains its importance, and the socio-ecological system continues to prevent any significant accumulation of individuals who, like the students, fail to maintain the situational barrier between the dialects and the standard.

Source: Blom, J.-P. and Gumperz, J.J. (1972) Social meaning in linguistic structure: code-switching in Norway. In J.J. Gumperz and D. Hymes (eds) *Directions in Sociolinguistics*. New York: Holt, Rinehart and Winston, pp. 407–34, by permission of the authors.

Chapter 6

Code-switching as indexical of social negotiations

CAROL MYERS-SCOTTON

THIS CHAPTER PROVIDES AN overall explanation of code-switching, using primarily an East African data base. A number of previous studies have dealt with code-switching in East African contexts. Their emphasis, however, has been different (Abdulaziz-Mkilifi, 1972; Whiteley, 1974; Abdulaziz, 1982; Scotton, 1982), or their explanations have not been comprehensive (Parkin, 1974; Scotton, 1976; Scotton and Ury, 1977). Some of these studies are mentioned in the synthesis given here.

The model developed here focuses on social consequences as motivating linguistic code choices and how speakers use conversational implicatures to arrive at the intended consequences. In this sense, it extends the markedness model of Scotton (1983), proposed to explain code choice in general, but its focus is more specific. The premise of Scotton (1983) is that in addition to relying on a cooperative principle, its associated maxims, and the conversational implicatures which they generate in understanding the content of what is said (Grice, 1975), speakers use a complementary negotiation principle to arrive at the relational import of a conversation. The negotiation principle directs the speaker to 'choose the form of your conversational contribution such that it symbolizes the set of rights and obligations which you wish to be in force between speaker and addressee for the current exchange' (Scotton, 1983: 116). A set of maxims referring to the choice of one linguistic variety rather than another relates to this principle, and the speaker's following or flouting the maxims generates implicatures about proposed interpersonal relationships.

While conveying referential information is often the overt purpose of conversation, all talk is also always a negotiation of rights and obligations between speaker and addressee. Referential content – what the conversation is about –

obviously contributes to the social relationships of participants, but with content kept constant, different relational outcomes may result. This is because the particular linguistic variety used in an exchange carries social meaning. This model assumes that all linguistic code choices are indexical of a set of rights and obligations holding between participants in the conversational exchange. That is, any code choice points to a particular interpersonal balance, and it is partly because of their indexical qualities that different languages, dialects, and styles are maintained in a community.

Speakers have tacit knowledge of this indexicality as part of their communicative competence (Hymes, 1972). They have a natural theory of markedness. The result is that all speakers have mental representations of a matching between code choices and rights and obligations sets. That is, they know that for a particular conventionalized exchange, a certain code choice will be the unmarked realization of an expected rights and obligations set between participants. They also know that other possible choices are more or less marked because they are indexical of other than the expected rights and obligations set. Their reference to other sets depends on their association with other conventionalized exchanges for which they are unmarked choices. While the theory is universal, actual associations are speech community specific, with speakers knowing what code choice is unmarked and which others are marked for exchanges conventionalized in the community.

A conventionalized exchange is any interaction for which speech community members have a sense of 'script'. They have this sense because such exchanges are frequent in the community to the extent that at least their medium is routinized. That is, the variety used or even specific phonological or syntactic patterns or lexical items employed are predictable. In many speech communities, service exchanges, peer-to-peer informal talks, doctor–patient visits, or job interviews are examples of conventionalized exchanges.

Exchanges themselves are realized as speech events consisting of specific participants, a code choice and a rights and obligations balance between the participants. The rights and obligations balance for a speech event is derived from whatever situational features are salient to the exchange, such as status of participants, topic, etc. The salient features will not be the same across all types of exchanges; they are, however, relatively constant across speech events under a single type of exchange. The following example shows a change in feature salience as the exchange type changes from an interaction between strangers to an interaction as ethnic brethren. Initial interactions with security guards at places of business in Nairobi constitute a conventionalized exchange in the speech community. The most salient feature in this exchange is the visitor's appearance of being a Kenyan African or not. If the visitor is apparently a local African, the unmarked choice is Swahili, a relatively ethnically neutral lingua franca widely used across the Kenyan populace. (Observations at a number of Nairobi places of business showed that Swahili is, indeed, the unmarked choice across a number of different speech events realizing this type of exchange.) However, if the conversation develops so that shared ethnic group membership is recognized, then the interaction is perceived as a speech event under a different conventionalized exchange type. It is not an exchange between strangers who are Africans, but an exchange between strangers who share ethnic identity. In this case the most salient of their social features is the shared ethnicity and the unmarked choice for such an exchange is the shared mother tongue. The following example illustrates changes in the salience of the social features of the situation. It also shows that the same uninterrupted sequence of conversational turns can constitute more than one exchange type.

(*Entrance to the IBM Nairobi head office. The visitor, who is a school principal in the Luyia area of Western Kenya, approaches. He speaks English and Swahili fluently in addition to his first language, a Luyia variety.*)

Security Guard (Swahili): Unataka kumwona nani?
(Whom do you want to see?)
Visitor (Swahili): Napenda kumwona Solomon Inyama.
(I want to see Solomon Inyama.)
Guard (Swahili): Unamjua kweli? Tunaye Solomon Amuhaya – nadhani ndio yule.
(Do you really know him? We have a Solomon Amuhaya – I think that's the one you mean.)
Visitor (Swahili): Yule anayetoka Tiriki – yaani Mluyia.
(The one who comes from Tiriki – that is, a Luyia person.)
Guard (smiles) (switches to Luyia): Solomon mwenuyu wakhumanya vulahi?
(Does Solomon know you?)
Visitor (Luyia): Yivi mulole umovolere ndi Shem Lusimba yenyanga khukhulola.
(You see him and tell him that Shem Lusimba wants to see you.)
Guard (Luyia): Yikhala yalia ulindi.
(Sit here and wait.)
(*At this point another visitor comes in.*)
Visitor 2 (Swahili): Bwana Kamidi yuko hapa?
(Is Mr. Kamidi here?)
Guard (Swahili): Ndio yuko – anafanya kazi saa hii. Hawezi kuiacha mpaka iwe imekwisha. Kwa hivyo utaketi hapa mpaka aje. Utangoja kwa dakika kama kumi tano hivi.
(Yes, he's here – he is doing something right now. He can't leave

until he finishes. Therefore you will wait here until he comes. You will wait about five or ten minutes.)
(*Then Guard goes to look for Solomon Amuhaya.*)

Speech events among white-collar office personnel constitute another type of conventionalized exchange in Nairobi. In this case, educational attainment is a more salient feature than simply being a Kenyan African or not. English is a frequent unmarked choice in such speech events, as extensive observation indicated. An example follows:

> (*The conversation takes place in a downtown office building. Herman, a young man who has finished secondary school and who comes from Western Kenya, is visiting a relative of his. They first converse alone in their shared mother tongue. Then, the relative switches to English as he shows him around within earshot of fellow workers.*)

> *Relative (to Herman)*: And, you, are you looking for employment or have you got a job already? You look very smart as someone who is working.
> *Herman*: I haven't got a job yet. I'm still looking for one.
> *Fellow worker of relative*: So you have visitors. I can see you're showing someone around.
> *Relative*: Yes, these are my visitors.

While I speak of an unmarked choice, the singular is used only as a convenience. The model calls for a markedness continuum: speakers operate with degrees of markedness, not categorical distinctions. They perceive one or more choices are more unmarked than others; and among marked choices some are more marked than others. Further, the same choice is not necessarily unmarked for all participants in the same exchange. For example, structured observations in many Nairobi offices showed that English and Swahili are both unmarked choices for conversation among fellow workers, although each one seems more unmarked under different conditions (see Scotton, 1982a).

Of course far from all exchanges are conventionalized. Very often, situations arise for which norms of behaviour are not established, or conflicting norms apply, and an unmarked choice is not clear. In such cases, community members have no communal sense of how individual participants are expected to carry out such an exchange, no sense of 'script'. Non-conventionalized exchanges typically include such situations as lengthy conversations with strangers (if their social identities remain unknown), interactions as the superior of a former peer, or conversation as a peer with someone of a much older generation. In such cases, both speaker and addressee recognize that any linguistic choice is exploratory, intended as a candidate to become the index of a mutually acceptable relationship, i.e. to become the unmarked choice.

Speaking of choices as marked or not assumes that they take place in a normative framework. Yet, norms do not determine choices. Rather, norms determine the relative markedness of a linguistic code for a particular exchange, given the association of the code with a specific rights and obligations set. What the norms do, then, is give all speakers a grammar of consequences. Speakers are free to make any choices, but how their choices will be interpreted is not free. The mental representations of the 'histories' of possible choices (and their associated rights and obligations sets) is the backdrop against which the choosing of one linguistic variety rather than another is played out. (This sets up a three-way association between the speaker, the addressee, and the speech event.)

The choices themselves are negotiations in the sense that, given the normative framework, speakers make their choices as goal-oriented actors. They weigh the relative costs and rewards of their choices in seeking a good outcome (Thibaut and Kelley, 1959; Brown and Levinson, 1978). In this way, choices are creative and 'localize' the construction of a speech event.

Three main types of choices are possible. Making the unmarked choice in a conventionalized exchange is a negotiation to recognize the status quo as the basis for the present speech event, since it is indexical of the rights and obligations balance which is expected, given the salient situational factors. But speakers also can make marked choices in conventionalized exchanges. Such a choice is a dis-identification with the expected. It is a call for some balance other than the expected one since it indexes a rights and obligations set which is unexpected, given the salient situational factors. Finally, far from all exchanges are conventionalized and choices in such cases are seen as the nominating of some rights and obligations set as, in effect, for the present exchange, i.e. as the unmarked basis pro temp.

It can be seen, then, that there is an interplay between societal factors and more dynamic, individual considerations in the choice of linguistic varieties as media for conversational exchanges. The mentally represented normative framework is the primary source of the consequences of choices. It makes speakers aware of the relative markedness of choices for a given exchange and likely outcomes. Speakers, however, are free to assert their individual motivations since, whatever their markedness, all choices are open to them. Finally, another dynamic aspect is that all choices, unmarked or not, are basically negotiations, requiring reciprocity from the addressee, making the construction of any speech event an ultimately cooperative enterprise.

Specifically in reference to code-switching, this markedness model has some of the same concerns as Scotton and Ury (1977). That is, both models stress switching as simultaneously a tool and an index. For the speaker, switching is a tool, a means of doing something (by affecting the rights and obligations balance). For the listener, switching is an index, a symbol of the speaker's intentions.

Switching, therefore, is both a means and a message. The model developed in Scotton and Ury (1977), however, treated all switching as a strategy to change social relationships. Within the terms of the markedness model, attempting to change relationships involves making a marked choice, but it is only one possible motivation for switching. The markedness model predicts switching as a realization of one of three negotiations: in conventionalized exchanges, switching may be an unmarked choice between bilingual peers, or with any participants it may be a marked choice; in non-conventionalized exchanges, switching is an exploratory choice presenting multiple identities.

The psychological reality of switching as encoding such negotiations has been demonstrated empirically in two studies of reactions of local speech community members to switching in contexts familiar to them (Scotton and Ury, 1977; Scotton, 1982). In both studies, facsimile audio recordings of actual conversations were played to subjects. Local persons served as amateur actors, with the identities of the original participants masked. Subjects were told they would hear possible conversations taking place in Western Kenya, their home area. They were told they would be asked questions 'about the relationships' of the people in the conversation, but their attention was not drawn to the code-switching, or even language usage in general.

Results were consistent with the explanations proposed here and were significant, according to certain statistical tests.[1] Also of interest is that subjects regularly attributed to speakers socio-psychological motivations with interpersonal consequences, based on their language use. That is, first of all, they regularly mentioned code choices and, second, they did not link switching to folk explanations taking account only of the speaker (rather than the interaction), such as 'he switches because he can't think of the right word' or 'he is just used to speaking different languages'.

Code-switching is defined as the use of two or more linguistic varieties in the same conversation, without prominent phonological assimilation of one variety to the other. Most studies have dealt with switching between two or more distinctive languages, but the same motivations account for switching between dialects (see Chapter 5 of this volume) or styles of the same language (Gumperz, 1978; Scotton, 1985); switching may be either intrasentential or intersentential and often (but not necessarily) involves stretches of more than one word. East African data, at least, show that the free morpheme constraint on switching proposed by Sankoff and Poplack (1979/81) does not apply.[2] In Scotton (1982a) numerous switches between a first language (L1) bound morpheme and a second language (L2) morpheme which is not integrated into L1 are shown. For example:

(Swahili) Ni nani alispoil kamba yetu?
(Who spoiled our rope?)

a-	-li-	-i-	-spoil
SUBJECT	PAST TENSE	OBJECT	VERB STEM

Such hybrid forms occur especially where an international language is used daily as a second language *and* is expanding into settings in which an indigenous language had been the dominant or exclusive unmarked choice. Among educated bilinguals in various African capitals, for example, or in other parts of the Third World, something approaching a melange of two varieties (an international language which either has official status locally or is the unmarked medium of international contacts and an indigenous mother tongue) is common, especially for informal interactions. (The discussion below on overall code-switching as an unmarked choice relates to such usage.)

Agreeing on labels for these innovating varieties is a problem, with the use of 'code-mixing' alongside 'code-switching' as somewhat unfortunate. This is so for two reasons. First, some writers use 'mixing' for what is referred to here as 'switching'; but others use mixing for intrasentential shifts only, reserving 'switching' for intersentential switches. The overlap of reference results in confusion. Second, others use 'mix' for what they see as a development beyond switching, with more integration of the two varieties than under switching (Kachru, 1978: 108). The problem is that the term 'mix' implies unprincipled chaos.

The fusion may be such that the two components form something distinct from either donor system. Gibbons speaks of the combination of English and Cantonese, used by some in Hong Kong in these terms, as 'an autonomous system' (1979: 116). (Within the model developed here, such a fused variety could develop from an overall pattern of switching as an unmarked choice, especially if it remains in place with frequent use over a period of time. However, this is not a necessary development, nor does it follow that the use of the innovating variety need convey the same social meaning as overall switching does. This is discussed below.)

In some (or in many?) cases, such amalgamating varieties may be ephemeral, associated with age grading in a way analogous to teenage slang. For example, such a variety called 'Sheng' is current today in Nairobi among the young. While it combines elements of Swahili and English (its name coming from the 's' and 'h' from Swahili and 'eng' from English), the results diverges from both. Sheng does seem to follow many of the syntactic rules of Swahili (but not all); but it has a new lexicon, including some Swahili morphemes (especially the inflectional ones), many English ones (but typically with new meanings), and also some entirely novel morphemes.[3]

Distinguishing code-switching from borrowing presents another problem.[4] Trying to resolve this problem on a structural basis, considering degree of assimilation, yields no useful results. First, assimilation is a gradient, not a categorical, concept, and can provide us only with a continuum as a metric for evaluation. Second, while an expected hypothesis is that borrowed morphemes are more assimilated phonologically into Ll than switched morphemes, what about the many clearly established borrowings which show little assimilation? (For example, *town* [taun] 'city center' shows next to no assimilation as a common loan into diverse Kenyan African languages spoken in Nairobi.) Third, what about the relative weight of phonological assimilation vs. morphological assimilation? One may or may not be accompanied by the other. Thus, an educated Tanzanian who knows both English and Swahili may say:

> *u-si-ni-misundastand.*
> (second person singular subject prefix-NEGATIVE prefix-first person singular object prefix-MISUNDERSTAND)
> ('Don't misunderstand me.')

As a verb stem *misundastand* shows little phonological assimilation (since Swahili does not permit closed syllables or consonant clusters such as *-st-*, but it shows deep morphological assimilation (i.e. it accepts Swahili verbal inflections). The fact the same person also might say *ni-ta-cheki mambo hayo* 'I will check on those matters', with *cheki* showing both types of integration does not make it easy to claim that categorical structural criteria identifying borrowings exist.

As I hope will become clear below, however, the problem of distinguishing borrowing and switching is solved if it is approached in terms of social content, not structure. Just as, for example, all phonological or syntactic features in a social dialect are not distinctive and therefore are not crucial defining features of the dialect (they are not all socially diagnostic of social group membership), all incorporations of L2 into L1 are not diagnostic of interpersonal negotiations. Those which carry social significance (as a negotiation) constitute code-switching while those which do not are borrowings. (The only complication is that a borrowing can appear as a code-switch when it is part of style-switching. But this development is entirely consistent with the model: any style (and its components) becomes socially meaningful when it is used in a marked way. For example, a speaker may switch in an informal discussion to a style interlarded with learned loan words. This is a marked choice, possibly to negotiate a position of erudition.)

Code-switching as an unmarked choice

As noted above, the markedness model most crucially consists of a negotiation principle and a set of maxims which participants in conversation use to calculate conversational implicatures about the balance of rights and obligations which the speaker proposes for the present speech event. The unmarked choice maxim is the keystone of these maxims, directing speakers to 'make the unmarked code choice when you wish to establish or affirm the unmarked rights and obligations set associated with a particular conventionalized exchange'. Making the unmarked choice, then, gives rise to the implicature that the speaker is negotiating a normative position, the status quo (Scotton, 1983:120).

Sequential unmarked choices

What Blom and Gumperz (see Chapter 5 of this volume) refer to as situational switching is seen within this model as a movement from one unmarked choice to another. Such sequences occur in a chain of conventionalized exchanges when participants wish to engage in normative behaviour and acknowledge that the change from one type of exchange to another has altered the expected rights and obligations balance, and therefore the relevancy of the indexical quality of one code vs. another. The example above of the security guard and visitor who first interact in Swahili and then, when their shared ethnic membership is known, in Luyia, shows sequential unmarked choices. New information (about ethnic identity) brought about a re-definition of the exchange. Another example makes even clearer how external factors are involved in changing the unmarked choice. Two East Africans from the same ethnic group will chat about personal affairs in their shared mother tongue if they are making the unmarked choice for such an exchange. But if they are joined by a friend from another ethnic group, the exchange is no longer the same. They will switch to a neutral lingua franca now if they are making the unmarked choice.

Because what stimulates the change in code is external to the participants themselves (situational features or their relative saliency are what change), calling this type of code choice situational switching clearly has its motivations. But within the model developed here, situations do not determine choices. Rather, speaker motivations do. Speakers make decisions within a framework of predictable consequences, with situations figuring only indirectly in that they alert speakers (they 'situate' them) to consequences since markedness of choices is determined by situational features. Characterizing such choices as sequential unmarked choices highlights speakers as actors and the element of predictability. While part of what happens is that the situation changes, what counts more is the change in the appropriateness of the present choice to encode the unmarked relationship between speakers, and then their decision (conscious or not) to recognize this new relationship.

Overall switching as the unmarked choice

When participants are bilingual peers, the unmarked choice may be switching with no changes at all in the situation. That is, the pattern of using two varieties for the same conventionalized exchange is itself unmarked. For example, many educated persons from the same Kenyan or Zimbabwean ethnic group alternate between their own first language and English in many conversations with peers.

The motivation for such switching is the same as that for choosing a single linguistic variety which is an unmarked choice: any variety is indexical of the speaker's position in the rights and obligations balance. When the speaker wishes more than one social identity to be salient in the current exchange, and each identity is encoded in the particular speech community by a different linguistic variety, then those two or more codes constitute the unmarked choice. In most parts of Africa, for example, speech communities are multilingual, with each language having particular associations. Ethnic identity is signaled by use of mother tongue. In addition, ability to speak the official language fluently is associated with membership in a multi-ethnic elite. Other associations are also possible. For example, speaking an indigenous lingua franca well, such as Swahili in East Africa, signals participation in a travel syndrome, usually involving experience in urban multi-ethnic areas. Knowing the language of another ethnic group is also indicative of a special social identity.

The unmarked choice for many speakers having two such identities, when talking with persons similar to themselves, is a pattern of switching between the two varieties indexical of the rights and obligations sets which the speakers wish to be in force for the speech event. The two varieties are both indexical of positively valued identities, but from different arenas, such as ethnic group membership and being part of an educated and/or urban elite.

Each switch need have no special significance; rather it is the overall pattern of using two varieties which carries social meaning (the negotiation of two different rights and obligations balances as simultaneously salient). Note that this feature distinguishes overall switching as an unmarked choice from all other forms of code-switching since, for them, each switch signals a new negotiation.

The following example (Scotton, 1982) shows switching as an unmarked choice.

> (1) *Setting: Veranda of a restaurant in Western Kenya. All participants are native speakers of Lwidakho, a Luyia variety. A staffing officer in the ministry of education, a local school teacher and his wife, who is also a school teacher, greet a secondary school headmaster who has just driven up.*
>
> *Staffing office (English)*: It's nice that we've met. I haven't seen you for long.
> *Headmaster (English)*: Yes, it's really long – and this is because I'm far from this way.
> *Staffing officer (Lwidakho)*: Yikhala yaha khulole nuva nuvula haraka.
>   (Sit down if you're not in a hurry. [Note: *haraka* is Swahili loan for 'hurry'])

Headmaster (English; Lwidakho): I'm not very much in a hurry. Nuva noveye na khasoda khambe.

(Lwidakho: If you have to offer some soda, let me have it.)

Male teacher (English): Tell us about X place. How are the people there treating you?

Headmaster (English; Lwidakho): X is fine, the people are OK, but as you know, they are very tribalistic. Nuwatsa kwanalani navo ni miima jiavo.

(Lwidakho: But now I am used to their behavior.)

Female teacher (Lwidakho): Kwahulda vakukuyagaku, gall ndi?

(Lwidakho: We heard they attacked you and beat you up. How was this?)

Headmaster (Lwidakho; English): Gali madinyu. (Lwidakho: It was very serious.) I've seen a place where men can beat up a headmaster. But now they can't tell me personally. Kalunu ku tsiharambe tsya khohola lwayumbaha. (Lwidakho: Due to harambee spirit, we've put up a modern dining hall to cater for all students at once) . . . Ndevahe, Peter – Kekokeka Kalmosi yiki? (Lwidakho: May ask, Peter – what's happening at Kaimosi?)

A fragment of a conversation between two University of Nairobi students shows a conventionalized exchange for which switching between Swahili and English is an unmarked choice for bilingual peers. This is the case even though the participants share the same first language (Luo) since the setting is a university dining room, with students from other ethnic groups also participating.

(2) *Onyango (Luo; Swahili; English)*: Omera, umesoma katika papers kwamba government imekuwa frozen.

(Luo: I say. Swahili: Have you read in the papers that the government is frozen? Meaning: there is a freeze on employment.)

Owino (Swahili): Kitambo sana.

(Swahili: Long ago.)

Onyango (Swahili; English): Na huoni kuna need ya kujaza zile forms za TSC badala ya kungojea zile za PSC?

(Swahili: And don't you think there's a need to fill in the forms of the Teacher Service Commission rather than wait for those of the Public Service Commission?)

Owino (English; Swahili): Yea, you have a point there. Singejali kuwa part-time cheater.

(Swahili: I wouldn't mind being a part-time teacher. [Note: cheater = 'teacher' in student word play.])

Onyango (Swahili; English): Hutaki kuwa full-time cheater.
(Swahili: You don't want to be a full-time teacher.)
Owino (English): No way.

Other writers in Heller (1988) – McConvell (1988) on switching among Gurindji Aborigines in Australia and Poplack (1988) on Spanish-English switching among Puerto Ricans in New York – recognize a type of switching matching these examples and the above characterization of overall switching as an unmarked choice. They do not, however, fit such switching into a model of code choice as a principled type, as is proposed here. When McConvell (1988) mentions this type of switching, though, it is in making a theoretical point which is – within my model – an important motivation for overall switching as an unmarked choice. His point is that the possibility of defining an interaction as belonging to more than one exchange type simultaneously (a 'nesting' of arenas in his terms) should be accommodated in any model. And Poplack's (1988) comment about some of the switching in New York, that 'it could be said to function as a mode of interaction similar to monolingual language use' (p. 217) is reminiscent of my claim that this type of switching is analogous to using a single code which is the unmarked choice for an exchange, the only difference being that using two codes in a switching pattern happens to be what is unmarked. Once more, her comments that this type of switching shows transitions between varieties and apparent unawareness of participants of the particular alternations between languages would apply to the type of prosody and lack of self-consciousness which would be expected when speakers are simply making the unmarked choice. Further, her description of this type of switching among Puerto Ricans in New York fits the examples from Kenya just cited. She notes that 'in the course of a single utterance the language of the discourse oscillated from English to Spanish and back to English; and during each stretch in one language there are switches of smaller constituents to the other'.

As for the function of such switches, Poplack's observation that 'individual switches cannot be attributed to stylistic or discourse functions' seems to support an important distinction this chapter makes above: that overall switching as an unmarked choice differs from other types of switching in that each switching is not socially meaningful on its own. (Rather, only the overall pattern has a discourse function.)

As noted above, overall switching as an unmarked choice seems to be the first step to what has been called the development of a semi-autonomous 'mix'. Overall switching, for example, seems to include more alternations at the bound morpheme level ('deep switching') than other types of switching, although this claim needs to be supported empirically. But typical examples are the following, taken from natural conversations of bilingual East and Central African university students:[5]

One student to another at the University of Nairobi:
Alikuwa amesit papa hapu tu . . .
(A-li-ku-wa a-me-sit = he/she-PAST-BE-VERBAL SUFFIX he/she-
PERFECT-sit)
(Swahili/English: He/she had been sitting just right here . . .)
[Note that SIT is used with Swahili inflectional morphemes, not
English -*ing*, to convey the progressive meaning 'sitting'.]

One student to another at the University of Zimbabwe:
Huana kuda ku-mbo-react-a zvokuda ku-mu-kis-a here kana kuti?
(Ku-mbo-react-a = INFINITIVE PREFIX-NEGATIVE INTENSIFIER
'sometimes'-react-VERBAL SUFFIX; ku-mu-kis-a = INFINITIVE PREFIX-
THIRD PERSON SINGULAR OBJECT PREFIX-kiss-VERBAL SUFFIX)
(Karanga dialect of Shona/English: Didn't you react by wanting to
kiss her or to . . .)

Does overall switching as an unmarked choice occur in all bilingual communities? The answer seems to be 'no'. Elsewhere (Scotton, 1986), I suggest that
overall switching as an unmarked choice would be hypothesized as unlikely in a
narrow diglossic community where there is strict allocation of the two varieties
involved. But not only is the degree of normative compartmentalization of the
varieties important, what must be considered is the evaluation of the varieties (as
vehicles of the identities they encode), as is discussed more fully below.

Let us first consider some data. Poplack (1988) notes that this type of
switching (she refers to it at times as 'skilled' switching but elsewhere as 'true'
switching) occurs only infrequently in an Ottawa–Hull study of French–English
switching. She says this is the case 'despite the fact that the participant constellation, mode of interaction and bilingual situation appear to be similar to those in
the Puerto Rican study' (p. 230). (Most of the switching she reports among the
French Canadians would be classified as making marked choices in terms of this
model.)

A similar lack of switching as an overall pattern for informal interactions was
reported for instructors of English at the University of Panama in the 1980s
(Alnouri, personal communication). Staff room interactions were almost all
entirely in Spanish for these native speakers of Spanish who taught English. One
possible reason for not switching to English was that such usage would provide
invidious comparisons among persons whose livelihood depended on their English
competence. But another reason may have been that there was hostility toward the
United States at the time over the Panama Canal. Therefore, a persona as an
English speaker was not valued for informal interactions with Panamanian peers.

These examples support the hypothesis that overall switching as an unmarked
choice between bilingual peers is only frequent when both varieties are indexical

of identities which are positively evaluated for the specific exchange type. For example, this means the point is not that English is never associated with positive values by French Canadians, or that they do not see themselves as bilinguals. Rather, this hypothesis would predict that an overall pattern of switching is infrequent because an identity encoded by English is not valued specifically for informal exchanges with French Canadian peers. Obviously, data from other communities, including attitudinal studies, would be necessary to support this hypothesis in any meaningful way. But the overall insight that the specific type of switching possible will depend on evaluations of the varieties involved (and that evaluations are not of one fabric, but are exchange specific) seems valid.[6]

Code-switching as a marked choice

Switching away from the unmarked choice in a conventionalized exchange signals that the speaker is trying to negotiate a different rights and obligations balance as salient in place of the unmarked one, given the situational features. Such switching constitutes a marked choice, a flouting of the unmarked choice maxim.

Because a marked choice is a violation, it is always disruptive, although it can be so in a positive or negative sense. That is, a marked choice can be positive by narrowing social distance if it is indexical of a relationship of solidarity, given the normative matrix of associations between varieties and social meanings in the community. Or, it can be negative in that it increases social distance because it encodes anger or the desire to make a power differential salient (when it would not be salient ordinarily). As noted above, marked choices are interpreted by matching them with the exchanges in which they would be unmarked choices. Thus, in the following speech event a passenger begins speaking to the bus conductor in the passenger's own native language, not in the unmarked choice for this event, Swahili. Everyone present laughs (including the passenger, who seemed to intend his use of his language as a joke). How is the choice of his own language to be interpreted? By reference to those exchanges in which it would be the unmarked choice. And those are largely exchanges in which solidarity is salient. Thus, as a marked choice, using his native language is a negotiation for solidarity with the bus conductor, if only facetiously. While the conductor rejects the bid for solidarity as such, he does give the passenger a discount, indicating the bid to alter the unmarked rights and obligations balance has worked.

> *Setting: A bus in Nairobi, with Swahili as the unmarked choice for the conventionalized exchange of passenger to conductor. A Luyia man who has just got on the bus speaks to conductor.*
>
> *Passenger (Lwidakho) (Speaking in a loud and joking voice)*: Mwana weru, vugula khasimoni khonyene.

(Dear brother, take only fifty cents.) *(Laughter from conductor and other passengers)*

Passenger (Lwidakho): Shuli mwana wera mbaa?

(Aren't you my brother?)

Conductor (Swahili): Apana. Mimi Si ndugu wako, kama ungekuwa ndugu wangu ningekujua kwa jina. Lakini sasa sikujui wala sikufahamu.

(No, I am not your brother. If you were my brother, I would know you by name. But, now I don't know you or understand you.)

Passenger (Swahili): Nisaidie, tu, bwana. Maisha ya Nairobi imen-ishinda kwa sababu bei ya kila kitu imeongezwa. Mimi ninaketi Kariobang'i, pahali ninapolipa pesa nyingi sana kwa nauli ya basi.

(Just help me, mister. The life of Nairobi has defeated me because the price of everything has gone up. I live at Kari-obang'i, a place to which I pay much money for the bus fare.)

Conductor: Nimechukua peni nane pekee yake.

(I have taken 80 cents alone.)

Passenger (English; Swahili): Thank you very much. Nimeshukuru sana kwa huruma ya huyu ndugu wango.

(I am very thankful for the pity of this one, my brother.)

Scotton and Ury (1977: 16–17) cite another example showing a marked choice in a conversation on a bus in Nairobi. But in this case, the passenger's marked choice is to encode authority and educational status, not solidarity. The conductor counters by matching the passenger's marked choice, showing that he too can compete in any power game (involving here ability to speak English):

Setting: A conductor on a Nairobi bus has just asked a passenger where he is going in order to determine the fare (in Swahili).

Passenger (Swahili): Nataka kwenda posta.

(I want to go to the post office.)

Conductor (Swahili): Kutoka hapa mpaka posta nauli ni senti hamsini.

(From here to the post office, the fare is 50 cents.)

(Passenger gives conductor a shilling from which there should be 50 cents in change.)

Conductor (Swahili): Ngojea change yako.

(Wait for your change.)

(Passenger says nothing until a few minutes have passed and the bus nears the post office where the passenger will get off.)

Passenger (Swahili): Nataka change yangu.
    (I want my change.)
Conductor (Swahili): Change utapata, Bwana.
    (You'll get your change, mister.)
Passenger (English): I am nearing my destination.
Conductor (English): Do you think I could run away with your change?

Another example shows how a marked choice is used to narrow social distance. Even though the speech event in this case is discontinuous, its parts constitute a single scenario and therefore show switching in a broad sense.

Setting: A young, well-educated Luyia woman is driving her car into a Nairobi athletic club where she is a member. She has stopped her car and wants the gatekeeper to open the club gate. A middle-aged man, the gatekeeper also turns out to be a Luyia, although that is not obvious until later. An ethnically neutral lingua franca, Swahili, is the unmarked choice for this speech event no matter whether speakers share ethnicity or not. This is probably so because, in the face of the substantial status differential between the gatekeeper (as an unskilled, little educated worker) and the upper middle-class club members, ethnicity has little or no salience as a factor in affecting the rights and obligations balance.

Gatekeeper (to young woman stopped in the middle of the gate) (Swahili):
    Ingla kwa mlango mmoja tu. (Enter by using only one gate.)
*Young woman (looks behind her and sees another car pulled up so that she
    cannot move easily) (Swahili)*: Fungua miwili. Siwezi kwenda
    revas! Kuna magari mengine nyuma.
    (Open both. I can't reverse! There are other cars behind me.)
    (Seeing the situation, the gatekeeper very grudgingly opens both gates.)
Young woman (driving by the gatekeeper, she says to him) (Swahili): Mbona
    wewe mbaya sana leo?
    (Why are you so difficult today?)
    *(She says to her companions in the car — in English — 'The man is a
    Luyia.' She determines this by his pronunciation.) (Several hours later,
    she drives through the gate as she leaves.)*
Young woman (to gatekeeper) (Maragoli, a Luyia variety): Undindiyange
    vutwa.
    (You were being unkind to me.)
Gatekeeper (Swahili; Maragoli): Pole, simbere nikhumany ta.
    (Sorry. I didn't know it was you.)

The young woman's use of Luyia for the final part of this interaction was a conscious effort to establish co-ethnic identity, she reported.[7] After all, she expected to have to deal with the gatekeeper again and did not want the next encounter to be as irritating as this one had started out to be. By switching from the unmarked choice of Swahili, encoding the neutral relationship of club member: club employee, to a Luyia variety, she is asserting common ethnicity and negotiating a different relationship. The gatekeeper's reply, 'I didn't know it was you,' was interpreted by the young woman as meaning 'I didn't know you were of my ethnic group' (since he definitely did not know her personally). Both his switch from Swahili to Luyia and the content of this utterance encode a movement away from the unmarked relationship for this exchange.

There are many variants of switching as a marked choice, with many of them relatively brief in duration – only a word or two. Yet, the same motivation characterizes such momentary switches as longer ones: a bid to dis-identify with the unmarked rights and obligations balance for the exchange. It is as if the switch is made to remind other participants that the speaker is a multi-faceted personality, as if the speaker were saying 'not only am I X, but I am also Y'. This ploy, in and of itself, is a powerful strategy because the speaker 'enlarges' himself or herself through marked choices in a mainly unmarked discourse, asserting a *range* of identities (Scotton, 1985: 113). In addition, of course, the specific associations of the variety making up the marked choice are also part of the attempted negotiation.

A very common type of momentary marked switching is change in code for emphasis.[8] Such switching often involves repetition (in the marked code) of exactly the same referential meaning conveyed in the unmarked code. The fact there is this repetition makes it very clear that the new information is the change in code and therefore its social associations. The following examples, both involving a refusal to give money, show this. In both, the marked choice is a negotiation to increase the social distance between the speaker and his supplicant, since the switch is to a variety symbolizing authority and also unmarked for formal interactions. Such a choice reinforces the speaker's denial.

> *Setting: A farmer in rural Western Kenya is asking money of a salaried worker who is in his home area on leave. The conversation takes place in a bar where all speak the same mother tongue, Lwidakho, the unmarked choice for this exchange* (Scotton, 1983: 128).

> *Farmer (finishing an oblique request for money) (Lwidakho)*: . . . inzala ya
>   mapesa, kambuli.
>   (Hunger for money. I don't have any.)
> *Worker (who had been speaking only Lwidakho before the request)*
>   *(English)*: You have got a land.
> *(Swahili)*: Una shamba.
>   (You have a farm/land.)

(Lwidakho): Uli mulimi.
      (You have land.)

Setting: A Zimbabwean university student is refusing to give a fellow student money. He has already refused once in their shared mother tongue, the Ndau dialect of Shona; but the petitioner persists. The student switches to English.

Student (English; Ndau): I said, 'Andidi'. I don't want!

'Permissible' marked choices

Marked choices under certain circumstances in conventionalized exchanges are allowable. These choices are marked because they do not encode the unmarked rights and obligations expected for the overall exchange. But at the same time, they are almost unmarked 'in context' because they signal what becomes a conventionalized suspension of the current rights and obligations balance. Two types seem universal: those which encode deference and those which take account of lack of ability to speak the unmarked choice.

Choices encoding deference

These choices are made when the speaker wishes special consideration from the addressee, or when the speaker wants to perform a 'face-threatening act' (Brown and Levinson, 1978) but also wants to maintain a good relationship with the addressee. Scotton (1983:123) refers to such choices as following a *deference maxim* which, in a revised form, is 'Show deference in your code choice to those from whom you desire something or to mitigate a face threatening act.'

A major way of expressing deference is to accommodate to the addressee by switching to the variety used in his or her turn, or to a variety otherwise associated with the addressee (e.g., his or her mother tongue). Many of the subtle shifts in phonological features which Giles and his associates refer to under their accommodation hypothesis would be included here (e.g. Giles and Powesland, 1975; Thackerar *et al.*, 1982). Another way of showing deference is to switch to a variety (or sub-variety) whose unmarked use is to express respect. For example, the use of an elaborate directive form — which is in a marked style for the expected rights and obligations balance — when performing a face-threatening act illustrates this (e.g. Professor to student: 'If it is not out of your way, I would appreciate it if you would please check on whether the library received my reserve list.').

The use of a term of respect, which is part of a style, dialect or language whose use is not called for by the unmarked rights and obligations balance, is also an instance of following the deference maxim. Scotton and Zhu (1984) report that many customers in Beijing service encounters call unskilled personal *shi fu*, a term whose meaning is now changing, but generally it means either 'elder craftsman' or at the very least 'skilled worker'. Scotton and Zhu refer to such switching as 'calculated respect' since the choice elevates the addressee so that the speaker can gain some advantage.

Choices taking account of lack of ability to speak the unmarked choice

A conversation starting out in the unmarked choice may shift into a marked choice because of limits on speaking abilities. Scotton (1983: 125) accounts for such choices as following the *virtuosity maxim*: 'Make an otherwise marked choice whenever the linguistic ability of either speaker or addressee makes the unmarked choice for the unmarked rights and obligations set in a conventionalized exchange infelicitous.'

Many times the switching away from the unmarked choice because of lack of fluency is overtly acknowledged by the speaker, who says, 'I'm sorry, but I can't speak X very well' meaning – in the terms of this model – 'I know the unmarked relationship calls for the use of X.' (Note that it seems to be a marked choice for the other participant – the one who *is* fluent in the unmarked choice – to initiate a switch under the virtuosity maxim. That is, the speaker following the virtuosity maxim must self-select. For another speaker to take the initiative often elicits a negative affective response.)

The following conversation (Parkin, 1974: 194–5) illustrates the use of a marked choice to show deference, as well as a switch to the unmarked choice because of lack of virtuosity. A Kikuyu market seller in Nairobi greets a Luo customer in his own language, clearly a move designed to flatter the Luo by acknowledging his personal distinctiveness. The customer accepts this accommodation, but it soon becomes apparent that the seller cannot speak much Luo. The customer switches to the unmarked choice of Swahili, jocularly accusing the seller of attempting flattery. Thus, the deference negotiation fails, showing that, as the model claims, code choices are made with normative expectations of consequences, but at the same time are negotiations whose success depends on the dynamics of the individual speech event.

> *Setting: A Kikuyu woman stallholder greets a Luo male customer in a Nairobi market. (Dashes indicate switching.)*

> *Seller (Luo)*: Omera, nadi!
>   (How are you, brother?)
> *Customer (Luo)*: Maber.
>   (Fine.)

Seller (Kikuyu; Swahili): Ati-nini?
       (What-what?)
Customer (Swahili): Ya nini kusema lugha ambao huelewi, mama?
       (Why (try) to speak a language you don't know, madam?)
Seller (English): I know Kijaluo very well!
       (English with Swahilized form, Kijaluo).
Customer (Swahili; English; Swahili): Wapi! — You do not know it at all
       — Wacha haya, nipe mayai mbili.
       (Go on! You do not know it at all — Let's leave the matter; give
       me two eggs.)
Seller (Swahili; Luo; Swahili): Unataka mayai — anyo, omera — haya ni —
       tongolo — tatu.
       (You want two eggs, brother. OK, that's thirty cents. Note:
       'two', 'brother', and 'thirty' are Luo.)

In his analysis of such conversational exchanges, Parkin uses games as an analogy, emphasizing the to-and-fro movement of turn taking and the influence of turns on each other. The dynamic nature of conversation and the possibility for a variety of choices are also important aspects of the markedness model presented here. This model, however, depicts more a 'grammar of consequence' than a 'grammar of choice'. While the speech event itself may be likened to a competition, with speakers making choices to accumulate points, the scoring is only incidentally dependent on the choice in a previous turn or someone else's choice, according to my model. Rather, the specific choices which are made and the outcome depends more on the indexicality of choices and, accordingly, their expected consequences. This is what makes it a grammar of consequences.

A marked choice or a sequence of unmarked choices?

One problem for the overall model is to distinguish a marked choice following or embedded in an unmarked choice from a sequence of two unmarked choices. They can be distinguished in two ways. First, as noted above, there is always some change in factors external to the ongoing speech event when there is a shift from one unmarked choice to another; the topic changes, or new participants are introduced, or new information about the identity of participants which is salient in the exchange becomes available, etc. Second, a sequence of unmarked choices is expected, given the change in factors. In contrast, a marked choice is unexpected. Furthermore, it evokes an affective response, as noted above.

The claim that the distinction between unmarked and marked choices has psychological reality can be empirically tested, although I know of no existing studies. Such expectations and affect are amenable to measurement. Significant differences between marked and unmarked choices would be predicted, although they would be gradient, not categorical.

Ervin-Tripp's discussion of expected vs. unexpected directive forms is relevant here (1976: 61–2). She notes, 'In normal circumstances, when an expected form occurs, *listeners need make no affective interpretation at all*' [italics in original]. She goes on to contrast this reaction with that of an unexpected directive:

> If social features are clear, but the form is unexpected by his own coding rule, the hearer assumes that the speaker is imputing different social features than he thinks he has, and reacts to the imputation as deference, sarcasm, arrogance, coldness, undifferentiated annoyance, or a joke. *These inferences appear to be relatively systematic to the point of being like marking rules* [italics added].

Switching to exclude? Permissible marked choices or not?

In many multilingual societies, switching to a language not known by all participants is a common means of exclusion, often conscious. At the least, it withholds information from those not knowing the language of switching. It may also contain negative comments about those excluded. Such switching is predicted to be most frequent when there is a sharp power differential between those participants who switch to the new code and those who are excluded; for example, parents vs. children. The switching itself conveys that the speakers share an identity others do not have and narrows the social distance between them while increasing that between speakers and those left out. Because of the relatively greater power of the speakers, others may not like this marked choice, but they must permit it.

When the power differential is less great, such switching may not be condoned, but considered rude. Among other things, the speakers are overtly accused of 'back-biting' and, of course, they are figuratively speaking behind the non-participants' backs. Given the unmarked rights and obligations balance, such switching is clearly a marked choice. Is it though? The markedness of exclusive switching in many parts of Africa, for example, seems very unresolved. Exclusive switching there is normally to an ethnic language. Those who accept such switching may do so because ethnic identity and giving priority in social relations to affinity with ethnic brethren are facts of life in many parts of Africa. Switching which is indexical of these facts simply seems unmarked to many. But not all agree. And, not surprisingly, it seems to be members of the larger, more powerful groups who do more exclusive switching.

This state of affairs indicates that there is not necessarily a categorical consensus including all speech community members on the relative markedness of varieties available. In this case, for example, an interethnic conversation may still be considered a conventionalized exchange by all concerned, but they may not agree on the markedness of a non-neutral ethnic language. (It remains a conventionalized exchange because participants do recognize unmarked choices; that is, they do recognize 'scripts' for the exchange. It is just that they do not recognize the same scripts. If the views about markedness become very fragmented, such exchanges may become unconventionalized. This seems to be what happened in Montreal in the late 1970s when the relative unmarkedness of French vs. English became a political issue, especially for exchanges in public institutions; Heller, 1982a: 116–17.[9])

A typical example of switching to exclude in a multi-ethnic conversation in Nairobi follows.

> *Setting: Four young Kenyan men who have completed secondary school and who work in the same government ministry in Nairobi are chatting. Two are native speakers of Kikuyu, one of Kisii and one of a Kalenjin language. Swahili and/or Swahili/English are unmarked choices.*

Kiikuyu 1 (Swahili): Sasa mumesema nini juu ya hiyo plan yetu? Naona kama siku kama siku zinaendelea kwisha.
(Now, what do you all say about the plan of ours? I think time is getting short.)

Kikuyu 2 (Swahili; English): Mlisema tu collect money, lakini hakuna mtu hata mmoja ambaye amenipatia pesa.
(You said collect money, but there isn't even one person who has got money for me.)

Kalenjin (Swahili): Makosa ni yako kama mweka hazina. Tulisema uwe ukitembelea watu mara kwa mara lakini hufanyi hivyo. Watu wengi hawawezi kufanya kitu bila kuwa harassed.
(The fault is yours as treasurer. We said you should visit people (us) from time to time but you don't do that. Many people can't do a thing unless they are harassed.)

Kikuyu 1 (Swahili; English): Mjue ni vibaya for the treasurer akimaliza wakati wake akiona watu ambao hawawezi kupeana pesa.
(You should know it's bad for the treasurer to waste his time if he sees people who can't give money.)

Kisii (Swahili): Mweka hazina hana makosa hata kidogo. Mtu anatakiwa lipe pesa bila kuulizwa.
(The treasurer hasn't made any mistakes. Each person is required to pay without being asked.)

Kikuyu 2 (Kikuyu): Andu amwe nimendaga kwaria maundu maria matari na ma namo.
(Some people like talking about what they're not sure of.)

Kikuyu 1 (Kikuyu): Wira wa muigi wa kigina ni kuiga mbeca. No tigucaria mbeca.

(The work of the treasurer is only to keep money. Not to hunt for money.)

Kisii (Swahili; English): Ubaya wenu ya Kikuyu ni kuassume kila mtu anaelewa Kikuyu.

(The bad thing about Kikuyus is to assume that everyone understands Kikuyu.)

Kalenjin (Swahili; English): Si mtumie lugha ambayo kila mtu hapa atasikia? We are supposed to solve this issue.

(Shouldn't you use a language which every person here understands? We are supposed to solve this issue.)

Kikuyu 2 (Swahili; English): Tunaomba msameha. Sio kupenda kwetu. Ni kawaida kwa most people kupendelea lugha yao.

(We are sorry. It isn't that we favor our side. It's normal for most people to prefer their own language.)

Code-switching as a strategy of multiple identities

In uncertain situations (non-conventionalized exchanges) when an unmarked choice is not apparent, speakers nominate an exploratory choice as the basis for the exchange. The nominated variety is recognized as indexical of a certain rights and obligations balance existing in the conventionalized exchange for which it is unmarked. By analogy, it is proposed that the 'new' exchange be treated as an instance of the 'old'.[10]

Many times, however, at the outset of a conversation a speaker is not sure that any one balance would be preferable to another, even as a candidate, for the exchange. In such cases, a speaker may open an exchange with one choice, but be prepared to switch to another choice, depending on the addressee's own code choice in his or her response. If the speaker changes in his or her second turn to the addressee's choice (first turn), this is a form of showing deference, or accommodation. By using two codes in two different turns, however, the speaker has also been able to encode two identities – and the breadth of experience associated with them. For this reason, participants may find it socially useful to treat certain speech events as non-conventionalized exchanges, if it is at all possible. (Scotton and Zhu (1983) discuss some other social advantages of maintaining various ambiguities in linguistic systems.)

Initial contacts with strangers in situations other than service encounters typically are treated as non-conventionalized exchanges. In the following example, a young man switches from Swahili to English, apparently in an effort to please the young woman with whom he wants to dance.

Setting: A dance at a Nairobi hotel. A young man (his native language is Kikuyu) asks a young woman to dance.

He (Swahili):   Nisaidie na dance, tafadhali.
                  (Please give me a dance.)
She (Swahili): Nimechoka. Pengine nyimbo ifuatayo.
                  (I'm tired. Maybe a following song.)
He (Swahili):   Hii ndio nyimbo ninayopenda.
                  (This is the song which I like.)
She (Swahili): Nimechoka!
                  (I'm tired!)
He (Swahili):   Tafadhali –
                  (Please.)
She (interrupting) (English):   Ah, stop bugging me.
He (English):   I'm sorry. I didn't mean to bug you, but I can't help it
                  if I like this song.
She (English): OK, then, in that case, we can dance.

Conclusion

An explanation for code-switching has been proposed which emphasizes linguistic choices as negotiations of personal rights and obligations relative to those of other participants in a talk exchange. This explanation follows from a markedness model of code choice which claims that speakers make choices and others interpret them by considering their probable consequences. This process involves a consensus concerning the relative markedness of any choice for a specific exchange and a view of all choices as indexical of a negotiation of rights and obligations between participants. Because all community members have this theory of markedness, they are able to use conversational implicatures to arrive at the intended consequences of any code-switching. (As has been noted, this explanation is not merely speculative but is based on studies of the social interpretation of switching by subjects in their own communities (Scotton and Ury, 1977; Scotton, 1982). However, as has also been mentioned, not all claims of the markedness model have been empirically tested, although the fact that they can be tested seems clear.)

The principle guiding some earlier explanations of code-switching in East Africa was the need to detail situational factors. For example, while Whiteley (1974) explicitly recognizes the failures of certain situational factors to account for switching in rural Kenya, his solution is only a more thorough study of the situation. Thus, he writes, 'It does not seem possible to correlate the choice of any particular language with a shift along the scale of formality', but then offers as a solution that 'much more needs to be known about the total social situation than can be gleaned from the language diaries' (1974: 331).

The point of view taken here is, of course, quite different. Situational factors *are* paramount in determining the unmarked choice in a conventionalized exchange: the unmarked rights and obligations set is derived from the salient configuration of social features for the exchange, and the unmarked linguistic choice as indexical of that set. But because not all exchanges are conventionalized and because the relevant features and their hierarchy will differ from exchange to exchange, it is impossible to provide any set of features as universally crucial independent variables. The features themselves even may be dependent variables in the sense that their saliency is context sensitive. In addition, feature salience is dynamically related to a specific exchange in that it may co-vary with content and linguistic choices in progressive turns by participants (for example, the example above involving the security guard and visitor, or Genesee and Bourhis, 1982).

Some other more general explanations do acknowledge personal motivations (as does Parkin (1974) for East Africa, mentioned above), although not exactly along the lines of the markedness model. For example, Blom and Gumperz (see Chapter 5 of this volume) recognize that non-situationally motivated switching occurs, referring to it generally as metaphorical switching. Their primary emphasis, however, remains on the concepts of setting, social situation, and social event to explain choice. In Gumperz' later work, however, switching is recognized much more as a strategy which the speaker employs at will to generate conversational inferences. He writes, 'Code-switching signals contextual information equivalent to what in monolingual settings is conveyed through prosody or other syntactic or lexical processes. It generates presuppositions in terms of which the content of what is said is decoded.' Specifically in relation to what he terms metaphorical usage, he writes:

> This partial violation of co-occurrence expectations then gives rise to
> the inference that some aspects of the connotations, which elsewhere
> apply to the activity as a whole, are here to be treated as affecting only
> the illocutionary force and quality of the speech act in question.
> (Gumperz 1982: 98)

While some aspects of the treatment here are reminiscent of such statements, more of an attempt is made in the markedness model to provide a comprehensive and principled treatment, explicitly assigning roles to a normative framework in implicating consequences and to individual, interactive choices as tools of specific negotiations.

Much more psychologically centered is the accommodation hypothesis and related hypotheses of Giles and his associates (mentioned above) which seek to explain switching and specifically subjective reactions to the process. The accommodation model handles very well switching motivated by a desire to narrow the social distance between the addressee or not, such as those choices encoding deference. However, it seems limited because it seeks to explain all choices in terms of either accommodation or non-accommodation to the addressee. It is argued here that choices have a broader range of motivations. Most important, many are much more speaker-centered (such as choices encoding authority or education). Further, a framework of markedness seems essential in order to deal with the consequences of choices.

In conclusion, this paper has argued that the guiding research question for studies of switching should not be so much, what social factors or interactional features determine code choice? But rather, what is the relation between linguistic choices and their social consequences, and how do speakers know this? From this, more specific questions follow: is there an unmarked choice for a specific exchange? Given that the unmarked choice will have dominant frequency, for what effect do speakers employ switching away from this choice? If there is not an unmarked choice, how do speakers make sense out of choices made?

The several hypotheses and the overall markedness model suggested here respond to these questions. First, it is claimed that choice is not so much a reflection of situation as a negotiation of position, given the situation. People make the choices they do because of personal motivations. Second, it is proposed that these motivations can be characterized and all switching explained parsimoniously in the framework of unmarked, marked, and exploratory choices outlined here. Finally and in general, it has been argued that expected consequence structures code choices. Speakers are restrained only by the possibility and attractiveness of alternative outcomes. This involves, of course, their own linguistic abilities and, more important, their framework of expectations.

Notes

1   In Scotton and Ury (1977), 70 subjects were asked open-ended questions about four audio-recorded conversations. In Scotton (1982), 35 subjects were played audio recordings of six conversations and then asked to select one of five possible answers from a fixed list. In both cases, it was stressed there were no 'right' or 'wrong' answers.

   Three of the four test conversations in the 1977 study illustrated switching as a marked choice. The majority of the subjects provided responses about 'what happened in the conversation' entirely consistent with the claims here about the social negotiation encoded by a marked choice; further, their interpretations were very similar. The fourth conversation showed switching in a non-conventionalized exchange. Perhaps not surprisingly, subjects did not cluster very well in their interpretations; however 69 per cent did mention the different social associations of the three languages involved as a reason for switching (Scotton and Ury, 1977: 14–16).

   The six test conversations used in Scotton (1982) were examples of overall switching as an unmarked choice and switching as a marked choice, including one showing deferential switching. In general, over 90% chose the same interpretation and this was the one consistent with the claims of this model (Scotton, 1982: 442–3). More details are available from the author, including statistical test results.

2   This finding is based on more than 100 hours of recordings of natural conversations made in Nairobi and about 20 hours of recordings in Harare in 1983.

3   'Sheng' is discussed in an article in the *Daily Nation* of 14 March 1984. One example cited is *Buda amenijamisha* 'Father has annoyed me' (as a reason for not going home). The origins of *buda* for 'father' are unclear. The verb stem *-jam* comes from the English but means 'feel stuck or annoyed'. It has Swahili inflections, including the causative suffix. Similar examples were found in my 1983 data corpus from recordings of pre-teens in certain areas of the city.

4   Overall switching as an unmarked choice is most difficult to separate from borrowing. For example, a Luo cooking teacher in Nairobi, addressing in Swahili a class of other teachers, peppered her presentation with such utterances as this:

> Wengine wanachemusha (sic), wengine wana*steam*, na mambo mengi
> mengi. Wengine wanakaanga kama mtu ambaye anakaanga nyama.
> (Some boil [bananas], some steam, and a lot of other things. Some fry
> like a person frying meat.)

The use of *steam* is probably motivated by the fact that 'to steam' in Swahili requires a longer expression, *kupika kwa nguvu ya mvuke*. Thus, *steam* seems best described as a loan, since it regularly replaces a longer Swahili expression. The same is true of Shona expressions of number, which have been almost totally replaced by English forms in urban Shona (more or less assimilated phonologically). To express number in Shona requires long phrases. I thank Kumbirai Mkanganwi for this observation.

But what about words such as *fry*? In the passage above, the teacher uses the Swahili verb -kaanga 'fry'. Yet, within five minutes she uses English *fry*:

> Yaondoke kidogo. Kama vile unatake kufry. Ni tamu isipokua (si) ni a
> bit dry. Sisi, hio ndio njia tuna preserve . . .
> (It [water] evaporates a bit. Just as if you want to fry. It is tasty except
> that it is a bit dry. This is the way we preserve . . .)

Is such a usage as *fry* switching or borrowing? Clearly, *fry* is not a replacement loan. Is this a *nonce* borrowing? Or is this passage simply an example of overall switching as an unmarked choice? Because the lesson in question contains many other English words and phrases, this does seem to be a case of switching (given the audience).

5   A Swahili poem by Kineene wa Mutiso (1983) contains a good deal of 'morphemic switching'. The poem is about a conversation between a secretary and someone who has come to her office. Here is one quatrain:

Brother sije ka *sorry*, *Bosie* utam*see*
Kwanza tupiga *story*, ama hauna *say*?
Hata ukiwa me*marry*, kwa nini tusi*enjoy*?
Sema ma*home* ku*how*, na kote kwenye ma*joint*.

(Brother, lest you worry, you'll see the boss
First let's talk, or do you have nothing to say?
Even if you are married, why can't we enjoy?
How are things at home and in all the nightspots?)

6   Nartey (1982) suggests, too, that the socio-cultural environment may impose constraints on the type of switching possible. He, however, refers specifically to
whether switching is possible after a bound constituent (providing data showing
such switching does occur in the conversations of young, educated Ghanaians).

7   Personal observation and interview on the spot.

8   Another type of momentary switching to a marked choice is to avoid taboo words.
For example, a Shona lecturer in Zimbabwe speaking about Shona marriage cus-
toms used Shona throughout his lecture to an audience of Shona-speaking university
students until he had to mention sexual relations. He switched to English for the
two words, *sexual intercourse*, and then went on in Shona. (I thank Caleb Gwasira for
this example.) Even within a single language, the use of euphemisms for semi-taboo
subjects or objects is a form of marked switching (from one style to a specialized
style), with the shift serving to distance the speaker from the taboo item.

9   Heller's comment (1982: 118) emphasizes how, through the use of exploratory
choices, a consensus is reached:

> This negotiation [of language] itself serves to redefine the situations in
> the light of ongoing social and political change. *In the absence of norms,*
> *we work at creating new ones* [italics added]. The conventionalization of
> the negotiating strategies appears to be a way of normalizing relation-
> ships, of encoding social information necessary to know how to speak
> to someone. . .

10 A related strategy, which encodes neutrality more than exploration, is the extended
use of two varieties in an uncertain situation so that some entire conversations may
be in one variety and some in another. Such a pattern is very similar to overall
switching as an unmarked choice because it simultaneously presents two identities
while also neutralizing them. Scotton (1976) explains the high incidence of
reported use of two languages (rather than either one alone) in urban work situations as such a strategy of neutrality. For example, in Kampala, Uganda many
educated persons reported speaking both English (the official language) and Swahili
(a widely used lingua franca) with fellow workers of different ethnic groups.
Speaking English signals a person is educated and has the necessary expertise for a
job, but English is also the language of formality in Uganda, and even pretentious-

ness. Speaking Swahili there signals an ethically neutral African identity and egalitarianism (since it is known by persons from diverse socio-economic backgrounds); but Swahili also has associations primarily as the lingua franca of the uneducated in Uganda. Which language to use with fellow workers? Results show that a middle choice is preferred: switching or alternating between the two.

Source: Myers-Scotton, C. (1988) Code-switching as indexical of social negotiations. In M. Heller (ed.) *Codeswitching*. Berlin: Mouton de Gruyter, pp. 151–86, by permission of Mouton de Gruyter. N.B. This paper was originally published under the name C.M. Scotton.

Chapter 7

A conversation analytic approach to code-switching and transfer

J.C. PETER AUER

Background of this study

This chapter summarizes some main findings of an analysis of code-switching and transfer (in the following, the term *language alternation* is used to cover both) carried out in Constance, West Germany,[1] among the children of Italian migrant workers with a Southern Italian background. (A more detailed analysis grounded in the transcripts is given in Auer, 1981; 1983; 1984a.) The investigation was part of a larger study on the native language of Italian migrant children (*Muttersprache italienischer Gastarbeiterkinder im Kontakt mit Deutsch*)[2] and is based on an extensive corpus of spontaneous and non-spontaneous speech used by these children interacting with each other, the field-workers, or their parents. Nineteen children between the ages of six and 16 formed the core group of this study. These children were observed to use (various varieties of) Italian and German alternately, in a number of situations. Four hundred instances of such alternations were submitted to conversation analysis; another 1,400 instances were used for quantitative-differential analysis.

In this contribution, I sketch the conversation analytic model that was developed out of the materials and that can account for the main types of interpretations that language alternation receives in the community under investigation. In addition, I briefly touch upon differential issues. Before going into details, however, some general remarks on the global linguistic and ethnographic situation of the Italian migrants in West Germany may be necessary.

The linguistic situation of the urban Italian 'communities' in Germany differs from what is known about other contexts of language contact after migration; it also differs from the linguistic situation of other ethnic groups in West Germany, such as the Turkish or the Yugoslavian communities.

The difference is due to the political status of the Italian migrants who, as members of the European Community, have the right to move relatively freely between Italy and Germany. Whereas the influx of adult workers from non-EC countries has been stopped, and those returning to their countries of origin are no longer allowed to come back, the Italian 'communities' are continuously reshaped by the arrival of new members, as well as by the multiple migration of those who came and go again. This comparatively high mobility, which, particularly in a southern German town like Constance, is still enhanced by geographical closeness to Italy, is one of the reasons for the weak or even absent positive self-definition of the Italians as one ethnic group or community. Although the first Italian migrants – in general, first men, later wives and families – arrived in Constance in the 1950s, the Italian population still lacks any political and almost any cultural infrastructure. Activities on the community level, such as attempts to create social foci (*centri italiani per i lavoratori*), have been treated with utmost suspicion; at the same time, the Italians' inability to create such foci is perceived by them as one of the few stable and widely accepted stereotypes that are part of the Italian population's negative self-image. In fact, if we can speak of a community at all, it is a largely negatively defined one.

The comparatively high degree of mobility led us to abandon the terms 'immigrant' and 'emigrant' in favour of the more neutral term 'migrant'. It applies not only to the first generation adults, but also to the second generation. Many Italian couples send their children back to Italy for a while to live with their relatives, and/or to go to an Italian school, before allowing them to stay in Germany again.

For the present study, this high degree of mobility was relevant in the following way. The children that form the core group of our investigation were either born in Germany or had moved to Germany early in childhood; although some of them returned to Italy for shorter periods, their dominant socialization took place in the host country. Nonetheless, the social environment of these children is not homogeneous, for the Italian 'community' in Constance includes children of varying biographical backgrounds. If they wish to, they can establish peer relationships with children and youngsters who have only come to Germany recently and are clearly dominant speakers of Italian (dialect). On the other hand, they, too, may choose their friends among those who have been socialized predominantly in Germany (and, for the most part, are dominant speakers of German (dialect)). Finally, they may, of course, avoid all ties to the Italian ethnic group to which they were born, and exclusively affiliate with Germans.

Accordingly, the children's and youngsters' linguistic repertoire is quite complex. The dominant language of pre-kindergarten socialization in the family is, in many cases, the parents' local, southern Italian dialect (in our materials, mostly dialects of the Basilicata, Calabria and Sicily). In kindergarten and primary school, the German dialect is acquired as the most important variety for inter-ethnic peer networks. Between five and eight, all the children we investigated had become German-dominant; their German was a more or less dialectal (Aleman-nic) variety. Regional or standard Italian comes latest in the acquisition process. It is used in the Italian *doposcuola* (a couple of hours per week), and heard in the Swiss Italian mass media. Most families are not in a position to act as a language mediator for the Italian standard, for even regional Italian only plays a peripheral role in family interaction.

After childhood, many young Italians develop a more positive, and more self-confident, attitude towards Italy and Italian. But although this change of attitude favours the acquisition of a more standard variety of this language, the problem of learning a language that, in the migrants' everyday world, hardly has any speakers, remains. Being, as it is, a diffusely perceived target, standard Italian is hard to acquire. Instead of showing progress towards that target, the speech of many young Italians continues to be characterized by a very high degree of fluctuation and variation.

However, questions of language acquistion are only part of the issue. The rich repertoire of the second generation Italians also opens up the possibility of func-tionally employing variation in their repertoire. We have investigated such functions via the analysis of complex variational signs such as code-switching, code-shifting, code-fluctuation (including *italiano stentato*) (cf., for instance, Auer and Di Luzio, 1983; 1983a).

Variation in the repertoire has to be dealt with in a way that is sensitive to the general social and linguistic situation of the 'community'. As this 'community' is heterogeneous, it is not very likely to have developed rigid regulations or norms of language use and language alternation. Within certain limits imposed by co-participants' linguistic competences, language choice is indeed open to nego-tiation quite regularly, often throughout an interactive episode. Patterns of language choice begin to emerge in small-scale network structures, but there are no larger scale 'domains' in Fishman's sense (see Chapter 3 of this volume). This calls for an analytic tool that is able to catch the subtlety of the ongoing linguistic and social processes; we think that this tool is available in the framework of a linguistically enriched conversation analysis.

Another consequence of this social and linguistic instability is that the patterns of language alternation found in the data can be expected to be related to the type of network in which they are being produced. It is reasonable to predict that language alternation of a different type will occur in networks whose members have diverging language preferences (due to their biographical background) than in those where such a divergence is absent, be it because all members share the same history of migration, be it because certain members of the network are dominant in the sense of imposing their preferences on the others. This calls for a differential account of language alternation on the basis of network types.

In our investigation, we focused on children and youngsters with a pre-dominantly 'German' socialization because we think that it is this group of second generation 'guest workers' who will decide the linguistic future of the migrant 'communities'. In order to make predictions about the future develop-ment of the Italian part of the speakers' repertoire, it was necessary to find out something about the role this Italian repertoire plays in the everyday life of the children when compared to the German part of the repertoire. Are the varieties of Italian at all necessary in Germany? If so, in what situations are they employed? One can look for an answer to these questions by closely observing linguistic behaviour, and, in fact, this was one line of procedure. A more rigorous answer to the question is possible, however, when small-scale linguistic behaviour is analysed on the basis of transcriptions of audio and visual recordings. The analyst of such recordings is in a better position than the participant observer to pay close attention to the small details involved in the organization of linguistic activities. The basic question facing the micro-analyst in the case of language alternation is this: If children regularly switch from variety A to variety B in order to organize linguistic activities X, Y, etc., and from B to A in order to organize linguistic activities V, W, etc., then what status is being attributed to these varieties by and because of the ways in which they are being employed in conversation? Regularities of language choice and language alternation, if treated in this way, reveal the status of the varieties contained in the linguistic repertoire of the speakers.

In addition, I had a more theoretical interest in the analysis of language alternation that relates to the notion of bilingualism itself. Linguistics owes an extensive and inconclusive literature to the futile discussion of how competent someone has to be in order to be considered 'bilingual'. Dozens of attempts have been made at a definition. The impasse reached can only be overcome if bilingual-ism is no longer regarded as something inside the speaker's head, but as a dis-played feature in participants' everyday behaviour. You cannot be bilingual in your head, you have to use two or more languages 'on stage', in interaction, where you show others that you are able to do so. I propose then to examine bilingualism primarily as a set of complex linguistic activities, and only in a secondary, derived sense as a cognitive ability. From such a perspective, bilingualism is a predicate ascribed to and by participants on the basis of their visible, inspectable behaviour. As a result, there is no one set definition of bilingualism. Being bilingual is turned into an achieved status, and how it is achieved, in different ways and by different speakers, is precisely what we need to investigate. We need a model of bilingual conversation which provides a coherent and functionally motivated picture of bilingualism as a set of linguistic activities.

A model of bilingual conversation

Two basic category pairs provide the 'underlying' procedural apparatus for arriving at local interpretations of language alternation embedded in their individual contexts. These are the category pairs *transfer* vs. *code-switching* and *participant-related* vs. *discourse-related* language alternation. From a hearer's point of view, the speaker has to indicate solutions to the following problems corresponding to the two category pairs:

1   Is the language alternation in question connected to a particular conversational *structure* (for instance, a word, a sentence, or a larger unit) (transfer), or to a particular *point* in conversation (code-switching)?
2   Is the language alternation in question providing cues for the *organization of the ongoing interaction* (i.e. is discourse-related), or about *attributes of the speaker* (i.e. is it participant-related)?

In answering these questions, and in providing indications that make them answerable, bilingual participants operate a basic category grid which provides a fundamental four-way differentiation of the signalling device under investigation. It is important to keep in mind that 'discourse-related code-switching', 'participant-related code-switching', 'discourse-related transfer' and 'participant-related transfer' are not generic categories grouping language alternation types; that is, they are not superordinates to subordinated alternation types such as addressee selection, citations, and so on. Instead, the latter should be seen as situated interpretations arrived at in context, whereas the former are generally available procedures designed to carry out these local interpretations. It is these more general procedures and not the types of language alternation which are used as interpretive resources by participants in the first place.

Let us begin by taking a look at the dichotomy *discourse-related* vs. *participant-related code-switching*. In the organization of bilingual conversation, participants face two types of tasks. First, there are problems specifically addressed to language choice. A given conversational episode may be called bilingual as soon as participants orient to the question of which language to speak. Second, participants have to solve a number of problems independently of whether they use one or more languages; these are problems related to the organization of conversation in general, e.g. to turn-taking, topical cohesion, 'key' (in Hymes' sense; see Hymes, 1974), the constitution of specific linguistic activities. The alternating use of two languages may be a means of coping with these problems. For illustration, let us turn to some data extracts:[3]

Extract (1) (VIERER G 37–39)

((Clemente is telling a story in order to prove how little respect German children have for their parents. He reports an interaction between a German boy and his mother.))

```
37: 14   m:    kom=è kome a fattë?
    15   Cl:   na - na - un - un kompan'o del - kë kë va nella
    16         klassë ko me a dettO ke io lO devO a - prendere
               nO: per g'oka : rë - io sono andantë dopë në -
    17         noi le volemë=mondare una - - Seifenkiste - -
38: 01   m:    mi devi spiegare kos=è sta Seifekiste hе̣ hе̣
    02         ((Agostino, Camillo and Alfredo laugh))
    03   Cl:   i weiß itte
    04   Al:             sag einfach na karrotsEllë ko le rO : të
    05   Cl:   aja: ja genau - - na dopë a venuta la la su
    06   Ag:                 u : nd?
    07   Cl:   ma : dre noi ab/ ehm - - e=nato a spannë i - - pannë
               no: nda dopë lei dOmanda ma : : ti: tu n eh de
    08         de=fattë i komptë - nda : : - nël suo fil'ë - -
    09         ditt
    10                                      (1.0)
    11         nientë
    12                                      (1.0)
    13         dopa heh? - ( ja it ìe a) sе̣ntsi=i: - kompti - -
    14         mae - h (tu : :) hе̣ hе̣ hе̣ hе̣ 'h dopẹ̈=kо̣mе̣=a̧=
                                   oo  oo
    15   Ag?:                      ḥ
    16   Cl:   =dе̣ttẹ̈; 'h=
    17   Al:   =sa̧gs in deutsch halt wenn=s et it
→   18   Cl:                           Mensch du̱ mit deiner
                                       ((high pitch, imitates
    19         mie̠se̠ La̠une fa̧hr do̧ch ab    ḥ  ḥ  ḥ ḥ
                 shouting))
    20                        ((Ca., Al. & Ag. laughing))
    21   m:                                  kome, kome?
    22         Mensch du mit? ki è - il bambino a detto
    23         alla mamma
    24   Cl:   e : : la dittë a la ma a – ditt=a : – tu=eh ke ke
    25   Al:         laut!
    26   Cl:   lei kwella : – ku – këlla La̠une –
```

```
39: 01  Al:   Cle – sags auf deutsch er wird scho verstehe=aber
    02  Ca:            (. . . . . . . . . . . . . . . . . . . . . . )
    03  Al:   deutlich!
    04  Cl:   nja –
    05  Ag:   Mensch du mit deiner miesen Laune fahr ab
```

TRANSLATION (Italian parts are in ordinary letters; German parts are in CAPITAL
LETTERS)

```
37: 14  m:    how did it what did he do?
    15  Cl:   a-a-a-a friend of the – who who goes in the class
    16          with me said that I have to – take him you know for
                playing – I went then (we) –
    17          we wanted to set up a – – SOAP BOX – –
38: 01  m:    you have to explain to me what that is this SOAP BOX
    03  Cl:   I DON'T KNOW
    04  Al:              JUST SAY a pram on wheels
    05  Cl:   OH YES I SEE – – a – then has came the the his
    06  Ag:              SO?
    07  Cl:   mother we ha/uhm – – she came to HANG UP the – –
                clothes you see in the then she asks but you you n uh ha
    08          have (to do) your homework – in – in her son – –
    09          he said
    11          nothing
    13          then eh? – (. . . . . . .) without=the – homework – –
    14          (but) – h (you : :) he he he he 'h then=what=did=she=
    16          =say; 'h=
    17  Al:   =SAY IT IN GERMAN IF YOU CANNOT (SAY) IT
→   18  Cl:                          HEY YOU AND YOUR
                                     LOUSY IDEAS
    19          PUSH OFF h h h h h
    21  m:                     what, what?
    22          YOU AND? who was – the boy said it to
    23          his mother
    24  Cl:   yes he said to his mo he – said to – you=eh who who
    25  Al:        SPEAK UP!
    26  Cl:   she this : – with – this IDEAS –
39: 01  Al:   CLE – SAY IT IN GERMAN HE WILL UNDERSTAND=BUT
    03          CLEARLY!
    04  Cl:   WELL –
    05  Ag:   YOU AND YOUR LOUSY IDEAS PUSH OFF
```

The interaction is between four youngsters – Clemente (13), Camillo (13), Alfredo (14) and Agostino (15) – and an Italian student and fieldworker (m.). The four form an insulated network cluster which is characterized by a high frequency of switching and transfer of all types. Clemente, the youngest, is also the most German-dominant of the four. In our extract, he tries to tell a story to m.. Many aspects of his way of talking suggest that he is having enormous difficulties formulating what he wants to express in Italian (see the hesitations, vowel lengthening, repetitions and reformulations, incomprehensible passages). The efforts he makes to speak (Standard) Italian for m. (a variety he hardly knows), and not to make use of German (which he speaks fluently), lead him into hybrid forms, transfer from German (cf. the *spannë* in 38: 07) and Italian dialect (cf. the *nda* instead of *nel*, 38: 08), hypercorrections (cf. *a venuta* in 38: 05 as the maximally distinct form from dialectal schwa-reduction *venutë*), and a generally wide range of variation.[4] Clemente's difficulties reach a climax when he attempts to translate what the German boy in his narrative said to his mother – the punch line of the story. He finally switches to German to make himself understood (line 38: 18f). In reconstructing the local interpretation of this instance of code-switching, the various hesitation phenomena and, on a grammatical level, the *italiano stentato* produced by the boy give us the decisive cues. They reveal that it is his competence in Italian which doesn't allow him to continue, and that switching into German rescues the narrative (if at all) because of his superior competence in this language. Switching thus displays an imbalanced bilingual competence. A second possible interpretation relating Clemente's switching to the direct speech he is about to report can be shown to be of no more than secondary relevance for participants, because another participant explicates how he interpreted Clemente's hesitations: Alfredo, in lines 38: 18 and 9: 01 appeals to Clemente to use German (in line 17, his *sags in deutsch halt* is to be continued with a 'if you can't . . . say it in Italian'). We can therefore be quite sure that our interpretation of the speaker's switching into German as being related to his lacking competence in Italian is also shared by the co-participants in this episode.

The second type of participant-related switching doesn't display a participant's competence, but his or her *preference* for one language over the other. Of course, the two are not always independent. For instance, participants often use self-ascriptions of incompetence as accounts for their preferences (for details, see Auer, 1981). Extract (2) is an instance of preference-related code-switching. Participants are Irma (11) and m., the field-worker. Irma lives in a German-dominated network, including only one Italian boy (her brother). She has a clear preference for German, whereas m. (as do almost all adult Italians) prefers Italian. Language alternation is due in this case to m.'s and Irma's insisting on and thereby displaying their respective preferences. While m. consistently uses Italian for all of his contributions, Irma only switches into Italian once (for the Italian variant of

her brother's name – *Tonio* instead of *Toni* – which answers m.'s *ki* in line 03).
Usually, she speaks German.[5]

Extract (2) (MG 10 I B, 2)

((talk about Irma's name))

```
      01  Ir.:   Toni ((=her brother)) nennt mich Makkaroni;
      02         – – Makkaronimännchen
                    ((lamenting))
→     03  m:     ˆki
      04  Ir.:   Tonio!
      05  m:     ki E/ ah:
→     06  Ir.:   de Toni eh (immer) Toni mi(t)=m=
→     07  m:     =E=pperkE? perke: ti kiama
→     08  Ir.:              früher hat=r immer gsagt
      09         Makkaronimännchen °wieviel Uhr und so,° – –
      10         jetz nennt=er mich au Irma: –
```

TRANSLATION
```
      01  Ir.:   TONI CALLS ME MACARONI; – – MACARONI
      02         MANNIKIN
→     03  m:     who
      04  Ir.:   TONIO!
      05  m:     who's that/ah:
→     06  Ir.:   TONI UH (ALWAYS) TONI WITH=THE=
→     07  m:     =and=why? why does he call you
→     08  Ir.:              HE USED TO SAY MACARONI
      09         MANNIKIN WHAT'S THE TIME AND SO ON, – –
      10         NOW HE CALLS ME IRMA TOO; –
```

Our interpretation that such a patterned usage of the two languages can tell
us (and participants) something about Irma's and m.'s preferences (at least, in the
given constellation) is based on the more general expectation that for two participants it is 'unmarked' to agree on a common language for interaction rather than
using languages at random. This is in fact the case in the sociolinguistic situation
we are dealing with, although certainly not a universal feature of bilingual
communities.

Extracts (3) and (4) illustrate *discourse-related code-switching* for certain conversational tasks which are relevant in monolingual contexts as well. (Luziano is
10, Pino is 9.)

Extract (3) (MG 3 I A 70/71)

((m. has taken Luziano and Pino in his car to his house. The car has stopped, the three are about to get out.))

	70:	06	m:	là là si apre, là sotto
		07	Lz.:	ah là.
→	71:	01		Pino – – willscht rau:s – wart mal
		02		wart mal Pino

– –

TRANSLATION:

70:	06	m:	here here you can open it, down there
	07	Lz.:	oh there.
71:	01		PINO – SO YOU WANT TO GET OUT – WAIT,
	02		WAIT PINO

Extract (4) (MG I A 50)

((in m.'s car, on the way to a city district called Wollmatingen))

	01	Lz.:	il mio dzio ahm – abita=pure a Wollmatingen
	02	m:	ah
	03		(0.5)
	04		lo vai a trovare on'i tanto?
	05	Lz.:	°ah° (.) kwalke vo:lta=
	06	m:	=mhm
	07		(5.0)
→	08	Lz.:	da kommt Luft raus
	09	m:	si: , – mhm,

– –

TRANSLATION:

01	Lz.:	my uncle uhm – also lives in Wollmatingen
02	m:	ah
04		do you go and see him now and then?
05	Lz.:	ah (.) sometimes=
06	m:	=mhm
08	Lz.:	HERE THE AIR COMES OUT
09	m:	yes, – mhm,

In Extract (3), Luziano's switching in line 71: 01 helps to bring about a change in the participant constellation. His *ah là* has acknowledged m.'s instruction on how to get out of the car; but in the following utterance, the boy takes on the role of the 'knowing adult' himself vis-à-vis Pino. The activities are set off by the use of different languages against each other. Together with non-linguistic cues such as gaze and gesture (which cannot be analyzed on the basis of the audio-tape), it is language alternation which effects this change in constellation. In (4), the discourse function served by code-switching is topic change. Luziano has been talking about his uncle in 01–06, but in 08, after a relatively long silence, he refers to the car. Again, switching from Italian into German is one of the means used to terminate one and to initiate the next stretch of talk.

If we compare participant and discourse-related language alternation we note that the main difference is the object of the signalling process. Whereas in the case of participant-related alternation, co-participants display or ascribe certain predicates to each other (competence, preference), they signal a change of conversational context in the case of discourse-related switching.[6] This is why language alternation of the second type is what Gumperz calls a contextualization strategy: a strategy by which participants signal what they are doing at a particular moment. We may also use Goffman's term *footing* and say that code-switching can effect a change from one footing to another when related to discourse (Goffman, 1979; Gumperz, 1982). Looked upon as a way of contextualizing verbal activities, code-switching can be compared to other contextualization cues such as change of loudness or tempo, change of body position or gaze, etc.

Some important types of discourse-related switching found in our materials are:

- change in participant constellation;
- change in mode of interaction (for instance, between a formal interview and a casual conversation, or between a move in a game and conversation);
- topic change;
- sequential contrast (for instance, between an on-going sequence and a subordinated repair sequence, or side-remark);
- change between informative and evaluative talk, for instance, after stories (including formulations and other summing-up techniques).

In addition to these local interpretations of code-switching occurring between or within single speakers' turns, there are others which overwhelmingly or even exclusively occur within turns, such as:

- marking of non-first firsts (e.g. of repeated questions or requests);
- marking of reformulations/elaborations;
- setting off prefaces from stories or other 'big packages' (Sacks, see Jefferson, 1989);
- setting of 'setting' and 'events' in narratives;
- distinguishing various types of information in an utterance (for instance,

'given' and 'new', or 'focus of contrast' and the rest of the contribution, to use Chafe's terms; Chafe, 1987).

The last types hold a middle position with regard to the second major distinction, that between *code-switching* and *transfer*. (Note that the two basic dichotomies provide bilingual participants with four prototypical cases of language alternation; between these prototypical cases, there are numerous less prototypical ones, to which is attributed conversational meaning on the basis of their distance from the prototypes. Heller (1988: 11, 15) is indeed right: category boundaries *are* fuzzy, and any attempt by the analyst to dissolve this fuzziness in favour of the Procrustean bed of clearly delimited categories will lead to a loss of realism in description.)

Looking at language alternation in conversation, especially in sequential terms, one notices two major patterns. According to the first, language alternation from language X to language Y is followed by further talk in language X, either by the same or by other participants. According to the second pattern, language alternation from language X to language Y is followed by further talk in language Y, by the same or other participants. Apparently, there is a difference in how language alternation affects the language of interaction (the 'base language'). In the first case, we speak of transfer: no renegotiation of the language of interaction is observed. The stretch of speech formulated in the other language has a built-in and predictable point of return into the first language. In the second case, we speak of code-switching: the new language invites succeeding participants to also use this new language. In fact, not using this language may be interpreted as disregarding the first speaker's language preference and/or competence (in the case of participant-related switching) or the new 'footing' (in the case of discourse-related switching).

Extracts (5) and (6) illustrate transfer from German into Italian. (Participants are the same as in Extract (1). The episode SCHNECKENFRESSER was recorded two years after VIERER. It will be noted that whereas Clemente still has a preference for German, Alfredo is quite willing to speak Italian (dialect) now.)

As in the case of code-switching (see Extracts (1) to (4)), we have to distinguish between participant-related and discourse-related transfers:

Extract (5) (VIERER B: 37–38)

((narrative about a typing test the speaker took))

37: 07   Al: skrivi dopo – kwandë la maestra vidë ke sai skrive
                 ((lento))   ((acc.))
     08   – molto ti fa komminc'are a skrive – h koll=o –
                 ((lento))

```
    09          l=oro10g' g' o=diec' I minutI kwante fai;
    10    m:    °aha,°
    11    Al:          dOppë – da tuttI kwelle pac' ine ke pë skrive
    12          sveltI c'E skrittë,
    13          tutti Anschläge kwandë/volte – 'hhh
    14    m:                                °mhm,°
    15    Al:    sin zum Beispeil: due mille=o – c'inke c'ento: –
    16    Ag:    due mille c'inkwe c'ento
                 ((pp e molto presto))
    17    m:     par ole
    18    Al:        Ansc hläge
    19    m:            Anschläge kwã=m (. . .)
                                 ((pp))
38: 01    Al:    arOppë – guarda le: – Fehler – allOrë i=errori
                 ((lento))
    02          e tutto sbal' c'i vonno lovare ventic'inkwe
                                    ((hesitating))
                 Anschläge – c'ai/ –
    03    m:     °o kapito°
```

- -

TRANSLATION:

```
37: 07    Al:    you write then – when the teacher sees that you can write
    08          – a lot she makes you start to write – h
                 with=the=w –
    09          the watch=when (?) you do ten minutes;
    10    m:     aha,
    11    Al:        then – of all the pages that you were able to
    12          write fast which you (?) have written,
    13          all the TOUCHES how many/times – 'hhh
    14    m:                                mhm,
    15    Al:    THERE ARE FOR INSTANCE
                 two-thousand=or – five hundred
    16    Ag:    two thousand five hundred ((corrects Al.'s pronunciation))
    17    m:     words
    18    Al:        TOUCHES
    19    m:            TOUCHES (. . . . . .)
38: 01    Al:    and then – she has a look at the – MISTAKES – I mean
                 the mistakes –
    02          and (for) every mistake they are going to subtract twenty-five
                 TOUCHES – which is/ –
    03    m:     I got it
```

Extract (6) (SCHNECKENFRESSER 91 : 25)

((Cl and Al are complaining about two older people living in their house))

```
02  m:   perke non lavorano però eh stanno tutto=il
03       g'orno a kasa
04  Al:  ke E vekkië e g'a pendzionann nun g'annë fil'ë,=
05  m:   =he : :
06  Cl:          na aber nicht der Mann; – der Mann schafft no;
07  Al:                      u mO u mO
08       u Mann E : : c' s' te: kiu s' – kiu schlimm angOrë;
09                              (1.0)
10  Al:  na vO : t (.)
11  m:   °°mhm°°
```

((follows Italian narrative))

_____

TRANSLATION:
```
02  m:   because they don't work eh they stay at home all day
03       long
04  Al:  because (s)he is old and retired already they don't have children;=
05  m:   =he : :
06  Cl:          NO BUT NOT THE HUSBAND; –
                 THE HUSBAND STILL GOES TO WORK;
07  Al:          the HUSBAND the HUSBAND
08       the HUSBAND is sometimes even wor – worse;
10       once ( . )
```

((follows narrative))
((Note: mo is dialectal for Mann))

In Extract (5), Alfredo is about to explain a rather complex matter, i.e. how the final results were calculated in a typing test. He runs into difficulties in the case of *Fehler/errori* and *Anschläge* ('touches') which are marked as such by vowel lengthening, hesitation, short silence and above all the self-repair in line 01 (*allorë i=errori*) and the initiated but uncompleted self-repair in line 02 (*c'ai* : /from *cioè i*. . .). The transfer from German is displayed as related to the speaker's (momentary) lack of competence in Italian: it is the German word which comes to his mind first. In Extract (6), we find one of the more important types of discourse-related transfer which I call anaphoric. Alfredo refers to the person introduced in Camillo's previous German turn and uses *Mann* as a topical link between the two utterances. *U Mann* here means 'this man you are talking about'.[7]

Certainly, this type of back-referencing could also have been accomplished by the Italian equivalent (*l=uomo*); however, anaphoric typing is based solely on semantic similarity in this latter case, whereas it is based on semantic and formal identity in the first.

Although most of the instances of transfer we find in our materials are on the lexical level (here, nouns are by far the most frequent), our definition of transfer does not restrict the term to this level. We only require that transfer not relate to a certain *point* in conversation (as code-switching does) but to a certain (well-defined) unit which has a predictable end that will also terminate the use of the other language. Accordingly, transfer on higher structural levels must be included as well; for instance, language alternation to set off citations, or even songs, sayings, poems, rhymes and other 'kleine Gattungen'. In all these cases, transfer is discourse-related.

Two additional remarks concerning the distinction between transfer and code-switching can be made. First, our expectation is that after code-switching it is the newly introduced language that will be taken up by the co-participant. This is only a conversational preference, not an absolute 'rule' or 'norm'. On the one hand, there are cases of code-switching in which recipients refuse to accept the new footing together with the new language; and cases in which recipients accept the new footing, but not the new language (a phenomenon which would have to be interpreted on the level of language preference ascription); on the other hand, there are cases of transfer which 'prepare' or 'trigger' switching into the other language. What is important is the distinction between switching *points* and transferred units.

Second, my notion of transfer does not correspond to, and is not to be confused with, the one usually met in the literature on language contact and second language acquisition. The latter is supposed to cover the phenomena subsumed under 'interference' before that concept went out of fashion. Let us call them transfer$_L$, where L stands for 'linguist'; for transfer$_L$ is defined and described from the linguist's point of view. He or she can take into account 'diachronic' and other facts that do not necessarily concern participants. Transfer$_L$ is in continuous danger of being a linguistic artifact, due to a monolingual point of view, that is, of taking the monolingual systems of the two languages in contact as the point of reference (German as spoken by Germans in, for example, Hanover and Italian as spoken, for example, in Milan). The (bilingual) speaker may not make a distinction between two independent and strictly separated systems. Often the varieties in the repertoires of bilingual speech communities show independent developments setting them off against the coexisting monolingual norms ('convergence'). Transfer$_P$ (P for participant) is defined from the member's perspective. Accordingly, if we want to claim that an item such as *Mann* is a transfer$_P$, we have to show that the speaker *makes use of* the other-language status of *Mann*. It is not enough that *Mann* can be found in a German dictionary and not in an Italian one. The 'proof procedures' for transfer$_P$ and transfer$_L$ are therefore quite different. Usually, transfer$_L$ is the weaker alternative with which we have to content ourselves if we cannot demonstrate that the production of an 'other'-language item has a function (be it of the discourse-related or of the participant-related type). Transfer$_P$ requires demonstrating how the participant displays a 'reason' for language alternation, in the way this alternation is produced, which is visible to his or her co-participants (as in Extracts (5) and (6)).

Transfer$_L$ is observed in the following utterances, also from our materials, but from a different speaker: Daniele is part of a network that is dominated by newly arrived Italian boys. Interaction in this network is characterized by the almost complete lack of code-switching. Language alternation occurs in the format of (mostly discourse-related) transfer$_P$, but most transfers are not marked as such by the speaker:

Daniele: mia (*sic*) padre fa: l=spazi:no: e: – mia madre fa: la Putzfrau
    (50:08/9)
TRANSLATION: my father is a road sweeper and – my mother is a CLEANING
    WOMAN

Daniele: o: vergon'atevi davanti $\begin{Bmatrix} il \\ al \end{Bmatrix}$ Mikrophón – 71:07)

TRANSLATION: or do you feel embarrassed in front of the MICROPHONE

Daniele: volete delle Kartoffel (73:11)
TRANSLATION: do you want CHIPS ((lit.: potatoes))

Daniele: mme l'i mettë tutti sopra al Sparbuch kwelli ke mi gwardan'o=ilà;
    (97:12)
TRANSLATION: (s)he puts them all on my SAVING ACCOUNT (the money)
    which I make there;

Here, we cannot speak of transfer$_P$ in the sense of (individually) functional language alternation, but only of transfer$_L$ in the sense of *code-fluctuation* (see Auer and Di Luzio, 1983a; 1983b) which is possibly interpretable in global terms. The distinction between language alternation and code-fluctuation is based on the way textual variation between two items presents itself to conversationalists.

Who switches how?

The following remarks on individual differences among the Italian children [. . .] need to be embedded in a wider linguistic and ethnographic description of the speakers than can be given here (for ethnographic details, see d'Angelo, 1984).

The first question we have to ask is: If Italian migrant children alternate between languages, what is the *direction* of code-switching and transfer? There is an enormous amount of evidence which supports the following hypothesis:

> *Hypothesis 1*: In the overwhelming number of cases, code-switching is from the Italian into the German part of the linguistic repertoire. Transfer is from German into Italian passages.

This clear dominance of German holds for more or less all types of alternation mentioned above, with the exception of turn-internal switching, which is unspecific with regard to direction. In the case of competence-related alternation, practically all transferred items are from German, and all instances of code-switching are from Italian into German. The conclusion to be drawn from this is that because the preponderance of German is not restricted to preference-related switching, all types of alternation, in addition to whatever else they may do in conversation, display an imbalance between the Italian and the German part of the repertoire. Most of the children have a much stronger tendency to switch codes when the 'base language' is Italian, and almost all children readily transfer lexical items from German into Italian, but rarely vice versa. If we look at the type of 'footing' that coincides with discourse-related switching, the much greater inter-actional 'value' of German as opposed to Italian is underlined even more. German is the switched-to language coinciding with a transition from formal to informal interaction or from giving information to evaluating it. German is used for ironic or humorous statements, for side-remarks, for the punchline of a story or a joke, etc.

The instances of language alternation that do not conform to this picture are often of a particular type. They are not from German into Regional Italian, but from German (or Regional Italian) into the local southern Italian dialect or its approximation. Without going into details (however, see Di Luzio, 1984) it can be said that for those children who (still) have the choice between more than one variety of Italian, the local dialect may have the same function in relation to German (or Regional Italian) as German does in relation to Regional Italian.

This is to say that a transition from more to less formal speech, from topical talk to side-remarks, or the setting off of humorous or funny statements, may either correspond to a switching from 'Regional' Italian to dialectal Italian, or to one from 'Regional' Italian to German (dialect); it does not coincide with a transition in the opposite direction, however. The third case (switching between Italian dialect and German (dialect)) is rare and less predictable: it may take either direction. Thus, in a maximally exploited repertoire, we can get the following switches:

'Regional' Italian

Southern Italian ←——————————— German

dialect ——————————→ (dialect)

A second hypothesis concerns the overall frequency of language alternation. Here, the following picture emerges:

Hypothesis 2: Frequency of language alternation is most often similar for members of the same interactional network.

It seems that members of the same network adapt to each other and develop a common style of linguistic behaviour which may or may not be characterized by code-switching and transfer. This is true independently of the quality of the particular network.

Types of network contacts are relevant for a more detailed characterization of the individual speaker's linguistic behaviour:

Hypothesis 3: If a child's primary network contacts are children of a similar biographical background, language alternation will mostly assume the format of discourse-related switching; otherwise, there may be discourse-related transfer, but most often language alternation is restricted to the participant-related types.

This means that children who do not have any contacts with other Italian children – or who are part of networks which incorporate children with different histories of migration (recently arrived Italian dominant speakers) – show the lowest percentage of discourse-related switching. Those who have their primary network contacts with children who have lived through a similar socialization process show a higher percentage of these switches. Thus, only the existence and the homogeneity of networks seem to provide the necessary conditions for the development of language alternation as a contextualization strategy. If a child who has been brought up and/or was born in Germany has close friends or siblings who have gone to Germany only recently, discourse-related switching is rare.

A final hypothesis concerns the internal differentiation of the largest group of alternations, i.e. discourse-related switching:

Hypothesis 4: The employment of code-switching as a contextualization strategy varies with age.

Among the earlier employments of discourse-related switching (most frequent between the ages of 10 to 13), switching to initiate a change of participant constellation is most likely because of its intimate relationship to preference-related switching. Quite often, changing the language when addressing a new partner is only the functional aspect of adapting to his or her language preference which diverges from that of the preceding addressee. More sophisticated uses of code-switching – for example, changing the topic, or the mode of interaction, or establishing sequential contrasts, etc. as well as the various types of turn-internal switching only become frequent at around age 13 or 14.

Conclusion

Language alternation can be approached from a number of perspectives. Three stand out in the literature: the grammatical, the macro-sociolinguistic and the conversation analytic approaches. From the grammatical perspective, a number of restrictions on code-switching within the sentence have been formulated (see Gumperz, 1982; Poplack, 1978/81; and others). These restrictions are important for a general theory of grammatical processing in bilinguals since they allow one to draw certain conclusions about the psycholinguistic reality of the bilingual's two grammars. However, they are only relevant in a minority of cases of language alternation in our materials. The Italian children we have investigated usually change languages either for individual lexical items, or for whole sentences. However, even in intrasentential switching, grammatical restrictions do not tell us anything about the interactional 'value' or 'meaning' of transfer and code-switching as conversational activities.

Surprisingly perhaps, the same applies to the macro-sociolinguistic perspective (see, for instance, Breitborde, 1983). Again, general statements are made, concerning the distribution of code-switching in certain situations, or among participants holding certain 'roles' and 'statuses' in a given society, but little or nothing is said about the contribution of language alternation to the ongoing interaction, that is, about its local functioning. Thus, although neither the value of the grammatical nor that of the macro-sociolinguistic perspective can be denied, it seems that both have to be incorporated into a third, more basic perspective which is to investigate the contribution of language alternation to members' sense-making activities. This may fruitfully be done in the framework of conversation analysis, which, taking into account grammatical restrictions where necessary, can work up and relate to larger scale sociolinguistic statements.[8] Some fundamental distinctions that are relevant for the production and interpretation of language alternation in conversation have been presented in this chapter.

On the basis of these distinctions, the place of language alternation between the German and the Italian part of the repertoire, in the speech of Italian migrant children in Germany, can be summarized as follows:

- The two parts of the repertoire are not kept distinct. There is a high degree of variation; in particular, a high degree of lexical transfer$_L$ was noted. These lexical transfers are not usually adapted to the phonology or grammar of the receiving language: indeed, I have argued that it would be mistaken to speak of a receiving language here at all. We are simply dealing with intra-repertoire variation.

- Code-switching is frequent, but mostly occurs at sentence boundaries. Sentence-internal switching is only relevant in some few, insulated and dense networks.
- Code-switching is not necessarily related to a metaphoric function (in Gumperz' sense). Often, it 'just' takes part in the organization of discourse. As a contextualization strategy, it is comparable to prosodic parameters, such as intonation, loudness or pitch level.
- Most speakers have a preference for German. By code-switching, they display this preference or, at least, their better competence in that language. Code-switching is always an attempt to renegotiate the language of interaction, at least temporarily.
- Both competence-related switching and competence-related transfer demonstrate that, in the present situation, typical aspects of language contact mix with aspects of second language acquisition (of 'Regional' Italian).

It is reasonable to conclude from all these indicators that, at the macro-level, the sociolinguistic situation of second-generation Italian migrants is still unstable and may develop in two directions: either complete linguistic adaptation including loss of Italian and Italian dialects in the repertoire, or stabilization as a bilingual community. This uncertainty certainly corresponds to the social mobility of the Italian 'communities' which, in turn, is to be seen against the background of political (European Community) and geographical (distance) factors. A more definite answer would be possible as the result of a comparison of different Italian communities abroad.

Notes

1   Constance was part of West Germany until German unification in 1990.
2   For an outline of the project, see Di Luzio, 1983; for some results see Auer and Di Luzio, 1983; 1983a; Bierbach, 1983; d'Angelo, 1984. The MIG project was located in the *Sonderforschungsbereich 99* at the *Fachgruppe Sprachwissenschaft* of the University of Constance from 1980 to 1985.
3   The usual transcription conventions of conversation analysis are employed. However, note that:

    /   phonetic break-off
    (.)   phonetic pause

—   pause not exceeding 0.2 sec.
h̲ h̲ h̲   laughing.

For the transcription of the Italian passages, quasi-phonetic symbols are used:

E, O, I   open variables of e̱, o̱, i̱
c', g'   alveo-palatal affricates
s', z'   alveo-palatal fricatives
l', n'   palatal laterals and nasals
ë   schwa.

English translations give a simplified version.

4   Cf. Auer and Di Luzio (1983; 1983a) for an analysis of this type of variation (*italiano stentato*).

5   Irma insists on German in initiative sequential positions (lines 01–02), in responsive sequential position (line 09) and in a contribution which disregards the co-participant's prior turn altogether (lines 8 ff). In a more extensive discussion of the data, it could be demonstrated that these three positions are not equivalent with regard to preference displays. Responsive utterances in the other language are stronger indicators of diverging preferences than initiative ones (where I mean by 'responsive' and 'initiative' the respective slots in sequential formats such as question/answer, etc.). Disregarding the preceding other-language contribution can be a way to avoid a responsive position in which switching would have under-lined one's preference, for the sake of an initiative contribution (for details, see Auer, 1983).

6   We are talking about primary levels of interpretation here. On a secondary, 'global' level, matters of competence and preference also relate to the organization of discourse, for finding a common language of interaction obviously is a prerequisite for interaction. Vice versa, discourse related switching can allow ascriptions of competence and of preference to individual speakers.

7   Apart from anaphoric transfer, lexical transfer is not very often employed for discourse-related purposes in our data. In rare cases, transfer is usually part of a contrast pair built up between a same-language and an other-language item.

8   Jordan and Fuller (1975), Heller (1982), Valdés and Pino (1981), and McClure (1977) belong to the few authors who have attempted to approach code-switching in conversation analytic terms, although the investigations are restricted to certain types of language alternation. More comprehensive accounts are given by Gumperz (1982), in his famous distinction between situational and meta-phorical code-switching, and by Zentella (1981). I have dealt with Gumperz' model elsewhere in detail (Auer, 1984a). Zentella's distinction between factors 'on the spot', (pertaining to the 'observables of interaction'; 1981: 147) and factors 'in the head' (which are not directly observable) leads into somewhat artificial classifications. For example, 'topic', 'psychological setting' and

addressee's language preference are grouped together as 'on the spot' factors, whereas a momentary loss for words, or a change of the speaker's role are said to be factors 'in the head'.

Source: Auer, J.C.P. (1988) A conversation analytic approach to code-switching and transfer. In M. Heller (ed.) *Codeswitching*. Berlin: Mouton de Gruyter, pp. 187–214, by permission of Mouton de Gruyter.

Chapter 8

A two-step sociolinguistic analysis of code-switching and language choice: the example of a bilingual Chinese community in Britain

LI WEI, LESLEY MILROY AND PONG SIN CHING

T HE EXTENSIVE LITERATURE ON bilingualism illustrates a range of (sometimes interdisciplinary) approaches to code-switching behaviour, some of which seem rather distant from the primarily social one which we shall present here. However, we would suggest that an adequate account of the social and situational context of code-switching behaviour is an important prerequisite even where the perspective of the researcher is (for example) psycholinguistic rather than social. This article attempts to develop a coherent account of the relationship between code-switching and language choice by individual speakers, and of the relation of both to the broader social, economic and political context. The exposition is presented both in general terms which emphasise its applicability to a range of bilingual situations, and with specific reference to the example of the bilingual Chinese–English-speaking community in Tyneside, north-eastern England.

It is evident from the abundant research literature that a wealth of data and analyses of code-switching behaviour from many very different communities is readily available (for a recent overview of such work, see Heller, 1988). What seems generally to be lacking is a coherent social framework within which to interpret these data and analyses. For example, Heller (1990) remarks that while John Gumperz, an important leader in the field, has always viewed code-switching as constitutive of social reality, he has perhaps been less successful in linking this interactional level with broader questions of social relations and social organisation. While Gumperz himself may not have intended to make this micro–macro link, it is important that those who develop his procedures should attempt to do so. Otherwise, insightful interactional-level analyses of data sets which cannot be compared with each other will continue to proliferate without any corresponding advance in understanding similarities and differences in the code-switching and language choice behaviours of different communities, or in explaining why rapid language shift is likely in one particular community but not in another.

Like Woolard (1985), Gal (1988; 1989) and Heller (1990), we take the starting point for any social or sociolinguistic model to be existing detailed socio-linguistic observations of code-switching behaviour. But such everyday behaviour of social actors and larger scale institutional analysis should be seen as related rather than as dissociated, as tends to be the case in the bilingualism literature (cf. the approaches of Fishman and Gumperz, which are generally considered quite separately). Giddens (1984) has developed a social theory based on the relation-ships between these two levels, commenting that 'the study of day-to-day life is integral to analysis of the reproduction of institutionalised practices' (1984: 282).

Any attempt to integrate micro and macro levels of analysis entails a con-sideration of patterns of *language choice* at the *community* (or even national) level, in conjunction with an analysis of *code-switching* at the *interactional* level. Myers-Scotton's (1986) remark that a model of code-choice needs to be in place before one can develop a model of code-switching is particularly relevant here, since it is important before attempting to account for code-switching behaviour to have some idea of how language choice is restricted for some speakers, or affected by social values assigned to community languages. For this reason, we shall have a good deal to say in this chapter about language choice, prior to our remarks on code-switching.

The following sections are structured as follows. First we shall outline rele-vant aspects of the concept of social network. We then relate the language choice patterns of the community to its informal social structure, considering separately relevant patterns of both inter-generational and intra-generational patterns of variation. We then examine the reflection of these patterns in code-switching behaviour at the interactional level; and, finally, we attempt to relate observations of behaviour at both community level and interactional level to a wider social, political and economic framework.

The network concept

Social network analysis of the kind which is most relevant to sociolinguists was developed in the 1960s and 1970s by a group of mainly British social anthropolo-gists. Personal social networks were generally seen as contextualised within a broader social framework, which was 'bracketed-off' to allow attention to be concentrated on developing less abstract modes of analysis which could account more immediately for the variable behaviour of individuals. However, it is import-ant to remember that such bracketing-off is wholly methodological and does not reflect an ontological reality. While no one claims that personal network structure is independent of the broader social framework which constantly constrains individual behaviour, a fundamental postulate of network analysis is that individuals create personal communities which provide them with a meaningful framework for solving the problems of their day-to-day existence (Mitchell, 1986: 74). This kind of focus has made the social network approach a useful one for sociolinguists investigating relatively clearly definable communities like the Tyneside Chinese, as well as for researchers from other disciplines. For example, Riley et al. (1990) describe the application of network analysis in an international project encompassing communities in Sweden, West Germany, the United States and Wales, where the capacities of urban social networks to provide support for families are considered. Many of the methods developed by the research team for investigating and comparing social networks are of relevance to field sociolinguists (see Cochran et al., 1990).

A social network may be seen as a boundless web of ties which reaches out through a whole society, linking people to one another, however remotely. But for practical reasons social networks are generally 'anchored' to individuals, and interest focuses on relatively 'strong' first-order network ties; i.e. those persons with whom ego directly and regularly interacts. This principle of 'anchorage' effectively limits the field of network studies, generally to something between 20 and 50 individuals.

It is, however, useful to distinguish between 'strong' and 'weak' ties of everyday life, using the notions of 'exchange' and 'interactive' networks elaborated by Milardo (1988: 26–36). Exchange networks constitute persons such as kin and close friends with whom ego not only interacts routinely, but also exchanges direct aid, advice, criticism, and support. Interactive networks, on the other hand, consist of persons with whom ego interacts frequently and perhaps over prolonged periods of time, but on whom ego does not rely for personal favours and other material or symbolic resources. An example of an interactive tie would be that between a shop owner and customer. In addition to exchange and interactive ties, we identified a 'passive' type of network tie. Passive ties entail an absence of regular contact, but are valued by ego as a source of influence and moral support. Examples are physically distant relatives or friends, such ties being particularly important to migrant families.

Our basic procedure for comparative analysis of the 'strong tie' exchange network structures of persons in the Chinese community was to compile for each individual a list of 20 others who comprised significant daily contacts. This information was obtained by a mixture of informal interviewing and observation. Once these various 'networks' of 20 had been identified, contrasts between them were examined with respect to the extent of their ethnic and peer orientation. It is their ethnic orientation, expressed by an ethnic index to represent the proportion of Chinese ties, which chiefly concerns us here. Ethnic indices were also compiled for interactive and passive networks. For passive networks, the index was based on a figure of 10 ties per individual, and for interactive networks, 20 or 30; the precise figure varied according to the interactional practices of individuals.

These differences in procedure for arriving at the three types of network index are not arbitrary. They reflect the abilities of persons to enumerate individuals with whom they have contracted different types of network tie (in the case of exchange and passive ties), and the capacity of the fieldworker to make reasonably reliable observations (in the case of interactive ties). We have adapted here the approach to network analysis described by Mitchell (1986) with respect to his study of the networks of homeless women in Manchester, Britain. It is quite a different procedure from the one described by Milroy (1987a) in a sociolinguistic study of inner-city Belfast where networks tended to be close-knit and territorially bounded.

Close-knit social networks seem to have a particular capacity to maintain and even enforce local conventions and norms, including linguistic norms. Thus, network analysis offers a basis for understanding the social mechanisms that underlie this process of language maintenance, the converse of language shift. This is true whether we are looking at maintenance in opposition to the publically legitimised code of a stigmatised urban vernacular as in Belfast, or maintenance of an ethnic language. Migrant and other communities are not all equally successful in maintaining their community languages, and they also apparently vary in their intergenerational communication practices; for example the Panjabi and Bengali speakers in Newcastle do not seem to be experiencing such a sharp intergenerational disjunction as the Chinese community (Moffatt and Milroy, 1992). We shall argue that network analysis can illuminate the social dynamics involved in this kind of inter-group difference.

It has sometimes been suggested that close-knit types of community network are nowadays marginal to urban life; for example, since the work of Georg Simnel there has been a large sociological literature on 'the stranger' and the marginal individual who is now often seen as typical of a modern city dweller (Harman, 1988). Wirth, an influential member of the Chicago school of urban sociologists, argued that urban conditions give rise to impersonality and social distance. All this may reflect some kind of truth about urban life, but it does not tell the whole story. Certainly the Italian American 'urban villagers' described by Gans (1962) or the close-knit Yorkshire mining communities described by Dennis et al. (1957) may now seem less salient in American and British cities. But such traditional working-class communities are apparently being replaced, in Europe and elsewhere, by similar types of community created by newer immigrants. Indeed, as Giddens (1989) points out, neighbourhoods involving close kinship and personal ties seem to be actually created by city life. Those who form part of urban ethnic communities, such as the Tyneside Chinese, gravitate to form ties with, and sometimes to live with, others from a similar linguistic or ethnic background. Such ethnic groups seem to use the close-knit network as a means of protecting their interests while the community develops the resources to integrate more fully into urban life. Few of the Tyneside Chinese, for example, want their children to inherit their catering businesses, but prefer them to integrate into British society and train for higher-status employment.

The chief point we wish to emphasise here is that the type of close-knit network structure which seems to help maintain community languages is likely to be a product of modern city life rather than a residue of an earlier type of social organisation. With regard to the associations between this level of social organisation and patterns of face-to-face interaction, we need to remember the role of such close-knit networks in renewing and maintaining local systems of norms and values within which discourse processes of the kind analysed by Gumperz (1982) are understood and enacted. Indeed, as Gumperz' work has suggested, language use is itself an excellent diagnostic of group collectivity.

The Chinese community

We shall examine in this section the relationship between network structure and language choice patterns in the bilingual Chinese community in Tyneside, before relating this analysis to code-switching behaviour at the interpersonal level. The material presented here is derived chiefly from participant observation carried out in the field by Li Wei. Most of the linguistic data was collected during mealtimes, which provided an excellent setting for intergenerational interaction. Code-switching could be observed particularly frequently in such an interactional context.

The Tyneside Chinese number somewhere between 5000 and 7000 persons, most of whom are bilingual in English and one of several Chinese languages for which we shall use the generic label 'Chinese'. Like other researchers who have worked with migrant communities, we are conscious of the need for a model of ongoing social and linguistic change since code-switching and language choice patterns need to be modelled very differently from those in well-established bilingual communities (Boeschoten, 1991). Network analysis can be carried out only after a period of ethnographic observation in the community, in order to discover basic patterns of interaction and informal social organisation. Two initial observations were made at this point, which were critical to a subsequent network analysis:

1   The family is the primary unit of social organisation, having a clear internal authority structure. Like most Chinese migrant communities, the majority of the Tyneside Chinese earn their living from family-based catering businesses which rely almost exclusively on family labour. They thereby avoid high wages, overtime payments and other potential drains on resources. To provide service for the maximum number of potential customers, they do not live in identifiable settlements with a centralised authority structure. In

this respect they contrast sharply with other linguistic minority communities in Britain, whose social organisation is less family-based and who cluster in specifiable urban areas. Generally speaking, Chinese caterers keep a low public profile and do not develop close personal ties with non-Chinese people. This dispersed settlement pattern and reliance on kin is important for subsequent network analysis.

2   Three groups were identifiable which are not always exactly isomorphic with the three-generation cohorts of grandparents, parents and children:

(a)   first-generation migrants;

(b)   sponsored immigrants, who are either immediate kin of the first-generation migrants or have personal connections with people already established in Britain;

(c)   the British-born.

Subsequent analysis revealed that these groups contract quite different kinds of interpersonal network ties, which need to be interpreted within the framework of a social organisation which gives primacy to the family and an economic dependence on the catering trade.

Over the years, most first-generation migrants and those sponsored immigrants who are actively involved in the food trade have contracted network ties with *mainly Chinese* non-kin who are associated with their business and professional activities. The rest of the sponsored immigrants, mostly women and the elderly, more or less confine themselves to the household and family. The British-born generation differs from both these groups in having developed extensive network ties outside the family and also often outside the Chinese community. The educational level of this group is much higher than that of the others, and most British-born Chinese seem to want to enter occupations other than the catering trade. Thus, the exchange networks of the economically active group – both men and women who belong mainly to the 'parent' generation cohort – are strongly Chinese-oriented but not restricted to kin; those of the economically less active adults are also Chinese-oriented but largely restricted to kin; and those of the British-born generation are less kin-oriented and less ethnically oriented than either of these groups. It was also clear from this preliminary period of observation that the patterns of language choice in the community corresponded to some extent to these groupings, varying from Chinese monolingualism in the 'grandparent' generation, through various proportions of Chinese–English bilingualism to the English-dominant bilingualism characteristic of the British-born Chinese.

We are now in a position to look at the linguistic consequences of these differing age-related social network types, drawing on analysis of a corpus of 23 hours of spontaneous conversation involving 58 speakers in 10 families. Tables 8.1 and 8.2 implicationally order these speakers (male and female analysed separately)

Table 8.1 Implicational scale for observed language choices by male speakers (scalability 98.2%)

A	B	C	a	b	c	Interlocutors											
						1	2	3	4	5	6	7	8	9	10	11	12
25	6GP	73	20	10	10	—	C	C	—	C	C	C	C	C	C	C	C
1	1GP	66	20	10	10	—	C	C	—	C	C	C	C	—	C	C	C
45	9P	53	15	4	10	C	C	C	—	—	C	C	C	—	CE	CE	CE
10	3P	47	18	5	10	C	C	C	—	—	C	C	C	—	CE	CE	CE
5	2P	41	16	0	10	—	C	C	—	—	C	C	C	—	CE	CE	CE
26	6P	56	17	6	10	C	C	C	C	—	C	C	C	CE	CE	CE	CE
20	5P	37	17	2	10	C	C	C	C	—	C	C	C	CE	CE	CE	CE
53	10P	44	15	2	10	C	CE*	CE*	C	—	CE*	C	C	CE	CE	CE	CE
2	1P	35	16	0	10	—	C	C	C	—	C	CE	CE	—	CE	CE	CE
32	7P	49	12	5	10	C	C	C	—	CE	CE	CE	CE	CE	CE	CE	CE
51	10GP	68	16	6	10	C	C	C	—	CE	CE	CE	CE	CE	CE	CE	CE
37	8GP	65	14	5	10	C	C	C	—	—	CE	CE	CE	CE	CE	CE	CE
39	8P	44	14	1	10	C	C	C	CE	—	CE	CE	CE	CE	CE	CE	CE
15	4P	40	2	6	10	C	C	CE	—	—	CE	CE	CE	CE	CE	CE	CE
28	6C	22	1	3	6	—	C	CE	C*	CE	CE	CE	CE	CE	CE	CE	CE
47	9C	24	2	1	7	C	C	CE	—	CE	CE	CE	CE	—	CE	CE	CE
48	9C	22	3	0	9	C	C	CE	—	CE	CE	CE	CE	CE	CE	CE	CE
12	3C	21	5	0	8	C	C	CE	—	CE	CE	CE	CE	—	CE	CE	CE
13	3C	19	0	0	8	C	C	CE	—	CE	CE	CE	CE	CE	CE	CE	CE
49	9C	18	0	0	6	C	C	CE	—	CE	CE	CE	CE	—	CE	CE	CE
7	2C	15	2	0	6	—	C	CE	—	CE	CE	CE	CE	CE	CE	CE	CE
8	2C	12	0	0	5	—	C	CE	—	CE	CE	CE	CE	—	CE	CE	CE
29	6C	17	0	1	5	—	CE	CE	C*	CE	CE	CE	CE	CE	CE	CE	CE
4	1C	10	0	0	4	—	CE	CE	C*	CE	CE	CE	CE	—	CE	CE	CE
34	7C	18	0	0	5	C	C	CE	—	CE	CE	CE	CE	CE	CE	E	E
17	4C	11	1	0	6	C	C	CE	—	CE	CE	CE	CE	CE	—	E	E
43	8C	16	0	0	4	C	C	CE	CE	CE	CE	CE	CE	CE	—	E	E
55	10C	16	0	1	5	C	CE	CE	CE	CE	CE	CE	CE	CE	—	E	E
35	7C	15	0	0	3	C	CE	CE	—	CE	CE	CE	CE	CE	CE	E	E
22	5C	14	2	0	3	C	CE	CE	—	CE	CE	CE	CE	—	—	E	E

Notes: A = speaker number; B = family membership (GP = Grandparent; P = Parent; C = Child; the numbers denote families 1–10) C = age; a = ethnic index of exchange network (total: 20); b = ethnic index of interactive networks (total: 10); c = ethnic index of 'passive' networks (total: 10); Interlocutors: 1 = grandparent, female; 2 = grandparent, female; 3 = grandparent generation, female; 4 = grandparent generation, male; 5 = parent, male; 6 = parent, female; 7 = parent generation, female; 8 = parent generation, male; 9 = child, female; 10 = child, male; 11 = child generation, male; 12 = child generation, female.
* These cells fail to conform to perfect scalability.

according to customary language choice with different addressees both within and outside the family. Also included is the ethnic index associated with all three types of network. Tables 8.1 and 8.2 adapt slightly Gal's (1979) application of the implicational scale technique to examine both the social and stylistic dimensions of language choice. In these scales, speakers are ranked on the vertical axis and interlocutors on the horizontal axis. Those who are listed towards the top of the scale are speakers who use Chinese (C) on more occasions (i.e. with more inter-locutor types), while those who use more English (E) are listed towards the bottom. Interlocutors are also ranked according to the language choices of the vertically ranked speakers. Those who are spoken to in Chinese by more speakers are listed towards the left, while those spoken to more in English towards the right. Thus, the use of C with any particular interlocutor implies that C will be used with all interlocutors to the left of the scale, while if E is used with any interlocutor, it will be used with all interlocutors to the right. The use of both C and E to the same interlocutor will appear between the use of only C and the use of only E, and these are the situations where code-switching may (but not neces-sarily) occur. Any choice that does not fit this pattern is considered 'unscalable'. Scalability is calculated as the percentage of cells that fit the scale model, and 85 per cent scalability is normally considered to be a sufficient approximation of perfect scaling (Gal, 1979; Fasold, 1990).

The language choice pattern of any individual speaker can be read across each row, while inter-speaker differences in language choice with particular interlocu-tors can be read down each column. The relationship between social networks and language choice patterns is indicated by the ethnic indices associated with the three types (exchange; interactive; 'passive'). Information on speaker age and generation cohort is provided in columns B and C.

On the horizontal axis, grandparents are listed at the far left and children at the far right, indicating that Chinese is generally used to grandparents and English to children. This addressee ranking largely corresponds with the speaker ranking on the vertical axis, where grandparents appear towards the top of the scales and children towards the bottom. Broadly speaking, therefore, Chinese tends to be used by grandparents and to grandparents, while English tends to be used by children and to children. Both Chinese and English may be used by parents and to parents.

Gal (1979) suggests that it is through this kind of association between language and interlocutor types that languages acquire their social symbolism. For example, since in the Tyneside community Chinese is associated primarily with the grand-parents, it may be described as the 'we code' for that generation and for older speakers generally; English, on the other hand, which is associated chiefly with British-born children, may be regarded as their 'we code'. Note that even this tentative generalisation, which takes some account of intergenerational change in patterns of language use, rejects any assumption that the ethnic language of the community is the 'we code' and the language of the majority the 'they code'.

Table 8.2 Implicational scale for observed language choices by female speakers (scalability 99.6%)

A	B	C	a	b	c	Interlocutors											
						1	2	3	4	5	6	7	8	9	10	11	12
44	9GP	72	20	10	10	—	C	C	C	C	C	—	C	—	C	C	C
9	3GP	70	20	10	10	—	C	C	C	C	C	—	C	—	C	C	C
31	7GP	67	20	10	10	—	C	C	C	C	C	—	C	C	C	C	C
14	4GP	65	20	10	10	—	C	C	C	C	C	C	C	C	C	C	C
52	10GP	63	20	10	10	—	C	C	C	C	C	C	C	C	C	C	C
38	8GP	61	20	10	10	—	C	C	C	C	C	—	C	C	C	C	C
19	5GP	58	20	10	10	—	C	C	C	C	C	—	C	C	C	C	C
46	9P	50	18	4	10	C	C	C	—	C	C	—	C	—	CE	CE	CE
11	3P	46	20	5	10	C	C	C	—	C	C	—	C	—	CE	CE	CE
6	2P	38	20	2	10	—	C	C	—	C	C	—	C	—	CE	CE	CE
21	5P	35	20	6	10	C	C	C	—	C	C	—	C	CE	CE	CE	CE
3	1P	32	18	7	10	—	C	C	—	C	C	—	C	—	CE	CE	CE
27	6P	52	17	6	10	C	C	C	—	C	C	C	C	CE	CE	CE	CE
33	7P	42	15	5	10	C	C	C	—	C	C	C	CE	CE	CE	CE	CE
54	10P	45	18	1	10	C	C	C	—	CE	C	CE	CE	CE	CE	CE	CE
16	4P	37	6	0	10	C	C	C	—	CE	CE	—	CE	CE	CE	CE	CE
40	8P	40	18	5	10	C	C	C	—	CE	CE	CE	CE	CE	CE	CE	CE
50	9C	22	2	6	8	C	C	CE	CE	CE	CE	—	CE	—	CE	CE	CE
56	10C	21	3	6	8	C	C	CE	CE	CE	CE	CE	CE	CE	CE	CE	CE
57	10C	18	2	0	5	C	C	CE	CE	CE	CE	CE	CE	CE	CE	CE	CE
41	8C	12	1	0	6	C	C	CE	CE	CE	CE	CE	CE	CE	CE	CE	CE
58	10C	12	1	1	4	C	C	CE	CE	CE	CE	CE	CE	CE	CE	CE	CE
42	8C	8	0	0	4	C	C	CE	CE	CE	CE	C*	CE	CE	CE	CE	CE
30	6C	20	1	1	7	—	CE	CE	CE	CE	CE	—	CE	—	CE	CE	CE
18	4C	15	0	0	5	C	C	CE	CE	CE	CE	—	CE	CE	CE	E	E
24	5C	9	1	0	4	C	C	CE	CE	CE	CE	—	CE	CE	CE	E	E
23	5C	11	0	0	3	C	C	CE	CE	CE	CE	—	CE	—	CE	E	E
36	7C	10	2	1	5	C	CE	CE	CE	CE	CE	—	CE	—	CE	E	E

Notes: see notes at Table 6.1

Closer examination of the implicational scales reveals, however, that the interaction between the social and stylistic dimensions of language choice needs a more sophisticated analysis than this. The first point is that not all speakers of the same generation share the same language choice patterns, and there are cases where speakers are ranked either higher or lower than other members of their generation on the horizontal scale. For instance, speakers 51 and 37 (from families 10 and 8, aged 68 and 65 respectively) are ranked much lower than the other grandparents in Table 8.1 and lower even than some of the parents, suggesting that they use relatively more English. Furthermore, those who are listed at the extreme bottom of the scales are not always the youngest speakers in the child generation. Because such variations in language choice patterns cannot be accounted for entirely by the variables of age and generation, the social network variable becomes relevant.

Relative to other members of the grandparent generation, speakers 51 and 37 have fewer ethnic ties in their networks, and relative to other members of the child generation those listed at the bottom of the scales have even fewer Chinese contacts. In other words, these 'anomalous' speakers seem to have contracted personal social network ties which are rather different from those characteristic of their generation peers and consequently have developed different behavioural patterns.

Interestingly, however, inter-speaker variations of this kind are closely associated with interlocutor types, in that speakers with different network patterns adopt different language choice patterns with particular interlocutors. For example, while speakers of the parent generation who have relatively more Chinese-oriented networks use Chinese for communication between spouses, those with relatively fewer Chinese ties may use both Chinese and English with this addressee type. And while all children use Chinese with grandparents (especially female grandparents) and both Chinese and English with parents, some (but not all) use only English with their peers. Thus, any attempt to infer the social symbolism of Chinese and English by identifying the generations with which they are associated is too simplistic. Tables 8.1 and 8.2 suggest that particular languages are associated with particular groups of speakers who have contracted similar types of social network, and the variable of social network is plainly associated with the variable of age and generation (and to a lesser extent that of sex). Social networks also vary between individuals, despite these associations. Li Wei (1994) reports the results of an initial statistical analysis (using Analysis of Variance and Rank Order Correlation procedures) which explores more systematically the effects of these interacting variables on patterns of language choice.

Network structure and language choice in the British-born generation

Parallel to Li's observational study of 59 persons from 10 families, some results of which we reported in the previous section, Pong (1991) carried out a questionnaire study of language choice of a further 20 three-generational families, comprising 101 persons. This questionnaire study confirmed the chief findings listed above, revealing the same sharp disjunction between the generations; for example, 24% of the 'children' generation cohort report themselves to be monolingual English speakers, while none were monolingual in Chinese. Although this general pattern of generational difference seems to be common in migrant communities, it is not clear how far details vary between communities; for example, it is less clearly evident in the Tyneside Panjabi-speaking community (see Moffatt and Milroy, 1992). The general social explanation which we are offering is based on the types of network contacts made by the children, which involve non-Chinese people much more than their parents' contacts. While this is not particularly startling in itself, the network variable emphasises the basis of variable language choice patterns in social interaction rather than in duration of residence or in opportunity to use English in any straightforward sense. The social symbolism of the languages and the sense of appropriateness which is felt in choosing a suitable language either for an addressee or an auditor is also involved; some of the children reported embarrassment at using Chinese in the presence of English friends. Following the analysis described above which focused on intergenerational differences, we shall look further at how the network concept can illuminate differences in language choice patterns *within* this British-born generation.

Pong's 20 families consisted of two sets, as follows. Ten of the 20 families had migrated from a group of villages on Ap Chau Island, close to Hong Kong and were associated with the so-called True Jesus Church. The other 10 families were not tied to each other in quite this way, sharing neither pre-migration network ties nor having a centralised institution where they might meet. The chief function of the True Jesus Church seems to be that of maintaining Chinese language and culture, and the activities in which the True Jesus families participate each Sunday do not resemble those of the church-going population of Britain generally. The families are all related to each other either closely or more distantly. They generally eat a meal together and attend one of two relatively short church services; one is conducted entirely in Chinese and one mainly in English with an interpreter (usually a bilingual teenager) translating the sermon. There are also lessons in Chinese language and culture for the children during the afternoon, and the families meet otherwise to celebrate special occasions like Chinese New Year or Christmas. Thus, they have ample opportunity to maintain their pre-existing network ties, which are strongly kin-oriented, and to maintain their knowledge of Chinese language, history and culture.

We might ask what effect this has on the language choice patterns of the True Jesus group. With respect to the older generations, the answer is very little, since there is a strong orientation to Chinese in both of them, a tendency which is related to the strongly Chinese- and kin-oriented network patterns of these groups. This kind of generational contrast has already emerged with respect to the 10 families whose language choice patterns are implicationally scaled in Tables 8.1 and 8.2. But the ability to speak Chinese as self-reported on a three-point scale and arranged implicationally in Table 8.3 shows that the children belonging to the True Jesus group (note *a*) tend to appear towards the top, while non-True Jesus children appear near the bottom. This positional variation reflects a stronger preference for Chinese by the True Jesus group. Interestingly, sex of speaker seems to have very little effect on this pattern, nor do other classic sociolinguistic factors such as difference in length of residence or educational attainment. But we would also want to argue that the formal teaching of Chinese is unlikely to have much effect on the spoken language; this is on the basis of our knowledge of the generally negligible effect of (for example) formal lessons in Urdu on the language competence of Pakistani teenagers, also noted in Tyneside. In short, it is the internal social organisation of the community, the persistence of pre-emigration networks and the strategies evolved by the community for maintaining these networks which seem to be the crucial factors. It seems likely that other communities which are trying to maintain their language and culture in opposition to a state or national language may create similar coalitions, which are effectively networks established for a particular purpose.

In the previous section, we suggested that the network variable could account for generation-specific differences in language choice, while in this section it was used to account for differences within a single generational sub-group. By its very nature, the network variable overlaps and interacts with a host of other social variables, but offers, we have argued, a more general and economical way of accounting for language choice if the relationship with these other variables is made explicit (see also Li Wei, 1993; 1996; Li Wei and Milroy, 1995).

Network-specific conversational code-switching patterns

The first part of our analysis of bilingual language behaviour in the Chinese community revealed a sharp intergenerational disjunction in language choice patterns between the children and the older generations, and has suggested that the network variable is a more accurate predictor of language choice than that of generation, with which it is closely associated but not isomorphic. The implicational scales presented in Tables 8.1 and 8.2 not only illuminate the interaction between inter- and intra-speaker linguistic variations, but also locate specifically the contexts (indicated by a CE pattern) where *conversational code-switching* is likely to occur.

Table 8.3   Implicational scale for language choice by children

Speakers	Age	Sex	Chinese-speaking ability	Interlocutors							
				1	2	3	4	5	6	7	8
1 [a]	28	M	Very well	C	C	C	C	C	C	CE	CE
2	22	M	Very well	C	C	C	C	C	C	CE	CE
3 [a]	21	F	Very well	C	C	C	C	C	CE	CE	CE
4 [a]	18	M	Very well	C	C	C	C	C	CE	CE	CE
5 [a]	16	M	Very well	C	C	C	C	C	CE	CE	CE
6 [a]	16	F	Very well	C	C	C	C	C	CE	CE	CE
7 [a]	25	M	Very well	C	C	C	C	C	CE	CE	CE
8 [a]	23	F	Very well	C	C	C	C	C	CE	CE	CE
9 [a]	20	F	Very well	C	C	C	C	C	CE	CE	CE
10 [a]	20	F	Very well	C	C	C	C	C	CE	CE	CE
11 [a]	16	M	Very well	C	C	C	C	C	CE	–	CE
12	20	M	Fairly well	C	C	C	C	–	–	CE	CE
13 [a]	21	F	Fairly well	C	C	C	C	–	–	CE	CE
14 [a]	12	M	Very well	C	C	C	C	C	CE	CE	E
15	18	F	Very well	C	CE [b]	CE [b]	C	C	CE	CE	E
16 [a]	10	M	Very well	C	C	C	C	CE	CE	CE	CE
17	18	M	Not well	C	C	C	C	CE	CE	CE	E
18	14	M	Not well	C	C	C	C	–	–	CE	E
19	12	M	Fairly well	C	C	C	C	CE	CE	CE	E
20	10	F	Fairly well	C	C	C	C	CE	E	E	E
21 [a]	16	M	Very well	C	C	C	CE	C [b]	CE	CE	E
22 [a]	11	M	Very well	C	C	C	CE	C [b]	CE	CE	E
23 [a]	9	F	Fairly well	C	C	C	CE	C [b]	CE	CE	E
24	16	F	Very well	C	C	C	CE	CE	CE	–	CE
25 [a]	7	M	Fairly well	C	C	C	CE	CE	CE	CE	CE
26 [a]	15	F	Very well	C	C	C	CE	CE	CE	E [b]	CE
27	8	F	Not well	C	C	C	CE	CE	E [b]	CE	CE
28	13	F	Not well	C	C	C	CE	CE	E [b]	CE	E
29	10	F	Not well	C	C	C	CE	–	–	E	E
30	6	F	Not well	C	C	C	CE	–	–	E	E
31	13	M	Fairly well	C	C	C	CE	CE	E	E	E
32	9	M	Fairly well	C	C	C	CE	CE	E	E	E
33	11	F	Not well	C	C	C	CE	CE	E	E	E
34 [a]	13	F	Fairly well	C	C	CE	CE	CE	CE	CE	E
35	11	M	Fairly well	C	C	E [b]	CE	–	–	E	–
36	15	M	Not well	C	E [b]	E [b]	C	CE	CE	CE	E
37	7	F	Fairly well	C	E [b]	E [b]	C	CE	CE	CE	CE
38	7	F	Not well	CE	E	E	E	E	E	–	E

Notes:
[a] Informants from the True Jesus Church.
[b] These cells fail to conform to perfect scalability; Interlocutors: 1 = Grandparents and their generation; 2 = Chinese shopkeepers; 3 = Chinese waiters/waitresses; 4 = Parents and their generation; 5 = Teachers at Chinese Sunday School; 6 = Schoolmates at Chinese Sunday School; 7 = Siblings; 8 = Chinese friends

Extracts (1) and (2) below are discussed by Pong (1991: 24, 99) as typical of the different kinds of language mixing behaviour of the child and the parent generations. Note, however, that the fluent code-switching of the bilingual teen-agers in (1) indicates a language choice pattern which is rather less English-oriented than that of the speakers listed at the very bottom of the scales in Tables 8.1 and 8.2. The parents in (2) regard themselves as monolingual Chinese speakers, so that whatever criteria we use for distinguishing borrowings from single-word code-switching (and we shall not consider this issue further here), it is reasonable to consider the English items *football hooligan* and *pub* as borrowings (see further Poplack and Sankoff, 1984).

(1) *Fieldworker*: Gem nei dei dou wui hao leu wen go ying guog yen zon peng yeo ne wo.
   (So you won't consider having an English girlfriend.)
   Anthony: Zou peng yeo wui, *but not a wife*.
   (Yes friends, but not a wife.)
   . . .
   Anthony: Yeu hou do yeo *contact*.
   (We have many contacts.)
   George: *We always have opportunities* heu xig kei ta dei fong gao wui di yen. Ngo dei xi xi dou *keep in contact*.
   (We always have opportunities to get to know people from other churches. We always keep in touch.)

(2) *Father*: Bed guo, Ying Guog di heo seng zeo kuai di la. Bin dou yeo Ying Guog gem do *football hooligan*.
   (But the teenagers in Britain are very badly behaved. Where else can you find so many football hooligans?)
   Mother: Ni dou di heo seng zung yi yem zeo. So yi ngo m bei di zei neu heu *pub* ga.
   (The teenagers here like to drink. That's why I never allow my children to go to pubs.)

These two extracts illustrate contrasting patterns of intergenerational conver-sational behaviour which partly derive from the language choice patterns we have described in the preceding sections. To a very large extent, these patterns are associated not only with the different socialisation patterns described above, but with differing levels of ability in the two community languages. However, inter-generational differences in the way the two languages are used in conversation are often subtle and seem to be better analysed as *socially symbolic discourse behaviours* rather than as following from these community-level social variables in any obvi-ous way. We shall examine this dimension of code-switching behaviour within a general *conversation analysis* framework (cf. Auer, 1991). Briefly, this involves searching the data for recurrent sequential patterns, which are then interpreted with reference both to the observable behaviour of participants and to generalisations derived inductively from previously observed conversational corpora (see Levinson, 1983; Atkinson and Heritage, 1984; Roger and Bull, 1989). Using this general framework, we shall look in this section at how speakers alternate their two languages in conversation as a procedure for the organisation of preference marking, repairs and insertion sequences.

Preference marking

Consider first the following conversational sequences:[1]

(3) (Dinner table talk between mother A and daughter B):
   A: Oy-m-oy faan a? Ah Ying a?
     (Want or not rice?)
   B: (No response)
   A: Chaaufaan a. Oy-m-oy?
     (Fried rice. Want or not?)
   B: (2.0) *I'll have some shrimps.*
   A: Mut-ye? (.) Chaaufaan a.
     (What? Fried rice.)
   B: Hai a.
     (OK.)

In extract (3), a mother, speaking Cantonese throughout, offers her daughter rice. The child first delays her response to the offer, and then in English requests an alternative to rice. Her final acceptance is in Cantonese. In extract (4), B, a 12-year-old boy, is playing with a computer in the family living-room. A is his mother.

(4) A: *Finished homework?*
     (2.0)
   A: Steven, yiu mo wan sue?
     (want to review (your) lessons)
   B: (1.5) *I've finished.*

In this extract, B does not respond to A's question. The mother then switches to Cantonese for a further question, which B apparently understands as an indirect request to review his lessons. His response is marked by a pause as 'dispreferred' and his language choice contrasts with that of his mother. In both (3) and (4), dispreferred responses seem to be marked by code-switching to a contrasting language, as well as by the more usual pause. A rather clear example of this pattern can be seen in (5), where A is the mother, B her nine-year-old daughter and C her 12-year old son:

(5) A: *Who want some?   Crispy a.*
     B: *Yes*
     A: Yiu me?
        (Want some?)
     B: Hai a
        (Yes.)
     (A handing over some spring-rolls to B.)
     A: (To C) *Want some, John?*
     C: Ngaw m yiu.
        (I don't want.)
     A: M yiu a? *Crispy* la.
        (Don't want?)
     C: (Shaking head) mm

In this sequence, B twice accepts A's offer of spring rolls, twice using the same language as A (English and Cantonese respectively) for this preferred response. However, when C declines A's offer we find a pattern similar to the one which is evident in (3) and (4). After a short pause, C selects a language different from the language used for the first pair part; A uses English for the offer whereas C uses Cantonese for the refusal. This example supports Auer's argument that the contrast is more socially meaningful than the actual choice of language. Switches marking dispreferred responses can be in either direction.

Dispreferred responses in monolingual English conversations (e.g. refusals and disagreements, as opposed to acceptances and agreements) are generally marked by various structural complexities including pauses before delivery, 'prefaces' such as *but* and *well*, token agreements, appreciations and apologies (see further Levinson, 1983: 334–5). These three sequences suggest that contrasting choices of language – with the second-part speaker choosing a language different from the first-part speaker – can be used to mark dispreference in bilingual conversation in much the same way as a wide range of markedness features in monolingual conversation. In fact, Auer (1991) argues that code-switching is the most significant discourse marker in bilingual conversations in the sense that marked language choices are more noticeable than other discourse markers (see also Lavandera, 1978; Gumperz, 1982). It is perhaps for this reason that code-switching may even replace some language-specific dispreference markers. For example, although we have shown that pauses accompany code-switching in this conversational context, we find that in our corpus English discourse markers such as *well* and *but* do not. These items commonly occur in monolingual discourse as prefaces to dispreferred second parts of pairs.

A general pattern which emerges from these examples and many others in the corpus is that code-switching to mark a dispreferred second part occurs chiefly in *intergenerational conversation*. Furthermore, it is usually *children* who use English to mark their dispreferred responses to the Chinese first pair parts of their parents or grandparents (although this is not invariably the case, as can be seen in (5) above). Code-switching seldom seems to be used to mark dispreference in conversations between speakers of the same generation and, where it is, the language direction of the switch is rather less predictable. The emergence of a general pattern of this kind lends support to the point made earlier, that the association between conversation structure and language choice varies according to speakers. Thus, in order to understand the social and discourse meaning of code-switching, we need to relate specific interactional strategies to the more general patterns of language choice and language ability at the inter-speaker (or community) level.

Repair

Consider now the following three sequences, which involve older speakers. A and B are both women in their early forties.

> (6) *A*: . . .koei hai yisaang.
>   (He's a doctor.)
>   *B*: *Is he?*
>   *A*: Yichin (.) hai Hong Kong.
>   (Before. In Hong Kong.)

In extract (6), B's utterance, in a language contrastive with that of A's preceding utterance, initiates a self-repair by A, prompting her to specify more accurately that the man mentioned in her first turn was formerly a doctor in Hong Kong, but is not currently a doctor in Britain.

In extract (7), where A and B again are both women, A in her forties and B in her mid-twenties, B similarly marks a repair initiator with a contrasting choice of language. Here she queries the accuracy of A's assertion that the person she is trying to contact on the telephone will ring in a short time.

> (7) *A*: Da m do. Koeige *telephone* gonggan. Koei dang yatjan joi da.
>   (Can't get through. Her telephone is engaged. She'll ring again in a short while.)
>   *B*: *She ring?*
>   *A*: Hai a, ngaw da.
>   (Yes, I'll ring.)

(8) A: *He's a* [ku:]. . . (.) *I don't know how to say* (.) *send message* (.)
      Nay ji-m-ji a?
      (Do you know?)
    B: *Oh, courier.*
    A: *Yes, courier.*

In extract (8), A, a woman in her late thirties, initiates a subsequent other-repair
by B, a man in his late twenties. Again the repair initiator is marked by a contrasting choice of language, as in the previous two examples. Researchers have frequently observed that code-switching can serve such functions as word-finding,
self-editing (with or without discernible errors), repetition, emphasis, clarification, confirmation and so forth. All these uses are parts of a more general repair
procedure, examples of which we have presented. Although they are difficult to
analyse quantitatively because of the multifunctional nature of specific conversational contributions, the association between code-switching and repair is a
common one in our corpus.

The role of code-switching in organising discourse can be seen also in conversation sequences which do not fit the adjacency pairs structure, to which we now
turn.

Presequences

Not all conversational sequences can be analysed as paired sets of utterances or as
chained to the preceding and following utterances in a linear fashion, as illustrated by our examples so far. The first utterance in (9) is an example of the first
part of a 'presequence', a type of conversational structure which prefigures or
clears the ground for a later interactional episode. Presequences simultaneously
mark the boundary of two interactive episodes (Levinson, 1983), and our data
suggest that this boundary is often marked by code-switching. In (9), A is talking
with his (female) cousin, B, about one of their friends who has been ill. Both
speakers are in their twenties:

(9) A: *Did you see Kim yesterday?*
    B: *Yeah.*
    A: Mou [mat si. . .
        (It's not serious. . .)
    B: [Yau di tautung je, Mou mat si ge.
        ((She) only has a little headache. It's nothing serious.)
    A: Ngaw jing yiu man nay.
        (I was just about to ask you.)

A's first utterance is a question checking the precondition for his subsequent enquiry about their friend's health. After B confirms that she is in a position to provide this information, A embarks upon his intended enquiry. The boundary between presequence and target sequence is marked by code-switching. In mono-lingual discourse, presequences are often marked prosodically or phonologically in various ways (Levinson, 1983: 345ff).

In this section we have cited examples designed to illustrate some of the conversational patterns marked by code-switching which recur in our corpus, and we have suggested that code-switching might plausibly be viewed as fulfilling some specifiable conversational functions. Probably because of the contrasting language preferences of the children, on the one hand, and the parents and grandparents, on the other, it seems to be particularly common in intergenerational communica-tion. In addition to the functions of preference marking, marking of repairs and presequence boundary marking illustrated here, code-switching seems to be used to regulate turn-taking in various ways (see Li Wei and Milroy, 1995). As we have hinted, the adoption by individuals of one or another of these discourse strategies seems to a considerable extent to be generation and network specific. For example, parents and grandparents generally do not code-switch during peer conversations, except to mark self-repairs. However, they sometimes switch from Chinese to English when they are addressing children, particularly to mark turn allocation and repair initiators. Children, on the other hand, tend to use English with their peers and to switch to Chinese to mark presequences and embedded sequences. However, it is characteristic of this generation to mark dispreferred responses by switching from Chinese to English.

These intergenerational differences in code-switching practices might be described as interactional reflexes of the network- and generation-specific language choice preferences in the Tyneside Chinese community. Although they can some-times be related to practical constraints arising from the language preferences and language abilities of different sub-groups, many code-switching practices such as those exemplified in extracts (3)–(8) cannot easily be related to such constraints, and are better interpreted as network-specific strategies of a socially symbolic kind.

Social network and the broader social framework

As well as relating interactional and community levels of analysis, network struc-ture can relate to social, economic and political structure. The main point we need to make here is that the various network types discussed in this chapter do not constitute themselves in a socially arbitrary fashion. Particularly, the charac-teristic occupational preferences of the economically active Chinese largely determine the nature of the ties which they contract with others. Similarly, the mainly kin-oriented ties which the economically dependent adults contract are a natural consequence of the Chinese family system. The British-born generation, for their part, by attending school and participating in life outside the community, will contract ties with non-Chinese peers.

A coherent theory of language choice and code-switching needs to make explicit the relationship between community networks – 'frames' within which language choice takes place – and large-scale social and economic structure. As Gal (1988) points out, the success, persistence and precise form of the 'opposition' to mainstream values symbolised by minority language maintenance depend not upon community-internal linguistic or interactional factors, but upon the relation of the group to the national economy and to like groups in other cities or states; we need both a socio-political and interactional level of analysis. The outcome in terms of language (or dialect) survival or shift in Belfast may be different from that in Paris or Copenhagen; in Catalonia it may be different from Gascony. It will be constrained by local variations in political, economic and social structure.

What seems to be required is a *social* (as opposed to a sociolinguistic) theory which can associate these network patterns with specifiable sub-groups which in turn emerge from larger scale social, economic and political processes. One useful integrated analysis is proposed by Giddens (1984), but the *life-modes* theory of the Danish anthropologist Thomas Højrup, which is grounded more firmly in systematic ethnographic work, is particularly helpful. Offering an analysis which is designed to be generally applicable to Western Europe but allows for local, historically contingent differences in social and economic systems, Højrup proposes a division of the population into sub-groups which are described in terms of three life-modes. These life-modes are seen as both social and cultural, as necessary and inevitable constituents of the social structure as a whole which spring from economic systems of production and consumption. Thus, like social network types, they are not socially or culturally arbitrary, but are the effect of 'fundamental societal structures which split the population into fundamentally different life-modes' (Højrup, 1983: 47). The precise way in which they split the population will, however, vary between nation-states, depending on local political and economic systems. Højrup's analysis focuses on the differing ideological orientation of the three sub-groups to work, leisure and family, and from the point of view of this research, the distinction between, on the one hand, Life-mode 1, the life-mode of the self-employed, and of the other, Life-mode 2, that of the ordinary wage-earner, is particularly important. The life-mode of a different kind of wage-earner, the high-powered Life-mode 3 executive, is quite different from either of these.

A close-knit family-centred network with a strong solidarity ideology and little distinction between work and leisure activities is characteristic of the self-employed. Conversely, ordinary wage-earners will be embedded in less kin-oriented and generally looser-knit networks. This analysis, to which we cannot do justice here, converges with our own. We would predict a more Chinese-oriented pattern of language choice by speakers who are embedded in close-knit networks, and would expect such a personal network structure to be characteristic of Life-mode 1. Indeed, this seems to be the case. For example, two speakers in our sample are a married couple who are both wage-earners, employed by a local computer company. They interact on a daily basis with English speakers, retaining contact with other Chinese only for a short time on Sundays. Their command of English is very much better than other economically active but self-employed (Life-mode 1) Chinese. Højrup does not see the life-mode of the self-employed as a relic of an earlier period but as highly efficient and competitive given its flexibility of operation and the commitment of the producers. He uses the Danish fishing industry as an example, but his description equally well applies to the Tyneside Chinese family catering businesses.

Conclusion

While we have used the Tyneside Chinese community to illustrate a social network perspective on code-switching and language choice, the analysis presented in this chapter is intended to be of more general application. We have tried to demonstrate that while network interacts with a number of other variables, it is capable of accounting more generally for patterns of language choice than the variables such as generation, sex of speaker, duration of stay and occupation with which it interacts. It can also deal in a principled way with differences within a single generational group. We have also suggested that it can form an important component in an integrated initial theory of language choice: it links with the interactional level in focusing on the everyday behaviour of social actors, and with the economic and socio-political level in that networks may be seen as forming in response to social and economic pressures. We briefly examined this latter link in terms of Højrup's life-modes analysis.

We can conclude by suggesting fruitful directions for future research. To some extent this has been done already in the argument for a more coherent approach to the economic and socio-political context of code-switching, without sacrificing detailed sociolinguistic analysis of code-switching behaviour. What is needed, however, is a more principled analysis of interacting social variables such as sex, age, class, generation cohort and network to see how they interact in their effect on language choice. However, there is a more general point which needs to be emphasised: rather than collecting ever more data which, while intrinsically interesting, cannot easily be interpreted, researchers need to devote some energy to developing a framework within which this interpretation can take place.

Note

1   We have kept the transcription conventions used in our samples of bilingual conversation as simple as possible. The romanised system for transcribing spoken
Cantonese was developed by Li Wei (see further Li Wei, 1994) in association with
colleagues at the University of Hong Kong. The chief conversational phenomena
provided for all our samples in this article are simultaneous speech (marked by [ )
and pauses (marked by (.) to indicate a micropause and by a series of dots to
indicate longer pauses).

Source: Li Wei, Milroy, L. and Pong, S.C. (1992) A two-step sociolinguistic analysis of
code-switching and language choice. *International Journal of Applied Linguistics* 2(1): 63–86,
by permission of Novus Press.

Notes for students and instructors

Study questions

1   What kinds of special communicative effect can be achieved through code-switching?
2   How do you decide which language is 'marked' and which is 'unmarked', in Myers-Scotton's sense of the terms, for specific situations in a specific community?
3   What are the key functions of 'discourse-related' code-switching in Auer's sense of the term?
4   In what way can code-switching be used as an organisational procedure for conversational interaction?

Study activity

Record an informal conversation involving two or more bilingual speakers on to an audio tape recorder. Transcribe the recording in detail, paying particular attention to any gap, false start, overlap and interruption. Examine the language choice of each individual speaker and see how a particular choice may be related to the co-participant's choice of language as well as his or her own in previous turns in the conversation. Can you describe particular instances of code-switching as 'situational', 'metaphorical', 'marked', 'unmarked', 'participant-related' or 'discourse-related'? What problems are there in using these terms? How is code-switching related to the overall organisation of conversation?

Further reading

Blom and Gumperz's approach to code-switching is further developed in J.J. Gumperz, 1992, *Discourse Strategies*, Cambridge University Press.

For Gumperz's contributions generally, see *Language in Social Groups: Essays by J.J. Gumperz*, selected by A.S. Dil, 1971, Stanford University Press.

For a more detailed exposition of the 'markedness' model of code-switching, see C. Myers-Scotton, 1993, *Social Motivations for Codeswitching: Evidence from Africa*, Oxford University Press.

A fuller account of Auer's analysis of conversational code-switching is in J.C.P. Auer, 1984, *Bilingual Conversation*, John Benjamins.

A detailed analysis of the code-switching patterns in the Tyneside Chinese community can be found in Li Wei, 1994, *Three Generations Two Languages One Family: Language choice and language shift in a Chinese community in Britain*, Multilingual Matters.

New perspectives on bilingual interaction are offered in B. Rampton, 1995, *Crossing: Language and ethnicity among adolescents*, Longman, and M. Sebba, 1993, *London Jamaican: Language systems in interaction*, Longman.

A state-of-the-art collection of sociolinguistic studies on bilingual interaction is given in *Code-Switching in Conversation: Language, interaction and identity*, edited by J.C.P. Auer, 1998, Routledge.

Linguistic dimensions of bilingualism

Introduction to Part Two

LI WEI

Part Two focuses on the linguistic aspects of bilingualism. Chomsky (1986) defined three basic questions for linguistics:

1   What constitutes knowledge of language?
2   How is knowledge of language acquired?
3   How is knowledge of language put to use?

For bilingualism research, these questions need to be rephrased to take in knowledge of more than one language:

1   What is the nature of language, or grammar, in the bilingual person's mind and how do two systems of language knowledge co-exist and interact?
2   How is more than one grammatical system acquired, either simultaneously or sequentially? In what aspects does bilingual language acquisition differ from unilingual language acquisition?
3   How is the knowledge of two or more languages used by the same speaker in bilingual speech production?

The articles reprinted in this part of the Reader cover approaches to bilingualism that are related to this particular agenda of linguistic research. They are further divided into two sections: Grammar of code-switching and Language acquisition of bilingual children.

Grammar of code-switching

The occurrence of code-switching – the alternation of two languages both between and within sentences – has been shown to be governed not only by extra-linguistic (or social and situational) but also intra-linguistic (or structural) factors. In her agenda-setting article, Shana Poplack (Chapter 9) proposes two grammatical constraints which seem to operate on code-switching:

1   the *free morpheme constraint* which states that codes may be switched after any constituent in discourse, provided that constituent is not a bound morpheme; and
2   the *equivalent constraint*, i.e. code-switching tends to occur at points in discourse where juxtaposition of two languages does not violate a surface syntactic rule of either language.

Poplack further argues that the equivalent constraints on code-switching may be used to measure degrees of bilingual ability. Using quantitative analysis, she demonstrates that fluent bilinguals tend to switch at various syntactic boundaries within the sentence, while non-fluent bilinguals favour switching between sentences, allowing them to participate in the code-switching mode without fear of violating a grammatical rule of either of the languages involved.

The article by Michael Clyne (Chapter 10) critically examines some of the assumptions underlying the constraints proposed by various researchers. In particular, Clyne questions the assumptions about the stability and 'standardness' of the bilinguals' grammatical systems. Using data from German–English and Dutch–English bilingual speakers in Australia, he argues that the grammatical constraints and the even more powerful grammatical models of code-switching cannot be substantiated universally. He further develops the idea of 'triggering', which he proposed in his earlier work (in particular Clyne, 1967); namely, an item of ambiguous affiliation – i.e. one belonging to the speaker's two systems – triggers off a switch from one language to another. He points out that trigger words are not part of the switch, but indicative of the psycholinguistic process by which the bilingual speaker plans and produces his or her speech.

A theoretical model of code-switching which focuses more specifically on psycholinguistic processes of bilingual speech production is presented in the article by Carol Myers-Scotton and Janice L. Jake (Chapter 11). This model, known as the Matrix Language Frame (MLF) model, is built on the hypothesis that the two languages involved in code-switching do not participate equally, the matrix language (ML) being more dominant and setting the grammatical frame while the embedded language (EL) provides certain elements to be embedded in the frame. Furthermore, only certain EL elements can participate in code-switching: they must be content morphemes *and* they must be congruent with the ML in terms of three levels of structure: lexical–conceptual, predicate–argument and morphological realisation. Myers-Scotton and Jake point out that the analysis of intra-sentential code-switching, using the MLF model, provides an empirical window on the viability of key theoretical claims about the structure of language and the nature and organisation of language production.

Language acquisition of bilingual children

The second section of this part of the Reader focuses on language acquisition of bilingual children. Despite the upsurge of case studies of bilingual children in the 1990s, the central theme has remained largely unchanged: do bilingual children have one undifferentiated linguistic system or two differentiated systems? The two articles reprinted in this section both focus on this issue.

The fact that bilingual children mix elements from their two languages is often interpreted as evidence for a unitary underlying language system. Fred Genesee's article (Chapter 12) examines the empirical basis for such a claim. He points out the serious methodological problems of some of the studies, and re-analyses selected case studies. He also offers new data from speech perception studies, arguing that young bilingual children are able to differentiate two languages from the earliest stages of bilingual development, and that they can use their two languages in contextually sensitive ways. He points out that code-mixing itself is not good evidence for the unitary system argument. In fact, children's mixing may be related to mixed input by parents. Genesee calls for more serious research on the possible role of parental input in the form of mixed utterances.

Jürgen M. Meisel's article (Chapter 13) addresses the 'one system or two' question by focusing on the syntactic and morphological development of bilingual children. However, instead of simply providing further evidence in support of the separate development argument, Meisel raises the theoretically more interesting question of whether the human 'language making capacity' (Slobin, 1985) could allow the bilingual individual to separate the two simultaneously acquired grammatical systems from early on, without going through a phase of confusion. Through a longitudinal study of simultaneous French–German bilingual children, he argues that grammatical processing is in fact possible much earlier than is usually assumed on the basis of analyses of monolingual child language. He further speculates that this early development of grammatical processing ability could be explained by the fact that the task of acquiring two language systems simultaneously requires more attention to problems of form, rather than relying on semantic–pragmatic strategies alone.

Grammar of code-switching

Sometimes I'll start a sentence in Spanish *y termino en español*: toward a typology of code-switching

SHANA POPLACK

Preface

Reprinting a 20-year old paper is a risky business, especially one interpreted or misinterpreted in as many ways as *Sometimes I'll start a sentence . . .* has been. I have none the less accepted the invitation to reproduce it virtually unchanged, prefaced only by this brief attempt to situate it in the context of what we know now, thanks to two decades of corroborative research in a variety of bilingual communities and language pairs, about code-switching and lexical borrowing.

   Sometimes I'll start a sentence . . . represented a first attempt to delineate, for quantitative analytical purposes, what has turned out to be the fundamental distinction in language mixing: that between code-switching and borrowing. This was manifest in the contrast between those English-origin items which, despite their etymology, function morphologically and syntactically as though they were Spanish (borrowings), and those retaining the inflections and syntactic characteristics of their lexifier language (code-switches) (Section 2, especially Table 9.1). It was also evident in the conception of the *free morpheme constraint* – essentially a preliminary formulation of the claim, now amply confirmed – that the (nonce) borrowings and the (single-word) switches in a corpus of bilingual discourse may be identified and operationally distinguished from each other.

   We know much more about the relevant criteria for delimiting borrowing and code-switching now than we did 20 years ago. For example, phonological integration need not go hand in hand with morphological integration, although this was usually the case in the Puerto Rican–English context studied here. In many bilingual communities, phonological integration of loanwords is highly variable, and this is also foreshadowed in Sections 2 and 6.3, disqualifying phonology as a (foolproof) criterion. Moreover, it has now been proved that loanword (vs. code-switch) status can be determined even for items featuring *no* overt linguistic indications (the 'zero forms' recently debated in the literature), at least in the aggregate. The key to disambiguating the status of such apparently ambiguous elements is recourse to the monolingual varieties that combined to produce the mixed utterance. Such comparison has revealed that even uninflected borrowed forms pattern along with their counterparts in the recipient language, which also show variable marking (see the papers in Poplack and Meechan, 1998). Code-switches (single-word as well as multiword code-switches) have similarly been shown to pattern according to the donor, or lexifier, language.

From this perspective, many of the lone other-language forms operationally classified as code-switches in *Sometimes I'll start a sentence . . .* would today be identified as borrowings. Despite the nomenclature, their quantitative patterning (Table 9.2) already revealed them both to outweigh by far the unambiguous multiword switches, and to behave differently from them, as has by now been confirmed for numerous other communities and contexts. For example it is the inclusion of large numbers of lone English-origin nouns (and a lesser number of other lone items) that is responsible for the apparent tendency in Table 9.2 for unidirectional (Spanish–English) 'code-switching'. When the lone items are treated separately from the unambiguous switches, any significant rate differences disappear.

Most of these lone other-language items have since been identified, after Weinreich (1953), as *nonce borrowings*. For such items, the Free Morpheme Constraint turns out to be a consequence of the *nonce borrowing hypothesis* (Sankoff *et al.*, 1990). As originally formulated, however, the free morpheme constraint also suggests that switches should not occur across a morpheme boundary where a morpheme appearing at the end of a multiword fragment in one language is bound to another at the beginning of a multiword fragment in the other language. Although there are still no published reports of the systematic occurrence of this type of counterexample – which would effectively falsify the free morpheme constraint in this context – we have no particular stake in this issue. The constraint was basically intended to account for the disproportionate number – now empirically confirmed in dozens of bilingual communities – of *lone* other-language lexical items in code-mixed discourse (Poplack and Meechan, 1998). This is more precisely formulated as the *nonce borrowing hypothesis*.

What of the *equivalence constraint*, adumbrated in Poplack (1978/81) and first tested empirically on a community-wide basis in *Sometimes I'll start a sentence . . .?* Once lone other-language items are identified as syntactically and morphologically part of the recipient-language fragments in which they are embedded, the analysis of intrasentential code-switching may proceed unimpeded by confusion between switching and borrowing. The equivalence constraint – which has since been formalized (Sankoff and Mainville, 1986) and shown to be a logical consequence of consistency conditions on speakers' production of hierarchically and linearly coherent sentences (Sankoff 1998; 1998a) – turns out to account for virtually all quantitatively significant patterns of switching in most large corpora. Patterns other than equivalence-point switching, such as 'repetition-translation', and 'constituent insertion' (Naït M'Barek and Sankoff, 1988) also occur, but these are confined to specific communities and are observed in only one or two quite specific constructions. It is by first recognizing all the data accounted for by the equivalence constraint that these other patterns are highlighted, detected and described. Thus the major conceptual preoccupations of *Sometimes I'll start a sentence . . .* – the avoidance by speakers of word-order conflicts at switch-points, and their patterned use of the fundamentally different processes of code-switching and borrowing – have provided the essential tools for dozens of studies of bilingual contexts that have followed.

No less important has been the community-based research protocol first exemplified here, inspired by the variation theory paradigm originating with Labov. It is evidenced not only in the delineation of the speech community through innovative participant-observation fieldwork techniques, but also in the quantitative analyses of the data collected there and, especially, adherence to the *principle of accountability* to those data. These have more recently been augmented by techniques of computational linguistics. Such research methods are onerous and often tedious compared with elicitation, intuition or reanalysis of previously published examples, but they continue to furnish the richest and by far the most valid material for the scientific study of bilingual discourse.

Shana Poplack
October 1999

1   Introduction

An overwhelming majority[1] of Puerto Ricans residing in the continental United States currently claim Spanish as their 'mother tongue'. This is true for young as well as older speakers, despite the fact that most of them were either born, raised, or spent a good part of their adult life in an English-speaking society.

Along with signs of vigour and renewal of the language, however, there is also some indication that use of Spanish is on the wane, especially among the younger generations of speakers who were born and raised in New York City (Pedraza, 1978). The present investigation is part of an interdisciplinary study which aims to examine the place of both Spanish and English in a Puerto Rican community in East Harlem through:

1   participant observation of their distribution in the daily life of the community;

2   analysis of attitudes of community members toward each of the languages; and

3   quantitative sociolinguistic analysis of selected linguistic behaviour.

Due, among other things, to a circulatory pattern of migration, this appears to be a stable bilingual community, rather than a transitional one where acquisition of a second language would eventually displace the first (Fishman, 1971). This pattern of displacement of the mother tongue has characterized several early twentieth-century immigrant groups in the United States, and has usually been brought to completion by the third generation. In contrast, the Puerto Rican community under investigation includes third-generation speakers of both Spanish and English.

102nd Street, a block in the heart of El Barrio, perhaps the oldest continuous Puerto Rican settlement in the United States, provides a unique setting to investigate these issues. Block residents are predominantly (95%) Puerto Rican, to the virtual exclusion of all other ethnic groups, an attribute which is not characteristic of the Puerto Rican community in the United States as a whole (Pedraza, 1978). If the Spanish language and Puerto Rican culture are to survive in the United States, their chances of doing so are presumably greatest in such an ethnically homogeneous environment.

This chapter is an attempt to integrate the results of the ethnographic and attitudinal components of the broader study into a specifically sociolinguistic analysis.

2   Code-switching

Long-term ethnographic observation of 102nd Street, carried out by Pedro Pedraza (1978), indicated three modes of communication among block members: English-speaking, Spanish-speaking and code-switching. While use of Spanish predominates in certain domains (such as in the home or while playing numbers), its exclusive use in any of these settings was not observed. Similarly, while use of English predominates in official settings, it is also possible to hear Spanish in these domains. Pedraza further observed that 'there were speakers who code-switched because they lacked full command of Spanish and those who code-switched because they lacked full command of English' (p. 33). However, as we will see, it is only by linking ethnographic observations with linguistic analysis that code-switching behaviour may be most adequately explained.

Code-switching is the alternation of two languages within a single discourse, sentence or constituent. In a report on an earlier study of a balanced bilingual speaker (Poplack, 1978/81), code-switching was categorized according to the degree of integration of items from one language (L_1) to the phonological, morphological and syntactic patterns of the other language (L_2).

Because the balanced bilingual has the option of integrating his utterance into the patterns of the other language or preserving its original shape, items such as those in (1) below, which preserve English phonological patterns, were considered examples of code-switching in that study, while segments such as those in (2) which are adapted to Puerto Rican Spanish patterns, were considered to be instances of monolingual Spanish discourse.[2]

(1) a. Leo un MAGAZINE. [mægə'ziyn]
       'I read a magazine'.
    b. Me iban a LAY OFF. [lɛ́y ɔ̀hf]
       'They were going to lay me off'.
(2) a. Leo un *magazine*. [maɣa'siŋ]
       'I read a magazine'.
    b. Me iban a dar *layoff* ['leiof]
       'They were going to lay me off'.

In the ensuing sections we explore code-switching on a community-wide basis, focusing on speakers of varying bilingual abilities. Inclusion in the sample of non-fluent bilinguals requires modifying our previous definition of code-switching. In the speech of non-fluent bilinguals, segments may remain unintegrated into L_2 on one or more linguistic levels, due to transference of patterns from L_1. This combination of features leads to what is commonly known as a 'foreign accent', and is detectable even in the monolingual L_2 speech of the speaker, as in (3) below, which was rendered wholly in Puerto Rican Spanish phonology:

(3) That's what he said. [da 'waɾi se] (58/100)[3]

In order to consider an utterance such as (3), which occurs in an otherwise entirely Spanish context, as a code-switch from Spanish into English, we have refined the criteria for identifying a code-switch in terms of the type of integration as in Table 9.1.

The example of Type I, *mogueen*, is phonologically (phon), morphologically (morph) and syntactically (syn) integrated into the base language, although etymologically a loan word from English 'mug'. It is here considered an instance of monolingual Spanish discourse. In contrast, Type 4 segments are totally unintegrated into the patterns of the base language. This sort of code-switch occurs most typically in the speech of balanced bilinguals. Type 2 follows English phonological and morphological patterns, but violates English syntactic patterns. The example shown follows the Spanish syntactic pattern of adjective placement. This type of segment is also considered a code-switch into English, although one which violates the 'equivalence constraint'. Although Type 3

Table 9.1   Identification of code-switching according to type of integration into the base language *

| Type | Levels of integration into base language | | | Code-switch | Example |
	phon	morph	syn		
1	✓	✓	✓	no	Es posible que te MOGUEEN. (They might mug you.) (002/1)
2	–	–	✓	yes	Las palabras HEAVY-DUTY, bien grandes, se me han olvidado. (I've forgotten the real big, heavy-duty words.) (40/485)
3	✓	–	–	yes	[da 'waɾi se] (58/100)
4	–	–	–	yes	No creo que son FIFTY-DOLLAR SUEDE ONES. (I don't think they're fifty-dollar suede ones.) (05/271)

Note: * We follow Hasselmo (1970) in designating as the 'base' language that language to which a majority of phonological and morphological features of discourse can be attributed.

involves phonological integration into Spanish (i.e. follows Puerto Rican Spanish phonological rules), it is morphologically, syntactically and lexically English. Thus the example of Type 3 is considered a code-switch into English, rendered with a 'foreign accent'. Spontaneous switches of words, sentences and larger units at a turn boundary, not involving any change in interlocutors, were also considered to be code-switches if they exhibited Types 2, 3 or 4 of integration in Table 9.1.

3   Theoretical background

Much of the literature on code-switching (e.g. Gumperz and Hernández-Chávez, 1970; Gumperz, 1971a; 1976; McClure, 1977; Valdés-Fallis, 1976; 1978) has focused on its social and pragmatic functions. While there is little doubt that functional factors are the strongest constraints on the occurrence of code-switching, it is clear that linguistic factors also play a role. This paper demonstrates how the incorporation of both functional and linguistic factors into a single model is necessary to account for code-switching behaviour.

Although in some of the earlier literature (e.g. Lance, 1975) the occurrence of code-switching was characterized as random, most investigators now appear to agree that in many aspects it is rule-governed, despite the fact that there is little agreement on the precise nature of the rules involved. Proposed grammatical rules have generally taken the form of categorical constraints based on acceptability judgments of invented instances of code-switching (Gingràs, 1974; Timm, 1975; Gumperz, 1976). While acceptability judgments provide a manageable way to tap community grammar norms, their use is questionable in the case of an overtly stigmatized sociolinguistic marker, as is the case of code-switching (Gumperz, 1971a). Moreover, studies of code-switching performance in two widely separated bilingual communities have independently yielded counterexamples to these categorical constraints (Pfaff, 1975; 1976; Poplack, 1978/81).

More importantly, the proposed constraints are not of the general nature one would wish to ascribe to linguistic universals.[4] In Poplack (1978/81) two syntactic constraints on code-switching were suggested, which together were general enough to account for all instances of code-switching in the Puerto Rican data on which that study was based, as well as the Chicano data on which the majority of the code-switching literature is based, and at the same time restrictive enough not to generate instances of non-occurring code-switches:

(a) *The free morpheme constraint*: Codes may be switched after any constituent in discourse provided that constituent is not a bound morpheme.[5] This constraint holds true for all linguistic levels but the phonological, for reasons explained above. Thus, a segment such as (4) may be produced, where the first syllable follows the Caribbean Spanish tendency to aspirate /s/ before voiceless consonants, while the second syllable follows English phonological patterns. This should be seen as aiming for, but missing, an English target, rather than a switch between two bound morphemes. However, items such as (5) where the Spanish bound morpheme -*iendo* ('-ing') is affixed to the English root 'eat', have not been attested in this or any other study of code-switching to my knowledge, unless one of the morphemes has been integrated phonologically into the language of the other.

    (4)   una buena EXCUSE [eh'kjuws]
           'a good excuse'
    (5)   *EAT – iendo
           'eating'

Included under this constraint are idiomatic expressions, such as *cross my fingers* [sic] *and hope to die* and *si Dios quiere y la virgen* ('God and the virgin willing') which are considered to behave like bound morphemes in that they show a strong tendency to be uttered monolingually.

(b) *The equivalence constraint*: Code-switches will tend to occur at points in discourse where juxtaposition of L_1 and L_2 elements does not violate a syntactic rule of either language, i.e. at points around which the surface structures of the two languages map onto each other. According to this simple constraint, a switch is inhibited from occurring within a constituent generated by a rule from one language which is not shared by the other.[6] This can be seen in Figure 9.1, where the dotted lines indicate permissible switch points and the arrows indicate ways in which constitutents from two languages map onto each other. The speaker's actual utterance is reproduced in (C).

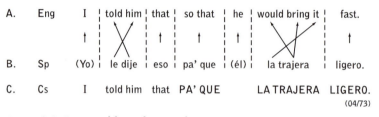

A.   Eng   I │ told him │ that │ so that │ he │ would bring it │ fast.

B.   Sp   (Yo) │ le dije │ eso │ pa' que │ (él) │ la trajera │ ligero.

C.   Cs   I   told him   that PA' QUE   LA TRAJERA LIGERO.
                                                                (04/73)

Figure 9.1 Permissible code-switching points

An analysis based on the equivalence constraint may be applied to the by now classical examples in (6) which were constructed by Gingràs (1974) and tested for acceptability on a group of Chicano bilinguals.

> (6) a. El MAN que CAME ayer WANTS JOHN comprar A CAR nuevo.
>   'The man who came yesterday wants John to buy a new car.'
>   b. Tell Larry QUE SE CALLE LA BOCA.
>   'Tell Larry to shut his mouth.'

Gingràs claims that (6a), in which codes are switched after almost every other word, is 'in some very basic sense different' from (6b), where the switching occurs between major constituents (1974: 170). While it is true, as we will see below, that major constituents are switched more frequently than smaller ones, we suggest that constituent size only partially explains the difference between the two sentences, and that the important distinction is with respect to the equivalence constraint.[7] The sentence structures in (6a) and (6b) are similar in that both include a verb phrase and a verb phrase complement. In each, the verbs belong to a class which in English requires that an infinitive complementizer rule apply to the verb phrase complement, while Spanish makes use of a subjunctive complementizer in this same construction.

Sentence (6a) violates the equivalence constraint because it applies an English infinitive complementizer rule, which is not shared by Spanish, to the verb phrase complement. Because the code switch did take place in this invented example, an

English rule was lexicalized in Spanish, yielding a construction which could not have been generated by a Spanish rule, and which is therefore ungrammatical by Spanish standards. On the other hand, the first portion of (6a) was generated by rules which are shared by English and Spanish (i.e. marked for both L_1 and L_2). The L_1 and L_2 versions map onto each other, constituent-by-constituent and element-by-element. A code-switch may therefore occur at any point within the main clause and the utterance remains grammatical by both L_1 and L_2 standards. Structures in discourse to which a rule from L_1 but not from L_2 must categorically apply were found to be avoided as switch points by the balanced bilingual. There were no cases like (6a) in our data, and furthermore, all 26 of Gingràs' Chicano informants found it to be unacceptable as well. Constituents whose structures are non-equivalent in L_1 and L_2 tend to be uttered monolingually in actual performance. This occurred in (C) in Figure 9.1 (as well as in Gingràs' example (6b)), where the verb phrase complements have undergone the Spanish subjunctive complementizer rule and are also lexicalized completely in Spanish. Ninety-four per cent of Gingràs' informants also found (6b) to be an acceptable utterance.

An additional site of non-equivalence in (6a) is the object noun phrase in the embedded sentence: A CAR *nuevo*. English and Spanish have non-equivalent rules for adjective movement. In English, attributive adjectives typically precede the head noun, whereas in Spanish they typically follow it. A closed set of Spanish adjectives may also precede the noun. Switching an adjective but not the noun within the noun phrase, by following *either* L_1 or L_2 adjective placement rules for adjectives other than those in the closed set, results in a construction which is judged unacceptable by Timm's Chicano informants (1975: 479) and 'fairly unacceptable' by Gingràs' informants (1974: 172). Such constructions occur very rarely in our own performance data.

Simultaneous operation of the free morpheme and the equivalence constraints permits only code-switched utterances which, when translated into either language, are grammatical by both L_1 and L_2 standards, and indicate a large degree of competence in both languages.

One might ask then whether the formulation of these constraints was not simply a consequence of having studied a balanced bilingual speaker: it is not surprising, although it required empirical proof, that an individual with an extensive repertoire in more than one language can manipulate them without violating the grammatical rules of either. But what happens in the case of non-fluent bilinguals? Being clearly dominant in one of the two languages, are they forced to switch into it from time to time because of lack of lexical or syntactic availability when speaking the other?

Weinreich (1953) characterized the ideal bilingual as an individual who 'switches from one language to the other according to appropriate changes in the speech situation (interlocutor, topics, etc.) but not in an unchanged speech situation, and CERTAINLY NOT WITHIN A SINGLE SENTENCE' (p. 73; emphasis added).

He further speculated that there must be considerable individual differences between those who have control over their switching and those who have difficulty in maintaining or switching codes as required (p. 73).

The phenomenon of code-switching has been a point of contention in assessing community identity. While intellectuals have seen language mixture as constituting evidence of the disintegration of the Puerto Rican Spanish language and culture (e.g. de Granda, 1968; Varo, 1971), community members themselves appear to consider various bilingual behaviours to be defining features of their identity (Attinasi, 1979). The opinion that code-switching represents a deviation from some bilingual 'norm' is also wide-spread in educational circles today (LaFontaine, 1975). It is our contention here that code-switching is itself a norm in specific speech situations which exist in stable bilingual communities. Furthermore, as we will demonstrate, satisfaction of this norm requires considerably more linguistic competence in two languages than has heretofore been noted.

The present study addresses these issues by analysing the code-switching behaviour of twenty Puerto Rican speakers of varying degrees of reported and observed bilingual ability.

4   Hypothesis

As documented in Poplack (1978/81), a single individual may demonstrate more than one configuration or type of code-switching. One type involves a high proportion of intra-sentential switching, as in (7) below.

> (7) a. Why make Carol SENTARSE ATRAS PA' QUE (sit in the back so) everybody has to move PA' QUE SE SALGA (for her to get out)? (04/439)
>
> b. He was sitting down EN LA CAMA, MIRANDONOS PELEANDO, Y (in bed, watching us fighting and) really, I don't remember SI EL NOS SEPARO (if he separated us) or whatever, you know. (43/412)

We refer to this as a more complex or 'intimate' type, since a code-switched segment, and those around it, must conform to the underlying syntactic rules of two languages which bridge constituents and link them together grammatically.

Another, less intimate type, is characterized by relatively more tag switches and single noun switches. These are often heavily loaded in ethnic content and would be placed low on a scale of translatability, as in (8).

> (8) a. Vendía arroz (He sold rice) 'N SHIT. (07/79)
>
> b. Salían en sus carros y en sus (They would go out in their cars and in their) SNOWMOBILES. (08/192)

Many investigators do not consider switches like those in (8) to represent true instances of code-switching, but rather to constitute an emblematic part of the speaker's monolingual style (Gumperz, 1971a; Wentz, 1977). It will also be noted that their insertion in discourse has few, if any, ramifications for the remainder of the sentence. Tags are freely moveable constituents which may be inserted almost anywhere in the sentence without fear of violating any grammatical rule. The ease with which single nouns may be switched is attested to by the fact that of all grammatical categories, they have been found to be the most frequently switched (e.g. Timm, 1975; Wentz, 1977).

It was found that the choice of intimate versus emblematic code-switching is heavily dependent on the ethnic group membership of the interlocutor in the case of the balanced bilingual, who has the linguistic ability to make such a choice. In-group membership favours intra-sentential code-switching, while non-group membership favours emblematic switching. In other words, that type of switch which all investigators agree to be 'true' instances of code-switching was mainly reserved for communication with another in-group member. In considering whether this pattern holds true more generally, we first note that the type of code-switching used by non-fluent bilinguals must be further constrained by bilingual ability. The research described in the following sections examines the extent to which the bilingual competence evinced by the skilled code-switching behaviour of a balanced bilingual is shared by the non-fluent bilinguals in the same speech community. This will have ramifications for the possible use of code-switching as an indicator of bilingual ability.

With the inclusion of non-fluent bilinguals in the sample, three alternative outcomes may be hypothesized. The speaker may engage in both intimate (intra-sentential) and emblematic switching, regardless of her competence in the two languages, thereby running the risk of rendering utterances which will be ungrammatical for L_1, L_2 or both (and hence providing a principled basis for the claim that code-switching represents a deviation from some norm). On the other hand, the speaker may avoid those intra-sentential switches which are syntactically risky. This might assure grammatical utterances. Such results would weaken the claims that code-switching occurs due to lack of availability in L_2. Logically, there is a third possibility, that the speaker will not switch at all. This need not be considered; although two members of the sample switched only once each in two-and-a-half hours of speech, there was no one who did not switch at all.

5   The sample

5.1   Block description

102nd Street is located in the heart of El Barrio, one of the oldest and until recently the largest Puerto Rican community in the United States. Although

Puerto Ricans have now dispersed to other areas of Manhattan and other boroughs in New York City, we estimate that the population on 102nd Street is still at least 95% Puerto Rican.

The block, which is identified by the census to be one of the lowest socio-economic areas of the City, is largely residential. It consists of 16 three- to five-storey tenements housing some 600 people, and is bounded by major avenues on the East and West. There is a small number of commercial establishments on the block, including two *bodegas*, an *alcapurria* stand, two Hispanic social clubs, a numbers parlor, a pet store, a vegetable market, and a plumbing supply shop.

Block life is active. It is not uncommon to see groups of people congregating on the stoops, and in the summer months, children play in the streets and adults set up tables on the sidewalks for domino games.

The block has had a stable Puerto Rican population since the 1930s, and today includes third- and even fourth-generation family members. Although uncharacteristically homogeneous with regard to ethnicity, block residents are heterogeneous with regard to personal history. About half of the block residents were born and raised in Puerto Rico. These are mostly older people, who tend to be Spanish dominant or monolingual. The younger people were generally born and raised in El Barrio, and most are either English dominant or bilingual. This fact and the low median age of the population (three-fourths are under 45 years of age) match the general demographic characteristics of the New York City Puerto Rican population in general (United States Department of Labor, 1975: 44).

Extended participant observation of 102nd Street indicates that block residents may be divided into nine social networks, which though not mutually exclusive, are seen to reappear consistently in the public life of the block. The informants for this study are drawn from two of the more closely observed of these networks.

Half of the sample belongs to a network centered around the *Gavilanes* social club. Participants in this network are linked through friendship or familial ties as well as participation in common club activities. The group is male-dominated, and its members are on public display more than other block residents since they are out on the street for large periods of the day. Members range in age from the early twenties to the fifties and most of the males were employed during the period of observation (1975–1977). (Only one female in the present sample had paid employment during this time.) The group includes both the Island-born and raised, who are Spanish dominant, and New York City-born and raised, who are English-dominant or bilingual. Group members generally accommodate to the older, Island-born members by speaking Spanish.

An additional eight informants belong to a network whose members congregate around the numbers parlor (*Banca*), a center of lively social activity on the block. Calling the numbers and passing them on by word-of-mouth (in Spanish) is a daily event in block life. Like members of the *Gavilanes* group, *Banca* group members range in age from the twenties to the fifties; however, both men and women participate in this network. Friendship and familial ties are less of a factor in linking group members than shared participation in activities in and around the *Banca*. Members of this network were all born and raised in Puerto Rico, and are Spanish-dominant or bilingual. *Banca* members were for the most part unemployed during the period of observation.

Of the two remaining informants, one does not participate in any network significantly more than in any other, and the second is a recent arrival to the block. Both are Spanish-dominant.

5.2   The informants

The twenty informants in the sample were selected primarily on the basis of two parameters: age of arrival in the United States, and (ethnographically) observed language preference. This choice was made in order to study the effects of bilingual ability and community influence on code-switching. Sample members are fairly evenly divided between:

- those who arrived as children or were born in the United States (0–6 years of age), when parental influence on child language use is greatest;
- those who arrived as pre-adolescents (7–12), when peer influence encroaches on parental influence;
- those who arrived as adolescents (13–17), when peer influence on language choice is greatest (Payne, 1976; Poplack, 1978); and
- those who arrived as adults, when patterns of language use tend to have crystallized.

About half of the speakers were observed to be Spanish-dominant; about 10% English-dominant; and the rest bilingual. With some exceptions these observations confirm the speakers' own self-reports (cf. Section 5.4 below).

In addition, several other demographic, ethnographic and attitudinal factors which could affect language use were studied.

5.3   Demographic characteristics of the sample

Eleven of the twenty informants are male, nine are female, and 75% of them are between 21 and 40 years of age. Regardless of age of arrival, all but two have spent ten years or more in the United States, and the majority (60%) has been there for more than twenty years. Since duration of stay is probably overshadowed by other influences on linguistic behaviour after about two years (Heidelberger Forschungsprojekt 'Pidgin-Deutsch', 1977), the level of competence in English of this group is not likely to change much with increased residence in the United States.

Most of the sample (65%) have also spent ten or more years in Puerto Rico, either early in life (only one informant was born in the United States), or including extended sojourns after having migrated to the continental United States. There is some correlation between speaker age and time spent in Puerto Rico: the older speakers are generally those who have spent most time on the Island. However, the majority of the sample (70%) visits the Island infrequently: less than every two years. In sum, it is reasonable to expect that these speakers have all also acquired some competence in Spanish, whether it is put to use at present or not.

Sample members report more years of schooling than the general Puerto Rican population in New York City. Seventy percent have had at least some high school education; this includes 20% who have either graduated high school or had some college education.

Slightly less than half the sample was employed at the time of the study, and these mainly in the service sectors of the workforce: baker, cook, medical technician, counterman, etc. Of these, the majority (70%) is employed off the block.

5.4   Language-oriented characteristics of the sample

The informants responded to a language-attitude questionnaire, designed to tap various aspects of language skill by self-report as well as community attitudes towards Puerto Rican language and ethnicity.

When asked if they considered themselves 'mainly Spanish speakers, English speakers, or bilinguals', slightly more than half (55%) of the sample claimed to be mainly Spanish speakers. The others considered themselves bilingual. No one claimed to be mainly an English speaker, reflecting the underrating on the part of speakers of their English language skills. There is doubtless some correlation between this finding and the fact that all speakers report having learned Spanish in early childhood (between the ages of two and seven), with the majority (75%) having learned it in Puerto Rico. On the other hand, only two informants learned English in early childhood. Sixty percent of the sample learned English between the ages of seven and 21, and all speakers report having learned English in the United States. When asked to rate their competence in both Spanish and English on a seven-point scale, speakers' ratings are consistent with their verbal self-description. Almost all (95%) rate themselves as having more than median proficiency in Spanish, while less than half (45%) claim this for English. If the hypothesis that code-switching is caused by lack of availability in L_2 were correct, it would appear that members of this sample population would favour switching into Spanish from an English base.

5.5   Attitudinal characteristics of the sample

Our language-attitude questionnaire also seeks to tap speakers' feelings towards language as it relates to Puerto Rican culture and ethnicity. Responses to attitude questions are less readily interpretable than reports of language use. On an ethnic-identity scale based on questions about pride in being Puerto Rican, feelings towards assimilation and speakers' characterization of nationality (e.g. Puerto Rican, *Nuyorican*, American, etc.), the majority (65%) revealed clear positive identification as Puerto Ricans. When asked to assess how important the Spanish language is to 'Puerto Ricanness', 90% felt that Spanish is 'important' or 'very important' to being a Puerto Rican. This attitude was summarized by Sally:

> SI TU ERES PUERTORRIQUEÑO (if you're Puerto Rican), your father's a Puerto Rican, you should at least DE VEZ EN CUANDO (sometimes), you know, HABLAR ESPAÑOL (speak Spanish). (34/25)

Nevertheless, a majority (60%) also felt that Puerto Rican monolingual English speakers did not represent a divisive force in the Puerto Rican community in New York City.

When asked if there was 'anything you could say in Spanish that you could not say in English', or vice-versa, 60% of the speakers felt that there was nothing that could be said in one language that could not be translated into the other. For the most part (75%), the speakers in this sample are also aware that code-switching is a frequent and wide-spread phenomenon in their community. When asked if they thought that 'few, some or many speakers mixed languages', three-fourths of the sample thought that many people code-switched. Such awareness of community and individual behavioural norms with regard to code-switching was again voiced by Sally, who provided the title for this paper.

> Sometimes I'll start a sentence in Spanish Y TERMINO EN ESPAÑOL [sic] ('and finish in Spanish'). (34/489)[8]

This opinion corroborates Pedraza's ethnographic observation that a majority of block residents code-switched somewhat or frequently.

In sum, although the Spanish language is overwhelmingly considered an integral part of being Puerto Rican, and in spite of the fact that only a minority feels that one or the other of the languages may be better for saying certain things, ethnographic observation, quantitative sociolinguistic analysis, and speakers' own self-reports all indicate that code-switching is an integral part of community speech norms on 102nd Street. Code-switches provoked by lack of availability or utilized as an emblem of ethnic identity appear, then, to be only weak factors in speakers' perception of their own behaviour.

6   Methodology

6.1   Data collection

The quantitative analyses which follow are based on recorded speech data in both interview and 'natural' settings. Pedraza's membership in the Puerto Rican community and his familiarity with the setting and participants allowed him to enter local network situations, such as domino games or *bochinche* (gossip) sessions, and simply turn on his tape-recorder without causing an apparent break in the conversational flow. In addition, he carried out a 'sociolinguistic interview'[9] with each informant aiming to elicit casual, undirected speech, and administered the detailed attitude questionnaire mentioned above. Our data, then, range from the vernacular speech of informal, intra-group communication, to the more formal discourse used in discussing concepts such as language and culture.

The importance of data-collection techniques cannot be overemphasized, particularly in the study of a phenomenon such as code-switching, which cannot be directly elicited. The actual occurrence of a switch is constrained, probably more than by any other factor, by the norms or the perceived norms of the speech situation. The most important of these norms for the balanced bilingual was found (Poplack, 1978/81) to be the ethnicity of the interlocutor, once other criteria (appropriateness, formality of speech situation) were met. The balanced bilingual speaker switched four times as frequently with an in-group interlocutor as with a non-member and, what is more, used a much larger percentage of intimate switches with the in-group member. Since the data utilized in this study are representative of in-group interaction only, they are presumably characterized not only by a higher rate of code-switching, but also by a larger proportion of intra-sentential switches, than would have been the case if they had been collected by a non-member.

6.2   Coding procedures

Sixty-six hours of tape-recorded speech in which each informant participated in each of the three speech situations provided 1,835 instances of code-switching. Transcription, coding and analysis of the data were carried out with the invaluable collaboration of Alicia Pousada. The informants appeared on tape, either alone or in a group, from a minimum of two-and-a-half hours to a maximum of eleven hours. Each instance of a switch was coded as to its syntactic function in the utterance, along with the syntactic categories of the segments which preceded and followed it. We also noted the language of the switch, whether it was preceded or followed by editing phenomena (hesitations, false starts, etc.), whether it constituted a repetition of the preceding syntactic category, whether it was a single noun switch in an otherwise L_2 base, and if so, whether it was an ethnically loaded item.

In each instance, the largest complete constituent next to the switch in the syntactic derivation of the utterance was considered to be the syntactic category of the segment adjacent to the switch. Thus, *con los puños* in (9a) was coded as a prepositional phrase preceded by an independent clause and followed by a tag. *Promising* in (9b) was coded as a verb preceded by an auxiliary and followed by an object noun phrase, since all of them are dominated by the same verb phrase node. *Que* in (9c) was coded as a subordinate conjunction preceded by an independent clause and followed by a subordinate clause. This method was used to determine syntactic category of the code-switch and segment following it as well.

(9) a. But I wanted to fight her CON LOS PUÑOS (with my fists), you know. (43/356)

b. Siempre está PROMISING cosas. (He's always promising things.) (04/408)

c. I could understand QUE (that) you don't know how to speak Spanish. ¿VERDAD? (right?). (34/24)

Other segments of varying syntactic make-up, but which exercised a consistent function in discourse, were coded according to that function. Examples of these are fillers, e.g. *este* (umm), *I mean*; interjections, e.g. ¡ay, Dios mio! (oh, my God!), *shit!*; tags, e.g. ¿entiendes? (understand?), *you know*; idiomatic expressions, e.g. *y toda esa mierda* (and all that shit), *no way*; quotations, e.g. put down '*menos*' (less). These are segments which are less intimately linked with the remainder of the utterance, insofar as they may occur freely at any point in the sentence. As will be seen, they contrast with the intra-sentential switches, which must obey sentence-internal syntactic constraints.

Certain switched segments were larger than a single constituent, as in (10) below. Hasselmo (1970) has called this 'unlimited switching'. These cases, which were relatively rare, required special coding conventions. The only type with non-negligible frequency involved moveable constituents like *sometimes* and *honey* in (10). Since these constituents do not form an integral part of the syntactic structure of the sentence, they were relegated to the category of intervening material between the switch and the adjacent syntactic categories, and the switches were considered to have occurred between the independent clause and the adverb in (10a), and between the verb phrase and the adverbial phrase in (10b).

(10) a. No tienen ni tiempo (they don't even have time) SOMETIMES FOR THEIR OWN KIDS, AND YOU KNOW WHO I'M TALKING ABOUT. (04/17)

b. Se sentó (he sat down), HONEY, AWAY FROM US. (04/433)

In a case like (11), utterances were divided by sentence boundary. *Pa' muchos sitios* was coded as a switched prepositional phrase in Spanish preceded by an independent clause and followed by a sentence.[10] *With my husband* was coded as a switched prepositional phrase in English preceded by an independent clause and followed by a pause.

> (11) And from there I went to live PA' MUCHOS SITIOS (in a lot of places). Después viví en la ciento diecisiete (then I lived on 117th) WITH MY HUSBAND. (42/76)

It will be noted that the analysis in (11) involves a change of base language. The first prepositional phrase is considered a switch into Spanish from an English base, while the second is considered a switch into English from a Spanish base. While speakers who are dominant in one language show a strong tendency to switch into L_2 from an L_1 base, more balanced bilinguals often alternate base languages within the same discourse.[11] An example of this can be seen in (12) which represents a single discourse, and where segments to the left of the slashes exhibit a base language different from those to the right of the slashes.

> (12) But I used to eat the BOFE, the brain. And then they stopped selling it because TENIAN, ESTE, LE ENCONTRARON QUE TENIA (they had, uh, they found out that it had) worms. I used to make some BOFE! / Después yo hacía uno d'esos (then I would make one of those) CONCOCTIONS: THE GARLIC con cebolla, y hacía un mojo, y yo dejaba que se curara eso (with onion, and I'd make a sauce, and I'd let that sit) FOR A COUPLE OF HOURS. / Then you be drinking and eating that shit. Wooh! It's like eating anchovies when you're drinking. Delicious! (04/101)

6.3   Non-code-switches

Certain borderline alternations between L_1 and L_2 were excluded from this study. One type involves switched items which have been referred to by Hasselmo (1970) as socially integrated into the language of the community: segments which are repeated often enough in a certain language to be regarded as habitualized. These may or may not be phonologically integrated into the base language; and should not be confused with the types of integration shown in Table 9.1:

> (13) a. Ay, ¡qué CUTE [kju] se ve! (34/202)
>   'How cute he looks!'
>   b. Eso es un TEAM [tiŋ]: 'Palo Viejo'. (37/42)
>   'That's a a team: "Palo Viejo".'

    c. En ese tiempo había muchos JUNKIES [jɔŋki]. (34/40)
       'At that time there were a lot of junkies.'

Switches into L_2 designating food names, proper names and place names were also omitted from this study, except when there was an acceptable L_2 alternative which was not used, e.g. *Puerto Rico* [pɔɔə'əiykow] ~ [pwɛrtə'xikɔ].

Also excluded were translations in response to requests for information, as in (14a), L_2 segments followed by an explanation in L_1, as in (14b), switches accompanied by metalinguistic comments, as in (14c), and instances of 'externally conditioned switching' (Clyne, 1972: 70) in which the interlocutor switched languages within the same discourse and the informant followed suit, as in (14d).

  (14) a. *A:* Lo pusieron un . . . ¿cómo se dice? ¿un tutone?
              (They gave him a – how do you call it? tuton?)
           B: TUTOR? (52/229)
        b. But I used to eat the BOFE, the brain. (04/101)
        c. I'm one of those real what you call in Spanish PENDEJAS
            (jerks), you know. (04/158)
        d. *A:* I had a dream yesterday, last night.
           B: ¿DE QUE NUMERO? (What number?)
           A: EL CERO SETENTA Y CINCO. (Zero seventy-five.) (34/040)

6.4   Quantitative analysis of the data

We are concerned here with both linguistic and extra-linguistic questions, and we shall attempt to incorporate the answers into a single analytic model. The linguistic questions concern the surface configuration of the switches. Are there some sorts of constituents in discourse which can be switched and others which cannot? Are there constituents which tend to be switched into one language rather than the other? In what ways do switched items combine with unswitched portions of discourse?

The extra-linguistic questions concern the code-switchers. Can the community as a whole be characterized by some code-switching type, or are there speakers who favour certain switch types over others? In the latter case, what are the demographic, attitudinal, and social factors which contribute to the occurrence of one type over another, and what is the comparative effect of each?

To answer these questions the following quantitative analyses were performed on the data. The syntactic category of the switched item was cross-tabulated first with the preceding and then the following syntactic category to ascertain whether certain points (as, for example, the point between determiner and noun) in discourse were more favourable to the occurrence of a switch than others. Also cross-tabulated were switched item by language, to see if certain switch types were favoured by one language over another, and switched item by speaker, to see if there was any difference in switching behaviour among speakers.

The cross-tabulations revealed that speakers could be divided into two groups: one which favoured extra-sentential switches, and another which tended towards the intra-sentential, or more intimate type. The code-switching data were subsequently collapsed into two categories: intra-sentential and extra-sentential switches. These categories were then cross-tabulated individually with the demographic, attitudinal and language-oriented characteristics of the informants to discover which, if any, have an influence on the choice of one code-switch over the other. Tests of association were applied to each of these cross-tabulations to determine the significance of the extra-linguistic factors for the occurrence of one code-switching type over the other.

Having thus been able to determine a dependent variable (in this case, code-switch type), its relevant variants (intra-sentential and extra-sentential code-switching), and the total population of utterances in which the variation occurs (i.e. the total corpus of switched items), the significance tests made it possible to suggest which extra-linguistic factors might reasonably be expected to affect the relative frequency of the two types of code-switches. Because these factors may be correlated among themselves within the sample and have correlated effects on code-switching type, it was then necessary to use multivariate statistical techniques to determine which factors made a significant contribution, independent of the effects of other factors, to the choice of code-switch type. Because of the binomial nature of the data and their uneven distribution among the different possible configurations of factors, a maximum likelihood approach was taken for the evaluation of factor effects, together with log-likelihood tests of significance.

7   Results

Perhaps the most striking result of this study is that there were virtually no instances of ungrammatical combinations of L_1 and L_2 in the 1,835 switches studied regardless of the bilingual ability of the speaker.

Our hypotheses as to the nature of syntactic constraints on code-switching in the speech of the balanced bilingual, i.e. the free morpheme constraint and the equivalence constraint, are generally corroborated by the present investigation of both balanced and non-fluent bilinguals. There were no examples of switches between bound morphemes of the type *eat -iendo mentioned in (5) above. A small number (five, or less than 1% of the data) of switches within idiomatic expressions did occur, however, as in (15a), where a Spanish expression is broken up, and (15b), where an English expression is broken up.

(15) a. Estamos como marido y WOMAN. (We are like man and wife.
          < Sp. Estamos como *marido y mujer*.) (05/141)
      b. Mi mai tuvo que ir a firmar y SHIT pa' sacarme, YOU KNOW.
          (My mom had to go sign *'n shit* to get me out, you know.)
          (07/058)

A small number of switches which violated the equivalence constraint also
occurred (11, or less than 1% of the data). The majority (7/11) of these involved
adjective placement, a rule which is not shared by L_1 and L_2. This can be seen in
(16a), where adjective placement follows Spanish but not English rules, and (16b),
where the reverse is true.

(16) a. Tenían patas flacas, pechos FLAT. (They had skinny legs, flat
          chests.) (09432)
      b. I got a lotta BLANQUITO (whitey) friends. (34/274)

A strong tendency to avoid non-equivalence is nonetheless manifested in the
fact that 88% (49/56) of the adjectival forms in the corpus are either predicate
adjectives, which have equivalent surface structures in Spanish and English, or
members of the subset of Spanish adjectives which precede the noun, as in
English.

The proportion of switched items which when combined with the rest of the
utterance did not follow grammatical rules shared by both L_1 and L_2 is negligible.
(Of this small number, NONE of the constructions was idiosyncratic, or based on
rules which were not drawn from one or the other of the grammars.) This finding
is strong evidence that alternation between two languages requires a high level of
bilingual competence. Code-switching involves enough knowledge of two (or
more) grammatical systems to allow the speaker to draw from each system only
those rules which the other shares, when alternating one language with another.
Surprisingly enough, this knowledge appears to be shared by even the non-fluent
bilinguals in the sample. The way in which these latter speakers are able to fulfill
the requirement of grammaticality, despite their limited competence in one of the
codes, is examined in Section 7.5 below.

7.1   Discourse functions of code-switching

The finding that code-switching constitutes the skilled manipulation of overlapping sections of two (or more) grammars is further corroborated by an examination of some of the ways in which a code-switch functions in discourse. One of
the characteristics of skilled code-switching is a smooth transition between L_1 and
L_2 elements, unmarked by false starts, hesitations or lengthy pauses. When we
examine the data we find that the transition between the preceding category and

the switched item is made smoothly, i.e. with no editing phenomena, 96% of the time, while the transition between switched item and following syntactic category is made smoothly 98% of the time. Other characteristics of skilled code-switching include a seeming 'unawareness' of the alternation between languages, i.e. the switched item is not accompanied by metalinguistic commentary, it does not constitute a repetition of all or part of the preceding segment, nor is it repeated by the following segment; switches are made up of larger segments than just single nouns inserted into an otherwise L_2 sentence; and code-switching is used for purposes other than that of conveying untranslatable items.

On examining the data for the sample as a whole, we find that these characteristics are strongly in evidence: the switched item only constitutes a repetition of the preceding segment 5% of the time, while the following segment repeats all or part of the switched item only 8% of the time. Single noun switches constitute only 10% of the data; of these, less than one-fourth represent items which are ethnically loaded.

In other words, features known to be characteristic of communication with a non-group member, such as high percentages of single noun switches used to convey notions which are difficult to translate, are not defining features of intra-group communication.

7.2   Linguistic properties of switched segments

Having established that switching occurs in a smooth fashion, we turn our attention to the nature of the switches themselves. Which constituents are switched, and in what ways do they combine with preceding and following segments? Do certain combinations tend to occur more regularly?

Fifteen syntactic categories whose occurrence is dependent on sentence-internal constraints were extracted from the data, along with seven extra-sentential, or freely distributable categories. These appear in Table 9.2.

The relative frequencies with which constituents may be switched, indicated in Table 9.2, largely confirm the findings of other studies (Gumperz, 1976; Wentz, 1977; Poplack, 1978/81). As can be seen, full sentences are the most frequently switched constituent, making up 20% of the data. Extra-sentential code-switching types, which require less knowledge of two grammars since they are freely distributable within discourse, together constitute about half the data.

Among the intra-sentential switches, we find single nouns to be the most frequently switched category, again confirming the findings of other studies. Table 9.2 also reveals a tendency to switch major constituents, which account for about 60% of the intra-sentential data, more frequently than smaller ones. This provides additional support for the equivalence constraint, which predicts that whole constituents will be switched rather than elements within them if the syntactic rule for generating the constituent is not shared by both L_1 and L_2.

Table 9.2 Code-switching by syntactic category and language *

Syntactic category of CS (code-switch)	Number of CS from English to Spanish	Number of CS from Spanish to English	Percentage of total CS	N
determiner	3	0	0.2	3
(single) noun	34	141	9.5	175
subject noun phrase	44	25	3.8	69
object noun phrase	62	78	7.6	140
auxiliary	0	0	0.0	0
verb	6	13	1.0	19
verb phrase	27	13	2.2	40
independent clause	44	35	4.3	79
subordinate (and relative) clause	53	23	4.1	76
adjective	3	12	0.8	15
predicate adjective	6	37	2.3	43
adverb	14	33	2.6	47
preposition	2	0	0.1	2
phrases (prep. adj. advb. inf)	55	39	5.1	94
conjunctions (subordinate, coordinate, relative pronoun)	33	16	2.7	49
sentence	201	171	20.3	372
filler	9	11	1.1	20
interjection	26	89	6.3	115
idiomatic expression	8	23	1.7	31
quotation	20	14	1.9	34
tag	9	403	22.5	412
Totals	659	1176		1835

Intra-sentential spans the rows from *determiner* through *conjunctions*. *Extra-sentential* spans the rows from *sentence* through *tag*.

Note: * Nouns and verbs were counted as noun phrases or verb phrases respectively if they functioned within the utterance.

7.3   Language of the switch

Table 9.2 also shows the frequencies with which the syntactic categories under investigation are produced in each language. As can be seen, with a few exceptions, segments are about as likely to be switched into English as into Spanish, providing further evidence for the suggestion that the code-switching mode proceeds from a single grammar.

Examining the data in Table 9.2 more closely, we may test whether the rate of occurrence of a given syntactic category of a switch is significantly different from one language to the other. For this we compared a log-likelihood of a rate estimate for the two languages separately compared to that for the combined data. Significantly more switches from Spanish into English were found for four categories: tags, interjections, single nouns, and predicate adjectives. The latter is probably an artifact of sparse data, but the results for tags, interjections, and single nouns have important interpretations.

It is not surprising that bilinguals residing in an English-speaking society should favour English noun switches over Spanish. Interjections and tags, as will be shown in Section 7.5, are precisely the switch types which are favoured by Spanish-dominant speakers. These speakers not only switch almost uniquely into English from a Spanish base, but are also distinguishable from the bilinguals by the type of constituents they switch.

The statistical analysis shows that aside from the four switch types which are favoured from Spanish into English, most of the rest tend to be switched significantly more from English into Spanish. This result is an artifact of the other, however, and when the tag, interjection, and noun switches are removed from the data, almost all of the remaining switches show no significant rate differences between the two languages.

7.4   Combinability of switched segments

In order to ascertain points within the sentence at which segments may be switched, intra-sententially switched items were cross-tabulated with segments preceding and following them. In a 225-cell table generated by the 15 possibilities of syntactic category preceding the code-switch versus 15 syntactic categories for the code-switch itself, about 40% were filled; i.e. 88 different combinations of some constituent and another switched one occurred. Of the non-occurrent combinations, 40% were syntactically impossible (e.g. auxiliary + preposition); the remainder of the cells were empty due most probably to the distribution of the data – cells corresponding to relatively rare switch types and/or relatively rare preceding categories would not be expected to occur with this sample size.

The two most frequently recurring switch points among 681 tokens of intra-sentential code-switch + preceding category were between determiner and noun

(19%) and between verb phrase and object noun phrase (12%). This is not surprising since we already have evidence that nouns and noun phrases are frequently switched. Other combinations which recur frequently include independent clause and subordinate clause (4%), verb and predicate adjective (4%), and subject noun phrase and verb phrase (3%). The remaining combinations each represent 2% or less of the data. Similarly, 63 (28%) of the possible combinations occurred among the 729 tokens of code-switch + following category, the overwhelming majority of which also individually represented very small proportions of the data.

Because of the size of the data set, it is statistically unlikely that clearer patterns could emerge from such a large-celled table. With more data we might be able to predict frequencies with which code-switched items precede and follow specific constituents. We hypothesize that such frequencies would simply reflect the frequency of any given combination of constituents (e.g. adverb + adjective, preposition + noun phrase) in monolingual speech. This hypothesis could only be confirmed by evaluating the frequencies of all the possible constituent combinations in a large sample of monolingual speech, a task beyond the scope of the present research.

What information we do have, however, indicates that there is a rather large number of points within the sentence at which it is permissible to switch codes. This is additional evidence that code-switching requires knowledge of two systems. Note that there is about as much intra-sentential as extra-sentential switching (Table 9.2) in the corpus. While extra-sentential switching could presumably be accomplished by alternately drawing on rules from two separate grammars, intra-sentential code-switching would appear to depend on the juxtaposition of constituents too intimately connected to be generated separately by rules from two distinct grammars. This, together with the finding that only a very small number of switches are accompanied by breaks in the speech flow, lends strong support to the hypothesis that code-switching is in fact a verbal mode distinct from English-speaking and Spanish-speaking, yet which consists of the overlapping elements from both.

7.5   Differential behaviour of informants

Let us now examine the individual code-switching behaviour of the informants in the sample.

Table 9.3 shows the frequency with which speakers switch into English. It is striking that the Spanish-dominant speakers switch almost uniquely into English from an unambiguously Spanish base. Bilingual speakers, on the other hand, cluster around the half-way mark, with some switching somewhat more into Spanish from an English base, others the reverse. It is clear that these bilinguals cannot be said to have a single base or dominant language of discourse, but rather two.

Table 9.3 Percentage of code-switches into English for Spanish-dominant and bilingual speakers

Spanish-dominants

Informant	% of CS from Spanish to English	N				
Eli	100%	9				
Gui	100	35	*Bilinguals*			
Tera	100	1				
Isi	100	45		% of CS from		
Rosa	100	1		Spanish to		
Fela	97	69	*Informant*	English	N	
Charlie	94	33	Cal	100%	35	
Sami	93	93	Edo	99	212	
Chito	92	89	Apache	91	63	
Shorty	71	40	Pearl	57	135	
Wilda	63	127	Garra	53	15	
Average	92%	542	Candy	52	81	
			Lola	43	309	
			Melo	39	89	
			Sally	37	354	
			Average	63%	1293	N = 1,835

Note that three bilingual and two Spanish-dominant speakers (according to self-reports) show patterns which contrast with the other members of their respective groups. As will be seen again in the next section, four of these are speakers whose self-report of language dominance conflicted with our ethnographic and linguistic observations in this regard. The fifth, Edo, is in fact bilingual, but has strong feelings towards speaking Spanish, and has been observed to do so almost uniquely when interacting on the block.

7.5.1 *Differential behaviour of informants: switch type*

Let us now examine another way in which bilinguals differ from Spanish-dominant speakers. The switches in Table 9.2 were listed according to the presumed degree of bilingual proficiency required to produce them, in decreasing order. Lowest on the scale are tag-like switches. These include interjections, fillers, tags, and idiomatic expressions, all of which can be produced in L_2 with only minimal knowledge of the grammar of that language. Next on the scale are full sentences or larger segments, which require much more knowledge of L_2 to produce, although hypothetically, not as much as is required by the third category, intra-sentential switches. As suggested above in order to produce this latter sort of switch, the speaker must also know enough about the grammar of each language, and the way they interact, to avoid ungrammatical utterances.

Figure 9.2 graphs the percentages of each of these switch types for the informants in our sample.[12]

Figure 9.2 shows that reported language ability (which in all cases but four corresponds to observed ability) is an excellent indicator of code-switching patterns. Figure 9.2a shows that most of those who report that they know, feel more comfortable in, and use more Spanish than English, tend to switch into L_2 by means of tag-like constructions, sometimes to the practical exclusion of sentential or intra-sentential switches. Those who claim to be bilingual, on the other hand, show a reversal (Figure 9.2b). They favour large amounts of the switches hypothesized to require most knowledge of both languages, sentential and intra-sentential switches. The most favoured switch type for bilinguals is clearly intra-sentential, while the least favoured is tag-like switching.

The few exceptions to these patterns are represented by the dotted lines on the graphs. Two speakers who claimed to be Spanish-dominant in fact show a similar code-switching configuration to the bilinguals, while two who claim to be bilingual show patterns similar to the Spanish-dominants. Strikingly enough, these are precisely the cases where ethnographic observation and linguistic analysis were previously found to conflict with self-report, because the speakers underrated or overrated their ability in English. Two additional speakers are actually Spanish-dominant, but also show a code-switching pattern similar to that of the bilinguals. They do, however, have a greater degree of competence in English than those who follow the 'Spanish-dominant' pattern. Their switches tend to distribute among the three switch types, rather than show a marked preference for any one, and they may be considered to exhibit code-switching behaviour intermediate to the bilinguals and the more clearly Spanish-dominant speakers.

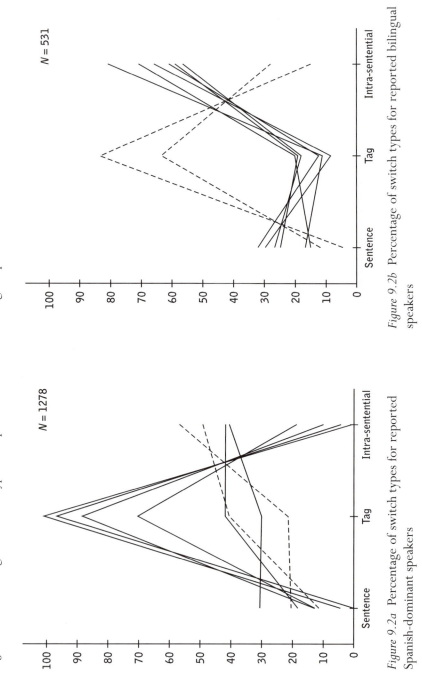

Figure 9.2 Percentages of switch types for Spanish-dominant and bilingual speakers

N = 1278

N = 531

Figure 9.2a Percentage of switch types for reported Spanish-dominant speakers

Figure 9.2b Percentage of switch types for reported bilingual speakers

8   Contribution of extra-linguistic factors to the occurrence of code-switch type

Having ascertained that reported and observed bilingual ability is an important factor in predicting the type of code-switch that will be uttered (a chi-square test shows this factor to be significant at the 0.001 level), we next attempted to determine which other extra-linguistic factors might have an effect on the occurrence of intra-sentential code-switching. Individual tests were performed on each factor group as well as each pair of factors within each group to determine their significance.

8.1   Sex

The sex of the speaker is a significant factor in predicting code-switch type at the 0.001 level. Women favour intra-sentential switching; over half (56%) of their switches are intra-sentential, while only one-third of the men's switches are of this type.

8.2   Age of L_2 acquisition and age of migration to the United States

These two factors were originally examined separately for each speaker. All informants learned Spanish in early childhood, though there was some variation in the age at which English was learned. Since there is a one-to-one correspondence between the age at which the speaker arrived in the United States and the age at which she learned English (not a surprising fact since all speakers report having learned English in the United States), these two factors were subsequently considered as one. On ethnographic grounds we had originally distinguished four ages of arrival/L_2 acquisition: early childhood (2–7), pre-adolescent (8–13), adolescent (14–18), and adult (over 18). Tests of association reveal that the difference between learning English/arriving in the United States as an adolescent or as an adult is not significant at the 0.05 level. Consequently, these two age groups were considered together. All the other age distinctions were significant at either 0.001 or the 0.01 levels.

Those speakers who learned both English and Spanish in early childhood, the 'true' bilinguals, show the highest percentage of intra-sentential switching (346/582, or 59%). Those who learned English between the ages of 8 and 13, show only a slightly lower percentage of this type of switch (309/593, or 52%), a small difference, but one which is nonetheless significant at the 0.01 level. Speakers who learned English after the age of 13, however, show a much lower percentage of intra-sentential switches (196/660, or 30%), a drop which is significant at the 0.001 level.

8.3 Reported bilingual ability

As we have already seen in Figure 9.1, reported (and observed) bilingual ability is an excellent predictor of code-switching type. Bilinguals produce a far greater percentage of intra-sentential switches (682/1293, or 53%) than those who are Spanish-dominant (169/542, or 31%). This difference is significant at the 0.001 level.

8.4 Education

Sample members were divided into three categories according to their educational attainment: those who had no more than primary school education (first through eighth grades), those who had some high school but did not graduate (ninth through eleventh grades), and those who graduated high school and/or attended some college. An initial test performed on this factor group revealed that it has an effect on code-switching which is significant at the 0.001 level. Speakers who had primary school education or less tended to switch intra-sententially slightly more (45%) than those who had some high school education (41%). This difference is not significant. High school graduates, however, switched intra-sententially more (60%) than either of the other two groups, a significant difference at the 0.001 level. Upon closer examination, however, it became apparent that although the category contained six speakers, all but five of the tokens (401/406) had been uttered by two bilingual women who had learned English as children. Sex, bilingual ability and age of L_2 acquisition are the three factors we have already seen to be highly correlated with choice of switch type.

8.5 Age

Sample members were divided into two groups: younger speakers (those between 20 and 40) and older speakers (those over 41). Speaker age was found not to be significant in predicting code-switch type.

8.6 Social network membership

All but two informants belong to two ethnographic networks we called the *Gavilanes* and the *Banca* groups, both of which include both Spanish-dominant and bilingual speakers. Network membership is not a significant factor in predicting code-switch type.

8.7 Ethnic identity

People were divided into those who scored low on a composite index measuring positive feelings towards Puerto Rican identity and those who obtained high scores. Those with positive feelings towards Puerto Rican ethnic identity switched codes intra-sententially somewhat more (446/881, or 51%) than those who had negative feelings (405/954). This difference is significant at the 0.001 level.

8.8   Continued contact with Puerto Rico

Sample members were also divided according to relative frequency of return visits to Puerto Rico. Those who return to the Island, where they must speak more Spanish than in New York, more frequently than once every two years, tend to switch intra-sententially far less (71/304, or 23%) than those who visit Puerto Rico less frequently than once every two years (780/1576, or 49%). This difference is significant at the 0.001 level. Further perusal of these categories, however, indicates that all speakers who migrated to the United States in early childhood (and hence tend towards bilingualism) return to Puerto Rico less frequently than once every two years, and that all those who return more frequently are Spanish-dominant, a distinction we have already seen to be significantly correlated with a low incidence of intra-sentential switching.

8.9   Workplace

A distinction was made between those informants who are employed off the block, where they must presumably interact in English, and those who are either unemployed or employed on the block, where they may communicate in English, Spanish or the code-switching mode. Those who work off the block switch intra-sententially only about a third of the time (167/460), while those who remain on the block engage in this switch type half of the time (684/1375), a difference which is significant at the 0.001 level. It is conceivable that those who spend the better part of the day in a speech situation where code-switching is not appropriate get less practice in switching and are therefore less skilled at it. More likely, however, since only Spanish-dominant speakers are employed off the block, it is this characteristic which undoubtedly accounts for the low percentage of intra-sentential switching by these speakers.

9   Multivariate analysis of code-switch type

Situations in which the data is poorly distributed, as is the case for the factors of education, continued contact with Puerto Rico, and workplace, can be as misleading. As we have seen, the apparently significant effect of one factor may really be mainly due to another, language dominance, a fact which is not brought out by looking at one factor at a time. Multivariate analysis can, within limits, separate out these overlapping effects, and extract the independent contributions proper to each of several related factors (Rousseau and Sankoff, 1978; Sankoff and Labov,

1979). It can also provide information on the statistical significance of the distinctions defining each factor group.

Let us now examine the comparative contribution of each extra-linguistic factor found by the factor-by-factor analysis to be significant in the prediction of code-switch type: sex, language dominance of speaker, age of arrival in the United States and age of L_2 acquisition, educational attainment, the speaker's feelings towards his own ethnicity, amount of continued contact with Puerto Rico, and location of work place.

To what extent are these extra-linguistic factors significant when considered simultaneously? To carry out this multivariate analysis we used VARBRUL 2 (Sankoff, 1975) to calculate factor effects and significance levels of factor groups. The factor effects combine to give the probability that a switch will be intra-sentential, according to the model $\dfrac{P}{1-p} = \dfrac{P_0}{1-p_0} \times \dfrac{P_1}{1-p_1} \times \ldots \times \dfrac{P_n}{1-p_n}$, where P_0 is a corrected mean parameter and $p_1, \ldots, p_n$ are the parameters representing the effects of factors $1, \ldots, n$ characterizing a given speaker. Factor probabilities vary between zero and 1, with figures higher than 0.5 favouring intra-sentential code-switching, and figures lower than 0.5 favouring extra-sentential code-switching. The higher the figure, the greater the contribution to rule application, so comparisons can easily be made between various factors and factor groups. The program also calculates the log-likelihood of the model under a given configuration of factor groups. Different analyses can then be compared to see whether the various factor groups contribute significantly to explaining the differential use of code-switching types among speakers.

In the preceding section we found seven factors that, when examined one by one, seemed to significantly affect code-switch type. Some of these factors, however, are clearly correlated among themselves. To see which ones could be considered to have an independent contribution to choice of code-switch type, we carried out 128 separate analyses, each one corresponding to a different combination of explanatory factors. By examining the log-likelihoods first of the seven one-factor analyses, then the 21 two-factor analyses, and so on, we could detect which factors contributed a significant independent effect to the explanation of the variation in the data.[13] The result of this was the four-factor analysis depicted in Table 9.4. Each of the four factors here has a strongly significant independent effect on choice of switch type, but the addition of any of the others: ethnic identity, education or continued contact with Puerto Rico, does not significantly increase the explanatory power of the model.

The comparative effect of the factors is of particular interest. As can be seen, reported and observed language dominance is the single factor which most affects the occurrence of this switch type. Bilinguals favour it the most, at 0.68, while those who are Spanish-dominant disfavour it, at 0.32. An almost equal effect is

Table 9.4 Contribution of extra-linguistic factors to the occurrence of intra-sentential code-switching; corrected mean: 0.36

Sex		Age of arrival L_2 acquisition		Language dominance		Work place	
Female	0.59	Child	0.55	Bilingual	0.68	On-block	0.67
Male	0.41	Pre-adolescent	0.55	Spanish	0.32	Off-block	0.33
		Adolescent	0.40				

shown by the factor of work place. Those who are unemployed or work on the block, where they engage in this discourse mode with other members of their social network, show a greater tendency to switch intra-sententially than those who work off the block. Table 9.4 shows that those speakers who acquired both languages in early childhood or pre-adolescence, a defining feature of the balanced bilingual, switch intra-sententially more (0.55) than those who learned L_2 at a later age.

Table 9.4 also indicates that women, who are often in the vanguard of linguistic change, favour intra-sentential switching more than men.

10   Discussion

We have shown how to incorporate both linguistic and extra-linguistic factors into a single analytical model to account for code-switching performance. The linguistic constraints on this phenomenon, the free morpheme and equivalence constraints, represent the basis on which the foregoing analysis was carried out.

The extra-linguistic factors contribute variably to the occurrence of one switch type over another. Choice of these factors arises from long-term familiarity with the members of the speech community, and on the basis of attitudinal and ethnographic studies carried out in the community.

An elementary, but crucial finding of this study is that there are virtually no ungrammatical combinations of L_1 and L_2 in the 1,835 switches studied, regardless of the bilingual ability of the speaker. This corroborates the hypothesis as to the nature of syntactic constraints on code-switching advanced in Poplack (1978/81), for both balanced and non-fluent bilinguals.

By showing that non-fluent bilinguals are able to code-switch frequently, yet maintain grammaticality in both L_1 and L_2 by favouring emblematic or tag-switching, we have also demonstrated empirically that code-switching is not monolithic behaviour. Three types of code-switching emerge in the speech performance studied, each characterized by switches of different levels of constituents, and each reflecting different degrees of bilingual ability. Multivariate analysis of extra-linguistic factors confirms that those speakers with the greatest degree of bilingual ability ('true' bilinguals) most favour intra-sentential code-switching, the type we had hypothesized to require most skill. The two Chicano code-switching studies of Gingràs (1974) and Pfaff (1975; 1976) also indirectly support these findings. Gingràs tested a group of Chicano and non-Chicano bilinguals on the acceptability of a series of constructed intra-sententially code-switched utterances. The Chicano bilinguals showed much higher rates of acceptance of his grammatical code-switches than the non-Chicanos. This led him to posit that there were probably code-switching norms peculiar to the Chicano community. While speech communities may be characterized by different code-switching norms, it was also the case that the Chicano group had learned both languages in early childhood, while the non-Chicano informants all learned English as adults. Bilinguals of the first type are precisely those we have shown to engage most in intra-sentential code-switching, a fact which concords with their high rate of acceptance of such switches. Similarly, of three samples of Chicano speakers studied, Pfaff found that those who engaged most in 'deep-s' (intra-sentential) switching were those whose speech was characterized by use of both Spanish and English.

Previous work (Gumperz 1971a; 1976; Valdés-Fallis, 1978; Poplack, 1978/81) has shown that code-switching may be used as a discourse strategy to achieve certain interactional effects at specific points during a conversation. The findings in the present chapter, together with the ethnographic observations that code-switching is a linguistic norm in the Puerto Rican community, suggest that this use is characteristic only of certain types of code-switching, which we call 'emblematic', including tags, interjections, idiomatic expressions, and even individual noun switches. On the other hand, a generalized use of intra-sentential code-switching may represent instead an overall discourse MODE. The very fact that a speaker makes alternate use of both codes itself has interactional motivations and implications beyond any particular effects of specific switches. Indeed, speaker attitudes toward use of Spanish, English and code-switching reported in Section 5.4 above do not offer any ready explanation for why a particular segment in discourse should be switched. McClure and Wentz (1975) have pointed out that 'there is apparently no real social motivation for, or significance attached to, the practice of code-switching [for example] subject pronouns alone' (p. 266). We agree that there is no 'good reason' (Wentz, 1977; e.g. pp. 143, 218) for switching subject pronouns, or lone determiners, etc. Nonetheless, such segments ARE switched by bilingual speakers. It may well be possible in some cases for the analyst to impute situational motivations or consequences to specific intra-sentential switches, but the evidence presented here suggests that this has little if any pertinence for the speakers themselves. More important, there is no need to require any social motivation for this type of code-switching, given that, as a discourse mode, it may itself form part of the repertoire of a speech community. It is then the choice (or not) of this mode which is of significance to participants rather than the choice of switch points. When these conditions are met, any segment in discourse may be switched, depending on the bilingual ability of the speaker, and provided it obeys the equivalence constraint. Thus, we cannot agree that switches of, say, object pronouns are 'non-sentences' of any language because 'they violate the social motivation for code-alternation in the first place' (McClure, n.d.: 265). They simply violate the equivalence constraint!

The suggestion that code-switching is itself a discrete mode of speaking, possibly emanating from a single code-switching grammar composed of the over-lapping sectors of the grammars of L_1 and L_2, is supported by several findings in the present study. We have shown that there is a large number of permissible switch points in the data, rather than a few favoured ones. Switching any given constituent in discourse does not necessarily entail continuation in the language of the switch, unless the surface structures are not equivalent in L_1 and L_2. Hence larger constituents are switched more frequently than smaller ones. It was additionally shown that all constituents are about as likely to be switched into L_1 as into L_2, with the few exceptions contingent upon the bilingual ability of the speaker.

In light of these findings, code-switching behaviour may be used to measure bilingual ability. Bilingual speakers might have expanding grammars of the type depicted in Figure 9.3, representing greater degrees of bilingual acquisition. Further empirical studies of code-switching performance in other bilingual communities would provide comparative data to test these hypotheses.

These findings, taken together and interpreted in terms of the equivalence constraint, provide strong evidence that code-switching is a verbal skill requiring a large degree of linguistic competence in more than one language, rather than a defect arising from insufficient knowledge of one or the other. The rule-governed nature of code-switching is upheld by even the non-fluent bilinguals in the sample. Their behaviour suggests at least enough passive competence in L_2 to switch codes by means of the few rules they know to be shared by both languages. It is also striking that precisely those switch types which have traditionally been considered most deviant by investigators and educators, those which occur within a single sentence, are the ones which require the most skill. They tend to be produced by the 'true' bilinguals in the sample: speakers who learned both languages in early childhood, and who have most ongoing contact with the monolingual English-speaking world.

  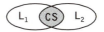

a. Inter-sentential switching   b. 'tag'-switching   c. Intra-sentential switching

Figure 9.3 Representation of bilingual code-switching grammars

Code-switching, then, rather than representing deviant behaviour, is actually a suggestive indicator of degree of bilingual competence.

Notes

1　92% (Bureau of the Census, 1973).

2　The reverse pattern, the insertion into an English base of Spanish items with English phonological or morphological patterns is non-existent in this community.

3　Numbers in parentheses identify speaker and code-switch.

4　For example, why should it be possible to switch codes between a subject and a verb, but not if that subject is pronominal, as suggested by Gumperz (1976) and Timm (1975)?

5　This constraint is confirmed by data from independent studies (Pfaff, 1975; 1976; Wentz, 1977; McClure, n.d.).

6　A condition similar to the equivalence constraint has been independently suggested by Lipski (1978).

7　Gingràs also claims that it is not obvious whether (6a) should even be considered an example of code-switching, mainly because 'in the formation of the complement it is not clear whether English transformations have applied in an otherwise Spanish structure' (Gingràs, 1974: 168). Whether or not an invented example should be considered a code-switch is questionable; in any event, it is one which is hardly likely to occur in actual speech, as operation of the equivalence constraint demonstrates.

8　This lapsus provides ground for interesting speculation, which we leave to the reader.

9　This questionnaire was developed for the Philadelphia speech community by the Project on Linguistic Change and Variation under the direction of William Labov, and subsequently adapted for use in the Puerto Rican community by the author.

10　Note that the sentence itself contains a switch. The switched segment was only coded for the following syntactic category if the category was produced in the language other than that of the switch. So an example like *Pa' muchos sitios* was not coded for following syntactic category.

11　A construct such as 'language of the sentence', which according to Wentz (1977: 182) is the one in which the determiner and main verb were produced, does not appear to be operative for these data, as they contain a good number of code-switched verbs (60, or 3% of the data) in a language other than that of the determiner.

12　Three Spanish-dominant and one bilingual speaker were omitted from these calculations as they each produced 15 tokens or less.

13　I would like to thank David Sankoff for making available a version of the variable rule program which facilitates this stepwise multiple regression procedure.

Source: Poplack, S. (1979/80) Sometimes I'll start a sentence in Spanish *y termino en español*. *Linguistics* 18: 581–618, by permission of Mouton de Gruyter.

Chapter 10

Constraints on code-switching: how universal are they?
MICHAEL CLYNE

1   Introduction

A welcome development of the past few years has been an awakening of interest among theoretical linguists in the potential of bilingual speech for the theory of language. In so doing, they have unwittingly reopened an issue that has interested researchers into bilingualism in the past (such as Haugen, 1953; 1956; 1973; Hasselmo, 1961; 1974; Gilbert, 1969; Shaffer, 1975; Clyne, 1969; 1971; 1980).

It goes without saying that, for the implications for linguistic theory to be valid, the assumptions on code-switching must be correct and verifiable from corpuses from as many bilingual situations as possible. In this chapter, I shall examine some of the claims made about code-switching constraints and their theoretical implications in recent studies by Di Sciullo, Muysken and Singh (1986), Joshi (1985), Klavans (1983), Pfaff (1979), Sankoff and Poplack (1979/81), and Woolford (1983), also taking account of a critical analysis by Romaine (1986) and various other studies. After reviewing some basic issues and assumptions underlying constraints on code-switching, I shall discuss actual constraints proposed in the literature under consideration. I shall then describe a corpus derived from 640 German–English and 200 Dutch–English bilinguals in Australia (Clyne, 1967; 1972a for German; Clyne, 1974 for Dutch) and test the validity of the constraints against this data. Among the points raised for consideration will be the definition of code-switching and its delineation from mixing/ borrowing/interference/transference; the relation between code-switching and syntactic interference/transference; and the significance of triggering (that is, psycholinguistically conditioned code-switching) rather than sociolinguistically conditioned code-switching.

2   The concept of code-switching

In this chapter, I shall employ *code-switching* in the sense of 'the alternative use of two languages either within a sentence or between sentences'. The speaker stops using language A and uses language B, so that syntactic connections are now with items from the speaker's language-B system. This contrasts with transference, where a single item is transferred from language B to A (or vice versa), whether integrated into the grammatical and/or phonological system of the recipient language or not. (Such distinctions were already established in the 1950s, for example by Haugen (1956: 40) in his three-fold differentiation 'switching', 'interference', and 'integration'.)

Although most of the papers I shall refer to (Woolford, 1983; Klavans, 1983; Joshi, 1985) agree with this definition to a large extent, most of them concentrating on *intrasentential* switching, this does not apply to all. A problem occurs when switching and mixing are employed contrastively. While Pfaff (1979) and Romaine (1986) use 'mixing' as a generic term to cover both 'borrowing' (my 'transference') and 'code-switching', Wentz and McClure (1977) employ 'code-switching' as the generic term with 'code-changing' (my 'code-switching') and 'code-mixing' (my 'transference') as the subcategories; and Di Sciullo, Muysken and Singh (1986) (hereafter DSMS) appear to use 'code-mixing' as a generic term and as the main term for the phenomenon under consideration, with 'switching' occasionally appearing as a synonym, and 'switches' and 'switching sites' employed throughout. While indicating distinctive features of 'borrowing' (integration, brevity of mix, absence of appropriate word known to speaker), and 'switching' (bilingualism of the user), Pfaff (1979: 297) refers to the 'indeterminacy of the distinction'. This is due to triggering of code-switching by 'borrowed' words, the beginning of code-switching being the same as the beginning of 'borrowing', and idiomatic expressions being similar to code-switching. In an earlier study, Hasselmo (1961; 1974) had designated some forms of code-switching as 'ragged' as opposed to 'clean' (see examples in Section 6.5). He also used acceptability tests to demonstrate the principles of ordered selection in the transference (rather than code-switching) of English lexemes and morphemes in Swedish in the US (that is, which parts of the sentence can be Swedish and which can be English).

Apart from generating confusion, vagueness in terminology can influence the results of research. For instance, Klavans (1983) reports complete indecision on the part of informants in acceptability tests where the verb alone is in one language (for example 'The dog *corría* quickly down the street'). However, this could be regarded as an unintegrated lexical transfer rather than code-switching and should not affect findings on the matrix language in code-switched sentences. Many of DSMS's (1986) examples of code-switching seem to be lexical transfers, such as

Ha ricevuto il diplôme.
'He (has) received the (Italian) diploma (French).'

This is conceded in another example where there is phonological integration. Most of their Hindi–English instances can be categorized as stabilized lexical transfers, as can Romaine's (1986) Panjabi–English mixed compounds, especially those using the operator *kərna* 'to do' (as in *phonam kərna* 'to telephone').

3 The studies in question

Of the main studies I shall discuss, four – Woolford (1983), Klavans (1983), Joshi (1985), and DSMS (1986) – deal with theoretical questions. Woolford and DSMS use language-contact data to support government theory. Klavans argues in favor of the notion of a 'matrix language' determined by the language of the verb while Joshi represents a computational formalization of a code-switching model. On the other hand, Pfaff (1979) and Sankoff and Poplack (1979/81) are sociolinguistic corpus studies of Spanish–English bilingualism in the United States with theoretical implications. Many of the constraints discussed in the recent theoretical literature are actually derived from these papers.

4 Basic issues and assumptions

4.1 Basic issues in general

There are a number of basic issues which recur in several of the papers under consideration.

4.1.1 The differentiation between code-switching and other language contact phenomena

As will be apparent from the brief summary in Section 2, above, most of the researchers agree with such a differentiation, though terminological confusion has somewhat obscured the issue. The main 'dissenter' is Pfaff, who stresses vague boundaries.

4.1.2 Relation between grammars

Woolford's (1983: 522) generative model of bilingual code-switching indicates how two monolingual grammars 'co-operate to generate code-switching sentences'. Code-switching occurs only where the two systems overlap. In DSMS's (1986) 'code-mixing', structural integrity of the components is also preserved. 'Mixed codes' for them 'remain phonologically and morphologically separate'. The limitations of this will be shown in Sections 5.4 and 5.5 below. They, like

Woolford, believe in the compatability of grammars as a prerequisite for code-switching. Pfaff sees clearly discernible junctures and independent syntactic structures as potential characteristics of both code-switching and transference. Sankoff and Poplack (1979/81) is probably the source of later postulations of syntactic integrity between the two constituent grammars in code-switching.

4.1.3   'Mixed grammar' or 'grammar for code-switching'

In view of the preference of most of the scholars for 'two independent grammars', arguments are also presented against a 'mixed' grammar (Pfaff, DSMS, Sankoff and Poplack). Klavans attempts to refute these by contending that if government holds over code-switched sentences, then these must be generated by a code-switching grammar (G c-s). Joshi assumes a system L x in terms of the grammars of the two languages (though *not* a third grammar for 'mixed' sentences).

4.1.4   The existence of general constraints

There is general agreement in the theoretical studies that there are general constraints on code-switching (between any pair of languages). This applies to Woolford, to DSMS – who, as we shall see below, subsume the constraints proposed by previous authors for Hindi–English code-switching under one general constraint – and to Joshi, whose constraints are also dependent on an all-embracing one. Klavans argues that code-switching is asymmetrical in that different constraints apply according to the direction in which it occurs. Joshi postulates a 'control structure' permitting shifting control from the Marathi to the English grammar (but not vice versa), an asymmetry necessary because of the nature of code-switching among the speakers.

4.1.5   Determination of 'matrix language'

Klavans's case for asymmetrical directionality rests on the notion of the 'matrix language', determined by the inflection-bearing element of the verb, which is supported by native-speaker judgments. (But see Pfaff (1979) and Sankoff and Poplack (1979/81) on difficulties with acceptability testing.) This enables her to establish constraints in languages with different case marking. Joshi also postulates a matrix language for each utterance, and the notion of the matrix language is implicit in Woolford and DSMS. The assumption of the matrix language developed by Klavans and Joshi is refuted by Sankoff and Poplack by reference to single sentences with several switches. However, the 'matrix language' has its parallels in their own labeling system, where superscripts on the symbols for various grammatical categories are introduced to avoid violations of code-switching constraints (as in NP + det N$^{s.p.N}$ Adj$^{sp:adj}$).

4.1.6   Code-switching: surface structure or deeper?

Sankoff and Poplack see code-switching constraints on the surface structure of the sentence, thus not generated in the deep structure, since there is no need for deep-structure neighbors to be in the same language. Both DSMS and Woolford postulate constraints within universal grammar. 'The problem, from the point of view of theoretical linguistics, is', according to Woolford (1983: 522), 'to look beyond surface strings to determine how one can switch grammars in mid-tree and still end up with a coherent and interpretable sentence.'

4.2   Assumptions in the discussion of constraints

At least the 'theoretical' papers imply a number of assumptions about languages in contact which I shall challenge in the second part of this article.

4.2.1   Standard languages

The assumption that there are two standard languages in contact which can be described in terms of standard norms.

4.2.2   Stability of grammatical systems

The assumption that the speaker has a stable grammatical language, without syntactic convergence. The papers make no attempt to see variation in the 'languages' between which code-switching occurs. Actually, Sankoff and Poplack see the syntactic integrity of Spanish and English in code-switched sentences as part of the case against convergence of Spanish toward English in the Puerto Rican community in New York.

4.2.3   The notion of grammaticality

A major difference between the sociolinguistic corpus studies (Pfaff, Sankoff and Poplack) and the theoretical ones is that the latter discard as 'ungrammatical' code-switched utterances which, in their experience or in the corpuses with which they are familiar, do not occur (Klavans) or contravene constraints (Woolford). The sociolinguistic studies, on the other hand, report 'tendencies'. (Pfaff uses words such as 'tend to', 'are favored', 'are infrequent'. It is clear that these are not absolutes, something that is not taken into account by those using her data and conclusions for theoretical discussions, in which the term 'ungrammatical' is generally employed.) It is a matter of doubt if the notion of grammaticality can be applied at all to data as variable as that of code-switching.

In her attempt to validate the constituent structure of NPs in X-bar theory, the lexical projection of parts of the constituent structure of VPs, and the cross-language nature of category labels, Woolford relies on the categorization of switched sentences as 'grammatical' and 'ungrammatical' and the clearcut determination of a grammar of language A and language B. Klavans resorts to the label 'gross ungrammaticality' for sentences that appear to be unusual (such as 'The boys have *recogido los juguetes*').

4.2.4   Triggering

In Clyne (1967; 1969; 1972), I developed the notion of 'triggering', where an item of ambiguous affiliation (that is, one belonging to the speaker's two systems) triggers off a switch from one language to another.

> (1)   Ich fahre an die <u>beach</u> *and I'll spend the rest of the day there.*
>   'I'll go to the beach and . . .'

The trigger word is frequently preceded by a hesitation pause – where an attempt is made to find a standard L1 word for an English transfer. This phenomenon is referred to briefly in the sociolinguistic studies (Pfaff and Sankoff and Poplack) but not in the 'theoretical' ones. Notable examples of trigger words are lexical transfers (words transferred from one language to the other), bilingual homophones (words from the two languages sounding the same), proper nouns (personal and place names, syntactically combinable with items from the two systems), and compromise forms between the two languages (see Section 6.5 below). The question here is, is the trigger word part of the switch? Through the examples cited, the literature tacitly assumes this to be the case.

4.3   Language-specific constraints

As many of the studies derive data from Spanish–English bilinguals, some of the constraints are specific to this pair of languages, though they may be presented in the theoretical papers as universals or as evidence in favor of a particular theoretical framework. For instance, Woolford discusses constraints on switching between noun and following (modifying) adjective,

> *the casa big
> 'the house big'

and on the language from which an object clitic pronoun,

> Yo it compré.
> 'I it bought.'

can be drawn – both questions of relevance to Spanish. This applies, to a lesser extent, to the language of the verb used with empty subject and that of the auxiliary with particular negatives.

> *Was training *para pelear*.
> '. . . to fight'
> *I am no *terca*.
> '. . . stubborn'

In her consideration of WH movement and Subj–Aux inversion, Woolford (1983: 532) hypothesizes that certain switched sentences can be deemed ungrammatical on the basis of a constraint resulting from a language-specific transformation rather than a language-specific phrase-structure rule. This accentuates the need for corpuses from many language-contact situations, for Spanish and English are both SVO languages and share many grammatical rules.

Klavans claims that conflicts in code-switching between differently structured languages cannot be explained in terms of constraints. She uses this to support her 'matrix language' concept.

DSMS deal, among other things, with Hindi–English code-switching, which involves a clash between SOV and SVO. They mention this language pair as one where code-switching could theoretically be constrained. This is not taken up in any detail or mentioned elsewhere in the literature, but DSMS do introduce examples from 'Hinglish' (which is actually Hindi plus lexical transference from English) to consider a 'language-specific' constraint that complements rather than one that overrides the general constraints. DSMS observe that, for example:

1   Switching may occur between subject and verb, but not in the same way between verb and object:

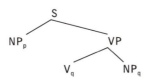

2   Complementizers can be in a different language from their sister subjects. Conjunctions are in the language of the constituent they conjoin to something else.
3   The relation between X and Y may be due to government (hence subject–object and complement–conjunction asymmetry):

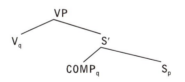

4   The complements of a preposition must have the same index as the preposition, as in 'sonata *for two violins*':

5   Elements inserted into the phrase-structure tree of a sentence must be drawn from the same lexicon.

On constraints, Pfaff's corpus enables her to come to the following conclusions:

1   Clitic pronoun objects must be in the same language as the verb (agreed with by Wentz and McClure (1977) and Timm (1975), both based on Spanish–English bilingual speech).
2   She also records the low occurrence of det + N mixes (which Wentz and McClure label ungrammatical).
3   Unlike Gumperz (1976) who reports the frequent switch of a full clause, P records a very rare use of this kind of switch in her data.
4   P records that the mixing of an entire PP is very rare in her corpus, and prepositions alone are never 'switched' (1979: 310). (In the case of prepositions, it is likely that the uncertainty of what is a switch and what is a transfer (borrowing) could be relevant.)
5   P disagrees with Gumperz's constraint that conjunctions must be in the language of the second of the conjoined sentences.

5   Constraints proposed in the literature

5.1   Structural-integrity constraint, also known as equivalence constraint

Sankoff and Poplack and Woolford postulate that the syntax on either side of the code-switch must be grammatical for the language concerned. This is the most basic constraint in terms of general theoretical implications. While it is, in a sense, subsumed in their government constraint, DSMS object to the 'equivalence constraint' on two grounds. It requires interlingual equivalence of grammatical categories and it is formulated exclusively in terms of linear sequence rather than structural relations, when most grammatical principles are formulated in terms of hierarchical relations.

5.2   Free-morpheme constraint

According to Sankoff and Poplack, no switch can occur between a bound morpheme and a lexical form unless that lexical form is phonologically integrated into the language of the bound morpheme, as in *flipeando*, **runeando*. This is supported by Wentz and McClure (1977: 706), who compare Spanish–English code-switching in bilinguals and switching between subcodes in English monolinguals.

5.3   Semantic constraint

Of the authors who raise semantic issues, only Pfaff formulates a semantic constraint: whole PP switches involve figurative or temporal, but not locative, switches. DSMS conclude that English manner adverbs (such as *quickly*, *reluctantly*) do not mix well with Hindi verbs, and other adverbs divide into those that occur freely with Hindi verbs (such as *unfortunately*, *frankly*) and those that do not (such as *yesterday*, *today*). This is probably a semantic constraint. Romaine (1986: 25) discusses whether sentences with *kərna* are '"implicated" in the semantics of causativity, and whether they are in any sense to be regarded as equivalent to the periphrastic causatives of English', such as *to make cry*.

5.4   Government constraint

DSMS postulate that switching is possible only between elements not related to government (for example V governs O and P governs the NP in a PP). This constraint, it is claimed, has precedence over all others, and it incorporates some of them (including the proscription of PP switching and Kachru's (1978) det and complementizer constraint). It predicts correctly for French–English–Italian code-switching and most of the constraints previously proposed for Hindi–English code-switching, although, according to Klavans, it disallows common sentences such as

> Los hombres comieron *the sandwiches* [switch between V and Obj.NP].
> 'The men ate (Spanish) the sandwiches (English).'

while allowing unusual switches – such as those between Subj.NP and VP:

> La plupart des canadiens *scrivono* 'c'.
> 'The majority of (the) Canadians (French) write (Italian) 'c'.'

DSMS claim universal validity for their government constraint though they admit that individual languages may impose additional constraints.

5.4.1   Switching sites

According to DSMS, switching takes place at points where items from each language can occur, at what they call 'neutralization sites'. A neutralization site had a node characterizable in the phrase structure of both languages involved, either in terms of universally defined categories or because, while language-specific, the characteristics are shared by the two languages. In addition, a neutralization site may also have no 'lexical sisters' which unambiguously index the node dominating them and their constituents.

Sankoff and Poplack propose actual switching sites on the basis of their quantitative study (between V and [Obj] NP and, to a lesser extent, between [Subj] NP and VP). Pfaff contends that surface structures common to both languages are favorable for switches (see Hasselmo, 1961; 1974).

5.5   Constraint on switchability of closed-class groups

In Joshi's schema, most constraints are dependent on a general constraint on the switchability of 'closed-class items' (determiners, quantifiers, prepositions, tense morphemes, complementizers, pronouns).

5.6   Summarizing remarks

Disagreement between scholars is recorded regarding the government constraint, the notion of the matrix language, whether code-switching is only a surface phenomenon, and the existence of a 'mixed grammar' to generate code-switched sentences.

6   The Australian corpus

6.1   The data and how they were collected

Our corpus is based on taped interviews in which bilinguals were asked to describe a number of clearly Australian pictures and one that could have been taken in Australia or Europe, to describe the events of a typical day in their lives and books read or films seen, and to discuss their first impressions of Australia (if they were immigrants themselves), or (if they had grown up in a rural settlement in Australia) what their district was like when they were children. These open-ended requirements minimized the influence of the interviewer. Apart from the description of the 'ambiguous' picture, the language in which they were asked to speak was German or Dutch. The Dutch speakers were postwar immigrants and their children, as were 200 of the German speakers. There are also tapes of later-generation descendants of nineteenth-century German settlers in former German *Sprachinseln* in Australia, of prewar refugees and their children, and of Templars

(Palestinian-Swabians) who were resettled in Australia during and after the Second World War.

For syntactic transference specifically, an analysis was made of 330 German–English bilinguals in Australia (200 postwar migrants and their children, 50 prewar refugees, and 80 descendants of nineteenth-century settlers).

This data is used to test the assumptions and constraints dealt with in the above-mentioned literature.

6.2   The two languages in contact with English

There is a substantial correspondence between the grammars of Dutch and English (Van Haeringen n.d.). The syntactic dissimilarities between English and either German or Dutch are different from those between English and Spanish. The reader is referred to the long controversy on whether German is an SOV or an SVO language (see, for example, Clyne, 1972: 37; the same would apply to Dutch). More recently, Dik (1978) has proposed a VSO order for Dutch, with a rule for placing the salient constituent first. Mallinson and Blake (1981: 129) argue that a language must not have one basic order for all types of clause, as transformationalists have postulated, and suggest that German and Dutch can be SOV for subordinate clauses while VSO or SVO for main clauses. In German and Dutch, the verb comes second in sentences in which direct object, indirect object, or adverb are focused by initial placement, such as

> Er hat seinem Bruder gestern einen Regenschirm geschenkt.
> He has his-DAT brother yesterday a-ACC umbrella given as a present
> 'He gave his brother an umbrella yesterday.'

> Seinem Bruder hat er gestern einen Regenschirm geschenkt.
> His-DAT brother has he yesterday a-ACC umbrella given as a present

> Gestern hat er seinem Bruder einen Regenschirm geschenkt.
> Yesterday has he his-DAT brother a-ACC umbrella given as a present

Aux + Vb are discontinuous if there are one or more adverbs or an object (see above examples). In embedded sentences, the main Vb is placed at the end:[1]

> Er weiß, daß er wenig Zeit hat.
> He knows that he little time has

> Hij Weet, dat hij weinig tijd heeft.
> He knows that he little time has

> Er wußte, daß er sich verspäten würde.
> He knew that he REFL be late-INF would

Hij wist, dat hij te laat zou komen.
He knew that he too late would come

On the other hand, German and Dutch do not have N + Adj or pro-drop constructions (except in the imperative) which are an important issue in Spanish–
English code-switching.[2]

6.3 Convergence and code-switching in the data

In contradistinction to the assumptions outlined in section 4.2 above, our studies
of German and Dutch in Australia suggest that (1) the syntactic system of L1 in
many individuals converges toward L2, and (2) syntactic convergence in specific
sentences often accompanies code-switching. If a particular speaker (or community) has taken over syntactic rules from English into L1 consistently, it could
be argued that, for that speaker (or community), the grammars remain independent and overlapping and the constraints on code-switching expressed by the
above-mentioned authors hold. However, the Australian material indicates considerable variation in syntax, with widespread syntactic transference, especially in
second- and later-generation Australians. The two main factors promoted by
syntactic transference are the following (Clyne, 1971):

- Proximity of immediate constituents.
    - (2) Jedes Jahr die Schafe werden geschert.
      'Every year the sheep are "sheared".'
      Standard German: Jedes Jahr *werden* die Schafe geschoren.
    - (3) Sie war geboren in Hamilton.
      'She was born in Hamilton.'
      Standard German: Sir war in Hamilton *geboren*.
- The SVO order generalized as in English.
    - (4) Natürlich die Landstraßen sind besser.
      'Of course the highways are better.'
      Standard German: Natürlich *sind* die Landstraßen besser.
    - (5) . . . was wir haben jetzt.
      '. . . what we now have.'
      Standard German: . . . was wir *jetzt* haben.

The data analysis shows that proximity accounts for 38.7% of syntactic transfers, SVO generalization for 38.2%, and the combination of the two factors for
4.6%. However, proximity-conditioned syntactic transfers predominate in the
first generation (50% of prewar, 74% of postwar migrants' syntactic transfers). In
the speech of both the second generation of post- and prewar migrants (51% of
syntactic transfers) and the rural settlers (45%) it is the SVO generalization that is

more prevalent. This represents only 9.6% and 20% respectively of pre- and postwar first-generation syntactic transfers (Clyne, 1971; 1972: 31–3). However, among 200 postwar Dutch-speaking migrants and their children, proximity accounts for only 14% of the first-generation syntactic transfers and 15% of the second-generation ones, while SVO generalization represents 60% of the first-generation instances and 66% of the second-generation ones.

There is a tendency in contemporary European German and Dutch to bring discontinuous constituents closer together (see, for example, Moser, 1968; Geerts *et al.*, 1984: 920–4, 1021–3).

It can be seen that SVO generalization is more advanced in our Dutch corpus than in the comparable German one (see Clyne, 1980). Some speakers will vary between 'standard' and 'nonstandard' (English-influenced) syntax:

(6) Typisch australische Bäume, welche wir im Continent nich' *haben*.

(7) Wir haben in Berlin eine Straße, welche *is'* Unter den Linden.
(Standard German verb to end)

Lexical transference ('borrowing') and code-switching are often accompanied by syntactic transference. Sometimes the speaker has apparently mapped out the sentence according to an English pattern and needs an English lexeme to produce a GRAMMATICAL construction, as in

(8) . . . if der Vater *hat* keine Farm.
'. . . if the father has no farm.'

where the German equivalent *wenn* would require verb-final placement, and

(9) Ich prefer *diese* Straße.
'I prefer this street.'

where *vorziehen* would entail discontinuous constituents.

A Dutch parallel:

(10) Ik was achtenzestig jaar *before* ik kon *get* mijn pension.
'I was sixty-eight before I could get my pension.'
Standard Dutch: Ik was achtenzestig jaar, voordat ik mijn pensioen *kon krijgen*.

Variation in syntax will thus occur because of surrounding transferred items:

(11) Und so packt *man* alles schnell ein.
'And so one packs everything quickly.'

(12) So *ich* prefer die self-service shops.
 'So I prefer the self-service shops' [same speaker].

Although Dutch is not a pro-drop language, subject pronouns are sometimes dropped where they are at the boundary of a switch and Dutch and English word order are different:

(13) Dan soms*times go* voor'n hour nog in bed.
 'Then (*I*) sometimes go back to bed for an hour.'
 Standard Dutch: Dan ga ik soms voor cen uur nog naar bed.
(14) Dan *make* the beds en dan doe ik afwas.
 'Then make the beds and then I do the washing up.'
 Standard Dutch: Dan maak *ik* do hoddun (op) on dan doe ik de afwas.

The transference of *remembern* as in *Ich kann es nicht remembern* saves the speaker (1) the planning and articulation of a reflexive pronoun, (2) the planning of preposition *an*, and (3) the transformation of *an* and NP to *daran*. Similarly, code-switching will sometimes enable a speaker to apply a preferred syntactic rule from the other language without being ungrammatical:

(15) Sollten sie da sch/geblieben weil es war besser because *it's* gutes Land, very reiches reiches Land.
 'They should have stayed there because it's good land, very rich rich land.'
 Standard German: Die hätten da bleiben sollen, weil es sehr fruchtbares Land war (SVO).
(16) *Before that* wir haben gewohnt about vier Meilen von hier.
 'Before that we lived about four miles from here.'
 Standard German: Vorher *haben* wir vier Meilen von hier gewohnt (SVO).
(17) want wij war . . . *coming to Australia.*
 'For we were coming to Australia.'
 Standard Dutch: Want wij kwamen naar Australië. [Progressive not possible in this context in Dutch.]
(18) En dan je realize dat this, dat farmleven . . .
 'And then you realize that this, that farm life . . .'
 Standard Dutch: En dan *besef* je dat dit, dat boerenleven . . .

Where word order is identical in the speaker's two languages (not necessarily the 'standard' languages), he/she can switch in and out of them (Clyne, 1971). Thus, the speaker's convergence of languages due to syntactic transference can also promote a swifter return to the pre-switch language:

(19) Das ist ein Foto, gemacht an der <u>beach</u>. *Can be, kann be, kann sein in Mount Martha.*
      'This is a photo taken on the beach. Can be in Mount Martha.'
      Standard German: Das ist ein Foto, das am Strand aufgenommen worden ist. (Es) kann in Mount Martha sein.

However, syntactic convergence will take place around the switch, apparently IN ORDER to ease code-switching:

(20) In nine neunzehnhundertundfourteen die erste War Tarrington *war* Hochkirch und das *the post-office war* registered als Tarrington 'cause es war ein englische Witwe . . . [non-inversion]

6.4   Marginal passages

Hasselmo (1961: 39–78) refers to older first-generation Swedish speakers in Swedish settlements in the US whose speech is marked by unlimited switching between the two languages at the grammatical and lexical levels, and a Swedish phonic pattern, promoted by an apparently large number of compromise forms. Hasselmo subsequently termed such speech 'marginal passages'.

The speech of five of our Dutch–English bilinguals falls into this category. Due to the combination of Dutch phonic transference in English, lexical transference both ways, and compromise forms, it is very difficult to identify the matrix language:

(21) Ja, *in de, in de* big place *is* het a lot, nou ja, je kan't, 't *is de same* als *hier.* Je h*a*bt Melbourne en *de* other places met *de* high flats and so. Dat heb je in Holland ook. Maar 'n, maar a lot of places *nou* (now), de same before we go. D'r is, we go to my sister in Apeldoorn, en [*zi hɛf*] de same place nog. [Overlapping items in italics]
      'Yes, in the, in the big place there is a lot, now yes, you can, it is the same as here. You have Melbourne and the other places with the high flats and so on. You have got that in Holland too. But, but a lot of places now, the same before we go. There is, we go to my sister in Apeldoorn and [zi hɛf] still the same place.'

The informant often generalizes the present uninflected form of the verb for other parts (including the past). An instance of a compromise form is:

English	ʃi hæːz
Dutch	zə heːft
Compromise	zi hɛf

Another example from a different informant:

> En dan [vi hɛf] nog een daughter in Zweden.
> 'And then [vi hɛf] another daughter in Sweden.'
> English   wiː hæːv
> Dutch   və hɛbə
> Compromise   vi hɛf

6.5   Triggering and the point of switching

In Section 4.2.4, I introduced the notion of triggering and raised the question whether the trigger word is part of the switch. The following examples may help illustrate the problem.

Lexical transfers:

> (22) Ich les' gerade eins, das handelt von einem alten <u>secondhand dealer</u> *and his son.*
> 'I am just reading one. It's about an old secondhand dealer and his son.

Bilingual homophones:

> (23) Meestal hier (here) *at the local shops* <u>en in Doncaster</u>.
> 'Mostly here at the local shops and in Doncaster.'

Proper nouns:

> (24) Es war Mr Fred Berger, der wohnte da in Gnadenthal *and he went there one day* . . .
> 'It was Mr Fred Berger, he lived there in Gnadenthal and . . .'
> [*Gnadenthal*, realized according to German phonological rules, is the name of an old German settlement in Western Victoria, Australia.]
>
> (25) Sie war in <u>New Guinea</u> *when the Japanese came there* and dann haben's mußten sie 'raus von <u>New Guinea</u> *at the time* of war.
> [N.B. *New Guinea* triggers two switches in one sentence.]
> 'She was in New Guinea . . . and then they had to get out of New Guinea . . .'

Compromise forms between two languages.

> (26) Wir haben se gehabt, but oh, großes Feuer [kʌm] *through and killed the trees.*

[kʌm] to cover German [kaːm], English [kɛːɪm].
'We had them but oh, big fire come . . .'

(27) Ieder ding waar je <u>ken</u> *think on it*.
[kɛn] to cover Dutch [kɑn], English [kæːn].
'Every thing where you [kɛn].'

In these cases the question can be asked, 'where does the switch start?' All the articles cited would include the trigger word in the switch; I would not. To one speaker, 'secondhand dealer' (or 'New Guinea') is just as much part of her vocabulary in both languages as *Gnadenthal* is to the other. If the switch in (24) begins at *and*, then so should the switch in (22). Even though *Gnadenthal* is a place-name in Australia and therefore common to both languages, New Guinea is part of the third speaker's English and German systems, so much so that it is used twice in one sentence in a German context. Example (26) shows that, in this category, it is impossible to define an item from the 'gray' area such as [kʌm] for both /kɛːɪm/ and /kaːm/. Sometimes the nature of the triggering is not clearcut, especially in Dutch–English language contact where the language distance is not great:

(28) Ik hebt een <u>kop of</u> *tea, tea or something*.

[kɔp ɔf] could be a phonologically integrated form of lexical transference from English. [kʌp ɔv] or [ɔf] could be a semantic transfer from English. Standard Dutch: *een kop(je) thee*; Dutch *of* (meaning 'or') may have taken on the meaning of English *of*.

Triggering, which is a psychologically rather than socially conditioned type of code-switching, occurs in two forms: (1) consequential triggering, following a trigger word (see examples above), and (2) anticipational triggering, anticipating a trigger word, usually at the beginning of a phrase of which the trigger word is the head word, as in:

(29) . . . und so arbeitet sie *at* <u>Monsanto</u>.
and so she works at Monsanto.'

(30) Hij staat *on the* <u>bridge</u>.
'He is standing on the bridge.'

While anticipational triggering can provide insights into sentence planning, consequential triggering appears to represent an exception to some of the constraints discussed (see below).

6.6   Switching within a word

There are not many instances in our corpus of switches between a bound morpheme and a phonologically unintegrated lexical form. However, the phenomenon is certainly not absent:

(31) That's what Papschi   *mein*   -s to say.
ENGLISH   PROPER N. GERMAN ENGLISH

(32) in meine Mutter *-s car.*
GERMAN   ENGLISH

(33) naar mijn vriendin *'s place.*
DUTCH   ENGLISH

Example (31) contains two switches, one (English to German) resulting from the name *Papschi* [papʃiː], the other a switch back to English (possibly due to awareness of the previous switch). In (32) and (33) the switch may be triggered off by an English grammatical pattern (possessive) which is ungrammatical in German and Dutch respectively. (A similar explanation can be given for

(34) Es waren hundert-*s* und hundert-*s of* Leute.)

Another instance of interlexical code-switching is (13), repeated here:

(13) Dan soms*times go* voor'n hour nog in bed.

Dutch *soms* already means sometimes and the switch is probably triggered off by *som(s)*. The speaker employs marginal passages and [ɔ] is the vowel she uses in both *soms* and *som(e)times*.

In the following example, a bilingual compound triggers off a switch, promoted by the 'ambivalence' of the following verb:

(35) . . . dat de arbeitspace *was very much slower than it is in Holland.*
'That the work pace was . . .'

6.7   Switching of PP

The incidence of switching of a PP is very high, especially among German–English bilinguals, due to anticipational triggering. Among 50 German–English bilinguals whose speech contains several examples of anticipational triggering, 43% of the instances occur at the beginning of a PP (compared with 33% at the start of a NP). Note the large proportion of locative switches and the relatively low incidence of figurative switches.

	GERMAN	DUTCH
LOCATIVE	66.67%	60%
(such as 'at Balcombe', 'out of bed')		
TEMPORAL	6.67%	20%
(such as 'in the afternoon', 'at playtime')		
MANNER	26.67%	nil
(such as 'on the telephone')		
FIGURATIVE	nil	10%

(In each case, the first example is from the German corpus, the second from the Dutch corpus.)

It is highly improbable that there are any semantic constraints involved here. Speakers anticipate the use of a lexical item from the 'overlapping area' between the two languages at the point of time when they are planning the phrase. This confirms the psychological reality of the phrase as an integral unit of planning.

7   Validity of constraints proposed

Let us now assess to what extent the constraints postulated in the literature are supported by the Australian data.

7.1   Structural-integrity constraint

On the whole, the data affirm the structural-integrity (equivalence) principle. However, it negates the tacit assumption of two stable (standard language) syntactic systems in contact. This does not affect the validity of the actual constraint because the SPEAKER's syntactic rules overlap at the point of switching. What our discussion has shown is that, in order for the structural-integrity constraint to be valid, adjustments are made to the syntax, after taking advantage of the syntactic convergence that has already taken place.

7.2   Free-morpheme constraint

As has been shown in Section 6.6, there are a small number of counterexamples to the free-morpheme constraint in our corpus. Evidence against the constraint has also been found in code-switching between Dutch and Turkish (Boeschoten and Verhoeven, 1985), Yoruba and English (Goke-Pariola, 1983), and Adãŋme and English (Ghana) (Nartey, 1982).

7.3   Semantic constraint

In Section 6.7, I have shown that in our corpus, the switching of an entire PP is very common (see Pfaff (1979: 310), who describes it as 'occurring very infrequently'). While Pfaff's 'whole PP switches involve figurative or temporal meanings' and 'literal locatives switch after the preposition' (1979: 314), locatives predominate in our corpus, with some temporal meanings in Dutch and some manner meanings in German.

7.4   Government constraint, including the 'depth' question

It will be recalled that PPs are crucial to DSMS's government principle, which constrains code-switching either at the beginning of a PP or in the middle of one. Anticipational triggering provides the conditions for a frequent, syntactically 'planned' major exception to the government constraint. Anticipational triggering provides utterances such as

> (36) Die sprechen *the language*
> 'They speak the language.'

and

> (37) Sie nehmen Geld für *the missions.*
> 'They take money for the missions.'

both of which are 'ungrammatical' according to the government constraint (DSMS).

Consequential triggering, being conditioned only by the lexical environment, can occur anywhere and can therefore be seen as a possible exception to all constraints, including the government constraint. (But note the point made earlier about syntactic convergence in switching or switch-back.)

In addition, our model permits us to account for other 'violations' of the government constraint which are quite normal:

> (38) You don't see dat in Australië.

[dat] is common to the speaker's English and Dutch (as is *in*). *Dat* and *in* together trigger off *Australië*. The switch at *Australië* (or at *in*) does not violate the constraints.

Some speakers tend to preserve the linguistic integrity of discontinuous constituents; others do not. I have already cited a Dutch example in another context in Section 6.3 above:

(17) Want wij war . . . *coming to Australia.*
      'Because we were . . . *coming to Australia.*'

And some examples from German–English language contact:

(39) Er zieht den Ropp die <u>rope</u> *down*.
      'He pulls the rope [integrated transfer] die rope down.'
(40) Sie nehmen sein furniture away.
      'They are taking his furniture away.'

In each of these two examples, the switch affects the surface level only, for the syntax is the same in both languages. In the two Dutch examples, syntactic transference has taken place and the speaker's grammar deviates from that of Standard Dutch. This supports Poplack and Sankoff's contention that code-switching constraints are constraints on the surface-structure syntax, which is one of the ways in which Romaine (1986) explains the contradictions of the government constraint. The examples may also be an indication of late lexicalization (Clyne, 1974). The inability of some speakers to deviate from (or avoid returning to) the lexemes (or lexeme groups) originally chosen – a type of perseveration preserving the integrity of the phrase – suggests that lexical insertions are connected with the sentence planning:

(41) *As far as* was m'modernes Leben und moderne Land *is concerned.*
(42) . . . nur im Moment bin ich *on* auf Urlaub auf *holiday.*
      '. . . only at the moment I am on on holiday on holiday.'

7.5   Conjunction constraint

Another instance of how compromise forms and triggering cast doubt on hard and fast constraints relates to the conjunction constraint. Gumperz (1976) postulates that the conjoined clause conjunctions must be in the language of the second, while Kachru (1978) claims that conjoined items must be from the language from which the conjoined sentence is introduced. Pfaff (1979) finds that conjunctions can come from either language at the point of code-switching, and THIS is supported by my corpus. However, in a sentence such as

(43) I don't know *wat* [vɑt] *ze doen.*
      '. . . what they are doing.'

w(h)at could be part of the switch, which would support Gumperz. In view of our earlier discussion, it is more likely to be an item common to English and Dutch due to Dutch phonological transference in English. It then triggers off the switch.

7.6   Matrix language

Klavans's and Joshi's claims that every sentence can be assigned to a matrix language according to the linguistic affiliation of the verb is not practicable in our corpus for two reasons:

- Some verbs are common to both systems:
    (44) Ja, in de, in de big places *is* het a lot.
- Some verbs are 'compromise forms' or lexical transfers promoted by partial phonological correspondence and are therefore common to both systems:
    (45) Dit <u>kan</u> *be anywhere.*
    (46) You don'I see *dat in Australië.*

In (46), *dat* has a triggering function. Example (45) could be interpreted as being entirely in the SPEAKER's English, or a switch could be postulated after the trigger word *kan*. Or, in accordance with our discussion under Section 6.5 above, *Dit kan* can be regarded as trigger words. Since *die* and *kan* (like *dat* in (46)) are part of the speaker's English and Dutch Systems, I would prefer the latter interpretation.

8   Encoding and decoding

The data cited in this paper are drawn from the PRODUCTION of bilinguals. PERCEPTION yields quite different results, as was shown using an experiment based on Forster's (1970) RSVP method. Thirty-two sentences with code-switching from German into English, spoken on tape by a bilingual, were played to 50 bilinguals (Clyne, 1972a). The four categories of eight sentences each (switch at clause boundary and potential trigger word; at clause boundary but not potential trigger word; at potential trigger word but not clause boundary; switch at neither) were presented in random order. Correct recall of actual words (rather than meanings) was very significantly better when the switch occurred at the clause boundary than when it came elsewhere. Potential trigger words did not seem to aid recall. The results support Kolers's (1966) results on code-switching that encoding and decoding are not mirror-symmetrical processes.

9   Conclusion

The evidence that we have considered appears to suggest non-language-specific processing on the part of bilinguals (at least), with mapping into one or the other language. Indexing and code-switching and its constraints are then surface-structure phenomena. Our data suggest that the structural-integrity/equivalence constraint applies, but only if we accept that the syntax of the two language systems may have already converged through transference, and even when it is violated by syntactic convergence at the point of code-switching. The interaction between triggering, syntactic transference, and syntactic convergence strengthens arguments in favor of a 'mixed grammar'. Some problems inherent in the notion of the 'matrix language' have been demonstrated from our corpus. While there is a general tendency favoring the government and free-morpheme constraints, there is also some evidence against the latter constraint, and far more against the former. In her excellent critique of DSMS's government principle through a study of Panjabi–English code-switching, Romaine (1986) proposes three possible explanations of violations and constraints:

1   Government relations are relaxed in certain types of contact situations.
2   Government relations have not been formulated correctly.
3   Code-switching sites are surface-structure properties, which are not base-generated and thus not determined by X-bar theory. (The language-indexing principle is an essentially surface-structure-level constraint.) Rather, 'language mixing' is governed by the kinds of structural constraints applying to monolingual performance.

On the strength of the Australian evidence, I would concur particularly with the third point. In addition, the assumptions about stability of the bilinguals' syntactic systems and about the trigger word being part of a switch have been found wanting. The triggering model (especially consequential triggering) defies many of the presuppositions of 'neatness' to which code-switching has been subjected. It also encourages the exercising of caution with such techniques as 'matched guise' for code-switching (see for example, Gibbons, 1983). The process is so individual (see Kolers, 1966; Clyne, 1972a) that we do not know what we are actually doing, let alone what sort of impression we are creating, by code-switching at a particular word or in a particular way.

The implications are that theoretical linguists wishing to use language-contact data must ensure that the data they have gathered or are taking over represent a typologically very wide range of language pairs. Otherwise they run the risk of developing and supporting powerful universal models which cannot be substantiated universally (see Nartey, 1982: 188).

Some of the difficulties in the discussion on code-switching constraints are due to the unclear division between code-switching and borrowing/interference/transference in the literature under consideration. Another problem is the use of the term 'ungrammatical' for nothing more than a tendency.

Notes

1   Note that the modal auxiliary precedes the infinitive in embedded sentences in Dutch and follow it in German.
2   But compare the alternative interpretation which distinguishes between languages with and without cross-referencing pronouns (Mallinson and Blake, 1981: 43).

Source: Clyne, M. (1987) Constraints on code-switching: how universal are they? *Linguistics* 25: 739–64, by permission of Mouton de Gruyter.

Chapter 11

Matching lemmas in a bilingual language competence and production model: evidence from intrasentential code-switching

CAROL MYERS-SCOTTON AND

JANICE L. JAKE

1 Introduction

This chapter has three related goals. First we show that how language pairs behave in code-switching provides evidence for certain types of salient congruence between languages. The analysis assumes the *matrix language frame model* (MLF model) for code-switching and provides elaborations and extensions of this model (Myers-Scotton, 1993a). Second, based on this evidence, we make proposals about the nature and organization of language production. Third, while the chapter focuses its discussion on production, proposals in this area imply details of a model of language competence. Many language production models include three levels; these are the conceptual, functional, and positional levels. At the conceptual level, intentions are "bundled" into semantic and pragmatic features associated with lexemes. At the functional level, morphosyntactic directions encoding the predicate–argument structure are activated. At the positional level, lexemes are realized in a surface structure. Our proposals deal largely with the first two levels and relate specifically to producing bilingual language. However, we argue that the same organization of language production holds for monolingual discourse.

Data discussed here come from code-switching (CS). Most briefly and generally, CS is defined as the use of two or more languages in the same discourse. From a structural point of view, there are two types of CS, intersentential and intrasentential. Our interest here is only in intrasentential CS, because it is only there that the grammars of the two languages are in contact. A more explicit definition of intrasentential CS follows below.

2   Designating the matrix language in CS

Central to our discussion of intrasentential CS is the claim that the two languages involved do not participate equally. One language, which we call the matrix language (ML), is more dominant in ways crucial to language production. This language sets the grammatical frame in the unit of analysis. The other language(s) is referred to as the embedded language (EL). However, both languages are "on" at all times during bilingual production; the difference is a matter of activation level.[1]

Although the subject here is intrasentential CS, it is as well to note that the constituent level that is relevant in the determination of either intersentential or intrasentential CS is the same. This is the CP (complement phrase) or S-bar (S'). The CP as the relevant unit of analysis in intrasentential CS will be discussed below. A CP is a syntactic structure expressing the predicate–argument structure of a clause, plus the additional syntactic structures needed to encode discourse-relevant structure and the logical form of that clause. Because CP explicitly assumes that the unit of structure includes COMP (complementizer) position, it is a more precise term than either clause or sentence.[2] Its use does not assume that the MLF model analyzes CS within a government and binding framework, and, in fact, some of our assumptions differ significantly from those of such a framework. We continue to use the term intrasentential CS because of its wide-spread use in the CS literature; however, intra-CP switching would be a more appropriate and precise term.

In contrast with intrasentential CS, intersentential CS involves switching BETWEEN CPs that are monolingual. For this reason, describing the INTERNAL structure of the CPs making up intersentential CS in terms of oppositions between an ML and EL is not appropriate.[3]

In order for the identification of an ML vs. an EL to be relevant in intrasentential CS, as we argue, morphemes from more than one language must occur under the same CP. In fact, a precise definition of intrasentential CS is this: if a CP includes morphemes from two or more languages in one or both of these patterns, the result is intrasentential CS: (1) the CP includes a mixed constituent, and/or (2) the CP includes monolingual constituents, but from two or more languages. In such a CP, one of the languages sets the grammatical frame and is the ML. The other language is the EL. This distinction between the ML vs. the EL is the basic principle structuring intrasentential CS within the MLF model (Myers-Scotton, 1993a) and its extended version followed here.

3   The role and nature of the matrix language

The decision of the interlocutors in a discourse to use intrasentential CS (cf. Section 7) is based on social, psychological, and structural factors. Consequently, a definition of the ML is based on a complex interaction of these factors. Two of the definitional criteria have a structural basis. The first criterion is this: the ML is the language that projects the morphosyntactic frame for the CP that shows intrasentential CS. A major aspect of this criterion is operationalized as the *morpheme order* and *system morpheme* principles of the MLF model:

- *The morpheme order principle*: In ML + EL constituents consisting of singly occurring EL lexemes and any number of ML morphemes, surface morpheme order (reflecting surface syntactic relations) will be that of the ML.
- *The system morpheme principle*: In ML + EL constituents, all system morphemes that have grammatical relations external to their head constituent (i.e. participate in the sentence's thematic role grid) will come from the ML (Myers-Scotton 1993a: 83).[4]

Second, the ML is defined generally, but not always, as the source of more morphemes in a sample of discourse-relevant[5] intrasentential CS. The structural basis of these two criteria will become clear under the discussion of the distinction between content vs. system morphemes and the issue of congruence.

Sociolinguistic factors provide a basis for psycholinguistic factors in the second set of definitional criteria. The ML is the unmarked or expected choice as the medium of communication in the interaction type in which the intrasentential CS occurs. Its unmarked status is generally empirically demonstrable: the ML is the language that contributes quantitatively more linguistic material in the entire discourse (including monolingual stretches). Based on this fact, speakers engaged in CS perceive the ML as "the language we are speaking" (cf. Stenson, 1990; Swigart, 1994); often they do not even recognize they are using another language in addition to the ML.[6]

4   The structural constituents in intrasentential CS

In a CP showing intrasentential CS, the distinction between ML vs. EL of the MLF model allows us to identify three types of constituents that are structurally different.[7] By constituent we mean any syntactic S-structure constituent. Within the CP of intrasentential CS, the most relevant constituent is the maximal projection. Two types of possible constituents in such a CP are made up entirely of one language or the other(s). These are either ML or EL islands. A third type of constituent is one consisting of morphemes from both languages, that is, an ML + EL constituent (hereafter a "mixed" constituent). All three types are found in most data sets showing intrasentential CS.[8]

5   Content/system morpheme distinction

In addition to the ML vs. EL opposition, a second crucial opposition in intrasentential CS is the distinction between content and system morphemes. This opposition is relevant to all linguistic structures in a number of ways, as evident in
monolingual speech-error data (cf. Garrett, 1988) as well as in other forms of
bilingual speech (Myers-Scotton, 1995c). As it is played out in intrasentential CS,
this opposition interacts with the ML vs. EL distinction (Myers-Scotton, 1993a;
Jake, 1994).

Nouns, adjectives, time adverbials, and most verbs and prepositions are
prototypical content morphemes. The feature shared by these lexical categories is
that they constitute the predicate–argument structure, by either receiving or
assigning thematic roles. Nouns and descriptive adjectives receive thematic roles;
verbs, predicate adjectives, and some prepositions assign thematic roles. Discourse markers (e.g. *well, because*) are content morphemes because they assign
thematic roles at the discourse level.

Failure to either receive or assign a thematic role prevents a member of these
categories from being designated as a content morpheme. For example, the
copula and some *do* matrix verbs fail to assign thematic roles. Similarly, some
prepositions only assign case, and not thematic role (e.g. English *of* in *student of
physics*).

A second feature characteristic of most system morphemes is the feature
[+Quantification] ([+Q]). Within the MLF model, a morpheme shows a plus
setting for quantification if it restricts possible referent(s) of a lexical category. For
example, articles restrict the possible reference of nouns, either to a smaller set
(*the boys* vs. *boys*) or to an individual (*the boy*). Similarly, tense and aspect restrict
the possible reference of predicates (i.e. verbs and adjectives) (Dowty, 1979).
Degree adverbs, such as *very*, also restrict the reference of events and adjectives.
More formally, a [+Q] morpheme quantifies (=restricts) across a variable
(=category).

6   Congruence and EL participation

The net result of the two principles of the MLF model, the morpheme order
principle and the system morpheme principle, is to restrict the role of the EL in
mixed constituents in intrasentential CS. Essentially, only EL content morphemes, not system morphemes, may occur, and these must occur in the frame
projected by the ML. Example (1) shows content morphemes from English, the
EL, inserted into a frame prepared by Irish, the ML.

> (1) Bíonn   sé ag   CONTRIBUT-áil do MAGAZINE
>   be-HAB he PROG contribute-PROG to magazine

atá PUBLISHED   in Sasana.
REL/be published in England
'He is contributing to a magazine that is published in England.'
(Irish/English; Stenson, 1990: 176)

However, not even all EL content morphemes can occur freely. A blocking hypothesis states that "a blocking filter blocks any EL content morpheme which is not congruent with the ML with respect to three levels of abstraction regarding subcategorization" (Myers-Scotton, 1993a: 120). Congruence refers to a match between the ML and the EL at the lemma level with respect to linguistically relevant features. Lemmas are entries in the mental lexicon and are discussed below.

In this chapter, we make the discussion from Myers-Scotton (1993a) more specific and introduce additional aspects of congruence. We propose that certain nonuniformities of lexical structure across languages mean that a mixed constituent may pass the blocking filter, but may not pass unscathed. For example, in many languages, the only way an EL verb appears in a mixed constituent is in a construction where an ML auxiliary verb carries all necessary inflections and the EL verb is a bare form. Such examples are discussed below in Section 11.

Various views of congruence have figured in many attempts to explain constraints on intrasentential CS. Many of these were stated in terms of surface structure (Pfaff, 1979; Poplack, 1979/80; Sridhar and Sridhar, 1980; Woolford, 1983; *inter alia*). Lack of congruence regarding lexical subcategorization has been discussed by others but is generally limited to subcategorization differences between specific language pairs (e.g. Azuma, 1991; Bentahila and Davies, 1983; Muysken, 1991). In this chapter, the nature of congruence as relevant to CS is seen as more complex because a more complex view of lexical structure is assumed (Jackendoff, 1983; Talmy, 1985). Here congruence is examined in terms of the different levels or subsystems comprising content lexemes. In addition, the relation of these subsystems to a model of production of a bilingual utterance is articulated.

7   A language production model: a first sketch

The language production model sketched here is specifically designed to accommodate "system decisions" regarding congruence. One of our hypotheses is that variation in congruence (complete, partial, or absent) in the levels of language restricts and therefore structures choices in CS. That is, variation in actual CS realizations reflects variation in congruence at more abstract levels of linguistic structure. We will be referring to these levels in terms of three types of structure: lexical-conceptual, predicate–argument, and morphological realization patterns.

The way in which the MLF model, as elaborated here, analyzes intrasentential

CS data makes important predictions about how types of linguistic information are organized in language production. In turn, these predictions imply certain aspects of the nature of linguistic competence.

A single mental lexicon is hypothesized for bilinguals, but with entries tagged for specific languages. The entries are not lexemes, but rather *lemmas*, more abstract elements that support the realizations of actual lexemes (Levelt, 1989). (In some cases they support idiomatic collocation of lexemes at the surface level, e.g. *keep tabs on* or *a fly in the ointment*). In this model, lemmas are characterized as containing abstract pragmatic information, in addition to semantic, syntactic, and morphological information. Incongruence in pragmatic messages in cross-language lemmas that are otherwise nearly identical often motivates mixed constituents in CS; other types of congruence problems motivate other CS patterns, such as EL islands, we will argue.

The information contained in lemmas is referred to at two levels: the conceptual level and the functional level. The conceptual level (i.e. *conceptualizer*) consists of the lexical-conceptual structure in which universally available semantic and pragmatic information is conflated as specific lexical-conceptual structures (referred to as semantic/pragmatic feature bundles, or *SP feature bundles*), which are necessarily language-specific. The functional level consists of the *formulator* and the morphosyntactic procedures that are activated by directions from the lemma. The formulator is a sort of "control central" in actual on-line production.

Initially, speakers make selections encapsulating the lexical-conceptual structures they wish to convey; for example, in choosing a lexical-conceptual structure in English to encode MANNER as well as MOTION, a speaker will select the structure supporting *roll* vs. *go*. Selections at this stage are abstract and result in the activation of abstract, but language-specific, lemmas in the mental lexicon.

In addition to lexical-conceptual structure, lemmas contain predicate–argument structure and directions for morphological realization patterns. This is how syntactic and morphological information is coded. When speakers select a particular conflation of semantic and pragmatic information, this involves selection of a language-specific lemma, which in turn specifies a particular predicate–argument structure and certain morphological realization patterns. Table 11.1 provides a schema of language production.

7.1   The nature of lemmas

A lemma can he defined as a carrier of lexical-conceptual structure and an associated predicate–argument structure and concomitant morphological realization patterns. What follows develops our view of lemmas and their relation to lexical entries. First, they are not concrete; that is, they are not lexical items with subcategorization features. Rather, they support such items. In order for this to be so, what is their nature? Each one includes the specific bundling of semantic and

Table 11.1   Speaker's intentions

Conceptual level:	Universally present lexical-conceptual structure in the conceptualizer.
	"Choices" made:
	If discourse includes CS, then select ML and semantic/ pragmatic feature bundles
	Language-specific semantic/pragmatic feature bundles activate entries in the mental lexicon (language-specific lemmas)
	Language-specific lemmas send directions to the formulator ↓
Functional level:	The "activated" formulator projects
	Predicate-argument structures (e.g. thematic roles) and
	Morphological realization patterns (e.g. word order, case marking, etc.) ↓
Positional level:	Morphological realization (surface structure after move-alpha, agreement inflections, etc.)

pragmatic features that encodes the lexical-conceptual structures that represent the speaker's communicative intentions. They also include information as to how these intentions are grammatically realized in a sentence. An example of such morphosyntactic information is lexical category (e.g. Noun vs. Verb) or grammatical gender. Note that such categories are not what speakers select at the conceptual level; rather, speakers are dealing in terms of notions such as "thing" or "process." This information (predicate–argument structure and morphological realization patterns) is something of a default choice; that is, selecting features in the conceptualizer that become a specific semantic/pragmatic bundle in language X entails selecting the predicate–argument structure and its morphological realizations associated with this bundle in language X. Thus, lemmas are what link conceptual intentions (=semantic and pragmatic features) to the predicate–argument structures and morphological realization patterns of a specific language.

7.2   Lemmas and lexical items

Do lemmas support specific lexical items? Yes, and no. In some cases, the abstract feature bundles do match up with a specific lexical entry. For example, an easily accessible concrete entity, such as *nose*, does match a lemma. Yet, this lemma is (most likely) language-specific, because of pragmatic considerations. For any one particular language, then, lexemes for concrete entities are supported by specific lemmas in the mental lexicon. This is also true for many more complex concepts. However, because the semantic and pragmatic features associated with them are more complex and less concrete, there may be less cross-linguistic congruence with the lemmas supporting such concepts than with concrete entities.

When there is sufficient incongruence between an EL lemma and its ML counterpart, inserting the EL lexeme supported by the EL lemma in a constituent framed by the ML may require the types of strategies to be discussed below. Cases of insufficient congruence are what give us an insight into the relative importance of features in lexical entries in defining the entries (in regard to pragmatic/ semantic matters) and in allowing for the occurrence of lexemes supported by these entries in specific types of constituents.

When there is a lack of correspondence in pragmatic force between lexemes, this state of affairs will be referred to as a "pragmatic mismatch." Most insertions of single EL lexemes in ML frames are motivated by pragmatic mismatches. That is, from the speaker's point of view, *le mot juste* is an EL lexeme, not the ML counterpart with like semantic features. Some pragmatic mismatches may be general (i.e. based on differences in connotations of semantically congruent lexemes); however, other cases of mismatches may only arise in specific interactions as a result of unique social and psychological factors.

Note how pragmatic mismatches are different from *lexical gaps*, which also may motivate the inserting of EL lexemes in ML frames. When there are gaps in the semantic correspondence between lexemes, we apply the term "lexical gap" to such cases. When the gap is large, such as in the case of EL lexicalizations for objects or concepts new to the ML culture for which the ML has no counterpart at all, the net result is typically a borrowing of the EL lexeme into the ML. For example, lexemes akin to *computer* now occur in many languages; that is, a gap has been closed through lexical borrowing so that both the donor and the recipient languages have lemmas supporting the equivalent lexeme.

In other cases, however, especially when the gap is only partial and thus there is sufficient cross-linguistic congruence, the ML does not borrow the EL lexeme, but bilingual speakers may insert the EL lexeme in CS discourse. For example, in French, *journal* refers to "daily news bulletins." A daily newspaper is a *journal* in French, but so is a daily television news broadcast (cf. *télé-journal*). In contrast, in English, while some daily news "bulletins" are referred to as *journals* (e.g. *The Wall Street Journal*), in English more prototypical as *journals* are academic or scientific publications that appear less frequently than daily. Thus, English *journal* is not an exact counterpart to French *journal*, nor is any other English lexeme. This lexical gap in English relative to the French lexeme *journal* remains, and when speakers engaging in English/French CS want to convey the specific semantic content of this French lexeme, they may insert it in an English frame, as long as the context makes clear that the intended referent is a daily *journal*.

When a lexical gap exists, this means that there is no lemma in the mental lexicon to support an actual surface lexeme. Yet, we argue that the potential to lexicalize any concept exists in any language as what we will call *lexical knowledge*.[9] Such lexical knowledge must be posited to provide for the possibility of languages bringing into existence lemmas to support new lexemes. Further, because in all languages it is possible to express all semantic and pragmatic intentions (while at the same time actual lexicalization patterns differ cross-linguistically), we propose that these intentions, located in the conceptualizer, must be available to all languages for configuring new lemmas. When these intentions are conflated into a "bundle," they can combine with the undifferentiated lexical knowledge present in the mental lexicon. This lexical knowledge includes universal as well as language-specific default information about predicate–argument structures and morpho-logical realization patterns. Universal default aspects of lexical knowledge cover such matters as the unmarked syntactic treatment of nouns and verbs. Language-specific lexical knowledge includes information about the unmarked syntactic realization of thematic roles (e.g. how experiencer is encoded) and the morpho-syntactic treatment of these roles. How congruence checks in CS may make use of undifferentiated lexical knowledge (i.e. when there is a lexical gap in the ML) is discussed further in Section 13.

8   The conceptual level

We now discuss in some detail the language production model motivated by our analysis of CS data. At the conceptual level speakers seek linguistic structures that satisfy their intentions. First they make decisions structuring the entire discourse. Second, speakers take account of other aspects of lexical-conceptual structure that apply at the level of specific lexemes; they consider which surface lexemes would best convey the semantic as well as the more purely pragmatic and sociopragmatic features of their intentions.

8.1   Overall discourse-level decisions

In reference to the overall discourse, speakers first consider socio- and psycho-linguistic aspects of lexical-conceptual structure. For example, of particular rele-vance to CS, speakers assess the feasibility of monolingual or bilingual discourse. This means that they take into account attitudes toward the linguistic varieties that the speakers have the potential to employ (i.e. sociolinguistic considerations); they also take account of their perceptions of proficiency of the interlocutors in these same linguistic varieties (i.e. psycholinguistic considerations). One consideration is simply the effect of their producing monolingual vs. bilingual speech. Possible attitudes toward even specific varieties of bilingual production are also considered (e.g. in a particular speech community, is intrasentential CS acceptable?). While interlocutors in a particular discourse setting weigh such matters, they are free to choose modes of speaking that may be characterized by others as marked (vs. unmarked; cf. Myers-Scotton, 1993).

If the interlocutors in a particular discourse choose to engage in bilingual speech involving intrasentential CS, they simultaneously select an ML to frame CPs to be produced. In Section 3, we referred to the socio- and psycholinguistic factors defining the ML. When speakers choose the ML, these are considered, but also salient are the more purely semantic (referential) features of a speaker's intentions. Based on some combination of these considerations, the ML is selected as the frame for the CP to be produced.

8.2   Semantic/pragmatic intentions

Also, again simultaneously, these same features come into play when individual content morphemes (lexemes) are considered to encode specific speaker intentions. That is, speakers consider which surface lexemes would best convey the semantic as well as the more purely pragmatic and sociopragmatic features of their intentions. The lexemes they select can be from either the ML or the EL. Recall, however, that at this abstract level of production, there are no lexemes accessed, but rather lemmas are activated in the mental lexicon that will support surface-level morphemes.

In summary, even though decisions made at the conceptual level refer to intentions, not utterance structures, the results of these decisions determine the language or languages to be activated and set their structural roles.

8.3   Semantic/pragmatic feature bundles

The particular semantic and pragmatic features associated with each lemma entry form its own specific lexical-conceptual structure. As indicated, the model assumes a universal set of semantic and pragmatic features that are available for the lexical-conceptual structuring of lemmas; yet, it also expects their presence and conflation to vary cross-linguistically. We see variation in lexicalization patterns across languages as evidence that there are different configurations of these features across related lemmas in different languages. As noted above, we refer to a lemma's configuration of these features as its *semantic/pragmatic feature bundle* (*SP feature bundle*).

Implicit in our discussion is the hypothesis that the structures appearing in intrasentential CS are evidence of the relative importance of lexical-conceptual DIFFERENCES in the nature of lexical entries. That is, when there is not an exact match across the language pairs involved in CS, there are consequences for the resulting CS structures. These conceptual structure differences may be simply pragmatic or semantic, or semantic with morphological consequences. When there are such differences across the languages involved in CS, the structures that are possible in CS give us information about the relative importance of specific conceptual differences as defining features of a lexical entry.

8.3.1   Differences in semantic/pragmatic features

A number of examples illustrate the nature of semantic/pragmatic features encoded in lexical-conceptual structure and how their conflation into SP feature bundles may differ cross-linguistically. First, in example (2), second-generation Turkish women immigrants in the Netherlands are alternating between Dutch and Turkish in discussing a traditional prewedding event and its attire (Backus, 1994). Related lexemes in Turkish and Dutch referring to "dress" are selected as appropriate at different points in the discourse; in (2a) the Turkish lexeme *elbise* is selected while in (2b) the Dutch lexeme *rok* is selected. Example (2a) occurs when the speakers are focusing on the traditional event, while much later in the conversation, the speakers produce (2b) as part of a general discussion of fashion ranging from velour trousers to LA Gear tennis shoes.[10]

> (2) a. als jij die   trouwjurk   zie-t, en die   KINA
>   if 2S DEM wedding dress see-2S and DEM henna
>   GECE-Sİ   ELBİSE-SI,
>   night-POSS dress-POSS
>   'if you see that wedding dress, and the "henna evening" dress,'
>   b. en die   gaa-t ze   drag-en   onder haar   KINA
>   and DEM go-3S she wear-INF under FEM/S/POSS henna
>   GECE-Sİ   rok.
>   night-POSS skirt
>   'and she will wear that under her "henna evening" skirt.'
>   (Turkish/Dutch CS; Backus, 1994)

Second, examples (3a) and (3b) and (4a) and (4b) show how semantic differences in the SP feature bundles of conceptually related lexemes have morphosyntactic consequences. For example, how the feature CAUSATION is conflated with other semantic features of a predicate determines the lexical-conceptual structure contained in a lemma (cf. Talmy, 1985). This affects the type of morphosyntactic procedures that the lemma calls from the formulator.

In English, agent causation is not distinguished from autonomous (non-) causation. In contrast, in Spanish and Japanese, the relevant semantic features are conflated into two distinct lexicalization patterns. In Spanish, CAUSATION is inherently part of the lexical conceptual structure of *abrir* 'open'. In order to express an autonomous, noncausative related event, a "morpheme satellite," the reflexive, is called up as part of the morphologically complex entry. In contrast, in Japanese, *aku* 'open' is inherently an autonomous, noncausative event, and a causative verb form *akeru* is required to add a semantic feature to the lexical-conceptual structure of intransitive 'open'.

(3) a. Spanish:

       Abrió la puerta.   La puerta se   abrió
       [he] opened the door.   the door REFL opened
       'He opened the door.'   'The door opened.'

  b. Japanese:

    Doa   ga   aita
    door SUBJ open (PAST)
    'The door was open.'
    Kare wa   doa   o   aketa
    he   TOP   door OBJ open (CAUS PAST)
    'He opened the door.'
    (Talmy, 1985: 85)

Another pair of examples illustrating how semantic features can be conflated differently into SP feature bundles (and consequently realized in lexical entries differently) involves the feature MANNER. English motion verbs can include MANNER as a semantic feature; Spanish motion verbs cannot. In (4a), MOTION and MANNER are conflated into *float*. The PP *into the cave* expresses PATH. In (4b), MOTION and PATH are conflated into *entró*. A present participle *flotando* expresses MANNER.

(4) a. The bottle floated into the cave.
  b. La botella entró a la cueva flotando.
    (Talmy, 1985: 69)

Similarly, one can argue that certain CS examples arise because of lack of congruence in semantic features. For example, the English verb *decide* occurs frequently in Swahili/English CS conversations (see example (5)), seemingly filling a semantic function not met by a Swahili counterpart. In a Swahili counterpart to *decide* (*-kata shauri*, literally 'cut/reduce problem'), the relevant semantic features of *-kata shauri* express (in Talmy's terms; 1985: 88) "inchoative *entering-into-a-state*." These contrast with those of *decide*, which express "agentive *putting-into-a-state*."

(5) Kwa vile zi-ko   ny-ingi,   si-wez-i   DECIDE
    because   CL10-COP CL10-many 1S/NEG-be able-NEG decide

i-le   i-na-fa-a   zaidi
CL9-DEM CL9-NON-PAST-be proper-FV[11] more
'Because there are many, I can't decide the most proper one.'
(Swahili/English; Myers-Scotton, 1993a: 114)

8.3.2 SP feature bundle congruence and CS examples

We now consider the consequences for CS structures of cross-linguistic variation in SP feature bundles. Example (6) illustrates a case of sufficient congruence across SP feature bundles to allow for near-complete morphosyntactic integration of an EL content morpheme in a surface string fully inflected by the ML (i.e. a mixed constituent).[12] We posit that English *come* can occur because it is projected from an EL lemma in the mental lexicon that has an SP feature bundle sufficiently congruent with an ML lemma counterpart. The ML lemma that has the most closely related SP feature bundle supports the Swahili verb stem -*j*- 'come'. At this point in our articulation of the model, what is "sufficiently congruent" is unknown. (The presence of "double morphology" (i.e. the English plural morpheme in *books*) is discussed in Section 9.2.)

(6) Leo   si-ku-COME   na   Ø-BOOK-S   z-angu.
    today 1S/NEG PAST/NEG-come with CL10-book-s CL10-my
    James a-li-end-a   na-zo   mpaka kesho
    James 3S-PAST-go-INDIC with-CL10(them) until   tomorrow
    'Today I didn't come with my books. James went with them until tomorrow.'
    (Swahili/English; Myers-Scotton, 1993a: 80)

8.4 Conceptual structure and compromise CS strategies

Two main alternatives to full ML inflection of an EL morpheme in a mixed CS constituent exist.

First, an EL content morpheme can occur as a *bare form*. That is, although the EL content morpheme does occur in the constituent slot project by the ML, it lacks the ML system morphemes to make it completely well formed according to the ML morphosyntax. (Note that bare forms do not violate the system morpheme principle, which requires that if syntactically active system morphemes are present, they must be from the ML.) We propose that uninflected EL content morphemes occur because there is not sufficient congruence at some level (Myers-Scotton, 1993a: 112–16). In (7), the lexical-conceptual structure of *underestimate* is not totally congruent with a Spanish counterpart. The result is that *underestimate* occurs as a bare form without the second person familiar suffix -*as*.[13] Possible Spanish counterparts have different semantic/pragmatic bundles;

menospreciar 'undervalue' has a negative connotation, and *desestimar* has more the sense of 'not esteem'.

> (7) Tú lo   UNDERESTIMATE a Chito
>   you him underestimate   to Chito
>   'You underestimate Chito.'
>   (Spanish/English; Pfaff, 1979: 301)

The second alternative strategy is more radical from the standpoint of the ML frame: an EL island is produced. Recall that an EL island consists only of EL morphemes and must be well formed according to EL well-formedness conditions. We hypothesize that the major reason EL islands are formed is a congruence problem across the CS language pair in regard to SP feature bundles. Examples (8), (9), and (10) illustrate such cases. The other major reason for their formation has to do with incongruence regarding predicate–argument structure, and that will be discussed below. Note that these hypotheses depart somewhat from the discussion of EL islands in Myers-Scotton (1993a). The ways in which the ML still frames the entire CP that includes EL islands are discussed in Section 11.5.

In example (8) the English lexeme *nonsense* is the head of an EL island posited to result because of differing SP feature bundles across the languages involved. According to our hypothesis, at the level of the mental lexicon where the lemma supporting *nonsense* is present, there is no ML counterpart in which the relevant semantic and pragmatic features are conflated into a sufficiently congruent SP feature bundle, that is, its lexical-conceptual structure. Still, since an EL rendition of a certain concept is preferred, the EL lemma supporting this concept is activated in the mental lexicon.[14] This lemma activates morphosyntactic procedures in the formulator, such that ML procedures are inhibited for the maximal category projection (here, NP) associated with that lemma. The result is an EL island. As in all EL islands, all of the system morphemes come from the EL.

> (8) Wewe u-li-ku-w-a   mlevi   sana jana.
>   You   2SG-PAST-INFIN-be-FV drunk person very yesterday
>   Karibu m-kosan-e   na kila   mtu.
>   nearly obj-make mistake-SUBJUNC with every person
>   U-li-ku-w-a   u-ki-onge-a
>   2SG-PAST-INF-COP-FV 2SG-ASP-chat-FV
>   A LOT OF NONSENSE
>   'You were very drunk yesterday. That you should almost make a
>   fool of yourself with every person. You were talking a lot of
>   nonsense.'
>   (Swahili/English; Myers-Scotton, 1993a: 44)

In line with our hypothesis, example (9) also arises because the SP feature bundles of the EL lemma are not sufficiently congruent with those of the ML lemma. *Bring it up* occurs as an EL island because the speaker chooses an EL lemma's lexical-conceptual structure. One of the consequences of selecting *bring up* with a pronominal object is that the EL lemma projects a morphosyntactic structure in which the pronominal object of English occurs before the particle satellite. This example illustrates that in EL islands, it is the EL lemma that calls up morphosyntactic procedures in the formulator. Notice that in a mixed constituent, while an EL lemma may support an EL lexeme, provided that the EL lemma is sufficiently congruent with the ML counterpart, it is always this ML counterpart that calls up the morphosyntactic procedures from the formulator, never the EL lemma. Compare (7) above, in which the EL lexeme *underestimate* occurs in a morphosyntactic frame projected by its ML counterpart. Evidence that it is the ML counterpart projecting the frame is that the object pronoun clitic occurs before the inflected verb in (7) while the object pronoun occurs according to English structural constraints in (9).

(9) No va-n   a BRING IT UP
      NO go-3PL to
      'They are not going to bring it up.'
      (Spanish/English; Pfaff, 1979: 296)

Thus, one reason EL islands result is that the speaker's intentions regarding lexical-conceptual structure cannot be adequately realized in the ML (i.e. SP feature bundles do not match sufficiently).

The above examples illustrate EL islands resulting from lack of congruence regarding content morphemes; however, because speakers can also have intentions regarding lexical-conceptual structure conveyed by system morphemes, they may produce EL islands because of congruence problems in such cases.

Quantifiers are good examples of system morphemes that may produce such problems. Quantifiers are system morphemes that clearly have semantic content. Recall that system morphemes with the feature [+ Q] identify a member or members of a set. Thus, in many examples of EL islands, it seems that a motivation for producing the island is to make a contrast to ensure UNIQUE specification of quantification. That is, there may well be a pragmatic or semantic mismatch cross-linguistically in quantifiers. In (10), the speaker's intention seems to be to draw attention to the contrast between her having completed a task as opposed to the addressee's more minimal accomplishments. The English construction, *all the x*, gives the quantifier *all* prominence not afforded by the Swahili counterpart *nguo zote* 'clothes all'. (Neither would a mixed constituent offer prominence to 'all' since it would follow Swahili order, e.g. *clothes zote*.) Her choosing to use English, partly because of the word order it affords, is made at the conceptual level; yet, this has consequences in terms of the morphological realization pattern.

(10)   Ni-me-maliz-a ku-tengenez-a vi-tanda ni-ka-WASH
       I have finished to fix [make] PL-bed 1SG-CONSEQ-wash
       ALL THE CLOTHING na   wewe bado   maliza na
                        and you   not yet finish   with
       KITCHEN. Ni nini   u-na-fany-i-a   hu-ko?
                   is   what you are doing there?
       'I finished making the beds and I've washed all the clothing and you aren't yet finished in the kitchen. What are you doing there?'
       (Swahili/English; Myers-Scotton, 1993a: 80)

8.5   The conceptual level and predicate–argument structure

As should be clear, the selection of the SP feature bundles is part of the conceptual level of this language production model. Yet, this selection can have consequences at another level. Recall that lemmas, which are located in the mental lexicon, send directions to the formulator to construct sentential frames at the functional level. The basis for most directions is the predicate–argument structure contained in lemmas. Yet the SP feature bundle may ultimately be the determining factor for some of these directions. The specifics of this argument will not be developed in this chapter; but such examples as the morphosyntactic consequences of selecting the nominalization version of a conceptual structure rather than the verbal version come to mind.

9   Insights into the complexities of lemma entries

CS data also provide empirical evidence about the nature of at least certain lemma entries and their relation to the conceptual structures activating them.

9.1   Nonfinite verb forms and their lemma entries

First, consider nonfinite forms, such as present and past participles. In all CS data sets available, such lexical items, although morphologically complex, act as if they are single units from the standpoint of the constituent frame.

For example, when an EL participle appears in a mixed constituent, evidence of its unitary nature is twofold.

1   The participle always appears in a multimorphemic form, as the verb stem plus the requisite EL affix(es) associated with well-formed participles in the

EL. Such "full category-identifying affixation" does not occur for other EL content morphemes in mixed constituents, with the exception of plurals in some cases, as noted above.

2   The formulator treats the EL participle as a "completed content morpheme" of the same order as an EL noun or adjective. That is, no further ML affixes relevant to category membership (i.e. participle, in this case) are applied (cf. for example Ten Hacken, 1994: 311–12). Example (11) illustrates an English past participle (*worried*) in a mixed constituent.

(11) ma ba'ti?id   innik   WORRIED bas
      no 1S/PRES/think COMP/2S worried   but
      inti   CURIOUS
      you   curious
      'I don't think that you are worried but you are curious.'
      (Arabic/English; Okasha, 1995: 2.50)

Recall that, as formulated in the MLF model, the system morpheme principle refers to "syntactically active" system morphemes. A syntactically active morpheme has relevance in a syntactic category beyond its head. This principle, therefore, allows for the possibility of EL system morphemes, but only if those morphemes do not control the signalling of syntactic relationships of the head in its larger constituent.

The fact that certain EL inflected forms occur in mixed constituents implies that there are two different kinds of procedures operating in the formulator. One is sensitive to directions INTERNAL to a lexical category. This is the procedure that accepts the English past participle *worried* as congruent with an ML modifier. Under this view, EL affixes on nonfinite verb forms are accessed via procedures providing morphology relevant only in a category-internal sense. One way of looking at those affixes that we refer to as category-internal is to say that they are best classified as derivational rather than inflectional. The other procedure in the formulator is sensitive to directions ACROSS lexical categories, including those regarding morphological realization patterns of surface phrase structure. Directions relevant across lexical categories must come only from the ML.

In terms of the inflectional procedures they undergo, participles are treated as single units in CS. Whether the lemma supporting the morpheme is complex or whether two lemmas are involved is open to question.

Yet CS data also provide evidence that the complexity of these lemmas – and presumably other lemmas as well – can vary cross-linguistically. For example, even though the lexical category Infinitive would have seemingly identical SP bundles cross-linguistically, the lemma supporting this category may be different from one language to another The evidence is at the morpheme level. English and

French infinitives differ in their realizations in CS mixed constituents when either language is the EL. The French infinitive is always bimorphemic (including an affix which apparently marks Infinitive), as in (12) below. In contrast English infinitives never include the free-form system morpheme *to*, which also marks Infinitive. This pattern suggests two things:

1   The French infinitive lemma entry is complex and distinctive, while the English one is the same as that for the verb stem.
2   English *to* is a system morpheme while the French infinitive marker serves more as a derivational affix.

Thus, the same conceptual structure (Infinitive) has different lemma histories cross-linguistically.

9.2   How does "double morphology" result?

Plurals in a number of language pairs show "double morphology," that is, plural affixes from both the ML and the EL. In fewer cases, infinitives also show infinitival affixes from both languages; this is usually the case when French is the EL, since, as noted above, a French infinitive always appears with the French infinitival affix.

The two different cases of double morphology arise in two different ways. When infinitives in CS show double morphology, it is because the EL lemma entry for Infinitive is the base form in that language. For example, in (12) the entire French infinitive *comprendre* is retrieved as a single unit because there is no other form in French that is congruent with the base form of the Lingala verb stem.

> (12) L'   HEURE ya kala TROIS QUARTS ya ba-JEUNE-S
>   DET hour   of past three   quarters of CL2-young-PL
>   ko-COMPREND-RE   AVENIR te . . .
>   INFIN-understand-INFIN future   not
>   'In the past three-fourths of the young people did not under-
>   stand what their future meant . . .'
>   (Lingala/French; Bokamba, 1988: 37)

The plural case is more problematic. Myers-Scotton discusses the phenomenon extensively (1993a: 110–12, 132–6) and concludes that there is "strong implicational evidence that double morphology may result from misfiring at some point in production" (1993a: 135). Under her argument, the plural affix is encoded in its own lemma and the EL affix is accessed by mistake when the lemma for the noun itself is called. Since the grammatical frame in which the EL noun is to appear is under ML control, the formulator then goes on to call the ML affix. The net result is two affixes for the same job.

The issue remains, however, what is the nature of the suggested "misfiring" and why should it come about frequently only with the plural affix and not affixes for inflections for other properties, such as gender or case?[15] We can make "misfiring" more specific in the following way. We suggest that plural has a conceptual structure setting it apart from other nominal affixes whose contribution has to do with structuring the nominal phrase, not adding semantic weight. While all system morphemes are "indirectly elected" at the conceptual level by the content lemma that projects them (Willem Levelt, personal communication), only an ML system morpheme should be elected (i.e. not a system morpheme from BOTH the ML and the EL). A possible reason both morphemes appear is that there may be a "mistiming" (rather than a "misfiring") such that the EL lemma supporting both the nominal concept and its indirectly elected plural are selected before the ML setting the grammatical frame is activated (Willem Levelt, personal communication). Then, when it turns out that the ML is not the same language as that of the nominal concept, in its frame-building function, the ML supplies its own rendition of plural.

10   Predicate–argument structure and the functional level

Recall that while intrasentential CS requires that morphemes from both languages be present in the same CP, it is only ML lemmas that send directions to the formulator to set the CP frame (except internally in EL islands). Setting the frame has several aspects for intrasentential CS. As in monolingual discourse, it means that the predicate–argument structure is realized (i.e. a schema with slots for the verb and its arguments) as well as morphological realization patterns (most crucially the requisite system morphemes). For the mixed constituents of intrasentential CS, setting the frame also means inhibiting EL lemmas at the functional level so that only ML lemmas will "call" procedures in the formulator setting up the schema (i.e. morpheme order and system morphemes will come from the ML). Yet, lemmas from BOTH languages are activated at some point in the production process.

Above we suggested how EL lemmas first come into play at the conceptual level. That is, speaker intentions that involve EL content morphemes activate the EL lemmas in the mental lexicon that support the morphemes. There, these lemmas are checked with ML counterparts for congruence with respect to lexical-conceptual structure; that is, their SP feature bundles are checked.

We now discuss CS data that motivate the claim that another checking procedure must take place before directions are sent to the formulator. The predicate–argument structures supported by EL lemmas and their ML counterparts are checked; that is, their *morphosyntactic feature bundles* (hereafter *MS feature bundles*) are compared.

Suppose that an EL lemma is selected at the conceptual level. If the MS feature bundle of its supported lexeme is congruent with the MS feature bundle of the ML lexeme whose lemma is directing the projection of the sentential frame, then the EL lexeme is morphosyntactically integrated into the ML frame.

As was the case with the conceptual level, there is internal complexity at the functional level. The predicate–argument structure encoded in the lemma "calls" two classes of morphosyntactic procedures in the formulator, an argument introduced in Section 9.1. First, some procedures result in structures internal to a single maximal category (e.g. regarding a noun and certain affixes – possibly those for gender and plural). There is some evidence that not only the ML but also the EL may be involved in calling these procedures that determine category-internal form. Specifically, we have in mind gender as a feature. Further discussion awaits more research, however. Second, there is another class of procedures that is called only by the ML. These determine the morphosyntactic relations between the projections of the various lexical categories. The examples that we cite now to demonstrate the role of congruence between EL and ML lemmas at the predicate–argument structure come from this second class.

Example (13) shows the prototypical case of close congruence between the lemmas underlying the realization of an EL content morpheme (the English verb stem *help*) in an ML frame. In this case, the thematic content of the lexical-conceptual structure and the grammatical argument structure are very similar across the ML and EL. In both the ML (Adaŋme) and the EL (English), a figure is a benefactive and the subject is the actor.

> (13) a   ŋɛ   mĩ   HELP-e
>   3PL COP 1S/OBJ help-PRES PROG
>   'They are helping me.'
>   (Adaŋme/English; Nartey, 1982: 185)

Example (13) contrasts with (12) from Lingala/French CS. In (12) the French verb includes the infinitive suffix. We argue that the difference between the EL verb in (12) and (13) lies in the difference between what is perceived as the base form of the verb in the EL (i.e. English and French differ in this regard).

11   Issues of congruence in verb phrase structure

In some cases, an EL verb may be congruent at the conceptual level, but not congruent in terms of the predicate–argument structure.

11.1   Congruence and predicate–argument structure

The lack of congruence between the EL and ML regarding the verbal phrase in example (14) shows clearly that it is the ML that projects the morphosyntactic frame. In this case, the lemmas supporting the notion of *graduate* in the ML (Japanese) and the EL (English) have similar enough lexical-conceptual structures for the EL lemma to project its lexeme in the surface. Yet, these structures are slightly different and this becomes evident when SOURCE is part of the proposition to be expressed. In English to express SOURCE with *graduate* requires a surface form of verb + prepositional phrase (*graduate + from*-NP). Its Japanese counterpart expresses the notion of SOURCE without a prepositional/ postpositional contentful phrase; it takes only a direct object with accusative case marking. While this may be only a slight difference, it still means the MS feature bundles of *graduate* are different in English and Japanese.

(14) a. *Watashi wa Waseda-kara   GRADUATE
          1S   TOP   from (ABL)
          shimashita
          did
     b. Watashi wa Waseda-(o) GRADUATE shimashita
                          ACC
          'I graduated from Waseda [University].'
          (Japanese/English; Azuma, 1991: 97–8; also cited in
          Azuma, 1993: 1078–9)

If the EL lemma supporting *graduate* were the one calling morphosyntactic procedures in the formulator for mixed constituents, then a sentence such as (14a) should be possible, since the system morpheme *-kara* 'from' comes from Japanese, and only the content morpheme *graduate* comes from English. Since (14a) is not attested, but (14b) is, such evidence supports the hypothesis that the ML (Japanese here) is the only one sending morphosyntactic directions of any kind to the formulator when mixed constituents are being constructed – even though EL lemmas (*graduate* here) can support content morphemes in these constituents.[16] (The use of an EL content verb with an ML auxiliary verb in a *do* verb construction is discussed in Section 11.2.)

The following example illustrates a similar situation in Turkish/Dutch. The main difference is that both the verb and its grammatical argument, the direct object, are EL lexemes. The Dutch direct object occurs with the ML suffix for accusative and plural, *gesprek-ler-i* 'conversations'. If the frame for this mixed constituent were projected from the EL, then this Dutch noun would occur in a comitative/instrumental PP (with *met*) and with a Dutch plural suffix. However, as is predicted, the formulator has projected an accusative-marked slot for the direct object, in line with the specifications of the ML. This is why the Dutch noun occurs without *met*, but with the Turkish accusative suffix.

(15) POLITIEK GESPREK-ler-i   OPHOUD-EN yap-ın
      political   conversation-PL-ACC stop-INF   do-IMP
      la
      INTENS
      'Stop this about politics, man!'
      (Turkish/Dutch; Backus, 1992: 99)

Example (16) shows how a lexical gap for a verb is handled by Turkish. Turkish has no equivalent for *uitmaken met* 'break up with' in Dutch. The Dutch verb itself is inserted as a nonfinite form into a mixed constituent by using the *do* construction discussed below. The verb "satellite" meaning 'with' (Dutch *met*) is rejected by the Turkish frame; yet a loan translation of *met* into Turkish is accepted, possibly because Turkish has no competing counterpart; thus, the question of ML congruency for the satellite does not arise. This is a remarkable example from the standpoint of showing the robustness of the ML frame in controlling system morphemes.

(16) O diyor ben UITMAK-EN   yap-tı-m   kız-ınam
      he said I   break up-INFIN do-PAST-1S girl-with
      'He said [that] I have broken up with [the] girl.'
      (Turkish/Dutch; Backus, 1994)

The following Swahili/English example contrasts with the Japanese/English and Turkish/Dutch examples above in that the lack of congruence across lexical categories of verbal complements is solved in a different way – without the system morpheme supporting the ML frame prevailing, but with no EL frame, either.

(17) Mbona ha-wa   Ø-WORKER-S w-a   EAST AFRICA
      why   dem-CL2 CL2-worker-PL CL2-of
      POWER AND LIGHTING wa-ka-end-a   STRIKE
                                3PL-CONSEQ-go-FV strike
      hata we-ngine na-siki-a
      even CL-other 1SG/NONPAST-hear-FV
      wa-sha-wek-w-a   CELL
      3PL-"PERFECTIVE"-put-PASS-FV
      'And why did these workers of the East African Power and
      Lighting [Company] go [on] strike? – I even hear [that] some of
      them have already been put [in] cell[s].'
      (Swahili/English; Myers-Scotton, 1993a: 96)

In this example, note the mixed constituents *wa-ka-end-a STRIKE* and *wa-sha-wek-w-a CELL*. The result is now a bare form; both *strike* and *cell* are EL content morphemes uninflected in either the ML or the EL. In the previous two examples, the ML inflections appeared. We propose that the full form vs. the bare form realization can be explained by the difference in the morphosyntactic requirements of the respective MLs. In Japanese, for example, all NPs must be overtly case marked (unless the accusative direct object immediately precedes its verb). In Swahili, however, specific word order and verbal extensions, as well as prepositions and postpositions, are required to realize thematic roles. In (17) word order seems to serve the function of identifying *cell* as locative goal, even though the NP is not well formed in Swahili without some functional element marking its class gender (i.e. an element corresponding to any of classes 16–18, the locative gender classes).

In the Swahili/English example, the MS feature bundle projected by the verb for both languages includes the thematic role of locative. In English, locative thematic roles occur as PPs; in Bantu languages, most locatives are NPs prefixed or suffixed with a locative class (= gender) marker. This example shows a compromise strategy. The EL locative NP occurs with neither the EL preposition nor the ML class marker (*-ni* in this case), with only word order as an indication of role.

11.2 A strategy to include EL verbs as nonfinite forms

Another type of compromise strategy already exemplified above is a *do* construction. This construction consists of the ML verb encoding *do* (or a similar auxiliary verb) inflected with all of the requisite ML system morphemes (tense/aspect, agreement, etc.) appearing with an uninflected EL content verb (often the infinitive). We propose that the structural properties of verbs (what constitutes an inflectible stem) are such that when these languages are MLs, these properties block the occurrence of an EL verb with ML inflections. Thus, if an EL verb best satisfies the speaker's intentions, a compromise strategy is to place it in a frame projected by the ML auxiliary, with the auxiliary taking all verbal inflections.

> (18) Avan enne CONFUSE paNNiTTaan
>   he   me   do-PAST
>   'He confused me.'
>   (Tamil/English; Annamalai, 1989: 51, cited in Myers-Scotton, 1993: 113)

Boeschoten (personal communication) argues that such constructions are an areal feature rather than a typological one. He makes two points: first, such constructions are a commonplace strategy for incorporating borrowed lexemes in

the geographical area extending from Turkey to India. Second, such *do* constructions are now being found in the Moroccan Arabic/Dutch CS of some Moroccans
living in the Netherlands, possibly by analogy with such constructions in Turkish/
Dutch CS. Example (19) shows this:

> (19) baš y-dir   AFKOEL-EN!
>   for 3-do/IMPERF cool down-INF
>   'In order to cool (himself) down!'
>   (Moroccan Arabic/Dutch; Boumans, 1994: 3)

In many of the data sets in which the *do* construction is attested, the ML is
verb-final. One could argue that this typological contrast seems to motivate the
use of an ML auxiliary verb (usually *do*) in final position preceded by a nonfinite
EL verb that carries the content. Language pairs in which the ML is verb-final
showing *do* constructions include various Indian languages/English (both Indo-
European and Dravidian), Japanese/English, and Turkish/Germanic languages.
Earlier examples from Japanese/English CS (14) and Turkish/Dutch CS ((15) and
(16)) include *do* constructions. No cases of EL verbs inflected with ML morphology, if the ML is verb-final, are reported in the literature. However, the *do*
construction is also found in other language pairs that do not show this directional
contrast in thematic role and case assignment, for example southern Bantu languages (e.g. Shona, Chewa) and English CS as well as Moroccan Arabic/Dutch CS
(see (19)).

Thus, as we have suggested above, directionality may be only a surface mani-
festation of a more basic distinction in what it takes for a verb to qualify for
projecting thematic roles onto the sentential frame. Lack of congruence at the
level of morphological realization patterns in terms of both thematic role and case
assignment seems to promote use of the *do* construction, but more research is
necessary.

11.3   When a lexical category is missing

Some passive constructions in CS illustrate the effects of lack of congruence cross-
linguistically when verbal derivations are encoded differently, For example, in
English, past participles function adjectivally (and are analyzed as adjectives within
most generative frameworks, having lost their case-assigning properties). That is,
English past participles can be viewed as [+N] and [+V], but Swahili lacks a past
participle and Swahili passive verbs are only [+V]. These passive verbs exhibit the
same morphosyntactic properties as active verbs; subject morphology and tense/
aspect morphology are identical. Furthermore, the passive suffix is a member of
the set of verbal suffixes that add to or alter the lexical-conceptual content of the
verb stem. Other characteristic members of the set are stative, causative, and

applied. Passive combines productively with many of these suffixes to produce modified SP feature bundles (for example, -andik- takes the passive suffix for the meaning 'be written', -andik-w-; combined with the applied suffix -andik-i-w- has the meaning 'to be written for'). In the example below, the lexical-conceptual structure associated with the SP feature bundle of *offered* has been selected. It could be argued that English *offered* fills a lexical gap; yet it seems the better argument is that *offered* and its Swahili counterpart are pragmatic mismatches. The Swahili semantic counterpart is -nunuliwa 'be bought for'; however, its use incorporates the sense of 'money being paid' much more so than does *offered*. At any rate, the EL lexeme most closely matches the speaker's intentions and occurs in the sentential frame projected by the ML counterpart lemma. The lexical category of the EL lexeme, however, does not fit into the morphosyntactic frame normally projected in the Swahili passive construction. It does, however, fit into a frame of *copula "be"* + *predicate adjective* in Swahili.

(20) A-li-ku-w-a   ha-zi-BUY   hi-zo
      3SG-PAST-INF-BE-FV 3SG/NEG-CL10/OBJ-buy those-CL10
      a-li-ku-w-a   a-na-ku-w-a   OFFERED tu
      3SG-PAST-INF-BE-FV 3SG-PROG-INF-be-FV offered   just
      'He didn't buy those, he was just being offered.'
      (Swahili/English; Myers-Scotton, 1993a: 115)

The use of a compromise strategy is common in Swahili/English CS when there is lack of congruence across derived verbal forms, here, a past participle. For example, in "popular Swahili" there is a construction consisting of the locative copula -ko inflected for subject plus a predicate adjective. English past participles occur readily in this construction (e.g. *tu-ko confused* 'we are confused'; Myers-Scotton, 1993a: 115). Recall that we argue in Section 9.1 that participles are morphologically complex single units supported by a single lemma.

11.4   Tailoring EL verb stems to meet ML requirements

Another compromise strategy is illustrated in the Swiss German/French example below. In order for French verbs to receive Swiss German subject-verb agreement, they are morphologically adapted to a Swiss German verbal paradigm. This is accomplished by attaching the derivational affix -ier- before the normal inflectional agreements. That is, in order for a verb to be recognized as an inflectible stem, it must satisfy certain morphological requirements of Swiss German. Without the German derivational affix, French verbs do not appear to do so, for reasons unknown as yet. Note that while *forcier-* occurs in Standard German, it does not occur in monolingual Swiss German.

(21) Die altere muen die jungere FORCIER-e, no die ander Sproch
      au no einisch hie und do . . .
      'The parents must force the children, to [use] the other language
      now and then . . .'
      (Swiss German/French; Lüdi, 1983)

11.5   EL islands: the radical solution to a mismatch

When predicate–argument structures across languages involved in CS show such
incongruence that the types of compromise strategies discussed above do not
seem to suffice, then a more radical strategy is followed: EL material selected at
the conceptual level appears in EL islands. All EL islands consist entirely of EL
morphemes and follow EL well-formedness conditions for internal structural
dependency. EL islands that are not internal EL islands (discussed below) are well-
formed maximal projections (e.g. NP, PP) in the EL; internal EL islands may or
may not be maximal projections. All EL islands are within a CP framed by the ML.
This is a more restricted definition of an EL island than that in Myers-Scotton
(1993a).

   Under the approach followed here, sometimes congruence at the lexical-
conceptual structure level provides a match between the EL lemma and its ML
counterpart, but the ML morphosyntactic frame does not accept the mapping
that the EL lemma would project. For example, in (22) from Shona/English CS,
the issue is lack of congruence in how a required locative NP (i.e. the verb is
subcategorized for it) is realized in the morphosyntactic frame. In Shona, to
convey the idea of movement along a PATH, a motion verb with an applied suffix
conveying directionality toward a figure realized as a postverbal NP is required.
English conveys such directionality with a PP. Because *ku-transfer* has been realized
without the requisite applied suffix, an EL island with PPs is required to convey
the notion of PATH. Note that we would argue that while *transfer* DOES trigger a
following constituent in English, the trigger is not the surface lexeme *transfer*.[17]
Rather, the reason is that *transfer* lacks the applied suffix that would allow for a
bare NP complement as projected by the ML counterpart. Thus it is the morphological realization encoding the predicate–argument structure that triggers an EL
island. Given *transfer* as a "bare verb" (without the applied suffix), the only alternative is to complete the projection of the locative thematic role with an EL island
PP.[18]

(22) . . . WHENEVER munhu kana-ada ku-TRANSFER FROM
      A   CERTAIN   DEPARTMENT   TO   A   CERTAIN
      DEPARTMENT . . .
      '. . . whenever a person wants to transfer . . .'
      (Shona/English; Crawhall, 1990: tape 16d)

The example above contrasts with the following one from English/Spanish CS. In English, an NP expressing the notion of PATH must be governed by a locative preposition, as in (22). However, an NP expressing the notion of BENE-FICIARY (MALEFACTIVE) can be directly governed by its verb, as in *accuse someone*. This contrasts with Spanish, in which a verb cannot directly govern a BENEFICIARY complement. Thus, if a speaker engaging in intrasentential English/Spanish CS selects Spanish to encode the BENEFICIARY, this NP can appear in an EL island, as in (23). The BENEFICIARY NP occurs in a PP EL island, properly governed in Spanish, by the case-assigning preposition *a*.

The argument that Spanish, not English, is the underlying ML was con-sidered, but discarded. On this view, a Spanish verb would project the PP and English *accused* is only an inserted EL lexeme (a sufficiently congruent counterpart of the Spanish verb). But if Spanish were the ML, then there is no explanation for the English pronoun (*he*), which is not congruent with a Spanish counterpart, or the English past tense inflection. Within the model, the only possible explanation is to argue that English is the ML and that there are two Spanish EL islands. The English verb *accuse* projects the beneficiary thematic role, but it need not project the surface phrase structure realizing the role; it can be realized in an EL island. Of course the speaker could have avoided using Spanish altogether. However, he/she has chosen to identify the beneficiary in Spanish; this is a decision made for pragmatic reasons at the lexical-conceptual level. As long as the constituent *a Mister Bigote* is a well-formed maximal projection in Spanish, it qualifies as an EL island. This constituent case-marked by a preposition is predicted (not an NP) because Spanish, not English, calls procedures in the formulator spelling out the morphosyntax. Thus, it is the content lexeme *Mister Bigote* that indirectly elects its requisite system morpheme *a*, not the case-marking preposition that is hierarchic-ally superior in surface phrase structure. As long as the projection of a beneficiary is congruent across Spanish and English (as it is), the Spanish PP following the English verb is possible. The presence of such a mixed CP implies that the realization of thematic roles is somehow a surface phenomenon, separable from the projection of those roles.[19]

(23) He accused A   MISTER BIGOTE DE DOBLE LENGUAJE.
           [to] mister   bigote   of   double   language
      'He accused Mister Bigote ["Mister Moustache"] of double talk.'
      (English/Spanish; Moyer, 1992: 55)

Finally, lack of congruence between two languages based on clitic proper-ties of definite articles may explain why NP EL islands occur in an asymmetric fashion. Data from a large corpus of Swiss German/Italian CS (Preziosa-Di Quin-zio, 1992) in which at times Swiss German is the ML and at other times Italian is the ML shows such an asymmetry. EL islands consisting of NPs from Italian occur freely, but not such islands from Swiss German when Italian is the ML. The EL island from Italian (DET + N) in (24a) exemplifies the many Italian NP EL islands that occur in this corpus, while (24b) illustrates a German noun occurring with an Italian determiner. There are no instances of German definite DET + N EL islands. This case illustrates lack of congruence at the functional level (morphological realization patterns), but it may also reflect congruence problems at the conceptual level (lexical-conceptual structure).

(24) a. Eba   dann simmer go LE   PENTOLE
        exactly then be-1PL go DET/FEM/PL pan-PL
        bringa
        take-INF
        'Exactly, and then we went to take the pans there.'
     b. Gli   italiani   sono   cosi
        the/MASC/PL italian/MASC/PL be/3PL so
        forti   con le   ABCHURZIGA,
        strong/MASC/PL with DET/FEM/PL abbreviations,
        ga?
        huh?
        'The Italians are so good at abbreviations, aren't they?'
        (Italian/Swiss German; Preziosa-DiQuinzio, 1992: xxx, vii)

11.6   Summary of effects of congruence on resulting phrase structures

All the examples in the preceding parts of Section 11 show some compromise strategy that seems necessary to accommodate the appearance of the EL material. In line with our overall claim, we hypothesize that there is insufficient congruence, regarding some aspect of predicate–argument structure, between an EL lemma and its ML counterpart for the EL lexeme supported by the EL lemma to appear with no modifications in a mixed constituent framed by the ML. In (14) an EL verb is stripped of its satellite (*graduate from = graduate*) but otherwise morphosyntactically integrated into the ML frame. In (15) the Dutch noun *gesprek* receives ML accusative marking rather than occurring in a PP headed by *met* 'with' as it would in Dutch. In (16) a "*do* construction" from the ML plus an ML loan translation of the Dutch verb satellite is employed to accommodate a Dutch verb for which the ML shows a lexical gap (i.e. *uitmaken met* 'to break up with' becomes *uitmaken* plus the Turkish suffix for 'with' on the Turkish direct object). Examples (14) through (20) and (22) show EL lexemes occurring in mixed constituents, but as bare forms, under a variety of conditions including the *do*-verb construction. Recall that a bare form is an EL noun or verb that appears in a mixed constituent, but without the requisite ML system morpheme that would make it a fully inflected noun in the ML or a finite verb in the ML. Another strategy for dealing with noncongruent EL material is shown in example (21); a derivational suffix added to an EL verb enables it to be read as an ML verb and therefore to receive ML verbal inflections. Finally, examples (22), (23), and (24) show the most extreme accommodation to lack of congruence between an EL lemma and an ML counterpart. In these cases, accommodating certain types of EL material in a mixed constituent seems impossible; the evidence is that the EL material appears only in an EL island.

12 EL islands further studied

In (6)–(24), we have shown how EL material can be treated in various ways when congruence involving its predicate–argument structure or morphological realization patterns is checked against that of its ML counterpart. As discussed above, one strategy for dealing with insufficient congruence is to produce an EL island that fits the requirements of both the ML and the EL as a maximal projection. Evidence that these islands are under some ML control, even while conforming to the well-formedness conditions of the EL (i.e. morphological realization patterns are those of the EL, not the ML) is twofold:

1   EL islands (which are not internal EL islands) must qualify as maximal projections in the ML as well as in the EL, but they need not be identical syntactic categories, a constraint proposed in Woolford (1983).
2   Placement of EL islands follows well-formedness conditions of the ML, not the EL.

For example, see (25) in which the French PP conforms with Brussels Dutch placement, not unmarked placement in French.

(25) Ja vijf of zes waren er   want die À FRONT DE RUE
       yes five or six were there for   who at end   of street
       waren
       were
       'Yes there were five or six, (for) who were at the end of the street.'
       (Brussels Dutch/French; Treffers-Daller, 1993: 223)

There is also another type of EL island. While these islands may be maximal projections within the EL, they are not according to ML well-formedness conditions. Rather, they occur as intermediate constituents within ML maximal projections. For this reason, we differentiate them by calling them "internal" EL islands. Such islands do meet well-formedness conditions of the EL. Yet, because they occur within ML maximal projections, ML morphosyntactic procedures govern into internal EL islands in ways that do not happen with EL islands that are not internal EL islands. Such an internal EL island (*dak la semaine*) is illustrated in (26).

(26) . . . jaɣni   w   kant dak LA SEMAINE djal   tajzawlu
    . . . I mean and it   was that-the-week where they take away
    LES PERMIS
    the driving licenses
    '. . . I mean, and it was [that] the week where they take away the
    driving licenses.'
    (Moroccan Arabic/French; Bentahila and Davies, 1992: 449)

Both *la semaine* 'the week' and *les permis* 'the driving licenses' are EL islands. That is, they are well formed according to French grammatical constraints; consequently, the determiners, which are system morphemes, are from French, not from Arabic, the ML. The one island of interest here is *la semaine* 'the week'. While it is well formed in French, it is within a larger NP constituent for which the ML projects the frame. For an NP introduced by the demonstrative *dak* to be well formed in Arabic, it must be followed by a determiner, not just a noun, resulting in the structure Demonstrative–Definite Article–Noun, or a triple bar structure. Thus, while **dak semaine* would not be predicted, *dak* plus *la semaine* does meet the ML specifications.

Contrastive evidence from other data sets involving French as an EL leads to the argument that while an internal EL island must be well formed in the EL, that is not enough. Rather, its particular form is governed by the constituent frame projected by the ML maximal projection containing it. In two other CS data sets with French as the EL, such internal EL islands as *la semaine* (consisting of a DET + N) do not occur (Wolof/French in Swigart, 1992); (Lingala/French in Kamwangamalu, 1989). See (27) for how a French noun is inserted into a Wolof frame and (28) for how one is inserted into a Lingala frame. In both cases, the NP has only a double bar structure (i.e. in Wolof the French noun only occurs with a single determiner and in Lingala the French noun has no determiner because there are no definite article determiners in Lingala).

(27) MÈRE bi, SIX la   am
    mother the six poss/existential has
    'The mother has six [a young man keeping score during a card
    game].'
    (Wolof/French; Swigart, 1992: 136)

(28) O-leki DIRECT na   CHAMBRE À COUCHER . . .
    2S-go direct   to [the] room of sleeping

'You go straight to the bedroom . . .'
(Lingala/French; Kamwangamalu, 1989: 138)

The argument here is that in these cases the ML frame does not call for a prenominal determiner, as do both Arabic and French. In Wolof, determiners follow their heads and Lingala does not have determiners. Thus, while a mixed constituent in these data sets may well include a French noun, internal EL islands of a French DET + Noun do not occur.

Another reason why an internal EL island of French DET + N is possible in an Arabic frame, but not in either a Wolof or a Lingala frame, is that determiners in Arabic are morphophonemically attached to their heads. Determiners in French are the same. Thus, again French meets Arabic structural requirements, but not those of the other two languages.

Finally, another example shows how the ML frame governs into an internal EL island. The ML in (29a) and (29b) is Turkish. Both instances of a Dutch ADJ + Noun may be considered internal EL islands; they are N-bar projections in Dutch, not maximal projections, and they are part of Turkish maximal projections. But note that the island in (29a) contains an overt agreement suffix on the adjective *blond*, while the one in (29b) does not. In Dutch, definite NPs including a noun from the neuter class take *-e* as an agreement suffix on their adjectives. However, indefinite NPs, as in (29b) in this class have no AGR suffix on adjectives. It seems clear here that whether the Dutch NP is considered definite or indefinite is controlled by a higher-level ML procedure, expressed on the surface by the appearance of either definite or indefinite Turkish specifier lexemes (definite is marked by *o*; indefinite by *birtane*).

(29) a. Ø   BLOND-E MEISJE afstuder-en   yap-tı
     DET blond-AGR girl   get-degree-INF do-PRET
     'That blond girl got her degree.'
   b. ENGELS-i   birtane BLOND MEISJE-dan
     English-ACC one   blond   girl-ABL
     alı-yor-dun
     take-IMPERF-2SG
     'You got the English [lessons] from a blond girl.'
     (Turkish/Dutch; Backus, 1992: 74, 44)

As in other EL islands, the EL directs the formulator to activate the EL morphosyntactic procedures in such internal EL islands. However, the choice of one EL procedure vs. another is determined by the larger ML frame. The semantic/pragmatic features of the ML phrasal category (NP, here) have certain morphological consequences for the entire NP. Thus, for example, if this SP feature bundle specifies the NP as definite, because the frame has been set at the maximal projection by the ML, the intermediate category (here, N′) also has this feature. Therefore, if the N′ is an internal EL island, it must also have this feature. Further research needs to be done as to what intermediate categories can be internal EL islands and whether morphosyntactic procedures of the ML always have consequences for the morphology of these EL islands.

13   The checking of ML and EL lemmas

While other hypotheses/principles of the MLF model refer to overall structural patterns in intrasentential CS, it is the blocking hypothesis and its "blocking filter" that determine how EL material is incorporated into these patterns. This hypothesis states that if an EL content morpheme has been chosen at the conceptual level as best conveying the speaker's intentions, the EL lemma supporting this morpheme must pass the blocking filter. That is, the EL lemma must be checked for congruency with an ML counterpart in the mental lexicon. The result is a determination of how that EL morpheme can be realized in a CP under ML control.

We propose that congruence checking is possible because whether or not languages show direct lexical correspondences, correspondences do exist (i.e. SP feature bundles), even if they are incompletely specified. As indicated above, our assumption is that the ML projects the frame for the entire CP in intrasentential CS. If, at the conceptual level, the speaker has chosen what is assembled as an EL SP feature bundle, then this will activate the EL lemma in the mental lexicon associated with that bundle. Of course an EL lemma also includes the predicate–argument structure and morphological realization patterns associated with such an EL bundle. But because the ML projects the overall CP frame, this EL lemma will be checked against an ML counterpart.

This checking may occur in one of two ways. First, if the counterpart ML lemma does support an ML lexeme, then the ML lemma is necessarily fully specified according to lexical-conceptual structure (i.e. semantic and pragmatic information) and predicate–argument structure and morphological realization patterns (i.e. what directions to send to the formulator).

A second possibility is that the ML lemma does not support an existing ML lexeme; that is, there is a lexical gap in the lexical entries of the ML. Or, speakers as "rational actors" may well exploit differences in SP feature bundles between ML and EL counterparts (i.e. these are pragmatic mismatches) when they select a particular lexical-conceptual structure (cf. Myers-Scotton, 1993c; Myers-Scotton, 1995). That is, they may choose an EL content morpheme with no close ML surface correspondent. Still, a checking is possible with ML material. In the case of a lexical gap in the ML or a serious pragmatic mismatch, no existing ML lemma is a ready-made counterpart. Yet checking may be done with "unbundled" ML material (i.e. undifferentiated ML lexical knowledge). Note that while this material is not bundled into specific lemmas, it is prototypical ML material.

Thus, because congruence is being checked with an EL lemma supporting a content morpheme, checking may be done with the ML lexical knowledge that is associated with content morphemes. Based on the EL lexical-conceptual information that has been activated, it is evident how a content morpheme supported by this lemma would fit into a semantic structure; for example, at the least it is clear whether it would receive or assign thematic roles. Also, because characteristic predicate–argument structure of the ML is available as part of ML lexical knowledge, this means that information about characteristic lexicalization patterns is available.

Thus, whether the ML lemma counterpart of the EL lemma selected (based on speaker intentions) is fully specified (i.e. supports an actually occurring lexeme) or must be matched with ML lexical knowledge, congruence can be checked. As already indicated, the result of this check has consequences for how the EL lexeme supported by the EL lemma in question will appear in intrasentential CS. In the examples of intrasentential CS cited here, we have illustrated degrees of congruence across ML and EL lemmas and their consequences for intrasentential CS. Most of the examples involve cases of congruence across lemmas supporting existing lexemes in both the ML and the EL; however, the case where an ML lexical gap exists has also been illustrated.

14   Summary

We conclude by recapitulating the type of language production model that CS data motivates. At the conceptual level, the speaker makes two types of decisions simultaneously. The first has discourse-general consequences. In brief, discourse decisions answer two related questions. Does the bilingual speaker wish to conduct the current discourse in a bilingual mode? If the answer is yes, then, does the speaker wish to use intrasentential CS? The development of the language production model in this chapter assumes that the speaker has answered yes to both of these questions.

These decisions having been made, the result is that both languages are "on" during production; however, the language to be designated the ML is more activated in specific ways, since it projects the overall frame for the relevant CP. In most discourses, the ML also supplies more of the morphemes than the EL.

The second type of decision made at the conceptual level concerns semantic intentions, as well as those pragmatic intentions in addition to the more specifically sociopragmatic intentions addressed in discourse-level decisions. In general, these intentions relate to answering two questions as well. Which of the languages to be used in bilingual speech will be the ML? Second, which content morphemes best convey specific semantic and pragmatic intentions? The discussion in this chapter has concerned itself largely with the consequences of satisfying these intentions by selecting an EL content morpheme as a potential entry in an ML frame. In summary, then, while lexical-conceptual structure in the conceptualizer is unspecified according to language, once selections are made regarding bilingual vs. monolingual modes, the ML, and the specific semantic/pragmatic feature bundle desired, these decisions are necessarily language-specific.

The intention to select an EL content morpheme activates an EL lemma in the mental lexicon. (Of course, intending to select an ML content morpheme would activate an ML lemma in the mental lexicon.) In order for an EL lemma to support an EL content morpheme in an ML frame, the EL lemma must be checked for congruency with an ML lemma counterpart.

This checking concerns lexical-conceptual structure (respective SP (semantic/pragmatic) feature bundles), but also the predicate–argument structure and morphological realization patterns associated with the lexical-conceptual structure (respective MS (morphosyntactic) feature bundles). These types of structures are what define lemmas.

At the functional level, lemmas send directions to the formulator in order to build the CP frame and support surface level lexemes. The directions calling frame-building morphosyntactic procedures are a response to the predicate–argument structure and morphological realization patterns encoded in lemmas. The evidence from intrasentential CS is that these procedures fall into at least two categories when they apply to mixed constituents. Directions affecting procedures internal to a single maximal category may come from both the ML and the EL. In general, a more systematic investigation of intrasentential CS is needed in order to determine which morphosyntactic procedures affecting surface morphology are sensitive to EL, as well as ML, directions. For example, in relation to double morphology, it seems that the procedure calling plural is one of these.

A second class of procedures is called only by the ML. These determine morphosyntactic relations between the projections of separate lexical categories. For example, while a noun may be marked for plural from both the ML and the EL, the agreement on any modifiers is supplied via directions from the ML.

As indicated above, when a speaker's intentions call for an EL content morpheme at the surface level, this selection activates the EL lemma in the mental lexicon supporting that morpheme. How the EL morpheme may appear in a CP framed by the ML depends on the extent to which there is congruence between its lemma and an ML counterpart in the mental lexicon.

If the ML counterpart supports an existing ML lexeme, its lexical-conceptual structure (i.e. semantic and pragmatic information) as well as its predicate–argument structure and morphological realization patterns are fully specified. These structures are checked against those of the EL lemma's entry.

If there is no existing ML lemma as a counterpart, the EL lemma is matched with relevant prototypical ML material that exists in the mental lexicon in an unbundled state as ML lexical knowledge. In order to form new words (fill lexical gaps) and change the meaning or grammatical patterning of existing lexemes, the existence of prototypical ML material as undifferentiated lexical knowledge, alongside fully specified lemmas, seems necessary. The undifferentiated ML lexical knowledge contains information at the same three levels as lemmas do (lexical-conceptual and predicate–argument structures, and morphological realization patterns). This is sufficient for both frame building and congruence checking.

Thus, based on such information contained in even undifferentiated ML lexical knowledge, congruence checking is possible.[20] If the result of the checking of counterparts is sufficient congruence, then the EL lemma meets the specifications of the ML frame, and the EL lexeme that this EL lemma supports can appear in a mixed constituent in this ML frame. If the result is insufficient congruence, one of a number of compromise strategies is necessary. Many of these have been discussed above, such as "bare" nouns, do-verb constructions and EL islands.

There is a second way in which an EL morpheme may appear in an ML frame.[21] As a discourse decision, the bilingual speaker makes the choice not to engage in intrasentential CS. Thus, the speaker intends to produce a monolingual CP framed by language X, a language chosen because it meets sociopragmatic and semantically based intentions, whatever they may be. Yet, the speaker is not successful in finding le mot juste in language X for a semantic/pragmatic feature bundle that he/she wishes to convey (i.e. in this case, finding le mot juste involves shifting from monolingual discourse). Thus, the speaker revises his/her plan and attempts to select a content morpheme from language Y (another entry in the speaker's linguistic repertoire). At this point, the speaker must also select either monolingual production in language Y (which may mean a "frame restart" at the conceptual level) or proceed with language X as the frame-building language. If he/she continues with language X, since this language was already framing the CP, the necessary adjustment is slight. Rather than framing a monolingual CP, language X becomes the ML of a bilingual CP, and the result is an instance of intrasentential CS. Further study may show that most of these searches for le mot juste result in the speaker staying with the original framing language; psycholinguistically, this would seem to be the easiest alternative to take. Of course the EL lemma supporting the morpheme from language Y (le mot juste) must be checked against its ML counterpart in the manner described above, even though most certainly the ML counterpart may support no actual surface ML morpheme.

Hesitation phenomena indicate that revision is possible at any point in the production process. Revisions are more minor if the speaker has chosen a candidate lexeme from language Y that is congruent with the requirements of an otherwise fully specified frame. Insertion is simply delayed but is accomplished with no change of the frame. More serious are revisions that require "restarting" the frame; these indicate that the predicate–argument structure or morphological realization patterns satisfied by the language X semantic/pragmatic feature bundle that was rejected are not congruent with what is projected by the new candidate from language Y.[22]

15   A window on language production and lexical entries

In this chapter, we have presented evidence from intrasentential CS to motivate a model of language production. We have dealt with only two levels of the model: the conceptual level and the functional level. Of course any complete discussion would also have to treat the surface, or positional, level. Our main interest has been in supporting the hypothesis that various types of congruence explain variation in structures found in intrasentential CS. Congruence involves lexical-conceptual structure, predicate–argument structure, or morphological realization patterns, or some combination of these three levels.

In turn, implicit in our discussion is the suggestion that how congruence issues are resolved in CS provides evidence about the nature of lexical entries. Specifically, this resolution implies how central certain aspects of lexical-conceptual structure and predicate–argument structure are to the specification of lexical entries. Put another way, how an EL content morpheme is accommodated by an ML frame tells us something about which features characterizing that morpheme (ultimately characterizing its supporting lemma) are critical and which may be peripheral in lexical entries. At this stage, we only claim to have shown the effects on CS of different aspects of lexical structure, but we do think it is clear how studying congruence in CS has implications far beyond the nature of CS itself.

Notes

1   Grosjean and Miller (1994) present experimental evidence that while both languages are activated during CS, a complete phonological shift from one language to another is possible.

2   Both "traditional" subordinate clauses and main clauses are CPs; however, most main clauses have a null element in COMP position as in the main clause of [I want [for him to do it]].

3   In contrast with the ML vs. EL distinction, relative dominance of languages at the discourse level does apply to both intersentential and intrasentential CS. First, one language usually contributes more material to the entire discourse (e.g. in intersentential CS, more CPs are in this language). Second, this same language sets various aspects of the discourse frame; however, we will have no more to say about them in this chapter. This more dominant language is often synonymous with "the unmarked choice" of the discourse, while the other language(s) are more or less "marked choice(s)" (Myers-Scotton, 1993; 1993c).

4   The examples below illustrate both the morpheme order and the system morpheme principles. In (a) the modifier of *plate* follows, as is required by Swahili, the
ML. Swahili also provides the system morpheme *ma-* on *home*.

(a)   Hata MIDTERM, wa-ki-pe-w-a   ha-wa-end-i
      even midterm,   3PL-CONDIT-give-PAS-FV neg-3PL-go-neg/FV
      ma-HOME. . . .
      CL6-home
      a-na-ku-l-a   PLATE m-bili   z-a   murram
      3S-NON-PST-INFIN-eat-FV plate   CL10-two CL10-of maize
      'Even at midterm, when they are given [breaks], they don't go home
      . . . He eats two plates maize.'
      (Swahili/English; Myers-Scotton, 1993a: 86)

In (b), the French past participle *recalé* precedes Alsatian *wurd*, following the Alsatian ML order, rather than following the inflected auxiliary verb, as would be
required by the EL grammar of French. (In Alsatian subordinate clauses, the
inflected auxiliary occurs in final position, although it may be followed by adjunct
PPs.) In the mixed constituents in this example, the system morphemes come from
Alsatian, the ML: the determiner *de*, the preposition plus determiner *am*, and the
passive auxiliary *wurd*. The constituent *panne d'essence* is an EL island; in EL islands,
all the morphemes, including system morphemes, come from the EL.

(b)   Noch schlimmer, wenn de CLIENT RECALÉ wurd
      Still   worse,   when the client   refused   become + 3SG/PAST
      am   PERMIS weje   de PANNE D' ESSENCE.
      to + DEF license   because the lack   of gas
      'Even worse is when the client has been failed because of the lack
      of gas.'
      (Alsatian/French; Gardner-Chloros, Appendix III, cited in Myers
      Scotton, 1993a: 89)

5   "Discourse-relevant" implies coherence; i.e. a relevant sample should include minimally two contiguous CPs, either from a single speaker or from an adjacency pair
produced by two speakers.
6   The socio- and psycholinguistic criteria mean that the ML is often the speaker's
first language; but this is not necessarily so, most obviously if the different speakers
have different first languages. It should be clear that neither is the ML necessarily
the speaker's "best" language, by either his/her own assessment or independent
evaluation, although it often is.
      ML assignment is not fixed across time or even for a single discourse. If the
sociolinguistic and psycholinguistic factors associated with ML choice in a community change over time (e.g. new sociopolitical divisions arise or language policies

change, etc.), what was the EL (or another language) may become the ML. Also, in many communities when situational factors are modified (e.g. the topic shifts or participants change, etc.), which language is the ML may change in "on-line" discourse.

7   Note that these are not the only types of constituents that are logically possible. Thus, certain types of constituents are ruled out by the MLF model.

8   There can be characteristic patterns of CS in particular communities or in particular language pairs. For example, intersentential CS may be the dominant or even exclusive pattern. Or, within intrasentential CS, there can be differences in the role of the EL that can be qualitative and quantitative.

   One type of qualitative difference is in the syntactic nature of the mixed constituents. For example, in some languages internal EL islands occur; these may or may not be maximal projections in the EL. However, from the point of view of the ML they are intermediate constituents or nonmaximal projections within an ML maximal projection. In Moroccan Arabic/French CS such islands consisting of Determiner + Noun occur relatively frequently (Bentahila and Davies, 1983; 1992). In some corpora, EL verb stems inflected with ML morphology occur frequently; (e.g. in Swahili/English CS (Myers-Scotton, 1993a) or in Irish/English CS (Stenson, 1990)).

   In addition, some differences are strictly quantitative. For example, how many singly occurring EL morphemes are found in mixed constituents? In some data sets, there are very few (e.g. Swiss German/French in Myers-Scotton and Jake, 1994). In other sets, single EL morphemes are very frequent (e.g. Turkish/Dutch in Backus, 1992).

   Finally, the difference in the role of the EL can be both quantitative and qualitative. For example, are there more EL islands or more mixed constituents? Another source of difference is the syntactic role of EL islands across corpora. However, equivalence, as discussed by Poplack (1979/80) does not determine what can occur as an EL island. In fact, as we argue here and as Myers-Scotton (1993a: 138) argues, "when there is NOT equivalence (= congruence) of an abstract nature, this is when there is a change in the basic procedures resulting in EL islands."

9   We thank Pim Levelt for suggesting *lexical knowledge* as a cover term for this material.

10   Note that *kina gece-si elbise-si* 'henna evening dress' is an internal EL island, discussed below. Turkish requires possessive suffixes in this type of compound noun construction.

11   FY = final vowel. Bantu languages have a characteristic phonotactics of CVCV.

12   From the standpoint of bilingual language production, whether they are borrowed forms or pragmatic mismatches, or have another semantic/pragmatic history, we argue that singly occurring EL lexemes in mixed constituents undergo the same processes.

   There is only "near-complete" morphological integration because the code-switched verb form lacks the final vowel characteristic of Bantu verbs and required by the Bantu CVCV phonotactics. This final vowel, however, carries no or very little morphological information independent of other elements in the verbal assembly.

13 Another possible analysis of example (7) would be to argue that *underestimate* is an internal EL island. That is, it could be claimed that it is inflected with an English present tense 2nd person suffix, realized as zero. This is implied in Pfaff (1979: 301, note 8). The idea was suggested to us by Mary Sue Sroda. Either as a base form or as an EL island, its treatment in this mixed constituent indicates less than total congruence between the EL lemma supporting the lexeme *underestimate* and an ML counterpart.

14 Reference to studies of expected collocations in English would test the claim that *a lot of nonsense* has a near idiomatic, unitary value.

15 Nominal plural morphemes are not structurally assigned, whereas some gender and case morphemes are. This leaves open the possibility that doubling of other inherently assigned system morphemes may occur. However, we hypothesize that structurally assigned system morphemes cannot double because, although their slot is prepared by the content lemma, structurally assigned system morphemes cannot be spelled out until the functional or positional level where morphological patterns are set. The matching of the SP feature bundle with a lemma takes place at the conceptual level and this is where mistiming can occur, not later in the production process.

16 Azuma (1993) also discusses this example, but to support a somewhat different argument.

17 This use of "trigger" differs from that of Clyne (1987), where triggering depends on the surface occurrence of a form in one language that is similar or cognate with a form in the other and therefore triggers a language switch.

18 The argument that the island occurs because the verb form really is an inseparable phrasal verb (*transfer* + a satellite *from*) does not go through. Recall example (18) where *graduate* appears without *from*.

19 Elsewhere (Jake and Myers-Scotton, 1994) we make a complimentary argument about EL islands in Spanish/English CS data. A quantitative analysis of 259 EL islands that are PPs in Pfaff (1979) shows that only three possible configurations are present in PP EL islands in CS involving these two languages: (1) the entire PP is in Spanish; (2) the entire PP is in English; or (3) there is a Spanish P and an English NP. That is, there are no cases of an English P and Spanish NP complement, even when English is apparently the ML. We explain this anomaly by arguing that Spanish nouns require "tighter" case markers than English prepositions assign, resulting in structural asymmetry in possible EL islands.

20 The matching process in CS has parallels in learner varieties in second-language acquisition. This means that there are natural similarities between CS and interlanguage phenomena. We thank Ad Backus for this suggestion. Jake *et al.* (1995) discuss interlanguage in these terms.

21 We thank Georges Lüdi for reminding us that this provision is necessary to the model.

22 A final comment about the overall model is this: while this information is repre-

sented in discrete modules of the grammar (as represented in most generative approaches to grammar), parallel processing of the information contained in these modules characterizes language production. That is, the projection of linguistic information from the lexical-conceptual structure is simultaneous to specification of the predicate–argument structure and morphological realization patterns in terms of many different modules of the grammar. Information regarding thematic roles, case, and government for example, is being processed at the same time.

Source: Myers-Scotton, C. and Jake, J.L. (1995) Matching lemmas in a bilingual competence and production model. *Linguistics* 33: 981–1024, by permission of Mouton de Gruyter.

Notes for students and instructors

Study questions

1   Give three examples of code-switching involving the languages you know to illustrate the 'free morpheme constraint', and give three examples to illustrate the 'equivalent constraint'.
2   What are the criteria for the identification of the 'matrix language'?
3   How do the concepts of 'system morpheme' and 'content morpheme', as defined by Myers-Scotton and Jake, apply to a language other than English that you know?

Study activity

Using a sample of code-switching data – either collected by yourself or documented in detail by others – find out to what extent the grammatical constraints proposed by Poplack and others work. Can you identify any trigger words in the sample? How do the examples of code-switching in the sample fit into the Matrix Language Frame (MLF) model?

Further reading

For an overview of the grammar of code-switching, see S. Poplack and D. Sankoff, 1987, Code-switching, in U. Ammon, N. Dittmar and K. Mattheier (eds), *Sociolinguistics: An international handbook of the science of language and society*, volume 2, Walter de Gruyter, pp. 1174–80; C. Myers-Scotton, 1997,

Codeswitching, in F. Coulmas (ed.), *The Handbook of Sociolinguistics*, Blackwell, 217–37; or Chapter 4 of S. Romaine, 1995, *Bilingualism*, 2nd edn, Blackwell.

For further discussion of Poplack's approach to grammatical constraints on code-switching, see S. Poplack, 1978/81, Syntactic structure and social function of code-switching, in R. Duran (ed.), *Latino Discourse and Communicative Behaviour*, Ablex, pp. 169–84; D. Sankoff and S. Poplack, 1979/81, A formal grammar for code-switching, *Papers in Linguistics* 14: 3–46; S. Poplack and D. Sankoff, 1984, Borrowing: the synchrony of integration, *Linguistics* 22: 99–135; S. Poplack, 1993, Variation theory and language contact: contact, concept, methods and data, in D. Preston (ed.), *American Dialect Research*, John Benjamins, pp. 251–86; S. Poplack and M. Meechan (eds), 1998, *Instant Loans, Easy Conditions*, Kingston Press. A state-of-the-art collection of studies which apply Poplack's model is published in a special issue of the *International Journal of Bilingualism* 2(2).

Clyne's notion of 'triggering' was first developed, and fully discussed, in M. Clyne, 1967, *Transference and Triggering*, Nijhoff.

A fuller exposition of the MLF model can be found in C. Myers-Scotton, 1997a, *Duelling Languages: Grammatical structure in code-switching*, Oxford University Press; C. Myers-Scotton and J.L. Jake (eds), 2000, *Testing a Model of Morpheme Classification with Language Contact Data*, Kingston Press. A state-of-the-art collection of studies which apply Myers-Scotton's model is published in a special issue of the *International Journal of Bilingualism*, 4(1).

Other studies of the grammar of code-switching include: C. Pfaff, 1979, Constraints on language mixing: intrasentential code-switching and borrowing in Spanish/English, *Language* 55: 291–318; A. Bentahila and E.E. Davies, 1983, The syntax of Arabic–French code-switching, *Lingua*, 59: 301–30; E. Woolford, 1983, Bilingual code-switching and syntactic theory, *Linguistic Inquiry* 14: 520–36; A.K. Joshi, 1985, Processing of sentences with intrasentential code-switching, in D.R. Dowty, L. Kartnnen and A.M. Zwicky (eds), *Natural Language Parsing*, Cambridge University Press, pp. 190–205; A.M. Di Sciullo, P. Muysken and R. Singh, 1986, Government and code-switching, *Journal of Linguistics* 22: 1–24; S. Berk-Seligson, 1986, Linguistic constraints on intrasentential code-switching, *Language in Society* 15: 313–48; H.M. Belazi, E.J. Rubin and J. Toribio, 1994, Code-switching and X-bar theory: the functional head constraint, *Linguistic Inquiry* 25: 221–37; S. Mahootian and B. Santorini, 1996, Code-switching and the complement/adjunct distinction, *Linguistic Inquiry* 27: 464–79; R.M. Bhatt, 1997, Code-switching, constraints and optimal grammars, *Lingua* 102: 223–51.

Recent book-length studies of code-switching which contain substantial grammatical analyses include: J. Nortier, 1990, *Dutch–Moroccan Arabic Code-Switching among Moroccans in the Netherlands*, Foris; J. Treffers-Daller, 1993, *Mixing Two Languages: French–Dutch contact in a comparative perspective*, Mouton; A. Backus, 1996, *Two in One: Bilingual speech of Turkish immigrants in the Netherlands*, Tilburg University Press; H. Halmari, 1997, *Government and Code-Switching: Explaining American Finnish*, John Benjamins; L. Baumans, 1998, *The Syntax of Codeswitching: Analysing Moroccan Arabic/Dutch conversation*, Tilburg University Press; and J. MacSwan, 1999, *A Minimalist Approach to Intrasentential Code-Switching*, Garland.

Pay attention to the *International Journal of Bilingualism* and *Linguistics*, which often carry articles on the grammar of code-switching.

Language acquisition of bilingual children

Chapter 12

Early bilingual language development:
one language or two?

FRED GENESEE

IT IS COMMONLY THOUGHT that children learning two languages simultaneously during infancy go through a stage when they cannot differentiate their two languages. In fact, virtually all studies of infant bilingual development have found that bilingual children mix elements from their two languages. Researchers have interpreted these results as evidence for an undifferentiated or unitary underlying language system. In this chapter I will examine the empirical basis for these claims and I will argue that they are questionable because of serious methodological shortcomings in the research. I will then offer some tentative evidence based on speech perception studies and re-analyses of selected bilingual case studies that young bilingual children are psycholinguistically able to differentiate two languages from the earliest stages of bilingual development and that they can use their two languages in functionally differentiated ways, thereby providing evidence of differentiated underlying language systems.

Before proceeding, it is necessary to define some terms that will be used in the remainder of this chapter. BILINGUAL DEVELOPMENT/ACQUISITION will be used to refer to simultaneous acquisition of more than one language during the period of primary language development. FIRST LANGUAGE DEVELOPMENT/ACQUISITION will be used when acquisition of only one language from birth is in question. SECOND LANGUAGE ACQUISITION will be used to refer to acquisition of a second language after the period of primary language development. Finally, the term MIXING will be used to refer to interactions between the bilingual child's developing language systems. Mixing has been used by other researchers to refer to the co-occurrence of elements from two or more languages in A SINGLE UTTERANCE. The mixed elements may be phonological, morphological, lexical, syntactic, phrasal or pragmatic. The definition is problematic when discussing childhood bilinguals because it pertains only to two-word and multi-word stages of development, thereby eliminating a consideration of mixing during the one-word-stage. For reasons that will become clear later, it is desirable to extend the definition of mixing to include single-word utterances from two languages during the same stretch of conversation between a child and caregiver.

Bilingual mixing

The majority of empirical investigations of bilingual development have found mixing (for a summary of early research see McLaughlin, 1984). Phonological, lexical, phrasal, morphological, syntactic, semantic and pragmatic mixing have all been reported. Examples of each type will be described.

Phonological mixing in the form of loan blends has been reported by Murrell (1966) and Oksaar (1971). Loan blends are words made up of phonemic segments from two languages. For example, Oksaar has recorded the loan blend *kats* from an Estonian/Swedish bilingual child: it consists of the Swedish word for 'cat' (*katt*) and the Estonian word for 'cat' (*kass*). Mixing of grammatical morphemes has been noted by Murrell (1966), Oksaar (1971), Burling (1978), Lindholm and Padilla (1978), and Redlinger and Park (1980). Redlinger and Park report instances of morphological mixing by a German/English bilingual: *pfeift*ING ('whistling') and *Die Mädchen's going night-night* ('The girl's going night-night'). Bergman (1976) reports that her Spanish/English bilingual daughter used the English possessive morpheme *'s* in Spanish utterances, apparently in imitation of her nursery school teacher's use of this mixed form.

By far the most frequent type of mixing to be reported involves whole lexical items, both content and function words (see Swain and Wesche, 1975; Burling, 1978; Leopold, 1978; Lindholm and Padilla, 1978; Redlinger and Park, 1980; Vihman, 1982; 1985; Goodz, 1989). Some investigators have found that content words, and especially nouns, are the most frequently mixed lexical items (Swain and Wesche; Lindholm and Padilla), while others have found that functors are the most frequently mixed (Redlinger and Park; Vihman, 1982; 1985). Redlinger and Park have reported specifically that adverbs, articles, pronouns, prepositions and conjunctions occurred in mixed utterances in descending order of frequency. Examples of lexical mixing can be found in Appendix 12.1.

Mixing at the level of the phrase has also been found. Redlinger and Park (1980) gave an example for a German/Spanish child: *Putzen Zähne* CON JABON ('Brushing teeth with soap'). Lindholm and Padilla (1978) cited an example from a Spanish/English bilingual child: *I ask him* QUE YO VOY A CASA ('I ask him that I go home'). They also reported that when phrasal mixing occurred, the structural consistency of the utterances was maintained so that there were no lexical redundancies or syntactic errors (see also Padilla and Liebman, 1975). To the extent that this is generally true, it would argue against an interpretation of mixing in terms of linguistic confusion.

Swain and Wesche (1975) have reported examples of syntactic mixing, or what they refer to as structural interactions, in the case of a three-year-old French/English boy:

1   *They open*, THE WINDOWS? (use of the noun apposition construction from French in an otherwise English utterance);
2   *A house* PINK (colour adjectives follow the noun in French).

Swain and Wesche also report instances of semantic mixing: *You want to* OPEN *the lights?* (in French, the verb *open* is used in comparison with the English verb *turn on* when referring to lights). It is difficult to interpret such utterances unequivocally as linguistic creations by the child that reflect an underlying lack of differentiation of language systems, since this usage is heard sometimes even among native English speakers in Quebec, where the Swain and Wesche study was conducted. It is possible that bilingual children mix because they have heard mixing by their parents or other speakers in the environment. This raises an important methodological issue that will be discussed in more detail later – it is necessary to study the language models to whom bilingual children are exposed in order to understand all possible sources of mixing.

An example of pragmatic mixing to elicit parental attention can be found in Goodz (1989). She reports that Nellie, an English/French bilingual, being concerned that her French-speaking father would take away a recently acquired set of barrettes, admonished him to leave them alone, initially in French (*Laisse les barrettes, touche pas les barrettes, Papa*), and then desperately in English (*Me's gonna put it back in the bag so no one's gonna took it*).

Rates of mixing vary considerably from study to study and from case to case. Mixed utterances are reportedly more frequent in early stages of bilingual development and diminish with age (Fantini, 1978; Volterra and Taeschner, 1978; Redlinger and Park, 1980; Vihman, 1982). Summarizing the results from four case studies, Redlinger and Park found 20% to 30% mixing during Stage I (Brown, 1973), 12% to 20% during Stage II, 6% to 12% during Stage III, and 2% to 6% during Stages IV and V. Vihman (1982) reports that the use of mixed utterances by her Estonian/English bilingual son dropped from 34% at 1;8, to 22% at 1;9, to 20% at 1;10, to 11% at 1;11 and to 4% at 2;0.

Reported rates of mixing are difficult to interpret or compare across studies owing to:

1   differential exposure to the languages in question;
2   the possibility of unequal or inequitable sampling of the child's language use in different language contexts and/or with different interlocutors;

3   the lack of an acceptable metric of language development with which to
     identify children at comparable stages;
4   different operational definitions of mixing; and
5   different language histories.

It is important to point out at this time that adult bilinguals also mix languages in the same sentence, a phenomenon referred to as code-mixing (Sridhar and Sridhar, 1980). Studies of code-mixing in adults show it to be a sophisticated, rule-governed communicative device used by linguistically competent bilinguals to achieve a variety of communicative goals, such as conveying emphasis, role playing, or establishing socio-cultural identity. It has highly structured syntactic and sociolinguistic constraints. In particular, mixing of linguistic elements from one language into another is performed so that the syntactic rules of BOTH languages are respected (Poplack, 1979/80). Poplack cites evidence to the effect that intra-sentential mixing increases in adult bilinguals as their competence in the two languages increases. Adult bilinguals also switch between languages as a function of certain sociolinguistic factors, such as the setting, tone and purpose of the communication or the ethnolinguistic identity of the interlocutor. This language behaviour is referred to as CODE-SWITCHING (Sridhar and Sridhar, 1980). What is thought to distinguish bilingual children's mixing from adult mixing is the lack of systematicity or compliance to linguistic rules in the case of children.

The period of language mixing just described is generally reported to be followed by linguistic differentiation. Investigators studying children with different language histories have reported that differentiation occurs during the third year of life (Murrell, 1966; Imedadze, 1978; Vihman, 1982). At this time, the child is thought to have developed or to be developing two separate representations of his/her language systems or, alternatively, to have overcome the linguistic confusion characteristic of the earlier stage. He or she begins to switch systematically between languages as a function of the participants, the setting, the function of the message (e.g. to exclude others), its form (e.g. narration), and to a lesser extent, the topic of conversation. Bilingual children are reported to be especially sensitive to their interlocutors so that initially when differentiation occurs they tend rigidly to use the language they associate with the speaker even though he or she may express a willingness to use the other language (Fantini, 1978; Volterra and Taeschner, 1978).

In sum, the fact that mixing of two languages occurs during bilingual development has been reported and is accepted by all investigators. More questionable are the explanations of it.

The unitary-language system explanation

Language mixing during the early stages of bilingual development has been interpreted in general terms as evidence of a unitary-language system with undifferentiated phonological, lexical and syntactic subsystems (except see Bergman, 1976; Lindholm and Padilla, 1978; Pye, 1986; Goodz, 1986; 1989). For example, Leopold, in one of the first and still most comprehensive studies of bilingual development, concluded that 'Words from the two languages did not belong to two different speech systems but to one . . .' (in Hatch, 1978: 27). In 1977, Swain postulated a 'common storage model' of bilingual development according to which all rules of both languages are initially stored in a common location. Even rules that are specific to each language are initially stored in common storage and subsequently tagged as appropriate for a particular language through a process of differentiation. More recently, Redlinger and Park (1980) write 'These findings suggest that the subjects were involved in a gradual process of language differentiation and are in agreement with those of previous investigators supporting the one system approach to bilingual acquisition' (p. 344). Volterra and Taeschner (1978) have interpreted mixing in terms of a three-stage model:

1   initial unification of both lexical and syntactic subsystems;
2   differentiation of the lexicon but continued unification of syntax;
3   finally, differentiation of both the lexicon and syntax.

The title of Swain's (1972) thesis – *Bilingualism as a first language* – exemplifies the unitary-system interpretation of early bilingual development.

There are empirical reasons to question this interpretation The evidence cited by the respective investigators is simply not sufficient to support such an interpretation. In order to uphold the unitary-system hypothesis one would need to establish that, all things being equal, bilingual children use items from both languages indiscriminately in all contexts of communication. In other words, there should be no differential distribution of items from the two languages as a function of the predominant language being used in different contexts. In contrast, support for the differentiated-language systems hypothesis would require evidence that the children use items from their two languages differentially as a function of context. Even in cases where the child might be more proficient in one language than the other, which is common, it would be possible to test the differentiated-systems hypothesis by observing the distribution of items from the weaker language. In particular, if the differentiated-language systems hypothesis were true, one would expect to find more frequent use of items from the weaker language in contexts where that language is being used than in contexts where the stronger language is being used, even though items from the stronger language might predominate in both contexts.

In fact, most proponents of the unitary-system hypothesis do not present or analyse their data by context. Therefore, it is impossible to determine whether the children are using the repertoire of language items they have acquired to that point in a differentiated way. For example, the evidence cited by Volterra and Taeschner (1978) in support of stage I of their model consists simply of isolated examples of lexical mixing in utterances addressed to the child's German-speaking mother. No evidence of language use with the child's Italian-speaking father is given. Redlinger and Park (1980) calculated the rate of mixing for four different bilingual children over a period varying from five to nine months and found a decline in mixing over time. No systematic data of differential mixing of each language as a function of language context are provided. Evidence of declining rates of overall mixing does not constitute sufficient proof that the child has only one language system. Mixing may decline with development, not because separation of the languages is taking place but rather because the children are acquiring more complete linguistic repertoires and, therefore, do not need to borrow from or overextend between languages.

Some investigators have examined mixing as a function of interlocutor or context, but their analyses are incomplete or questionable. Vihman (1985), for example, reports the percentage use of English in English contexts versus an Estonian context, but she does not report corresponding values for Estonian. That the child used English utterances in the Estonian context, which was the home, is perhaps not surprising given that the child's sister and parents all spoke English and were undoubtedly overheard using English in their home in Palo Alto, California (see also Pye, 1986). More convincing evidence of a unitary language system would include examples of Estonian multiword utterances in English contexts (the daycare centre, for example). Swain (1972) cites evidence of mixing in bilingual children who were asked to translate messages from one monolingual adult stranger to another, neither of whom spoke the other's language. Mixing under such conditions may reflect the peculiarities of such language use rather than lack of differentiation of language *per se*. In the absence of sound and complete data on language use in different language contexts, an explanation of bilingual mixing in terms of undifferentiated language systems is open to serious question.

Other explanations of mixing

A number of other more specific explanations of bilingual mixing have been suggested. By far the most frequent of these is that bilingual children mix because they lack appropriate lexical items in one language but have them in the other language and, effectively, they borrow from one language for use in the other (see, for example, Fantini, 1978; Lindholm and Padilla, 1978; Volterra and Taeschner, 1978; Redlinger and Park, 1980). Vihman (1985: 313) has argued that this is an unsatisfactory explanation of mixing, and that, alternatively, mixing declines as the child 'comes to recognize adult-imposed standards of behaviour and shows awareness of his own ability to meet them'. If this is indeed the case, then differentiation would be more an issue of developing sociolinguistic competence than of underlying psycholinguistic separation of the language systems.

Mixing has also been reported in cases of overly restricted use of specific lexical items. Imedadze (1978) and Swain and Wesche (1975) have suggested that in some cases bilingual children identify a referent with the lexical item in the language that was first or most frequently used to label it. They might insist on using that word at all times when talking about that referent regardless of the linguistic context. A particularly striking example is described by Volterra and Taeschner (1978: 317–18) in which a German–Italian girl insisted on using the Italian word *occhiali* to refer to her Italian-speaking father's eyeglasses when speaking with her German-speaking mother. The mother had to make repeated attempts to get the child to refer to her father's glasses as *Brillen* when speaking German.

Yet a third explanation of mixing has been suggested in terms of structural linguistic factors (Tabouret-Keller, 1962; Murrell, 1966; Vihman, 1985). Vihman, for example, claims that her bilingual son used English function words in otherwise Estonian utterances because the English words were simpler and more salient than the corresponding Estonian words.

In contrast to the unitary-language system explanation which implicates the nature of the representational system underlying the bilingual child's developing language competence, these more specific explanations implicate the nature of the acquisitional process underlying bilingualism. All three of these explanations of bilingual mixing can be interpreted in terms of acquisitional processes that have been identified in monolingual acquisition. Thus, instances of mixing due to lexical borrowing could be viewed as overextensions of the type observed in monolingual children (Griffiths, 1986), with the difference that bilingual children overextend inter-lingually as well as intra-lingually while monolingual children overextend intra-lingually only. In the case of first-language acquisition, it has been observed that particular overextensions of nominals usually cease once the child has learned what mature speakers of the language would consider a more appropriate word (Griffiths, 1986). In other words, monolingual children make use of whatever vocabulary they have acquired; as their vocabulary grows, they use increasingly appropriate, less overextended words. This also seems a reasonable interpretation of bilingual overextensions (see also Goodz, 1989) and, in fact, accords with the tendency for bilingual children to mix less as their proficiency increases, as noted earlier.

Overly restricted use of particular lexical items has been observed in monolingual children in the form of underextensions (Stross, 1973; Reich, 1976). Anglin (1977) has suggested that in fact underextensions are more frequent than overextensions in monolingual development, but they often go unnoticed because they do not violate adult usage. It has been suggested further that 'the character-istic early path is for nominals to be underextended first and only later to apply to a wider range of entities (perhaps then going as far as overextension)' (Griffiths, 1986: 300). Bilingual children may overextend longer than monolingual children because they hear more instances of particular nominals being used in specific contexts (e.g. the German nominal for 'glasses' being used in German contexts or with German-speaking interlocutors), whereas monolingual children are likely to hear the same nominals used in extended contexts (e.g. *glasses* used in all contexts in which the referent occurs). Moreover, bilingual children's use of specific nomi-nals in specific language or interlocutor contexts is accepted by bilingual parents, whereas monolingual parents are not as likely to accept underextended usage, if they notice it.

Finally, Slobin (1973) has argued for a set of universal operating principles which every child brings to bear on the problem of language acquisition, and for a number of language-specific strategies which are involved in the acquisition of aspects of a given native language. According to Slobin, the order of development of various grammatical devices is determined by the child's cognitive and per-ceptual development and by characteristics of the languages to be learned. It follows that children learning two languages simultaneously may be expected to mix aspects of their languages because of acquisitional strategies that are independent of language representation *per se*. More specifically, language mixing might occur in any given utterance of a bilingual child, even though his/her two languages are represented separately, for two possible reasons. In one case, mixing might occur because the language system in use at the moment is incomplete and does not include the grammatical device needed to express certain meanings. If a device from the other language system that serves the same purposes were avail-able, it might be used at that moment. In the other case, the grammatical device required to express the intended meaning is available in the language currently in use, but it is more complex than the corresponding device in the other language system and its use strains the child's current ability. Therefore, the simpler device from the other system might be used at that moment. In both cases, developing bilingual children can be seen to be using whatever grammatical devices they have in their repertoire or whatever devices they are able to use given their current language ability. In neither of these cases is it necessary to assume that the languages are represented in a unified system.

Issues concerning acquisitional strategies in bilingual development are independent of the issue of language representation. That particular acquisitional strategies may result in differences in the utterances of bilingual and monolingual children obscures what is perhaps a more important implication, namely that bilingual development is characterized by the same processes of acquisition as monolingual development. Indeed on theoretical grounds one would expect bilingual and monolingual acquisition during infancy to be the same (see Genesee, 1987). To date, researchers have not seriously examined the nature of bilingual acquisition in infancy and, in particular, whether it is the same as or different from monolingual acquisition. There has been much speculation about a possible relationship between bilingualism and metalinguistic awareness and the effect this might have on language acquisition (Cummins, 1976; Diaz, 1983; Hakuta, 1986). While there is some evidence of such relationships, it is inconsistent and pertains to older bilinguals, either school-age children or adults (Ben-Zeev, 1977; Ianco-Worrall, 1972), and not infant bilinguals.

The role of input

Notwithstanding the possible significance of specific acquisitional processes in accounting for some instances of mixing, an alternative general explanation of mixing that has not been examined seriously is that bilingual children's mixed utterances are modelled on mixed input produced by others (see also Goodz, 1989). Modelling could affect the child's language mixing in two ways – in specific ways, such that particular instances of modelled mixed utterances are used by the child, or in a general way, such that frequent mixing by adults or linguistically more mature children will result in the child mixing frequently and generally. Bergman's speculation, noted earlier, that her daughter's use of the English possessive marker *'s* in otherwise Spanish utterances could be traced to her nursery school teacher's use of this same construction is consistent with the first possibility. Also in this regard Goodz (1989) cites evidence of parents using mixed utterances in response to their children's language choices. She notes that parents might thereby present specific examples of mixing that children are particularly sensitive to since they are made in response to the children's solicitations.

Certainly one would expect children exposed to frequent and general mixing to mix frequently, since there is no reason for them to know that the languages should be separated. Indeed, there are fully formed dialects which consist of elements of two languages (e.g. so-called Spanglish in the southern US, or Franglais in Quebec). Conversely, it is commonly advocated, although not well documented, that the best way to avoid bilingual mixing in children is to have each parent speak only one language to the child – the so-called rule of Grammont, after the individual who first espoused this principle (Ronjat, 1913). In fact, it appears from the published evidence that more mixing does occur among children who hear both languages used freely and interchangeably by the same interlocutors (Murrell, 1966; Redlinger and Park's case Danny 1980), and less in children who hear the languages separated by person and/or setting (Fantini, 1978; Redlinger and Park's case Marcus 1980).

It is difficult, however, to ascertain the exact relationship between input and rate or type of mixing from the available research, since descriptions of the language-input conditions are either totally lacking (Padilla and Liebman, 1975; Lindholm and Padilla, 1978) or, at best, are general and impressionistic (Volterra and Taeschner, 1978; Vihman, 1982). In a study of parental language use in bilingual families, Goodz (1989) found that even parents 'firmly committed to maintaining a strict separation of language by parent, model linguistically mixed utterances to their children', but are unaware of doing so. Thus, impressionistic reports are probably inaccurate. Garcia (1983) has studied what he refers to as bilingual switching in 12 children in interaction with their mothers. The children were aged 2;0–2;8 at the beginning of the study, which lasted 12 months, and the mothers were part-time teachers in their children's co-operative pre-school where the study took place. He found that switching could be classified as serving three different communicative functions – instructional, translation or other – and that it occurred relatively infrequently (11%). It is difficult to know whether these results are typical of younger bilingual children and of less linguistically sensitive mothers in more natural, home conditions.

The most extensive study to date of the relationship between parental mixing and children's mixing is that of Goodz (1989). She has studied some 17 children raised in French/English bilingual families longitudinally for over three years in some cases. Of particular relevance to the present discussion, she reports that the frequency of occurrence of children's mixed utterances is correlated with the frequency of occurrence of parental mixing, especially in mother–child dyads. Parental mixing may occur for a number of different reasons, all of which are motivated to maintain and encourage communication:

1   use whatever lexical items the child understands;
2   as part of linguistic expansions and repetitions of their children's two- and three-word utterances; and
3   to attract attention, emphasize or discipline. Goodz points out that children may be particularly attentive to such parental mixing given its communicative context and intention.

There are reasons to believe that all of the children examined by the research under review here heard some mixed input – a number of researchers indicate obliquely that the parents did not separate their languages completely, and others even allude to the possible role of mixed input as an explanation of mixed output, thereby implying that mixed input was present (e.g. Tabouret-Keller, 1962; Burling, 1978; Redlinger and Park, 1980; Vihman and McLaughlin, 1982). The problem is that virtually all researchers to date (cf. Goodz, 1989) accept their own general impressions or parental reports that the languages are used separately, and on this basis do not seriously consider mixed input as a major contributor to the children's use of mixed utterances. Evidence that mixing by bilingual children can be traced in part to mixed input would weaken arguments that mixing during early bilingual development NECESSARILY reflects an underlying undifferentiated language system. Bilingual children with differentiated language systems may still mix because the input conditions permit it or because the verbal interaction calls for it. We will see examples of this shortly. Clearly, careful, detailed research examining input to bilingual children is needed (see Goodz, 1989).

The unitary-language system hypothesis re-examined

So far I have argued that the extant evidence on bilingual development is inadequate to conclude, as most researchers have to date, that bilingual children have an undifferentiated representation of their two languages. The question arises: what kind of evidence would be necessary? First, since one cannot examine the underlying representation of language directly, evidence for differentiation would necessarily be based on functional separation of the languages, that is, how the languages are used. Second, data on language use would need to be collected in different language contexts in order to determine the relative functional distribution of elements from the two languages, as already noted. Third, detailed documentation of the input conditions, both during specific interactional episodes and more generally, is needed in order to correlate the incidence and type of mixed output with mixed input. Finally, as was also noted earlier, children who mix during the early stages of bilingual development do so less with age as their lexical systems and presumably their other linguistic subsystems expand, making overextensions and overgeneralizations between languages less necessary. Therefore, it would be necessary to examine their language use prior to this stage of development; that is, from the one-word stage on.

In the absence of adequate data, how plausible is the differentiated-language systems hypothesis and what do existing data tell us? Differentiation of two languages during bilingual development minimally requires that children be able to discriminate perceptually between the spoken languages. Research on the perceptual abilities of infants suggests that they possess many, if not all, of the necessary prerequisites for speech perception (Jusczyk, 1981) and that they are capable of fairly sophisticated perceptual discriminations (Jusczyk, 1982). In this regard, Jusczyk (1982: 361) has commented that 'today, some researchers in the field . . . have been moved to comment that the most interesting kind of result would be to discover some aspect of speech perception that infants were incapable of'.

Relevant to bilingual development, Trehub (1973) has found that infants of 6–17 weeks are able to differentiate phonetic contrasts in languages (Czech and Polish) that they have never been exposed to. Also, Mehler *et al.* (1986) report that 4-day-old infants from French-speaking families were able to discriminate between French and Russian and that they showed a preference for French. That this was not simply a novelty effect is suggested by an earlier study by Mehler *et al.* (1978) in which 4- to 6-week-old infants were found to discriminate between their mothers' voices and those of strangers, but only if the speech was normally intonated; they were unable to make this discrimination when both voices were monotone. Thus, it would appear that it is the linguistic properties and qualities of speech, or at least their complex acoustic properties, that infants are sensitive to. These studies do not tell us whether children can differentiate between two languages they have heard, which is the appropriate test case for bilingual children, but they are certainly suggestive of such discriminative capacity. At the very least, the extant evidence suggests that bilingual-to-be infants are capable of discriminating between different unfamiliar spoken languages at the point in development when they begin to utter single words.

Re-examination of a number of published language samples of interactions between children and their parents suggests that in fact bilingual children may use their languages differentially. Three such samples will be examined briefly at this time (Murrell, 1966; Volterra and Taeschner, 1978; Redlinger and Park, 1980). These interactions have been reproduced in Appendix 12.1. The point of this re-examination is not to prove the differentiated-language systems hypothesis, since the available data are inadequate, but rather to establish its tenability.

Volterra and Taeschner (1978) (see Appendix 12.1) report a conversation between a German/Italian bilingual girl, Lisa, and her German-speaking mother, along with three isolated utterances by Lisa to her mother. Lisa was 1;10 at the time of the recordings. With the exception of Lisa's use of *la* (Italian for 'there'), all items used by Lisa could be German. The authors interpret Lisa's use of *da* in the last utterance as mixing from Italian *dare* ('to give'); an alternative interpretation is that it is the German *da* ('there'), which Lisa had used previously.

Redlinger and Park (1980) report conversations between a German/Spanish bilingual boy, Marcus, and both his German-speaking father and Spanish-speaking mother (see Appendix 12.1). Marcus was between 2;4.23 and 2;5.20 and had an MLU [mean length of utterance] of 2.21 at the time of the recording. German was used by the parents with one another; the father used only German with Marcus; and the mother used predominantly Spanish (70%); the family resided in Germany. It can be conjectured from the parents' reported language use that Marcus had learned more German than Spanish, and indeed, German predominated in both conversations. Of particular interest is Marcus's use of Spanish – he used four different Spanish lexical items with his Spanish-speaking mother and only two with his German-speaking father. These data could be interpreted as functional differentiation of his limited Spanish. The authors' interpretation was that 'Marcus appeared to have basically one lexical system consisting of words from both languages' (p. 340).

Finally, Murrell (1966) reports conversations between a Swedish/Finnish/English trilingual child, Sandra, and the author and her mother (see Appendix 12.1). According to the author 'At the nursery only Finnish was spoken. Her mother spoke mostly Swedish to her at home, while I spoke partly Swedish and partly English. Her mother and I spoke mostly English together' (p. 11). The recordings were made almost three months after the family had moved to England when Sandra was between 2;3.25 and 2;4.1. Examination of the transcripts indicates that Sandra's lexical usage with the author is predominantly in English. The only non-English lexical items used by Sandra are references in Finnish to a cat in a picture (*kia*) and responses in Swedish to utterances initiated by the author in Swedish. To illustrate this, in Appendix 12.1 transcript (3b), turn S1, Sandra utters a word (*kekka*) that the author interprets to be Swedish ('to lick') but acknowledges that it might have been the corresponding English verb. As a result of this interpretation, apparently, the author responded in SWEDISH in turn F1 to the child's otherwise ENGLISH string of lexical items. Sandra then responded in Swedish (*kikka*) in turn S2. The author then responded in turn F2 in Swedish (apparently intending to provide a corrected imitation of Sandra's previous Swedish utterance) AND in English (apparently providing an English translation of his own previous utterance). Sandra then proceeded with a combination of English and Swedish in turn S3. In short most, and it could be argued all, of the child's Swedish utterances are made in response to Swedish modelled by the author; otherwise, the child used English. Even the child's use of the Finnish lexical item *kia* is equivocal in that it might actually function as a proper noun or name for her cat. Contrary to evidencing a lack of linguistic differentiation, Sandra appears to have used Swedish and English differentially in contextually sensitive ways during the same conversation with an interlocutor who switches back and forth, somewhat in confusion.

Analysis of Sandra's conversation with her mother yields a similar impression. In this case, Sandra uses predominantly Swedish except for three English-content words (i.e. *pull*, *bucket* and *faggit*) and the demonstrative adjective *that*. The child's use of *faggit* here is not at all clear from the transcript. It is not clear whether the child is really confused over the use of English *bucket* for spade and Swedish *ambare* for bucket as the author's notations would seem to imply or, alternatively, whether she is not underextending her use of the English lexical item *bucket* to a specific referent (i.e. a 'spade'); admittedly this is an incorrect lexical usage.

The preceding analysis focused on differentiation of language according to lexical distribution. One final piece of evidence which focuses on the use of different syntactic features will be offered here in support of the differentiated-language systems hypothesis. Meisel (1990) reports on the syntactic development of two French/German bilingual children. The children were observed between 1;0 and 4;0. The parents claimed to use their respective native languages exclusively with their children. Meisel examined the children's use of word-order sequences and verb inflections in French and German; these syntactic features were examined because they differ in mature forms of the target languages and in monolingual children's acquisition of the target forms. In brief, Meisel found that the bilingual children used different word orders in French and German as soon as they produced multiword utterances, and they correctly inflected verbs to agree with subjects according to the rules of each language as soon as they consistently filled the subject slot in their utterances.

Conclusion

In sum, I have argued that, contrary to most interpretations of bilingual development, bilingual children are able to differentiate their language systems from the beginning and that they are able to use their developing language systems differentially in contextually sensitive ways. As well, I have suggested that more serious research attention needs to be given to parental input in the form of bilingual mixing as a possible source of influence in children's mixing. Evidence that children's mixing may indeed be related to mixed input by parents was presented. This evidence, however, was limited to lexical mixing, and more attention to phonological, morphological and other kinds of mixing by parents and children is clearly needed. The available evidence is obviously inadequate to come to confident conclusions regarding these points, and my re-examination of other researchers' transcriptions must be regarded as preliminary and tentative pending more adequate research. What is clear from this review is that the case for undifferentiated language development in bilingual children is far from established.

Appendix 12.1

(1)   Volterra and Taeschner (1978: 355–16)

Lisa with German-speaking mother

(a)   L: Miao miao.
       M: Wo ist miao? ('Where is meow?')
       L: *La* miao. ('There meow.')
       M: Wo ist miao? ('Where is meow?')
       L: Da ist miao. ('There is meow.')

(b)   L: Daki Buch. ('Thanks book.') (*Her mother had just given her a book.*)

(c)   L: Daki. ('Thanks.') (*while giving the pencil to her mother.*)

(d)   L: Mama tita daki. ('Mommy pencil thanks.') (*She wants her mother to give her the pencil.*)

(e)   L: *Da.* (authors: interpret this as variant of Italian *dare* 'to give'; could be German *da* 'there') (*offering a sweet to her mother.*)

(2)   Redlinger and Park (1980: 340–41)

(a)   *Marcus with German-speaking father*
       F: Und was macht er hier? ('And what's he doing here?')
       Ms: Haare putzen ('Hair cleaning.')

F: Ja, er wäscht die Haare, und dann auch? ('Yes, he washes his hair, and then also?')

Ms: ¡Jabón! ('Soap!')

F: Bitte? ('What?')

Ms: ¡Jabón! ('Soap!')

F: Mit der Seife. Und was macht er denn hier? ('With the soap. And what is he doing then here?')

Ms: Putzen Zähne *con jabón*. ('Brushing teeth with soap.')

(b)   *Marcus with Spanish-speaking mother*

M: ¿Qué hacen los niños? ('What are the children doing?')

Ms: Müd. Die Kinder da müde. ('Tired. The children there tired.')

M: ¿Están cansados? No juegan los niños? ('Are they tired? Aren't the children playing?')

Ms: Das *no juegan*. ¡*Arboles!* ('That not playing. Trees!')

M: ¿Qué hay en los árboles? ('What are on the trees?')

Ms: *Manzanas*. Hund schlafen. ('Apples. Dog sleeping.')

(3)   Murrell (1966: 19–22)

Sandra with father
Situation: *Looking at two pictures, the first (a) showing a woman with a cat, the second (b) showing the same cat, this time covered with milk, and a dog licking the milk off the cat's back.*

(a)   F1: What else have you got there? ('What other pictures have you got there?')

S1: [ˌmami]
     See comment on S3.

F2: Is that Mummy?

S2: [n̩ ˈkʰinˌɛə]
     ([n̩] often preceded utterances at this stage (it did not apparently derive from Finnish *on* 'is' or English *and*)

F3: Kia.

S3: [n̩ ˈkʰia ˌmami]
     With [ˈkʰia] compare S2. This utterance meant 'Kia's mummy', i.e. 'the cat's owner'. The word *mummy* was still used to designate any older female in cases where a relationship was implied.

F4: Pussy-cat.

(b)   S1: [n̩ ˋdɛə [ˈ. . .] ˋbɔββa . . . ˋkʰekka . . . ˋuːː ˋkʰia]
     [dɛə] English *there* (Swedish *där*). S2 [ˈbɔββa] English *bow-wow*, Swedish *vovve*. Swedish *slicka* '(to) lick' (the English word was less well known than the Swedish). [uːː] was an exclamation of feigned shock and disapproval and real delight at seeing the cat covered with milk.

F1: Vad gör han?
     Swedish 'What's he doing?' (I did not understand [ˈkʰekka] but assumed, partly because of the form [ˈbɔββa], that it was Swedish rather than English she was speaking.)

S2:   ['kikka]

Swedish *slicka* (the gemination and final [-a] suggest the Swedish word).

F2:   ['kʰɪk . . . he's licking.

I may have thought she was using English *kick*.

S3:   [ˌlikiŋ . . . ['ʋaɣʋa] ˋkikkan ˋkikin ['ʋaɣʋa] ˋkikin ['ʋaɣʋa ˋkikiŋ] ['ʋaɣʋa]

Swedish *vovve* 'bow-wow'; cf. S1. The diphthong now more closely resembles my own (dialect) equivalent of standard British-English /ɑu/; but cf. Finnish *hauva* 'Bow-wow' and Finish *vauva* 'baby'. All four words were at first used indiscriminately for both 'dog' and 'baby'.

F3:   Licking pussy-cat.

I repeat the verb and add the object.

S4:   ['kiki ˋbɔββa]

The final nasal is lost in ['kiki]. The diphthong in ['bɔββa] suggests the English word. She is now excited, whereas in S3 she was speaking more deliberately. She assumes I have contradicted her, that I mean it is the cat that is doing the licking.

F4:   Bow-wow licking pussy-cat.

I misunderstand her, too prematurely attributing to her a knowledge of English syntax. Two-item utterances were still maximal and the order arbitrary.

Sandra with Swedish-speaking mother

Situation: *looking at two pictures, the first* (c) *showing a monkey pulling a girl's hair, the second* (d) *showing the girl with a bucket.*

(c)   *M1*:   Och vad är det?

Swedish 'And what's that?'

S1:   ['ɑːpa]

Swedish *apa* 'monkey'.

M2:   Apa. Vad gör apan?

Swedish 'Monkey. And what's the monkey doing?'

S2:   [ˌpu ˌsika ɟje]

English *pull*, Swedish *flicka* 'girl' and Swedish *håret* 'the hair'. (= 'He's pulling the girl's hair.')

M3:   Ja, han drar flickan i håret, så dum apa! Fy! dum apa.

Swedish 'Yes, he's pulling the girl's hair [lit. 'the girl in the hair'], what a naughty monkey! Tut, tut! naughty monkey.'

S3:   ['eː hɛ e ˋkɔkkea]

Finnish *ei saa koskea* 'mustn't touch'

M4:   Ei saa koskea . . . 'ei ta kokia'.

Her mother repeats the sentence in its correct form and then in mimicry of a common version of the child's.

S4:   [ˌei saː ˋkɔkkia]

(d)   *M1*:   Vad har flickan?

Swedish 'What's the girl got?'

S1:   [ˌemˌen ˋembala]

Swedish *ämbare* 'bucket'.

M2: Och vad har hon mera – i andra handen?
      Swedish 'And what else has she got – in her other hand?'

S2: ˌbakit . . . 'dat ˌembala]
      English *bucket* and English *that*. Both *bucket* and *ämbare* were used for both 'bucket' and 'spade', but here she seems to be making a distinction between *bucket* (= 'spade') and *ämbare* (= 'bucket').

M3: Det år *spade*.
      Swedish 'That's 'spade'.

S3: [ˋpaːde]

M4: Det där är *ämbare*.
      Swedish *'That's "bucket".'*

S4: [ˋembala . . . ˌfaggit]
      The child repeats the Swedish word, then, after a pause, the English.

Source: Genesee, F. (1989) Early bilingual language development: one language or two? *Journal of Child Language* 16: 161–79, by permission of Cambridge University Press.

Chapter 13

Early differentiation of languages in bilingual children

JÜRGEN M. MEISEL

THE SIMULTANEOUS ACQUISITION OF two (or more) "first languages"
can be of particular interest for language acquisition studies. By analyzing the
development of two linguistic competences in one individual, we may be capable
of sorting out more easily to what extent the underlying logic of development is
determined by the grammatical system to be acquired, or the particular way of
human language processing as opposed to properties of the individual or of the
communicative situation. There is, in fact, a steadily increasing amount of research
in this area (for fairly comprehensive overviews including more recent studies, see
McLaughlin, 1984 or Taeschner, 1983).

Much of this work is largely descriptive in its orientation, and theoretical
questions are not always discussed explicitly. One question which is, however,
pursued very frequently is whether bilinguals are able to "differentiate their two
linguistic systems" (Lindholm and Padilla, 1978: 334). (For some recent contributions to this discussion, see, for example, Volterra and Taeschner, 1978; Redlinger
and Park, 1980; Vihman, 1982; 1985; 1998.)

The emerging picture is somewhat flawed by terminological confusions,
especially with respect to those concepts underlying the terms "language mixing"
and "code-switching." To avoid problems of this kind, I will use *code-switching* to
describe the bilingual's ability to select the language according to the interlocutor,
the situational context, etc. This choice is constrained by the properties of the
linguistic system, among other things, much in the same way as with adults
(compare Pfaff, 1979; Poplack, Chapter 9 of this volume). *Language mixing*, on
the other hand, will be used to designate a bilingual's "indiscriminate combinations of elements from each language" (Redlinger and Park, 1980: 337), not
being able to differentiate the two languages. In my conclusions, I will suggest
some modifications to this terminology.

With this terminological distinction in mind, one may try to summarize[1] very briefly the large body of research available as follows:

1   Code-switching is a common phenomenon, among young bilinguals as well as among adults. Bilingual children often appear to use it as a kind of "relief strategy" when the necessary linguistic material is more easily available in the other language, e.g. when the topic of conversation normally falls within the domain of the other language. Children frequently seem to be aware of the fact that they are switching languages, and they tend to correct themselves in situations of this kind. Normally, however, when switching is used not only as a relief strategy, it becomes more frequent as the child acquires more proficiency in *both* languages, i.e. its use increases with age and with developing competence in the two languages. Code-switching, in other words, is thus regarded as part of the bilingual's pragmatic competence.

2   Mixing seems to occur most frequently in the lexicon whereas it is most unlikely to happen in the sound system. As for morphological and syntactic mixing, the reports given in the available literature are contradictory. This is partly due to theoretical and methodological differences. It is not even possible to distinguish, in all cases, between switching and mixing if the authors themselves do not make this distinction nor give the necessary information. At any rate, mixing is most likely to occur if (a) one of the two languages is very dominant in the child's competence, and if (b) the adults in the child's environment mix or switch quite freely in their own speech. As McLaughlin (1984: 95) phrases it: "interference . . . can be held to a minimum if the domains are clearly defined and if the two languages are maintained somewhat in balance."

3   Assuming the developmental perspective, we may summarize that mixing is reported to happen most frequently during a very early phase of language acquisition, before or around age 2;0 (years;months), whereas later on, bilingual children easily separate the two linguistic systems.

Findings of this kind have led Volterra and Taeschner (1978) to propose a three-stage model for early phases of language development in bilingual children. These stages can be characterized in the following way:

I   the child has only one lexical system comprising words from both languages

II   development of two distinct lexical systems although the child applies "the same syntactic rules to both languages" (Volterra and Taeschner, 1978: 311)

III   differentiation of two linguistic systems, lexical as well as syntactic.

In this chapter, I merely discuss the alleged stage II, focusing on syntactic and morphological aspects. For reasons of space, lexical development is not discussed, although it should be noted that the claim that bilingual children initially use only one lexicon is by no means non-controversial, as can be seen when looking at the data presented by Ronjat (1913), Pavlovitch (1920), Leopold (1939–49) and others. (For a more detailed discussion I refer to Jekat, 1985.)

With regard to a possible phase characterized by a single syntactic system underlying performance in both languages, the issue is even more controversial, as has been mentioned above. (See also Mikès, 1967; Bergman, 1976; Lindholm and Padilla, 1978; Hoffmann, 1985.) Nevertheless, the three-stage model appears to have been widely accepted. In discussing its stage II, I will assume that certain factors (e.g. mixing in the linguistic environment, dominance of one language, social-psychological biases in favor of one language, etc.) may indeed lead to mixing and will certainly render language differentiation more difficult.

In my opinion, however, the theoretically more interesting question is whether the human "language making capacity" (Slobin, 1985) could allow the bilingual individual, in principle, to separate the two simultaneously acquired grammatical systems from early on, without even going through a phase of confusion.

Discussion of the theoretical issues involved

Before turning to empirical data in an attempt to answer this research question, it is necessary to examine a number of problems related to the following three issues:

1   the definition of stage II, as suggested by Volterra and Taeschner (1978);
2   the kind of empirical evidence necessary to support or refute claims connected with the alleged stages I–III;
3   theoretical assumptions about whether language processing in young children is grammatical (or "syntactic") in nature.

A clarification of these issues should help to avoid the currently common confusion whereby authors arrive at contradictory conclusions about language differentiation and mixing – as a result of using apparently similar terms which are, in fact, defined quite differently.

1 The *definition of the three stages*, especially that of stage II, as proposed by Volterra and Taeschner (1978), is surprisingly vague. In fact, concerning stage II, one does not learn any more than the above quoted claim that the child "applies the same syntactic rules to both languages" (Volterra and Taeschner, 1978: 312). No independent criterion is mentioned, like age, mean length of utterances (MLU), or any other feature which is not itself part of the definition of this stage.

Note that not even for the children studied by Volterra and Taeschner themselves (children acquiring Italian and German simultaneously) are we given precise indications delimitating these stages. There exists only one remark[2] to the effect that "until the age of 2;9 she (Lisa, JMM) appears to have acquired only one syntactic system" (p. 322). If, however, age, MLU, etc. are considered to be unreliable indicators of stage, other defining criteria could have been found. The most likely candidates would be syntactic phenomena, especially since stage II is defined in terms of syntactic features. Use of syntactic criteria is common practice in language acquisition studies, both for natural second language acquisition (see Meisel *et al.*, 1981) as well as for first language acquisition (see Clahsen, 1982). The case for "stage II" would be much stronger if it could be stated that syntactic mixing occurred during developmental phases, for instance independent of age and MLU, when word order phenomenon X has already been acquired but phenomenon Y has not yet been acquired. (For a convincing example using verb placement as an independent variable in assessing the order of acquisition of case markings, see Clahsen, 1986.)

This is not to say, however, that using instances of "mixing" to define a stage of mixing must necessarily lead to circularity in the argument. But it may be – and in fact is, I will claim – a non-sufficient definition. For one thing, if one does not find such mixing, one may simply have overlooked it, it may not yet have begun or already be abandoned by the child – or it may not exist at all. More seriously, Volterra and Taeschner (1978) themselves show, in the course of their discussion, that instances of mixing do not constitute evidence in favor of the stages under discussion. They found (p. 319) that children at stage II "keep mixing words of the two languages" (Lisa at age 2;5). If, however, mixing of words may still occur after "the child distinguishes two different lexicons" (p. 312), how do we know s/he has already reached stage II; and vice versa, if this can be accounted for, how can we make sure that similar examples at stage I do indeed indicate that the child operates with only one lexical system for both languages? Even more intriguingly, would we have to allow for the possibility that the three stages need not be ordered chronologically? In that case, they would merely represent logical entities which need not appear in reality as discrete phases. Note that Vihman (1985), who adopts the three-stage model, concludes that these "stages" may surface in a parallel fashion.

All this is far from being clear and things become no clearer even after looking at the empirical evidence given by Volterra and Taeschner (1978). Examples quoted from the speech of Lisa, one of the children studied, fall into the following age ranges:

stage I: 1;6–1;11
stage II: 2;5–3;3
stage III: 2;9–3;11

Bearing in mind that stage II is said elsewhere in their text to last until age 2;9 (see quote above), it seems that stage I ends around 2;0 and stage II lasts from 2;5 to 2;9, allowing, however, for features of stage I to appear at II, and features characteristic of II to be used at III.

Another fact is still more confusing: the tables given by Volterra and Taeschner (1978: 321ff.) indicate that for at least one of the three syntactic constructions discussed (i.e. placement of adjectives), the Italian examples, which apparently indicate the use of one syntax for both languages, occur without exception at age 2;9 or later, and the German examples are all modeled on the adult norm. How could these speech samples then be used as evidence in favor of a developmental phase which is said to end at about 2;9? In addition, all constructions but one quoted from German utterances that look like "Italian syntax" appear at 2;9 or later. Whatever the explanation of this phenomenon may be, it certainly cannot be used as evidence in favor of stage II, since this child is said to have achieved the differentiation of the two systems at this point of development.

To sum up, I do not believe that the empirical evidence and/or the theoretical justification given is sufficient to support the hypothesized phase II of the three-stage model. One might add that the arguments given by Volterra and Taeschner (1978) in favor of a stage at which a single syntactic system is used, are based on data from only one child, Lisa. It appears that she was the only one of the children studied to use constructions which could be interpreted in this fashion. Yet, as becomes evident from what we are told about her, Italian is clearly Lisa's dominant language. In fact, Taeschner (1983: 102, 107) mentions that Lisa strongly preferred Italian and had less contact with German for a considerable period of time. This happened at exactly the same time when she was said to be at stage II, namely from (at least) age 2;6 until 3;0.

In other words, these facts suggest that social-psychological factors may lead to language mixing or code-switching, as has been mentioned above. They do not, however, represent convincing evidence in favor of an early phase of mixing through which all children would have to go. One might add that Redlinger and Park (1980) also offer – although unwillingly – good evidence against "an initial mixed stage in language production" (p. 337). They studied the speech of four bilingual children (two German–French, one German–Spanish, and one German–English), who were between the ages 2;0 and 2;8 and with MLU of 1.39 to 2.66 at the onset of the investigation. They conclude that "the children whose language was more advanced produced fewer mixed utterances than the children at earlier stages of development," but they also admit that "Various linguistic and sociolinguistic factors seem to have influenced the degree of mixing" (p. 340). In fact, only one boy in their sample, Marc, used practically no mixed utterances; and this was also the only child for whom two languages were clearly separated in the environment, the mother speaking French with the boy, the father using German (adhering to the well-known principle "one person – one language").

Unfortunately, this boy's linguistic development was already fairly advanced (MLU 2.66) at the beginning of the study. In spite of claims made by Redlinger and Park (1980), however, language development does not explain what they call "mixing."[3] First, for each individual, it is not true that the percentage of mixes would decrease parallel to increasing MLU values. For Marc, no such correlation exists; his "mixes" even drop to zero at a point where his MLU also drops. Second, interpersonal comparison does not support the hypothesis by Redlinger and Park (1980). In other words, MLU values do not allow one to make predictions about frequency of "mixing." For example, at MLU 3.3, one child, Danny, uses 14.6 percent of mixed utterances, whereas Marc uses 2.1 percent. Thirdly, the nature of the input (i.e. separation of the two languages, dominance of one language, etc.) *does* make it possible to predict occurrence or non-occurrence of mixing. In other words, what Redlinger and Park (1980: 340) call "sociolinguistic factors" seem to be the crucial ones. And I would like to emphasize their conclusion – which they limit to only one child (*sic!*) – that "the lack of strict language separation by person in Marc's linguistic environment may have had an effect on his overall high rate of mixing" (p. 341).

To conclude, I want to claim that the evidence offered by Volterra and Taeschner (1978), Redlinger and Park (1980), and others is not sufficient to support the hypothesis that bilingual children must pass through an initial stage of syntactic mixing which, in turn, would have to be explained as a result of their processing both languages as a single system.

2 The question which then arises is what *kinds of empirical evidence* could be accepted as instances of syntactic mixing or of differentiation between syntactic systems. Volterra and Taeschner, quite correctly, remark that the "mixed system" may be different from each of the two adult monolingual systems involved.

This should, indeed, be interpreted as a necessary condition: one should only consider those aspects of grammar where the two *adult target systems differ*. If, for example, both languages acquired by the child allow for SVO (subject–verb–object) ordering (as is the case in Italian–French–German), SVO sequences in the speech of bilinguals do not support one or the other claim. In fact, I would even like to suggest that one should try to find evidence in favor of, or against, a "common, non-differentiated" syntax in structural areas where language *uses of monolingual children* acquiring each of the languages under consideration also *differ*. Otherwise, one has two separate systems to consider which do, however, overlap with regard to just these structural properties, rather than one common system. As far as I can see, an empirically based method of deciding which of the two hypotheses is the correct one does not exist. The placement of negators (NEG), to give one example, proceeds through what may well be universally similar or identical phases (see Wode, 1977; 1981); preverbal placement of NEG is common even for languages where the adult norm allows only for postverbal position. If, therefore, German–Italian or German–French bilinguals use preverbal negation in both languages, there is no way of deciding whether they are processing both languages as one system or whether the two systems underlying this kind of language use merely overlap in this structural domain at the given point of linguistic development.

A different problem arises if the supposed common system is identical to one of the two adult systems in a given structural area. Even if the two target languages do differ in this respect, it is difficult to decide whether one really has only one underlying grammar. Instead, the commonalities in the use of the two languages may be the result of transfer from the dominant language. If one system interferes with the other, this is, by definition, not the same as when only a single grammar exists. To give another example, Lisa, the child studied by Volterra and Taeschner (1978) and by Taeschner (1983), initially seems to prefer what looks like "German syntax" in all three structural domains analyzed (possessor + possession (N + N) patterns, adjective + noun sequences,[4] and placement of negators in final position) in German and in Italian. This does not imply that these structures must always correspond to the German adult norm, as was observed by Volterra and Taeschner (1978: 324). Later on, at approximately age 2;9 (sic!), Lisa apparently uses "Italian" surface structures more frequently. This shift corresponds to changes in the linguistic environment of the child where Italian strongly prevails after 2;6.

Note that I do not want to claim that whenever a structural pattern appears in both languages spoken by the bilingual, but only in one of the corresponding target languages, that this should necessarily be interpreted as evidence for transfer processes. In fact, I would argue that transfer occurs much less frequently than is commonly assumed (see Meisel, 1983). But I do want to claim that such phenomena cannot easily be interpreted as evidence in favor of the "one common system" hypothesis; especially not if sociolinguistic factors indicate that the language from which the "common" structures are taken appears to be dominant in the child's language environment.

3 In view of the methodological problems, which make it very difficult to find positive evidence in support of the one-system stage, it appears to be more promising to look for evidence in favor of the hypothesis that bilinguals do differentiate between the two grammatical systems from early on. If it can be shown that they use structures in which the two target systems (including the respective child languages) differ, then this obviously also constitutes evidence against the alternative one-system hypothesis. Yet, whatever the empirical evidence may look like, it can only be interpreted if a crucial theoretical question is answered first, a question which, amazingly enough, is not even asked, let alone answered, in the literature on bilingual first language acquisition: at what point of language development may one reasonably assume that the child is *able to use syntactic* (or, more generally *grammatical*) *modes* of language processing?

In (monolingual) child language research, this is one of the most crucial theoretical questions. It suffices to look at recent collections of papers dealing with child language and theories of language development (e.g. Fletcher and Garman, 1979; Wanner and Gleitman, 1982; or Slobin, 1985) to come up with a picture which can roughly be sketched as follows. It is generally assumed that child language is initially organized according to semantic–pragmatic principles. Only through a gradual process of "syntactization" will grammatical ways of processing come in. In other words, it is believed that after a period of semantic–pragmatic primacy, syntactic categories and relations develop which resemble (or are identical with) those in mature grammars. Givón (1979; 1985), for example, suggests a distinction between a "pragmatic" and a "syntactic" mode of language processing, and he furthermore claims that the former chronologic- ally precedes (in ontogenesis as well as in phylogenesis) the latter. In fact, some authors would not even exclude the possibility that mature language com- petence, as well, could be described in terms of semantic–pragmatic principles without the use of specific grammatical categories or rules (e.g. Bates and MacWhinney, 1982).

In the light of these discussions, at least two possible interpretations of the single-system hypothesis exist. First, during this developmental phase the bilingual children do not (yet?) have access to grammatical categories and prin- ciples. Rather, they rely entirely on semantic–pragmatic strategies of language use. This "pragmatic mode" of language processing would operate in exactly the same way for both languages of the bilingual and thus account for the structural similarities which are claimed to exist in their speech.

However, this interpretation is evidently not the one intended by those who defend the three-stage model since they clearly refer to *syntactic categories* and *rules*, *grammatical systems*, and so forth (see Volterra and Taeschner, 1978; Redlinger and Park, 1980; among others). To speak of syntactic rules, etc. obvi- ously only makes sense if one presupposes that the child is capable, at this particu- lar point in time, of returning to a syntactic mode of processing. Note that this first version of the model would also be neutral with regard to the current discussion since it does not imply any prediction or claim specific to bilingual language acquisition. Nor could it answer our initial question as to whether the language-making-capacity of humans allows for the simultaneous acquisition of two grammatical systems. It would merely state that monolinguals and bilinguals alike start out with a mode of processing which follows general pragmatic principles, rather than more language-specific grammatical ones.

We may thus take it for granted that the second possible interpretation is the one assumed by those researchers who support the single-system hypothesis: once the child has begun to use the grammatical (or syntactic) mode of language processing, s/he will initially develop only one syntax which is used to process both languages.[5]

From these considerations it follows that we cannot separate our initial question from a second one concerning the onset of grammatical processing. The answers given to this second question vary enormously if one looks at mono-lingual child language research. Maratsos (1982), for example, summarizes rele-vant findings and concludes that syntactic categories may not be acquired until the end of the preschool years, while Valian (1986) presents good evidence that this may actually happen much earlier, namely at approximately age 2;6 (MLU 3.0–4.0). Garman (1979) views the period around age 3;0 as the crucial one for grammatical developments. This is only to mention some reports which are, I believe, based on broad and reliable empirical research. We need not try to solve this problem, however, before addressing our initial question. Neither need we take a stand on the issue of whether grammatical processing is indeed preceded by a phase of pragmatic primacy. Instead, we may search for evidence in favor of *syntactic* categories and rules – and then work our way back into earlier develop-mental phases. In fact, if one can show that a bilingual child uses different gram-matical means for expressing the same or similar semantic–pragmatic functions in both languages, this not only indicates that s/he is indeed differentiating the two grammatical systems, but also constitutes what I believe to be the clearest evi-dence that one can and, indeed, must attribute to the child – the ability to use the *grammatical mode*.

Subjects and data collection methods

In what follows, I will present some results from a study analyzing the acquisition of French and German by children of preschool age. The present analysis focuses on the speech of two children who were 12 months of age (1;0,0 – years; months, days) at the beginning of the data collection period and includes the period from age 1;0,0 until 4;0,0. One child (C) is a girl, the other (P) is a boy. So far, from 1980 to 1986, a total of eight children have been studied longitudinally by our research group DUFDE;[6] currently (1986–88), three children are being recorded and studied. The children are videotaped every second week while interacting with adults and occasionally with other children. The recordings consist mainly of free interactions in play situations; they last for approximately 50–60 minutes each, half in German and half in French. The well-known principle of "une personne, une langue" is observed. At least one recording per month is tran-scribed and analyzed.

Both children are growing up in middle-class families. The native language of the mothers is French while the fathers' first language is German. Each person uses his/her respective native tongue with the children; the language of com-munication between father and mother is German.

C is her parents' only child. At the age of 9 months, she started going to a German day-care center. She is, thus, exposed to German more often than to French, the language primarily spoken with her mother and with some French friends. The family usually spend their holidays in France, where French is then spoken almost exclusively. On average, this happens three times a year. During a period of several months, beginning at the age of about three years, C stopped speaking French. Even when communicating with her mother, she would respond in German. The recording sessions with C were stopped when she was 5;0,6.

P, the second child, usually speaks French with his sister who is three years older. At the age of 2;8 he started going to a French kindergarten. Since their mother works, a young person frequently takes care of the children in the afternoons. P and his sister speak German with their sitter as with their father, and French with their mother and in the kindergarten. Every year, the family spends approximately six or seven weeks in a French-speaking country. During these weeks, the children speak French almost exclusively. P was recorded twice per month until he was 6;6; since then, he is part of a group which is videotaped every three months.

It should be added that P's linguistic development is very slow, as compared to many other children who are described in language acquisition studies. Contrasting his development with C's, one finds that he is about six months behind, although he catches up after the period under investigation. This can already be noted towards the end of the investigation period. For both children, French initially appears to be the dominant input language and it is also the language preferred by the children at this time. This preference is clearly changing for C between 2;6 and 3;0, when she begins to favor German. As for P, his bilingualism seems to be fairly balanced.

To give an approximate idea of the degree and rate of development in both languages, MLUs are given in Table 13.1. In spite of the well-known shortcomings of this type of measurement, it should at least allow for comparison of our results with those from other studies. By and large, we are using procedures to establish MLU values that are suggested by Brown (1973) and Bloom and Lahey (1978). Unlike many other child language studies, we do in fact count morphemes, not words, as soon as we have evidence that the child uses a certain morpheme productively. In the case of plurifunctional morphemes, each form is only counted once; that is, a flexive is not counted three times for case, number, and gender.

Discussion and results

In this section, I will try to test the research guidelines developed above empirically. I will thus examine some linguistic phenomena which are sufficiently distinct in French and German, to serve as test cases for the problem of language differentiation. If possible, they should also be distinguishable in French and German monolinguals' linguistic development. It will furthermore be necessary to investigate whether these phenomena may rightly be regarded as syntactic in nature.

Table 13.1   Age and MLU of the children

C: Age	German	French	P: Age	German	French
2;01,13	1.93	2.09	2;03,16	1.19	1.31
2;03,11	2.30	2.50	2;07,06	1.43	1.86
2;04,08	2.12	3.23	2;09,02	2.06	2.30
2;07,20	3.08	3.16	2;11,10	2.17	3.00
2;10,28	3.62	3.68	3;01,09	3.37	3.59
3;00,02	3.96	—	3;02,03	2.57	3.00
3;02,10	3.65	4.08	3;05,03	4.13	4.32
3;03,10	4.30	3.78	3;06,14	3.59	4.34
3;06,11	4.86	—	3;11,02	4.60	5.90
3;10,20	5.99	5.61			

Word order phenomena

Word order is a grammatical area which does, in fact, fulfill all the requirements mentioned. German word order, as compared to French, is rather variable. There is even disagreement as to whether German is an SOV or an SVO language. Unmarked order in main clauses is SVO, whereas the canonical order in subordinate clauses is SOV. Non-finite verbal elements, however, always appear in final position: in main clauses at the very end, in subordinate clauses followed by the finite part of the verb phrase. This is the case with auxiliary (Aux + Past Participle) and with modal (Modal + Infinitive) constructions, but also with compound verbs (Particle + V). Some examples are:

> (1) a. Ich schrieb einen Brief
>   'I wrote a letter'
>   b. dass ich einen Brief schrieb
>   'that I wrote a letter'
>   c. Ich habe einen Brief geschrieben
>   'I have written a letter'
>   d. dass ich einen Brief geschrieben habe
>   'that I have written a letter'

The finite verb obligatorily assumes the second position of a main clause, as in (1c). Placement of the finite verb in second position is also required if some other element (NP, Adverbial, WH-word, embedded S, etc.) is fronted. Compare the examples in:

(2) a. Heute schrieb ich einen Brief
       'Today I wrote a letter'
    b. Einen Brief schrieb ich heute
       'A letter I wrote today'

In other words, verb placement is specifically interesting. It depends on whether the verb is finite or not, and on whether it appears in an embedded clause or not.

French word order, on the other hand, is almost strictly SVO. Problems arise with clitic object pronouns which are placed in preverbal position, resulting in SoV sequences. This type of construction, however, does not yet appear during very early phases of child language. Another phenomenon is also quite important for it is rather frequent in spoken colloquial French, i.e. *dislocation* of subjects and objects. Reliable quantitative evidence is not available, but it may be taken for granted that dislocation of subjects is far more frequent than dislocation of objects. As for the latter, placement to the left is more common than to the right, and direct objects are more likely to be dislocated than indirect ones. In any case, a pronominal copy must be left standing.

(3) a. Il a tout bu, notre chat
       'He has drunk all of it, our cat'
    b. Notre chat, il a tout bu
       'Our cat, he has drunk all of it'
    c. Ce livre, je l'ai lu il y a longtemps
       'This book, I read it a long time ago'

Furthermore, very specific situational conditions allow for placement of objects in initial position without leaving a pronominal copy behind. But this is a marginal case which is apparently not reflected in child language. Finally, it should be kept in mind that subject–verb inversion, a very frequent phenomenon in German, has virtually disappeared in spoken French, although it does exist in the grammar of the standard language.

To summarize these remarks: French is a fairly strict SVO language but other sequences are possible and appear in the child's linguistic environment, especially "double subjects" in dislocated constructions such as sVOS, but also those with cliticized objects (SoV).

Let us now look very briefly at monolingual acquisition of German and French. Clahsen (1982; 1984) and Mills (1985) give evidence of the following developmental pattern in German. During phase 1 – roughly equivalent to Brown's (1973) stages I–II – word order is highly variable, but final position of the verb is preferred, and children soon begin to front objects and adverbials. During phase 2 – approximately stage III suggested by Brown – copula and modal constructions appear and the non-finite verbal element is regularly placed in final position, as required by the target grammar. Finite verbs, however, continue to be used in second as well as in final position. During phase 3 (Brown's stage IV), child word order follows largely the same regularities as the language use of adults. Subordinate clauses, however, do not show up until phase 4 (stage V). Interestingly enough, this is a case of error free acquisition: the verb is always placed correctly in final position, right from the beginning. In contrast to this apparent ease of acquisition of verb placement in embedded clauses, second position placement of verbs in main clauses represents a major acquisitional difficulty. Thus, in utterances with an initialized interrogative pronoun, or those with a topicalized complement, the verb sometimes appears in third position.

As for monolingual acquisition of French, we unfortunately lack information on some crucial aspects. Following the state-of-the-art paper by E. Clark (1985), one may nevertheless draw the following picture. During the two- and three-word phases, word order is fairly variable, but V(O)S sequences seem to be preferred. Some authors claim that children prefer SV(O) rather early. At any rate, this becomes the predominant pattern later on. Left and right dislocation of subjects appears quite early, and at least some children tend to use such sequences in the majority of their utterances.

Let us now turn to the development of word order phenomena in bilingual children, using data obtained from C and P (see example (2) above). Some of the results of these analyses are summarized in Figures 13.1 and 13.2. (For more details see Meisel, 1986: 143ff.) The analysis begins with what Brown characterized as stage II, having an MLU around 1.75, since it is during this period that children start using a larger number of multi-word utterances. Only declarative sentences are considered here, leaving aside the peculiarities of imperative and interrogative sentences.

First of all one can observe that SVO is largely predominant in both languages, from the beginning of the multi-word phase through all of the period investigated. Word order is thus markedly less variable than in the speech of monolingual French and German children. There is, however, a difference between French and German for both bilingual children which reflects properties of the two target languages. In French, frequency values for SV(O) order rarely drop below 0.8, and they often reach 1.0. Word order use in German is more variable, although SV(O) is also clearly dominant during the entire period. Note that SOV patterns, the preferred order in monolingual German child language, are not used except with the non-finite verb in final position, as required by the target norm. It goes without saying that this does not appear in French either with finite or with non-finite verbs. We thus find less variability in bilinguals as compared to monolinguals and, more interestingly, a quantitative difference between French and German for each bilingual child in the use of SV(O) sequences.

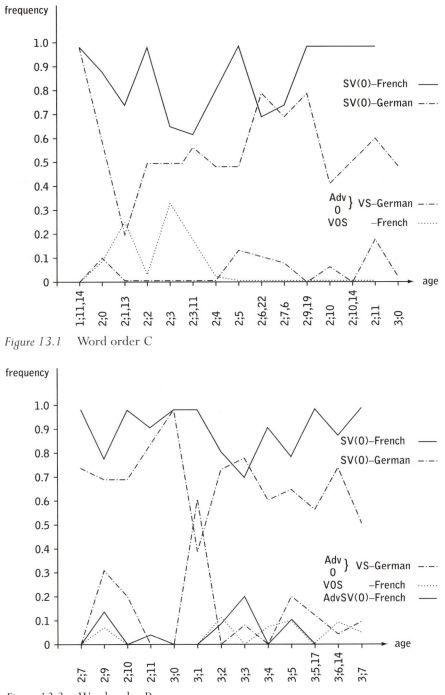

Figure 13.1 Word order C

Figure 13.2 Word order P

Another difference between French and German in bilingual language use results from the dislocation of subjects to the right in French. Since children during these developmental phases tend to omit subject pronouns, such uses may surface as VOS patterns. They only exist in French and never in German. In addition, the subject in French is also dislocated to the left occasionally; this is not shown in the figures, since these uses are rather infrequent.

Whereas so far the differences between the uses of the two languages have only been quantitative in nature, or resulted from the non-appearance of certain phenomena in one of the two languages, more convincing evidence for the early differentiation between languages consists in the application of grammatical devices specific for French or German. This is the case with the verb-second position required by the German system. Objects and adverbials may be fronted in both languages in order to topicalize these constituents. In French, this results in sequences with the verb in third position: AdvSV(O) or OSV(Adv). Fronting of objects is not used by the children during the period under consideration. Fronted adverbs, however, appear in P's speech. In these cases, the order of elements correctly follows the adult norm. Fronting of these constituents in German, on the other hand, necessarily triggers subject-verb inversion, leading to AdvVS or OVS sequences; compare example (2) above. As can be seen from the figures, both children use such structures in German but never in French. In fact, they never deviate from the adult norm. In other words, whenever they do front a constituent in German, the verb appears in second position whereas in French the verb remains in third position. This is especially remarkable since monolingual German children, as has been mentioned above, tend to leave the verb in third position for some time, thus violating the target norm. Note that verb-second position is only motivated by the grammatical system; it does not serve stylistic purposes, nor does it express specific semantic or pragmatic functions. In the light of this observation, it is even more revealing to observe that both children use constructions of this type from the very beginning of the multi-word phase onwards, beginning within Brown's stage II, approximately at MLU 2.0. I therefore want to claim that this is strong evidence in support of the hypothesis that bilingual children are, in fact, able to differentiate between two languages as soon as they use what may be interpreted as *syntactic* means of expression.

A similar argument can be used to explain the observation already mentioned that non-finite verbs in German are placed in final position. In the French utterances of the children, such constructions do not exist.

Let me add one remark concerning word order in subordinate clauses. It has been mentioned above that verb placement in German which requires clause final position, in this case does not cause acquisitional difficulties. Rather, monolinguals always use these constructions as prescribed by the adult norm. The bilingual data available are not unambiguous. First of all, subordinates are rather rare during this period. Secondly, C uses a few utterances which might be interpreted as – incorrect – SVO orders. And similar examples can be found in the literature for bilingual children acquiring German as one of their languages (e.g. Park, 1981; Taeschner, 1983). P, on the other hand, behaves quite like monolinguals and uses correct SOV sequences in embedded sentences. This seems to indicate that subordinate constructions might also be used as evidence in favor of the differentiation hypothesis since both children always use SVO order in French.

In sum then, I believe I have adequately shown that bilingual children use different word order sequences in both languages as soon as they begin to produce multi-word utterances. The two target systems are distinct in these cases; and monolingual children also use different orders in the respective languages. In addition, there are very good reasons to assume that these phenomena may rightly be called syntactic ones. If semantic and/or pragmatic functions were determining these uses, one would have to expect that similar or identical functions should be expressed similarly in both languages. This is definitely not the case in these instances. Instead, the children follow the requirements of the grammatical systems of both target languages quite closely, even when these merely express grammatical necessities without any apparent semantic–pragmatic motivation. In other cases, certain constructions may well be motivated pragmatically, such as the topicalization of complements, yet their formal properties are merely determined by the respective grammatical system, e.g. verb in second or third position after fronting of complements.

Subject–verb agreement

Another promising area to find evidence in support of the differentiation hypothesis is the use of subject pronouns and of subject–verb agreement. It is generally agreed that these phenomena are grammatical ones. Even Bates (1976), who otherwise argues against syntactic explanations, states that rigid adherence to SVO order (in Italian) and the use of such devices should be "explained by the possibility that the child has just discovered the concept of syntactic subject" (p. 209). The function of person and number markings on the verb is thus primarily a syntactic one, namely to encode the grammatical function of *subject*. And the respective coding devices are sufficiently distinct in German and in French.

A very brief look at the two adult target systems reveals that German uses a fairly rich system of suffixes to encode person and number, whereas French has lost most of its suffixes serving similar purposes. We may restrict this discussion to present-tense forms, since other tenses appear later in child language and are used much less frequently. The German paradigm for main verbs and modals is as follows:

sagen (to say)			*können* (to be able)	
(4) ich sage ich sag'	I say		ich kann	I am able to
do sagst	you say		du kannst	you are able to
er sagt	he says		er kann	he is able to
sie sagt	she says		sie kann	she is able to
wir sagen	we say		wir können	we are able to
ihr sagt	you say		ihr könnt	you are able to
sie sagen	they say		sie können	they are able to

Consequently there is a difference between main verbs and modals. The zero suffix for the first person singular is the one commonly used in colloquial speech. The suffixes, in other words, carry the following functions:

		main verbs	*modals*
(5)	ø	1st sg. (coll)	lst/3rd sg.
	e	1st sg.	—
	st	2nd sg.	2nd sg.
	t	3rd sg. 2nd pl.	2nd pl.
	en	1st/3rd pl. infinitive	1st/3rd pl. infinitive

In French, the corresponding suffixes have mainly survived in the writing system. In spoken language, only some plural forms are left:

parler (to speak)	
(6) je parle	I speak
tu parles	you speak
il parle	he speaks
elle parle	she speaks
nous parlons/on parle	we speak
vous parlez	you speak
ils parlent	they speak
elles parlent	they speak

In colloquial speech where the 1st person plural is regularly realized as "on," we are therefore normally left with only two forms, zero and *-ez* (2nd person plural). Certain additional variants may be ignored here, for they are unlikely to appear in early child speech, for example the 3rd person plural form of certain "irregular" verbs. Merely with the auxiliary and the copula do we find a pattern of verbal markings for person and number which is used in early phases of language development. But this cannot be generalized as a productive system of verb inflection.

Given this situation, the study of subject pronouns in French turns out to be of prime importance. In fact, it could be argued that the clitic subject pronoun in French forms part of the verb rather than being a syntactic subject. Similar proposals have been put forward repeatedly in studies on French syntax: for example see the discussion in Joly (1973). Recent generative analyses conclude that the subject clitic should be regarded as a constituent of the auxiliary in the INFL node but not of the subject NP (see Jaeggli, 1982). A number of phonological, morphological and syntactic facts lend support to analyses of this kind. Its status as a clitic already points in this direction. The frequency of patterns like (7a) in colloquial speech also supports this hypothesis. Note that in cases like (7b) where a non-clitic subject pronoun is used, the clitic cannot be omitted:

(7) a. Lui il mange tout
       'He, he eats everything'
    b. * Lui mange tout
    c. Pierre il mange tout
       'Pierre, he eats everything'

For reasons of space, this problem will not be discussed in any detail. It is enough to notice that the clitic pronoun in subject position cannot simply be treated as a variant of the usual subject NP. Rather, it is possible to argue that it is part of the subject–verb agreement system in French. Syntactically, it can be regarded as a constituent of INFL or of V'; a slightly more radical version of this hypothesis would claim that it functions as a prefix of the verb.

Monolingual German children's acquisition of verb inflection has been studied recently by Clahsen (1986); in addition, results from a few other studies are summarized by Mills (1985). They all seem to agree that -ø, -(e)n, and -t are the first suffixes used. Leaving aside phonological variants (e.g. -ø replacing -e, -e replacing -en) and non-finite forms (infinitives and past participles), -t is clearly the first form which may be interpreted as a suffix of a finite verb. In a second step, most or all other forms come into play within a relatively brief period of time. There is some disagreement as to whether the early uses of -t can be regarded as syntactic markings of agreement. Clahsen (1986: 95ff.), for example, argues that they encode a semantic function, namely non-transitivity. Although I do not find this suggestion very plausible, I will not pursue the problem any further for the time being (see Meisel, 1990). What matters for the present discussion is that all authors apparently agree that subject–verb agreement as a syntactic phenomenon emerges quite early (probably no later than at stages III–IV, as defined by Brown). And this development parallels another one, namely the acquisition of finite verb placement in second position. Mills (1985) as well as Clahsen (1986: 91) suggest that these two phenomena are logically connected. This is in accordance with the claims made by Bates (1976), alluded to above.

As for monolingual acquisition of French, we actually know very little about the phenomena discussed in this section of the chapter (see Clark, 1985). It has been mentioned above that the crucial issue here concerns clitic pronouns in "subject" position. A short glance at the relevant literature indicates that subject pronouns appear quite early in the speech of French children, approximately at age 2;0. *Il* is usually the first pronoun attested, but the others follow within a brief time span of a few months. Apart from the fact that plural forms emerge later than the singular forms, a clear developmental pattern apparently does not exist. To my knowledge, the use of these forms in French child language has never been studied in connection with the problem of subject–verb agreement. In fact, even the general question of when and how syntactic functions such as "subject" are acquired by French-speaking children is still wide open.

Analyzing the speech of the bilingual children reveals that they acquire *each* of the two languages very much like monolingual children. In German, they begin using verbs at age 1;9 (C) and 2;6 (P), respectively. The first forms which are modeled on adult finite verb inflection appear at age 1;11 (C) and at 2;7 (P). Most of these emerge within a relatively short period of time, as is evidenced by Table 13.2 (for more details, see Meisel, 1990).

It is easy to see that for each child there are two phases during which most of the suffixes are acquired. The late appearance of some forms of *sein* "to be" is not pertinent to the present discussion. And the fact that C begins to use the *-e* suffix only after everything else has been acquired, can probably be accounted for by means of phonological arguments. This form competes with the colloquially pre-ferred zero marking; it is in fact not used frequently. On the other hand, P occasionally overgeneralizes the *-e* suffix to modals.

This brings us to the crucial point of this discussion: apart from overgeneral-izations in P's speech such as *man kanne* "one can," both children make almost *no errors* in person marking on verbs. There are a few errors in number marking, where singular is used instead of plural (3 in C's speech and 2 in P's), but this happens fairly late, for C at 2;8 and for P at 3;10–3;11. Indeed, I find only three errors where P uses an inappropriate form to encode person, but this, too, happens long after verb inflection has already been firmly established in the child's grammatical competence, at 3;5 and at 3;11:

(8) a. nein du nimmt nicht
         'no you take – 3rd sg. – not'
     b. der hab aufgegessen
         'this one have – 1st sg. – eaten all up'
     c. der hab ja gesagt
         'this one have – 1st sg. – said yes'

Table 13.2   Order of acquisition of German verb forms

C 1;11–2;1		P 2;6–2;9	
is	3rd sg. "to be"	*is*	3rd sg. "to be"
-*t*	3rd sg.	-*t*	3rd sg.
C 2;4–2;6		**P 2;9–2;11**	
ø	1st sg.	-*e*	1st sg.
ø	3rd sg. (modals)	*ø*	1st sg.
-*st*	2nd sg.	*ø*	3rd sg. (modals)
-*en*	3rd pl.	-*st*	2nd sg.
sind	3rd pl. "to be"	-*en*	3rd pl.
C 2;8–2;10		**P 3;3–3;11**	
-*en*	1st pl.	-*en*	1st pl.
bin	1st sg. "to be"	*bin*	1st sg. "to be"
sind	1st pl. "to be"	*sind*	1st pl.
		sind	3rd pl. "to be"
-*e*	1st sg.		

It seems to be safe to assume that these examples may be interpreted as performance errors. At any rate, there can be no doubt that verb inflection is acquired early, within a brief time span, and virtually without errors. As with monolingual children, -*t* is the first marking to appear, together with the colloquial *is*, replacing the standard variant *ist*. Note, however, that P acquires 3rd sg. -*t* and 1st sg. -*e* almost simultaneously. The former is attested only once at age 2;7 and then again at 2;9; from then on, it is used productively. As a conclusion, I would like to suggest that inflectional markings for finite verbs develop at about age 1;11 (C) and 2;9 (P), respectively. This corresponds to an MLU value of approximately 2.0, thus to stage II, as defined by Brown. It remains to be seen whether these forms do in fact serve a *syntactic* function at this point, i.e. whether they are used to encode subject–verb agreement.

It is important to realize that the same children have been found to use the first *grammatical* tense markings at exactly the same point of development (see Meisel, 1985). Also, we have seen above that language-specific word order patterns – and particularly verb-second placement in German – begin to appear during this phase.

Concerning verb inflection in French, as mentioned before, one has to rely on rather scanty evidence. By examining the contrast between finite and non-finite forms, and by evaluating the amount of variability in form across the whole range of verbs used by one child at a given time, we do, nevertheless, have two criteria which enable us to decide whether and when the children are using a form class *verb*.

Candidates for this syntactic label appear much earlier in French than in German. The first examples are attested at about age 1;3–1;4. But these are probably the result of rote learning; they never vary in form and they all belong to a small set of items reflecting certain routine patterns in adult–child interaction, e.g. *tiens, donne, attends* "hold/take," "give," "wait." The first type which appears in different forms is documented for C at age 1;10. Using the two criteria just mentioned (finite *versus* non-finite contrast; variability in form), leads us to the conclusion that C is in fact using the syntactic category of verbs and verb inflection no later than at age 2;0. At this point, some twenty different verbs are used, and they are marked for *present tense, past participle, imperative,* and *infinitive.* Applying the same criteria in the analysis of P's speech, shows that he uses verbs and verb inflection at about age 2;9. In other words, this syntactic category develops during the same period of time, in French as well as in German.

It should not be overlooked, however, that we used defining criteria for what might be syntactic entities, which makes it impossible *per definitionem* to find evidence for *syntactic* operations before a child reaches stage II (MLU 1.75–2.25). It remains to be seen whether a less restrictive definition would not allow us to identify instances of grammatical categories and processes much earlier than has been possible here. For the time being, we will assume that both children have access to the syntactic mode of processing no later than at stage II.

At this point, it is necessary to look at the emergence of subjects and to examine the question whether early verb morphology is indeed used to encode agreement with the subject. I will be very brief here, referring again to Meisel (1990) for a more detailed discussion. The following remarks apply to multi-word utterances; infinitives and imperatives will not be included in this discussion for the obvious reason that they do not require subject–verb agreement.

At about age 1;11 (C) and 2;8 (P), subjects are normally supplied by both children in contexts where the adult norm requires them in German. C omits them only occasionally. These instances can be interpreted as elliptic utterances, most of which are perfectly normal in adult casual speech, e.g. *geht nicht* "doesn't work." Most of these omissions occur with the verbs *is/ist* "is" and *will* "want." P omits subjects more frequently, but he tends to leave out other obligatory elements as well. I would like to suggest that once an element is used productively, such omissions should be interpreted as resulting from a performance strategy. This claim is supported by the fact that, as in C's omissions, this is restricted to a small set of verbs: *ist, gehen,* and *will.* In fact, all but one of the omissions in P's speech at age 2;10 occur with *geht kaputt* "goes broken = is breaking" (see Figure 13.4). Similarly, all but one of the missing subjects at 3;5 (P) occur with the construction *will* + verb. In other words, omissions are highly predictable and

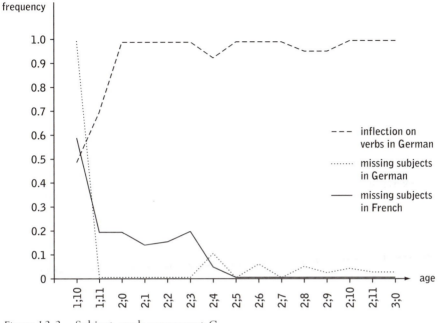

frequency

1.0

0.9

0.8

0.7

0.6

0.5

0.4

0.3

0.2

0.1

0

age

1;10 1;11 2;0 2;1 2;2 2;3 2;4 2;5 2;6 2;7 2;8 2;9 2;10 2;11 3;0

- - - inflection on
      verbs in German

.... missing subjects
         in German

——— missing subjects
       in French

Figure 13.3   Subject–verb agreement C

usually happen in very specific contexts. In conclusion, subjects are used productively in German by C and P from age 1;11 and 2;8 respectively. It should be noted that up to age 2;9 (C) and 3;3 (P), these are almost exclusively pronominal subjects.

Analyzing the use of subjects in French leads to very similar conclusions. The subject position is frequently not filled until age 1;10 (C) and 2;9 (P). Missing subjects after this point of development can be interpreted as in the German data, i.e. as resulting from performance strategies. And again, this only happens in connection with a small set of verbs, i.e. almost exclusively with *veux/veut* "will/wants." The observed preference for pronominal subjects is even more marked in French than in German. The children either use only a clitic pronoun in subject position, or they dislocate the subject (preferably to the left) and leave a clitic copy in subject position. Non-pronominal subjects in a position adjacent to the verb *never* occur in C's speech and only very rarely in P's. Note that this reflects to a large degree the use of such constructions in colloquial adult French. But this observation, too, indicates that the children adhere to the respective target systems. This again leads to a differentiation between the two languages.

Some of the most crucial facts discussed above are shown in Figures 13.3 and 13.4. They indicate that verb inflection in German develops very rapidly. Once it is attested, it is almost without exception used in all contexts where it is required

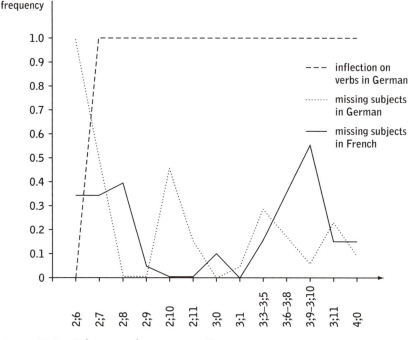

Figure 13.4   Subject–verb agreement P

in the adult language. At the same time, the frequency of omitted subjects drops in both languages – except for some instances in P's speech which have been explained above as a phenomenon peculiar to his language use. Most importantly, the two figures show quite clearly that constructions where the subject position is not filled, fade out as inflected verbs come in. If one bears in mind that markings for the grammatical person on the verb always agree correctly with the subject, these facts represent strong evidence in favor of the claim that the children's use of language can be described adequately as being organized according to *syntactic* categories and processes. The function of early verb inflection is thus to encode subject–verb agreement. The correct use of these devices in each of the bilingual's two languages implies that they are differentiated from early on.

Conclusions

In the introduction to this chapter, the question was raised whether it might be possible, in principle, that an individual exposed to two languages from early on should be capable of separating the two grammatical systems without going through a phase of temporary confusion. I believe that our findings lend strong support to the claim that this is indeed possible. The evidence provided here is of the sort required above. In addition, a strong effort has been made to back up the further claim that early differences in the use of the two languages may correctly be qualified as *syntactic* in nature, as discussed above. In fact, I want to suggest that grammatical processing is possible much earlier than is usually assumed on the basis of analyses of monolingual child language. I would guess that this might be explained by the fact that the task of acquiring two grammatical systems simultaneously will be easier if the child focuses his attention on problems of form, rather than relying on semantic–pragmatic strategies alone. This, however, is rather speculative for the time being. At any rate, I believe I have shown that bilingual children consistently use different word order in both languages no later than with the appearance of two – or more – word utterances. At about the same time, they begin to mark for case (see Meisel, 1986) and they also start using verb inflection to encode grammatical person, number, and tense (see Meisel, 1985). In doing so, they use what may reasonably be labeled syntactic subjects, and whenever a subject is supplied, the verb agrees with it in person and usually also in number.

Before concluding, I would like to add a terminological remark. In the introduction, I suggested that some of the contradictory claims concerning language "mixing" are due to the fact that "mixing" is not clearly distinguished from "code-switching." Rather superficial definitions, as suggested by Redlinger and Park (1980), cannot but result in a terminologically motivated confusion. In fact, the few researchers who do distinguish the two phenomena and who then explicitly ask which of the two occurs in specific contexts, seem to agree that in most cases even lexical "mixing" has to be interpreted as code-switching which frequently helps to improve communication (for example, Oksaar, 1971; 1978; Saunders, 1982).

As I have used the two terms, *mixing* was defined as the fusion of two grammatical systems, i.e. a possible characteristic of a bilingual's *grammatical competence. Code-switching*, on the other hand, was defined as a specific skill in the bilingual's *pragmatic competence*. These two definitions, however, do not cover a third phenomenon which should be distinguished from the two others.[7] Namely, the child may well use two different grammatical systems, as evidenced by distinct word order patterns, etc., and yet may still choose the "wrong" language occasionally. (Which language is the "right" or wrong one is usually determined by the same sociolinguistic factors as in code-switching, e.g. interlocutor, topic, etc.) This may correspond to an error in what Grosjean (1982: 127) calls "language choice", or it may be a case of "code-mixing" (Grosjean, 1982: 204), i.e. the child switches "to express a word or an expression that is not immediately accessible in the other language" (Grosjean, 1982: 206). In any case, it is a phenomenon which would have to be explained by the bilingual's *pragmatic competence*. From this it follows that language differentiation is a necessary but not a sufficient prerequisite for successful code-switching. Even though two grammatical systems have been internalized, the child might still violate the rules which govern choice or switching, e.g. in the case of the children discussed here, speaking German to the French-speaking mother. If we want to call *this* "mixing," we should find a different term to refer to the phenomenon treated in this chapter, i.e. the alleged inability to separate two grammatical systems. I would suggest calling this *fusion* (of grammatical systems).

Terminological quarrels are certainly boring. And I will not necessarily insist on the terminology proposed above. But I would urge keeping the three phenomena apart, whatever labels one may finally use to refer to them. If, however, one adopts these terms, the results of this chapter can be phrased in the following way: bilinguals are capable of differentiating grammatical systems; fusion is not necessarily a characteristic of bilingual language development, but mixing may occur until code-switching is firmly established as a strategy of bilingual pragmatic competence.

Notes

1   This summary draws on the studies which are also included in the overviews given by Taeschner (1983) and McLaughlin (1984). A number of other studies have been included in this survey, for example: Fantini, 1982; Hoffmann, 1985; Kadar-Hoffmann, 1983; Kielhöfer and Jonekeit, 1983; Porsché, 1983; Pupier *et al.*, 1982.

2   In fact, one finds a second but contradictory statement on this issue; see Volterra and Taeschner (1978: 320): "It is at the end of this stage [stage II], that bilingual children amaze observers because of their extraordinary skill in passing from one language to another during the same verbal interaction" – followed by an example to illustrate this point, taken from Lisa, age 3;3!

3   In fact, "mixing," as used by Redlinger and Park (1980), is a rather ill-defined term. The vast majority of the "mixes" are "single lexical substitutions" (pp. 345ff.). It is quite unlikely that these may adequately be treated as syntactic phenomena. I would suspect that most instances of "mixing" in their data could easily be explained as lexical transfer from the dominant language, probably even as code-switching (compare "code-mixing," as defined by Grosjean, 1982: 204). Redlinger and Park (1980: 342) themselves observe that at least in some cases, the children were consciously aware of the fact that they were switching.

4   I find it somewhat strange to argue (see Volterra and Taeschner, 1978: 324) that the child uses a common syntax for adjective constructions, based on the observation that during this phase (i.e. up to age 2;9) one does not find a single example of this construction in Italian; and the German examples stick perfectly to the target norm.

5   Traute Taeschner (personal communication) confirmed, in fact, that this is the intended interpretation. I should also point out that she apparently does not defend the single-system hypothesis any more. It is only lexical development which is described in Taeschner (1983) in the same fashion as in Volterra and Taeschner (1978). As for morphology and syntax, Taeschner (1983) also mentions three

stages, but those are not defined in terms of one single grammatical system. Rather, she suggests that, by and large, development is very similar in bilingual and in monolingual children. (See chapters 3 and 4, and Table 7.1 in chapter 7 of Taeschner, 1983.) She concludes that the simultaneous acquisition of two languages is "the formation of two linguistic systems under conditions of complex interaction which are both based or depend upon the same process of cognitive, linguistic, social, and emotional maturation" (Taeschner, 1983: 113). Nevertheless, I find her statements to this effect somewhat confusing. To mention one example, in section 4.13 (Taeschner, 1983: 166f.) she claims that the child "believes that both languages have the same rules." And "During the second period, the child very gradually realizes that the rules involved in linguistic processing must be separated." It would have been helpful if she had stated explicitly which claims contained in the Volterra and Taeschner (1978) model have now been abandoned. Unfortunately, this previous model is not discussed in any detail.

6   This study forms part of a research project which was started in 1980 as an enterprise of the research group DUFDE (Deutsch und Französisch – Doppelter Erstspracherwerb). During the period when this chapter was written, the researchers in this team were Swantje Klinge, Teresa Parodi, and Suzanne Schlyter. Students collaborating as research assistants were Marianne Dieck, Pascale Guénard, Martina Jürgens, Caroline Koehn, Marie-France Lavielle, Natascha Müller, and Anke Sigerist. Elvira Behrend was kind enough to lend me her intuitions as a native speaker. I want to thank all of them for their most valuable help. Furthermore, I want to thank those friends and colleagues who commented on an earlier version of this chapter, Harald Clahsen, Kathleen Connors, Charlotte Hoffmann, Annick de Houwer, Kenneth Hyltenstam, and Loraine Obler. I also acknowledge gratefully that the Deutsche Forschungsgemeinschaft has given a research grant (1986–88) to the author of this study to support this research project.

7   This was pointed out to me by Suzanne Schlyter. I want to thank her for her persistence and her patience, for it took me quite a while, I must confess, to accept this.

Source: Meisel, J.M. (1989) Early differentiation of languages in bilingual children. In K. Hyltenstam and L. Obler (eds) *Bilingualism across the Lifespan*. Cambridge: Cambridge University Press, pp. 13–40, by permission of Cambridge University Press.

Notes for students and instructors

Study questions

1   What are the main developmental stages in a bilingual child's language acquisition?
2   What factors can cause a child to mix two languages in an utterance? Why is code-mixing *not* good evidence for the 'one system hypothesis'?

Study activity

Observe a bilingual child in different situations (e.g. at home with parents, with siblings, outside home with other children, and with other adults). Pay special attention to his or her language choice with different people. Note down the occasions when the child makes a 'wrong' choice, i.e. using Language A when the addressee only understands or prefers Language B. Is there any particular reason for the 'wrong' choice (e.g. accidental, deliberate)? Does the child realise he or she has made a 'wrong' choice? What does the child do when he or she realises he/she has made a 'wrong' choice?

If time permits, design a case study of a bilingual child under the age of three. Either ask the parents to keep a weekly record of:

1   their own language choice to the child; and
2   the child's speech over an extended period of time (no less than six months);

Or tape-record the child's speech at weekly intervals. (If the keeping of a weekly record is not realistic, negotiate with the family to see how often they can keep such a record.) Analyse the speech data of the child, paying particular attention to any sign of under-differentiation (i.e. when two features in Language A for which counterparts are not distinguished in Language B are confused) and over-differentiation (i.e. the imposition of distinctions from Language A on the system of Language B in which they are not required) of his or her two languages. To what extent can the child's mixing of two languages be attributed to the language mixing in the parents' speech?

Further reading

A good general introduction to childhood bilingualism is Chapter 5 of S. Romaine, 1995, *Bilingualism*, 2nd edn, Blackwell. A comprehensive review of the field of bilingual language acquisition can be found in A. De Houwer, 1995, Bilingual language acquisition, in P. Fletcher and B. MacWhinney (eds), *The Handbook of Child Language*, Blackwell, pp. 219–50.

An early classic is W. Leopold, 1939–49, *Speech Development of a Bilingual Child: A linguist's record*, 4 volumes, Northwestern University Press.

Recent studies that specifically address the issue of language differentiation in bilingual children include: F. Genesee, E. Nicoladis and J. Paradis, 1995, Language differentiation in early bilingual development, *Journal of Child Language* 22: 611–31; R. Koppe, 1996, Language differentiation in bilingual children, *Linguistics* 34: 927–54; M. Deuchar and S. Quay, 1998, One vs. two systems in early bilingual syntax: two versions of the question, *Bilingualism: Language and Cognition* 1: 231–43.

Book-length studies of language acquisition of bilingual children include: J.M. Meisel (ed.), 1990, *Two First Languages: Early grammatical development in bilingual children*, Foris; A. De Houwer, 1990, *The Acquisition of Two Languages from Birth: A case study*, Cambridge University Press; S. Dopke, *One Parent One Language: An interactional approach*, John Benjamins; J.M. Meisel (ed.), 1994, *Bilingual First Language Acquisition: French and German grammatical development*, John Benjamins; G. Extra and L. Verhoeven (eds), 1994, *The Cross-Linguistic Studies of Bilingual Development*, North-Holland; J. Lyon, 1996, *Becoming Bilingual: Language acquisition in a bilingual community*, Multilingual Matters; E. Lanza, 1997, *Language Mixing in Infant Bilingualism: A sociolinguistic perspective*, Oxford University Press; M. Deuchar and S. Quay, 2000, *Bilingual Acquisition: Theoretical implications of a case study*, Oxford University Press.

A state-of-the-art collection of studies on the language acquisition of bilingual children is given in A. De Houwer, 1998 (ed.), *Bilingual Acquisition*, Kingston Press, as a special issue of *International Journal of Bilingualism*, 2(3).

Psycholinguistic dimensions of bilingualism

Introduction to Part Three

LI WEI

Part Three of the Reader focuses on the psycholinguistic aspects of bilingualism. It consists of two sections: The bilingual brain and Bilingual speech processing.

The bilingual brain

One of the most controversial and most discussed issues in the psycholinguistic studies of bilingualism has been the notion that the languages of bilingual speakers are less asymmetrically represented in the cerebral hemispheres than the language of unilingual speakers. The first two papers in this part address this issue.

In Chapter 14 Loraine K. Obler, Robert J. Zatorre, Linda Galloway and Jyotsna Vaid review the literature on lateralisation for language in bilinguals, which seems to suggest conflicting positions. One is that left hemispheric dominance, which is clearly evident in most monolinguals, applies to bilinguals too. A second proposes weaker left lateralisation for language in bilinguals, while a third maintains that there is differential lateralisation for the two languages. Obler *et al.* discuss a broad range of methodological parameters which need to be considered in carrying out, analysing and interpreting studies of language lateralisation in bilinguals. These include issues of subject selection, language and stimulus selection, testing procedure, data analysis and theoretical questions around interpreting dichotic and tachistoscopic measures of lateralisation.

While Obler *et al.* plead for caution in research design and conclusion, Michel Paradis (Chapter 15) calls for a complete stop to what he regards as a fruitless pursuit. In his article, Paradis critically reviews previous studies on language lateralisation in bilinguals and points out the many methodological flaws. He urges researchers to 'move on to something more productive'. However, evidence seems to suggest that inappropriately designed experiments and implausible interpretations have continued to appear, and as Paradis has already warned in his article, recommendations have continued to be made for applications of the alleged findings of increased participation of the right hemisphere to foreign language teaching, the treatment of mental illness, or the rehabilitation of bilingual aphasia.

Bilingual speech processing

An area of psycholinguistic research on bilingualism which has, indeed, been highly productive is bilingual speech production and perception. The first two articles in the second section of this part of the Reader, by David W. Green (Chapter 16) and Kees de Bot (Chapter 17), present two theoretical models of bilingual speech production. Green examines the way in which bilinguals control the use of their two languages. In view of the fact that bilingual speakers can choose which language they want to use in a given context, he suggests that the bilinguals' languages are organised in separate sub-systems which can be activated to different extents. He argues that a bilingual speaker who wishes to speak a particular language must ensure that activation exceeds that of competing languages. Green pays much attention to the resources that are needed to regulate, or control, the activation levels. The theoretical framework proposed by Green is meant to account for the performance of normal as well as brain-damaged bilinguals.

The model presented in de Bot's article is based on Levelt's (1989) 'Speaking' model, in which a number of information-processing components, or levels, are postulated. Because Levelt's model has a firm empirical basis, de Bot's adaptation made very few changes to the original. It is concluded that the first component, the conceptualiser, is partly language-specific and partly language-independent. Further it is hypothesised that there are different formulators for each language, while there is one lexicon where lexical elements from different languages are stored together. The output of the formulators is sent to the articulator which makes use of a large set of non-language specific speech motor plans. The adapted version of Levelt's model provides a good explanation of various aspects of bilingual speech production, especially with respect to code-switching and the storage and retrieval of lexical elements.

The third article in this section by François Grosjean (Chapter 18) is a state-of-the-art survey of the issues, findings and models in the study of bilingual speech processing. Grosjean focuses on the phenomenon that bilingual speakers can, and, indeed, often do, mix their two languages. He argues that the under-lying source of the amount of language mixing that a bilingual produces at a given time is the 'language mode' which the speaker is in: more mixing occurs when the speaker is in a bilingual mode than in a monolingual one. Grosjean agrees with other researchers in the field that the language system of the bilingual is organised into two subsets that can be activated and deactivated independently of one another, or activated simultaneously, each to a particular degree. In the bilingual mode, both of the bilingual speaker's two languages are activated, although one to a relatively higher level than the other, whereas in the monolingual mode, only one language is activated and the other is deactivated as best as possible. Grosjean substantiates his claims with empirical data from both production and perception studies and proposes an interactive-activation model of bilingual language processing.

The bilingual brain

Chapter 14

Cerebral lateralization in bilinguals: methodological issues

LORAINE K. OBLER, ROBERT J. ZATORRE, LINDA GALLOWAY AND JYOTSNA VAID

THE QUESTION OF INTEREST regarding cerebral lateralization for language in bilinguals is whether it differs from that in monolinguals. If lateralization is the same in both groups, one could expect it to be so for both languages of the bilinguals; if not, there are a number of theoretical possibilities; namely:

1   language is more left lateralized in the bilingual than in the monolingual
    (a)   for one language or
    (b)   for both; or
2   language is less left lateralized for the bilingual than for the monolinguals
    (a)   for one language or
    (b)   for both languages.

As with the studies of cerebral lateralization for language among children, elderly individuals, women, and musicians, conflicting findings have been reported around the issues of lateralization for language(s) in bilinguals. While lateralization data from bilinguals have been construed to support most of the theoretical possibilities mentioned above, the crux of recent debate has been whether or not there is greater right-hemisphere participation in the processing of one or both languages in the bilingual than in the monolingual. In order to appropriately interpret apparently contradictory findings, it becomes necessary to discuss a number of variables of potential importance to studies of cerebral lateralization with bilinguals. These include methodological variables such as subject selection, language and stimulus selection, test procedures, and data analysis, as well as theoretical questions around interpreting dichotic and tachistoscopic measures of lateralization. Many of the issues which arise in the literature on bilinguals have not yet been resolved with respect to monolingual subjects. Hence in this chapter we have undertaken to document a broad range of parameters which must be considered in carrying out, analyzing, and interpreting studies of language lateralization in bilinguals, with the conviction that focus on bilinguals will shed light on issues pertinent to testing lateralization in other normal and exceptional populations.

Subject selection

Handedness

It has repeatedly been observed that the "standard" pattern of left-hemisphere (LH) superiority for verbal, and right-hemisphere (RH) superiority for visuospatial processing more strongly characterizes right- than left-handed individuals, and, in particular, right-handed individuals with no family history of left-handedness (Andrews, 1977). Whether the factor of handedness has a similar effect in monolinguals and bilinguals, or whether it interacts with parameters of bilingualism to exert a different effect is a question of theoretical interest.

Unfortunately, evidence bearing on this issue is minimal, insofar as all but two of the experimental studies in the bilingual laterality literature considered only right-handed individuals. (It is doubtful, however, whether any of the early studies employing right-handers screened familial sinistrality.) Moreover, two methodologically similar studies in which the factor of handedness was specifically examined differed in their results with respect to handedness. In a tachistoscopic task, Gaziel *et al.* (1978) found no significant differences in the performance of right- and left-handed Hebrew–English bilinguals on either of their languages. Orbach (1967), however, obtained group differences related to handedness and interacting with language; his 21 strongly left-handed subjects (native speakers of Hebrew who were proficient in English) showed a significant right-visual-field effect (RVFE) for English stimuli, and a nonsignificant left-visual-field effect (LVFE) in Hebrew. By contrast, his 25 right-handers with the same language history showed significant RVFEs in both languages, greater for English than for Hebrew.

Gender

Evidence has accumulated in the literature on monolinguals suggesting that the standard pattern of cerebral lateralization is more characteristic of males than females (Waber, 1977; McGlone, 1978). Although similar evidence has been obtained in the bilingual literature as well (Gordon, 1980; Vaid and Lambert, 1979), the potential contribution of the factor of gender differences in lateralization has generally been ignored. A majority of the bilingual literality studies do not report whether or not significant gender differences were present. Indeed, a third of all the studies do not even report the gender composition of their subject samples. Of those studies in which gender composition was reported, less than one-third employed an equal number of males and females; where the gender ratio was unequal, it was in the direction of more females than males in three-quarters of the studies. In view of this bias in the literature, it is possible that at least some of the claims of differential lateralization made in the bilingual literature (e.g. Obler *et al.*, 1975) may be attributable to gender differences rather than, or in addition to, effects associated with bilingualism per se.

Age at the time of testing

Since it remains unresolved whether there is a developmental course toward left lateralization in childhood or in aging (Clark and Knowles, 1973; Borod and Goodglass, 1979; Johnson *et al.*, 1979), it would be premature to conclude that a finding which holds true for one group of bilinguals will necessarily hold true for bilinguals of different ages (but see Piazza and Zatorre, 1981).

Level of second-language proficiency

A great number of studies in the bilingual laterality literature have not specified the criteria, if any, used to screen individuals for proficiency in their two languages. In the earliest study, native English speakers were selected as subjects on the basis that "they had some knowledge of Yiddish" (Mishkin and Forgays, 1952). Recent studies have not necessarily used more objective criteria for subject selection. As a result, subjects within and across studies may have varied considerably in their levels of second-language proficiency.

Proficiency has itself become the focus of several recent investigations which have centered around the "stage hypothesis" first suggested by Obler *et al.* (1975) and then amended by Krashen and Galloway (1978; Galloway and Krashen, 1980). The hypothesis maintains that bilinguals will initially rely to a greater extent on the RH but will, with increasing second-language proficiency, engage the LH in second as in first-language processing. This hypothesis is consistent with demonstrated RH linguistic capabilities (Galloway, 1980; Galloway and Krashen, 1980) and compatible with general processing strategies of the RH (Vaid and Genesee, 1980).

A direct test of the stage hypothesis of Albert and Obler (1978) would require comparing the neuropsychological performance of second-language learners of varying ages and at different stages in their acquisition of the second language with that of monolingual and balanced bilingual controls. Such a test has yet to be undertaken. However, studies that have employed a cross-sectional paradigm to examine the question of right-hemispheric involvement in the initial stages of second-language acquisition lend some support to the stage hypothesis (Silverberg *et al.*, 1979; Schneiderman and Wesche, 1980; Hardyck, 1980). The findings of several other studies are inconsistent with the predictions of the hypothesis as stated, finding no differences between early and late learners (Galloway, 1980; 1980b; Gordon, 1980; for a review, see Vaid and Genesee, 1980).

Krashen and Galloway (1978; Galloway and Krashen, 1980) have proposed a modified version of the stage hypothesis whereby the second language, L_2, would be less lateralized than the first language, L_1, only among adults acquiring the second language in a naturalistic setting without any formal language instruction. Their test of this, however (Galloway, 1980; Galloway and Scarcella, 1982), did not yield evidence in support of this modification.

Age of L_2 acquisition

A number of studies employing proficient and nonproficient bilinguals have tended to confound the variable of proficiency with that of age of second-language acquisition (Obler *et al.* 1975; Albert and Obler, 1978). Whereas proficient bilinguals in these studies had typically acquired both languages during infancy, nonproficient bilinguals had begun second language acquisition during adolescence and/or in adulthood. However, as recent studies of proficient early and late bilinguals have demonstrated, age of onset of bilingualism may also be a factor responsible for differential hemispheric processing of language. Early bilinguals showed faster averaged evoked responses (AERs) in the left hemisphere on a language recognition task, whereas late bilinguals (who had acquired their second language in adolescence) evinced faster AERs in the right hemisphere for both languages (Genesee *et al.*, 1978). This finding has subsequently been replicated in an evoked-responses study of late Polish–Russian bilinguals (Kotik, personal communication). A similar early–late group difference was obtained from a monaural Stroop study of French and English balanced bilinguals (Vaid and Lambert, 1979). The Sussman *et al.* (1982) study of interference in tapping rate by concurrent speech production in fluent bilinguals likewise showed a strong tendency for more left-hemisphere dominance in subjects who were bilingual from birth, and more right-hemisphere language processing in subjects who learned their second language later. How the purported effects of second language proficiency (as discussed in the previous section) interact with the factor of age of onset of bilingualism is, as yet, unclear.

Manner of L_2 acquisition

The putative differential laterality of bilinguals would imply that lateralization for language is not entirely determined at birth. If we assume language experience may influence laterality, we must then ask:

1   Whether a second language is learned formally or acquired naturalistically.
2   The extent to which individual differences in learning style may interact with lateralization.
3   If a second language is learned in a classroom, what instructional method is used predominantly, e.g. one emphasizing the visual modality (reading) vs. one exclusively relying on the auditory modality.

With regard to the issues of formality and individual learning style, some researchers hypothesize that individuals with more "analytic" cognitive styles would presumably show a greater left lateralization, perhaps reflecting their use of a conscious monitor in second-language processing, as compared to children, who acquire the second language informally (Krashen and Galloway, 1978). One might imagine, likewise, that formal teaching could speak to more analytically inclined students, while informal acquisition would succeed with those less analytically inclined. Two studies with L_2 learners (Krashen *et al.*, 1974; Hartnett, 1975) reported that direction of conjugate lateral eye movements correlated with success in a particular method of instruction in the second language; specifically, individuals who tended to look more consistently toward the right (taken to indicate more left-hemisphere involvement, Kinsbourne, 1972 vs. Gardner and Branski, 1976) also tended to adopt a deductive, "analytic" approach to L_2 learning.

With respect to the method of L_2 instruction, it has been suggested that reading and writing may contribute to increased left-hemisphere control of language (cf. Wechsler, 1976; 1977). In the case of bilinguals who learned one of their languages via the written mode, as did Kotik's (1975) subjects, one would, accordingly, expect greater left lateralization of that language as compared to the language acquired and used auditorily.

Environment of L_2 learning

One must consider whether the learner is in a second-language environment, where the target L_2 is also the predominant language used in the L_2 performer's surroundings (e.g., an Icelandic student in the U.S.), or in a foreign language environment where the target L_2 is not the predominant language around the L_2 performer (e.g., an American studying Yoruba at a U.S. university). Suggestions are found in several studies of a lower overall language laterality in relatively advanced L_2 performers in a second-language environment (Galloway, 1977; 1980a). For example, Gordon's dichotic listening study (1980) found that Americans who learned Hebrew after puberty in Israel showed a trend toward a lower laterality in both Hebrew and English. In contrast, a comparable group of native Hebrew speakers, who had studied English after puberty as a foreign language in Israel, did not evidence lower overall language laterality. However, native Hebrew speakers who had spent many years abroad in English-speaking countries and/or were currently using English extensively (e.g., communicating with a spouse at home) also showed lower laterality scores in both languages.

Language stimuli

Familiar methodological issues arise in selecting word stimuli for laterality studies in monolinguals; the stimuli must be adequately screened in terms of word length, frequency, grammatical class, abstractness, imageability, and phonetic composition. In the case of studies of bilingual laterality, difficulties may arise in preparing comparable sets of stimuli from structurally different languages, especially regarding such dimensions as word length or phonetic composition. To the extent that the stimulus sets are not comparable, differences in lateralization patterns across languages may simply reflect such stimulus differences. Moreover, as language pairs will differ with respect to their genetic relatedness (e.g., Spanish and French are more related than are Spanish and Turkish), it is unrealistic to assume that any particular pairing of two languages is representative of all bilingual combinations. Similarly, orthographic differences between languages (e.g., type and/or direction of script) may contribute to the overall pattern of lateralization observed (Albert and Obler 1978; Vaid, 1981a). It has also been proposed that certain languages reflect more appositional (or "gestalt"), as compared to propositional (or analytic) cultural, modes of thinking (Rogers *et al.*, 1977; Scott *et al.*, 1979) which, in turn, may be reflected in differential hemispheric processing in bilingual speakers of these languages.

Testing procedures

Technical issues

Certain technical issues must be considered since, if stimuli or procedures differed for the two language conditions, artifactual response asymmetries or lack of dominance might result. Eye fixation must of course be controlled in tachistoscopic testing. If the decision is made to require report of a central digit, the "overlearned" status of L_1 numbers even in highly fluent bilinguals must be evaluated. Stimulus duration and displacement of stimuli from center must be equal, as must size of stimulus, tasks which are complicated if two very different orthographies are being studied. Orientation of display may interact with the direction of reading in a given language on tachistoscopic tasks (Bryden, 1970). In the bilingual laterality literature, only Gaziel *et al.* (1978) have contrasted vertical and horizontal displays. With their balanced Hebrew–English bilinguals, they found no visual effect for either language with vertical presentation, and a trend toward RVFE for each language with horizontal presentation.

In dichotic listening, temporal alignment of stimuli is crucial, as it happens that when one word in a dichotic pair precedes another by an interval as short as 20 msec, an accuracy advantage accrues to the delayed stimulus (Berlin *et al.*, 1973). This lag effect could well cancel or interact with the ear advantage of interest, thus making results very difficult to interpret. Of course, when one stimulus tends to predominate in a dichotic pair for any of several reasons (e.g., clarity of one stimulus over another, amplitude, degree of fusion, dichotic masking, etc.; see Repp, 1977), this effect will also interact with any ear advantage that may be present, underscoring the importance of having each dichotic pair appear in both channel-ear assignments. When word length differs between two languages, a dichotic test pitting one language against the other would thus be impossible.

Task differences

Level of processing

Task differences enter not only into comparisons between studies, but also within a single study if, for example, the fact that one language is less well known may mean it is being processed differently (Hardyck, 1980; Schneiderman and Wesche, 1980). As to differences among studies, one must ask what levels of processing are accessed by a task. For example, word recognition, word identification, or language recognition (e.g, reporting whether the stimuli were French or English words) may differ with respect to the type of processing they demand (see Vaid, 1981).

Perception vs. production

Most studies in the laterality literature have presented stimuli to subjects and asked for recognition, recall, etc. These studies are measuring predominantly perceptual capabilities. Productive abilities are also important, however, and tasks can be designed to measure them. This issue may be particularly important in comparing experimental results to clinical results. For example, studies of polyglot aphasia (Albert and Obler, 1978; Galloway, 1980) have suggested some laterality differences between bilinguals and monolinguals. However, the aphasia reports focus on production much more than perception. Therefore, caution must be exercised in comparing experimental results with clinical studies. The only lateralization study to date in the bilingual literature using a production paradigm is that of Sussman *et al.* (1982), who measured finger tapping rates with concurrent verbalization. It is unclear at this point whether their finding of greater right-hemisphere participation in language of bilinguals is due to the use of production in their experiment or to some other variable. Again, an experiment separately testing perceptual and productive tasks would be very helpful in disentangling these variables.

Language set

If two languages are mixed during presentation, subjects with greater proficiency in one language may process all stimuli as if they were in that language. Thus one would not want to claim there was no differential lateralization between the two languages merely because in the testing situation stimuli were not being treated as belonging to two different languages.

Memory constraints

If recall is immediate, the subject may be reading out of a short-term sensory store with little phonetic or semantic processing, whereas with a few seconds' delay, short-term memory proper may come into play. A less than balanced bilingual subject may process the items in his/her two languages differently to the extent that they require different levels of effort in processing.

Dependent measure

Various studies have used different response measures, e.g., accuracy, reaction time, errors, and order of report by ear/visual field. Future studies should investigate more than one response measure in a given study of bilingual laterality, since response time and accuracy means, for example, may give conflicting pictures of performance. Moreover, responses should be analyzed both qualitatively and quantitatively, since the types of errors subjects make may reveal important information about the processing strategies they are employing.

Practice effect

Since left lateralization may increase over the course of a test (Samar, 1980), or with practice with stimuli (Bentin, n.d.), we must question whether studies showing *no* differences in lateralization between the two languages (e.g., Barton *et al.*, 1965) achieved this finding because of much prestudy familiarization with a limited number of stimuli. Note, however, that Schneiderman and Wesche (1980) found differential results despite a very limited stimulus corpus and considerable prestudy familiarization.

Monolingual controls

It should be pointed out that many of the problems described thus far might be greatly alleviated in a bilingual experiment by the appropriate use of monolingual controls. If an interesting effect is found among a bilingual group then the use of a monolingual control group would permit an experimenter to ensure that methodological problems were not confounding the results. Unfortunately, it is often difficult or impossible to obtain matched controls in this situation, since in predominantly bilingual societies, monolingualism may reflect learning disabilities or severe educational deprivation.

Analysis

Measurement and reliability

An issue which can only be touched on here is the use (or lack of use) of *a laterality index* as a measure of hemispheric specialization (Marshall *et al.*, 1975; Repp, 1977; Bryden, 1980), rather than some raw score or simple difference score. Such indices should indeed be used, as without them comparisons across groups (especially groups of bilinguals whose proficiency in their two languages may differ significantly) are questionable at best. A second analytical issue has to do with the *reliability* of dichotic and tachistoscopic tests. Low test–retest reliability may well introduce artifacts into comparisons across subject groups and across languages. The reliability of dichotic tests with monolinguals has been reported to be anywhere from .74 (Blumstein *et al.*, 1975) to .80 (Ryan and McNeill, 1974). To the extent that they may employ differing strategies, bilinguals may be less reliable than other groups if they are more proficient in one language than the other. Moreover, if reliability is low then it makes little sense to single out a few subjects from a group just because they may have an interesting laterality pattern in their two languages, as only the group effect can be considered stable (Hamers and Lambert, 1977). Repp (1977) points out that a remedy for low reliability is to increase the length of the test; however, then factors such as fatigue and over-familiarity with the stimulus set enter.

Continuous vs. discrete laterality effects

A further analytical issue involves the question of degree of laterality effects. If significant differences are found in degree (but not direction) of laterality between two groups or between languages, this does not guarantee that such differences reflect the underlying functional lateralization. Indeed, as Colbourn (1978) has pointed out, it is not necessarily valid to assume a one-to-one correspondence between the magnitude of an observed effect and the corresponding cerebral function it purports to measure. Colbourn believes it may be more prudent to consider the outcome of an experiment in terms of right, left or no difference rather than as a matter of degree. There are many reasons for differences to appear in estimates of a continuous variable, and these reasons (some of which are discussed elsewhere in this chapter) must be taken into account before the conclusion can be drawn that true differences in laterality exist.

Multiple independent significance tests

If a standard statistical test is significant at the $p = .05$ level, we may claim that such a result would be due to chance about one time in 20. The problem is that with more than a single comparison, multiple independent tests will yield true significance levels much less stringent than .05. For example, the probability that at least one comparison of two will be significant is .0975 if each is set to .05. An experiment with, say, six comparisons of interest will yield a true significance level of .26 if six independent tests are performed, each with the significance level set at .05. Therefore, if a significant result is found we can in no way conclude that such a result was not due to chance. Although this is an elementary problem, it appears repeatedly in the lateralization literature in bilinguals as well as monolinguals (Obler and Albert, 1978; Gordon, 1980). One solution to this problem is obvious and simple: either set the significance level for each test at a much more stringent level, or perform some test such as the analysis of variance which takes all factors into account. The analysis of variance has the added advantage that it allows tests of interaction effects, which may not be apparent with multiple independent tests. A second solution is to run independent replication studies of only those effects that are significant.

Interpretation of nonsignificant intrahemispheric differences results

In cases where no laterality difference is found, the lack of significant results would be important if it were substantiated, since it could indicate equal processing of language in both hemispheres. However, caution must be exercised in interpreting nonsignificant laterality results, for they can arise from any of the numerous technical and methodological issues noted above. Moreover, there are also several statistical reasons for nonsignificant results. Foremost among these are violations of the assumptions underlying parametric tests, viz., normality and homogeneity of variance. Violation of either of these assumptions would be likely to obscure a result and make tests invalid. (In such cases nonparametric techniques may be preferable as there is no dependence on normality or homogeneity of variance.) Other reasons for overall negative results could simply be high dispersion of scores and ceiling and floor effects. The former problem can often be tackled by judicious elimination of outlying scores; also, certain transformations (e.g., logarithms) often help to reduce excessive variability. Ceiling and floor effects can only be corrected by adjusting the difficulty of the task.

The "language-as-fixed-effect fallacy"

Results of an experiment using a set of stimuli chosen from a larger group of possible stimuli must be generalizable to that larger set and not just to the specific examples that were used in the experiment (Clark, 1973). The majority of studies in the field of laterality and bilingualism have not utilized appropriate statistics for this purpose, and therefore their results are not, strictly speaking, applicable to new sets of stimuli. Furthermore, by failing to consider the variance attributable to words, artifactual results can be obtained. Consider, for example, a typical tachistoscopic experiment in which bilingual subjects are given two tests, one in each of their languages, with the appropriate counterbalancing. The analysis of variance should have the following three factors: visual field (fixed, with two levels, right and left), language (fixed, if only the two languages are of interest, and two levels), and also the third factor which must be taken into account: words. Since different words are presented on each trial they too will be a source of variance Further, words must be considered a random factor because the particular words chosen for an experiment can only be a small subset of all the words in a language. (Note that this is independent of whether or not the words were chosen randomly.) Moreover, the words factor must be nested into the language factor because each language (necessarily) has a different set of words; therefore, there can be no interaction of words with language (i.e., the unique effect due to words cannot be separated from an effect due to language). The correct variance components due to each factor and the expected mean squares are given in Table 14.1 for the more general case of an experiment with p languages, q words, r visual fields, and n subjects, with words nested within language, and with words and subject being random factors.

If the words factor is ignored the F ratio for the visual field factor, would be:

$$F = \frac{MS_V}{MS_{V \times S}}$$

Note that this ratio would leave two sources of variance in the numerator: one attributable to visual field, and one to the interaction of words and visual fields. Thus, a significant F ratio might be obtained even though the variance due to the visual field factor may have been very small or zero. The appropriate F ratio can be constructed from several of the mean squares, but it must result in only one source of variance remaining in the numerator. This statistic is known as a quasi-F, and in this case it would be:

$$F'' = \frac{MS_V + MS_{W \times V \times S}}{MS_{W \times V} + MS_{V \times S}}$$

Table 14.1   Within-subject variance components for a tachistoscopic experiment using p languages, q words, r visual fields, and n subjects; words are nested within the language factor; both words and subjects are considered to be random factors

Factor	Expected mean squares
Language (L)	$\sigma_e^2 + rn\sigma_{W\times S}^2 + qrn\sigma_{L\times S}^2 + rsn\sigma_W^2 + qrsn\sigma_L^2$
Words within language (W)	$\sigma_e^2 + rn\sigma_{W\times S}^2 + rsn\sigma_W^2$
Visual field (V)	$\sigma_e^2 + n\sigma_{W\times V\times S}^2 + pqn\sigma_{V\times S}^2 + sn\sigma_{W\times V}^2 + pqsn\sigma_V^2$
Language × Visual field (L × V)	$\sigma_e^2 + n\sigma_{W\times V\times S}^2 + qn\sigma_{L\times V\times S}^2 + sn\sigma_{W\times V}^2 + qsn\sigma_{L\times V}^2$
Words × Visual field (W × V)	$\sigma_e^2 + n\sigma_{W\times V\times S}^2 + sn\sigma_{W\times V}^2$
Language × Subject (L × S)	$\sigma_e^2 + rn\sigma_{W\times S}^2 + qrn\sigma_{L\times S}^2$
Words × Subject (W × S)	$\sigma_e^2 + rn\sigma_{W\times S}^2$
Visual field × Subject (V × S)	$\sigma_e^2 + n\sigma_{W\times V\times S}^2 + pqn\sigma_{V\times S}^2$
Lang. × Visual field × Subject (L × V × S)	$\sigma_e^2 + n\sigma_{W\times V\times S}^2 + qn\sigma_{L\times V\times S}^2$
Words × Visual field × Subject (W × V × S)	$\sigma_e^2 + n\sigma_{W\times V\times S}^2$
Experimental error (e)	σ_e^2

The degrees of freedom for this test may be calculated from formulas given by Clark (1973) or from any standard text (such as Winer, 1971). Using the appropriate test here allows the obtained result to be generalizable to a new set of stimuli. Some conflicting results in the bilingual literature may be due, then, to this lack of generalizability. Also, if the words factor is ignored or treated as a fixed effect in the above example, it could result in a spurious language × visual field effect, which would lead to the erroneous conclusion that the two languages were differently lateralized, when in fact the contribution of the variance due to words may be the reason for the obtained significant effect.

Interpretation

As with monolinguals, questions arise with bilinguals as to the discrepancy between lateralization as evidenced (or not evidenced) via instrumental measures compared with lateralization as evidenced via sodium amytal testing or incidence of aphasia. These discrepancies may reflect the insensitivity of the paradigms involved (Colbourn, 1978), or the added complexity of tasks beyond "pure" language processing, or the fact that we tend to generalize from tasks employing single words to speak about language in general (Galloway, 1980). Findings of differential lateralization for a set of language stimuli or for a group of bilinguals cannot be understood as "greater right-hemisphere participation in language processing than normal," i.e., than in monolinguals until all artifactual explanations can be ruled out. In the event that greater right-hemisphere involvement in L_2 acquisition and use can reliably be demonstrated, it will prove of interest to determine the extent to which "linguistic" capacities of the right hemisphere are being tapped; we may find as some suspect (e.g., Genesee *et al.*, 1978) that the right hemisphere contributes cognitive abilities such as effort (Hardyck, 1980), or specialization for novel stimuli (Bentin, n.d.) which while not strictly "linguistic," may be necessary to, or at least linked to, linguistic processing. In any event, the complexity of the factors involved in study of language lateralization in bilinguals must certainly caution us not to assume that any given study can speak for all bilingual individuals, nor for all bilingual populations.

Source: Obler, L.K., Zatorre, R.J., Galloway, L. and Vaid, J. (1982) Cerebral lateralization in bilinguals. *Brain and Language* 15: 40–54, by permission of Academic Press.

Chapter 15

Language lateralization in bilinguals: enough already!

MICHEL PARADIS

THE OBSTINACY WITH WHICH psycholinguists continue to look for differences in hemispheric asymmetry between bilinguals and unilinguals is nothing short of astounding. Given the dead-end that the issue is faced with after over two decades of contradictory results, why would researchers want to carry out one more of the same type of inconclusive experiments? Yet the topic seems as popular as ever and scores of experiments continue to be submitted for publication with increasingly implausible interpretations, and, more disturbingly, with recommendations for application of the alleged finding of increased participation of the right hemisphere to foreign language teaching, the treatment of mental illness, or the rehabilitation of bilingual aphasia.

It is not the intention of this chapter to provide one more review of the literature on language lateralization in bilinguals. The reader will find comprehensive treatments in Vaid and Genesee (1980), Vaid (1983), and, more recently, critical reviews in Mendelsohn (1988) and Solin (1989). Suffice it to say that laterality differences have been reported for very specific subgroups of bilinguals and/or under very specific conditions, such as only for early (Orbach, 1967) or for late (Sussman *et al.*, 1982; Albanèse, 1985) bilinguals, early or late bilingual women but only late bilingual men (Vaid and Lambert, 1979), or only when eyes are closed (Moss *et al.*, 1985). Decreased asymmetry has been claimed to hold (exclusively) for just about every possible subgroup of bilinguals and its opposite: proficient late bilinguals having learned their second language formally (Bergh, 1986) as well as only those late bilinguals that are at the beginning stages of acquiring their second language informally (Galloway and Krashen, 1980). In other words, one author claimed to have found differences only in proficient late bilinguals (as opposed to beginners) who have learned their second language in a formal setting, and another found no difference in such a group (nor in beginners) but found differences only in those at the beginning of an informal acquisition of a second language. Not only can we not generalize to all bilinguals from any given subgroup, but given the contradictory nature of the results on the same type of bilingual subgroups, we cannot even generalize to any subcategory of bilinguals, no matter how subcategorized by sex, degree of proficiency, age, and manner of acquisition. We must not forget that, in addition to the contradictory results among studies that did find some difference between bilinguals and unilinguals, about an equal number of studies found NO difference.

If the experimental paradigm is considered a variable (and within the paradigm methical, procedural, or statistical considerations) that explains the contradictory results, then the validity of the various paradigms (dichotic listening, tachistoscopic presentation in half visual fields, task-sharing experiments, EEG [electroencephalogram]) that yield these results must be seriously questioned. How could they be a reflection of laterality of language function if so many variables can have an effect on the results? On what basis could we select the one that would be indicative of the actual state of affairs? Equal involvement in each language, and more as well as less involvement of the right hemisphere have been claimed for the first language (L1) only, for the second language (L2) only, and only for early or late stages of informal acquisition or of formal learning.

For instance, Bergh (1986) interprets the results of his study as showing right-hemisphere (RH) participation in L2 processing increasing as a function of increasing proficiency in a formally learned L2. These results are in direct conflict with the predictions of the manner-of-acquisition hypothesis and the modified stage hypothesis. The former predicts that formally learned languages will not be less lateralized than L1 (only those acquired informally will); the latter predicts that greater participation of the right hemisphere will obtain only at the EARLY stages of INFORMAL acquisition of an L2. Yet both had claimed empirical support. Such reports contribute to the widening of the credibility gap associated with dichotic, tachistoscopic, and time-sharing studies of bilingual cerebral laterality of language functions. Such a situation invites one to seriously question the validity and reliability of the paradigm.

Evidence contradictory to the stage hypothesis abounds (see Vaid, 1983). There is now also evidence inconsistent with both the manner of acquisition and the stage of acquisition (Bergh, 1986). Not to mention all the studies that have reported no difference between various sub-populations of bilinguials and unilinguals (e.g., Barton et al., 1965; Kershner and Jeng, 1972; Kotik, 1975; Schönle, 1978; Walters and Zatorre, 1978; Carroll, 1980; Gordon, 1980; Hynd et al., 1980; Piazza and Zatorre, 1981; Soares and Grosjean, 1981; Galloway and Scarcella, 1982; Soares, 1982; Rapport et al., 1983; McKeever and Hunt, 1984;

Soares, 1984; Hoosain and Shiu, 1989) or even GREATER asymmetry in bilinguals (Starck *et al.*, 1977; Ben Amar and Gaillard, 1984). Yet in the face of such ever-increasing contradictory evidence, in spite of repeated denunciations of the lack of validity and reliability of current procedures, including those made by the very experimenters themselves (see Obler *et al.*, 1982; Vaid, 1983: 328; Mendelsohn, 1988; Solin, 1989; Sussman, 1989, Zatorre 1989), and remarks about the lack of significance of the published data on bilingual crossed aphasia (by those same authors who then go on and report old selected cases at length in support of their experimental findings), and in the view of recently published reports of unselected cases of crossed aphasia showing no greater incidence in bilinguals than unilinguals, dichotic, tachistoscopic, and tapping experiments nevertheless continue to be published at an alarming rate. What is the rationale for continuing to run and to publish experiments that the experimenter KNOWS yield uninterpretable conflicting results and ADMITS are neither reliable nor valid?

There was a time when it was possible to legitimately seek for subgroups within the bilingual population once it had been shown that the differential RH participation hypothesis did not hold for bilinguals at large. But why should we now wish to show at all cost that there must be some small subset of bilinguals such as proficient female late acquirers in informal settings, provided they keep their eyes closed (Moss *et al.*, 1985) or block one nostril (Shannahoff-Khalsa, 1984), when it is conceded that "it is questionable whether, even if properly tested, the predicted differences in the extent of hemispheric involvement in the two languages of bilingual subgroups can be reliably detected by current procedures, especially since the size of ear or visual field asymmetries may be influenced by factors other than degree of cerebral lateralization" (Vaid, 1983: 328). On the basis of statistical reanalysis of available data, Sussman (1989) concludes that previous findings and theoretical conclusions based on time-sharing laterality results may be meaningless, and he seriously questions the continued use of the time-sharing paradigm as a behavioral index of language lateralization. In addition, experiments with commisurotomized patients have shown that following section of the corpus callosum, under dichotic stimulation, the left ear score drops to near zero whereas in monaural stimulation it is normal (Milner *et al.*, 1968), which strongly suggests that the left ear score reflects the amount of information successfully transferred from the left ear to the left hemisphere – not information processed by the right hemisphere.

The interpretation of all these results as based on the unproven premise that reduced difference between the ears, or between half visual fields, or between tapping disruption, is indicative of increased RH participation or of a more bilateral contribution from both hemispheres. If left ear or right visual field scores were an index of RH linguistic processing, how would one interpret the 40–45% correct answers generally reported from the LEFT ear or visual field? How would one account for intraindividual variation over time within the same session or between sessions? When a difference between groups (unilinguals vs. bilinguals) is detected, what could the difference be indicative of, as opposed to when no difference is detected (i.e., in about half the studies) or when the difference is supposed to be present only in one specific population (e.g., late bilinguals) in one study, and the reverse (i.e., only in early bilinguals) in another?

It can no longer be assumed to be the case that "taken together, the available clinical and experimental studies suggest that competence in more than one language may influence brain functioning so that it differs from that characterizing speakers of a single language" (Vaid, 1983: 315). Most authors who speculate on a greater participation of the right hemisphere are aware of (and even explicitly mention) the reasons why the literature on which such a presumption is founded is not reliable. Obler *et al.* (1982) and Zatorre (1989) are even cited for providing methodological, theoretical, and statistical problems with these studies, but then authors go ahead anyway. Likewise, mention is made that published selected clinical cases are of no statistical use, but then authors go on to cite percentages anyhow.

In support of the manner of acquisition hypothesis, Hartnett's (1975) study is often cited by authors who have not read the original thesis, but only its published abstract. Had they read the original thesis, they would have realized to what extent the results were unreliable because of severe shortcomings in the areas of design, execution, data analysis, and interpretation (see Stieblich, 1983: 1–5 for details). Likewise, Nair and Virmani's (1973) study has been cited by many authors over the past 10 years as reporting a high incidence of crossed aphasia among bilinguals without having been read, for if these authors had read the original study rather than relying on the incidental misquoting of it in 1978, they would have realized that there was no way that one could have derived any percentage of bilingual crossed aphasics among the reported cases, since the number of bilinguals in their sample is nowhere mentioned.

As for the evidence from clinical reports, it is not just "equivocal" (Vaid, 1983: 317) with respect to the role of the right hemisphere in language mediation, it is simply *nonexistent*. There is not a shred of clinical evidence in support of less asymmetry of language representation in bilinguals for either or for both of their languages. There is NO statistically significant higher incidence of crossed aphasia in bilinguals than in unilinguals (for a review, see April and Han, 1980; Chary, 1986; Solin, 1989). Karanth and Rangamani (1988) report an incidence of crossed aphasia that is actually lower in bilinguals than in unilinguals. That study has been replicated by Rangamani (1989) on an unselected sample of CVA [cerebrovascular accident] patients, reporting crossed aphasia in 2/12 unilinguals and 0/26 bilinguals. Wada testing results are equally clear: both languages are affected only by left-hemisphere (LH) injection (e.g., Rapport *et al.*, 1983).

Given the extreme degree of variation within and between individuals, within and between groups of similar populations, and given that all available clinical evidence (incidence of crossed aphasia, Wada test) unequivocally shows identical LH involvement for both languages, whatever these experimental studies show, it is unlikely to be a lesser asymmetry of language cerebral representation and/or processing.

What is it then that these studies report a greater right-hemisphere participation of? One may in fact seriously question whether any of these paradigms are an index of *language* lateralization, when the stimuli used are nonsense syllables or isolated words. To start with, it seems legitimate to ask oneself what could possibly be the nature of this alleged increased participation of the right hemisphere. At least four possibilities come to mind (Paradis, 1987).

Let us call the first *the redundant participation hypothesis*. According to this hypothesis, both hemispheres process information in identical ways, though the participation of the left hemisphere may be quantitatively greater. The processing by the right hemisphere is redundant and hence the removal of the right hemisphere is of little consequence for language.

Another possibility would be *the quantitatively complementary participation hypothesis* according to which, as above, each hemisphere processes the same stimuli in the same way, with greater participation of the left hemisphere. However, there is a mass effect and the whole is necessary for normal language processing. A lesion to homologous parts of either the right or the left hemisphere will cause qualitatively identical deficits proportional to the extent of the damage.

One can also conceive of *a qualitatively parallel participation hypothesis*. According to this hypothesis the same stimulus is processed in a qualitatively different way by each hemisphere. Each hemisphere processes all aspects of a stimulus in accordance with its own inherent mode of functioning. The participation of the right hemisphere is thus qualitatively complementary to that of the left hemisphere in processing utterances.

Still another plausible candidate is *the qualitatively selective participation hypothesis*. Each hemisphere, in accordance with its intrinsic functional capacities, specializes in the processing of a different aspect of a complex stimulus. In this case, as in the previous one, the participation of the right hemisphere is qualitatively complementary to that of the left hemisphere. However, while in the qualitatively parallel participation hypothesis complementarity is with respect to each aspect of an utterance, in the qualitatively selective participation hypothesis it is with respect to the utterance as a whole.

The qualitatively parallel participation hypothesis predicts that a lesion in the right hemisphere will affect all aspects of the utterance (albeit in a specific way, distinguishable from the effects of a homologous left-hemisphere lesion; e.g., global vs. analytic-sequential decoding of the meaning of a word or phrase), whereas the qualitatively selective participation hypothesis predicts that a right-hemisphere lesion will affect certain aspects of the utterance (a homologous left-hemisphere lesion will affect the other aspects of the utterance; e.g., prosody related to emotional states vs. grammatical stress pattern of lexical tone).

The redundant and the quantitatively complementary participation hypotheses assume an identical processing of the same aspects of an utterance; the qualitatively parallel participation hypothesis assumes a different processing of the same aspects while the qualitatively selective participation hypothesis assumes a different processing of different aspects. Among the most often mentioned intrinsic processing modes attributed to each hemisphere, one finds the analytic/ global, sequential/concomitant, logical/analogical, context-independent/ context-dependent, and deductive/inductive. Aspects of an utterance that have been involved as likely to be processed separately by each hemisphere are, among others, grammatical/paralinguistic, phonemic/prosodic, and syntactic/ pragmatic.

To the extent that right-hemisphere damage is known to cause speech, language, and communication deficits (Alexander et al., 1989) bilinguals will exhibit such symptoms, but only to the extent and in the same form that unilinguals will. Subsequent to right-hemisphere lesions bilinguals may be expected, as unilinguals, to exhibit impairment of affective prosody, of the ability to handle humor, sarcasm, irony, inference, analogy, nonexplicit speech acts, and, in general, any nonliteral meaning. But they should not be expected to exhibit impairment in linguistic aspects of prosody or in grammatical usage; at any rate, not to a greater extent than that which has been reported in unilinguals (Joanette et al., 1983; 1990).

Now, it happens that language teachers are turning more and more to the neuropsychological literature for guidance. This is a commendable endeavor that may ultimately prove fruitful. However, one cannot be too cautious in applying to classroom methodology what are at best hypothetical and often quite controversial theoretical constructs. In the face of contradictory experimental results and the total absence of clinical evidence, the claim of lesser asymmetry of language representation and/or processing in bilinguals is absolutely unfounded, and should therefore not serve as a basis for researchers in neuropsychology to make any recommendation in the fields of pedagogy, psychiatry, or language therapy.

For example, Shannahoff-Khalsa (1984) reports having observed alternating periods of greater relative amplitudes of EEG activity in one hemisphere, and then in the other. At the same time, measures of airflow in the right and left nostril have shown a similar alternation between the use of each nostril. Rhythms of the nasal cycle and hemispheric cycle have been observed to be tightly coupled. Since this balance of hemispheric dominance can be shifted by forcibly altering the phase of the nasal cycle, it is suggested that we could exert control over cognitive functions by forced breathing through the right nostril to increase our mathematical capacity, or through the left nostril to enhance our creativity. It might neverthe-less be premature to recommend that foreign language teachers require their students to block their left nostril to activate their right hemisphere in the hope of forcing language processing in that hemisphere (or the reverse).

Even if it were the case that the right hemisphere played a major role in the acquisition and/or learning of a second/foreign language, it might very well do so in spite of whatever method of presentation of the second/foreign language is used. One cannot force a language to be represented or prevent it from being represented where it is natural for it to be represented (save for the removal of the left hemisphere early in life – which I hope no one would advocate!).

Song, dance, instrumental music, or blocking one's left nostril will not force the grammar to be processed and/or represented in the right hemisphere, if that is not where it is naturally processed and/or represented. The mode of presenta-tion might at best encourage particular processing strategies, but even these are not demonstrably beneficial. The fact (if it is a fact) that second language learning usually does involve the right hemisphere is no assurance that utilizing the right hemisphere is the most efficient way of learning a second language. Indeed it might be a main factor in failure to acquire native-like proficiency since, once higher proficiency has been attained, greater asymmetry is reported. Goodglass (1978: 103) suggests that, while in the early stages of first language acquisition neurons are recruited bilaterally, in the course of language development, the most compact, rapidly acting systems of the left hemisphere survive, while the slower, less efficient components of the neural network of the right hemisphere drop out of the processing of language. It might then be considered more efficient to try to get the left hemisphere to process the second language as soon as possible (if one knew how to do that).

But even if it were beneficial for the second/foreign language to be processed in the right hemisphere, one might argue that any competing right-hemisphere function concurrently activated might be a hindrance (as the time-sharing tasks experimental paradigm would indicate if it were valid; finger tapping is reported to be more disrupted when it is performed by the right hand by right handers). The moral should then be: "Do not overload the right hemisphere with materials (melody, choreography, etc.) that might require its attention." To the extent that the right hemisphere is normally engaged in (first) language process-ing, it will be engaged in second/foreign language processing as well – but no more. If it is a question of the extent to which certain bilinguals tend to use RH-based strategies in language processing (Gordon and Weide, 1983; Vaid, 1983), then we no longer are looking at a phenomenon characteristic of bilinguals *per se* (or groups of bilinguals) but of some unilinguals as well. The extent of reliance on strategies of the right hemisphere is a function of individual cognitive style, and there is no evidence that this style is more prevalent among bilinguals than unilinguals.

Has the inadequacy of dichotic, tachistoscopic, and time-sharing paradigms in reflecting laterality of language functions in bilinguals not yet been sufficiently attested? How many additional repeated failures to demonstrate differential laterality in increasingly specific subgroups of bilinguals will it take for neuropsychologists to move on to something more productive?

Source: Paradis, M. (1990) Language lateralization in bilinguals. *Brain and Language* 39: 570–86, by permission of Academic Press.

Notes for students and instructors

Study questions

1   In Obler *et al.*'s view, how do the following variables affect experimental results on language lateralisation in bilingual speakers:
    (a)   age of acquisition;
    (b)   manner of acquisition;
    (c)   test language stimuli; and
    (d)   experimental task?
2   What are the reasons for Paradis to suggest that language lateralisation in bilinguals is a 'dead-end issue'?

Study activity

Review the literature on language lateralisation in bilingual speakers and sort the studies according to the subjects and experimental paradigms used. Can you see any patterns which may suggest a link between the experimental results and the methods chosen?

Further reading

A general introduction to the bilingual brain can be seen in Chapter 3 of S. Romaine, 1995, *Bilingualism* (2nd edn), Blackwell; and also in F. Fabbro, 1999, *The Neurolinguistics of Bilingualism*, Psychology Press.

    For an overview of research on the bilingual brain, see M. Paradis, 1997,

The cognitive neuropsychology of bilingualism, in A. de Groot and J. Kroll (eds), *Tutorials in Bilingualism,* Lawrence Erlbaum, pp. 331–54.

A collection of earlier studies of the bilingual brain is M.L. Albert and L.K. Obler, 1978, *The Bilingual Brain,* Academic Press.

Bilingual speech processing

Control, activation, and resource: a framework and a model for the control of speech in bilinguals

DAVID W. GREEN

O NE EXPLANATION FOR THE effects of brain damage on speech is that it destroys, or isolates, one or more of the components of the system required for intact performance. Such an explanation lacks generality. It does not account for the speech errors of normal speakers and it fails to explain certain phenomena within the clinical literature itself, such as the recovery patterns of two bilingual aphasics recently reported by Paradis *et al.* (1982). This chapter develops a framework which accommodates the performance of normal as well as brain-damaged individuals, and it provides a specific model of the bilingual speaker. The framework and model describe a conceptual nervous system and make no claims as to the nature of the underlying neural mechanism.

The chapter presents three main ideas. The first is that the impaired performance of aphasic patients, and of bilingual aphasics specifically, reflects a problem in controlling intact language systems. Problems of control also seem the best way of explaining the kinds of speech error observed in normal bilinguals. Hence such an idea offers a way to accommodate both normal and pathological data.

The second idea concerns how control is effected. It is assumed that speech production can be understood in the same way as skilled action in general. In particular, the selection of a word, like the selection of a particular action, involves regulating a single underlying variable of the amount of activation. Choosing an appropriate word requires ensuring that its activation exceeds that of any competitors.

The third idea is that regulation involves the use, and hence possible depletion, of the means to increase or to decrease the activation of some internal component. Most functional models of speech production ignore this energy dimension and yet we would not normally consider the description of a working device as complete without some account of how it is powered. (A blueprint for a car ignores the fuel and braking systems at some peril.) A system needs energy to work and operating it consumes energy. Thus, if the means required to regulate a system are insufficient for whatever reason then, even though the system is intact, control will be imperfect. Brain damage, it is suggested, affects the availability of resources. These three ideas (control, activation, and resource) allow an explanation of the recovery patterns of the bilingual aphasics reported by Paradis *et al.*

The chapter considers each of these ideas in turn and develops a specific model within the overall framework. It begins by considering a functional model of bilingual performance based on certain typical case reports and then describes the data reported by Paradis *et al.* which are so problematic for such a model.

Albert and Obler (1978) cite the case reports of a number of brain-damaged polyglot speakers who understood speech in all their languages but who were either unable to speak, or who had severe difficulty in speaking, at least one of them (e.g., Cases 14, 41, 81, and 94). Such patterns indicate that the subsystems mediating the comprehension and production of language are separable and that different functional systems underlie different languages. Figure 16.1 presents a simple model for a bilingual speaker compatible with such data and it is apparent that the destruction or isolation of one output system is a reasonable explanation of the effects of brain damage on such patients. Such a model is a variant of the kind of model proposed by Morton (1980) and restricts itself to the recognition and production of words. Although not included in the figure it is perfectly possible to complicate the output systems by separately specifying the syntactic,

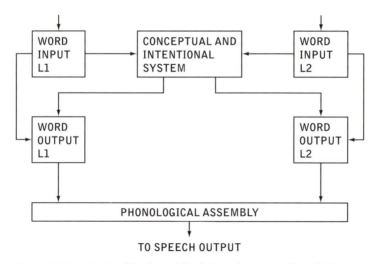

Figure 16.1   A simplified model of the subsystems for a bilingual speaker.

prosodic, and lexical components. Information from these converges at the stage of phonological assembly. Such a model can be used to account not only for the selective loss of a language but also for the recovery of a lost language. It can be assumed that the individual has either relearned or is using a novel strategy which bypasses the damaged subsystem, or even that damage has allowed a previously subordinate system to take over. However, major fluctuations in performance within brief periods of time are outside its scope. Just such fluctuations have been reported by Paradis *et al.* The case of A.D. is the better documented of the two cases cited and so her report is used to illustrate the phenomena of interest.

A.D. was a 48-year-old nun, fluent in French and Arabic, who was in charge of various child care clinics in Morocco. She spoke French with the other sisters and the doctors, and Arabic with the nursing aids, patients, and the local population. Following a moped accident, she suffered a right-parietal fracture and, in consequence, a contusion in the left temporoparietal area. After a period of total aphasia and a period where she spoke only a few words of Arabic, she was flown to a hospital in France, where the phenomena termed "alternate antagonism" and "paradoxical translation" were observed.

Eighteen days after the accident, she showed little spontaneous use of French but she was able to name objects in Arabic and to speak Arabic spontaneously. On the following day, naming and spontaneous speech were good in French and poor in Arabic. This pattern, "alternate antagonism," coincided with good comprehension in both languages.

Correlated with this pattern was the second phenomenon of "paradoxical translation." On the day when she could speak Arabic spontaneously, i.e., 18 days postonset, she was unable to translate into it, even though she was able to translate from Arabic into French, which was the language she was unable to speak spontaneously. On the following day, when her spontaneous speech in Arabic was poor, she was able to translate into Arabic but was unable to translate into French which she could use spontaneously.

As Paradis *et al.* point out, the phenomenon of "alternate antagonism" establishes the functional dissociation of the two languages. Indeed, A.D. exhibits a "double-dissociation" – a fundamental type of evidence for neuropsychology (Shallice, 1979). The two phenomena cannot be explained by the destruction, or isolation, of an output component, rather, as Paradis *et al.* phrase it, one language becomes "restrictively inaccessible" for a period of time but only under certain conditions.

The idea of control: errors and impairment

Temporary disruption of varying degrees of severity is a feature of the speech of normal monolingual and bilingual speakers. Indeed normal speech can be seen as the successful avoidance of error. Transient failures include errors where we blend two or more words together. Within a language we find blends such as "strying" (blended from "trying" and "striving") and across languages we find ones such as "Springling" (blended from "spring" and "Frühling"). In such cases, it is evident that the normal speaker can recognize that an error has been made and can also produce an appropriate utterance. There is no reason to suppose that some part of the speech system has been destroyed or isolated. On the contrary, the error is best seen as one of a failure to exercise full control over an intact system. A number of factors such as temporary distraction or stress may occasion such a failure and a number of detailed accounts of specific phenomena have been developed that explain how they may arise (e.g., Shattuck-Huffnagel, 1979; Butterworth, 1981). What is important for present purposes is that such errors occur as a result of a problem in controlling intact systems.

If a problem of control can offer a way to explain normal speech errors it may also account for aphasic performance. Freud (1891/1953) noted that the paraphasias observed in aphasic patients do not differ from the incorrect use and distortion of words healthy persons can observe in themselves when they are tired or distracted. Recent support for the idea comes from analyses of the neologisms of jargon aphasics that indicate that these may reflect a strategy for coping with *temporary* difficulties in retrieving words (Butterworth, 1985). At least, for temporary problems (i.e., ones where on other occasions a person does use the right word), it seems reasonable to suggest that the difficulty arises from a problem of controlling an intact system. This claim is sufficient for present purposes, but in order to apply it we need to consider how such control is exercised.

The idea of activation

The notion that the internal representation of words can vary in their level of activation is a relatively common assumption in recent theorizing. Combined with the notion that a word must reach a certain threshold of activation in order to become available as a response, it is possible to explain why, for example, speakers pause longer before producing less predictable words (Goldman-Eisler, 1958) – the less predictable word is at a lower level of activation. In the case of naming an object the appropriate name must be activated and come to dominate over other possible candidates. A picture of a car, for instance, may lead to the internal representations of the names for "car," "cab," "truck" becoming active since they all share some of the perceptual and functional properties that define a car. The appropriate name comes to dominate other possible candidate names by reducing their level of activation, i.e., by suppressing or inhibiting them. Empirical and experimental evidence further suggests that this process of word production may be divided into a stage at which the speaker activates words of a certain meaning and a second stage where the actual sound or phonological form of these is retrieved (see, for example, Garrett, 1982; Kempen and Huijbers, 1983) though for reasons of simplicity, these stages are not separately illustrated in the figures. On occasions two names labeling the same referent or idea may both reach threshold and give rise to a blend. Our primary concern is not the mechanics of producing words from a single language system but the nature of the control requirements when two such systems are involved.

Since a normal bilingual speaker can elect to speak one language rather than another it might be thought that this is achieved by completely deactivating the nonselected language. In fact, some early accounts did presume some internal on–off switch (e.g., Penfield and Roberts, 1959); others (e.g., Ervin and Osgood, 1954) raised the issue but failed to offer any sufficient explanation. In fact, experimental evidence using a variety of techniques, such as a bilingual version of the Stroop test (Preston and Lambert, 1969) and a lexical decision task (Altenberg and Cairns, 1983), indicates that in normal bilinguals although only one language may be selected, the other is nonetheless active, at least when both languages are in regular use. In the case of naming, one consequence of such activation is that bilinguals take longer to name any single object (Mägiste, 1979). The joint activation of both systems is also apparent in the case of errors of interference. A French–English bilingual talking to his son who speaks only English and pointing to a truck says: "Look at the camion" where "camion" is pronounced as if it were an English word (Grosjean, 1982). Indeed the effort to avoid interference can be extremely demanding (see Clyne, 1980a) and become almost impossible under severe stress (Dornic, 1978).

However, delay or interference are not the only outcomes of knowing two languages. Where two bilinguals share the same two languages they can switch between them (see Sridhar and Sridhar, 1980). In code-switching, elements from one language are embedded in those of another. At least part of the reason for such switching is the availability of expressions in one language compared to another. Speakers can output whichever expression first achieves threshold. Hence, code-switching need not involve dysfluency.

But why should a nonselected language remain active? It may be used frequently in daily life and its activation will, accordingly, be maintained both because the language is spoken and because it is heard. It would also continue to receive input from the conceptual system. However, it seems implausible to assume that a language system remains active when unused for long periods. Unused, its level of activation is likely to fall. We may distinguish, then, between three states of a language system, viz.:

1   selected (and hence controlling speech output);
2   active (i.e., playing a role in ongoing processing); and
3   dormant (i.e., residing in long-term memory but exerting no effects on ongoing processing).

These three states have been identified previously by Norman and Shallice (1980) and Shallice (1982) in the context of nonverbal motor skills. Our primary concern, of course, is to deal with circumstances in which both languages are active, or conceivably active, and here the idea that naming and speech production involves controlling the activation of the internal representations of words is useful because it offers a general way to account for both the fluent and the dysfluent aspects of normal speech in bilinguals.

The idea of a resource

In order to be able to activate or to suppress the activity of a component in a system it is necessary that some means exist for doing so. Within the activation framework (e.g., Collins and Loftus, 1975) it has been assumed that activation is limited and therefore that only one part of a system can be highly activated at any one time. Other researchers have postulated that each cognitive processor (e.g., a device for recognizing words or for producing them) has its own limited pool of resources (e.g., McLeod, 1977; see also Navon and Gopher, 1979). The present proposal links the resource idea to the actual process of controlling or regulating a system. A resource may be used either to excite a system (an excitatory resource) or to inhibit one (an inhibitory resource) and any act of control consumes resources. The resource idea makes explicit the fact that a system needs energy to operate – a fact which is invariably ignored in functional models of language and cognition. Now an inevitable consequence of the resource notion is that unless resources are replenished at the right rate, control will be impaired. We presume, then, a "resource generator" that manufactures such resources at a certain rate.

Controlling two language systems: an inhibitory control model

Where a person wishes to speak one language only, this language must be selected and the output from the other language system inhibited. Such selection and suppression requires that the relevant outputs be identified.

One solution to this problem, and the one adopted here, is to suppose that words possess particular "tags," where a tag can be thought of, following Albert and Obler (1978), as "a feature label associated with each individual item." (Such tagging may not be restricted to distinguishing words or structures in different languages. Some form of tagging may also be used to label vocabulary or structures associated with particular "registers" or styles of speech within a language.)

Since a bilingual can speak one or other language and can translate from one to the other, or switch between them, there must be a device (a "specifier") that specifies how the system must be controlled if a person is to act in one or other of these ways. The general scheme is presented in Figure 16.2.

Let us consider first of all the control requirements for speaking one language (L1) rather than the other language (L2). It is evident that the devices for recognizing words in L1 must be active and that the device for producing them must be selected. Selection is partially a matter of increasing the activation of L1 but, principally, it is a matter of suppressing the activation of L2 words so that words from that system do not get produced. The output from L2 could be suppressed within the system itself (internal suppression) or by the L1 system externally suppressing the activity of L2 (external suppression). Internal suppression, indicated in Figure 16.2 by an inhibitory loop, restricts the retrieval of word sounds from L2. External suppression, indicated by an inhibitory link to the output of L2 at the stage of phonological assembly, suppresses the activation of L2 words at the assembly stage.

It is proposed that the suppression of L2 is achieved *externally* in spontaneous use. This proposal predicts that dysfluencies in L1 will occur whenever there is an L2 expression of a concept which is more available than one in L1. For instance,

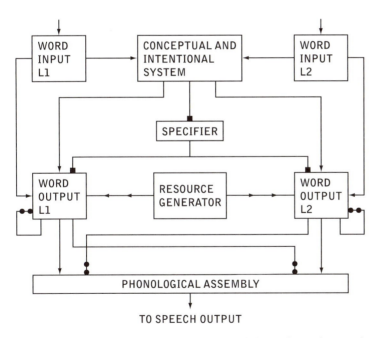

Figure 16.2 An inhibitory model for a bilingual speaker within the control, activation and resource framework

Notes: →, flow of activation; ▬, control instructions; →→, resource input; ●━●, inhibitory control.

L2 may possess a single word or idiom which expresses an idea that demands a novel phrase in L1. In order to produce the L1 phrase, the alternative in L2 must be suppressed.

In the case of code-switching, there need be no external suppression of L2 at all; at least in the simplest case, such as continuous word association, the output can be free to vary according to which words reach threshold first. Indeed in this circumstance, mixing languages is certainly no slower than producing associations in only one language (Taylor, 1971). In the case of normal speech a word cannot be produced unless it fits the syntax of the utterance. Accordingly, for example, an adverb will not be produced in a slot requiring a noun. Switches then will obey the syntactic properties of the two languages although no special device or grammar is required to achieve this goal. Code switches most often involve single words, especially nouns (Pfaff, 1979), though ones involving phrases or entire clauses also occur. In these latter cases, we suppose that structures from L2 reach threshold earlier. Since any words produced must meet the structural conditions, such a scheme predicts that code switches will preserve the word order in both languages (see Chapter 9 of this volume).

A more complex form of regulation is needed in the case of translation. Both language systems are required and when translating from L2 to L1 the output system for L2 must be suppressed. In principle, such suppression may be achieved internally or externally (as noted above). In practice, however, since translation into L1 requires that the speaker does not simply repeat the message in L2, it is proposed that suppression of the output from L2 is achieved internally in the same way as a monolingual speaker might avoid simply repeating a word or a phrase just heard. To recap, when speaking L1 spontaneously, L2 is *externally* suppressed, whereas when translating from L2 to L1 the output of L2 is *internally* suppressed.

Since distinct inhibitory means are used in spontaneous speech and in translating, it follows from the claim that resources are consumed in such activities that speaking may be affected by the nature of the previous activity. For example, in a paced task where the rate at which resources are used exceeds the rate at which they are replaced, there should be a "fatigue effect." A bilingual will be slower to name pictures in L1 after a session of such naming compared to a session where L2 names had to be translated into L1. In the latter case no L1 inhibitory resources would have been used to regulate the L2 system and hence would be available for naming in L1 in the second session.

The model outlined above can be generalized to account for language control in trilingual or polyglot speakers. In fact, these groups provide a further way of testing the model. As the number of languages increases, so should the problems of control. For instance, the time required to name simple objects should be greater for the trilingual compared to the bilingual speaker, as L1 must externally suppress the activity of the third language (L3) system as well as that of L2. Translation would involve the same control requirements for translating L1 into

L2 (i.e., internal suppression of L1) but, in addition, L2 must externally suppress L3. Assuming that the rate of generating inhibitory resources is the same for bilingual and trilingual speakers, when the latter are engaged in translation they should suffer impaired performance earlier than bilingual speakers. It may be that there is some limit on the number of language systems that can be active at the same time, which would reduce the problem of control. But such an empirical constraint is not part of the current model.

More generally, if other nonlinguistic systems also consume the resources provided by the generator then the use of such systems would affect the control of speech. So, for example, as stress or anxiety increase, speech should be disrupted especially in a person's weaker language. As remarked earlier, empirical research supports this expectation (Dornic, 1978). A further factor which may exert a profound effect on the availability of resources is brain damage.

Alternate antagonism and paradoxical translation: control and the limitation of resources

Brain damage may limit the availability of both the means to excite as well as the means to inhibit a system. This assumption is compatible with accounts of the working brain proposed by Luria (1973) and the account of memory disorders discussed by Talland (1965). Without sufficient activation no output could be achieved. On the other hand, unless there are sufficient means for L1 to inhibit L2, the person would be unable to use L1 spontaneously since the output of this system would be unable to dominate that of L2. This line of reasoning underlies some of the predictions of the model for normal speakers as well. In general, the kinds of output produced depend on the relative balance of the means to excite or to inhibit a system. Assume, though, that there are sufficient resources to activate the various systems but that brain damage in aphasics limits, at least initially, the availability of the means to inhibit these systems. Difficulties in inhibiting responses have been mooted before as one of the aspects of aphasia (Hudson, 1968; Yamadori, 1981). Such a view allows the inhibitory control model to explain in a unified way both of the central phenomena (alternate antagonism and paradoxical translation) reported by Paradis *et al.* (1982).

Suppose that there is an initial imbalance in the amount of inhibitory resource available to the two systems such that L1 has more of these means than L2 but that both receive resources. We have, then, the state depicted in Figure 16.3. According to the present framework, L1 can be used spontaneously because it can externally suppress outputs from L2, whereas L2 cannot meet this requirement and externally suppress L1. Since operating L1 consumes resources, and given the rate at which resources are generated is less than the rate at which they are consumed, the inhibitory resource available to L1 will cease to be adequate. Meanwhile, the inhibitory resources available for use by L2 will increase.

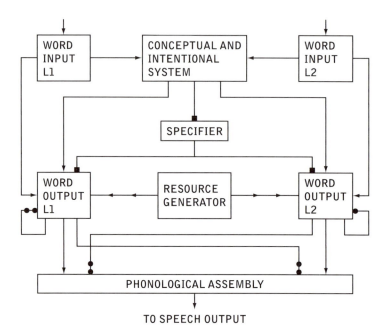

Figure 16.3   A state of the system in the inhibitory control model during alternate antagonism and paradoxical translation

Notes: →, flow of activation; ▬■, control instructions; →→, resource input; ●−●
adequate inhibitory control; −●, inadequate inhibitory control.

Behaviorally, this entails a shift from A.D. being able to use L1 spontaneously to a state where she can only use L2 spontaneously. Similarly, if the rate of generation continues to be insufficient to replenish resources as they are consumed, L2 will in turn cease to dominate and the system will flip back into the previous state where L1 but not L2 could be used spontaneously. Thus, a limitation on the inhibitory means available to a system can explain the pattern of alternate antagonism. It is a strong claim of the present account that even when one language cannot be used spontaneously, it is not because it is inactive but because it is unable to suppress sufficiently the activation of the other system.

The claim that L2 output is in fact active is consistent with the second phenomenon of paradoxical translation in which A.D. was unable to translate into the language which she used spontaneously but could translate into the one she could not use. How might this pattern be explained by the model? On the one hand, translation into L1 (the language of spontaneous use) would be precluded when L2 could not suppress its own activity sufficiently. On the other hand, when L1 can suppress its own activity, L2 would be free to translate. On this account, then, at one time each language system was able to externally suppress the other system as well as to internally suppress its own activity, whereas at another time it could meet neither of these control requirements. Thus, both alternate antagonism and paradoxical translation can be seen as outcomes of a system with limited inhibitory resources.

These phenomena are really a subset of those that could be produced by a system with insufficient regulatory means. There is no necessary reason why a system that can suppress the activity of another need have the means to suppress its own activity sufficiently to allow translation. External and internal suppression are distinct forms of control and adequacy in that one does not guarantee adequacy in another. Table 16.1 documents the alternative outcomes when there are adequate or inadequate means of internal and external control for two languages.

The third row in the table corresponds to the case of paradoxical translation. When, as in the fourth row, only one language can be used spontaneously, but the means for internal suppression in that language are inadequate, we have an outcome in which the speaker can only translate into the language of spontaneous use (nonparadoxical translation). Where neither language can suppress its own output sufficiently, translation is precluded entirely and we have the outcome such as that

Table 16.1   Speech outcomes for two languages as a function of the adequacy (+) or inadequacy (−) of the means for internal and external suppression

Suppression				
External		*Internal*		
L1	*L2*	*L1*	*L2*	*Outcome*
1 +	+	+	+	Spontaneous use of both languages and translation in either direction
2 +	+	−	−	Spontaneous use of both languages; translation impossible
3 +	−	+	−	Spontaneous use of one language and paradoxical translation
−	+	−	+	
4 +	−	−	+	Spontaneous use of one language and nonparadoxical translation
−	+	+	−	
5 +	−	−	−	Spontaneous use of one language; translation impossible
−	+	−	−	
6 −	−	−	−	No output although systems are active

listed in the second row. Later in her recovery A.D. evinced both of these phenomena.

The present model then explains such outcomes by postulating an underlying problem of control whose precise outcome depends on the relative availability of inhibitory means. Although a variety of outcomes can thereby be accommodated, each outcome is a direct consequence of a failure of a specific control requirement.

Some generalizations, predictions, and limitations

One of the surprising claims of the model is that the absence of speech following brain damage does not entail that some subsystem has been destroyed (see row 6, Table 16.1). The regulatory means, specifically the inhibitory resources, may be inadequate. If this is the case, then there should be evidence of activity (for example, EEG recordings) in those areas normally associated with language production. But such a measure is unlikely to tell us about the status of a specific language system. In cases where, following damage, only one language is recovered (selective recovery; Paradis, 1977), if the nonrecovered language is active then this fact should be detectable using such tasks as bilingual Stroop, since a color word in L2 (the nonrecovered language) should interfere with naming the ink color in L1.

In the case of antagonistic recovery, the disappearance of one language (L2) may be attributed to inadequate means to suppress the other system and this problem would be revealed by increasing problems in performing a bilingual Stroop task in L2 in the presence of an L1 color word. Mixing and differential recovery patterns may also be explained on the basis of insufficient inhibitory means. In the case of mixing it is a lack which extends to both systems, whereas in the case of differential recovery it is restricted largely to one system. The most widespread recovery pattern is one where both languages recover in parallel (see Paradis, 1977). If such recovery reflects the gradual increase in inhibitory means then recovery should be accompanied by a gradual decrease in bilingual Stroop interference as the means for suppressing alternative names improves.

We have supposed that recovery solely produces a change in the availability of inhibitory resources. As these increase it becomes possible to regulate active systems more effectively. The crucial determinant of the output of the system is this balance of the means to excite and the means to inhibit. But a change in excitatory means would also influence this balance. Perhaps as recovery progresses other areas become activated and require regulation. The problem of control is still one of the relative sufficiency of inhibitory means, but the model would need extending to incorporate such changes in excitatory means. However, such an extended model would still remain part of the general framework being proposed.

Conclusion

One of the primary aims of this chapter has been to describe a framework based on the ideas of control, activation, and resource which can increase the scope of functional models and establish a link between the normal and the pathological. The framework predicts that there are at least some cases in which language impairment following brain damage is not caused by the destruction or isolation of some functional subsystem but is the result of a problem in regulating the activity of an intact system. No speech can mean no activity, but the present framework encourages the search for cases where such activity does in fact exist. The major problem in coping with the effects of brain damage on this view is one of reestablishing control over intact systems. The longitudinal study of the recovery patterns of bilingual aphasics promises to provide insight into the means by which a person regulates alternative systems of expression.

Many alternative models are possible within this framework and one, in particular – an inhibitory control model – was proposed which makes specific predictions about both normal and pathological performance.

Source: Green, D.W. (1986) Control, activation, and resource. *Brain and Language* 27: 210–23, by permission of Academic Press.

Chapter 17

A bilingual production model: Levelt's 'speaking' model adapted

KEES DE BOT

WHILE RESEARCH INTO BILINGUALISM increased dramatically in the 1980s, there was remarkably little research aimed at the development of a model of bilingualism. The linguistic performance of bilinguals has been used to support syntactic theories – for example, Woolford's (1983) study of government and binding and code-switching and White's research into the relationship between Universal Grammar and second language acquisition (1989) – but there are no theories about the bilingual speaker that aim at a description of the entire language production process. There are of course partial descriptions of the process, as in Krashen's Monitor theory (1981), Bialystok's Analysis/Control approach (Bialystok, 1990), and the global description of the production process in Færch and Kasper (1986), but a full model which covers the whole process from message generation to articulation is still lacking.

In this article it is assumed that the single most important entity we are concerned with in model-construction is the individual speaker in whom we see all factors and influences combined. In language behaviour research there have traditionally been reasonably sharp dividing lines between linguistic, psycholinguistic, and sociolinguistic research. In a good production model these dividing lines fade; the model should be able to cope with universal characteristics of language as well as cognitive processes and situational factors in interaction and their consequences for language use. The individual speaker is seen as someone in whom all sorts of influences on language use are expressed, influences of a microsociological nature (influences resulting from the situation in which interaction takes place) as well as those of a macrosociological nature (such as language repression and language contact). In such an approach, societal concepts such as language vitality, ethnicity, and social mobility have, to use

Hakuta's words (1986: 192) 'psychological reality as concepts in bilingual individuals'.

Levelt's 'Speaking' model (1989) is very promising in all respects. Although the model has been developed explicitly to describe the unilingual speaker – the only thing that has anything at all to do with multilingualism is a reference to Perdue (1984) – it might also be useful, after adaptations, to describe the bilingual speaker. Clearly, many aspects of speaking are the same for monolingual and bilingual speakers, and a single model to describe both types of speaker is to be preferred over two separate models for different types. It could be argued that because every unilingual speaker has the potential to become bilingual, the validity of a model can be tested by examining whether it is suitable for bilingualism. Or, to push this point even further: given the fact that bilingualism or multilingualism is the rule all over the world and unilingualism the exception, especially if we include bidialectism as a form of bilingualism, one could argue that the basic model should be concerned with bilingualism, with an option to have a unilingual version.

As Meara (1989) points out, there is a real need for a model to describe the bilingual language user. Even if the model used may ultimately turn out to be inadequate, it can still serve to structure and organize research and data: 'Using a model as a starting point makes clear what problems we are addressing, what problems we are ignoring, and forces us to make explicit some of our central assumptions' (Meara, 1989: 12).

There are several reasons for taking Levelt's model as a starting point. The model is based on several decades of psycholinguistic research and is based on a wealth of empirical data, obtained through experimental research and the observation of speech errors. The present model is a further development of earlier proposals by Garrett (1975), Dell (1986), and Kempen and Hoenkamp (1987). A major advantage of the model is that it is not restricted to parts of the production process: its strength lies in the integration of the different parts.

In the following sections I will give a brief and global description of Levelt's model, subsequently I will consider how such a model should be adapted to make it suitable to describe the bilingual speaker, and finally some alternatives are presented for parts of the model. A full description of the model in only a few pages is impossible: it takes Levelt (1989) some 500 pages of rather dense text to present the model in full.

The bilingual version of the model presented here is not completely new or unique. It shares a number of characteristics with earlier proposals by Macnamara (1967), Dechert (1984), Hieke (1986), and Perecman (1989).

Levelt's model

The model aims at describing the normal, spontaneous language production of adults. It is a 'steady-state' model, and not a language learning model, and it

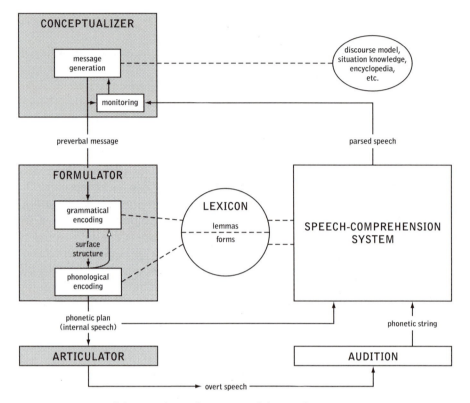

Figure 17.1   Levelt's speech production model (Levelt, 1989: Fig. 1.1.)

hardly says anything about language perception. The model is not concerned with reading and writing and it is not aimed at the explanation of language disorders of a central or peripheral nature.

A distinction is made between declarative knowledge – which includes encyclopaedic knowledge (conceptual and lexical knowledge in particular) and situational discourse knowledge – and procedural knowledge, which is relevant to the processing of declarative knowledge. Procedural knowledge forms part of the different processing components. A final general characteristic is that the same lexicon is used for production and perception.

Figure 17.1 presents a blueprint for the speaker. Boxes represent processing components, circles and ellipses represent knowledge stores. In this model the following components are distinguished:

- *A knowledge component* which is more or less separate from the production system and where general knowledge of the world and more specific knowledge about the interactional situation is stored. Levelt's description of this part of the model is not very extensive, and it is not really clear what it actually does or does not contain.

- *A conceptualizer*: this is where the selection and ordering of relevant information takes place and where the intentions the speaker wishes to realize are adapted in such a way that they can be converted into language. The output of this component is so-called 'preverbal messages', in other words messages which contain all the necessary information to convert meaning into language, but which are not themselves linguistic. In the planning of preverbal messages two stages can be distinguished: macroplanning and microplanning. Macroplanning involves the elaboration of communicative goals/intentions and the retrieval of the information needed to express these goals, while microplanning is 'the speaker's elaboration of a communicative intention by selecting the information whose expression may realize the communicative goals' (Levelt, 1989: 5).

- *A formulator*, where the preverbal message is converted into a speech plan (phonetic plan) by selecting the right words or lexical units and applying grammatical and phonological rules. According to several researchers (Kempen and Huijbers, 1983; Levelt and Schriefers, 1987) lexical items consist of two parts: the lemma and the morpho-phonological form or lexeme. In the lemma, the lexical entry's meaning and syntax are represented, while morphological and phonological properties are represented in the lexeme. In production, lexical items are activated by matching the meaning part of the lemma with the semantic information in the preverbal message. Accordingly, the information from the lexicon is made available in two phases: semantic activation precedes form activation. The lemma information of a lexical item concerns both conceptual specifications of its use, such as pragmatic and stylistic conditions, and (morpho-)syntactic information, including the lemma's syntactic category and its grammatical functions, as well as information that is needed for its syntactical encoding (in particular: number, tense, aspect, mood, case, and pitch accent). Activation of the lemma immediately provides the relevant syntactic information which in turn activates syntactic procedures. The selection of the lemmas and the relevant syntactic information leads to the formation of the surface structure. While the surface structure is being formed, the morpho-phonological information belonging to the lemma is activated and encoded. The phonological encoding provides the input for the articulator in the form of a phonetic plan. This phonetic plan can be scanned internally by the speaker via the speech-comprehension system, which provides the first possibility for feedback.

- *An articulator* which converts the speech plan into actual speech. The output from the formulator is processed and temporarily stored in such a way that the phonetic plan can be fed back to the speech-comprehension system and the speech can be produced at normal speed.

- *A speech-comprehension system* connected with an auditory system which plays a role in the two ways in which feedback takes place within the model: the phonetic plan as well as the overt speech are guided to the speech-comprehension system to find any mistakes that may have crept in.

In order to try to clarify the workings of this model I will illustrate the various components by using an example. Imagine we want to say: *The train from Amsterdam arrives at platform four*. We know from our knowledge of the world that trains regularly arrive at platforms and stop there, and that there is more than one platform. The communicative intention is pre-processed in the conceptualizer, after which the contextual information is passed on to the formulator in manageable chunks in the preverbal message. How this information is passed on is not exactly clear. It is possible that we have some sort of mental image of trains, platforms, and arrivals which is then transformed into interpretable information. The preverbal message also contains information about topic and comment assignment. In other words, it specifies whether the sentence will become *It is on platform four that the train from Amsterdam will arrive* or *It is the train from Amsterdam that will arrive on platform four*. Now the formulator becomes involved in the process. An important characteristic of this model is that the lexical items needed in the utterance are retrieved first and that the characteristics of these items determine the application of grammatical and phonological rules. In other words, the selection of the verb *arrive* automatically entails that there is a subject, something or some one that arrives, but that there is no object, and that adverbials of time and place are optional. Furthermore, information has been processed which says that only one train will arrive, so the verb is provided with the relevant morphological information which ensures the correct use of the inflectional suffix (–(e)s). Selecting these items also entails that information about their pronunciation is included so that what comes out of the formulator is a grammatical unit, as well as clues as to the pronunciation of the words of that sentence. The phonetic plan is temporarily stored in the buffer and fed back to the speech-comprehension plan, and sent on to the articulator which makes sure it is actually pronounced by activating and driving the entire speech mechanism, which leads to the production of the sentence *The train from Amsterdam arrives at platform four* with the right segmental and suprasegmental cues.

In the model, production takes place 'from left to right', i.e. the next processor will start working on the output of the current processor even if this output is still incomplete. In addition, there is no need to look back continually in time to see what has already been produced. This means that when a part of an utterance has left the conceptualizer and is being formulated, it cannot in any way influence the construction of parts that follow: each part of the utterance that leaves the conceptualizer passes through the whole system more or less by itself; without taking account of what may follow later on. Furthermore, production is incremental, so as soon as the information which goes with one part of the utterance is passed on to the formulator, the conceptualizer does not wait for that chunk to go through the whole system but immediately starts on the next part. In this way various parts of the same sentence will be at different processing stages: when the first part is being produced by the articulator, the last part may not have left the conceptualizer. Consequently the different components are at work simultaneously. Processing is largely automatic. Greatest attention is paid to conceptualizing and some attention is paid to the feedback mechanisms, but the remainder functions without conscious control. Production has to be incremental, parallel, and automatized in order to account for the enormous speed at which language is produced.

Requirements which a bilingual version of this model should meet

The requirements which a unilingual version of the model should meet are already relatively high, and a bilingual version has to meet additional requirements. In general it should provide an explanation for all phenomena associated with balanced and non-balanced bilinguals' speech. To be more specific, the most important demands are as follows:

- The model must account for the fact that the two language systems can be used entirely separately or mixed depending on the situation. Extensive literature on code-switching (for reviews, see Giesbers, 1989; Nortier, 1989) shows that all degrees do occur: from complete separation to extensive mixing of the two systems. The issue of code-switching will be dealt with later on in this article.
- Cross-linguistic influences have to be accounted for in the functioning of the model. There is a host of literature on cross-linguistic influences (see, for example, Kellerman and Sharwood Smith, 1986; Odlin, 1989). Research in this field was, of course, not set up to test the present model, but the outcomes of that research should not be at odds with the model.
- The fact that a bilingual uses more than one language should not lead to a significant deceleration of the production system. It is very likely that the production system has sufficient over-capacity to deal with language production problems. Mägiste (1986) observed a slight slowing down in language processing of multilinguals in a very demanding experimental setting, but there is no research which compares the speed of normal language production of unilinguals and bilinguals.

- Assuming that people seldom achieve 'total' bilingualism, the model should be able to deal with the fact that the speaker does not master both language systems to the same extent. First and second language proficiency can vary from very low to (near-)native. These differences in proficiency can be the result of incomplete acquisition, but also of loss of language skills in the first or the second language (cf. Weltens, 1989; de Bot and Clyne, 1989). It would be reasonable to assume that the extent to which the speaker has command of the two systems has consequences for the organization within the model and the way in which the model works.

- The model should be able to cope with a potentially unlimited number of languages, and must be able to represent interactions between these different languages. Typological differences between languages should therefore not cause problems. The languages of a bilingual may be typologically closely related or completely unrelated. However, this does not imply that the structural differences between the bilingual's languages are irrelevant for the workings of the model.

Single or double components?

For each of the components represented in Figure 17.1, the question should be asked whether these components are able to play their role in the production of the bilingual's speech without fundamental changes being made to them. Our aim is to keep the original model intact as much as possible and to revert to adaptations only if empirical findings on language production cannot be explained with the existing model. As compared to unilingual speech, the amount of empirical research on bilingual language production is rather sparse. For different components relevant data is still missing, therefore the model as described below invokes at least as many questions as it answers.

The knowledge component and the conceptualizer

We assume that the knowledge component is not language specific, and that a single system will suffice. This system is aware, for example, that conventions in conversation in Thailand are different to those in Great Britain and will supply the conceptualizer with the appropriate information. There is a crucial question to be asked here: which part of the system is involved in choosing the language to be used in an utterance, and what information is this choice based on? One possibility would be to assume that the knowledge component is involved in this choice: it contains a 'discourse model', a list of limiting conditions for the speech which is to be generated. We may assume that the choice of language depends on these conditions. However, the role of the knowledge component is not very clear.

Indirectly, Levelt gives some indication as to the place where the choice is made: he repeatedly points to the use of 'registers' which he defines as 'varieties which may have characteristic syntactic, lexical and phonological properties' (1989: 368). In adopting such a broad definition registers are no longer clearly distinguishable from 'varieties' and 'languages'. The same idea is found in the work of Paradis (1987) who also assumes that there is no difference, theoretically, between the different registers used by a unilingual speaker and the languages spoken by a multilingual speaker. Although Levelt explicitly refuses to go into the question of whether the use of a register is conceptually conditioned (Paradis, 1987: 183), the description of 'registers' (Paradis, 1987: 368) leads unambiguously to the conclusion that information about the register is already present in the preverbal message and subsequently plays a role in the selection of register-specific lexical items as well as the way in which these items are encoded. For the moment we therefore assume that information about the language to be chosen is included in the preverbal messages. This assumption is supported by the fact that in conversation between bilinguals, the language choice expresses communicative intentions and therefore carries meaning (Giesbers, 1989: 317).

Levelt assumes that the conceptualizer is language-specific (1989:103–4). He argues this point by referring to differences in concepts between languages. In the case of spatial reference, for example, Dutch, like English, only makes one conceptual distinction (proximal/distal: *hier/daar* (*here/there*), *dit/dat* (*this/that*)) where Spanish makes two such distinctions (proximal/medial/distal: *aquí/ahí/allí*). These distinctions would have to be defined in the preverbal message. Because Dutch does not make these distinctions and Spanish does, the preverbal messages for the same speech intention should be different for each of these two languages. One possibility is to assume that the first of the two processes that take place in the conceptualizer, the macroplanning, is not language-specific, while microplanning is language-specific, in accordance with Levelt's proposals. It could of course be argued that the preverbal message should contain all the possible relevant information for all possible languages, thus the proximal/medial/distal distinction for Spanish, tense and aspect for languages like English and Dutch, and shape characteristics for Navaho. Although this is not impossible in principle, it is not a very economic solution. It is more likely that in the first phase, the macroplanning, the language to be used is selected on the basis of information from the discourse model and that accordingly language-specific encoding takes place in microplanning.

A language production problem that unilinguals are not often faced with, but which is quite normal for non-balanced bilinguals, is that a concept has to be expressed in a particular language which does not have the lexical items needed to express that concept, or for which the relevant item cannot be found (in time). This will lead to problems in the formulator during the grammatical encoding stage, i.e. when the lemmas are selected from the lexicon. In the present version of the model this problem is still unsolved, not only for bilingual but also for unilingual production. In one way or another the conceptualizer should 'know' that a given concept cannot be lexicalized properly, but it is absolutely unclear how this takes place. At the same time, studies using introspective techniques suggest that foreign language learners anticipate lexical problems and use different strategies to avoid them (Poulisse, 1990).

The formulator and the lexicon

For both procedural grammatical/morpho-phonological knowledge and for declarative lexical knowledge there must be systems for every language that can be called upon. There are two explanations we can think of to account for this:

1   There is a separate formulator and a separate lexicon for each language. This solves the problem of having to separate the two systems. It will cost some storage capacity, but it is economical because there is no need to have a system that controls the co-ordination and separation of the two languages. It is, however, unclear how the two languages can be used simultaneously, during code-switching for example.
2   There is one large system which stores all the information, linguistically labelled in some way, about all the different languages. The problem which results from this solution is that it does not explain how the systems are separated in bilinguals without this causing apparent problems.

When we take into account research which has been done on storage and retrieval of lexical and syntactic information by bilinguals, we could imagine a probable solution somewhere between these two extremes. Elements/knowledge of the two languages may be represented and stored separately for each language or in a shared system depending on a number of factors. The most important of these seem to be the linguistic distance between the two languages and the level of proficiency in the languages involved. Although linguistic distance is a notion which still remains problematic (for a discussion, see Hinskens, 1988), it does seem possible to place languages along a continuum based on formal character-istics such as the number of cognates in languages or sets of shared syntactic characteristics.

It would not be unreasonable to assume that the linguistic difference between Dutch dialects is smaller than the distance between the standard Dutch variety and other standard languages, and that French is more closely related to Dutch than Moroccan Arabic. Based on neurolinguistic research, Paradis (1987: 16) formulates the hypothesis of coherence between linguistic distance and separate or joint storage as follows: 'According to such a view cerebral representation of bilingualism would be on a language pair-specific continuum, ranging from a bi- or multiregister unilingualism to a bilingualism involving two related languages.'

So this means that the speaker who speaks two closely related languages will for the most part use the same procedural and lexical knowledge when speaking either of the two languages, while in the case of languages which are not related, an appeal is made to much more language-specific knowledge.

The level of proficiency is an obvious factor where separate or jointly stored knowledge about the two languages is concerned (Grosjean, 1982; Hakuta, 1986). A person who knows a few words and sentences in a foreign language will not have a separate system for this. The first-language system is flexible enough to add an additional register to those already in existence. How the organization of the two languages develops as second language proficiency increases remains a crucial question. There has been very little research into the relationship between the level of proficiency and the organization of the bilingual lexicon. Kerkman (1984) found that balanced bilinguals (lecturers of English at university) store the two languages separately to a greater extent than non-balanced bilinguals (students of English at secondary school and at university). It is, however, not exactly clear what 'stored separately' means. This point will be discussed later on in this chapter.

The mental lexicon

Information about the words in a speaker's language is stored in the mental lexicon. The right words, that is to say the lexical items which express the intended meanings, are retrieved based on the conceptual information which is contained in the preverbal message. A lexical item is retrieved on the basis of its meaning. In the lemma the relevant syntactic information is activated, and in the form part of the item the relevant morphological and phonological information is activated as well. It is assumed that idioms and phrases can be entries in the mental lexicon.

The link between meaning and syntactic information in the lemma is a crucial aspect of Levelt's model. If the syntactic information does not become available via the meaning, the surface structure cannot be constructed. This essential point is also important when the model is applied to bilingualism: if we do not take a very Whorfian position, the idea could be defended by stating that the meaning part of the lemma is not language-specific, and could therefore be shared by more than one language. At the same time meaning and syntax are so closely linked that single storage is only conceivable when lemmas are exactly similar in both meaning and syntax in both languages. The situation is somewhat different for the morpho-phonological information of the lexical item which is retrieved during the formation of the surface structure: there may be single or dual storage depending on the similarity of form of the two items. For example: when a Dutch/German cognate like *Antwort/Antwoord* is retrieved, different lemmas may be called upon because of differences in syntax (gender), despite the great similarity in form. Usually these different lemmas will be connected with different morpho-phonological forms, but this is not necessarily the case. When two lexical items only differ syntactically, then a reference to the same form is conceivable. In the same way as ambiguous words in a language are connected with the same form from different lemmas, reference to cognates may take place from language-specific lemmas to forms that are not language-specific. These considerations make it clear that the prevailing ideas about the organization of the bilingual lexicon in terms of one or two lexicons are gravely oversimplified.

A lot of research has been done to answer the question of how the bilingual lexicon is organized, ever since Kolers' work in the early sixties (Kolers, 1963). For Kolers the question was simply: are the words of two different languages stored in one big container or in two separate ones? The answer to this question is not simply 'one' or 'two', because various factors appear to play a role in the way in which words are stored. Now the question is no longer whether the systems are separated or not, but under what conditions and for which parts of the lexicon they are separated. Based on neurolinguistic research with bilinguals, Paradis (1987) mentions four different options to explain storage of the two languages in the brain.

1   The 'Extended System Hypothesis': there is no separate storage for each language; elements from a second language are simply stored with what is already there.
2   The 'Dual System Hypothesis', which assumes that there are separate systems for each language, with separate sets of phonemes, rules, and words.
3   The 'Tripartite System Hypothesis', which assumes that language-specific elements are stored separately and joint elements, such as cognates, together.
4   The 'Subset Hypothesis', which assumes the use of a single storage system where links between elements are strengthened through continued use. This implies that, in general, elements from one language will be more strongly linked to each other than to elements from another language, which results in the formation of subsets which appear to consist of elements from the same language, and which can be retrieved separately. At the same time links between elements in different languages will be just as strong as links between elements in one language in bilingual speakers who employ a 'code-switching-mode', and who live in a community where code-switching is a normal conversational strategy.

The Subset Hypothesis is in line with Levelt's description of items in the mental lexicon in general: '[A lexical item] may have particular pragmatic, stylistic, and affective features that make it fit one context of discourse better than another' (Levelt, 1989:183).

The Subset Hypothesis is closely related to current models of the lexicon which are based on 'activation spreading' (for a survey, see Dell, 1986). In an approach such as this the basic question of whether there are one or two systems has become irrelevant. Research should be aimed at factors which influence the extent of the relationship between elements and how these links work: the extent to which the elements are semantically related doubtless plays a role, but the question remains whether relationships between elements in different languages are equally close in both directions. It is possible that a non-balanced bilingual speaker of Dutch (first language, i.e. L1) and English (second language, i.e. L2) is less inclined to think of the Dutch *paard* (*horse*) when faced with the English *horse* than vice versa (for a discussion, see Kerkman and de Bot, 1989; supportive evidence is also provided by Keatly *et al.*, 1989).

The enormous speed at which speech is processed, in relation to the size of the data-set (i.e. the total of the declarative and procedural knowledge) on which production is based, is one of the most important issues in the construction of a speech production model. This is especially true for lexical processes. It is not known, and not very easy to measure, how big the average speaker's lexicon actually is. Oldfield (1963) estimates that the average first-year university student in Great Britain has a passive lexicon of about 75,000 words at his disposal. Although the number of words we use actively is smaller, the active lexicon may still consist of about 30,000 words. The language user continually has to make the right choice from this enormous collection of words. When we consider that the average rate of speech is 150 words per minute, with peak rates of about 300 words per minute, this means that we have about 200 to 400 milliseconds to choose a word when we are speaking. In other words: 2 to 5 times a second we have to make the right choice from those 30,000 words. And usually we are successful; it is estimated that the probability of making the wrong choice is one in a thousand.

The above-mentioned is relevant for the hypothetical unilingual speaker. The situation is even more complex for the bilingual speaker. Even if we assume that the bilingual's lexicon is smaller for each language than the unilingual's lexicon, and that a proportion of the words are the same in different languages (cognates such as *television* or *multinational*), the total lexicon, even the active lexicon, would easily contain more than 60,000 elements. In order to get an idea of the complexity of the task one might think of someone who has to find a specific marble of a particular colour in a container with 60,000 different marbles 2 to 5 times a second.

Obviously, it is not the case that for the word selection process each individual lexical item is looked at to see if it is suitable every time a choice has to be made. There is no doubt that our brain is a very powerful calculator, but this is probably too demanding a task. The lexicon must be organized in such a way that a choice can be made quickly and accurately. In order to achieve this, irrelevant words have to be eliminated as quickly as possible in the search process. One possibility is that for the bilingual, the lexical items from one language can be retrieved as a separate set. The question is how this is achieved. In order to find the answer, it would be useful at this point to examine a few contemporary theories about the lexicon (for a survey, see Kerkman, 1984). A distinction is made between active and passive models. In active models the characteristics which words should comply with are defined, and subsequently the lexicon is scanned until the right candidate is found. An active retrieval process like this is very time-consuming because the entire lexicon has to be scanned. There are alternative versions of this active model, one alternative being, for example, that words are ordered according to frequency of occurrence, or on the basis of semantic field characteristics. Such orderings make lexical searches far more efficient: after all, we usually use frequent words because we talk about a limited number of topics. Yet this type of model does not seem very suitable because it is reasonably slow.

A more promising type of model is the passive model. The workings of this type can be explained as follows. A lexical element has a number of characteristics and must be stimulated to a certain level in order to become activated. The lexical element has detectors for all these characteristics which continuously monitor the preverbal message to see if these characteristics are present. If this is the case, the element is stimulated. As soon as a number of characteristics belonging to one element are asked for, it will become active: it will present itself as a candidate for a given slot. For example: suppose we are looking for the word *sampan*. This word has many characteristics, such as 'inanimate', 'made of wood', 'ship', 'sailing the Sea of China', but for some people also 'one of those words they use in the tip-of-the-tongue experiments'. If these characteristics are asked for, each characteristic stimulates a number of lexical items, but it is only when the number of characteristics is sufficiently large that the search is completed and *sampan* is retrieved. These types of models, of which Morton's 'logogen model' (Morton, 1979) is the best known, are called passive because there is no active lexical search: candidates automatically present themselves as a result of the information that is given. Passive models have an important advantage: they are extremely fast; by giving a number of characteristics, the number of possible candidates is narrowed down very quickly. Although this solution also presents some problems (for example, the Hypernym problem, see Levelt, 1989: 212–14), it is by far the best model available at the moment.

The main question to be answered with respect to the bilingual lexicon is: how does the selection of lexical items take place in bilinguals? This entails the question of how the systems are kept apart or mixed depending on the situation. A major advantage of the Subset Hypothesis presented earlier in this article is that the set from which the choice has to be made has been reduced dramatically as a result of the fact that a particular language/subset has been chosen. Research on code-switching, cross-linguistic influences, and aphasia has shown however that bilinguals cannot simply switch their language 'on' and 'off'. Green (1986) makes a plausible suggestion by saying that language spoken by bilinguals or multilinguals can have three levels of activation:

1   *Selected*: The selected language controls the speech output.
2   *Active*: The active language plays a role in ongoing processing, works parallel to the selected language and does the same things in fact, but has no access to the outgoing speech channel.
3   *Dormant*: A dormant language is stored in long-term memory, but does not play a role in ongoing processing.

Depending on the situation (the discourse model) languages are selected, active or dormant. One language is always selected, but more than one language can be active or latent. In many situations there is only one selected language and a number of latent languages. During speaking, the words will initially be chosen from the selected language, or from the active language if necessary, and as a last resort from the dormant language, with considerable loss of time as a result. Extreme cases of dormant languages are the mother tongues of immigrants, like the Dutch in Australia: the Dutch immigrants have spoken English almost exclusively for years and they are faced with retrieval problems when they attempt to reactivate their knowledge of the mother tongue. Once they succeed, it is surprising how much knowledge of the language they have retained (de Bot, 1990).

Green's idea of different levels of activation is in line with Færch and Kasper's (1986) suggestions for 'primary' (≈ selected) and 'secondary' (≈ active/dormant) knowledge. An important aspect of Green's proposals is that the active language does everything the selected language also does: it selects lexical items, forms sentences, generates surface structures, and eventually even makes a phonetic plan. The only difference is that the phonetic plan of the active language is not fed into the articulator. Phenomena associated with fluent and frequent code-switching can be explained as a result of this type of parallel production. The notion of parallel production is supported by findings from unilingual research into ambiguous words and speech errors which shows that more candidate-items are available in speaking (Swinney, 1979). For bilinguals Macnamara had already suggested this solution in 1967: 'The most likely solution [for code-switching] is that the bilingual has the capacity to activate the L2 system, carry out the semantic encoding, the selection of words and the syntactic organization while more or less mechanically producing in L1 material which has already been prepared for production' (Macnamara, 1967: 70). Similar ideas have been put forward by Lipski (1978) and Altenberg and Cairns (1983).

Summarizing, a useful extension of the model would be to assume that there is a separate system for every language as far as the processing components in the formulators are concerned. Lexical items are selected from one common lexicon in which items are connected in networks which enable subsets of items to be activated. One such subset can be the items from a specific language.

Following Green's ideas, we assume that there are two speech plans. In order to explain why a particular language is used at a specific time we have to assume that for each part of the preverbal message information is included as to the language in which this part should be articulated.

One of the most salient characteristics of a non-balanced bilingual is the occurrence of lexical retrieval problems. Those problems can have various causes: the words may never have been acquired in the first place or retrieval takes more time than the production system will allow ('speech need'). Based on research by Levelt and Maassen (1981) and Bock (1986; 1987), Levelt assumes that during production retrieval problems are not directly reported to the conceptualizer, in other words, when the preverbal message is being generated, the possibility that one or more of the lexical items needed may not be available (on time) is not taken into account. With respect to the form characteristics of a lexical item which has already been activated the situation is probably different: it would appear that problems during phonological encoding lead to a revision of syntactic frames in such a way that the time involved in generating speech is not affected. Whether feedback takes place directly or via the speech plan's internal feedback mechanism is not very clear. Lexical retrieval problems are fairly rare in a unilingual non-aphasic speaker. For a bilingual speaker who does not have a perfect command of one of the languages these problems are commonplace, and the question is whether a bilingual speaking-model can do without a mechanism that provides information about the availability of lexical items (i.e. both lemma and form characteristics) when the preverbal message is being generated. The alternative is that for each item that cannot be found a new feedback loop has to be initiated which inevitably leads to a major delay in speech production. The existence of a checking system like this will be brought to light by adapted versions of Levelt and Maassen's and Bock's experiments.

Languages differ in both the nature and size of the lexicon, not only because the number of lemmas may be different but also because the morphological characteristics of a language lead to a higher or lower lexical productivity in a particular language. In agglutinative languages such as Turkish and Finnish (as opposed to English) there will be fewer letter/sound combinations which have the status of 'lexical item', because in those languages stem–suffix combinations, which may be constructed every time they are used, express the meaning and function of lexical items in languages like English. It is not clear when a string of letters/sounds is assigned the status of 'lexical item'. It is conceivable that a certain combination which 'started off' as a stem–suffix combination eventually becomes an independent lemma through frequent use and because of reasons of efficiency. In a number of ways the production process of 'conservative' languages such as English is different from that of agglutinative languages. These differences in the relationship between lemma/information about meaning and morpho-phonological information provide support for the postulation of separated formulators for each language.

Phonological encoding and articulation

The next step in the production process is the phonological encoding. For unilingual speakers there is substantial evidence to show that sounds are not the units of speech planning. It is more likely that speech is encoded and produced in larger units. Levelt assumes that syllables are the basic units of articulatory execution. In fact, phonetic plans for words consist of a number of syllable programs. The speaker has an inventory of syllables that need not be generated from scratch every time a word is produced. Syllable programs are stored for articulatory patterns. The phonetic plan consists of a string of syllable programs. The number of syllable programs for a specific language is not too large. It is estimated that a non-syllabic language such as English has between 6,000 and 7,000 different syllables that actually appear in words. This concerns a count on written language, however, so it does not take into account all sorts of allophones which result from regional and social variation. This number of syllables is small enough to allow for their storage in the lexicon. For syllabic languages such as Chinese, the number of syllables is much smaller.

For the bilingual speaker the situation may depend on the level of proficiency attained in the two languages. Syllable programs are typically automatized, and the level of automaticity is likely to be correlated with level of proficiency. For the more advanced bilingual it is not inconceivable that there is one large set of syllable programs for all languages. The number of different syllables to be stored may become very large, but analogous to what has been said before about the lexicon, syllable programs that are the same for two languages will not be stored twice, while language-specific ones will be uniquely represented. A question not easily answered is, what is meant by 'the same for two languages'. Syllables are supposed to be the smallest relatively invariant articulatory units in speech production (Fujimura and Lovins, 1978), but it is unclear how invariant syllables are for the bilingual. Flege (1986) presents data that suggest that bilinguals tend to classify sounds from the second language in categories of the first language as much as they can.

In his chapter on articulation Levelt, after considering a number of theories, opts for a 'model referenced control' model. In this model, speakers have an internal model ('sensory images') of the sounds which are to be produced (or actually of the syllables, the units of speech production). The speaker has an internal model of his own speech system and knows how it should be adjusted in order to produce a particular sound. The sound itself does not actually need to be pronounced to achieve this. The speaker is able to simulate the sound internally and to check whether the chosen configuration is applicable in the situation or phonological context. Any possible deviations from the normal situation, such as talking while smoking a pipe, are accounted for when the system is adjusted. The internal model is not a system of innate values, but it is based on extensive experience in listening to one's own speech. Oller and MacNeilage (1983) show that the model has not yet been perfected in four- to nine-year-olds and that deviations from the normal situation do not always result in optimal accommodation.

The bilingual speaker must have models for all sounds/syllables in the different languages. If the units of production were sounds, then it is unnecessary to assume double/separated systems for the articulator: the existing collection of normalized sounds in L1 can be extended with additional sounds when a new language is acquired, and it is not inconceivable that the L1 norms apply to the L2 as long as possible. This could mean that for the advanced L2 speaker, the sounds which are similar in the two languages are represented by one single norm, while language-specific sounds develop their own norm. Cross-linguistic influence at the phonological level can be explained by the fact that the L1 norm is maintained when L2 sounds are being realized. The quality of the L2 norm will depend on the frequency of use of the language, the amount and quality of language contact, and the extent to which subtle differences between L1 and L2 sounds can be perceived. It is interesting to note that we do not know whether the absence of a perfect model for an L2 sound has repercussions for speech planning at other levels: does (the awareness of) the absence of a particular norm lead to the avoidance of word forms in which this sound occurs? As indicated above, Levelt's model is characterized by the absence of direct feedback mechanisms. It will have to be made clear experimentally whether this type of form-driven avoidance does in fact take place.

Prosody is one of the most important characteristics of speech. Information about prosodic aspects is generated mainly by the formulator. The phonological encoding module (see Figure 17.1) contains a prosody generator. This generator processes four types of input:

- 'intonational meaning', which includes the meaning of a particular intonational pattern, in particular the illocutionary functions;
- information about the surface structure, including the assignment of stress;
- information about the metrical structure of utterances;
- information about the segmental structure of utterances.

Based on information from these four sources, the prosody generator constructs a temporal structure and a pitch contour for the utterance. It is not known how the different components lead to the choice of a specific pitch contour (Levelt, 1989:

398). It seems likely that a choice is made from a restricted set of relevant pitch movements ('nuclear tones'). This set may be different for different languages or for different dialects of one language (Pijper, 1983; Willems, 1983).

How should this part of the model be adjusted to make it suitable to be used for bilingual speakers? The prosody generator's input is largely language-specific. The relationship between certain intonational patterns and their related meanings/connotations (for example, 'disbelief', 'joy') are different in each language (Keijsper, 1984; Bolinger, 1989: 26). Languages also differ with respect to metrical rules. A well-known distinction in this respect is the difference between 'stress-timed' languages like Dutch and English and 'syllable-timed' languages like French, Spanish, and Hungarian (Dauer, 1983). Information on the surface structure and segmental structure is also to a considerable extent language-specific. And, finally, the intonation contours from which the prosody generator can make a choice show differences between languages. If there were separate systems for the above-mentioned components for each language then it would be reasonable to assume that these systems would not influence one another; they function only when 'their language' is asked for. Although relatively little research has been carried out to examine cross-linguistic influences in prosody, and research in this field has been rather impressionistic (for a survey, see de Bot, 1986), it is clear that this dual system hypothesis is hardly tenable. Successive bilinguals in particular, that is to say people who were not brought up bilingually, appear to have many intonational characteristics from their L1 in their L2. Their foreign accent is highly determined by prosodic cues. The undeniable fact that only very few bilingual speakers completely master the prosodic aspects of the two languages must be accounted for in a bilingual model. A tentative conclusion would seem justified for the articulator. There is only one articulator for bilingual speakers which has an extensive set of sounds and pitch patterns from both languages to work with. The extent to which these sounds and patterns are more or less perfect models depends on the frequency and quality of contact with the L2. Extensive evidence of cross-linguistic influences at the pronunciation and phonological level suggests that L1 models continue to play a role even when the speaker has excellent command of the L2. This evidence makes the existence of two separate systems very improbable.

If we propose that each language has its own formulator, it would seem natural to assume a separate speech-comprehension system for each language as well. A discussion on this topic is outside the scope of this chapter.

Testing the adapted model against the requirements

Earlier in this chapter we set a number of requirements which the bilingual model should meet. In this section we explore to what extent the adapted model meets these requirements.

Separation of systems, code-switching, and cross-linguistic influence

By assuming that there are separate formulators and lexical subsets for each language and by adopting Green's ideas regarding the activation of different languages, it is plausible that the bilingual can keep the two language systems separate.

Accounting for the fact that bilinguals are capable of switching from one language to another very quickly and without much difficulty is less easy. Very relevant in this respect is Giesbers' study (1989). In his investigations into code-switching between a dialect and the standard language he tries to link different types of code-switching to components of a language production model, in his case the model developed by Kempen (Kempen and Hoenkamp, 1987). This model shares many of the characteristics of Levelt's model. One essential difference is that Kempen assigns an important role to the system which monitors all the subsystems' output, while Levelt assumes that it is only in the last/lower stages of the production process that monitoring or feedback takes place.

Giesbers distinguishes three basic forms of code-switching:

- intended, situationally motivated switches;
- contextual switches which are connected with the topic of conversation; and
- performance switches which include code-switching as a speech style or a speaking-mode.

Intended switches result from a choice at the conceptual level: through the choice of the language additional information is conveyed. Contextual switches originate in the grammatical encoding component and occur more particularly during the selection of lemmas. In Kempen's model this takes place in the 'lexico-syntactic module'. One of the mechanisms could be that the level of activation of particular lexical items in another language than the one being spoken is increased to such an extent by the conversational topic for example, that these lexical items will become more readily available. Another possibility is that the discourse model conveys the information that the conversational setting allows for any switching to take place, and that accordingly in the macroplanning no strict indications as to language choice are added, which may lead to more or less random switching. Performance-switches are justified by Kempen's morpho-phonological module which corresponds to Levelt's phonological encoding component. Giesbers assumes that these performance-switches are the result of form characteristics being more or less randomly linked to lemmas in the surface structure. In their research on L2 production by Dutch learners of English, Poulisse and Bongaerts (1990) found the same type of switches, which they call 'automatic switches'.

Although Giesbers' proposed linking of types of code-switching and modules in the language production system is definitely a crucial step forward, this does not mean that all problems are automatically solved. As he indicates himself, a sharp division between types cannot always be maintained (Giesbers, 1989: 319), and there are sentences in his corpus which seem to indicate that the switching occurring in these utterances was planned at the conceptual level even though they have the form of a non-intended switch. Contextual switches present an additional problem. There must be a specific subset in the lexicon in which lexical elements within one language can be activated but also a subset which contains lexical elements from different languages. This means that there must be separate subsystems which decrease or increase the extent of code-switching depending on the conversational setting and topic. If we adhere to the subset hypothesis we can provide an explanation for what happens with so-called triggerwords. These words which appear to trigger code-switching because they are similar in form in different languages typically figure in more than one subset/network and activation of this subset in language A leads to activation of another subset which includes this word in language B. Or, to put it more simply, the wrong turn is taken at the crossing.

In research on code-switching, several universal linguistic constraints have been postulated. Clyne (1987) reviews these constraints and concludes that basic assumptions for them are wanting and that therefore the basis for most of these constraints is rather weak. This also holds for what has been called the 'equivalence constraint', which postulates that the syntax on either side of a switch must be grammatical for the language concerned. In his study on bidialectal code-switching, Giesbers (1989) found that in general the equivalence constraint was met in his corpus, while Nortier's (1989) study on Dutch/Moroccan-Arabic code-switching showed that this constraint was not valid for her data. For languages that are structurally similar, as in Giesbers' study, there is equivalence, which is not very surprising, while for less related languages there is no equivalence.

One of the explanations given by Clyne for the occurrence of equivalence in code-switched sentences is that bilinguals actively converge in order to facilitate code-switching. In the terms of the present model this could suggest that in cases where a speaker can make a choice between two possible constructions in a language, that construction will be selected that is closest to the equivalent in the other language.

Many instances of cross-linguistic influences are related to code-switching and cannot be simply separated from this on theoretical or empirical grounds. Theoretically it is possible to restrict the term code-switching to cases where the speaker has a good command of both languages and is thus able, in principle, to convey the relevant information in both languages. In her research on Dutch/ Moroccan-Arabic code-switching, Nortier (1989) showed that for a large proportion of the L2 words that appear to cause a switch to L1, her informants actually used these words correctly in other parts of the conversation. It could still be the case that these words were not readily available at that very moment, but they were certainly neither lost, nor never acquired.

Cross-linguistic influences can be indicative of a lack of knowledge. When the knowledge of the L2 is insufficient, the speaker may 'borrow' from the L1.

Slowing down of the production process

Slowing need not occur as a result of more than one language being active in the model as we have described it. Separately used the languages do not get in each other's ways or paths. In addition, languages may differ by convention with respect to the speed of delivery. Möhle (1984) has shown that native speakers of French take longer to describe a given set of cartoons than native speakers of German, and her conclusion is that French speakers are apparently faced with more processing problems than German speakers. This interpretation is not really convincing. The stylistics of German and French may simply differ for that kind of language-use situation. Direct comparisons of native speakers and less proficient speakers of the language is complicated by the fact that L2 learners may indeed have processing problems that cause a deceleration of the speech rate, but at the same time these learners may not be fully acquainted with stylistic conventions. For code-switching comparable problems arise. There has been no research into the difference in the rate of production for subjects who do or do not code-switch. Research by Giesbers (1989) on timing aspects of bidialectal code-switching suggests that there is indeed a tendency to pause before switches, but the same holds for other structural aspects. In fact, he concludes that pausing behaviour is not typically different for code-switching sites. Furthermore a slower speech rate could be part of the 'code-switching mode'. In such a mode the slower rate does not result from capacity problems the system might have; it is instead a more or less consciously chosen style.

Lower speech rates for bilinguals as compared to monolinguals are to be expected for the 'minor' language. For perceptual tasks such a difference in speed has been reported repeatedly in the literature. It is quite obvious that a lower level of proficiency leads to less automatized processing and accordingly to a lower speech rate.

Unequal command of the two languages

As indicated, the model is not aimed at describing and explaining the acquisition process; it is a 'steady-state' model. It should be capable, however, of describing the bilingual system at any moment and at all stages of development. The model does not have to justify how development from stage A to stage B takes place. The majority of bilinguals will not have a complete command of both languages, whatever that may mean. If the above-mentioned extensions to the model (in particular the doubling of the formulator and the development of language-specific subsets in the lexicon) turn out to be valid, then we must determine which level of proficiency brings about the doubling of components (or conversely: which changes in the processing allow the development of higher levels of proficiency). It is clear that when the speaker has very little knowledge of the L2 he can still make utterances in that L2 by making some (internal) extensions to the L1 system. In this way it is plausible to think that it is only the morpho-phonological information for lexical items in the L2 which is L2 specific, while syntactic information from the L1 translation equivalent is activated.

The number of languages and typological differences

In principle the model is infinitely extendable to accommodate any number of additional languages, if we assume that each language has its own microplanning and formulator. The tiny amount of research that has been done into polyglots suggests that a good command of a large number of languages is possible (cf. the classic case studies of aphasics examined in Paradis, 1987).

I have indicated before, as regards typological differences, that the possibility that an individual speaks two typologically unrelated languages justifies the assumption that there is a separate formulator for each language. It would seem unlikely that languages which differ in the way in which intentions are formed syntactically, in particular with respect to the amount of semantic information conveyed through morphological means, can be processed by the same system.

How the model can be applied to explain various kinds of language disorders is outside the scope of the model we have described. However, it is useful to note that a considerable number of possibilities offered here have come about as a result of research into disorders (in particular the work done by Paradis and Green).

Conclusion

In this article an attempt is made to adapt a recent model of language production, Levelt's 'Speaking' model for bilingual speakers Given the adequacy of the model for unilingual language production, it was intended to change the model as little as possible.

The conclusion is drawn that with respect to the conceptualizer, Levelt's ideas had to be modified: rather than assuming that the conceptualizer is completely language specific, it is likely that in the first of the two production phases in the conceptualizer, the macroplanning is not language-specific, whereas in the second phase, the microplanning is language-specific. In the conceptualizer communicative intentions are given form in the preverbal message, which contains information about the language in which (part of) an utterance is to be produced. Through this information the relevant language-specific formulator is activated. In the formulator the preverbal message is converted into a speech plan very much in the same way as unilingual processing takes place in Levelt's model. There is one lexicon where lexical elements in different languages are stored together. It has been suggested that the relationship between the lemma and form characteristics in bilinguals is not one to one as in the unilingual case: a lemma can be linked to various form characteristics depending on the language or languages involved. Within the lemma, meaning and syntactic information may not be inextricably linked. The different formulators submit their speech plan to an articulator which is not language specific and which stores the possible sounds and prosodic patterns of the languages.

As indicated, the empirical basis for an evaluation of a bilingual production model is rather small at the moment. Therefore, the proposed model should be seen as a first attempt that will be adapted by future research and by reinterpretation of research findings from the past.

Source: de Bot, K. (1992) A bilingual production model: Levelt's 'speaking' model adapted. *Applied Linguistics* 13: 1–24, by permission of Oxford University Press.

Chapter 18

Processing mixed language: issues, findings, and models

FRANÇOIS GROSJEAN

In a previous paper on mixed language processing in bilinguals (Grosjean and Soares, 1986), we stated that psycholinguistic models of language processing in bilinguals have to account for the perception and production of language in the bilingual's different language modes: the monolingual mode, that is, when the bilingual is communicating with a person who only knows one of the bilingual's languages; and the bilingual mode, that is, when the interlocutors share two or more languages, and language mixing is taking place between them. Such a model has to describe the ways in which bilinguals in the monolingual mode differ from monolinguals in terms of perception and production processes, and it has to explain the actual interaction of the two (or more) languages during processing in the bilingual mode.

Ten years later, this statement is still at the center of my research on language processing in bilinguals. We have concentrated our efforts during this period on trying to understand the underlying processes that govern processing during mixed (as opposed to monolingual) language production and perception. One reason for doing this is that the psycholinguistics of mixed language is still in its infancy (unlike the linguistics and sociolinguistics of language mixing that have been studied extensively; for reviews, see Baetens Beardsmore, 1982; Grosjean, 1982; Romaine, 1989). A second reason is that studying the bilingual in the monolingual mode has been the object of much research (e.g., Harris, 1992; Schreuder and Weltens, 1993), although one can question whether subjects were really always in a monolingual mode in many of these studies. Ultimately, bilingual processing models have to account for the full range of bilingual behavior, from the monolingual to the bilingual mode of processing.

In the first part of this chapter, I raise a number of methodological issues that have to be taken into account when experimenting with bilinguals – subjects, language modes, stimuli, tasks, and models. We have had to struggle with such issues in our research and, by discussing them here, I may he able to help others set up studies or interpret experimental results – be it theirs or those of others. In the second part, I describe two production studies we have undertaken to better understand mixed language production. The first looks at the impact of the topic and the person addressed on the type of speech produced by the bilingual speaker, and the second examines the phonetics of code-switching. In the third part of the chapter, I turn to perception and examine guest word recognition in bilinguals. First, I examine the monolingual and bilingual factors that appear to play a role in word recognition and review studies that examine some of them. I then present a bilingual model of word recognition that can account for our findings so far. The studies I report on were conducted with a number of collaborators, both in the United States and in Switzerland, and primarily involve two languages – English and French.

Methodological issues

As is well known to researchers in the field of bilingualism, experimenting with bilinguals is a much more difficult enterprise than experimenting with monolinguals because one has to deal with such problems as choosing appropriate bilingual participants, controlling for language mode, choosing the right stimuli, using appropriate tasks, and so forth. Because of these difficulties, participants, language mode, stimuli, and tasks may be very different from one study to another, in turn producing divergent or even contradictory results. This can lead to the near impossibility of making sense of certain research topics (e.g., the unending debate that surrounds the independence or interdependence of the bilingual's language systems, the selective versus nonselective lexical access question, or the number of lexicons in the bilingual). In what follows, I first describe a number of methodological issues, discuss the problems they may cause if they are not dealt with appropriately and, then, state how, in our own research, we have attempted to deal with them.

Subjects

Bilinguals, by definition, are complex. When choosing them for an experiment and analyzing their data, it is important to take the following factors into account:

1   language history: When and how were the languages acquired, number of years of language use, and so forth;
2   language stability: Are one or several languages still being acquired (or restructured) or has a certain language stability been reached?

3   number and type of languages known and global competence in these languages;

4   competence in each of the four skills (reading, writing, speaking, listening) in each language;

5   function of the languages: Which languages are used, when, with whom, and for what?

6   language modes: How often and for how long do the subjects find themselves in a monolingual and in a bilingual mode in their everyday lives;

7   amount of code-switching and borrowing normally done;

8   age, sex, socioeconomic and educational status, and so forth.

It could be that some of these factors are more important than others, but, until we know more about them, it is crucial to control for them. As stated earlier, different results across studies are often due to the different types of participants used – some are still in the process of acquiring one of their languages (they have not stabilized); others do not share the same skills in their different languages; others have very different levels of fluency in these skills; others still do not find themselves in the same language modes in their everyday lives. It is important, therefore, to use groups of participants that are similar on as many of these factors as possible (unless, of course, the type of subject is an independent variable) and to describe them fully so as to allow for comparisons across studies.

In our own studies, described herein, we use stable, adult bilinguals who share the same language history and have similar global and specific competences in their languages (they acquired one language first and then the second in school before migrating to the country of their second language). Although more fluent in their first language, all the participants use both languages in their spoken and written forms on a regular daily basis, move in and out of the monolingual and bilingual language modes, depending on the situation, interlocutor, topic, and so forth, and all feel they are members of the bilingual community to which they belong (for one such group, see Grosjean, 1988). I make no claim as to the prototypicality of these bilinguals, but I do consider it important that they have stabilized their bilingualism (i.e., that they are no longer acquiring one of their languages) and that they use their two languages, separately or together, in their everyday lives.

Language modes

As has been proposed on numerous occasions (e.g., Grosjean, 1985; 1989; 1994), bilinguals find themselves in their everyday lives at various points along a situational continuum that induces different language modes. At one end of the continuum, bilinguals are in a totally monolingual language mode, in that they are interacting with monolinguals of one – or the other – of the languages they know.

At the other end of the continuum, bilinguals find themselves in a bilingual language mode, in that they are communicating with bilinguals who share their two (or more) languages and with whom they normally mix languages (i.e., code-switch and borrow). These are endpoints, but bilinguals also find themselves at intermediary points, depending on such factors as who the interlocutors are, the topic of conversation, the setting, the reasons for the exchange, and so forth. Figure 18.1 is a visual representation of the continuum. The base languages (A or B) are located in the top and bottom parts of the figure, and the continuum is in the middle. Additional dimensions can be introduced when more than two languages are involved. At the monolingual end of the continuum, bilinguals adopt the language of the monolingual interlocutor(s) and deactivate their other language(s) as best as possible. Thus in Figure 18.1, speaker X, whose position on the continuum is represented by a discontinuous vertical line, is using language A as the base language (represented by the black-filled circle) and has deactivated language B (white-filled circle). In fact, deactivation is rarely total, as is clearly seen in the interferences bilinguals produce, that is, the speaker-specific deviations from the language being spoken, due to the influence of the other, deactivated, language. At the bilingual end of the continuum, when bilinguals are interacting with other bilinguals, they usually first adopt a language to use together, that is a base (or matrix) language. Once it has been chosen, bilinguals can bring in the other language (the guest language) whenever they need or wish to. Thus, in Figure 18.1, speaker Y is using language B as the base language (black-filled circle) and brings in language A from time to time (gray-filled circle). There are two ways of bringing in the other language. One of these is to

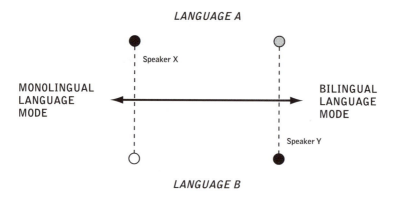

Figure 18.1   Visual representation of the language mode continuum.

Note: The speaker's position on the continuum is represented by the discontinuous vertical lines and the level of language activation by the shade of the circles (black is active, gray is partly active, and white is inactive).

code-switch, that is, to shift completely to the other language for a word, a phrase, or a sentence. The other way is to borrow a word or short expression from the other (less activated) language and to adapt it morphologically (and often phonologically) into the base language. Thus, unlike code-switching, the juxtaposition of two languages, borrowing is the integration of one language into another. Most often, both the form and the content of a word are borrowed, but some borrowings, called loanshifts, consist of either taking a word in the base language and extending its meaning to correspond to that of a word in the other language or rearranging words in the base language along a pattern provided by the other language and, thus, creating a new meaning. In what follows, we use the term *mixed language* to refer to both code-switching and borrowing. Note that, in terms of bilingual perception and production, a particular position on the language mode continuum corresponds to various levels of activation of the two languages (represented by the degree of darkness of the circles in Figure 18.1). When the bilingual is in a monolingual mode, one can assume that the other language is not activated (light circle). Green (1986) even proposed that the other language is inhibited. However, when the bilingual is in a bilingual mode, both languages are activated, but one – the base language – is more strongly activated than the other (as can be seen by the difference in darkness of the circles representing speaker Y's languages). Different positions along the continuum correspond to different levels of activation of the two languages but, particularly, of the guest language, as the base language probably never descends much below full activation.

The language mode factor does not seem to have been controlled carefully enough in many bilingual studies. We know very little about the participants' movement along the language mode continuum in their everyday lives, and it is particularly unclear which point along the continuum they were at when they were tested. Some may have been put in a *language set* (thus favoring a particular base language), but the fact that they knew they were being tested as bilinguals, that they were in a laboratory that worked on bilingualism, that they were run by a bilingual experimenter or that they were given stimuli in both languages, probably moved them toward the bilingual end of the continuum. Note that *hiding* one's own bilingualism when interviewing or running participants simply does not work; bilinguals pick up on the other person's bilingualism and shift to the bilingual end of the continuum. (The fields of bilingual language acquisition and neurolinguistics are particularly affected by this lack of control; for a criticism, see Grosjean, 1989.)

One consequence of not controlling for the language mode is that a lot of ambiguous data is obtained, as some participants may be in a monolingual mode, others in a bilingual mode, and others still between the two. The other, more serious, consequence is that, if, indeed, participants are in a bilingual mode, then both language systems are active (albeit to different degrees; see previous discussion), and no claims can be made about the independence or interdependence of the bilingual's language systems or about the *automatic* influence of one language on the other. It is only when participants are in a truly monolingual mode that such claims can be made. If the aim of a study is to show underlying shared representations or non-selective processing, and the participant is not run in a strictly monolingual mode (this, in itself, raises interesting, and probably insolvable, methodological issues), then the results almost certainly reflect a confound between the activation of the two languages, caused by the experimental situation, and the representational or processing issues being studied.

In our research on mixed language processing, we control for the language mode factor simply by making sure participants are indeed in a bilingual language mode. We tell them that we are doing research on mixed language (code-switching, borrowing), we interact with them in mixed language, and we ask them to keep their two languages *on* at all times (even though, of course, one language is more active than the other as it serves as the base language).

Stimuli

Much research on bilingualism focuses on lexical access and lexical representation and often involves similar words from the two languages, such as homographs, homophones, or cognates. What is striking, though, is that researchers do not seem to agree on what they mean by these terms. In the case of cognates, for example, one finds some researchers using words that are similar in meaning, phonology, and orthography, whereas others only use words that are similar in meaning and phonology. (An additional problem is that researchers do not seem to agree on what they mean by *similar*.) Homographs can vary on any number of linguistic variables. For example, English *pays* and French *pays* (*country*) are certainly homographs, but the English word, pronounced /peɪz/, is a verb with four meanings, a noun with two meanings, and an adjective with two meanings, whereas the French word not only has quite a different pronunciation, /pei/, but is only a noun and shares no meaning with its English counterpart. When such a word pair is used alongside another pair, where the elements share syntactic categories and meanings (in addition to being closer in pronunciation), one must expect a lot of noisy data. Among the variables that need to be controlled for, when making up pairs of words from the two languages, one finds graphic form, phonetic form, frequency and neighborhood of the graphic form, frequency and neighborhood of the phonetic form, syntactic categories and their frequencies, meanings of the various syntactic forms, and concreteness–abstractness of the meanings.

Because the *similar stimuli* used in various experiments are often not controlled for on the above variables, it is difficult to compare studies that are examining the same issue as, for example, the lexical representation of cognates or of homographs in the bilingual lexicon. One solution would be to establish a set of normalized stimuli for language pairs that researchers could use, much like word association and frequency lists in monolingual research. In our own research, we control for many of these factors and generally make words their own control, so as to avoid the difficulty of equating words across languages.

Tasks

It is well known that psycholinguists are constrained by the experimental tasks that exist in their field but two issues need to be kept in mind when testing bilinguals. The first is how a task, originally developed for monolingual research, is best used with bilinguals. Some do not cause too many problems, but others are more problematic. For example, if one is interested in the selective versus nonselective processing issue or the independent versus interdependent representation issue, one should be careful not to activate the other language by using a task that does just that (e.g., using a bilingual Stroop test, a word priming task with primes and probes in different languages, a bilingual association task, etc.). When such tasks are, in fact, used, it becomes difficult to disentangle normal, bilingual representation and processing, and the kind of bilingual processing required by the task. It is probably premature to conclude from the data obtained with these bilingual tasks that representations are organized interdependently or that processing is nonselective.

The second issue relates to what the task is reflecting. For example, a domain of much interest concerns lexical representation in bilinguals and tasks, such as picture naming, word translation, word association, Stroop, and so forth, are used to study the representation. The question is to what extent the task reflects processing operations that are involved in input and output (getting in and out of the system) and to what extent it reflects actual representation. If it is reflecting representation only (something that one can doubt), then what level of representation is it reflecting: the lexeme level, the lemma level, the conceptual level, or the encyclopedic level? It is important that we understand our tasks better not only to be able to tap into the process or level of representation that we are interested in but also to be able to compare studies among themselves. In our own research, we have only studied processing and not representation, as we agree with many researchers working on lexical access in monolinguals that most of the tasks used in the field mainly reflect processing.

Models

A final issue concerns the models that underlie our research. Until recently, the models available to the psycholinguistics of bilingualism were inspired by a monolingual view of bilingualism (e.g., the on–off switch models of the 1970s that allowed a language to be on or off, but not partly on) and were rather simple (e.g., bilinguals could be coordinate or compound or subordinate, but not a bit of each). Current models are much more elaborate and promising. As concerns the lexicon, the proposals made by researchers, such as Bierwisch and Schreuder (1992), Roelofs (1992), and Myers-Scotton and Jake (Chapter 11 in this volume), render the full complexity of the lexicon (be it monolingual or bilingual), with its different levels (lexeme, lemma, semantic, encyclopedic) and with the rich nature of its elements at each level (e.g., the fact that the lemma contains lexical structure, predicate–argument structure, and morphological realization patterns). On the level of language production, the influence of Levelt's "Speaking" model (1989), its bilingual adaptation by de Bot (Chapter 17 of this volume), and its enrichment by de Bot and Schreuder (1993), Poulisse and Bongaerts (1994), and Poulisse (1997), augur well for future bilingual research. This is true also of Myers-Scotton's Matrix Language Frame (MLF) model (1993a), which claims that a number of hierarchies, hypotheses, and principles govern the structuring of sentences containing code-switches. Finally, on the level of perception, the influence of connectionism has led to interesting new models, such as the BIA (Bilingual Interactive Activation) model of visual word recognition proposed by Grainger and Dijkstra (1992) and the BIMOLA model of spoken word recognition in bilinguals (Grosjean, 1988). These new models have influenced our research over the past few years. Thus, at the level of production, the results I present herein are best explained by a bilingual version of Levelt's model enriched by Myers-Scotton's MLF model, and at the level of perception, we have abandoned the language monitoring device (discussed in Grosjean and Soares, 1986, and criticized in Grosjean, 1988) in favor of our current interactive activation model.

In concluding this first part, I stress once again the importance of the methodological issues raised earlier. Although they are admittedly difficult to resolve at all times, I firmly believe that choosing participants, language modes, tasks, and stimuli with great care and using contemporary models as a basis of our research will enable us to understand results better and to compare them to those of other studies in a more fruitful way.

Production of mixed speech

Although code-switching and borrowing have continued to be studied extensively by linguists and sociolinguists the past few years (e.g., Di Sciullo *et al.*, 1986; Muysken, 1995; Myers-Scotton, 1993; 1993a; Poplack *et al.*, 1988; Romaine, 1995), and, although new models (or variants of models) of bilingual language production have been proposed recently (de Bot, Chapter 17 in this volume; de Bot and Schreuder, 1993; Green, 1986; Myers-Scotton, 1993a; Poulisse, 1997; Poulisse and Bongaerts, 1994), there is surprisingly little experimental work in the domain of bilingual language production. Most of the data obtained come from spontaneous conversations with naturally occurring code-switches and borrowings. Although these data are necessary for model building and testing, it is also important to be able to manipulate various psychosocial and psycholinguistic variables and to study their impact on bilingual production. In the long run, both experimental and naturally occurring data will be needed to build and test models of bilingual language production. In the two studies I present, we have purposefully designed production experiments in order to manipulate a number of variables and to study their impact on language production.

Manipulating the language mode

In a recent study we wanted to obtain experimental evidence for the language mode continuum (see also Grosjean, 1985; 1989; 1994). In particular, we wished to study two factors that appear to control where the bilingual is along the continuum – the topic of the exchange and the person addressed. We also wanted to examine the production strategies employed when language mixing is not appropriate on one factor (person addressed) but is required by the other (topic), and we wished to obtain code-switches and borrowings in good recording conditions for further analysis in the laboratory. The method used was to ask French–English bilingual participants, who live in Boston, to summarize stories they had heard in French, as well as to describe cartoons to persons not actually present. The participants, 15 in all, were told that they were taking part in a *telephone chain* experiment and that we were interested in the amount of information that could be conveyed from one person to another. (The persons they were speaking to would, in turn, convey the same information to other persons, and so on.) The first factor manipulated was the topic of the stories or cartoons that were given to them. Half the stories were in French only (they were monolingual) and concerned situations found in France. As for the accompanying cartoons, they depicted typically French scenes. The other half of the stories and cartoons were bilingual. The stories, in French, concerned typical American activities and, hence, contained a number of English code-switches. Here is an extract from one of the stories (code-switches are in caps, and the translation is in italics):

> L'autre jour, nous sommes allés APPLE PICKING avec les enfants. (*The other day we went apple picking with the kids.*) Il faisait vraiment très beau et le FOLIAGE virait au rouge. (*The weather was really beautiful and the foliage was turning red.*) Il y avait des YARD SALES un peu partout le long des routes et on s'arrêtait parfois pour voir s'il n'y avait pas de REAL BARGAINS. (*There were some yard sales all along the roads and we stopped from time to time to see if there weren't any real bargains.*) On a trouvé des SECOND-HAND CLOTHES pas chers du

tout pour les enfants. (*We found some quite cheap second-hand clothes for the kids.*) Marc avait tellement envie d'une DIRT BIKE qu'on la lui a finalement achetée, et Eric est reparti avec un SNOW SUIT presque neuf. (*Marc wanted a dirt bike so badly that we finally bought him one, and Eric came back with a snow suit that was practically new.*)

As for the *bilingual* cartoons, they depicted typical American scenes (e.g., Thanksgiving Day) and could not easily be described in French without reverting to code-switching and borrowing.

The second factor manipulated was the person to whom the participants spoke. The three persons were described to the participants before the experiment started in a short biographical sketch. The first person (referred to as French) had just arrived in the United States to do a postdoc. He could read and write English quite well but still had difficulties speaking it. He was still adapting to life in America and spoke French at home. The second person (Bilingual A) had lived in the United States for 7 years and worked for a French government agency. He taught French and organized French cultural events. His children went to a bilingual school, and he only spoke French at home, although he was bilingual in French and English. As for the third person (Bilingual B), he, too, had been in the United States for 7 years. He worked for a local electronics firm, had French and American friends, and spoke both languages at home. His children went to the local school. No mention was made of the three persons' practice of language mixing, but the answers to a questionnaire filled out by each participant at the end of the experiment clearly showed that they had inferred what this behavior was for each addressee. The French listener was not considered fluent in English and, as a consequence, was not seen as code-switching much. Bilingual A was considered fluent in English, but was also seen as a purist, and so did not code-switch very much either (although slightly more than the French listener). As for Bilingual B, he was seen as being very fluent in English and having a positive attitude to code-switching and, hence, as someone who code-switched a lot.

The participants were run individually, and the summaries and descriptions were transcribed. The amount of French and English spoken (in terms of number of syllables uttered in each language) and the hesitation pauses produced were tabulated for each story and cartoon. Although the results are still being analyzed, we already have evidence for the importance of the two variables tested. Bilingual stories and cartoons produced about 10 times more English, in the form of code-switches and borrowings, than monolingual stories and cartoons. As for the second variable, Figure 18.2 presents the distribution of the mean number of French, English (code-switches, borrowings), and hesitation syllables produced for the bilingual stories (i.e., the ones with code-switches) as a function of the person addressed. If one uses the results obtained for Bilingual B as the bilingual standard (right-hand bar), one notices, as expected, a large mean number of French

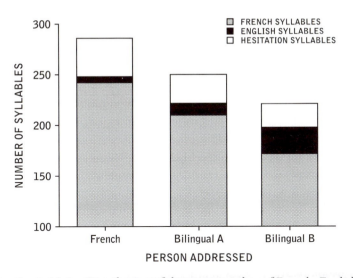

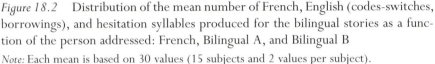

Figure 18.2   Distribution of the mean number of French, English (codes-switches, borrowings), and hesitation syllables produced for the bilingual stories as a function of the person addressed: French, Bilingual A, and Bilingual B

Note: Each mean is based on 30 values (15 subjects and 2 values per subject).

syllables (173; recall that the base language was French), some English syllables (25) that reflect the code-switching and borrowing taking place, and a certain number of hesitation syllables (23). When one examines the results for Bilingual A (middle bar), one observes far fewer English syllables (12), more French syllables (211), and more hesitation syllables (27). This difference in distribution seems to be due to the fact that participants did not feel they could code-switch as much with this person because of his purism. As a consequence, the information had to be given in French, and this entails hesitating more (while one finds a way of conveying the information) and producing rather lengthy translations. It is interesting to note that participants did not wish to code-switch with this addressee but, sometimes, gave way so as not to have to find roundabout ways of conveying the information, given in English, in the stories. As for the French addressee who knew very little English (left-hand bar), participants had little choice but to try to say everything in French; hence, the large number of French syllables (245) and hesitation syllables (36). One or two code-switches were produced (5 syllables on average), but they were invariably explained in French to the addressee. Separate one-way analyses of variance on the number of syllables (French, English, and hesitation), produced for each addressee, all show main effects at the 0.01 level, with all differences being significant.

This study, which we are currently completing, clearly shows that it is possible to manipulate factors that account for the point where bilinguals find themselves on the language mode continuum and, hence, how much they code-switch and borrow. (For converging evidence, see Weil (1994) who has run Swiss-German–French bilinguals, and Treffers-Daller (1998), who uses a more natural-istic approach to study language mode variability in Turkish–German bilinguals.) In terms of a Levelt-type production model (for details, see Poulisse, 1997), one can suppose that both the addressee and the topic have an impact on the level of activation of the guest language (set by the conceptualizer) and that the actual choice of lemmas is based not only on this level but also on the information sent to the lexicon. For Poulisse and Bongaerts (1994), lemmas are activated by conceptual information and a language cue sent by the conceptualizer; for Myers-Scotton and Jake (Chapter 11 of this volume), they are activated by language-specific, semantic–pragmatic feature bundles that also come from the conceptualizer; and for de Bot and Schreuder (1993), lemmas are activated by pieces of conceptual structure sent by the verbalizer. Whatever the origin and the nature of the information received, the system must find appropriate lemmas (in one or the other language) in order to convey, as best as possible, the meaning intended. This is more difficult when code-switching is either not possible or not appropriate, as in certain conditions of our study, and this produces a greater number of hesitation pauses and translations.

The phonetics of code-switching

A well-known effect in the domain of bilingual speech perception, originally proposed by Macnamara and Kushnir (1971), is the base language effect. This effect (which I study in more detail in the last part of this chapter) concerns the impact that the base language has on the guest language during the perception of code-switches. It has been shown repeatedly that there is a momentary dominance of base language units (phonemes, syllables, words) at code-switch boundaries that can, in turn, slightly delay the perception of units in the guest language (Soares and Grosjean, 1984; Grosjean and Soares 1986; Grosjean, 1988). The question asked by Grosjean and Miller (1994) is whether there is also a base language effect in production. Could it be that, in speaking, the phonetic momentum of the base language carries over into the guest language and, hence, affects at least the beginning of code-switches? How complete is a code-switch, therefore? The fact that 80% to 90% of linguistic units normally belong to the base language in a mixed utterance could lead to the expectation that there is some base language influence at code-switch onset (during the first phoneme or the first syllable). On the other hand, because of the inherent differences between perception and production, there could well be no clear equivalent of the base language effect in production. Given the flexibility of the production mechanism, a switch between languages might involve a total change not only at the lexical but also at the phonetic level. In order to test these alternatives, Grosjean and Miller measured the onsets of code-switches by means of a well-established variable, voice onset time (VOT) (Lisker and Abramson, 1964), and compared the results with those obtained when the same bilinguals were speaking only one language or the other.

In the first experiment, they asked French-English bilingual adults, with little if any foreign accent in either language, to retell stories in French, in French with English code-switches, and in English. These stories involved a number of characters with names that could be said in English and in French and that started with the three unvoiced stop consonants, /p/, /t/ and /k/ (e.g., *Paul, Tom, Carl*). The stories were written in such a way that the names of the characters appeared a number of times (between seven and nine). For each test word, said in French or in English (as code-switches in the French plus code-switches version of the story, or as base language words in the monolingual English version), the VOT of the initial consonant was measured, that is, the interval of time between the release of the stop and the onset of voicing of the following vowel (Lisker and Abramson, 1964).

Figure 18.3, taken from Grosjean and Miller (1994), presents the mean VOT durations for the three stop consonants /p, t, k/ at the onset of the stimulus words (*Paul, Tom*, and *Carl*). Each consonant is represented by three bars depicting the mean values obtained in the English condition, in the French, with English code-switches, condition (henceforth the English CS condition), and in the French condition. An expected, VOT difference between the two languages was obtained (79 vs. 24 msec for /p/, 77 vs. 19 msec for /t/, and 95 vs. 28 msec for /k/). Given that the participants showed a clear difference between English and French VOT values, Grosjean and Miller examined whether there was a base language effect in the production of code-switches and, more specifically, at their onset. As can be seen in Figure 18.3 (middle bar of each consonant set), the answer was clearly negative. The English CS values (91, 85, and 101 msec for /p/, /t/ and /k/, respectively) were quite different from the French values and were similar to the English values. One-way analyses of variance based on the subject means for each consonant set showed a main effect in each case (at the 0.01 level), and post hoc tests revealed, again in each case, a significant difference between English and French, and English CS and French, but no difference between English and English CS.

These results suggest that, in bilingual speech production, there is no phonetic momentum of the base language that carries over into the guest language (at least when bilinguals master the phonetics of the two languages). Switching from one language to another appears to involve a total change not only at the lexical but also at the phonetic level. Grosjean and Miller (1994) confirmed this in a second study where they tracked the phonetic shift from one language to another. They accounted for their findings in terms of a model inspired in large part by Levelt (1989), de Bot (Chapter 17 of this volume), and Myers-Scotton

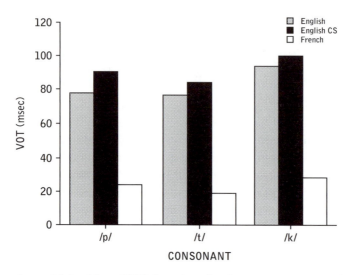

Figure 18.3   Mean VOT durations for the stop consonants /p, t, k/ at the onset of the stimulus words (*Paul*, *Tom*, and *Carl*) in the retelling task

Notes: Each consonant is represented by three bars depicting the values obtained in the English monolingual condition (English), the French, with English code-switches, condition (English CS), and the French monolingual condition (French). Each bar is the mean of 30 values (5 subjects and 6 values per subject).

Source: From Grosjean and Miller, 1994.

(1993a), which shows that pronouncing a code-switch is no different from pronouncing another word within the base language (a position that Paradis (1977; 1986) has maintained for a long time).

Perception of mixed speech

In this last part, I review the work we have undertaken over the last few years to try to understand how bilingual listeners, in a bilingual language mode, process the incoming utterance and recognize the guest words (code-switches, borrowings) that it contains. As is well known, word recognition (also called lexical access) plays a crucial role in language processing as the syntactic, semantic and pragmatic information needed by the higher level modules becomes available only when the lexicon is accessed. I first review some of the factors that are involved in guest word recognition and, whenever possible, give experimental evidence for their importance. I then present the interactive activation model that I first proposed in Grosjean (1988), which is now being implemented on computer.

Factors involved in the recognition of guest words

Guest word recognition by bilinguals has received very little attention. The litera-ture most closely related to this question dates back a number of years and examines the perception and production of language mixtures, most of them ungrammatical (e.g., Kolers, 1966; Macnamara and Kushnir, 1971; Neufeld, 1973). In an exploratory study (Soares and Grosjean, 1984), we investigated the lexical access of base language words and code-switched words by means of the Phoneme Triggered Lexical Decision task (Blank, 1980). English–Portuguese bilingual participants were presented with sentences and were asked to listen for a word or a nonword within them that began with a prespecified phoneme. Once this word (or nonword) was found, the participants had to indicate, as quickly as possible, whether the item was a real word. English monolingual participants were run on the English sentences only, whereas bilingual participants were tested on three separate sets of sentences (English, Portuguese, and Portuguese with code-switches).

Two main findings emerged from this study. The first was that, although bilinguals accessed real words in English as quickly as English monolinguals, they were substantially slower at responding to nonwords. This finding provided ad-ditional evidence for the residual activation of the other language when the bilingual is in a monolingual language mode (Obler and Albert, 1978; Altenberg and Cairns, 1983). We hypothesized that a nonword triggers a complete search (or activation) of the base language lexicon that is then immediately followed by, at least, a partial search (or partial activation) of the other, less active, lexicon. This takes place before the stimulus is classified as a nonword, hence the longer reaction times. The second finding was that bilinguals took longer to access code-switched words in the bilingual language mode than they did base language words in the monolingual language mode. Although, at first, we accounted for this by suggesting that bilinguals always search the base language lexicon before the less activated lexicon, in a later publication (Grosjean and Soares, 1986) we suggested that a number of factors could account for the delay, irrespective of the access strategy. Our research since then has been aimed at obtaining a better understand-ing of these factors.

Figure 18.4 presents a list of factors that appear to be involved in the recogni-tion of guest words (experimental evidence exists for some, as we will see, but not for others). In the top part of the figure are monolingual factors, that is, factors that play a role in lexical access, both in monolinguals and bilinguals; in the bottom part, are bilingual factors, that is, factors that are important when the bilingual listener is being presented with mixed speech. The horizontal line in the middle of the figure represents continuous speech, and the rectangles represent the presence of guest words. The darkened rectangle (to the right) is the guest word that the listener is currently processing. Regarding monolingual factors, we

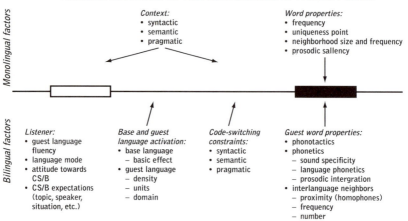

Figure 18.4   Factors that appear to be involved in the recognition of guest words

Notes: Monolingual factors are presented in the top part of the figure and bilingual factors in the bottom part. The horizontal line represents continuous speech, and the rectangles depict the presence of guest words. The darkened rectangle to the right is the guest word that the listener is currently processing.

know that certain properties of words affect their recognition, for example, their frequency of use, their uniqueness point, their neighborhood size and frequency (although the evidence is still tentative here), and their prosodic saliency. We also know that, when words are presented in context, their lexical properties interact with various sources of knowledge (syntax, semantics, pragmatics) to speed up or slow down the recognition process (for a review see Frauenfelder and Tyler, 1987). The exact nature of the *interaction* between the properties of the words and the sources of knowledge remains to be described adequately, and the controversy concerning the moment at which *top-down* information enters the lexical access process has yet to be resolved (Forster, 1976; Swinney, 1982; McClelland and Elman, 1986; Marslen-Wilson, 1987). One conclusion that emerges from this research is that recognizing a word may not be a simple mapping between its acoustic-phonetic properties and its entry in the mental lexicon (although see Klatt, 1979). Instead, it may well be a rather complex process that involves various narrowing-in and monitoring stages, correcting strategies, postaccess decision stages, and even look-ahead and look-back operations (Grosjean, 1985a; Grosjean and Gee, 1987; McClelland and Elman, 1986).

I have organized bilingual factors into four main categories: those that pertain to the listener, those that concern the level of activation of the base and the guest language, those that involve various code-switching constraints, and those that concern the properties of the guest word being heard.

The listener

Among the factors pertaining to the listener, one finds: the listener's fluency in the guest language, the language mode the listener is in (one expects slower recognition of guest words when the listener is not totally in the bilingual language mode), the listener's attitude toward code-switching and borrowing (a negative attitude will usually have an inhibitory effect on the guest lexicon), the listener's expectations for code-switches and borrowings (CS/B) based on the topic, speaker, situation, and so forth. The higher the expectation, the easier will be guest word recognition. Although these various factors are probably important, empirical evidence for the role they play during guest word recognition is still lacking.

Base and guest language activation

As seen in Figure 18.4, this category is divided into two parts: base language activation and guest language activation. Concerning base language activation, Macnamara and Kushnir (1971) showed empirical evidence that the bilingual listener has certain expectations for strings of words and that one such expectation is that all words should be in a single language. Although the terminology has changed a bit today (one would speak in terms of activation and/or inhibition), there is considerable evidence that the base language being spoken (which normally makes up some 80% to 90% of the utterance) has a strong effect on language processing. It is more strongly activated, and, hence, base language units (phonemes, syllables, words) are favored over guest language units, at least momentarily. Grosjean and Soares (1986) reported a set of short studies in which code-switched nonwords were gated (i.e., presented in segments of increasing duration) alone or embedded in a base language, and invariably the language identification results showed the impact of the base language. The first segments were always perceived as belonging to the base language, and as the segments became longer, the effect either continued to be assimilative (the segment was perceived as belonging to the base language) or became contrastive (the segment was perceived as belonging clearly to the guest language). The base language effect was also investigated by Bürki-Cohen et al. (1989) who used a categorical perception paradigm. In this study, French–English bilinguals identified stimuli from a computer-edited series that ranged from an English to a French word. A base language effect was again found, that is, the ambiguous stimuli in the series were perceived as belonging to one language or the other, depending on the base language. (The effect depended on the specificity of the sounds contained in the items, as discussed in more detail later.) Finally, in a gating study using real words,

Grosjean (1988) found that participants invariably proposed base language candidates for guest words when presented with very short gates preceded by a base language context.

Regarding guest language activation, we are starting to find some evidence that the density of the code-switches (i.e., the number of code-switched words in a sentence) has an impact on their recognition. Soares and Grosjean (1984) found a −0.45 correlation between code-switch density and access time to the targets, thereby showing that the more code-switching there is, the more the guest language is activated and, hence, the more easily a code-switched word can be recognized. In a more recent study, Leuenberger (1994) used the gating task to explore how code-switch density influences the recognition of French code-switches in Swiss-German sentences. Two levels of density were used:

1   no code-switch in the sentence leading up to the stimulus guest word (itself a code-switch); and
2   one prior code-switch.

A code-switch density effect was found, that is, a code-switch was identified more rapidly when it was preceded by another code-switch than when it was not. Despite these two promising results, a number of questions remain concerning guest language activation. First, what is the nature of this activation? In other words, how much code-switching is needed to activate the guest language lexicon? Second, what modifies the level of activation of the guest language lexicon more: guest language elements spread throughout the utterance or compact groups of these elements? Third, which elements play a greater role in guest language activation: words, phrases, or larger units? Finally, over what domain does activation take place: the sentence or the utterance as a whole? All these questions have to be studied in future research on guest language activation in bilingual lexical access.

Code-switching constraints

In this category, we find the higher order constraints (syntactic, semantic, and pragmatic) that govern code-switching. These have been studied extensively by linguists and sociolinguists (Di Sciullo et al. 1986; Poplack et al. 1988; Myers-Scotton, 1993a; Muysken, 1995; Romaine, 1989) but have not been the object of many word recognition studies. One exception is Leuenberger (1994), who manipulated semantic context and showed that a reference to a situation, in which the guest language is normally brought in by means of code-switching (e.g., Swiss-German students of French bringing French code-switches into Swiss-German when speaking about their studies), can speed up the recognition of code-switched words. Another exception is Li (1996) who used both a gating task and a naming task to show that English guest words in Chinese sentences were recognized sooner when they were preceded by a more constraining context (defined in terms of syntax, semantics, and sentence length). However, a lot more work needs to be done on this topic, using current linguistic research on code-switching constraints and principles (e.g., those of the Matrix Language Frame model).

Guest word properties

This final category concerns the properties of guest words that affect their recognition. The first is the word's phonotactics, that is, the sequential arrangements (or groupings) of the word's units, such as consonant sequences, syllables, and so forth. It is hypothesized that, the more phonotactic cues there are that the word belongs to the guest language, the easier it should be to recognize. The second concerns the actual phonetics of the word. If it contains sounds that are specific to the guest language, if it is said clearly and fully in the phonetics of the guest language (and not in that of the base language), and if it is said with the prosody of the guest language, then all this should speed up its recognition, as the appropriate word will be activated more easily in the less activated lexicon. We should note that one difference between code-switches and borrowings is their degree of phonetic integration into the base language. A code-switch is not usually integrated into the base language (unless the speaker has an accent in that language), whereas a borrowing is. We can, therefore, expect differences in the recognition of code-switches and borrowings. Finally, the presence of interlanguage neighbors (i.e., words that are phonologically similar in the base language) should have an impact on the recognition of guest words. If the guest word has a close homophone in the base language and, if this homophone is more frequent than the guest word, then the latter should be recognized with more difficulty.

In a gating study (Grosjean, 1988), I studied a number of guest word properties either by manipulating them as independent variables or by studying them in subanalyses. In Figure 18.5, I present the general characteristics of the study. Various types of English guest words, preceded by a French neutral context (*Il faudrait qu'on* [*We should*]), were heard. The words were presented in segments of increasing duration (depicted by short vertical bars on the figure) and then with their following context whose purpose was to resolve any remaining ambiguity problem the listener may have had. Our exploration revolved around the role of three variables: language phonetics, phonotactics, and interlanguage neighbor proximity. As to language phonetics, we asked the following question: Would guest words that retain a phonetic cue as to which lexicon they belong (by being pronounced clearly in the guest language, represented by E in Figure 18.5)

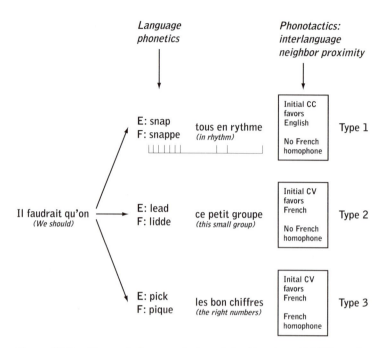

Figure 18.5   General characteristics of the Grosjean (1988) study

Notes: The experimental variables are presented in the top part of the figure and the type of words along the right-hand side. Examples of the three types of words are shown in the middle. The two phonetic forms of each word, English (E) and French (F), are represented in the spelling of each language.

be easier to process than words that are integrated phonetically into the base language (i.e., by being pronounced in the phonetics of the base language, represented by F and written with French-like spelling)? In other words, would code-switched words, which normally retain a phonetic cue as to the lexicon they are a part of, be accessed more easily than borrowings that are usually integrated into the base language and, hence, have lost some of their cues pertaining to their lexicon of origin? Concerning phonotactics, we asked whether guest words that are marked phonotactically as belonging to the guest language lexicon (e.g., English *snap, slash, blot, drop*) would be recognized sooner and with more ease than words not marked in this way. Thus, in the example presented in Figure 18.5. would *snap* be recognized more easily than *lead* and *pick*, as the initial consonant cluster of *snap* favors English? Finally, regarding interlanguage neighbor proximity, we asked whether guest words that have near homophones in the base language would be recognized with more difficulty than other guest language words (e.g., *pick [pique], knot [note], sit [cite]*)? Thus, in Figure 18.5, would *pick* take more time to be recognized than *snap* and *lead* which have no close French homophone? A combination of these two variables gave three types of words:

- Type 1 words that favor English phonotactically and that only exist in English;
- Type 2 words that favor French phonotactically but only exist in English; and
- Type 3 words that also favor French phonotactically but have a close homophone in the other language.

The sentences were recorded by a French–English bilingual with no apparent accent in either language. Then, by means of computer editing, a series of segments of increasing duration were gated, starting with *Il faudrait qu'on* (*We should*) and going all the way to the end of the sentence (Grosjean, 1980). Bilingual subjects (French–English) listened to the segments and, after each presentation, they were asked to guess the verb being presented, to give a confidence rating, and to finish off the sentence. In the data analysis, we examined both the isolation point of each word, that is, that point (defined as the percentage of the way through a word) at which participants correctly proposed the stimulus word and did not subsequently change their opinion, and the erroneous candidates proposed prior to the isolation point.

The results confirmed the importance of the variables under study. First, words that are marked phonotactically as belonging to the guest language only (e.g., *slash, blot*) were identified sooner than words not marked in this way. Subjects needed 66% of Type 1 words to identify them, as opposed to 78% for Type 2 words. (Li, 1996, has replicated this finding with English guest words in Chinese; and Grainger and Beauvillain, 1987, found an analogous result in the visual modality with language-specific orthographic cues.) Second, words that belong solely to the guest lexicon (Type 1 and 2 words) were recognized sooner than words that did not belong to just one lexicon (Type 3): 97% of Type 1 words and 92% of Type 2 words were identified before their ending, whereas only 43% of Type 3 words fell into this category. Third, words in the guest language lexicon that have close homophones in the base language (Type 3 words) were processed with more difficulty than other guest language words: 37% of Type 3 words were isolated after their acoustic offset but before the end of the sentence, and a full 20% were never identified at all.

In regard to the language phonetics variable, it appeared from our data that the way a guest word is said (i.e., as a code-switch or as a borrowing) affects more the narrowing-in process that leads to word identification than the actual point in time at which the word is identified (at least for Type 1 and 2 words). We found that, during the selection phase, the proportion of guest language candidates was greater for code-switches than for borrowings. We also noted an interaction between the language phonetics variable and the interlanguage homophone variable. The candidates proposed for Type 3 words were quite different, depending on whether they were said as borrowings (i.e., in French) or as code-switches (i.e., in English). In the former case, participants invariably chose the base language homophone (*pique* for *pick*, *note* for *knot*) but, in the latter case, only 16% fell into this category. The majority (71% of the candidates for Type 3 code-switches) involved the addition, omission, or substitution of one or more phonemes (e.g., *set* proposed for *sit*, *fourre* for *fool*, *coure* for *cool*). This indicated the very real difficulties participants had with items in which the language phonetics activate one lexicon (in this case, the English one), but the base language context and the presence of a near homophone in that language activates the other (the French lexicon). We should note that Li (1996) has found an even greater recognition difference between code-switches and borrowings in Chinese–English bilinguals.

In addition to showing the impact of phonotactics, the proximity of interlanguage neighbors, and language phonetics on guest word recognition, the study allowed us to examine two other variables – sound specificity and interlanguage neighbor frequency. As for sound specificity, an analysis of the proposed candidates showed that strong language phonetic cues (such as those of a plosive or a lateral) strongly activated either the English or the French lexicon, depending on the phonetics of the guest word, and affected the language of the candidates proposed. Thus, when guest words that began with /t/ or /l/ were said as code-switches, listeners invariably proposed English candidates, whereas, when they were said as borrowings (in French, therefore), they wrote down French candidates. It was only at the fourth or fifth gate of the borrowings (i.e., some way into the word itself) that listeners realized that no word with that beginning existed in the French lexicon and they started proposing English candidates. Of course, the impact of sound specificity will probably be even greater when a sound exists in the guest language only.

It is interesting to note that sound specificity appears to interact with the base language effect. In their categorical perception study, Bürki-Cohen *et al.* (1989) found that the base language had a contrastive effect on the perception of the ambiguous items when the endpoints of the between-language series were phonetically marked as English and French as in *ray* and *ré* but it had no effect when the endpoints were phonetically less marked and, thus, compatible with either language, as in *day* and *dé*. They found a contrastive effect with the *ray–ré* continuum but no assimilative effect with the *day–dé* continuum, although this effect had been observed with other paradigms (Soares and Grosjean, 1984; Grosjean, 1988). It should be noted that since then Handschin (1994), using German–French bilinguals, has investigated the impact of the base language (German and French) on the identification of elements taken from a between-language continuum ranging from German *Tee* to French *thé* (these are language marked end points but less so than *ray–ré*). She found a lot of variability in the responses: Nine subjects did not show a base language effect (the identification curves fell one on top of the other) but seven did; four showed a contrastive effect, and three showed an assimilative effect. More work is needed, therefore, on the relationship that exists between sound specificity and the base language effect.

Finally, concerning interlanguage neighbor frequency, there was a great deal of variability in the results of Type 3 words (i.e., those that had close homophones in the base language). Some were isolated before their offset, others after their offset, and some never at all. We hypothesized that this could be explained by the *frequency pull* of the guest words (i.e., the English items), as compared to their base language counterparts (the French words). (For research on interlanguage neighbors in the visual modality, see Grainger and Dijkstra, 1992; van Heuven *et al.*, 1995.)

In summary, a number of studies have shown that the recognition of guest words in bilingual mixed speech is a highly complex process governed by a number of factors pertaining to the listener, the degree of activation of the two languages, the linguistic constraints underlying code-switching, and the properties of the guest words. Research on these factors and on the relationship they have with one another will need to continue in the years to come.

BIMOLA: a Bilingual Model of Lexical Access

As I indicated in Grosjean (1988), the type of model that can best account for spoken word recognition during mixed speech processing is an interactive activation model such as the TRACE model proposed by McClelland and Elman (1986). According to this type of model, language processing takes place through the excitatory and inhibitory interactions of a large number of processing units, each working continuously to update its own activation on the basis of the activation of other units to which it is connected. In TRACE, the units are organized into three levels: features, phonemes, and words. Throughout the course of processing, each unit is continually receiving input from other units, continually updating its activation on the basis of these inputs and, if it is over threshold, it is continually sending excitatory and inhibitory signals to other units. Connections between levels are bidirectional, and there is no between-level inhibition (inhibition only exists within one level, between units that are inconsistent with one another). Although neither word frequency nor context effects are at present accounted for by the model, these can be built in quite easily: Word frequency can be accommodated in terms of variation in the resting activation level of word units, and contextual influences can be thought of as supplying activation to word units from higher levels of processing.

In 1988, I proposed an interactive activation model of word recognition in bilinguals (Grosjean, 1988), which has since been named BIMOLA (Bilingual Model of Lexical Access). It was strongly inspired by TRACE and is governed by two basic assumptions. First, I assume that bilinguals have two language networks (features, phonemes, words, etc.) that are both independent and interconnected. They are independent in the sense that they allow a bilingual to speak just one language, but they are also interconnected in that the monolingual speech of bilinguals often shows the active interference of the other language and in that bilinguals can code-switch ancl borrow quite readily when they speak to other bilinguals. This view has long been defended by Paradis (1981; 1986; 1989; 1997), who proposes that both languages are stored in identical ways in a single extended system. Because elements of each language normally appear only in different contexts, they form separate networks of connections and, thus, a subsystem within a larger system. According to this *subset hypothesis*, bilinguals have two subsets of neural connections, one for each language (each can be activated or inhibited independently because of the strong associations between elements). At the same time, they possess one larger set from which they are able to draw elements of either language at any time. The second assumption is that, in the monolingual language mode, one language network is strongly activated and the other is activated very weakly (the resting activation level of the units of this other network is, therefore, very low), whereas, in the bilingual language mode, both language networks are activated, but one more than the other (for a similar assumption see Green, 1986; Myers-Scotton, 1993a). In Figure 18.6, I present a visual representation of the model as it stands today (based on Grosjean, 1988). As can be seen, the feature level is common to both languages, but the next two levels – phonemes and words – are organized according to the subset hypothesis, that is, both independently (each language – Language A and Language B – is represented by a subset of units) but also interdependently (both subsets are enclosed in a larger set). At both the word and phoneme levels, units can have close or distant form neighbors, both within a language and between languages. This is depicted by the degree of darkness of the units; darkly shaded units have close neighbors in the other language, whereas lightly shaded units do not. At the word level, word frequency is represented by the size of the units: the larger the unit, the more frequent the word. Connections (mainly excitatory) are uni-directional between features and phonemes and bidirectional between phonemes and words. Features activate phonemes that, in turn, activate words. Descending connections, bearing information about the listener's base language and language mode and information from the higher linguistic levels (semantic, syntactic), serve to activate words that, in turn, can activate phonemes. Language activation (reflected by the overall activation of one language system over the other) takes place through these descending connections but also through within-language connections at the phoneme and word levels. Finally, at the phoneme level, between phoneme connections within a language can allow for phonotactic activation.

In Grosjean (1988) I presented a number of activation characteristics that can

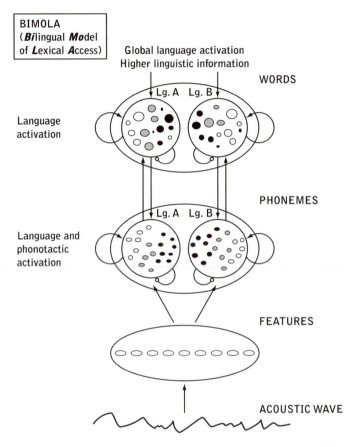

Figure 18.6   Visual representation of the BIMOLA model of lexical access in bilinguals

account for some of the effects found when bilinguals are in a bilingual language mode.

1   Both language networks (features, phonemes, words, etc.) are activated, but the base language network is more strongly activated (this accounts for the base language effect). The resting activation level of the language that is not being used as the base language (i.e., the guest language network) can be increased or decreased, depending on the amount of mixed language (code-switching, borrowing) that occurs during the interaction (via bottom-up and lateral activation) or by a change of the global language activation level (top-down activation).

2   The activation of a unit in one network and of its counterpart in the other

depends on their degree of similarity. Thus, at the phoneme level, if English /b/ is activated, French /b/ will also be activated (to some extent, at least), as the consonants in the two languages are quite similar. On the other hand, the activation of English word initial /p/ will lead to a much lower level of activation of French word initial /p/, as the two consonants are quite different. When English /r/ is activated, its French counterpart should receive very little activation (apart from some possible top-down lexicon activation, due to the fact that the two sounds have the same orthography). Cross-language activation of counterpart units concerns phonemes and words.

3   The activation of units (or of a combination of units, such as consonant clusters) that are specific to one language increases the overall activation of that language network and speeds up the recognition of words in that language (this accounts for the phonotactic effect and the language phonetics effects found in Grosjean, 1988).

4   The activation of words that are specific to just one language increases the overall activation of that network and speeds up the recognition of the words from that language (this accounts for the single lexicon effect of Type 1 and 2 words in Grosjean, 1988).

5   The activation of words that are similar in the two lexicons will normally slow down the recognition of guest language words (this explains the cross-language homophone effect). The frequency pull of cross-language homophones (reflected in their different resting activation levels) and the language phonetics of the input will interact with the recognition process of guest words to speed up or slow down their access (this accounts for the word frequency and language phonetics effects of Type 3 words).

As I noted in Grosjean (1988), such a model does away with the switch or monitor mechanism that has been proposed by a number of researchers (Macnamara, 1967; Obler and Albert, 1978) but rightly criticized by Paradis (1980; 1989). According to the proponents of this mechanism, its role is to tell the processing system which language is being spoken so as to direct the incoming signal to the processors of the appropriate language. The evidence for this mechanism is based mainly on studies that have shown that it takes bilinguals more time to process mixed speech than monolingual speech. This evidence is both insubstantial and indirect. It is not because bilinguals may, at times, process code-switches more slowly than base language words that researchers can conclude there is a language switch/monitor involved in the processing; the delay could be due to numerous other factors (see previous discussions). In addition, the proponents of the mechanism do not address pertinent questions such as: Is the switch/monitor an essential part of language processing or does it *fall out* of the processing? If the former, at what stage does it come in: during the acoustic to phonetic mapping of the speech sounds or after this mapping? Of course, existing data and the model I have presented do not prove the absence of a language switch or monitor, but they do show that the processing system can do without it and that language decisions (e.g., Was that word English or French?) can simply emerge from the process. Having heard a particular sound, syllable, or word, we can then make the metalinguistic statement that language X or language Y is being spoken. That the system needs to make this decision in order to process the incoming signal is highly unlikely. I should note that many of the arguments presented against a language switch/monitor are also valid for arguing against a language node, as proposed by the BIA (Bilingual Interactive Activation) model of visual word recognition (Grainger and Dijkstra, 1992; van Heuven *et al.*, 1995). There is no empirical evidence that this node exists and that what it does cannot also be done by varying the levels of activation of the language system as a whole (as in BIMOLA).

BIMOLA is currently being refined and implemented on computer. We have already spent much time developing a combined French and English feature system that will be used to activate phonemes of one or both languages, depending on their similarity. We are now working on the higher levels, interconnecting phonemes and words in the languages. Once the model has been implemented, we plan on assessing it by comparing its behavior to the data obtained experimentally and to that of the BIA model. Although also an interactive activation model, BIA has been developed for visual word recognition and is different in a number of ways from ours (e.g., presence of a language node, many inhibitory connections). It will be interesting to compare our results with those proposed by the BIA model.

Conclusion

As we have seen in this chapter, the psycholinguistics of mixed language processing in bilinguals is still very much in its infancy. Methodological issues have to be resolved, more experimental studies have to be run (especially in the domain of production), and models of production and perception have to be elaborated and tested, both empirically and through simulation. It is important that, in the years to come, psycholinguists work in close collaboration with linguists and sociolinguists in order to make full use of the very rich research, both data-driven and theoretical, that their domains are producing on mixed language. The ultimate challenge for the psycholinguist working in this area will be to account for how mixed language processing takes place so rapidly and so efficiently, despite, as we now know, many intricate underlying operations.

Source: Grosjean, F. (1997) Processing mixed language: issues, findings, and models. In A.M. de Groot and J.F. Kroll (eds) *Tutorials in Bilingualism*. Mahwah, NJ: Lawrence Erlbaum, pp. 225–54, by permission of Lawrence Erlbaum Associates.

Notes for students and instructors

Study questions

1 What are the three levels of activation, as identified by Green? What is the role of the *specifier*?

2 Review Levelt's original 'speaking' model. What changes has de Bot made to Levelt's model to accommodate bilingual speech production?

3 What is *language mode*? How does *language mode* differ from Fishman's concept of *domain*?

Study activities

1 Ask a bilingual speaker to retell two pieces of personal experience with traditional cultural festivals, one for each of his/her language cultures, to two imagined monolingual friends, one in each of his/her two languages. That is, the bilingual speaker tells the same experience twice, once in each language. Can you detect any difference in the *amount* and *type* of code-switching in each of the retells? Relate the findings to the notion of *language mode* discussed by Grosjean.

2 Select two groups of second/foreign language learners (learning the same second/foreign language and having the same first language/mother tongue), one beginner's group and one advanced group. Present them with 10 sentences in their first language, either on computer screen or on paper. Ask the learners to translate the sentences orally. Measure the speed of their translation and analyse the accuracy. For more accurate measures

of the speed, you will need a specially designed computer programme. Compare the results between the two groups of learners to see if the advanced learners produce faster and more accurate translations. Relate the findings to the control, activation and resources model proposed by Green.

Further reading

For a general introduction to bilingual speech production and perception, see Chapter 3 of S. Romaine, 1995, *Bilingualism* (2nd edn), Blackwell.

For individual studies, see J. Vaid (ed.), 1986, *Language Processing in Bilinguals*, Lawrence Erlbaum; R.J. Harris (ed.), 1992, *Cognitive Processing in Bilinguals*, North-Holland; R. Schreuder and B. Weltens (eds), 1993, *The Bilingual Lexicon*, John Benjamins. For a book which focuses on speech production and perception of bilingual children, see E. Bialystok (ed.), 1991, *Language Processing in Bilingual Children*, Cambridge University Press.

A state-of-the-art overview of the psycholinguistic studies of bilingual speech processing is A. de Groot and J. Kroll (eds), 1997, *Tutorials in Bilingualism*, Lawrence Erlbaum.

Conclusion

Methodological questions in the study of bilingualism

LI WEI

The papers collected in this Reader represent a diversity of approaches to various aspects of bilingualism. I have deliberately excluded work on language planning, language attitude and bilingual education, as there are already good collections of papers on these topics (e.g. Garcia and Baker, 1995; Coupland and Jaworski, 1997; Trudgill and Cheshire, 1997). Consequently, most of the papers included in this Reader focus on the language behaviour of bilingual speakers. I have tried to highlight the various theoretical stances of the papers in my sectional introductions. The differences in theoretical stances often lead to the use of different methods in data collection and data analysis. In this final chapter of the Reader, I discuss some of the methodological issues in the study of bilingualism.

It should be pointed out that this chapter is not a user's manual for any specific method, such as questionnaire, interview, tape-recording, transcription or quantification. There are abundant guidebooks on research methods for teachers and students to take their fancy. My main aim here is to raise a number of questions which I believe need to be considered either when we are preparing a study or when we are reading other people's findings.

Who is the researcher?

The identity of the researcher is extremely important, as it affects the aims and objectives of the research, the relationship with the people being studied and the choice of theoretical and methodological perspectives. Unfortunately, we do not always think about this question when we read other people's findings, or for various reasons the identity of the researcher is not made explicit in the research report. In studying the language behaviour of bilingual speakers, it is particularly useful to consider the following issues:

- Is the researcher monolingual or bilingual (in the appropriate languages for the study)?
- What is the ethnic origin and nationality of the researcher?
- Is the researcher male or female?
- What age group does the researcher belong to?
- What is the educational level of the researcher?
- What is the disciplinary background of the researcher (e.g. linguistics, psychology, neuroscience, speech therapy, sociology, education, administration and government, etc.)?
- What is the researcher's attitude towards bilingualism?

In the existing literature, there is very little detailed documentation of how the linguistic background and competence of the researcher affects his or her relationships with the people and their language behaviour being studied, although it is generally accepted that if the linguistic competence of the researcher is compatible with that of the people being studied, data collection should be smoother and more successful. Native competence certainly helps the research to reveal some of the minute linguistic details, particularly of non-standard language varieties (e.g. Trudgill, 1974). It may well be, however, that the number of researchers who can claim such competence is relatively small and that the majority of the existing studies of the language behaviour of bilingual speakers are carried out by non-native speakers of one of the languages. Some researchers are lucky enough to obtain sufficient funding to employ a team of temporary assistants to carry out data collection and data analysis. However, problems of comparability may then arise, as different researchers may impart their own perspectives to the phenomenon being investigated into the data collection and analysis. While such different perspectives are themselves interesting and provide valuable information worthy of studying, they create difficulties in interpreting the research findings.

Sometimes even if a researcher with the appropriate linguistic background is located, he or she may not be of the ethnic origin or nationality appropriate or necessary for the study. This often happens when the language boundary crosses ethnic or religious boundaries, i.e. the same language is used by members of different ethnic or religious groups. Bilingual researchers with North American or European nationalities may not be readily accepted by some of the people being studied in Africa, Southeast Asia or the Middle East even though they may be of the same ethnic origin.

The effects of age, gender and educational background of the researcher on the data that he or she collects and ultimately analyses have been discussed extensively by sociolinguists (e.g. Milroy, 1987). It is important to remember that there is no ideal candidate for carrying out bilingualism research. Successful investigation requires the researcher's sensitivity to the context of the study, willingness to overcome difficulties, and honesty about his or her identity, attitude and research agenda.

Two related examples from our work with the Pakistani and Chinese communities in Tyneside in the north-east of England may serve to illustrate the points I have made so far. Suzanne Moffatt, a white female researcher of university education, was a non-native speaker of Panjabi who was particularly interested in the bilingual behaviour of young children at the critical kindergarten stage, when they were faced with their first extensive exposure to English. She had previously travelled to Pakistan and had extensive personal contacts within the Pakistani community in Tyneside, partly due to her job as a community speech therapist. Nevertheless, it was impossible to claim the identity of a community member on the grounds of ethnic origin and religious beliefs. She had the further difficulty of having to deal with the male folks of the community who tended to be heads of the household. Subsequently she decided to concentrate on a variety of situations in kindergarten and infant school, where she doubled as a teacher's helper and was, in fact, accepted as such. Her social role was quite clear and she was able to carry out a participant observation study which gave her systematic evidence of the language switching behaviours of young incipient bilinguals (for a fuller description of this study and discussions of the findings, see Moffatt, 1990).

In the meantime, I myself was interested in the language shift from Chinese monolingualism in the grandparent generation to English-dominant bilingualism in the British-born children's generation which was taking place within the Tyneside Chinese community. Although I was of the same ethnic origin as members of the local Chinese community, my first language was Mandarin and I had only a working knowledge of Cantonese, the lingua franca of the community. Like Suzanne Moffatt, I had built up extensive personal contacts within the community during a three-year period of residence in Tyneside prior to our study. Because I was the only Chinese in the area who had a degree in English language and literature at the time, I was often asked by the families to help with English language problems when they went to see their doctors and solicitors. I also taught in the Chinese community language school and helped organise Mandarin Chinese and English language classes there. Where my situation differed from that of Suzanne Moffatt was that I did have access to the family setting which was usually closed to outsiders. In fact, I was often invited to their homes for meals; many of them offered me lodging, daily necessities and even odd jobs in their restaurants and take-aways! However, I did also have certain difficulties which Suzanne Moffatt did not encounter. Intra-generational interaction amongst Chinese adults was normally exclusively in Chinese, and inter-generational communication between adults and children was in both English and Chinese. Since I was accepted by most families as a friend of the parent generation, my use of English was confined to conversations with the British-born children. Most adults refused to speak to me in English, even if it meant that they sometimes had to switch to Mandarin, a non-native variety of Chinese to them, to accommodate my needs. Indeed, our assessments of the English language abilities of the adult Chinese in Tyneside had to be carried out by a non-Chinese researcher (see further discussions in Li Wei, 1994; Milroy, Li Wei and Moffatt, 1993). The main point that I want to make with these two related examples is that there is no point in trying to conceal the 'incompatible' aspects of one's identity in data collection. Instead, we should take into consideration the effect of the researcher's identity during data analysis and make it explicit in the discussions of the findings.

As well as the linguistic background, age, gender and educational level of the researcher, the issue of the disciplinary background of the researcher is equally important, not because different disciplinary traditions tend to have different research methods (e.g. sociologists tend to use questionnaires and interviews, and psychologists controlled experiments, and linguists tape-recordings of conversation) but because their views are not always in agreement on what language is. For example, psychologists and neuroscientists may see languages as fairly clearly defined, discrete systems, each having its own name tag; in contrast, linguists, especially those with a sociolinguistic inclination, see language boundaries as fuzzy and problematic (see discussions in the section 'Language as a socio-political issue' of the Introduction). Even among the broad category of linguists, some maintain a distinction between 'language' and 'speech', whereas others believe such a distinction is unnecessary and fallacious. Consequently, some researchers insist that bilingual speakers possess two more or less discrete grammatical systems, while others argue that bilinguals have their own coherent system which cannot be judged by any monolingual norm (see Chapters 9–13 in this volume). In practice, some researchers attempt to study bilinguals in two separate monolingual modes as well as a bilingual mode, while others believe such an endeavour is completely fruitless and misguided (see Chapter 16 in this volume).

Perhaps the most important issue related to the identity of the researcher is his or her attitude towards bilingualism. This is not a simple matter of seeing bilingualism as advantageous or disadvantageous to the individuals and the society. It is much subtler. Depending on their social and professional positions and personal interests, some bilingual researchers may believe that a generally positive portrayal of the speakers' bilingual ability is more desirable, and their investigations are designed in such a way that the results will highlight 'better' skills of bilingual speakers. Others may insist that only certain types of bilingualism are acceptable. For instance, some bilingual researchers believe that speakers with high proficiency levels in both of their languages do not engage in code-switching; in other words, code-switching is a sign of linguistic deficiency. It is therefore important to have a clear understanding of the ideology of the researcher when reading published research. This leads us to our second question about research objectives, which is clearly affected by the researcher's ideology.

What does the analyst want to find?

Although most published papers and books on bilingualism give fairly clear descriptions of the aims and objectives of the studies being reported, we, as readers, do not often make the link between the research agenda and the researcher's identity, background, personal interests and attitudes towards bilingualism. However, it is quite clear from the vast quantity of published work that, from a socio-political point of view, bilingualism research can never be truly 'value-free'. During my own fieldwork in the Tyneside Chinese community, I came across two groups of community leaders with rather different views: one group wanted to emphasise the problems and disadvantages of being speakers of a 'minority' language in an English-dominant environment; they wanted the central and local governments to provide more support by funding community language schools, translating policy documents and public notices into their language and providing bilingual assistants in public services. In contrast, the other group of community leaders wanted to highlight the success story of the Chinese community: their self-reliance and self-efficiency, assimilation into the mainstream society and harmonious relationships both within the community and with other social groups. Both groups tried to influence our research agenda by giving us only the examples that they thought would support their views. I have also encountered researchers who had already decided even before the study began that bilingual children, especially those from an ethnic minority background, would have serious difficulties at school because their English was not up to standard. They then set out to find evidence only to confirm their ideas. It is therefore necessary both for those who are planning a research project and those who are reading published results to be aware of such ideological influences on the aims and objectives of the research.

In addition, researchers of different disciplinary backgrounds often have different research agendas, even though they may be working with the same language pairs, the same speakers, or the same data corpus. For example, a number of researchers have looked at Spanish–English bilingualism in the US. Coming from a variationist tradition, Poplack and her associates have used quantitative methods to examine grammatical structures of mixed code utterances. They maintain there is a distinction between 'borrowing' and 'switching' and such a distinction shows different degrees and processes of integration (see, for example, Chapter 9 in this volume). Zentella (1997), on the other hand, adopts the 'interactional sociolinguistics' (Gumperz, 1982) approach and focuses on code-switching as an act of identity in a New York Puerto Rican community. In the meantime, Pearson and her team have developed a bilingual vocabulary checklist and other measures to investigate lexical development of Hispanic children (e.g. Pearson *et al.*, 1993; Pearson, 1998). Kroll and her associates also included Spanish–English bilinguals in their studies of bilingual memory. They asked the speakers to perform translation recognition tasks to examine the lexical mediation hypothesis, i.e. less fluent bilinguals were more reliant on a lexical translation strategy (for a review, see Kroll and de Groot, 1997). It is only natural that findings from these studies are not always compatible, as the research questions and methods of data collection and analysis are so radically different. When reading such work, we need to be particularly aware of the fact that researchers from different disciplinary backgrounds may use the same terms – such as *process* or *strategy* – with rather different meanings. A lot of the arguments among researchers on bilingualism about findings and interpretations are in fact a result of having different terminologies and research agendas.

Differences in the research agendas lead to different choices of a specific media for research. For example:

- studies of the language development of bilingual children can be based on parental diaries, video-recording or audio-recording of children's play and conversation, or standardised tests and checklists;
- studies of the language attitudes and language ideologies can be based on analyses of written documents or interview data;
- studies of language processing of bilingual speakers, on the other hand, are normally based on experiments.

There is no one method that is intrinsically better than others. Good methods are those that are appropriate for the research agenda and can provide evidence for answering the research questions.

We should be particularly aware of the possibility that style of research (e.g. ethnographic, experimental, survey, systematic observation) and use of tools (such as questionnaires, interviews, tape-recordings, tests, attitude scales) can carry with them a political ideology, a view of the person and a philosophy of knowledge. For example:

- surveys often aim for participative democracy, whereas experiments are often about control;
- qualitative ethnographic observation aims for a holistic view of the person, while quantitative variationist studies tend to fragment the person into variables;
- tape-recordings and detailed transcription of them aim for a 'mirror reflection', or a 'positivist' picture, of what actually happens, whereas in-depth interviews and critical analyses of them want to (re)construct particular versions of experience and reality.

We should also be aware of the fact that some researchers from specific disciplinary backgrounds (e.g. cognitive science, artificial intelligence) are carrying out research on bilingual speakers not with any interest in their bilingualism *per se*, but in order to validate theoretical models for some other purposes and contexts. Some of their findings may be interesting and relevant to bilingualism research generally, but they should be read with particular caution, as their methodologies are often driven by agendas which are not related to bilingualism at all.

Who is the speaker?

Researchers from different disciplinary backgrounds also sometimes use different terms for the same referent. As we have seen in the articles collected in this Reader, sociolinguists usually refer to the people whose language behaviour is under investigation as 'speakers', while psycholinguists call them 'subjects' or 'participants'.

Although most researchers have certain criteria for choosing the speakers, they are not always explained clearly, nor are they always taken into account during data analysis. Grosjean (1998: 133) suggests that the following questions should be considered in choosing the speakers:

- *Language history and language relationship*: Which languages (and language skills) were acquired, when and how? Was the cultural context the same or different? What was the pattern of language use? What is the linguistic relationship between the bilingual's languages?

- *Language stability*: Are one or several languages still being acquired? Is the bilingual in the process of restructuring (maybe losing) a language or language skill because of a change of linguistic environment? Has a certain language stability been reached?
- *Function of languages*: Which languages (and language skills) are used currently, in what context, for what purpose and to what extent?
- *Language proficiency*: What is the bilingual's proficiency in each of the four skills (listening, speaking, reading and writing) in each language?
- *Language modes*: How often and for how long is the bilingual in a monolingual mode (i.e. when only one language is active) and in a bilingual mode (i.e. when both languages are active)? When in a bilingual mode, how much code-switching and borrowing is taking place?
- *Biographical data*: What is the bilingual's age, sex, socio-economic and educational status, etc.?

Although Grosjean formulated these questions primarily to help experimental psycholinguists with their research design, they should be considered carefully by everyone who does or reads bilingualism research. Often, conflicting study results are a consequence of using different types of speakers for the study. Theoretical models built on the basis of one group of speakers do not always work on other groups of speakers.

Researchers from a sociolinguistic background may also be interested in power and status relationships between speakers, their subjective constructions of their language situation, as well as the biographical data. Such information is sometimes the subject of investigation in itself, but would impact on the data collected and the conclusions made.

What is the relationship between the researcher and the speaker?

A related question is that of the relationship between the researcher and the speaker. We have mentioned earlier that the researcher's identity, such as linguistic profile, ethnic origin, age, gender, occupation and education, can significantly affect the research agenda. Perhaps the most significant and noticeable effect of the researcher's identity is on the relationship that he or she can build up with the speaker whose language behaviour he or she intends to study. The fact that Suzanne Moffatt was a white, female, non-native Panjabi speaker from an educated background determined that she could not possibly be an 'insider' of the Pakistani community in Tyneside; and the fact that I was ethnically Chinese and spoke the language meant that I could not pretend to be completely detached from the local Chinese community. This does not mean that Suzanne Moffatt could not make friends with the Pakistani families; in fact, she was highly successful in building up an appropriate relationship with the children and their families which gave her a large amount of extremely interesting and useful data. However, I had to be very careful not to let my personal relationships with the Chinese families interfere with the research in a negative way (e.g. I was sometimes asked to do things for the families which either cost valuable research time or affected my relationships with other families in the community). The important point here is that we need to establish an appropriate and mutually acceptable relationship with the people whose language behaviour we are studying, which will be beneficial not only to the individuals involved but also to the fulfilment of the research aims and objectives.

There seems to be a tradition in the study of childhood bilingualism that the researchers are in fact parents of the children whose language development is being observed. Parents as researchers have the advantage of being able to make video-recordings and audio-recordings and/or to keep a diary record over an extended period of time, which a researcher without this relationship may not be able to do. It is nevertheless important for parent-researchers to state explicitly their relationships with the children under investigation, the context of the study, and the normal, daily routine activities of the family which may not be recorded for analysis. It is equally important to avoid idiosyncratic interpretations of the data which are not apparent to the general reader.

At a more micro level, we need to be particularly aware of the fact that the speaker's language behaviour is subject to change according to the relationships with the researcher and with any other people present. Bell (1984) calls this 'audience design', i.e. speakers choose their language and style primarily in response to audience types (e.g. addressee, auditor, overhearer and eavesdropper), including their social characteristics (e.g. age, gender, ethnicity and occupation) and their relationships with the speaker (e.g. stranger, acquaintance, colleague, neighbour, friend and family).

What is the research context?

The context of research includes the wider socio-political background as well as the more immediate physical setting of the study. Changes in the socio-political climate often lead to changes in research priorities. When new immigration legislation was introduced in the USA and Britain in the 1950s and 1960s, there was an upsurge of interest in ethnic minority communities. Military conflicts, natural disasters and economic crises, which contributed to language contacts in the first place, may also prompt renewed interest in bilingualism. The development of information and communication technologies and the reforms of the educational systems may also lead to increased awareness of the multilingual nature of modern life. Funding opportunities for bilingualism research may change drastically as the socio-political context changes. Certain types of research may be favoured at one time, but neglected or even forbidden at another. Some researchers are better, or quicker, than others in developing research projects which suit the current policy initiatives. It would be useful to bear in mind the wider context and conditions of the research when reading the findings and arguments.

The wider social context also has an impact on the specific research methods we use for studying the language behaviour of bilingual speakers. In some societies, one-to-one interviews are not an acceptable form of investigation unless the person being interrogated has committed a criminal offence, while in some others interviews are preferred over written questionnaires. In some cases speakers need to be paid to participate in laboratory experiments, while in others payment of any kind is not acceptable. In Singapore, a postal questionnaire survey can obtain a return rate of up to 98 per cent, especially if the research is funded and supported by government agencies. In most other countries a 30–40 per cent return would be considered a success for a questionnaire study. These 'external' factors need to be considered in both designing a research project and reading study results.

At a more immediate level, bilingualism research can be conducted in various physical settings, ranging from laboratory conditions to community-based participant observations. The specific setting of the study is determined by the aims and objectives of the research. It is important to remember that the same speakers may display very different behaviours in different settings. For example, results from a laboratory experiment on the reaction time of the bilingual speaker to language switching must be interpreted as such and should not be understood as indicating their naturally occurring code-switching behaviours in face-to-face interaction.

There are of course many other issues that need to be considered. But the central methodological question in bilingualism research, especially research on the language behaviour of the bilingual speaker, is that of the 'representativeness' of the data. Ideally, the data being collected and ultimately analysed should be characteristic of the normal behaviour of the speaker in everyday life. However, as Labov (1972: 209–10) points out, there exists a basic scientific quandary in linguistic research where, in almost every possible situation, there is one variable that cannot be controlled in every possible way, namely, the observer-researcher himself or herself. if language varies as much as it does, the presence of an observer will have some effect on that variation. Labov calls this the 'observer's paradox', that is, the aim of linguistic research is to find out how people talk when they are not being systematically observed, but the data are available only through systematic observation. Bell (1976: 187–91), drawing extensively on the work of Labov, suggests eight principles as worthy of consideration in linguistic research. Although the eight principles are phrased in terms of sociolinguistic research, particularly studies of language variation and change, they are nevertheless important to all types of research on bilingualism. The eight principles are:

1   *The cumulative principle*: The more that we know about language, the more we can find out about it, and we should not be surprised if our search for new knowledge takes us into new areas of study and into areas in which scholars from other disciplines are already working.

2   *The uniformation principle*: The linguistic processes which we observe to be taking place around us are the same as those which have operated in the past, so that there can be no clean break between *synchronic* (i.e. descriptive and contemporary) matters and *diachronic* (i.e. historical) ones.

3   *The principle of convergence*: The value of new data for confirming or interpreting old findings is directly proportional to the differences in the ways in which the new data are gathered; particularly useful are linguistic data gathered through procedures needed in other areas of scientific investigation.

4   *The principle of subordinate shift*: When speakers of a non-standard (or subordinate) variety of language, e.g. a dialect, are asked direct questions about that variety, their responses will shift in an irregular way towards or away from the standard (or superordinate) variety, e.g. the standard language, so enabling investigators to collect valuable evidence concerning such matters as varieties, norms and change.

5   *The principle of style-shifting*: There are no 'single-style' speakers of a language, because each individual controls and uses a variety of linguistic styles and no one speaks in exactly the same way in all circumstances.

6   *The principle of attention*: 'Styles' of speech can be ordered along a single dimension measured by the amount of attention speakers are giving to their speech, so that the more 'aware' they are of what they are saying, the more 'formal' the style will be.

7   *The vernacular principle*: The style which is most regular in its structure and in its relation to the history of the language is the *vernacular*, that relaxed, spoken style in which the least conscious attention is being paid to speech.

8   *The principle of formality*: Any systematic observation of speech defines a context in which some conscious attention will be paid to that speech, so that it will be difficult, without great ingenuity, to observe the genuine 'vernacular'.

My main purpose in this chapter is to raise awareness of the various methodological questions that need to be considered in both designing and reading bilingualism research. Bilingualism has become an enormous, multi-dimensional and multi-disciplinary research area. Researchers of diverse interests and agendas are using a variety of methods to study different aspects of bilingualism. Confusions and misunderstandings are only natural, given the diversity and multiplexity of bilingualism research. However, it is hoped that an awareness of the identity of the researcher, the aims and objectives of the research, the characteristics of the speaker, the relationship between the researcher and the speakers, and the research context will help to reduce confusions and misunderstandings and produce less ambiguous and more *truthful* research results.

Notes for students and instructors

Study questions

1 What are the advantages and disadvantages of being a member of the bilingual speech community when carrying out research on the language behaviour of the speakers in that community?
2 How do ideological and socio-economic changes in society affect the agenda of bilingual research?
3 In what way does the research agenda of the investigator affect the methods he or she chooses to use?

Study activity

Carry out a critical analysis of a chosen piece of research on the language behaviour of bilingual speakers. Can you identify the identity of the researcher, the objectives of the research, the methods used, and the socio-political context in which the research was done? How do the presentation and interpretation of research findings reflect the researcher's own beliefs and attitudes towards bilingualism?

Further reading

Ideological issues in linguistic research and how they affect the specific methods used in research are discussed in D. Cameron, E. Frazer, P. Harvey, B. Rampton and K. Richardson, 1992, *Researching Language: Issues of power and methods*, Routledge.

A general introduction to specific research methods in linguistics (including sociolinguistics and psycholinguistics) is A. Wray, K. Trott and A. Bloomer, 1999, *Projects in Linguistics: A practical guide to researching language*, Arnold.

RESOURCE LIST

State-of-the-art collections

A general book containing recent papers by some of the leading figures in bilingualism research is L. Milroy and P. Muysken (eds), 1995, *One Speaker Two Languages: Cross-disciplinary perspectives on code-switching*, Cambridge University Press.

On sociolinguistic aspects of bilingualism, see J.C.P. Auer (ed.), 1998, *Code-Switching in Conversation*, Routledge.

On linguistic aspects of bilingualism, see S. Poplack and M. Meechan (eds), 1998, *Instant Loans, Easy Conditions*, Kingston Press; and C. Myers-Scotton and J. Jake (eds), 2000, *Testing a Model of Morpheme Classification with Language Contact Data*, Kingston Press. These are special issues of the *International Journal of Bilingualism*.

On psycholinguistic aspects of bilingualism, see A. de Groot and J. Kroll, 1997, *Tutorials in Bilingualism*, Lawrence Erlbaum.

On childhood bilingualism, see A. De Houwer (ed.), 1998, *Bilingual Acquisition*, Kingston Press, a special issue of the *International Journal of Bilingualism.*

Key reference books

By far the most comprehensive account of bilingualism is C. Baker and S. Prys Jones, 1998, *Encyclopedia of Bilingualism and Bilingual Education*, Multilingual Matters.

A useful reference containing detailed definitions and discussions of key concepts is H. Goebl, P. Nelde, Z. Stary and W. Wolck (eds), 1996, *Contact Linguistics: An international handbook of contemporary research*, Walter de Gruyter.

A practical guide to professionals (e.g. speech therapists, doctors, psychologists, counsellors, teachers) working with bilingual children is C. Baker, 2000, *The Care and Education of Young Bilinguals*, Multilingual Matters.

Very useful practical advice on bilingual children is given in C. Baker, 2000, *A Parents' and Teachers' Guide to Bilingualism* (2nd edn), Multilingual Matters.

An early but still useful, practical guide to bilingualism in the family is E. Harding and P. Riley, 1986, *The Bilingual Family*, Cambridge University Press.

Other guides for parents include: A. Arnberg, 1987, *Raising Children Bilingually: The pre-school years*, Multilingual Matters; E. de Jong, 1986, *The Bilingual Experience: A book for parents*, Cambridge University Press; and U. Cunningham-Andersson and S. Andersson, 1999, *Growing up with Two Languages*, Routledge.

Research tool

The LIDES Coding Manual, compiled by the LIPPS Group (Language Interaction in Plurilingual and Plurilectic Speakers) is a document for preparing and analysing language interaction data, published in 2000 by Kingston Press as a special issue of the *International Journal of Bilingualism*.

Key textbooks

Perhaps the most comprehensive introductory text on bilingualism is S. Romaine, 1995, *Bilingualism* (2nd edn), Blackwell. It contains discussions of all aspects of bilingualism ranging from the bilingual brain and code-switching to bilingual education and attitudes towards bilingualism.

An introduction to bilingualism from a linguistic perspective and a particularly suitable book for use by students of linguistics is H. Bataens Beardsmore, 1986, *Bilingualism: Basic principles* (2nd edn), Multilingual Matters.

A user-friendly introductory text, focusing on bilingual education is C. Baker, 1996, *Foundations of Bilingual Education and Bilingualism* (2nd edn), Multilingual Matters. It has a companion reader, which is: O. Garcia and C. Baker (eds), 1995, *Policy and Practice in Bilingual Education*, Multilingual Matters.

An introductory text written from a bilingual speaker's point of view and in a highly readable style is F. Grosjean, 1982, *Life with Two Languages*, Harvard University Press.

The English translation of a successful French textbook, from a primarily psycholinguistic perspective, is J. Hamers and M. Blanc, 2000, *Bilinguality and Bilingualism* (2nd edn), Cambridge University Press.

An introduction to social aspects of language contact is J. Edwards, 1994, *Multilingualism*, Routledge.

The English translation of the Italian introductory textbook on neurolinguistic aspects of bilingualism is F. Fabbro, 1999, *The Neurolinguistics of Bilingualism*, Psychology Press.

Another two general introductory texts on bilingualism are C. Hoffman, 1991, *An Introduction to Bilingualism*, Longman; and R. Appel and P. Muysken, 1987, *Language Contact and Bilingualism*, Edward Arnold.

A jargon-free introduction to bilingualism, suitable for general reading, is K. Hakuta, 1986, *Mirror of Language: The debate on bilingualism*, Basic Books.

Journals

Journal of Multilingual and Multicultural Development (Multilingual Matters, Clevedon) is a long established international journal, focusing particularly on the sociological and socio-linguistic aspects of language contact. It is published six times a year.

International Journal of Bilingualism: Cross-disciplinary cross-linguistic studies of language behaviour (Kingston Press, London) is the first international, refereed quarterly journal which is devoted to the study of language behaviour of bilingual and multilingual individuals. It also covers crosslinguistic studies of language development and impairment.

Bilingualism: Language and cognition (Cambridge University Press), published three times a year, focuses on bilingualism from a cognitive science perspective. It contains keynote articles with invited commentaries, research articles and notes.

International Journal of Bilingual Education and Bilingualism (Multilingual Matters, Clevedon) focuses particularly on bilingual education and other applied areas of bilingualism research. It is published three times a year.

Bilingual Research Journal is the official publication of the National Association for Bilingual Education in the USA and is published by the Center for Bilingual Education and Research of Arizona State University.

Bilingual Family Newsletter (Multilingual Matters, Clevedon) is an informal publication, six issues a year, exchanging news and views from bilingual people. It contains useful advice and lists of contacts.

The following journals often carry articles on various aspects of bilingualism:

Applied Linguistics (Oxford University Press)
Applied Psycholinguistics (Cambridge University Press)
Brain and Language (Academic Press)
English World-Wide (John Benjamins)
International Journal of Applied Linguistics (Novus Press)
International Journal of the Sociology of Language (Mouton de Gruyter)
Journal of Child Language (Cambridge University Press)
Journal of Neurolinguistics (Elsevier Science)
Journal of Psycholinguistic Research (Plenum Press)
Journal of Sociolinguistics (Blackwell)
Language in Society (Cambridge University Press)
Language Problems and Language Planning (John Benjamins)
Language Learning (Blackwell)
Multilingua (Mouton de Gruyter)
Studies in Second Language Acquisition (Cambridge University Press)

Book series

Multilingual Matters, published by Multilingual Matters, is a companion series of the *Journal of Multilingual and Multicultural Development* and focuses on the sociological and socio-linguistic aspects of language contact.

Bilingual Education and Bilingualism, published by Multilingual Matters, is a companion series of the *Journal of Bilingual Education and Bilingualism* and focuses on bilingual education and applied areas of bilingualism research.

Child Language and Child Development: Cross-linguistic and cross-cultural perspectives, published by Multilingual Matters, is a new book series focusing on the language development of bilingual children and children speaking languages other than English.

Studies on Bilingualism, from John Benjamins, publishes research monographs on various aspects of bilingualism.

Studies in Multilingualism, from Tilburg University Press, publishes dissertations on linguistic studies of bilingualism.

Plurilingua, published by Dummler, Bonn, is a series of publications from the Brussels Research Centre on Multilingualism and focuses on social aspects of language contact.

Websites and electronic mailing lists

The Bilingual List, run by the Center for Bilingual Education and Research of Arizona State University, is the most popular electronic discussion service for bilingualism research. For archive, see http://lists.asu.edu/archives/biling.html. For subscription, contact: listserv@asu.edu.

The Linguist List is a worldwide electronic discussion forum on a variety of issues related to language and linguistics. For further information, see: http://linguistlist.org/

The Human Languages Page contains a catalogue of language-related internet resources (htp://www.june29.com/HLP/).

Speech on the Web links important sites related to phonetics and speech sciences (http://fonsg3.let.uva.nl/Other_pages.html).

National Council for Bilingual Education's homepage (http://www.ncbe.gwu.edu/) contains information about NCBE and links to important websites.

Clearinghouse for Multicultural/Bilingual Education has a homepage with useful links to important sites (http://www.weber.edu/mbe/Htmls/MBE-resource.HTML).

Bilingual Families Web Page provides practical information about raising children with two languages (http://www.nethelp.no/cindy/biling-fam.html).

Bilingual Education Resources on the internet (http://www.edb.utexas.edu/coe/depts/ci/bilingue/resources.html) offers links to other pages which have information on bilingual education.

The American Speech–Language–Hearing Association (ASHA) produces a number of fact sheets on multilingual and multicultural issues in speech-language therapy. They can be viewed on-line at: http://www.asha.org/professionals/multicultural/fact_hp.html

Centre for Applied Linguistics (USA): http://www.cal.org

Centre for Information on Language Teaching and Reseach (CILT, UK): http://www.cilt.org.uk

GLOSSARY

acculturation The process whereby an individual adjusts to a new culture, including the acquisition of the language(s) of that culture. See also *assimilation*.

achieved bilingualism Acquisition of bilingualism later than childhood. See also *late bilingualism*.

additive bilingualism A situation in which a bilingual's two languages combine in a complementary and enriching fashion.

ambilingualism Same as *balanced bilingualism*.

anomie A bilingual's state of anxiety resulting from an inability to resolve the conflicting demands from two cultures.

ascendant bilingualism A situation in which a bilingual's ability to function in a second language is developing due to increased use.

ascribed bilingualism Acquisition of bilingualism early in childhood. See also *early bilingualism*.

assimilation A process whereby an individual or group *acculturates* to another group often by losing their own ethnolinguistic characteristics.

asymmetrical bilingualism Same as *receptive bilingualism*.

attrition The gradual loss of a language within a person over time.

baby talk Distinctive linguistic characteristics found in the speech of adults when addressing very young children.

back translation A translation is translated back into the original language, usually to assess the accuracy of the first translation.

balanced bilingualism A situation in which a bilingual's mastery of two languages is roughly equivalent. Also called *ambilingualism*, *equibilingualism* and *symmetrical bilingualism*.

base language The language which provides the morphosyntactic structure of an utterance in which *code-switching* and *code-mixing* occur. Also called *matrix language*.

biculturalism A situation in which a bilingual individual or group identifies with and participates in more than one culture.

BICS Basic Interpersonal Communicative Skills.

bidialectalism Proficiency in the use of more than one dialect of a language, whether regional or social.

bilinguality A psychological state of the individual who has access to more than one linguistic code as a means of social communication.

biliteracy   Reading and writing in two languages.

borrowing   The taking over of linguistic forms (usually lexical items) by one language from another, either temporary or permanent. See also *loan blend*.

CALP   Cognitive/Academic Language Profiency.

code alternation   A general term for the communication strategy of alternate use of two languages in the same utterance or conversation. cf. *code-mixing* and *code-switching*.

code-mixing   A communication strategy used by bilinguals in which the speaker of language X transfers elements or rules of language Y to X (the *base language*); unlike *borrowing*, however, these elements are not usually integrated into the linguistic system of X.

code-switching   A bilingual communication strategy consisting of the alternate use of two languages in the same phrase or utterance.

codification   A systematic description of a variety of a language, e.g. vocabulary, grammar.

cognate   A linguistic form which is historically derived from the same source as another.

community language   A language used by speakers of a specific, usually minority, community. See also *heritage language*.

compound bilingualism   A situation in which a bilingual's two languages are learnt at the same time, often in the same context.

consecutive bilingualism   Same as *successive bilingualism*.

continuum   Continuous linguistic variation between two or more languages or speech varieties; at each pole of this continuum are situated two distinct linguistic entities which may be mutually unintelligible.

co-ordinate bilingualism   A situation in which a bilingual's two languages are learnt during childhood in different and separate contexts.

corpus planning   Language planning which focuses on the linguistic aspects of a language.

covert bilingualism   A situation in which a bilingual conceals his or her knowledge of a given language due to an attitudinal disposition.

critical age   Age at which acquisition or learning is achieved in an optimal way; before that age the individual has not reached the necessary maturation stage; after that age he or she has partially or totally lost the capacity for acquisition or learning. Also called *optimal age* and *sensitive age*

deculturation   The process by which an individual adapts to a new culture at the expense of his or her first.

diagonal bilingualism   A situation in which someone is bilingual in a non-standard language or a dialect and an unrelated standard language.

diglossia   A situation where two different varieties of a language or two distinct languages co-occur in a *speech community*, each with a distinct range of social functions.

domain   A group of social situations typically constrained by a common set of behavioural rules.

dominant bilingualism   A situation in which a bilingual has greater proficiency in one of his or her languages and uses it significantly more than the other language(s).

dormant bilingualism   A situation in which a bilingual has emigrated to a foreign country for a considerable period of time and has little opportunity to keep the first language actively in use.

double immersion   Schooling where subject content is taught through a second and third language.

early bilingualism   A situation in which someone has acquired two languages early in childhood. See also *ascribed bilingualism*.

embedded language   The language which provides lexical items which are inserted into the utterance in which *code-switching* and *code-mixing* occur.

enculturation   A part of the socialisation process by which a child acquires the rules of behaviour and the values of his or her culture.

endogenous language   A language that is used as mother tongue within a speech community.

equilingualism   Same as *balanced bilingualism*.

ethnolinguistic   A set of cultural, ethnic and linguistic features shared by a cultural, ethnic or sub-cultural social group.

exogenous language   A language not used as mother tongue but only as official or institutionalised language in a speech community.

first language   The linguistic code(s) corresponding to the individual's first language experience; also the linguistic code(s) used as *mother tongue* by most members of a speech community.

foreign language   Second and subsequently learned language(s) which are not widely used by the speech community in which the learner lives.

foreigner talk   A bilingual communication strategy in which the speaker simplifies his or her mother tongue to make himself or herself understood by another speaker who has limited competence in it.

functional bilingualism   A situation in which a speaker can operate in two languages with or without full fluency for the task in hand.

heritage language   Native language of ethnic minority communities. See also *community language*.

horizontal bilingualism   A situation in which someone is bilingual in two distinct languages which have a similar or equal status.

immersion   An educational program in which a second language is used as a medium of instruction.

incipient bilingualism   A situation in which someone is at the early stages of bilingualism where one language is not fully developed.

independence   A psychological state which enables a language mechanism or a linguistic code to function independently of another language mechanism or linguistic code.

interdependence   Relationship between two linguistic systems or psychological mechanisms which means that one cannot function or develop without reference to the other.

interference   A situation in which one piece of learning or one association inhibits another.

interlanguage   Successive stages in the processes of acquisition of a second language in which the linguistic productions of the learner represent systematic approximations to the target language.

language aptitude   A particular ability to learn a language as separate from intelligence and motivation.

language awareness   A comprehensive term used to describe knowledge about and appreciation of the attributes of a language, the way a language works and is used in society.

language dominance   One language being the stronger or preferred language of an individual.

language loyalty   The purposeful maintenance and retention of a language when it is viewed as being under threat.

language maintenance   The continued use of a language, particularly amongst language minorities.

language shift   Process in which a speech community gives up a language in favour of another one.

late bilingualism   A situation in which a bilingual has become a bilingual later than childhood. See also *achieved bilingualism*.

leaky diglossia   A situation where one variety or language spreads into the functions formerly reserved for another.

lect   A collection of linguistic phenomena which has a functional identity within a speech community.

lingua franca   An auxiliary language used between groups of people who speak different native languages for the purpose of routine communication.

linguistic community   Same as *speech community*.

loan blend   A type of *borrowing* in which the loan word is modified according to the rules of the borrowing language.

machine translation   Translation from one language to another by computer.

majority language   A language used by a socio-economically dominant group in society, or one which has received a political or cultural status superior to that of other languages in the community.

matrix language   Same as *base language*.

maximal bilingualism   A situation in which a bilingual has near native control of two or more languages.

metalinguistic   Using language to describe language. Thinking about one's language.

minimal bilingualism   A situation in which a bilingual has only a few words and phrases in a second language.

minority language   A language used by a socially subordinate group, or one which has received a social or cultural status inferior to that of another (dominant) language in the community.

monocultural   Individual/group identifying with and being identified by only one culture. Also called *unicultural*.

monolingual   Individual/group having access to only one linguistic code. Also called *unilingual*.

mother tongue   Same as *first language*.

native language   The language or languages which have been acquired naturally during childhood.

native speaker   An individual for whom a particular language is a *native language*.

natural bilingualism   A situation in which a bilingual has not undergone any specific training and is often not in a position to translate or interpret with facility between two languages. See also *primary bilingualism*.

official language   A language which is legally adopted by a state as its language of communication.

optimal age   Same as *critical age*.

partial immersion   Immersion program in which both the first and the second language are used as media of instruction.

passive bilingualism   Same as *receptive bilingualism*.

pluralism   A cultural and linguistic policy by which ethnolinguistic minority groups are integrated into the wider society while being allowed to maintain their linguistic and cultural characteristics to varying degrees.

preferred language   The language chosen by a bilingual speaker in a given situation from among his or her *repertoire*.

primary bilingualism   A situation in which two languages have been learnt naturally, i.e. not via school teaching. See also *natural bilingualism*.

productive bilingualism   A situation in which a bilingual not only understands but also speaks and possibly writes in two or more languages.

receptive bilingualism   A situation in which a bilingual understands a second language, in either its spoken or written form, or both, but does not necessarily speak or write it. Also called *asymmetrical bilingualism* and *passive bilingualism*.

recessive bilingualism   A situation in which a bilingual begins to feel some difficulty in either understanding or expressing himself or herself with ease, due to lack of use.

repertoire   The range of languages or varieties available for use by a speaker, each of which enables him or her to perform a particular social role; the range of languages or varieties within a *speech community* .

second language   The language learned by an individual after acquiring his or her first or native language. A non-native language which is widely used in the speech community.

secondary bilingualism   A situation in which a bilingual's second language has been added to a first language via formal instruction.

semilingualism   A situation in which a bilingual has insufficient knowledge of either language.

sensitive age   Same as *critical age*.

simultaneous bilingualism   A situation in which a bilingual's two languages are present from the onset of speech.

source language   The language in which a message is transmitted and which is decoded by the interpreter/translator with the aim of recoding it in another language. The first language of the second language learner.

speech accommodation   The process by which interlocutors modify their speech style or switch codes in order to converge towards, or diverge from, each other in communication interactions.

speech community   Any regionally or socially definable human group identified by the use of a shared linguistic system(s) and by participation in shared sociolinguistic norms. Also called *linguistic community*.

standard language   A language variety which has been accorded a status which is socially and culturally superior to other varieties and is used officially.

standardisation   The attempt to establish a single standard form of a language particularly in its written form, for official purposes, literature, school curriculum, etc.

status planning   Language planning which focuses on the existing status relationships between languages in contact in a given territory.

submersion   A form of education in which children are schooled in a language other than their mother tongue.

subordinate bilingualism   A situation in which a bilingual exhibits *interference* in his or her language usage by reducing the patterns of the second language to those of the first.

subtractive bilingualism   A situation in which a bilingual's second language is acquired at the expense of the aptitudes already acquired in the first language.

successive bilingualism   A situation in which a bilingual's second language is added at some stage after the first has begun to develop. Also called *consecutive bilingualism*.

switch mechanism   A psychological mechanism by which the bilingual is enabled to shut out one of his or her linguistic systems while using another.

symmetrical bilingualism   Same as *balanced bilingualism*.

target language   The language into which a message in another language is translated or interpreted. The language which is the goal of second language acquisition.

teacher talk   A variety of communication used by teachers in classroom, specific to the needs of instruction and learning.

territorial bilingualism   Co-occurrence of two or more languages which have official status within a geographical area. Co-existence of two or more unilingual areas within a single political structure (e.g. unilingual regions in a multilingual state).

transfer   The effect of one language on the learning or production of another.

translation equivalent   A linguistic unit in one language corresponding to that in another language at the semantic level.

transliteration   The notation of one language in the writing system of another language.

unicultural   Same as *monocultural*.

unilingual   Same as *monolingual*.

variety   Any system of linguistic expression whose use is governed by situational variables, such as region, occupation, etc.

vernacular   The indigenous language or dialect of a *speech community*.

vertical bilingualism   A situation in which someone is bilingual in a standard language and a distinct but related language or dialect.

BIBLIOGRAPHY

Abdulaziz, M.H. (1982) Patterns of language acquisition and use in Kenya: rural-urban differences. *International Journal of the Sociology of Language* 34: 95–120.

Abdulaziz-Mkilifi, M.H. (1972) Triglossia and Swahili–English bilingualism in Tanzania. *Language in Society* 1:197–213.

Al-Toma, S.J. (1957) The teaching of Classical Arabic to speakers of the colloquial in Iraq: a study of the problem of linguistic duality. Doctoral dissertation, Harvard University.

Albanèse, J.F. (1985) Language lateralization in English–French bilinguals. *Brain and Language* 24: 284–96.

Albert, E.M. (1972) Cultural patterning of speech behaviour in Burundi. In J.J. Gumperz and D. Hymes (eds) *Directions in Sociolinguistics*. New York: Holt, Rinehart and Winston, pp. 72–105.

Albert, M.L. and Obler, L.K. (1978) *The Bilingual Brain: Neuropsychological and neuro-linguistic aspects of bilingualism*. New York/London: Academic Press.

Alexander, M.P., Benson, D.F., and Stuss, D.T. (1989) Frontal lobes and language. *Brain and Language* 37: 656–91.

Altenberg, E. and Cairns, H. (1983) The effects of phonotactic constraints on lexical processing in bilingual and monolingual subjects. *Journal of Verbal Learning and Verbal Behavior* 22: 174–88.

Andrews, R. (1977) Aspects of language lateralization correlated with familial handedness. *Neuropsychologia* 15: 769–78.

Anglin, J.M. (1977) *Word, Object, and Conceptual Development*. New York: Norton.

Annamalai, E. (1989) The language factor in code mixing. *International Journal of the Sociology of Language* 75: 47–54.

Appel, R. and Muysken, P. (1987) *Language Contact and Bilingualism*. London: Edward Arnold.

April, R.S., and Han, M. (1980) Crossed aphasia in a right-handed bilingual Chinese man: a second case. *Archives of Neurology* 37: 342–6.

Arnberg, A. (1987) *Raising Children Bilingually: The pre-school years*. Clevedon: Multilingual Matters.

Atkinson, J.M. and Heritage, J. (eds) (1984) *Structures of Social Action: Studies in conversation analysis*. Cambridge: Cambridge University Press.

Attinasi, J. (1979) Results of a language attitude questionnaire administered orally to an ethnographically chosen sample of 91 residents of a block in East Harlem. New York, 1977–78. Unpublished ms.

Auer, J.C.P. (1981) Bilingualism as a members' concept: language choice and language alternation in their relation to lay assessments of competence. *Papiere des SFB 99*, Constance, No. 54.

Auer, J.C.P. (1983) Zweisprachige Konversationen. *Papiere des SFG 99*, Constance, No. 79.

Auer, J.C.P. (1984) *Bilingual Conversation*. Amsterdam: John Benjamins.

Auer, J.C.P. (1984a) On the meaning of conversational code-switching. In J.C.P. Auer and A. Di Luzio (eds), *Interpretive Sociolinguistics: Migrants – children – migrant children*. Tübingen: Narr, pp. 87–112.

Auer, J.C.P. (1988) A conversation analytic approach to code-switching and transfer. In M. Heller (ed.), *Codeswitching*. Berlin: Mouton de Gruyter, pp. 187–214.

Auer, J.C.P. (1991) Bilingualism in/as social action. *Papers for the Symposium on Code-switching in Bilingual Studies: Theory, significance and perspectives, Vol.2*. Strasbourg: The European Science Foundation.

Auer, J.C.P. (ed.) (1998) *Code-Switching in Conversation: Language, interaction and identity*. London: Routledge.

Auer, J.C.P. and Di Luzio, A. (1983) Structure and meaning of linguistic variation in Italian migrant children in Germany. In R. Bäuerle, Ch. Schwarze and A. von Stechow (eds), *Meaning, Use and Interpretation of Language*. Berlin, pp. 1–21.

Auer, J.C.P. and Di Luzio, A. (1983a) Three types of variation and their interpretation. In L. Dabène, M. Flasaquier and J. Lyons (eds), *Status of Migrants' Mother Tongues*. Strasbourg: ESF, pp. 67–100.

Auer, J.C.P. and Di Luzio, A. (eds) (1984) *Interpretive Sociolinguistics: Migrants – children – migrant children*. Tübingen: Narr.

Azuma, S. (1991) Processing and intrasentential code-switching. Unpublished doctoral dissertation, University of Texas at Austin.

Azuma, S. (1993) The frame–content hypothesis in speech production: evidence from intrasentential code switching. *Linguistics* 31: 1071–93.

Backus, A. (1992) *Patterns of Language Mixing*. Wiesbaden: Harrassowitz.

Backus, A. (1994) Turkish/Dutch corpus. Unpublished data.

Backus, A. (1996) *Two in One: Bilingual speech of Turkish immigrants in the Netherlands*. Tilburg: Tilburg University Press.

Baetens Beardsmore, H. (1982, 2nd edn 1986) *Bilingualism: Basic principles*. Clevedon: Multilingual Matters.

Baker, C. (1993, 2nd edn 1996) *Foundations of Bilingual Education and Bilingualism*. Clevedon: Multilingual Matters.

Baker, C. (1995, 2nd edn 2000) *A Parents' and Teachers' Guide to Bilingualism*. Clevedon: Multilingual Matters.

Baker, C. (2000) *The Care and Education of Young Bilinguals*. Clevedon: Multilingual Matters.

Baker, C. and Prys Jones, S. (1998) *Encyclopedia of Bilingualism and Bilingual Education*. Clevedon: Multilingual Matters.

Bakker, P. and Mous, M. (eds) (1994) *Mixed Languages: Fifteen case studies in language intertwining*. Amsterdam: Institute for Functional Research in Language and Language Use.

Balken, L. (1970) *Les effets du bilinguisme français–anglais sur les aptitudes intellectuelles*. Bruxelles: Aimav.

Barber, C. (1952) Trilingualism in Pascua: social functions of language in an Arizona Yaqui Village. Unpublished MA Thesis, University of Arizona, Tucson, AZ.

Barker, G.C. (1947) Social functions of language in a Mexican–American community. *Acta Americana* 5: 185–202.

Barnes, J.A. (1954) Class and committees in a Norwegian island parish. *Human Relations* 8: 39–58.

Barth, F. (1964) Ethnic processes in the Pathan–Buluchi boundary. In *Indo–Iranica: Mélanges présentés à Georg Morgestierne à l'occasion de son soixante-dixième anniversaire*. Wiesbaden: Otto Harrassowitz.

Barth, F. (1966) *Models of Social Organisation*. Royal Anthropological Institute of Great Britain and Ireland Occasional Papers, London.

Barton, M., Goodglass, H., and Shai, A. (1965) Differential recognition of tachistoscopically presented English and Hebrew words in right and left visual fields. *Perceptual and Motor Skills* 21: 431–7.

Bates, E. (1976) *Language and Context: The acquisition of pragmatics*. New York: Academic Press.

Bates, E. and MacWhinney, B. (1982) Functionalist approaches to grammar. In E. Wanner and L.R. Gleitman (eds), *Language Acquisition: The state of the art*. Cambridge: Cambridge University Press, pp. 173–218.

Baumans, L. (1998) *The Syntax of Codeswitching: Analysing Moroccan Arabic/Dutch conversation*. Tilburg: Tilburg University Press.

Belazi, H.M., Rubin, E.J. and Toribio, J. (1994) Code-switching and X-bar theory: the functional head constraint. *Linguistic Inquiry* 25: 221–37.

Bell, A. (1984) Language style as audience design. *Language in Society* 13: 145–204.

Bell, R.T. (1976) *Sociolinguistics*. London: Batsford.

Ben Amar, M., and Gaillard, F. (1984) January–June. Langage et dominance cérébrale chez les monolingues et les bilingues au seuil de l'école. *Les Sciences de l'Education pour l'ère nouvelle* 1–2: 93–111.

Bentahila, A. (1983) *Language Attitudes among Arabic–French Bilinguals in Morocco*. Clevedon: Multilingual Matters.

Bentahila, A. and Davies, E.E. (1983) The syntax of Arabic–French code-switching. *Lingua* 59: 301–30.

Bentahila, A. and Davies, E.E. (1992) Code-switching and language dominance. In R.J. Harris (ed.), *Cognitive Processing in Bilinguals*. Amsterdam: Benjamins, pp. 443–58.

Bentin, S. (n.d.) Right hemisphere role in reading a second language. Unpublished manuscript.

Ben-Zeev, S. (1977) The influence of bilingualism on cognitive development and cognitive strategy. *Child Development* 48: 1009–18.

Bergh, G. (1986) *The Neuropsychological Status of Swedish–English Subsidiary Bilinguals*. Göteborg: Acta Universitatis Gothoburgensis.

Bergman, C.R. (1976) Interference vs. independent development in infant bilingualism. In G.D. Keller, R.V. Taeschner and S. Viera (eds), *Bilingualism in the Bicentennial and Beyond*. New York: Bilingual Press.

Berk-Seligson, S. (1986) Linguistic constraints on intrasentential code-switching. *Language in Society* 15: 313–48.

Berlin, C.I., Lowe-Bell, S.S., Cullen, J.K. and Thompson, C.L. (1973) Dichotic speech perception: an interpretation of right ear advantage and temporal offset effects. *Journal of the Acoustical Society of America* 53: 699–709.

Bernstein, B. (1961) Social structure, language and learning. *Educational Research* 3: 163–76.

Bernstein, B. (1964) Elaborated and restricted codes: their social origins and some consequences. *American Anthropologist* 66, 6 Part II: 55–69.

Bhatt, R.M. (1997) Code-switching, constraints and optimal grammars. *Lingua* 102: 223–51.

Bialystok, E. (1990) *Communication Strategies. A psychological analysis of second language use*. Oxford: Basil Blackwell.

Bialystok, E. (ed.) (1991) *Language Processing in Bilingual Children*. Cambridge: Cambridge University Press.

Bierbach, C. (1983) 'Nun erzähl' mal mas!' Textstruktur und referentielle Organisation in elizitierten Erzählungen italienischer Kinder. In E. Gülich and T. Kotschi (eds), *Grammatik, Konversation, Interaktion*. Tübingen: Niemeyer.

Bierwisch, M. and Schreuder, R. (1992) From concepts to lexical items. *Cognition* 41: 23–60.

Blanc, H. (1964) *Communal Dialects of Baghdad*. Cambridge, MA: Harvard University Press.

Blank, M. (1980) Measuring lexical access during sentence processing. *Perception and Psychophysics* 28: 1–8.

Blom, J.-P. and Gumperz, J.J. (1966) Some social determinants of verbal behavior. Unpublished paper presented at the annual meeting of The American Sociological Association.

Blom, J.-P. and Gumperz, J.J. (1972) Social meaning in linguistic structure: code-switching in Norway. In J.J. Gumperz and D. Hymes (eds), *Directions in Sociolinguistics*. New York: Holt, Rinehart and Winston, pp. 407–34.

Bloom, L. and Lahey, M. (1978) *Language Development and Language Disorders*. New York: Wiley.

Bloomfield, L. (1927) Literate and illiterate speech. *American Speech* 2: 432–9.

Bloomfield, L. (1933) *Language*. New York: Holt.

Blumstein, S., Goodglass, H. and Tartter, V.C. (1975) The reliability of ear advantage in dichotic listening. *Brain and Language* 2: 226–36.

Bock, J. (1986) Meaning, sound and syntax: lexical priming in sentence production. *Journal of Experimental Psychology: Learning, Memory, and Cognition* 12: 575–86.

Bock, J. (1987) An effect of the accessibility of word forms on sentence structures. *Journal of Memory and Language* 26(2): 119–37.

Bock, P.K. (1964) Social structure and language structure. *Southwestern Journal of Anthropology* 20: 393–403.

Boeschoten, H. (1991) Asymmetrical code-switching in immigrant communities. In European Science Foundation (ed.), *Workshop on Constraints, Conditions, and Models*, Strasburg: European Science Foundation, pp. 85–104.

Boeschoten, H.E. and Verhoeven, L.T. (1985) Integration niederländischer lexikalischer Elemente ins Türkische. *Linguistische Berichte* 98: 437–64.

Bokamba, E. (1988) Code-mixing, language variation, and linguistic theory: evidence from Bantu languages. *Lingua* 76: 21–62.

Bolinger, D. (1989) *Intonation and its Uses: Melody in grammar and discourse*. London: Edward Arnold.

Borod, J. and Goodglass, H. (1980) Hemispheric specialization and development. In L. Obler and M. Albert (eds), *Language and Communication in the Elderly: Experimental clinical and therapeutic issues*. Lexington, MA: Heath.

Boumans, L. (1994) L'Arabe marocain et le néerlandais en contact: quelques particularités syntaxiques. Paper presented at conference on Mouvements migratoires Magrebine en Europe. Ouida, March.

Braunshausen, N. (1928) Le bilinguisme et la famille. In *Le Bilinguisme et l'Education*. Geneva–Luxemburg, Bureau International d'Education.

Breitborde, L.B. (1983) Levels of analysis in sociolinguistic explanation. *International Journal of the Sociology of Language* 39: 5–43.

Brown, P. and Levinson, S. (1978) Universals in language usage: politeness phenomena. In E. Goody (ed.), *Questions and Politeness*. New York: Cambridge University Press, pp. 56–310.

Brown, R. (1973) *A First Language: The early stages*. Cambridge, MA: Harvard University Press.

Bryden, M.P. (1970) Left–right differences in tachistoscopic recognition as a function of familiarity and pattern orientation. *Journal of Experimental Psychology* 84: 120–22.

Bryden, M.P. (1980) *Strategy and attentional influences on dichotic listening and tachistoscopic lateralization assessments*. Paper presented at the annual meeting of the International Neuropsychological Society. San Francisco, February.

Bureau of the Census (1973) *Puerto Ricans in the United States*. Publication PC(2)-1E.

Bürki-Cohen, J., Grosjean, F. and Miller, J. (1989) Base language effects on word identification in bilingual speech: evidence from categorical perception experiments. *Language and Speech* 32: 355–71.

Burling, R. (1978) Language development of a Garo and English-speaking child. In E. Hatch (ed.), *Second Language Acquisition: A book of readings*. Rowley, MA: Newbury House.

Butterworth, B. (1981) Speech errors: old data in search of new theories. *Linguistics* 19: 627–81.

Butterworth, B. (1985) Jargon aphasia: processes and strategies. In S. Newman and R. Epstein (eds), *Current Perspectives in Dysphasia*. London: Churchill Livingstone.

Cameron, D., Frazer, E., Harvey, P., Rampton, B. and Richardson, K. (1992) *Researching Language: Issues of power and methods*. London: Routledge.

Carman, J.N. (1962) Personal communication regarding a forthcoming second volume of *Foreign Language Units of Kansas: Historical Atlas and Statistics*. Lawrence, KS: University of Kansas Press.

Carroll, F. (1978) Cerebral dominance for language: a dichotic listening study of Navajo–English bilinguals. In H. Key, S. McCullough and J. Sawyer (eds), *The Bilingual in a Pluralistic Society: Proceedings of the Sixth Southwest Area Language and Linguistics Workshop*. Long Beach: California State University, pp. 11–17.

Carroll, F. (1980) Neurolinguistic processing in bilingualism and second language. In R. Scarcella, and S. Krashen (eds), *Research in Second Language Acquisition*. Rowley, MA: Newbury House, pp. 81–86.

Chafe, W. (1987) Cognitive constraints on information flow. In R.S. Romlin (ed.), *Typological Studies of Language, Vol. 11: Coherence and Grounding in Discourse*. Amsterdam: John Benjamins, pp. 21–51.

Chao, Y.R. (1947) *Cantonese Primer*. Cambridge, MA: Harvard University Press.

Chary, P. (1986) Aphasia in a multilingual society: a preliminary study. In J. Vaid (ed.), *Language Processsing in Bilinguals: Psycholinguistic and neuropsychological perspectives*. Hillsdale, NJ: Erlbaum, pp. 183–97.

Chejne, A. (1958) The role of Arabic in present-day Arab society. *The Islamic Literature* 10(4): 15–54.

Chomsky, N. (1986) *Knowledge of Language: Its nature, origin and use*. New York: Praeger.

Christiansen, H. (1962) *Malet I Rana*. Oslo: Institut for Sociologi, Universitete I Oslo.

Clahsen, H. (1982) *Spracherwerb in der Kindheit*. Tübingen: Narr.

Clahsen, H. (1984) Der Erwerb der Kasusmarkierung in der deutschen Kindersprache, *Linguistische Berichte* 89: 1–31.

Clahsen, H. (1986) Verb inflections in German child language: acquisition of agreement markings and the functions they encode. *Linguistics* 24: 79–121.

Clark, E. (1985) Acquisition of Romance: With special reference to French. In D. Slobin (ed), *Crosslinguistic Study of Language Acquisition*. Hillsdale, NJ: Erlbaum, pp. 687–782.

Clark, H.H. (1973) The language-as-fixed-effect fallacy: A critique of language statistics in psychological research. *Journal of Verbal Learning and Verbal Behavior* 12: 335–59.

Clark, L. and Knowles, J. (1973) Age differences in dichotic listening performance. *Journal of Gerontology* 28: 173–8.

Clyne, M. (1967) *Transference and Triggering*. The Hague: Nijhoff.

Clyne, M. (1969) Switching between language systems. *Actes du 10. congrès internationale des linguistes*, Vol. 1: 343–9. Bucharest: Editions de l'Académie de la République Socialiste de Roumanie.

Clyne, M. (1971) German–English bilingualism and linguistic theory. In V. Lange and

H.G. Roloff (eds), *Dichtung, Sprache und Gesellschaft. Akten des 4. internationalen Germanistenkongresses*, 503–11. Frankfurt: Athenäum.

Clyne, M. (1972) *Perspectives on Language Contact*. Melbourne: The Hawthorne Press.

Clyne, M. (1972a) Perception of code-switching in bilinguals. *ITL Review of Applied Linguistics* 16: 45–8.

Clyne, M. (1974) Lexical insertions in a performance model: evidence from bilinguals. *Proceedings of the 11th International Congress of Linguistics*. Bologna: Mulino.

Clyne, M. (1980) Zur Regelmäßigkeit von Spracherscheinungen bei Bilingualen. *Zeitschrift für germanistische Linguistik* 8: 22–33.

Clyne, M. (1980a) Triggering and language processing. *Canadian Journal of Psychology* 34: 400–6.

Clyne, M. (1982) *Multilingual Australia*. Melbourne: River Seine Publications.

Clyne, M. (1987) Constraints on code-switching: how universal are they? *Linguistics* 25: 739–64.

Cochran, M., Larner, M., Riley, D., Gunnarsson, M. and Henderson, C.R. (eds) (1990) *Extending Families*. Cambridge: Cambridge University Press.

Colbourn, C. (1978) Can laterality be measured. *Neuropsychologia* 16: 283–90.

Collins, A.M. and Loftus, E.F. (1975) A spreading activation theory of semantic processing. *Psychological Review* 82: 407–28.

Comhaire-Sylvain, S. (1936) *Le Créole haitien*. Wetteren and Port-au-Prince.

Coulmas, F. (1992) *Language and Economy*. Oxford: Blackwell.

Coupland, N. and Jaworski, A. (eds) (1997) *Sociolinguistics: A reader and coursebook*. Houndmills: Macmillan.

Crawhall, N. (1990) Unpublished Shona/English data set.

Crystal, D. (1987, 2nd edn 1997) *The Cambridge Encyclopaedia of Language*. Cambridge: Cambridge University Press.

Cummins, J. (1976) The influence of bilingualism on cognitive growth: a synthesis of research findings and explanatory hypotheses. *Working Papers on Bilingualism* 9: 1–43.

Cummins, J. (1981) The role of primary language development in promoting educational success for language minority students. In *Schooling and Language Minority Students: A theoretical framework*. Los Angeles: Evaluation, Dissemination, and Assessment Center.

Cunningham-Andersson, U. and Andersson, S. (1999) *Growing up with Two Languages*. London: Routledge.

d'Angelo, D. (1984) Interaktionsnetzwerke und soziokultureller Hintergrund italienischer Migranten und Migrantenkinder in Konstanz. *Papiere des SFB 99*, Constance.

Darbelnet, J. (1957) La couleur en français et en anglais. *Journal des Traducteurs* 2: 157–61.

Darcy, N.T. (1953) A review of the literature on the effects of bilingualism upon the measurement of intelligence. *Journal of Genetic Psychology* 82: 21–57.

Dauer, R. (1983) Stress-timing and syllable-timing reanalyzed. *Journal of Phonetics* 11: 51–62.

de Bot, K. (1986) Transfer of intonation and the missing data basis. In F. Kellerman and

M. Sharwood Smith (eds), *Cross-Linguistic Influence in Second Language Learning*. Oxford: Pergamon Press.

de Bot, K. (1990) Metalinguistic awareness in long-term Dutch immigrants in Australia. Paper presented at the annual meeting of the Australian Association of Applied Linguistics, Sydney, September.

de Bot, K. (1992) A bilingual production model: Levelt's 'speaking' model adapted. *Applied Linguistics* 13: 1–24.

de Bot, K. and Clyne, M. (1989) Language reversion revisited. *Studies in Second Language Acquisition* 11: 167–77.

de Bot, K., and Schreuder, R. (1993) Word production and the bilingual lexicon. In R. Schreuder and B. Weltens (eds), *The Bilingual Lexicon*. Philadelphia: John Benjamins, pp. 191–214.

Dechert, H. (1984) Second language production: six hypotheses. In H. Dechert, D. Möhle, and M. Raupach (eds), *Second Language Productions*. Tübingen: Gunter Narr.

de Groot A. and Kroll, J. (eds) (1997) *Tutorials in Bilingualism: Psycholinguistic perspectives*. Mahwah, NJ: Lawrence Erlbaum.

De Houwer, A. (1990) *The Acquisition of Two Languages from Birth: A case study*. Cambridge: Cambridge University Press.

De Houwer, A. (1995) Bilingual language acquisition. In P. Fletcher and B. MacWhinney (eds), *The Handbook of Child Language*. Oxford: Blackwell, pp. 219–50.

De Houwer, A. (ed.) (1998) *Bilingual Acquisition*. London: Kingston Press (also available as a special issue of *International Journal of Bilingualism*, 2(3)).

de Jong, E. (1986) *The Bilingual Experience: A book for parents*. Cambridge: Cambridge University Press.

Dell, G. (1986) A spreading activation theory of retrieval in sentence production. *Psychological Review* 93: 283–321.

Dennis, N., Henriques, F.M. and Slaughter, C. (1957) *Coal is Our Life*. London: Eyre and Spottiswoode.

Deuchar, M. and Quay, S. (1998) One vs. two systems in early bilingual syntax: two versions of the question. *Bilingualism: Language and Cognition* 1: 231–43.

Deuchar, M. and Quay, S. (2000) *Bilingual Acquisition: Theoretical implications of a case study*. Oxford: Oxford University Press.

Di Luzio, A. (1983) Problemi linguistici dei figli dei lavoratori migranti. In G. Braga (ed.), *Problemi linguistici e unità europea*. Milano: Angeli, pp. 112–19.

Di Luzio, A. (1984) On the meaning of language alternation for the sociocultural identity of Italian migrant children. In J.C.P. Auer and A. Di Luzio (eds), *Interpretive Sociolinguistics: Migrants – children – migrant children*. Tübingen: Narr.

Di Sciullo, A.M., Muysken, P. and Singh, R. (1986) Government and code-mixing. *Journal of Linguistics* 22: 1–24.

Diaz, R. (1983) Thought and two languages: the impact of bilingualism on cognitive development. In E. Norbeck, D. Price-Williams and W. McCord (eds), *Review of Research in Education*. Vol. 10. Washington DC: American Educational Research Association.

Diebold, Jr. A.R., (1961) Incipient bilingualism. *Language* 37.

Dieth, E. (1938) *Schwyzertütsch Dialäkschrift*. Zurich.

Dik, S. (1978) *Functional Grammar*. Amsterdam: Noord-Holland.

Dohrenwend, B.P. and Smith, R.J. (1962) Toward a theory of acculturation. *Southwest Journal of Anthropology* 18: 30–9.

Dopke, S. (1992) *One Parent One Language: An interactional approach*. Amsterdam: John Benjamins.

Dorian, N. (1981) *Language Death: The life cycle of a Scottish Gaelic dialect*. Philadelphia, PA: Pennsylvania University Press.

Dornic, S. (1978) The bilingual's performance: Language dominance, stress and individual differences. In D. Gerver and H. Sinaiko (eds), *Language Interpretation and Communication*. New York: Plenum.

Dowty, D. (1979) *Word Meaning and Montague Grammar*. Dordrecht: Reidel.

Dufour, R. (1997) Sign language and bilingualism. In A. de Groot and J. Kroll (eds), *Tutorials in Bilingualism: Psycholinguistic perspectives*. Mahwah, NJ: Lawrence Erlbaum, pp. 301–30.

Edwards, J. (1994) *Multilingualism*. London: Routledge.

Edwards, V. (1986) *Language in a Black Community*. Clevedon: Multilingual Matters.

Ervin, S.M. (1964) An analysis of the interaction of language, topic and listener. *American Anthropologist* 66, Part 2: 86–102.

Ervin-Tripp, S. (1976) Is Sybil there? The structure of some American English directives. *Language in Society* 5: 25–66.

Ervin, S.M. and Osgood, C.E. (1954) Second language learning and bilingualism. *Journal of Abnormal and Social Psychology* 49, Supplement: 139–46.

Extra, G. and Verhoeven, L. (eds) (1994) *The Cross-Linguistic Studies of Bilingual Development*. Amsterdam: North-Holland.

Færch, C. and G. Kasper (1986) Cognitive dimensions of language transfer. In E. Kellerman and M. Sharwood Smith (eds), *Cross-Linguistic Influence in Second Language Learning*. Oxford: Pergamon Press.

Fabbro, F. (1999) *The Neurolinguistics of Bilingualism*. Hove: Psychology Press.

Fantini, A.E. (1978) Bilingual behavior and social cues: case studies of two bilingual children. In M. Paradis (ed.), *Aspects of Bilingualism*. Columbia, SC: Hornbeam Press.

Fantini, A.F. (1982) *La adquisición del lenguaje en un niño bilingue*. Barcelona: Editorial Herder.

Fasold, R. (1984) *The Sociolinguistics of Society*. Oxford: Blackwell.

Fasold, R. (1990) *The Sociolinguistics of Language*. Oxford: Blackwell.

Ferguson, C.A. (1957) Two problems in Arabic phonology. *Word* 13: 460–78.

Ferguson, C.A. (1959) Diglossia. *Word* 15: 325–40.

Ferguson, C.A. (1960) Myths about Arabic. *Monograph Series on Language and Linguistics* 12: 75–82, Georgetown University.

Fernandez, M. (1994) *Diglossia: A comprehensive bibliography 1960–1990 and supplements*. Amsterdam: John Benjamins.

Fischer, C. (1984) *The Urban Experience*. 2nd edn. New York: Harcourt, Brace, Jovanovitch.

Fishman, J.A. (1956) The process and function of social stereotyping. *Journal Social Psychology* 43: 27–64.

Fishman, J.A. (1964) Language maintenance and language shift as fields of inquiry. *Linguistics* 9: 32–70.

Fishman, J.A. (1965) Who speaks what language to whom and when? *La Linguistique* 2: 67–88.

Fishman, J.A. (1965a) Language maintenance and language shift in certain urban immigrant environments: the case of Yiddish in the United States. *Europa Ethnica* 22: 146–58.

Fishman, J.A. (1965b) Bilingualism, intelligence and language learning. *Modern Language Journal* 49: 227–37.

Fishman, J.A. (1965c) Language maintenance and language shift: the American immigrant case. *Sociologus* 16: 19–38.

Fishman, J.A. (1965d) *Yiddish in America*. Bloomington, IN: Indiana University Research Center in Anthropology, Folklore and Linguistics. Publication 36. (Also: *International Journal of American Lingustics* 31, Part II, (2).)

Fishman, J.A. (1965e) Varieties of ethnicity and language consciousness. *Monograph Series on Languages and Linguistics* (Georgetown University) 18: 69–79.

Fishman, J.A. (ed.) (1966) *Language Loyalty in the United States*. The Hague: Mouton.

Fishman, J.A. (1966a) Language maintenance in a supra-ethnic age; summary and conclusions. In J.A. Fishman (ed.), *Language Loyalty in the United States*. The Hague: Mouton, pp. 392–411.

Fishman, J.A. (1966b) Bilingual sequences at the societal level. *On teaching English to speakers of other languages* 2: 139–44.

Fishman, J.A. (1966c) Some contrasts between linguistically homogeneous and linguistically heterogeneous polities. *Sociological Inquiry* 36: 146–158.

Fishman, J.A. (1967) Bilingualism with and without diglossia; diglossia with and without bilingualism. *Journal of Social Issues* 23(2): 29–38.

Fishman, J.A. (1968) Sociolinguistic perspective on the study of bilingualism. *Linguistics* 39: 21–49.

Fishman, J.A. (1971) The sociology of language: an interdisciplinary approach. In J.A. Fishman (ed.), *Advances in the Sociology of Language*. Vol. 1. The Hague: Mouton.

Fishman, J.A. (1972) *Language in Sociocultural Change: Essays by J.A. Fishman*, selected by A.S. Dil, Stanford, CA: Stanford University Press.

Fishman, J.A. (1985) *The Rise and Fall of the Ethnic Revival: Perspectives on language and ethnicity*. Berlin: Mouton.

Fishman, J.A. (1989) *Language and Ethnicity in Minority Sociolinguistic Perspective*. Clevedon: Multilingual Matters.

Fishman, J.A. (1991) *Reversing Language Shift*. Clevedon: Multilingual Matters.

Flege, J. (1986) Effects of equivalence classification on the production of foreign language sounds. In A. James and J. Leather (eds), *Sound Patterns in Second Language Acquisition*. Dordrecht: Foris.

Fletcher, P. and Garman, M. (eds) (1979) *Language Acquisition: Studies in first language development*. Cambridge: Cambridge University Press.

Forster, K.I. (1970) Visual perception of rapidly presented word sequences of varying complexity. *Perception and Psychophysics* 8: 215–21.

Forster, K.I. (1976) Accessing the mental lexicon. In R.Wales and E.Walker (eds), *New Approaches to Language Mechanism*. Amsterdam: North-Holland, pp. 257–87.

Frauenfelder, U. and Tyler, L. (eds) (1987) *Spoken Word Recognition*. Cambridge, MA: MIT Press.

Frei, H. (1936) Monosyllabisme et polysyllabisme dans les emprunts linguistiques. *Bulletin de la Maison franco-japonaise* 8.

Freud, S. (1891/1953) *On Aphasia* (E. Stengel, trans.). London: Imago.

Frey, J.W. (1945) Amish triple talk. *American Speech* 20: 85–98.

Friedrich, P. (1972) Social context and semantic feature. In J.J. Gumperz and D. Hymes (eds), *Directions in Sociolinguistics*. New York: Holt, Rinehart and Winston, pp. 270–300.

Fujimura, O. and Lovins, J. (1978) Syllables are concatenative phonetic units. In A. Bell and J. Hooper (eds), *Syllables and Segments*. Amsterdam: North Holland.

Gage, W.W. (1961) *Contrastive Studies in Linguistics: A bibliographical checklist*. Washington, DC: Center for Applied Linguistics.

Gal, S. (1979) *Language Shift: Social determinants of linguistic change in bilingual Austria*. New York: Academic Press.

Gal, S. (1988) The political economy of code choice. In M. Heller (ed.), *Codeswitching: Anthropological and Sociolinguistic Perspectives*. Berlin: Mouton de Gruyter, pp. 245–64.

Gal, S. (1989) Language and political economy. *Annual Review of Anthropology* 18: 345–67.

Galloway, L. (1977) The brain and the bilingual. Unpublished manuscript, University of California, Los Angeles.

Galloway, L. (1980) The cerebral organization of language in bilinguals and second language learners. PhD dissertation, University of California, Los Angeles.

Galloway, L. (1980a) Neurological correlates of language in second language performance. II. An overview and future perspectives. Paper presented at the Third Los Angeles Second Language Research Forum. University of California, Los Angeles, February/March.

Galloway, L. (1980b) Towards a neuropsychological model of bilingualism and second language performance: a theoretical article with a critical review of current research and some new hypotheses. In M. Long, S. Peck and K. Bailey (eds), *Research in Second Language Acquisition*. Rowley, MA: Newbury House.

Galloway, L. (1980c) Clinical evidence: polyglot aphasia. Presented at the Symposium on Cerebral Lateralization in Bilingualism. BABBLE Conference. Niagara Falls, Ontario.

Galloway, L. and Krashen, S. (1980) Cerebral organization in bilingualism and second language. In R. Scarcella and S. Krashen (eds), *Research in Second Language Acquisition*. Rowley, MA: Newbury House, pp. 74–80.

Galloway, L. and Scarcella, R. (1982) Cerebral organization in adult second language acquisition: is the right hemisphere more involved? *Brain and Language* 16: 56–60.

Gans, H.J. (1962) *The Urban Villagers: Group and class in the life of Italian-Americans*. 2nd edn. New York: Free Press.

Garcia, E.E. (1983) *Early Childhood Bilingualism*. Albuquerque: University of New Mexico Press.

Garcia, O. and Baker, C. (1995) *Policy and Practice in Bilingual Education*. Clevedon: Multilingual Matters.

Gardner-Chloros, P. (1991) *Language Selection and Switching in Strasbourg*. Oxford: Clarendon.

Gardner, E. and Branski, D. (1976) Unilateral cerebral activation and perception of gaps: a signal detection analysis. *Neuropsychologica* 14: 43–53.

Garfinkel, H. (1972) Remarks on ethnomethodology. In J.J. Gumperz and D. Hymes (eds), *Directions in Sociolinguistics*. New York: Holt, Rinehart and Winston, pp. 301–24.

Garman, M. (1979) Early grammatical development. In P. Fletcher, and M. Garman (eds), *Language Acquisition: Studies in first language development*. Cambridge: Cambridge University Press, pp. 177–208.

Garrett, M. (1975) The analysis of sentence production. In G. Bower (ed.), *Psychology of Learning and Motivation: Vol. 9*. New York: Academic Press.

Garrett, M. (1982) Production of speech: observations from normal and pathological language use. In A.W. Ellis (ed.), *Normality and pathology in cognitive functions*. New York/London: Academic Press.

Garrett, M. (1988) Process in sentence production. In F. Newmeyer (ed.), *The Cambridge Linguistics Survey III*, Cambridge: Cambridge University Press, pp. 69–96.

Gaziel, T., Obler, L. and Albert, M. (1978) A tachistoscopic study of Hebrew–English bilinguals. In M. Albert and L. Obler (eds), *The Bilingual Brain*. New York: Academic Press.

Geerts, G., *et al.* (eds) (1984) *Algemene Nederlandse Spraakkunst* (ans). Groningen: Wolters.

Genesee, F. (1987) *Learning through Two Languages: Studies of immersion and bilingual education*. Cambridge MA: Newbury House.

Genesee, F. (1989) Early bilingual language development: one language or two? *Journal of Child Language* 16: 161–79.

Genesee, F. and Bourhis, R. (1982) The social psychological significance of code switching in cross-cultural communication. *Journal of Language and Social Psychology* 1:1–28.

Genesee, F., Hamers, J., Lambert, W.E., Mononen, L., Seitz, M. and Starck, R. (1978) Language processing in bilinguals. *Brain and Language* 5: 1–12.

Genesee, F., Nicoladis, N. and Paradis, J. (1995) Language differentiation in early bilingual development. *Journal of Child Language* 22: 611–31.

Gibbons, J. (1979) Code-mixing and koineising in the speech of students at the University of Hong Kong. *Anthropological Linguistics* 21:113–23.

Gibbons, J. (1983) Attitudes towards languages and code-mixing in Hong Kong. *Journal of Multilingual and Multicultural Development* 4: 129–48.

Giddens, A. (1984) *The Constitution of Society*. Cambridge: Cambridge University Press.

Giddens, A. (1989) *Sociology*. Cambridge: Polity.

Giesbers, H. (1989) *Code-switching tussen dialect en standaardtaal*. Amsterdam: P. Meertensinstituut.

Gilbert, G.G. (1969) The linguistic geography of the colonial and immigrant languages in the United States. Paper presented to the Linguistic Society of America, December.

Giles, H. and Powesland, P. (1975) *Speech Style and Social Evaluation*. New York: Academic Press.

Gingràs, R. (1974) Problems in the description of Spanish–English intra-sentential code-switching. In G.A. Bills (ed.), *Southwest Areal Linguistics*. San Diego: Institute for Cultural Pluralism.

Givón, T. (1979) *On Understanding Grammar*. New York: Academic Press.

Givón, T. (1985) Function, structure and language acquisition. In D.I. Slobin (ed.), *The Crosslinguistic Study of Language Acquisition*. Hillsdale, NJ: Erlbaum, pp. 1005–27.

Goebl, H., Nelde, P., Stary, Z. and Wolck, W. (eds) (1996) *Contact Linguistics: An international handbook of contemporary research*. Berlin: Walter de Gruyter.

Goffman, E. (1959) *The Presentation of Self in Everyday Life*. New York: Doubleday.

Goffman, E. (1979) Footing. *Semiotica* 25:1–29.

Goke-Pariola, A. (1983) Code-mixing among Yoruba–English bilinguals. *Anthropological Linguistics* 25: 39–46.

Goldman-Eisler, F. (1958) Speech production and the predictability of words in context. *Quarterly Journal of Experimental Psychology* 10: 96–106.

Goodglass, H. (1978) Acquisition and dissolution of language. In A. Caramazza and E. Zurif (eds), *Language Acquisition and Language Breakdown*. Baltimore: Johns Hopkins Press, pp. 101–8.

Goodluck, H. (1987) *Language Acquisition and Linguistic Theory*. In P. Fletcher and M. Garman (eds), *Language acquisition*. 2nd edn. Cambridge: Cambridge University Press.

Goodz, N.S. (1986) Parental language in bilingual families: a model and some data. Paper presented at the Third Congress of the World Association of Infant Psychiatry and Allied Disciplines, Stockholm, Sweden.

Goodz, N.S. (1989) Parental language mixing in bilingual families. *Journal of Infant Mental Health* 10: 25–44.

Gordon, H.W. (1980) Cerebral organization in bilinguals. Vol. 1. Lateralization. *Brain and Language* 9: 255–68.

Gordon, H.W. and Weide, R. (1983) La contribution de certaines fonctions cognitives au traitement du langage, à son acquisition et à l'apprentissage d'une langue seconde. *Langages* 73: 45–56.

Grainger, J. and Beauvillain, C. (1987) Language blocking and lexical access in bilinguals. *The Quarterly Journal of Experimental Psychology* 39A: 295–319.

Grainger, J. and Dijkstra, T. (1992) On the representation and use of language information in bilinguals. In R. Harris (ed.), *Cognitive Processing in Bilingualism*. New York: North-Holland, pp. 207–20.

Grammont, M. (1902) Observation sur le langage des enfants. *Mélanges Meillet*. Paris.

Granda, G. de (1968) *Transculturación e Interferencia Lingüística en el Puerto Rico Contemporáneo (1898–1968)*. Bogotá: Instituto Caro y Cuervo.

Green, D.W. (1986) Control, activation, and resource: a framework and a model for the control of speech in bilinguals. *Brain and Language* 27: 210–23.

Greenberg, J.H. (1954) A quantitative approach to the morphological typology of language. In R. Spencer (ed.), *Method and Perspective in Anthropology*. University of Minnesota Press, pp. 192–220.

Greenfield, L. (1968) Spanish and English usage self-ratings in various situational contexts. In J.A. Fishman, R.L. Cooper and R. Ma (eds), *Bilingualism in the Barrio*. New York: Yeshiva University. Reissued by Indiana University Press, 1971.

Greyerz, O. von (1933) Vom Wert und Wesen unserer Mundart. *Sprache, Dichtung, Heimat*, Berne, pp. 226–47.

Grice, H.P. (1975) Logic and conversation. In P. Cole and J. Morgan (eds), *Syntax and Semantics: Speech Acts*. New York: Academic Press, pp. 41–58.

Griffiths, P. (1986) Early vocabulary. In P. Fletcher and M. Garman (eds), *Language Acquisition*. 2nd edn. Cambridge: Cambridge University Press.

Grosjean, F. (1980) Spoken word recognition processes and the gating paradigm. *Perception and Psychophysics* 28: 267–83.

Grosjean, F. (1982) *Life with Two Languages: An introduction to bilingualism*. Cambridge, MA: Harvard University Press.

Grosjean, F. (1985) The bilingual as a competent but specific speaker–hearer. *Journal of Multilingual and Multicultural Development* 6: 467–77.

Grosjean, F. (1985a) The recognition of words after their acoustic offset: evidence and implications. *Perception and Psychophysics* 38: 299–310.

Grosjean, F. (1988) Exploring the recognition of guest words in bilingual speech. *Language and Cognitive Processes* 3: 233–74.

Grosjean, F. (1989) Neurolinguists, beware! The bilingual is not two monolinguals in one person. *Brain and Language* 36: 3–15.

Grosjean, F. (1994) Individual bilingualism. *The Encyclopedia of Language and Linguistics*. Oxford: Pergamon, pp. 1656–60.

Grosjean, F. (1997) Processing mixed language: issues, findings, and models. In A.M. de Groot and J.F. Kroll (eds), *Tutorials in Bilingualism*. Mahwah, NJ: Lawrence Erlbaum, pp. 225–54.

Grosjean, F. (1998) Studying bilinguals: methodological and conceptual issues. *Bilingualism: Language and cognition* 1: 131–49.

Grosjean, F. and Gee, J. (1987) Prosodic structure and spoken word recognition. *Cognition* 25: 135–55.

Grosjean, F. and Miller, J. (1994) Going in and out of languages: an example of bilingual flexibility. *Psychological Science* 5: 201–6.

Grosjean, F. and Soares, C. (1986) Processing mixed language: some preliminary find-ings. In J. Vaid (ed.), *Language Processing in Bilinguals: Psycholinguistic and neuro-psychological perspectives*. Hillsdale, NJ: Lawrence Erlbaum Associates, pp. 145–79.

Gross, F. (1951) Language and value changes among the Arapho. *International Journal of American Linguistics* 17: 10–17.

Gumperz, J.J. (1961) Speech variation and the study of Indian civilization. *American Anthropologist* 63: 976–88.

Gumperz, J.J. (1962) Types of linguistic communities. *Anthropological Linguistics* 4(1): 28–40.

Gumperz, J.J. (1964) Linguistic and social interaction in two communities. *American Anthropologist* 66, 6 Part II: 137–54.

Gumperz, J.J. (1964a) Hindi–Punjabi code-switching in Delhi. In M. Halle (ed.), *Proceedings of the International Congress of Linguists*. The Hague: Mouton.

Gumperz, J.J. (1966) On the ethnology of linguistic change. In W. Bright (ed.), *Socio-linguistics*. The Hague: Mouton, pp. 27–38.

Gumperz, J.J. (1971) *Language in Social Groups: Essays by J.J. Gumperz*, selected by A.S. Dil. Stanford, CA: Stanford University Press.

Gumperz, J.J. (1971a) Bilingualism, bidialectalism and classroom interaction. In *Language in Social Groups*. Stanford, CA: Stanford University Press.

Gumperz, J.J. (1976) The sociolinguistic significance of conversational code-switching. *University of California Working Papers* 46. Berkeley: University of California.

Gumperz, J.J. (1978) Dialect and conversational inference in urban communication. *Language in Society* 7: 393–409. (Revised as Ethnic style as political rhetoric, in J.J. Gumperz, *Discourse Strategies*. New York: Cambridge University Press, pp. 187–203.)

Gumperz, J.J. (1982) *Discourse Strategies*. Cambridge: Cambridge University Press.

Gumperz, J.J. and Hernández-Chávez, E., *et al.* (1970) Cognitive aspects of bilingual communication. In E. Hernández-Chávez et al. (eds), *El Lenguaje de los Chicanos*. Arlington Center for Applied Linguistics.

Gumperz, J.J. and Naim, C.M. (1960) Formal and informal standards in the Hindu regional language area. *International Journal of American Linguistics* 26, Part 3: 92–118.

Hakuta, K. (1986) *Mirror of Language: The debate on bilingualism*. New York: Basic Books.

Hall, R.A., Jr. (1953) *Haitian Creole*. Menasha: WIS.

Halliday, M.A.K. (1964) The users and uses of language. In M.A.K. Halliday, A. McIntosh and P. Strevens, *The Linguistic Sciences and Language Teaching*. London: Longmans-Green, pp. 75–110.

Halmari, H. (1997) *Government and Code-Switching: Explaining American Finnish*. Amsterdam: John Benjamins.

Hamers, J. and Blanc, M. (1989, 2nd edn 2000) *Bilinguality and Bilingualism*. Cambridge: Cambridge University Press. (Original French edition *Bilingualité et bilinguisme*, 1983; Bruxelles: Liege.)

Hamers, J. and Lambert, W. (1977) Visual field and cerebral hemisphere preferences in bilinguals. In S. Segalowitz and F. Gruber (eds), *Language Development and Neurological Theory*, New York: Academic Press.

Handschin, K. (1994) L'influence de la langue de base dans la perception des alternances codiques: le cas de la consonne initiale du mot [Base language influence in the perception of code-switches: the case of a word's initial consonant]. *Travaux neuchâtelois de linguistique (TRANEL)* 21: 51–60.

Hansegard, N. E. (1975) Tvasprakighet eller halvsprakighet? *Invandrare och Minoriteter* 3: 7–13.

Harding, E. and Riley, P. (1986) *The Bilingual Family*. Cambridge: Cambridge University Press.

Hardyck, C. (1980) Hemispheric differences and language ability. Paper presented at Conference on Neurolinguistics of Bilingualism: Individual Differences, Albuquerque, NM, August.

Harman, L.D. (1988) *The Modern Stranger: On language and membership*. Berlin: Mouton de Gruyter.

Harris, R.J. (ed.) (1992) *Cognitive Processing in Bilinguals*. Amsterdam: North-Holland.

Hartnett, D. (1975) The relation of cognitive style and hemisphere preference to deductive and inductive second language learning. Unpublished MA thesis, University of California, Los Angeles, CA.

Hasselmo, N. (1961) American Swedish. Unpublished PhD dissertation, Harvard University.

Hasselmo, N. (1970) Code-switching and modes of speaking. In G. Gilbert (ed.), *Texas Studies in Bilingualism*. Berlin: Walter de Gruyter and Co.

Hasselmo, N. (1972) Code-switching as ordered selection. In E. Finchow *et al.* (eds), *Studies for Einar Haugen*. The Hague: Mouton.

Hasselmo, N. (1974) *Amerikasvenska*. Lund: Esselte.

Hatch, E. (1978) *Second Language Acquisition: A book of readings*. Rowley MA: Newbury House.

Hatzidakis, G.N. (1905) *Die Sprachfrage in Griechenland*. Chatzedaka, Athens.

Haugen, E. (1950) Analysis of linguistic borrowing. *Language* 26.

Haugen, E. (1953) *The Norwegian Language in America*. Philadelphia, PA: Pennsylvania University Press. Reissued by Indiana University Press in Bloomington, 1969.

Haugen, E. (1956) *Bilingualism in the Americas: A bibliography and research guide* (= Publication Number 26 of the American Dialect Society). Montgomery, AL: University of Alabama Press.

Haugen, E. (1973) Bilingualism, language contact and immigrant languages in the United States. *Current Trends in Linguistics* 10: 505–92.

Haugen, E. (1977) Norm and deviation in bilingual communities. In P. Hornby (ed.), *Bilingualism: Psychological, social and educational implications*. New York: Academic Press.

Heidelberger Forschungsprojekt 'Pidgin-Deutsch' (1977) The acquisition of German syntax by foreign migrant workers. In D. Sankoff (ed.), *Linguistic Variation: Models and methods*. New York: Academic Press.

Heller, M. (1982) Language strategies and ethnic conflict in the workplace. Manuscript, Ontario Institute for Studies in Education.

Heller, M. (1982a) Negotiations of language choice in Montreal. In J.J. Gumperz (ed.), *Language and Social Identity*. Cambridge: Cambridge University Press, pp. 108–18.

Heller, M. (ed.) (1988) *Codeswitching: Anthropological and sociolinguistic perspectives*. Berlin: Mouton de Gruyter.

Heller, M. (1990) The politics of codeswitching: processes and consequences of ethnic mobilisation. Paper presented at the third workshop of the European Science Foundation Network on Codeswitching and Language Contact, Brussels.

Heller, M. (1994) *Crosswords: Language, education and ethnicity in French Ontario*. Berlin: Mouton de Gruyter.

Heller, M. (1999) *Linguistic Minorities and Modernity: A sociolinguistic ethnography* (with the collaboration of M. Campbell, P. Dailey and D. Patrick). Harlow: Longman.

Herdan, G. (1960) *Type–Token Mathematics: A textbook of mathematical linguistics*. The Hague: Mouton de Gruyter.

Hieke, A. (1986) Absorption and fluency in native and non-native casual English speech. In A. James and J. Leather (eds), *Sound Patterns in Second Language Acquisition*. Dordrecht: Foris.

Hill, J.H. and Hill, K.C. (1986) *Speaking Mexicano: Dynamics of syncretic language in Central Mexico*. Tucson, AZ: University of Arizona Press.

Hinskens, F. (1988) Enkele gedachten over de notie 'structurele afstand'. *Mededelingen NCDN* 20: 89–100.

Hoffmann, C. (1985) Language acquisition in two trilingual children. *Journal of Multilingual and Multicultural Development* 6: 479–95.

Hoffmann, C. (1991) *An Introduction to Bilingualism*. Harlow: Longman.

Højrup, T. (1983) The concept of life-mode: a form-specifying mode of analysis applied to contemporary western Europe. *Ethnologia Scandinavica*: 1–50.

Hoosain, R. and Shiu, L.-P. (1989) Cerebral lateralization of Chinese–English bilingual functions. *Neuropsychologia* 27: 705–12.

Hudson, A.J. (1968) Perseveration. *Brain* 91: 571–82.

Hudson, R.A. (1980, 2nd edn 1996) *Sociolinguistics*. Cambridge: Cambridge University Press.

Hudson, R.A. (1992) Diglossia: A bibliographic review. *Language in Society* 21: 611–74.

Hymes, D. (1962) The ethnography of speaking. In T. Gladwin and W.C. Sturtevand (eds), *Anthropology and Human Behavior*. Washington, DC: Anthropology Society of Washington, pp. 13–53.

Hymes, D. (1964) Introduction: towards ethnographies of communication. *American Anthropologist* 66, 6 Part II: 1–34.

Hymes, D. (1972) On communicative competence. In J. Pride and J. Holmes, *Sociolinguistics*. Harmondsworth: Penguin, pp. 269–93.

Hymes, D. (1972a) Models of the interaction of language and social life. In J.J. Gumperz and D. Hymes (eds), *Directions in Sociolinguistics*. New York: Holt, Rinehart and Winston, pp. 35–71.

Hymes, D. (1972b) *Towards Communicative Competence*. Philadelphia, PA: University of Pennsylvania Press.

Hymes, D. (1974) *Foundations in Sociolinguistics*. Philadelphia, PA: University of Pennsylvania Press.

Hynd, G., Teeter, A. and Stewart, J. (1980) Acculturation and lateralization of speech in the bilingual native American. *International Journal of Neuroscience* 11: 1–7.

Ianco-Worrall, A.D. (1972) Bilingualism and cognitive development. *Child Development* 43: 1390–400.

Imedadze, N. (1978) On the psychological nature of child speech formation under conditions of exposure to two languages. In E. Hatch (ed.), *Second Language Acquisition: A book of readings*. Rowley MA: Newbury House.

Jackendoff, R. (1983) *Semantics and Cognition*. Cambridge, MA: MIT Press.

Jaeggli, O. (1982) *Topics in Romance Syntax*. Dordrecht: Foris.

Jake, J.L. (1994) Intrasentential code switching and pronouns: on the categorial status of functional elements. *Linguistics* 32: 271–98.

Jake, J.L. and Myers-Scotton, C. (1994) Embedded language islands in intrasentential code-switching: variation and compromise at two linguistic levels. Poster presented at annual meeting, NWAV (New Ways of Analyzing Variation), October.

Jake, J.L., Lüdi, G. and Myers-Scotton, C. (1995) Predicting variation in interlanguage. Paper presented at annual meeting, American Association of Applied Linguistics, March.

Jakobson, R. (1960) Closing statement: linguistics and poetics. In T.A. Sebeok (ed.), *Style in Language*. New York: Technology Press of MIT and Wiley, pp. 350–77.

Jefferson, G. (ed.) (1989) *Harvey Sacks Lectures, 1964–65*. Dordrecht: Kluwer Academic.

Jekat, S. (1985) Die Entwicklung des Wortschatzes bei bilingualen Kindern (Frz.-Dt) in den ersten vier Lebensjahren. Master's Thesis, University of Hamburg, Department of Romance Languages.

Joanette, Y., Goulet, P. and Hannequin, D. (1990) *Right Hemisphere and Verbal Communication*. New York: Springer Verlag.

Joanette, Y., Lecours, A. R., Lepage, Y. and Lamoureux, M. (1983) Language in right-handers with right-hemisphere lesions: a preliminary study including anatomical, genetic, and social factors. *Brain and Language* 20: 216–49.

Johnson, R., Cole, E., Blowers, J.K., Foiles, S.V., Nikaido, A.M., Patrick, J.W. and Woliver, R.E. (1979) Hemispheric efficiency in middle and later adulthood. *Cortex* 15: 109–19.

Joly, A. (1973) Sur le système de la personne. *Revue des Langues Romanes* 80: 3–56.

Jones, F.E. and Lambert, W.E. (1959) Attitudes toward immigrants in a Canadian community. *Public Opinion Quarterly* 23: 538–46.

Jones, I. (1960) *Bilingualism: A bibliography with special reference to Wales*. Aberystwyth: University College.

Joos, M. (1962) The five clocks. *International Journal of American Linguistics* 28, 2 Part V.

Jordan, B. and Fuller, N. (1975) On the non-fatal nature of trouble: sense-making and trouble-managing in *lingua franca* talk. *Semiotica* 13: 11–31.

Joshi, A.K. (1985) Processing of sentences with intrasentential code-switching. In

D.R. Dowty, L. Kartnnen and A.M. Zwicky (eds), *Natural Language Parsing*. Cambridge: Cambridge University Press, pp. 190–205.

Journal of the American Oriental Society (1955) vol. 75, pp. 124ff.

Jusczyk, P. (1981) Infant speech perception: a critical appraisal. In P.D. Eimas and J.L. Miller (eds), *Perspectives on the Study of Speech*. Hillsdale, NJ: Erlbaum.

Jusczyk, P. (1982) Auditory versus phonetic coding of speech signals during infancy. In J. Mehler, E. Walker and M. Garrett (eds), *Perspectives on Mental Representation*. Hillsdale, NJ: Erlbaum.

Kachru, B. (1978) Toward structuring code-mixing: an Indian perspective. *International Journal of the Sociology of Language* 16: 27–46.

Kadar-Hoffmann, G. (1983) Trlingualer Spracherwerb: Der gleichzeitige Erwerb des Deutschen, Französischen und Ungarischen. Dissertation, Kiel University.

Kahane, H., Kahane, R. and Ward, R.L. (1945) *Spoken Greek*. Washington.

Kamwangamalu, N. (1989) Theory and method of code-mixing: a cross-linguistic study. Unpublished doctoral dissertation, University of Illinois at Urbana.

Kaplan, R.B. and Baldauf, R.B. Jr. (1997) *Language Planning: From practice to theory*. Clevedon: Multilingual matters.

Karanth, P. and Rangamani, G.N. (1988) Crossed aphasia in multilinguals. *Brain and Language* 34: 169–80.

Keatly, C., Spinks, J. and de Gelder, B. (1989) Cross-language facilitation on the primed lexical decision task: Chinese–English and Dutch–French. Paper presented at Psychonomiecongres Noordwijkerhout, December.

Keijsper, C. (1984) Vorm en betekenis in Nederlandse toonhoogte contouren. *Forum der Letteren* 25(1, 2).

Kellerman, E. and Sharwood Smith, M. (eds) (1986) *Cross-linguistic Influence in Second Language Learning*. Oxford: Pergamon Press.

Kempen, G. and Hoenkamp, G. (1987) An incremental procedural grammar for sentence formulation. *Cognitive Science* 11: 201–58.

Kempen, G. and Huijbers, P. (1983) The lexicalisation process in sentence production and naming: indirect election of words. *Cognition* 14: 185–209.

Kerkman, H. (1984) Woordherkenning in twee talen. In A. Thomassen, L. Noordman and P. Eling (eds), *Het Leesproces*. Lisse: Swets and Zeitlinger.

Kerkman, H. and de Bot, K. (1989) De organisatie van het tweetalige lexicon. *Toegepaste Taalwetenschap in Artikelen* 34: 115–21.

Kershner, J. and Jeng, A. (1972) Dual functional hemispheric asymmetry in visual perception: effects of ocular dominance and post-exposural processes. *Neuropsychologia* 10: 437–45.

Kielhöfer, B. and Jonekeit, S. (1983) *Zweisprachige Kindererziehung*. Tübingen: Stauffenberg Verlag.

Kineene, M. wa (1983) Vioja afisini. *Mwanko*. Nairobi: Swahili club of the University of Nairobi.

Kinsborne, M. (1972) Eye and head turning indicates cerebral lateralization. *Science* 176: 539–41.

Klatt, D. (1979) Speech perception: a model of acoustic-phonetic analysis and lexical access. *Journal of Phonetics* 7: 279–312.

Klavans, J.L. (1983) The syntax of code-switching. Spanish and English. In *Proceedings of the Linguistic Symposium on Romance Languages*, Vol. 18. Amsterdam: Benjamins.

Kloss, H. (1929) Sprachtabellen als Grendlage für Sprachstatistik, Sprachenkarten und für eine allgemeine Sociologie der Sprachgemeinschaften. *Vierteljahrschrift für Politik und Geschichte* 1(7): 103–17.

Kloss, H. (1952) *Die Entwicklung neuer germanischer Kultursprachen von 1800 bis 1950.* Munich: Pohl.

Kloss, H. (1966) Types of multilingual communities, a discussion of ten variables. *Sociological Inquiry* 36.

Kolers, P. (1963) Interlingual word associations. *Journal of Verbal Learning and Verbal Behavior* 2: 291–300.

Kolers, P. (1966) Reading and talking bilingually. *American Journal Psychology* 3: 357–76.

Koppe, R. (1996) Language differentiation in bilingual children. *Linguistics* 34: 927–54.

Kotik, B. (1975) Lateralization in multilinguals. Thesis. Moscow State University, USSR.

Krashen, S. (1981) *Second Language Acquisition and Second Language Learning.* Oxford: Pergamon Press.

Krashen, S. and Galloway, L. (1978) The neurological correlates of language acquisition: current research: *SPEAQ Journal* 2: 21–35.

Krashen, S., Seliger, H. and Hartnett, D. (1974) Two studies in adult second language learning. *Kritikton Litterarum* 3: 220–8.

Kroll, J. and de Groot, A. (1997) Lexical and conceptual memory in the bilingual. In A. de Groot and J. Kroll (eds), *Tutorials in Bilingualism: Psycholinguistic perspectives.* Mahwah, NJ: Lawrence Erlbaum, pp. 169–200.

Krumbacher, K. (1902) *Das Problem der modernen griechischen Schriftsprache.* Munich.

Kulick, D. (1992) *Language Shift and Cultural Reproduction: Socialisation, self and syncretism in a Papua New Guinean village.* Cambridge: Cambridge University Press.

Labov, W. (1963) Phonological indices of stratification. Paper presented at the Annual Meeting of the American Anthropology Association, San Francisco.

Labov, W. (1964) Phonological correlates of social stratification. *American Anthropologist* 66, 6 Part II: 164–76.

Labov, W. (1966) *The Social Stratification of English in New York City.* Washington DC: Center for Applied Linguistics.

Labov, W. (1972) *Sociolinguistic Patterns.* Philadelphia, PA: Pennsylvania University Press.

Lado, R. (1961) *Language Testing.* London: Longman.

LaFontaine H. (1975) Bilingual education for Puerto Ricans: ¿si o no? Paper presented at the National Conference on the Educational Needs of the Puerto Rican in the United States, Cleveland, Ohio.

Lambert, W.E. *et al.* (1958) Evaluation reactions to spoken language. *Journal of Abnormal and Social Psychology* 60: 44–51.

Lance, D. (1975) Spanish–English code-switching. In E. Hernández-Chávez *et al.* (eds), *El Lenguaje de los Chicanos.* Arlington: Center for Applied Linguistics.

Lanza, E. (1997) *Language Mixing in Infant Bilingualism: A sociolinguistic perspective*. Oxford: Oxford University Press.

Laurie, S.S. (1890) *Lectures on Language and Linguistic Method in School*. Cambridge: Cambridge University Press.

Lavandera, B. (1978) The variable component in bilingual performance. In J. Alatis (ed.), *International Dimensions of Bilingual Education*. Washington DC: Georgetown University Press, pp. 391–411.

Lecerf, J. (1932) *Littérature Dialectale et renaissance arabe moderne* (Damascus, 1932–3), pp. 1–14; *Majallat al-majma'al-'ilmī al-'arabī* (Dimashq), vol. 32, no. 1 *'Adad xāṣṣ bilmu'tamar al-'awwal lilmajāmi' al-lugawiyyah al-'ilmiyyah al-'arabiyyah* (Damascus, January 1957).

Leopold, W. (1939–49) *Speech Development of a Bilingual Child: A linguist's record*, 4 volumes. Evanston, IL: Northwestern University Press.

Leopold, W. (1978) A child's learning of two languages. In E. Hatch (ed.), *Second Language Acquisition: A book of readings*. Rowley, MA: Newbury House.

Le Page, R. and Tabouret-Keller, A. (1985) *Acts of Identity: Creole-based approaches to language and ethnicity*. Cambridge: Cambridge University Press.

Leuenberger, M. (1994) L'accès au lexique de code-switches chez le bilingue: Effets de la densité et du contexte [Lexical access of code-switches in the bilingual: The effect of density and context]. *Travaux neuchâtelois de linguistique (TRANEL)* 21: 61–72.

Levelt, W. (1989) *Speaking: From intention to articulation*. Cambridge, MA: MIT Press.

Levelt, W. and Maassen, B. (1981) Lexical search and order of mention in sentence production. In W. Klein and W. Levelt (eds), *Crossing the Boundaries in Linguistics: Studies presented to Manfred Bierwisch*. Dordrecht: Reidel.

Levelt, W. and Schriefers, H. (1987) Stages of lexical access. In G. Kempen (ed.), *Natural Language Generation: New results in artificial intelligence, psychology and linguistics*. Dordrecht: Martinus Nijhoff.

Levinson, S. (1983) *Pragmatics*. Cambridge: Cambridge University Press.

Li, P. (1996) Spoken word recognition of code-switched words by Chinese–English bilinguals. *Journal of Memory and Language* 757–74.

Lieberson, S. (1966) Language questions in census. *Sociological Inquiry* 36: 262–79.

Lindholm, K.J. and Padilla, A.M. (1978) Language mixing in bilingual children. *Journal of Child Language* 5: 327–35.

LIPPS Group (Language Interaction in Plurilingual and Plurilectic Speakers) (ed.) (2000) *The LIDES (Language Interaction Data Exchange System) Coding Manual*. London: Kingston Press. (Also available as a special issue of the *International Journal of Bilingualism*.)

Lipski, J. (1978) Code-switching and the problem of bilingual competence. In M. Paradis (ed.), *Aspects of Bilingualism*. Columbia: Hornbeam Press.

Lisker, L., and Abramson, A. (1964) A cross-language study of voicing in initial stops: acoustical measurements. *Word* 20: 384–422.

Li Wei (1993) Mother tongue maintenance in a Chinese community school in Newcastle upon Tyne. *Language and Education* 7: 199–215.

Li Wei (1994) *Three Generations Two Languages One Family: Language choice and language shift in a Chinese community in Britain*. Clevedon: Multilingual Matters.

Li Wei (1996) Network analysis. In H. Goebl, P. Nelde, Z. Stary and W. Wolck (eds), *Contact Linguistics: An international handbook of contemporary research*. New York: Walter de Gruyter, pp. 805–11.

Li Wei and Milroy, L. (1995) Conversational code-switching in a Chinese community in Britain: a sequential analysis. *Journal of Pragmatics* 23: 281–99.

Li Wei, Milroy, L. and Pong, S.C. (1992) A two-step sociolinguistic analysis of code-switching and language choice. *International Journal of Applied Linguistics* 2(1): 63–86.

Lüdi, G. (1983) Unpublished Neuchatel data corpus on French/Swiss German language use.

Luria, A. (1973) *The Working Brain: An introduction to neuropsychology*. London: Penguin.

Lyon, J. (1996) *Becoming Bilingual: Language acquisition in a bilingual community*. Clevedon: Multilingual Matters.

McClelland, J., and Elman, J. (1986) The TRACE model of speech perception. *Cognitive Psychology* 18: 1–86.

McClure, E. (1977) Aspects of code-switching in the discourse of bilingual Mexican-American children. In M. Saville-Troike (ed.), *Linguistics and Anthropology*. Washington, pp. 93–115.

McClure, E. (n.d.) The acquisition of communicative competence in a bicultural setting. NIE Grant NE-G-00-e-0147 final report.

McClure, E. and Wentz, J. (1975) Functions of code-switching among Mexican-American children. In *Papers from the Parasession on Functionalism*. Chicago: Chicago Linguistics Society.

McConnell, H.O. and Swan, E. (1945) *You Can Learn Creole*. Port-au-Prince.

McConvell, P. (1988) Mix-Im-Up: Aboriginal codeswitching, old and new. In M. Heller (ed.), *Codeswitching*. Berlin: Mouton, pp. 97–150.

McGlone, J. (1978) Sex differences in functional brain asymmetry. *Cortex* 14(1): 122–8.

McKeever, W. F. and Hunt, L. (1984) Failure to replicate the Scott *et al.* findings of reversed ear dominance in the Native American Navajo. *Neuropsychologia* 22: 539–41.45.

Mackey, W.F. (1952) Bilingualism and education. *Pédagogie-Orientation* 6: 135–47.

Mackey, W.F. (1953) Bilingualism and linguistic structure. *Culture* 14: 143–9.

Mackey, W.F. (1956) Toward a redefinition of bilingualism. *JCLA* 2.

Mackey, W.F. (1959) Bilingualism. *Encyclopaedia Britannica*.

Mackey, W.F. (1962) The description of bilingualism. *Canadian Journal of Linguistics* 7: 51–85.

Mackey, W.F. (1965) Bilingual interference: Its analysis and measurement. *Journal of Communication* 15: 239–49.

Mackey, W.F. and Noonan, J.A. (1952) An experiment in bilingual education. *English Language Teaching* 6: 125–32.

McLaughlin, B. (1984) *Second Language Acquisition in Childhood. Vol. 1: Preschool Children.* Hillsdale, NJ: Erlbaum.

McLeod, P. (1977) A dual task response modality effect: support for multi-processor models of attention. *Quarterly Journal of Experimental Psychology* 29: 651–67.

Macnamara, J. (1967) The bilingual's linguistic performance: a psychological overview. *Journal of Social Issues* 23: 59–77.

Macnamara, J. and Kushnir, S. (1971) Linguistic independence of bilinguals: the input switch. *Journal of Verbal Learning and Verbal Behavior* 10: 480–7.

MacSwan, J. (1999) *A Minimalist Approach to Intrasentential Code-Switching.* New York: Garland.

Mägiste, E. (1979) The competing language systems of the multilingual: A developmental study of decoding and encoding processes. *Journal of Verbal Learning and Verbal Behavior* 18: 79–89.

Mägiste, E. (1986) Selected issues in second and third language learning. In J. Vaid (ed.), *Language Processing in Bilinguals: Psycholinguistic and neuropsychological perspectives.* Hillsdale: Erlbaum.

Mahootian, S. and Santorini, B. (1996) Code-switching and the complement/adjunct distinction. *Linguistic Inquiry* 27: 464–79.

Mak, W. (1935) Zweisprachigkeit und Mischmundart in Oberschlesien. *Schlesisches Jahrbuch für deutsche Kulturarbeit* 7: 41–52.

Mallinson, G. and Blake, B.J. (1981) *Language Typology.* Amsterdam: Noord-Holland.

Marçais, W. (1930–31) Three articles. *L'Enseignement Public* 97: 401–9; 105: 20–39, 120–33.

Maratsos, M. (1982) The child's construction of grammatical categories. In E. Wanner and L. Gleitman (eds), *Language Acquisition: The state of the art.* Cambridge: Cambridge University Press, pp. 240–66.

Marouzeau, J. (1951) *Lexique de la terminologie linguistique.* Paris: Geuthner.

Marshall, J.C., Caplan, D. and Holmes, J.M. (1975) The measure of laterality. *Neuropsychologia* 13: 315–21.

Marslen-Wilson, W. (1987) Functional parallelism in spoken word recognition. *Cognition* 25: 71–102.

Martin-Jones, M. and Romaine, S. (1986) Semilingualism: a half-baked theory of communicative competence. *Applied Linguistics* 6: 105–17.

Meara, P. (1989) Models of the lexicon in English and other funny languages. *Toegepaste taalwetenschap in Artikelen* 34(2): 7–12.

Mehler, J., Bertoncini, J., Barrière, M. and Jassik-Gerschenfeld, D. (1978) Infant recognition of mother's voice. *Perception* 7: 491–7.

Mehler, J., Lambertz, G., Jusczyk, P. and Amiel-Tison, C. (1986) Discrimination de la langue maternelle par le nouveau-né. *Académie des Sciences* 3: 637–40.

Meisel, J.M. (1983) Transfer as a second-language strategy. *Language and Communication* 3(1): 11–46.

Meisel, J.M. (1985) Les phases initiales du développement de notions temporelles, aspectuelles et de modes d'action. *Lingua* 66: 321–74.

Meisel, J.M. (1986) Word order and case marking in early child language: evidence from simultaneous acquisition of two languages. *Linguistics* 24(1): 123–83.

Meisel, J.M. (1989) Early differentiation of languages in bilingual children. In K. Hyltenstam and L. Obler (eds), *Bilingualism across the Lifespan: Aspects of acquisition, maturity and loss*. Cambridge: Cambridge University Press, pp. 13–40.

Meisel, J.M. (ed.) (1990) *Two First Languages: Early grammatical development in bilingual children*. Dordrecht: Foris.

Meisel, J.M. (ed.) (1994) *Bilingual First Language Acquisition: French and German grammatical development*. Amsterdam: John Benjamins.

Meisel, J.M., Clahsen, H. and Pienemann, M. (1981) On determining developmental stages in natural second language acquisition. *Studies in Second Language Acquisition* 3(2): 109–35.

Menarini, A. (1939) L'italo-americano degli Stati Uniti. *Lingua Nostra* 1: 154–6.

Mendelsohn, S. (1988) Language lateralization in bilinguals: facts and fantasy. *Journal of Neurolinguistics* 3: 261–92.

Mikès, M. (1967) Acquisition des catégories grammaticales dans le langage de l'enfant. *Enfance* 20: 289–98.

Milardo, R.M. (1988) Families and social networks: an overview of theory and methodology. In *Families and Social Network*. Newbury Park, CA: Sage.

Mills, A.E. (1985) The acquisition of German. In D.I. Slobin (ed.), *The Cross-Linguistic Study of Language Acquisition*. Hillsdale, NJ: Erlbaum, 141–254.

Milner, B., Taylor, L. and Sperry, R.W. (1968) Lateralized suppression of dichotically presented digits after commissural section in man. *Science* 161: 184–6.

Milroy, J. and Milroy, L. (1985, 2nd edn 1991, 3rd edn 1999) *Authority in Language*. London: Routledge.

Milroy, L. (1987) *Observing and Analysing Natural Language*. Oxford: Blackwell.

Milroy, L. (1987a) *Language and Social Networks*. 2nd edn. Oxford: Blackwell.

Milroy, L. and Li Wei (1995) A social network approach to code-switching. In L. Milroy and P. Muysken (eds), *One Speaker Two Languages: Cross-disciplinary perspectives on code-switching*. Cambridge: Cambridge University Press, pp. 136–57.

Milroy, L. and Muysken, P. (eds) (1995) *One Speaker Two Languages: Cross-disciplinary perspectives on code-switching*. Cambridge: Cambridge University Press.

Milroy, L., Li Wei and Moffatt, S. (1993) Discourse patterns and fieldwork strategies in urban settings. *Journal of Multilingual and Multicultural Development* 12: 287–300.

Mishkin, M. and Forgays, D. (1952) Word recognition as a function of retinal locus. *Journal of Experimental Psychology* 43: 43–8.

Mitchell, J.C. (1986) Network procedures. In D. Frick *et al.* (eds), *The Quality of Urban Life*. Berlin: de Gruyter.

Mitchell, J.C. (1987) The components of strong ties among homeless women. *Social Networks* 9: 37–47.

Moffatt, S. (1990) Becoming bilingual: a sociolinguistic study of the communication of young mother tongue Panjabi-speaking children. Unpublished PhD thesis, Department of Speech, University of Newcastle upon Tyne.

Moffatt, S. and Milroy, L. (1992) Panjabi/English language alternation in the classroom in the early school years. *Multilingua.*

Möhle, D. (1984) A comparison of the second language speech production of different native speakers. In H. Dechert, D. Möhle and M. Raupach (eds), *Second Language Productions.* Tübingen: Gunter Narr.

Morton, J. (1979) Word recognition. In J. Morton and J. Marshall (eds), *Psycholinguistic Series 2: Structures and processes.* London: Elek.

Morton, J. (1980) Two auditory parallels to deep dyslexia. In M. Coltheart, K. Patterson and J.C. Marshall (eds), *Deep Dyslexia.* London: Routledge & Kegan Paul.

Moser, H. (1968) Wohin steuert das heutige Deutsch? In H. Moser (ed.), *Satz und Wort im heutigen Deutsch.* Düsseldorf: Schwann, pp. 15–35.

Moss, E.M., Davidson, R.J. and Saron, C. (1985) Cross-cultural differences in hemisphericity: EEG asymmetry discriminates between Japanese and Westerners. *Neuropsychologia* 23: 131–5.

Moyer, M.G. (1992) Spanish–English code-switching in Gibraltar. In European Science Foundation (ed.), *Code-Switching Summer School.* Strasbourg: European Science Foundation, pp. 51–67.

Murrell, M. (1966) Language acquisition in a trilingual environment: notes from a case-study. *Studia Linguistica* 20: 9–35.

Muysken, P. (1991) Needed: a comparative approach. In European Science Foundation (ed.), *Papers for the Symposium on Code-Switching in Bilingual Studies: Theory, significance and perspectives*, Vol. 1. Strasbourg: European Science Foundation, pp. 253–72.

Muysken, P. (1995) Code-switching and grammatical theory. In L. Milroy and P. Muysken (eds), *One Speaker Two Languages.* Cambridge: Cambridge University Press, pp. 177–98.

Myers-Scotton, C. (1986) Diglossia and code-switching. In J.A. Fishman *et al.* (eds), *The Fergusonian Impact.* Berlin: Mouton de Gruyter.

Myers-Scotton, C. (1988) Code-switching as indexical of social negotiations. In M. Heller (ed.), *Codeswitching.* Berlin: Mouton de Gruyter, pp. 151–86.

Myers-Scotton, C. (1992) Constructing the frame in intrasentential codeswitching. *Multilingua* 11: 101–27.

Myers-Scotton, C. (1993) *Social Motivations for Codeswitching: Evidence from Africa.* Oxford: Oxford University Press.

Myers-Scotton, C. (1993a, paperback edition with new Afterword 1997) *Duelling Languages: Grammatical structure in codeswitching.* Oxford: Oxford University Press.

Myers-Scotton, C. (1993c) Common and uncommon ground: social and structural factors in codeswitching. *Language in Society* 22: 475–503.

Myers-Scotton, C. (1995) What do speakers want? Codeswitching as evidence of intentionality in linguistic choices. In P. Silberman and J. Loftin (eds), *SALSA II*, Austin: Department of Linguistics, University of Texas, pp. 1–17.

Myers-Scotton, C. (1995a) A lexically-based model of codeswitching. In L. Milroy and P. Muysken (eds), *One Speaker Two Languages.* Cambridge: Cambridge University Press, pp. 233–56.

Myers-Scotton, C. (1995b) Language processing and the mental lexicon in bilinguals. In R. Dirven and J. Vanparys (eds), *New Approaches to the Lexicon*. Frankfurt: Peter Lang, pp. 73–100.

Myers-Scotton, C. (1995c) 'Matrix language recognition' and 'morpheme sorting' as possible structural strategies in pidgin/creole formation. In A. Spears and D. Winford (eds), *Pidgins and Creoles: Structure and Status*. Amsterdam: Benjamins.

Myers-Scotton, C. (1997) Codeswitching. In F. Coulmas (ed.) *The Handbook of Socio-linguistics*. Oxford: Blackwell, pp. 217–37.

Myers-Scotton, C. (1997a) *Duelling Languages: Grammatical structure in code-switching*. Oxford: Oxford University Press.

Myers-Scotton, C. and Jake, J.L. (1994) Swiss German/French and Swiss German/Italian corpora. Unpublished data.

Myers-Scotton, C. and Jake, J.L. (1995) Matching lemmas in a bilingual competence and production model. *Linguistics* 33: 981–1024.

Myers-Scotton, C. and Jake, J.L. (eds) (2000) *Testing a Model of Morpheme Classification with Language Contact Data*. London: Kingston Press. (Also available as a special issue of the *International Journal of Bilingualism*, 4(1).)

Nader, L. (1962) A note on attitudes and the use of language. *Anthropological Linguistics* 4(6): 24–9.

Nahirny, V.C. and Fishman, J.A. (1965) American immigrant groups: ethnic identification and the problem of generations. *Sociological Review* 13: 311–26.

Nair, K. and Vermani, V. (1973) Speech and language disturbances in hemiplegics. *Indian Journal of Medical Research* 61: 1131–8.

Naït M'Barek, M. and Sankoff, D. (1988) Le discours mixte arabe/français: des emprunts ou des alternances de langue? *Revue Canadienne de Linguistique* 33 (2): 143–54.

Nartey, J.N.A. (1982) Code-switching, interference or faddism? Language use among educated Ghanaians. *Anthropological Linguistics* 24: 183–92.

Nation, P. (1984) Sheng, new urban language baffles parents. Wednesday *Nation* magazine, 14 March 1984.

Navon, D. and Gopher, D. (1979) On the economy of the human processing system. *Psychological Review* 86: 214–55.

Neufeld, G. (1973) The bilingual's lexical store. *Working Papers on Bilingualism* 1: 35–65.

Norman, D. and Shallice, T. (1980) *Attention to Action: Willed and automatic control of behavior*. San Diego: Center for Human Information Processing, University of California, Chip 99.

Nortier, J. (1989) Dutch and Moroccan-Arabic in Contact: code-switching among Moroccans in the Netherlands. PhD dissertation, University of Amsterdam.

Nortier, J. (1990) *Dutch–Moroccan Arabic Code-switching among Moroccans in the Netherlands*. Dordrecht: Foris.

Obler, L.K. and Albert, M. (1978) A monitor system for bilingual language processing. In M. Paradis (ed.), *Aspects of Bilingualism*. Columbia, SC: Hornbeam Press, pp. 105–13.

Obler, L.K., Albert, M. and Gordon, H.W. (1975) Asymmetry of cerebral dominance in

Hebrew–English bilinguals. Paper presented at the Academy of Asphasia, Victoria, October.

Obler, L.K., Zatorre, R.J., Galloway, L. and Vaid, J. (1982) Cerebral lateralization in bilinguals: methodological issues. *Brain and Language* 15: 40–54.

Odlin, T. (1989) *Language Transfer: Cross-linguistic influence in language learning*. Cambridge: Cambridge University Press.

Okasha, M. (1995) Unpublished Arabic–English codeswitching corpus.

Oksaar, E. (1971) Code switching as an interactional strategy for developing bilingual competence. *Word* 27: 377–85.

Oksaar, E. (1978) Preschool trilingualism: a case study. In F.C. Peng and W. v. Raffler-Engel (eds), *Language Acquisition and Developmental Kinesics*. Tokyo, pp. 129–37.

Oldfield, R. (1963) Individual vocabulary and semantic currency: a preliminary study. *British Journal of Social and Clinical Psychology* 2: 122–30.

Oller, D. and MacNeilage, P. (1983) Development of speech production. In P. MacNeilage (ed.), *The Production of Speech*. New York: Springer.

Orbach, J. (1967) Differential recognition of Hebrew and English words in right and left visual fields as a function of cerebral dominance and reading habits. *Neuropsychologia* 50: 127–34.

Padilla, A.M. and Liebman, E. (1975) Language acquisition in the bilingual child. *Bilingual Review* 2: 34–55.

Paradis, M. (1977) Bilingualism and aphasia. In H. Whitaker and H. Whitaker (eds), *Studies in Neurolinguistics*, Vol. 13. New York: Academic Press.

Paradis, M. (1980) The language switch in bilinguals: psycholinguistic and neurolinguistic perspectives. In P. Nelde (ed.), *Languages in Contact and Conflict*. Wiesbaden, Germany: Franz Steiner Verlag, pp. 501–6.

Paradis, M. (1981) Contributions of neurolinguistics to the theory of bilingualism. In R. Herbert (ed.), *Applications of Linguistic Theory in the Human Sciences*. East Lansing: Michigan State University Press, pp. 180–211.

Paradis, M. (1985) On the representation of two languages in one brain. *Language Sciences* 61(7): 1–40.

Paradis, M. (1986) Bilingualism. *International Encyclopedia of Education*. Oxford: Pergamon, pp. 489–93.

Paradis, M. (ed.) (1987) *The Assessment of Bilingual Aphasia*. Hillsdale, NJ: Lawrence Erlbaum.

Paradis, M. (1988) Review of G. Bergh, 1986: The neuropsychological status of Swedish–English subsidiary bilinguals. *Linguistics* 25: 886–92.

Paradis, M. (1989) Bilingual and polyglot aphasia. In F. Boller and J. Grafman (eds), *Handbook of Neuropsychology*, Vol. 2. Amsterdam: Elsevier, pp. 117–40.

Paradis, M. (1990) Language lateralization in bilinguals. *Brain and Language* 39: 570–86.

Paradis, M. (1997) The cognitive neuropsychology of bilingualism. In A. de Groot and J. Kroll (eds), *Tutorials in Bilingualism*. Mahwah, NJ: Lawrence Erlbaum, pp. 331–54.

Paradis, M., Goldblum, M-C. and Abidi, R. (1982) Alternate antagonism with paradoxical translation behavior in two bilingual aphasic patients. *Brain and Language* 15: 55–69.

Park, T.-Z. (1981) *The Development of Syntax in the Child: With special reference to German*. Innsbruck: Innsbrucker Beiträge zur Kulturwissenschaft 45.

Parkin, D. (1974) Language switching in Nairobi. In W.H. Whiteley (ed.), *Language in Kenya*. Nairobi: Oxford University Press, pp. 189–216.

Pavlovitch, M. (1920) *Le langage enfantin: L'acquisition du serbe et du français par un enfant serbe*. Paris: Champion.

Payne, A. (1976) The acquisition of the phonological system of a second dialect. Unpublished PhD dissertation, University of Pennsylvania.

Peal, E. and Lambert, W.E. (1962) The relation of bilingualism to intelligence. *Psychological Monographs*.

Pearson, B.Z. (1998) Assessing lexical development in bilingual babies and toddlers. *International Journal of Bilingualism* 2: 347–72.

Pearson, B.Z., Fernandez, S.C. and Oller, D.K. (1993) Lexical development in bilingual infants and toddlers. *Language Learning* 43: 93–120.

Pedraza, P. (1978) Ethnographic observations of language use in El Barrio. Unpublished ms.

Penfield, W. and Roberts, L. (1959) *Speech and Brain-Mechanisms*. Princeton: Princeton University Press.

Perdue, C. (ed.) (1984) *Second Language Acquisition by Adult Immigrants: A field manual*. Rowley, MA: Newbury House.

Perecman, E. (1989) Language processing in the bilingual: evidence from language mixing. In K. Hyltenstam and L. Obler (eds), *Bilingualism Across the Lifespan*. Cambridge: Cambridge University Press.

Pernot, H. (1898) *Grammaire Grecque Moderne*. Paris, pp. vii–xxxi.

Pfaff, C. (1975) Syntactic constraints on code-switching: a quantitative study of Spanish–English. Paper presented at the Linguistic Society of America annual meeting.

Pfaff, C. (1976) Functional and structural constraints on syntactic variation in code-switching. *Papers from the Parasession on Diachronic Syntax*. Chicago, IL: Chicago Linguistic Society.

Pfaff, C. (1979) Constraints on language mixing: intrasentential code-switching and borrowing in Spanish/English. *Language* 55: 291–318.

Piazza, D.M. and Zatorre, R.J. (1981) A right-ear advantage for dichotic listening in bilingual children. *Brain and Language* 13: 389–96.

Pijper, J.R. (1983) *Modelling British English Intonation: An analysis by resynthesis of British English intonation*. Dordrecht: Foris.

Pike, K.L. (1967) *Language in Relation to the Unified Theory of the Structure of Human Behaviour*. The Hague: Mouton.

Pillai, M. (1960) Tamil: literary and colloquial. In C.A. Ferguson and J.J. Gumperz (eds), *Linguistic Diversity in South Asia*. Indiana University Research Center in Anthropology, Folklore and Linguistics, Publication 13, pp. 27–42.

Pong, Sin Ching (1991) Intergenerational variation in language choice patterns in a Chinese community in Britain. Unpublished MPhil thesis, University of Newcastle upon Tyne.

Poplack, S. (1978) Dialect acquisition among Puerto Rican bilinguals. *Language in Society* 7(1): 89–103.

Poplack, S. (1978/81) Syntactic structure and social function of code-switching. In R. Duran (ed.), *Latino Discourse and Communicative Behaviour*. Norwood, NJ: Ablex, pp. 169–84.

Poplack, S. (1979/80) Sometimes I'll start a sentence in Spanish *y termino en español:* toward a typology of code-switching. Working Paper No. 4. New York: Centro de Estudios Puertorriquenos. Also in *Linguistics* 18: 581–618.

Poplack, S. (1988) Contrasting patterns of codeswitching in two communities. In M. Heller (ed.), *Codeswitching*. Berlin: Mouton, pp. 215–44.

Poplack, S. (1993) Variation theory and language contact: contact, concept, methods and data. In D. Preston (ed.), *American Dialect Research*. Amsterdam: John Benjamins, pp. 251–86.

Poplack, S. and Meechan, M. (eds) (1998) *Instant Loans, Easy Conditions: The productivity of bilingual borrowing*. London: Kingston Press. (Also available as a special issue of the *International Journal of Bilingualism* 2(2).)

Poplack, S. and Sankoff, D. (1984) Borrowing: the synchrony of integration. *Linguistics* 22: 99–135.

Poplack, S. and Sankoff, D. (1987) Code-switching. In U. Ammon, N. Dittmar and K. Mattheier (eds), *Sociolinguistics: An international handbook of the science of language and society*, volume 2. Berlin: Walter de Gruyter, pp. 1174–80.

Poplack, S., Sankoff, D. and Miller, C. (1988) The social correlates and linguistic processes of lexical borrowing and assimilation. *Linguistics* 26: 47–104.

Porsché, D.C. (1983) *Die Zweisprachigkeit während des primären Spracherwerbs*. Tübingen: Narr (TBL 218).

Poulisse, N. (1990) *The Use of Compensatory Strategies by Dutch Learners of English*. Dordrecht: Foris.

Poulisse, N. (1997) Language production in bilinguals. In A.M. de Groot and J.F. Kroll (eds), *Tutorials in Bilingualism*. Mahwah, NJ: Lawrence Erlbaum, pp. 201–24.

Poulisse, N. and Bongaerts, T. (1990) A closer look at the strategy of transfer. Paper presented at the AILA World congress, Thessaloniki.

Poulisse, N. and Bongaerts, T. (1994) First language use in second language production. *Applied Linguistics* 15: 36–57.

Preston, M. and Lambert, W. (1969) Interlingual interference in a bilingual version of the Stroop Colour Word Test. *Journal of Verbal Learning and Verbal Behaviour* 8: 295–301.

Preziosa-DiQuinzio, I. (1992) Teoreticamente la firma fa indietro. Lavoro di licenza inedito in linguistica italiana. Zurich: University of Zurich.

Psichari, J. (1928) Un Pays qui ne veut pas sa langue. *Mercure de France*, 1 October: 63–121. (Also in Psichari *Quelque travaux* . . . Paris, volume 1, pp. 1283–337.)

Pupier, P., Connors, K. and Lappin, K. *et al.* (1982) *L'acquisition simultanée du français et de l'anglais chez des petits enfants de Montréal*, Gouvernement du Québec, Office de la Langue Française.

Pye, C. (1986) One lexicon or two? An alternative interpretation of early bilingual speech. *Journal of Child Language* 13: 591–3.

Ramanujan, A.K. (1967) The structure of variation: a study in caste dialects. In B. Cohn and M. Singer (eds), *Social Structure and Social Change in India*. London: Aldine.

Rampton, B. (1995) *Crossing: Language and ethnicity among adolescents*. Harlow: Longman.

Rangamani, G.N. (1989) Aphasia and multilingualism: clinical evidence toward the cerebral organization of language. Unpublished PhD dissertation, The University of Mysore, India.

Rapport, R.L., Tan, C.T. and Whitaker, H.A. (1983) Language function and dysfunction among Chinese- and English-speaking polyglots: cortical stimulation. Wada testing, and clinical studies. *Brain and Language* 18: 342–66.

Redlinger, W.E. and Park, T. (1980) Language mixing in young bilinguals. *Journal of Child Language* 7: 337–52.

Reich, P. (1976) The early acquisition of word meaning. *Journal of Child Language* 3: 117–23.

Repp, B.H. (1977) Measuring laterality effects in dichotic listening. *Journal of the Acoustical Society of America* 62: 720–37.

Riley, D., Cochran, M., Henderson, C.R., Gunnarsson, L. and Larner, M. (1990) Settings and methods. In M. Cochran *et al.* (eds), *Extending Families*. Cambridge: Cambridge University Press.

Roelofs, A. (1992) A spreading activation theory of lemma retrieval in speaking. *Cognition* 42: 107–42.

Roger, D. and Bull, P. (eds) (1989) *Conversation: An interdisciplinary perspective*. Clevedon: Multilingual Matters.

Rogers, L., Ten Houten, W., Kaplan, C. and Gardiner, M. (1977) Hemispheric specialization of language: an EEG study of bilingual Hopi Indian children. *International Journal of Neuroscience* 8: 1–6.

Romaine, S. (1986) The notion of government as a constraint on language mixing: some evidence from the code-mixed compound verb in Panjabi. In D. Tannen (ed.), *Linguistics and Language in Context. The interdependence of theory, data and application*. Washington, DC: Georgetown University Press.

Romaine, S. (1989, 2nd edn 1995) *Bilingualism*. Oxford: Blackwell.

Ronjat, J. (1913) *Le développement du langage observé chez un enfant bilingue*. Paris: Champion.

Rousseau, P. and Sankoff, D. (1978) Advances in variable rule methodology. In D. Sankoff (ed.), *Linguistic Variation: Models and methods*. New York: Academic Press.

Rubin, J. (1962) Bilingualism in Paraguay. *Anthropological Linguistics* 4: 52–8.

Rubin, J. (1963) Stability and change in a bilingual Paraguayan community. Paper presented at the Meeting of the American Anthropological Association, November 21. San Francisco, CA.

Rubin, J. (ed.) (1968) *National Bilingualism in Paraguay*. The Hague: Mouton.

Ryan, W.I. and McNeil, M. (1974) Listener reliability for a dichotic task. *Journal of the Acoustical Society of America* 56: 1922–3.

Saer, D.J. (1923) An inquiry into the effect of bilingualism upon the intelligence of young children. *Journal of Experimental Psychology* Part I 6: 232–40; Part II 6: 266–74.

Saer, D.J. (1924) The effect of bilingualism on intelligence. *British Journal of Psychology* 14: 25–38.

Samar, V. (1980) Evoked potential and visual half-field measures of celebral specialization. Paper presented at BABBLE, Niagara Falls.

Sankoff, D. (1975) VARBRUL 2. Unpublished program and documentation.

Sankoff, D. (1998) A formal production-based explanation of the facts of code-switching. *Bilingualism: Language and Cognition* 1(1): 39–50.

Sankoff, D. (1998a) A production model for code-mixed discourse. In *Proceedings of the 17th COLING Congress and 36th Meeting of the Association for Computational Linguistics*, Montreal.

Sankoff, D. and Labov, W. (1979) On the uses of variable rules. *Language Society* 8(2).

Sankoff, D. and Mainville, S. (1986) Code-switching of context-free grammars. *Theoretical Linguistics* 13(1/2): 75–90.

Sankoff, D. and Poplack, S. (1979/81) A formal grammar for code-switching. *Centro Working Papers 8*. New York: Centro de Estudios Puertoriquenos. Published in *Papers in Linguistics* 14: 3–46.

Sankoff, D., Poplack, S. and Vanniarajan, S. (1990) The case of the nonce loan in Tamil. *Language Variation and Change* 2(1): 71–101.

Saunders, G. (1982) Dee Erweb einer 'zweiten' Muttersprache in der Familie. In J. Swift (ed.), *Bilinguale und Multikulturelle Erziehung*. Königshausen: Neumann, pp. 26–33.

Schermerhorn, R.A. (1963) Toward a general theory of minority groups. Paper presented at the 58th Annual Meeting, American Sociology Association, Los Angeles, CA, August 28.

Schmid, K. (1936) Für unser Schweizerdeutsch. *Die Schweiz: ein nationales Jahrbuch 1936*. Basle, pp. 65–79.

Schmidt-Rohr, G. (1932, reissued 1963) *Muttersprache*. Jena: Eugen Diederichs.

Schneiderman, E. and Wesche, M. (1980) Right hemisphere participation in second language acquisition. Paper presented at the Third Los Angeles Second Language Acquisition Research Forum, Los Angeles, February.

Schönle, P. (1978) Otität versus lingualität: Dichotische Untersuchungen zur Prävalenz der Ohrigkeit und Sprachigkeit bei deutschen and russischen Studenten. Unpublished doctoral dissertation, Tübingen, Germany.

Schreuder, R. and Weltens, B. (eds) (1993) *The Bilingual Lexicon*. Amsterdam: John Benjamins.

Scott, S., Hynd, G., Hunt, L. and Weed, W. (1979) Cerebral speech lateralization on the native American Navajo. *Neuropsychologia* 17: 89–92.

Scotton, C.M. (1976) Strategies of neutrality: language choice in uncertain situations. *Language* 52: 919–41.

Scotton, C.M. (1982) The possibility of switching: motivation for maintaining multilingualism. *Anthropological Linguistics* 24: 432–44.

Scotton, C.M. (1982a) An urban-rural comparison of language use among the Luyia in Kenya. *International Journal of the Sociology of Language* 34: 121–31.

Scotton, C.M. (1983) The negotiation of identities in conversation: a theory of markedness and code choice. *International Journal of the Sociology of Language* 44: 115–36.

Scotton, C.M. (1985) What the heck, sir: style shifting and lexical colouring as features of powerful language. In R.L. Street and J.N. Capella (eds), *Sequence and Pattern in Communicative Behaviour*. London: Edward Arnold, pp. 103–19.

Scotton, C.M. (1986) Diglossia and code switching. In J.A. Fishman *et al.* (eds), *The Fergusonian Impact*. Berlin: Mouton.

Scotton, C.M. and Ury, W. (1977) Bilingual strategies: the social function of codeswitching. *International Journal of the Sociology of Language* 13: 5–20.

Scotton, C.M. and Zhu, W. (1983) *Tongzhi* in China: language change and its conversational consequences. *Language in Society* 12: 477–94.

Scotton, C.M. and Zhu, W. (1984) The multiple meanings of *shi. fu*, a language change in progress. *Anthropological Linguistics* 26: 325–44.

Sebba, M. (1993) *London Jamaican: Language systems in interaction*. Harlow: Longman.

Senn, A. (1935) Das Verhältnis von Mundart und Schriftsprache in der deutschen Schweiz. *Journal of English and Germanic Philology* 34: 42–58.

Shaffer, D. (1975) The place of code-switching in linguistic contacts. Paper presented at the Linguistics Association of Canada and the United States, Toronto.

Shallice, T. (1979) Case study approach in neuropsychological research. *Journal of Clinical Neuropsychology* 1: 183–211.

Shallice, T. (1982) Specific impairments in planning. In D. Broadbent and L. Weiskrantz (eds), *The Neuropsychology of Cognitive Function*. London: The Royal Society.

Shannahoff-Khalsa, D. (1984) September. Rhythms and reality: the dynamics of the mind. *Psychology Today*: 72–3.

Shattuck-Huffnagel, S. (1979) Speech errors as evidence for a serial-ordering mechanism in sentence production. In W.E. Cooper and E.C.T. Walker (eds), *Sentence Processing Psycholinguistic studies presented to Merrill Garrett*. Hillsdale, NJ: Erlbaum.

Shouby, E. (1951) The influence of the Arabic language on the psychology of the Arabs. *Middle East Journal* 5: 280–302.

Silverberg, R., Pollack, S. and Bentin, S. (1980) Shift of visual field preference for Hebrew words in native speakers learning to read. *Brain and Language* 11: 99–105.

Silverberg, R., Bentin, W., Gaziel, I., Obler, L. and Albert, M. (1979) Shift of visual field preference for English words in native Hebrew speakers. *Brain and Language* 8: 184–91.

Skutnabb-Kangas, T. (1981) *Bilingualism or Not: The education of minorities*. Clevedon: Multilingual Matters.

Slobin, D. (1973) Cognitive prerequisites for the development of grammar. In C.A. Ferguson and D. Slobin (eds), *Studies of Child Language Development*. New York: Holt, Rinehart & Winston.

Slobin, D. (ed.) (1985) *The Crosslinguistic Study of Language Acquisition*. Hillsdale, NJ: Erlbaum.

Smith, M.E. (1935) A study of the speech of eight bilingual children of the same family. *Child Development* 6: 19–25.

Soares, C. (1982) Converging evidence for left hemisphere language lateralization in bilinguals. *Neuropsychologia* 20: 653–60.

Soares, C. (1984) Left-hemisphere language lateralization in bilinguals: use of the concurrent activities paradigm. *Brain and Language* 23: 86–96.

Soares, C. and Grosjean, F. (1981) Left-hemisphere language lateralization in bilinguals and monolinguals. *Perception and Psychophysics* 29: 599–604.

Soares, C. and Grosjean, F. (1984) Bilinguals in a monolingual and a bilingual speech mode: the effect on lexical access. *Memory and Cognition*, 12: 380–6.

Solin, D. (1989) The systematic representation of bilingual crossed aphasia data and its consequences. *Brain and Language* 36: 92–116.

Sridhar, S.N. and Sridhar, K.K. (1980) The syntax and psycholinguistics of bilingual code mixing. *Canadian Journal of Psychology* 34: 407–16.

Starck, R., Genesee, F., Lambert, W. and Seitz, M. (1977) Multiple language experience and the development of cerebral dominance. In S.J. Segalowitz and F.A. Gruber (eds), *Language Development and Neurological Theory*. New York: Academic Press, pp. 48–55.

Steinmetz, A. (1936) Schrift und Volksprache in Griechenland, Deutsche Akademie (Munich), *Mitteilungen*: 370–9.

Stenson, N. (1990) Phrase structure congruence, government, and Irish–English code-switching. In P. Hendrick (ed.), *Syntax and Semantics 23: The syntax of the modern Celtic languages*, San Diego and New York: Academic Press, pp. 167–97.

Stieblich, C. (1983) Language learning: a study on cognitive style, lateral eye-movement and deductive vs. inductive learning of foreign language structures. Unpublished PhD dissertation, McGill University, Montreal, Canada.

Stross, B. (1973) Acquisition of botanical terminology by Tzeltal children. In M.S. Edmondson (ed.), *Meaning in Mayan Languages*. The Hague: Mouton.

Sussman, H.M. (1989) A reassessment of the time-sharing paradigm with ANCOVA. *Brain and Language* 37: 514–20.

Sussman, H.M., Franklin, P. and Simon, T. (1982) Bilingual speech: bilateral control? *Brain and Language* 15: 125–42.

Swain, M. (1972) Bilingualism as a first language. Unpublished PhD dissertation, University of California, Irvine.

Swain, M. (1977) Bilingualism, monolingualism and code acquisition. In W. Mackey and T. Andersson (eds), *Bilingualism in Early Childhood*. Rowley, MA: Newbury House.

Swain, M. and Wesche, M. (1975) Linguistic interaction: case study of a bilingual child. *Language Sciences* 17: 17–22.

Swigart, L. (1992) Two codes or one? Codeswitching in Dakar. *Journal of Multilingual and Multicultural Development* 13: 83–102.

Swigart, L. (1994) Cultural creolization and language use in post-colonial Africa: the case of Senegal. *Africa* 64: 175–89.

Swinney, D. (1979) Lexical access during sentence comprehension: (re)consideration of context effects. *Journal of Verbal Learning and Verbal Behavior* 18: 645–60.

Swinney, D. (1982) The structure and time-course of information interaction during speech comprehension: lexical segmentation, access and interpretation. In J. Mehler, E. Walker, and M. Garrett (eds), *Perspectives on Mental Representations*. Hillsdale, NJ: Lawrence Erlbaum Associates, pp. 151–67.

Tabouret-Keller, A. (1962) Vrais et faux problèmes du bilinguisme. In M. Cohen, J. Rezine, F. Kocher, A. Brauner, L. Lentin and A. Tabouret-Keller (eds), *Etudes sur le langage de l'enfant*. Paris: Les Editions du Scarabée.

Taeschner, T. (1983) *The Sun is Feminine: A study of language acquisition in bilingual children*, Berlin: Springer.

Talland, G.A. (1965) *Deranged Memory: A psychonomic study of the amnesia syndrome*. New York/London: Academic Press.

Talmy, L. (1985) Lexicalization patterns: semantic structure in lexical form. In T. Shopen (ed.), *Language Typology and Syntactic Description III*, New York: Cambridge University Press, pp. 51–149.

Taylor, D.W. (1943) Learning telegraphic code. *Psychological Bulletin* 40: 461–87.

Taylor, I. (1971) How are words from two languages organised in bilinguals' memory? *Canadian Journal of Psychology* 25: 228–40.

Ten Hacken, P. (1994) *Defining Morphology*. Hildescheim: Olms.

Thakerar, J.N., Giles, H., and Cheshire, J. (1982) Psychological and linguistic parameters of speech accommodation theory. In C. Fraser and K.R. Scherer (eds), *Advances in the Social Psychology of Language*. New York: Cambridge University Press, pp. 205–55.

Thibaut, J. and Kelley, H. (1959) *The Social Psychology of Groups*. New York: Wiley.

Timm, L.A. (1975) Spanish–English code-switching: el porqué y how-not-to. *Romance Philology* 28(4).

Tits, D. (1959) *Le mécanisme de l'acquisition d'une langue se substituant à la langue maternelle chez une enfant espagnole âgée de six ans*. Brussells: Veldeman.

Treffers-Daller, J. (1993) *Mixing Two Languages: French–Dutch contact in a comparative perspective*. Berlin: Mouton de Gruyter.

Treffers-Daller, J. (1998) Variability in code-switching styles: Turkish–German code-switching patterns. In R. Jacobson (ed.), *Code-switching World-Wide*. Berlin: Mouton, pp. 177–200.

Trehub, S. (1973) Auditory-linguistic sensitivity in infants. PhD dissertation, McGill University, Montreal.

Trudgill, P. (1974) *The Social Differentiation of English in Norwich*. Cambridge: Cambridge University Press.

Trudgill, P. and Cheshire, J. (eds) (1997) *The Sociolinguistics Reader*, 2 volumes. London: Arnold.

United States Department of Labor (1975) *A Socio-Economic Profile of Puerto Rican New Yorkers*. New York: Bureau of Labor Statistics.

Vaid, J. (1981) Hemispheric differences in bilingual language processing: A task analysis. PhD dissertation, McGill University, Montreal.

Vaid, J. (1981a) Cerebral lateralization of Hindi and Urdu: A pilot tachistoscope Stroop study. Paper presented at the South Asian Language Analysis Conference, Stony Brook, NY.

Vaid, J. (1983) Bilingualism and brain lateralization. In S. Segalowitz (ed.), *Language function and brain organization*. New York: Academic Press, pp. 315–39.

Vaid, J. (ed.) (1986) *Language Processing in Bilinguals*. Hillsdale, NJ: Lawrence Erlbaum.

Vaid, J. and Genesee, F. (1980) Neuropsychological approaches to bilingualism: a critical review. *Canadian Journal of Psychology* 34: 417–45.

Vaid, J. and Lambert, W.E. (1979) Differential cerebral envolvement in the cognitive functioning of bilinguals. *Brain and Language* 8: 92–110.

Valdés, G. and Pino, C. (1981) Muy a tus ordenes: compliment responses among Mexican-American bilinguals. *Language in Society* 10: 53–72.

Valdés-Fallis, G. (1976) Social interaction and code-switching patterns: a case study of Spanish–English alternation. In G. Keller *et al.* (eds), *Bilingualism in the Bicentennial and Beyond*. New York: Bilingual Press.

Valdés-Fallis, G. (1978) Code-switching as a deliberate verbal strategy: a microanalysis of direct and indirect requests among bilingual Chicano speakers. In R. Duran (ed.), *Latino Language and Communicative Behavior*. New Jersey: Ablex Publishing Corp.

Valian, V. (1986) Syntactic categories in the speech of young children. *Developmental Psychology* 22: 562–79.

van Haeringen, C.B. (n.d.) *Nederlands tussen Duits en Engels*. The Hague: Servire.

van Heuven, W., Dijkstra, T., and Grainger, J. (1995) Neighborhood effects in bilingual word recognition: the BIA model and experiments. Unpublished manuscript, NICI, University of Nijmegen, The Netherlands.

Varo, C. (1971) *Consideraciones Antropológicas y Políticas en Torno a la Enseñanza del 'Spanglish' en Nueva York*. Rio Piedras: Ediciones Librería Internacional.

Vihman, M.M. (1982) The acquisition of morphology by a bilingual child: a whole-word approach. *Applied Psycholinguistics* 3: 141–60.

Vihman, M.M. (1985) Language differentiation by the bilingual infant. *Journal of Child Language* 12: 297–324.

Vihman, M.M. (1998) A developmental perspective on codeswitching: conversations between a pair of bilingual siblings. *International Journal of Bilingualism* 2(1): 45–84.

Vihman, M.M. and McLaughlin, B. (1982) Bilingualism and second language acquisition in preschool children. In C. Brainerd and M. Pressley (eds), *Verbal Processes in Children*. New York: Springer.

Vildomec, V. (1963) *Multilingualism*. Leyden: Sijthoff.

Vinay, J.-P. and Darbelnet, J. (1958) *Stylistique comparée du français et de l'anglais*. Paris: Didier; Montreal: Beauchemin.

Volterra, V. and Taeschner, T. (1978) The acquisition and development of language by bilingual children. *Journal of Child Language* 5: 311–26.

Waber, D. (1977) Biological substrates of field dependence: implications of sex differences. *Psychological Bulletin* 84: 1076–87.

Walters, J. and Zatorre, R. (1978) Laterality differences for word identification in bilinguals. *Brain and Language* 2: 158–67.

Wanner, E. and Gleitman, L. (eds) (1982) *Language Acquisition: The state of the art*. Cambridge: Cambridge University Press.

Wardhaugh, R. (1986, 2nd edn 1992, 3rd edn 1998) *An Introduction to Sociolinguistics.* Oxford: Blackwell.

Wechsler, A. (1976) Crossed aphasia in an illiterate dextral. *Brain and Language* 3: 164–72.

Wechsler, A. (1977) Dissociative alexia. *Archives of Neurology* 34: 257.

Weil, S. (1994) Choix de langue et alternances codiques chez le bilingue en situations de communication diverse: étude expérimentale [The bilingual's language choice and code-switches in various communication modes: an experimental study]. *Travaux neuchâtelois de linguistique (TRANEL)* 21: 97–109.

Weinreich, M. (1959) Inveynikste tsveyshprakikeyt in a skenaz biz der haskale; faktn un bagrifn [Intragroup bilingualism in Ashkenaz until the enlightenment; facts and concepts]. *Goldenc Keyt* 35: 3–11.

Weinreich, U. (1951) Research problems in bilingualism, with special reference to Switzerland. Unpublished PhD dissertation, Columbia University.

Weinreich, U. (1953) *Languages in Contact: Findings and problems.* New York: The Linguistic Circle of New York. Reissued by Mouton in The Hague, 1968.

Weinreich U. (1962) Multilingual dialectology and the new Yiddish atlas. *Anthropological Linguistics* 4(1): 6–22.

Weltens, B. (1989) *The Attrition of French as a Foreign Language.* Dordrecht: Foris.

Wentz, J. (1977) Some considerations in the development of a syntactic description of code-switching. Unpublished PhD dissertation, University of Illinois at Urbana-Champaign.

Wentz, J. and McClure, E. (1977) Monolingual 'codes': some remarks on the similarities between bilingual and monolingual code-switching. In *Papers from the 13th Regional Meeting, Chicago Linguistics Society, April 1977*, 706–13. Chicago: Chicago Linguistics Society.

West, M. (1958) Bilingualism. *English Language Teaching* 12: 94–7.

White, L. (1989) *Universal Grammar and Second Language Acquisition.* Amsterdam and Philadelphia: John Benjamins.

Whiteley, W.H. (1974) Some patterns of language use in the rural areas of Kenya. In W.H. Whiteley (ed.), *Language in Kenya.* Nairobi: Oxford University Press, pp. 319–50.

Willems, N. (1983) *English Intonation from a Dutch Point of View: An experimental investigation of English intonation produced by Dutch native speakers.* Dordrecht: Foris.

Winer, B.J. (1971) *Statistical Principles in Experimental Design.* New York: McGraw-Hill.

Wirth, L. (1938) Urbanisin as a way of life. *American Journal of Sociology* 44: 1–24.

Wode, H. (1977) Four early stages in the development of L1 negation. *Journal of Child Language* 4: 87–102.

Wode, H. (1981) *Learning a Second Language: An integrated view of language acquisition.* Tübingen: Narr.

Woolard, K. (1985) Language variation and cultural hegemony: toward an integration of sociolinguistic and social theory. *American Ethnologist* 12(4): 738–48.

Woolard, K. (1989) *Double Talk: Bilingualism and the politics of ethnicity in Catalonia.* Stanford, CA: Stanford University Press.

Woolford, E. (1983) Bilingual code-switching and syntactic theory. *Linguistic Inquiry* 14: 520–36.

Wray, A., Trott, K. and Bloomer, A. (1999) *Projects in Linguistics: A practical guide to researching language*. London: Arnold.

Yamadori, A. (1981) Verbal perseveration in aphasia. *Neuropsychologia* 19: 591–4.

Zatorre, R.J. (1989) On the representation of multiple languages in the brain: old problems and new directions. *Brain and Language* 36: 127–47.

Zentella, A.C. (1981) Hablamos los dos. We speak both. Growing up bilingual in El Barrio. Unpublished PhD dissertation, University of Pennsylvania.

Zentella, A.C. (1997) *Growing up Bilingual: Puerto Rican children in New York*. Malden, MA: Blackwell.

INDEX